A History of Shakespeare on Screen

A CENTURY OF FILM AND TELEVISION

Kenneth S. Rothwell

Second Edition

CAMBRIDGE
UNIVERSITY PRESS

PUBLISHED BY THE PRESS SYNDICATE OF THE UNIVERSITY OF CAMBRIDGE
The Pitt Building, Trumpington Street, Cambridge CB2 1RP, United Kingdom

CAMBRIDGE UNIVERSITY PRESS
The Edinburgh Building, Cambridge CB2 2RU, UK
40 West 20th Street, New York, NY 10011-4211, USA
477 Williamstown Road, Port Melbourne, VIC 3207, Australia
Ruiz de Alarcón 13, 28014 Madrid, Spain
Dock House, The Waterfront, Cape Town 8001, South Africa

http://www.cambridge.org

First published 1999
Second edition 2004

Printed in the United Kingdom at the University Press, Cambridge

Typefaces Palatino 9.5/12.5 pt.   *System* LATEX 2ε   [TB]

A catalogue record for this book is available from the British Library

ISBN 0 521 83537 2 hardback
ISBN 0 521 54311 8 paperback

The publisher has used its best endeavours to ensure that the URLs for external
websites referred to in this book are correct and active at the time of going to
press. However, the publisher has no responsibility for the websites and can
make no guarantee that a site will remain live or that the content is or will remain
appropriate.

A HISTORY OF SHAKESPEARE ON SCREEN

A History of Shakespeare on Screen: A Century of Film and Television chronicles how film-makers have re-imagined Shakespeare's plays from the earliest exhibitions in music halls and nickelodeons to today's multi-million dollar productions shown in megaplexes. Topics include the silent era, Hollywood in the Golden Age, the films of Laurence Olivier and Orson Welles, the television scene to include the BBC plays, the avant-garde cinema of Jarman and Greenaway, and non-Anglophone contributions from Japan and elsewhere. This second edition updates the chronology to the year 2003 and includes a new chapter on such recent films as John Madden's *Shakespeare in Love*, Kenneth Branagh's *Love's Labour's Lost*, Michael Almereyda's *Hamlet*, and Billy Morrissette's *Scotland, Pa*. An up-to-date filmography, bibliography, and index of names make it invaluable as a one-volume reference work for specialists, while the accessible style will ensure that it also appeals to a wider audience of Shakespeareans and cinephiles.

KENNETH S. ROTHWELL is Professor of English Emeritus at the University of Vermont, Burlington. He was the co-founder and co-editor with Bernice W. Kliman of the *Shakespeare on Film Newsletter*. He co-chaired the Shakespeare on Film Seminar at the Tokyo 1991 World Shakespeare Congress, and he produced the Shakespeare on Film Festival at the Los Angeles 1996 World Shakespeare Congress. He compiled with Annabelle Henkin Melzer *Shakespeare on Screen: An International Filmography and Videography* (1990), and 'Occasional Paper no.8', a monograph on Shakespeare silent films for the International Shakespeare Association (2000) series.

For my grandchildren,
Rosalind Springs Rothwell
Sara Mei-Ping Davis
James Waddell Rothwell
Charlotte Zhong-Xue Rothwell Davis
Phoebe Ming-Ming Davis

– CONTENTS –

[vii]

– ILLUSTRATIONS –

The need for a second edition of *A History of Shakespeare on Screen* goes beyond the obvious requirement of updating the chronology. As thousands of classroom teachers through readily available VHS and DVD recordings have refocused student attention from text to performance, a minor revolution has occurred in academic attitudes toward Shakespeare on screen. Once universally scorned as "dumbing down," Shakespeare films are now often credited with both preserving and redefining a cultural heritage. The latest pedagogy has been accompanied by theoretical contributions from new wave academics, whose enthusiasm for both Shakespeare and mass culture has persuaded them to expand the limits of the Shakespeare movie from text to "paratext." In the beginning filmmakers deferred to Shakespeareans; nowadays Shakespeareans defer to filmmakers. Subservience has yielded to subversion.

This shift in the center of gravity has toppled the sovereignty of text over performance to the point that the term, "transgressive," which I used in the first edition of this book as a label for bizarre adaptations, has become meaningless. Post-modernism collapses the distinctions between high and low culture so that Will Shakespeare becomes just another working screen writer subject to "the spurns That patient merit of th' unworthy takes." The ancient cry of protest "But is it Shakespeare?" is heard now only from diehard Luddites, who have in the sweep of events ironically themselves been made over into the counter-revolutionary transgressors. This volume's cover illustration from Billy Morrissette's *Scotland, PA* illustrates how Shakespeare's *Macbeth* has been reincarnated in the context of that most American of mass cultural institutions, the MacDonald's hamburger.

Actually there is nothing new about any of this tug of war between text and performance. The grudge in Jacobean times between Ben Jonson and Inigo Jones over whether in the court masque the text (*Lexis*) or the scenery (*Opsis*) should be given priority has been displaced forward into the struggle between author and *auteur*. This "dismemberment" of Shakespeare, as explicated by theorists like Richard Burt, Linda Charnes, Barbara Hodgdon, Douglas Lanier, Courtney Lehmann, Laurie Osborne, Lisa S. Starks, W. B. Worthen, and others, has not yet destroyed the powerful force of Shakespeare's work as a theogony, a kind of creation epic for western civilization. It has instead infused the parts like a sacramental wafer into the body and blood of the masses who partake of the feast. The old fashioned textual scholar remains on the high altar guarding the holy relics of folio and quarto. Never mind that only a faithful few still attend Mass.

In the newly drafted chapter 11, I have more or less erased the sharp distinction between film and video in order to solve a difficult organizational problem as well as to acknowledge the way that technology has increasingly blurred the distinction between them. I have also corrected and amended errors and misjudgments in the first edition. For their detailed and exhaustive criticism, I am especially grateful to José Ramón Díaz Fernández, Thomas A. Pendleton, Stanley Wells, and my editor Sarah Stanton. I would also like to thank Peter Balderstone, Peter Donaldson, Juana Green, Nicholas Jones, and Elsie Walker, for allowing me to draw on their unpublished papers, all but Walker's having been presented to the " Shakespeare and the Movies" seminar at the 2003 Shakespeare Association meeting in Victoria, BC. I am indebted to the staffs of the Butler/Howe Library at the University of Vermont, the Library of Performing Arts of the New York Public Library at Lincoln Center, and the Museum of Modern Art Film Library. Gary Crowdus has allowed me to draw on my reviews of *Elizabeth* and *Much Ado about Something* in *Cineaste*; Jim Welsh authorized me to echo things I have already said in his journal, *Literature/Film Quarterly*; the editors of *Shakespeare Bulletin* have not objected to my incorporating traces of work published in its pages; Lot 47 Films granted permission to use the cover photo from *Scotland, PA*; for some production data about recent film releases I have used by permission http://pro.imdb.com., © 1990–2001 Internet Movie Database Limited. Individual Web sites for specific films have occasionally been drawn on as well. "Photofest" has been indispensable in locating stills.

Throughout all these perturbations, my faithful wife, Lyn, has never hesitated to take time out to help me, even in the midst of her own heroic struggle to bring a single payer universal health system to Vermont and the United States.

K.S.R.
September 2, 2003
Burlington, Vermont

– PREFACE TO FIRST EDITION –

This book has been at least a quarter of the century in the making and along the way I have accumulated staggering debts from many generous and wonderful people. At the top of the list are the veteran members of the Shakespeare on Film Seminar at the meetings of the Shakespeare Association of America and the International Shakespeare Association who from Tokyo to Cleveland and Los Angeles to Stratford-upon-Avon have patiently read and critiqued my annual contributions. They include H. R. Coursen, Samuel Crowl, Anthony Davies, Peter S. Donaldson, Lawrence Guntner, Russell Jackson, Jack J. Jorgens, James H. Lake, R. Thomas Simone, Robert F. Willson, Jr., and many others whose friendship and collegiality have become especially meaningful to me.

To Dr. Bernice W. Kliman I owe a special debt for having co-founded and co-edited with me from 1976 to 1992 the *Shakespeare on Film Newsletter*. Dr. Nancy Hodge, formerly executive director of the Shakespeare Association of America, underwrote my three-day Shakespeare Film Festival at the 1996 World Shakespeare Congress in Los Angeles, which became the launching pad for this long-delayed book. Sarah Stanton of the Cambridge University Press added another incentive when in Los Angeles she encouraged me to submit an outline for evaluation. An anonymous reader for the Cambridge University Press did me an enormous favor by ferreting out errors of fact and judgment in an earlier draft and his/her industry has been matched by Jocelyn Pye's meticulous copy editing.

The Research Committee of the University of Vermont Graduate College generously contributed toward underwriting the book's movie stills, and other permissions fees. Many on the staff of the University of Vermont Library aided me, among them James T. Barickman, Nancy Crane, Martha T. Day, Barbara T. Lambert, and Roger F. Wiberg. I also have debts to the staff of the British Film Institute Library and National Film and Television Archive, especially Luke McKernan and Olwen Terris. Helpful persons like Rosemary Hanes at the Library of Congress Motion Picture Division, and Terry Geesken of the Museum of Modern Art went out of their way for me. In the pre-videocassette era, Barry M. Parker, Joseph G. Empsucha, and Candace Bothwell initiated me into the mysteries of the Steenbeck at the Folger Shakespeare Library film archive. Ken Wlaschin of the American Film Institute made some rare silent film materials available. I'm grateful to the lively film department at Burlington College, Chairman Ken Peck, and my Orson Welles teacher, Susan Henry, for helping me to make the crossover from Shakespeare to movies.

Among others who either advertently or inadvertently have helped along the way are the late Robert Hamilton Ball, Thomas Berger, Lynda E. Boose, Richard Burt, Mary Courtney, José Ramón Díaz-Fernández, Christina Egloff, Barbara Freedman, Kathy Grant, Kirk Hendershott-Kraetzer, Kathy Howlett, Michael Klossner, Patricia J. Lennox, Andrew M. McLean, Frank Manchel, Michael Manheim, the late Roger Manvell, Marjorie Meyer, Michael Mullin, Laurie Osborne, the late Ed Ruhe, Lisa S. Starks, Steve Toth, the late Sam Wanamaker, Stanley Wells, and Sara Woods. If I have overlooked anyone, I am truly sorry. Any errors in the pages that follow are of course entirely my responsibility.

Not least, I am grateful to my faithful and loving wife, Lyn, who put up with my becoming a grouchy recluse for two years.

– ACKNOWLEDGMENTS –

On behalf of Neal-Schuman Publishers, Michelle Rivera Rodriguez has granted permission to quote from, and/or paraphrase and rework sections (particularly in chapter five, on television) of my previously published commentaries in *Shakespeare on Screen: An International Filmography and Videography* (New York: Neal-Schuman, 1990). I owe thanks to James Welsh, editor of *Literature/Film Quarterly* for permission to draw on my "Zeffirelli's *Romeo and Juliet*: Words into Picture and Music," *LFQ* 5.4. (Fall 1977), 326–32; Bege K. Bowers, co-editor of CEA Publications, for use of excerpts from my "Roman Polanski's *Macbeth*: the 'Privileging' of Ross," *CEA Critic* 46, 1&2 (1983–84), 50–55; Luis Gmaz for permitting some use of my review essay, "Kenneth Branagh's *Henry V*," in *Comparative Drama* 24.2 (1990), 173–78; and Jason Arthur of Routledge for authorizing borrowings from my "In Search of Nothing: Mapping *King Lear*," in Lynda E. Boose and Richard Burt (eds.), *Shakespeare*, *The Movie* (London and New York: Routledge, 1997), pp. 135–47. Frequently I have also relied on the *Shakespeare on Film Newsletter* for relevant data. Jacqueline Kavanagh of the BBC Written Archives Centre, Caversham Park, Reading, allowed access to materials stored there and has given me helpful advice.

Excerpts from film reviews in *The New York Times* are: Copyright © 1896, 1921, 1922, 1927, 1929, 1947, 1949, 1950, 1952, 1954, 1960, 1966, 1967, 1971, 1974, 1980, 1983, 1985, 1990, 1991, 1993, 1996, by the New York Times Company. Reprinted by permission. In addition, Brian Whittaker, publishing director of *Sight and Sound* and *Monthly Film Bulletin*, has kindly consented to my quoting from film reviews.

Shakespeare quotations are from: G. Blakemore Evans (ed.), *The Riverside Shakespeare*. Copyright © 1974 by Houghton Mifflin Company. Used with permission.

– ABBREVIATIONS –

BBC	British Broadcasting Company
BFI	British Film Institute
BUFVC	British Universities Film & Video Council
CD	*Comparative Drama*
CSM	*Christian Science Monitor*
ETJ	*Educational Theatre Journal*
FM	*Film Music*
FQ	*Film Quarterly*
FR	*Films in Review*
LFQ	*Literature/Film Quarterly*
MFB	*Monthly Film Bulletin*
MG	*Manchester Guardian*
MPW	*Moving Picture World and View Photographer*
NFTVA	*National Film and Television Archive*
NYHT	*New York Herald Tribune*
NYO	*The New York Observer*
NYRB	*New York Review of Books*
NYT	*The New York Times*
PMLA	*Publications of the Modern Language Association*
QFRT	*The Quarterly of Film, Radio, and Television*
RSC	Royal Shakespeare Company
SB	*Shakespeare Bulletin*
SFNL	*Shakespeare on Film Newsletter*
SN	*Shakespeare Newsletter*
SQ	*Shakespeare Quarterly*
SS	*Shakespeare Survey*
S&S	*Sight and Sound*
TA	*Theatre Arts* (previously Theatre Arts Monthly)
TN	*The Nation*
TNY	*The New Yorker*

TRS	*The Riverside Shakespeare*
TS	*Theatre Survey*
VV	*Village Voice*
WAC	BBC Written Archives Centre
WP	*Washington Post*

- 1 -

Shakespeare in silence: from stage to screen

Nickelodeons, penny gaffs, and fair grounds

How best to imagine Shakespeare's words in moving images? The challenge to auteurial ingenuity began in September 1899 when William Kennedy-Laurie Dickson, an early collaborator with Thomas Edison, teamed up with actor/director Sir Herbert Beerbohm Tree to film excerpts from *King John*, then playing at Her Majesty's Theatre in London.[1] Sir Herbert might have hesitated if he had realized how Dickson's technology would one day make waiters out of thousands of unemployed actors. The mechanical reproduction of art was in the air, however. Over the next three decades, film makers would grind out an estimated 150,000 silent movies, though but a tiny fraction, fewer than one percent, perhaps 500, would draw on Shakespeare. With their newly patented Cinématographe, the Lumière brothers had already projected on a screen at a Parisian café one-minute "actualities" of workers leaving a factory.[2] After a rival Edison movie exhibition on April 23, 1896, at New York City's Koster & Bial's Music Hall, Charles Frohman magisterially declared that "when art can make us believe that we see actual living nature, the dead things of the stage must go."[3]

Photographed in widescreen 68 mm at the Thames embankment open-air studio of Dickson's British Mutoscope and Biograph Company, Tree played the dying King John in act five, scene seven, against a studio backdrop for Swinstead Abbey. He was flanked by Prince Henry (Dora Senior) and the Earl of Pembroke (James Fisher), and by Robert Bigot (F. M. Paget), all in period costumes. As the poisoned king, Tree's writhing and clutching and gyrating and swiveling and squirming mime the agony of a human being whose "bowels [are crumbling] up to dust" and whose inner torment is akin to "hell" (5.7.30–45).[4] In King John's death, however, Tree breathed life into an upstart rival to Shakespeare on stage – Shakespeare on screen in moving images. Ironically Shakespeare's *King John* also proleptically deals with the economic forces that would drive this fledgling art from its very beginnings – the curse of "tickling commodity," that "smooth-fac'd gentleman," which Philip the Bastard describes as "this bawd, this broker" that forces even kings to "break faith"

[1]

1 In *King John* (UK 1899), Sir Herbert Beerbohm Tree as the dying monarch writhes in agony at Swinstead Abbey, while Pembroke (James Fisher), Prince Henry (Dora Senior), and Bigot (F. M. Paget) look on.

(2.1.573–85). The most cash-driven art form in history, film from the beginning has been enslaved to "tickling commodity." Marx's insight that capitalism's gains for humanity's material comfort often come at the price of its soul needs no better illustration. The iron rule of profit or perish has commodified Shakespeare, dictating the scope, size, frequency, and even the artistry of filmed plays, and at the same time forced the Shakespeare director into an inevitable synergy with popular culture.

At the start of this century, however, no one envisioned the revolutionary potential of the movie industry. Movies were working-class entertainment at England's penny gaffs and music halls, American vaudeville, sideshows at European country fairs, and entr'acte diversions. Since by 1905, France controlled 60 percent of the world's film business, not surprisingly the next Shakespeare "movie," produced by the Phono-Cinéma-Théâtre, emerged, complete with "sound," at the 1900 Paris Exposition. It photographed Sarah Bernhardt in moving images energetically fighting Laertes (Pierre Magnier) in the duel scene from *Hamlet*, with synchronized Edison cylinders providing the sound of clashing epées.[5] Having played Hamlet on stage thirty-two times in 1899 alone, as well as performing in other earlier Shakespearean roles, and with an extraordinary flair for publicity,[6] Sarah Bernhardt was a natural choice to star in this second ever Shakespeare movie. In her career, frustrated by the dearth of first-rate female parts and encouraged by the French stage tradition for cross-dressing, she acted in over two dozen *travesti* ranging from minor (a page boy) in *Phèdre* to a truly *grand premier travesti rôle* as in *Hamlet*.[7] Moreover, contrary to prevailing ideas about "Hamletism" that stressed the prince's inward femininity, "revenge permeated the production of the Bernhardt *Hamlet*."[8] In silent movies, Bernhardt's famous silvery voice was stilled but on the other hand the French accent that prevented her from playing Romeo against Ellen Terry's Juliet became irrelevant, for by substituting images for words her personality crossed international language barriers. As Carl Laemmle proclaimed in a trade journal advertisement, "Universal pictures speak the Universal language." The spectacle of Shakespeare performed in a déclassé venue at a fairground may have shocked the bourgeois, who probably felt as did Oscar Wilde's Dorian Gray at a cheap London theatre that "I must admit I was rather annoyed at the idea of seeing Shakespeare done in such a wretched hole of a place." Bernhardt's *Hamlet*, like Tree's *King John,* as the extant frame enlargements show, went no further than being a record of a theatrical performance on a conventional stage set, a first step in the evolution of the Shakespeare movie from theatre into film.[9]

The sound effects for a fencing duel in Bernhardt's *Hamlet* remind us that "silent" films were really never silent. As David A. Cook has noted, silent film was an "aberration," and "movies were intended to talk from their inception."[10]

Thomas Edison's plan for a "coin-operated entertainment machine" envisioned motion pictures illustrating sound from a phonograph, not the other way around. Live musicians quickly showed up in theatres to fill out the awful silences, and typically theatre owner Lyman H. Howe of New York City advertised in a trade journal for "an imitator to create sound effects back of the screen . . . a man [with the] natural ability to produce animal and mechanical sounds."[11] A manager in Clear Lake, Iowa, needed a "singer and piano player combined," to whom he would pay "a good salary,"[12] for he subscribed to the universal belief that "a good piano player is essential to the success of . . . electric theatre."[13] Female pianists could now use their previously unmarketable talents "by earning an honest living playing in a public place."[14] Audiences soon became so accustomed to sound that when the unfortunate John Riker, a projectionist isolated in his booth, mistakenly grabbed a live wire, his shrieks of agony as 1,000 volts surged through him were interpreted as splendid sound effects and wildly applauded. Rescued by the piano player, Riker's roasted hand had "to be pried loose from the wire."[15]

By 1908 the Kleine Optical Company was advertising its "remarkable consignment of film subjects" showing "famous French actors."[16] Like everyone else, the French rejoiced in finding literary properties by famous authors like Shakespeare whose "public domain" status meant freedom from any unpleasantness about royalties. Mesmerized by the prestige of the Comédie Française, French film makers developed the Film d'Art movement to glorify French theatrical tradition, which nurtured high culture but inhibited the growth of film art. In America, some companies like Adolph Zukor's Famous Players, anxious to earn the cachet of high art, imitated the French, their movies often being lower-cased as "film d'art," and the creation in Italy of the Film d'Arte Italiana added further confusion for filmographers. The assumption was that movies were not themselves an art but had to have art put into them with literary classics. Jean Mounet-Sully, "the greatest French actor of the period," who played Hamlet at the Comédie Française, as well as Othello opposite Bernhardt's Desdemona, soon followed, or even preceded Bernhardt, with a vignette from the *Hamlet* graveyard scene;[17] and Georges Méliès, the inventor of trick photography, who put flying machines into space and showed people floating on air, performed the title role in a *Hamlet* segment (1907), as well as a cameo William Shakespeare in *Shakespeare Writing Julius Caesar* (1907), a portrayal of the assassination.[18] Paul Mounet, younger brother of Mounet-Sully, was cast in the lead of *Macbeth* (c.1909). A Pathé semi-Shakespearean *Cleopatra* (1910) starring Madeleine Roch anticipated a long line of films about the Egyptian witch that had little to do with Shakespeare's tragedy, culminating in the mega-budget 20th-Century Fox *Cleopatra* (1963) with superstars Elizabeth Taylor and Richard Burton. A derivative *Romeo Turns Bandit* (1910), which though only marginally indebted to Shakespeare, broke with and moved away from the merely presentational by employing a rudimentary film grammar. In general, however, the Film d'Art obsession with theatrical models distracted continental cinéastes from the main challenge of envisioning Shakespeare in cinematic tropes. The history of Shakespeare in the movies has, after all, been the search for the best available means to replace the verbal with the visual imagination, an inevitable development deplored by some but interpreted by others as not so much a limitation on, as an extension of, Shakespeare's genius into uncharted seas. In the United States, on the other hand, the trek westward to Hollywood sufficiently disconnected the movies from Broadway theatre to make possible by 1929 the thoroughly liberated Pickford/Fairbanks *The Taming of the Shrew.*

The economic engine in North America driving the production of cheap, one-reel movies was the "nickelodeon," a term coined by John P. Harris of McKeesport, Pennsylvania, by cleverly merging his admission price with the Greek word for music hall.[19] There were no cinemas and then suddenly there were hundreds, and thousands. Like the 1576 opening of James Burbage's professional theatre in Shoreditch, the new movie theatres revolutionized the entertainment industry. An editorial writer in the trade journal *Moving Picture World* observed that "there is a new thing under the sun...It is the 5-cent theatre...it came unobtrusively in the still of the night," and had multiplied "faster then guinea pigs."[20] By 1907 North America alone could tally 2,500 to 3,000 "nickelodeons," or "5-cent theatres," or "electric theatres," as they were variously labeled. It did not take much to get a 5-cent theatre started – an empty store with enough space to cram in 200 to 500 chairs; phonographs; a cashier; a "cinematograph" with a reliable non-smoking operator; a canvas for a screen; a piano; a leather-lunged barker; and of course a manager to oversee all this. Predictably the respectable classes sniffed at the honky-tonk flavor and spurned the upstart.

Such heady success did not go unchallenged. In the midst of its severe growing pains, the movie industry became a lightning rod for hostility. It threatened the praetorians of culture and morality who intuited how these new "site[s] of cultural contagion associated with the 'lower orders'"[21] would one day destroy the iron control of church and school over the masses. The Reverend E. L. Goodell stopped a showing of the Edison *Nero and the Burning of Rome* (1908) because the school children were worked into "a frenzy of fear when they saw men seized, choked, stabbed and their limbs twisted by their torturers."[22] Some little girls covered their faces with their hats to shut out the sight. An Episcopal bishop deplored the "demoralizing influence" of the nickelodeons.[23] Harassing fly-by-night theatre operators, many of whom were eastern European Jewish immigrants, for showing movies on Sunday became a favorite pastime of New York's Finest, but then also it might be a charge of "imperiling the morals of young boys," as in the lamentable case of George Watson who allowed juveniles to watch the drugging of Evelyn Nesbitt in *The Great Thaw Trial*.[24]

With Machiavellian cunning, the vaudevillians and other theatre people who were at risk of redundancy, calculating that politicians would more gladly listen to men of the cloth than to men of the motley, manipulated the clergy into lobbying against 5-cent theatres. In a last-ditch effort they also undercut the scruffy nickelodeons by incorporating movies into their vaudeville programs in real theatres.[25] The actors' clandestine scheming achieved dizzy success on Christmas Eve, 1908, when in a spasm of self-righteousness New York City's Mayor George B. McClellan shut down 500 nickelodeons, ostensibly because they were fire traps, which they indubitably were, but also possibly to appease those who saw them as dens of iniquity. An editorial in *Moving Picture World* accused the actors of chicanery and sarcastically thanked the Mayor for his "unexpected Christmas present."[26] In Los Angeles saloon keepers complained that the nickelodeons were stealing customers away.[27] In London, the penny gaffs competed with the public houses.

In the first decade of film, however, for a brief shining hour the Vitagraph Company's Brooklyn, New York studio emerged as a world hub for Shakespeare films. In 1908, J. Stuart Blackton's Vitagraph Company[28] entered into this rough-and-tumble marketplace with a series of one-reel Shakespeare movies. The cultural politics of turn-of-the-century America made this marriage of elitist Shakespeare with the populist nickelodeons inevitable. Seeing a compelling need for "quality" motion pictures to attract "classier" audiences, and perhaps inspired by France's Film d'Art movement, Blackton made public domain Shakespeare a pawn in a bid for higher social status. "Class," "classy," and "classier" became the mantras of the early film makers as they fought to gain respectability, envisioning a mythical audience for high-mimetic Shakespeare made up of Margaret Dumont types out of the Marx Brothers movies. Shakespeare movies were a small part of the campaign to obliterate socially aware films sympathizing with the plight of the exploited workers.[29] Movies became the sites of contestation for nothing more or less than the American soul. The Vitagraph line of "quality" products included films about George Washington, Dante's Francesca da Rimini, and biblical tales, though its trade journal puffs also listed low-brow material like *The Cook Makes Madeira Sauce* right alongside its "high art" *Midsummer Night's Dream*.[30] Another ideological agenda behind all this do-goodism was the need to civilize the hordes of eastern and southern Europeans disembarking at Ellis Island by exposure to solid Anglo-American values. Through beatifying George Washington, who was after all only transplanted English country gentry, and showcasing Shakespeare, the tired and huddled masses who jammed the nickelodeons could more quickly be melted into the pot.

Vitagraph's Shakespeare movies were highly compressed one-reelers of ten to fifteen minutes in duration that privileged tableaux, such as the assassination of Julius Caesar, or the balcony scene from *Romeo and Juliet*, which were familiar even to the unscrubbed masses. Vitagraph Shakespeare titles, all released between about 1908 and 1912, in addition to *A Midsummer Night's Dream* included *Antony and Cleopatra, As You Like It, Henry VIII [Cardinal Wolsey], Julius Caesar, King Lear, Merchant of Venice, Othello, Richard III, Romeo and Juliet,* and *Twelfth Night. A Comedy of Errors* used only the title, and *Hamlet* was planned but never completed. Often directed by William V. Ranous, a veteran stage actor, or Charles Kent, they were mass produced in a row of rooftop stalls, or in glass-roofed indoor studios in Flatbush. Sometimes the company went out on location in New York City's Central and Prospect Parks, or, in one instance on the beach at Bay Shore, Long Island, for Viola's emergence from the sea.[31] By all accounts there was a wonderful, almost amateurish atmosphere. Scenery and costumes were likely to have been borrowed from Broadway or slapped together by a makeshift crew, including the actors, who weren't yet high-paid superstars.[32] They also moonlighted from theatrical jobs on Broadway, a powerful and inhibiting influence on the new art that weakened when the studios moved west to Hollywood.

The Shakespeare and other "high art" films demanded a story-telling grammar that went far beyond the filmic strategies of the earlier "actualities." Film scholars disagree over which film to credit as the "first" to tell a story but Edwin S. Porter's *The Great Train Robbery* (1903) is generally held up as a milestone event,[33] along with D. W. Griffith's subsequent *The Lonedale Operator* (1911) that carried editing to new heights. Porter's railway thriller may not have been the first to do everything but it pointed the way to a rhetoric that would eventually include all the tricks of the trade, such as shifting camera angles, editing in the cutting room, dramatic lighting, full shots, close-ups, intercutting of sequences, slow motion, rhythm in editing, and so forth.

Like the other Vitagraph Shakespeare films, Blackton's *Romeo and Juliet* (1908), starring Florence Lawrence and Paul Panzer, went beyond the primitive "actualities" by using the camera not just as a recorder of but as a participant in the cinematic story telling. The struggle of these early movies was to break out of the prison house of the proscenium stage on nearby Broadway and make a film that did not look as if it had been photographed with a camera nailed to the floor in the sixth-row orchestra. The camera needed to be released to close in on the action. The two principals, Lawrence and Panzer, later became big stars, Lawrence as a D. W. Griffith favorite, and then as the famed "Biograph Girl" and "IMP girl," the first beneficiary of the new star system that allowed actors to cash in on their fame. After her breakthrough, by 1916 Sir Herbert Beerbohm Tree commanded $100,000 for six weeks' work, and by 1919 Mary Pickford was demanding $675,000 a year plus 50 percent of the gross.[34] Paul Panzer subsequently flourished as the villain in the Saturday-morning thriller serial, *The Perils of Pauline* (1914).

Seventeen different camera set-ups, or shots, thirteen title cards, and noticeable editing off camera make up Vitagraph's 15-minute compression of *Romeo and Juliet*. There is occasional cross-cutting, movement from indoor to outdoor settings, and a minimum of obviously fraudulent painted canvas backdrops. A long shot may interrupt the monotony of mid-shots, or actors are filmed from varied angles, but the close shot is not yet in the vocabulary. Title cards with dialogue and bridging explanations help out in the losing battle to make the aural entirely visual. The movie opens with the sonnet-prologue on a card reading "Two households, both alike in dignity, In fair Verona, where we lay our scene," and so forth. Other bridging cards offer helpful but slightly misleading comments such as "Capulet introduces his daughter, Juliet, to Paris, her future husband." For the Capulet ball and balcony scene, the laconic words "Love at First Sight" suffice, following which Romeo mimes his love for Juliet, while Tybalt's ever-widening mouth signals outrage. Another card reads "The Secret Marriage of Romeo and Juliet in Friar Laurence's Cell" just prior to a sequence showing the Friar, who resembles George Bernard Shaw, joining the couple in matrimony. The camera completely broke with theatre when the crew went out on location for the balcony scene at a house near Fort Hamilton, Brooklyn; for the duel between Romeo and Tybalt to the Boat Lake in Central Park; and for Verona's streets to Central Park's Bethesda Fountain.[35] Even without sound-recording equipment, to stay in character old-time Shakespeareans of the stature of Forbes-Robertson and Frederick Warde scrupulously spoke the lines but some of the lesser sort of actors may have been uttering gibberish.

Interiors were more likely to be thrift-shop stage sets with curtains and cardboard for doors and walls. Harsh lighting was a problem, as when Juliet emotes before drinking off the vial of potion and collapses too heavily on the bed. "Tickling commodity" intrudes in Juliet's bedroom, and elsewhere, with the Vitagraph logo, "V," inscribed over her bed. A precursor to today's FBI warnings on videocassettes against illegal copying, the logo was a relic of the rancorous patent wars that pitted the "Edison group," which included Vitagraph, against such upstarts as Carl Laemmle of the IMP group (Independent Motion Picture Company of America). The movie industry's endless law suits must have made many attorneys rich and happy.[36] A more satisfactorily realistic scene in *Romeo and Juliet* is the apothecary shop, which boasts a window apparently stocked with a skull, bat, alembic, and beakers, though they may only be good *trompes-l'oeil*. The director himself, William Ranous, played the apothecary.

The Vitagraph *Julius Caesar* (1908) shows no striking advance in film grammar over the *Romeo and Juliet*. It breaks with theatricality by moving outdoors. There is much *Aida*-like parading around of Roman soldiers in papier-mâché helmets who brandish wooden swords and carry placards reading "SPQR," but the "Forum" looks suspiciously like the steps of a Carnegie public library. Almost without exception the movie's fifteen setups are in mid-shot, without changing camera angles or using close-ups and long shots. Freed from the spatial and temporal restrictions of the stage, the camera shows events that are only reported in the play, such as the proffering of the crown to Caesar three times. The assassination of Caesar, a plausibly mimed Antony's funeral oration, and an out-of-doors funeral pyre for Brutus create familiar tableaux for a mass audience. Truly cinematic in its early use of special effects is the Méliès-like materializing of Caesar's ghost from thin air in Brutus' tent before Philippi. The battle field at Philippi is something of a disappointment, a flat arid landscape, boring even as the site of carnage. Brutus and Cassius stomp around followed by tiny detachments of soldiers. Costuming is rudimentary. When Brutus' Portia pledges fidelity to her husband, she is only vaguely Roman, being swathed in the yards of material thought chic for ladies traveling first class on liners like the *Titanic*. This cover-up was necessary because a "reverend gentleman" actually objected to costumes showing the men's legs. Ball also quotes a story of actors' bare legs being disastrously painted to avoid the expense of tights.[37]

Julius Caesar failed to impress Mr. W. Stephen Bush, America's earliest critic of filmed Shakespeare, who often waxed ecstatic over other Vitagraph movies. Bush, a frequent correspondent for *Moving Picture World* and its British counterpart, *Bioscope*,[38] regularly advertised his services as a lecturer to supplement "high art" films,[39] and in that way, like the pianists, he compensated for a film's unbearable silence. He uncharitably noted that the funeral pyre at the end of *Julius Caesar* "had a fatal resemblance to a Rhode Island clambake"; neither did he miss out on the opportunity to plug his own profession by pointing out that these plays on screen "are [little] more than a bewildering mass of moving figures to the majority of the patrons of electric theatres, but none stands more emphatically in need of a good lecture than *Julius Caesar*."[40]

The seeds of filmic greatness lie deeply buried in the Vitagraph *King Lear* (1909),[41] which strives for a realism that can only be achieved with enormously expensive sets. Actualities showing the Household Brigade on parade are one thing, but underfunded actualities of a Shakespearean play only succeed in becoming non-actualities. The movie begins innovatively by identifying the characters (but not the players) with their names superimposed below them. About thirteen different set-ups show events from the old king's testing of his daughters to his dying lamentations over the body of Cordelia. The parallel Gloucester plot and the scandalous love triangle among Goneril, Regan, and Edmund collapse under the weight of compression and would require W. Stephen Bush's lecturing service to sort out the story line for the bewildered audience. Exterior shots are non-existent. The white cliffs of Dover are painted on canvas and the storm scenes take place inside a studio with a fake hollowed-out tree for mad Tom to hide in. To spare the audience, and appease the enemies of nickelodeons, when Cornwall gouges out the old man's eyes, "Lest it see more, prevent it. Out vild jelly!" (3.7.83), Gloucester's back is to the camera. In the foreground, the indignant servant stabs the wicked Cornwall, and in a magical flash of pure film, Oswald breaks loose from an irate Kent, runs directly toward the camera, and with a wild look on his face almost invades the audience's space.

The festive *Midsummer Night's Dream* (1909) and *Twelfth Night* (1910) forced Vitagraph's director Charles Kent out of the studio and into the parks with happy results. Not only is the lighting cheerful but also then and future famous actors like Maurice Costello as Lysander and his two little daughters, Dolores and Helene, project high spirits, immensely enjoying themselves. Like all the Vitagraph one-reelers, *Midsummer Night's Dream* moves at the pace of a fast-forwarded videocassette, or as if the Reduced Shakespeare Company had made a movie for Vitagraph, an outcome that sometimes happens when a silent film is projected at the wrong speed. Notwithstanding technical glitches, certain scenes capture the spirit of the play. William V. Ranous, about whom little seems to be known except that he was a journeyman actor, makes a hilarious Bottom as he mimes the weaver's blustering attempts to show how he can roar or play any role in the Pyramus/Thisby skit better than anyone else. The antics of Puck and the emplacement of an ass's head on Bottom are made to order for tricky visuals. There's quite a charming scene by a pond as Puck (Gladys Hulette) is suddenly lifted up into the air to search for the magic flower. An unaccountable switch in casting occurs when a young woman called Penelope replaces Oberon. It's Penelope, not Oberon, that Titania quarrels with and Penelope who sends Puck out to look for the potion. Perhaps the director feared that the pedophile subtext about the Indian boy might upset the censorious classes.

The same story gets told twice, once in pictures when the rude mechanicals come to the forest and again with explanatory cards: "The tradesmen come to the forest to rehearse their play. Puck changes the weaver into an ass. Titania awakens and falls in love with him." Later, at the peak of the silent era, F. W. Murnau's famous *The Last Laugh* (1924) eschewed title cards in favor of telling the story only in pictures, a virtuoso feat wildly acclaimed by purists. A *Moving Picture World* reviewer congratulated Vitagraph on its success with

Midsummer Night's Dream: "We wondered . . . who amongst the American film-makers would be the first to strike into the rich preserve of material which Shakespeare offers the producer." He praised the Vitagraph director for his skill in compressing the scenes into "a continuous and intelligible story which does not destroy the narrative."[42]

Vitagraph's *Twelfth Night* (1910) showed increasing cinematic sophistication. Florence Turner, "The Vitagraph Girl," plays a saucy little Viola who, as the first explanatory card tells us, is "separated from her twin brother Sebastian by a shipwreck [and] finds herself in the realm of Duke Orsino." Cross-dressed as Cesario, Turner contrasts nicely with Julia Swayne Gordon's Olivia, who is muffled under the layers of garments that turned Victorian actresses into Volumnia lookalikes. Something close to a deep-focus shot occurs when in Olivia's mansion, courtiers retreat and exit in the background even as in the foreground Viola woos Olivia: "Make me a willow cabin at your gate, / And call upon my soul within the house" (1.5.268). Charles Kent's miming of Malvolio's pomposity when he intercepts the forged letter captures the essence of the dialogue. The audience sees the letter in close-up on a title card: "be not afraid of greatness. Some are [born] great, some [achieve] greatness, and some have greatness thrust upon 'em" (2.5.144). Then as the gulled Malvolio in close mid-shot devours the contents of the letter, the conspirators, Maria, Sir Toby and Aguecheek, gleefully hop and skip. The closing sequence accelerates as the twins are reunited, Maria confesses, the duke discovers Cesario is a girl, and Olivia finds solace in the arms of Sebastian. There is a moment allowed for Charles Kent as the abused and rejected Malvolio to vent his spleen on his tormentors. Decades later, Nigel Hawthorne as Malvolio would have a greater opportunity to wring the full poignancy out of Malvolio's downfall in Trevor Nunn's full-length film of *Twelfth Night* (1996).

Disputes about the nature of the audience for these Vitagraph Shakespeare films ironically recapitulate the many studies of the audience at Shakespeare's Globe playhouse. Lower class? Upper class? Both? There is no simple answer. More in the audience hailed from the huddled masses rather than the coddled classes, but the "class" of the audience tended to correlate with the style of neighborhood that the "nick" was situated in. It should not be forgotten, however, that even the most wretched of the earth had heard of and respected Shakespeare. From Mark Twain's rednecks in *Huckleberry Finn*, residents of sad, little towns along the Mississippi, to the eastern European immigrant Jews in New York City who revered the Shakespeare of Yiddish theatre, Shakespeare possessed enormous cultural capital. For America's nouveau riche, there was no more prestigious cultural trophy than a leather-bound complete Shakespeare for display in the parlor, even if the pages were uncut. The people who paid their nickels to see Shakespeare on screen were schoolboys who giggled at the overacting in *Julius Caesar*, outside salesmen resting between their appointed rounds, persons who simply delighted to see something more enlightening than the morning drill of the king's household guards in London, and totally perplexed and confused immigrants glad to be in out of the cold. When a law suit over an unauthorized movie of General Lew Wallace's *Ben Hur* struck fear into the movie industry, Shakespeare's status as public domain intellectual property made him all the more attractive.[43]

Film critic W. Stephen Bush saw through bourgeois pretensions and found hope in the nickelodeons. Bush attacked the "fashion in certain quarters to look upon the electric theatre as chiefly the poor man's amusement."[44] A high-minded foe of elitism, he rhapsodized that the poor woman's nickel at the movie was the equal of the rich woman's gold at the opera, and predicted that one day the carriage trade would be drawn to movies. He was also sensitive to the difficulties involved in "condensation and arrangement" but believed that the Vitagraph films were probably as "good as any that could have been made." Like many after him, he warned that "to condense or in any way to alter Shakespeare is as delicate and dangerous a task as meddling with an overture by Mozart or a painting by Rembrandt."[45] Still, he believed that "there is no play of Shakespeare that cannot be told in moving images," and that "the notion that Shakespeare, as the half-educated put it, is 'too deep' is altogether wrong."[46]

Bush's professional stake in explanatory lectures and recitations at silent Shakespeare movies may have fueled his zeal for the new art. As we have seen, he firmly believed that the solution to the oxymoron of Shakespeare on silent film was to flesh out the title cards with an "epilogue" in a kind of lecture/performance. That way the "best class of people" would flock to the Shakespeare movies, the "banal, the vulgar and the foolish"[47] would stay away, and high culture would be served. Unfortunately a lecturer like Bush was an extra expense and it's not at all clear how many 5-cent theatres bought his lofty services. As for Vitagraph studios, its "high art" Shakespeare films survive today only in archives, more often than not the targets for brainless laughter, though they should be respected not so much for what they did as for doing anything at all. The Vitagraph empire eventually was swallowed up by Warner Brothers, which purchased it in 1924 for $735,000.[48]

From nickelodeon to palace

While Vitagraph cranked out its one-reelers in New York, cinéastes in England, France, and Italy made Shakespeare films until World War I dictated a read-justment in priorities. After the war, the Germany of the Weimar Republic produced ambitious movies of *Hamlet, Othello*, and *The Merchant of Venice*. The movies increasingly expanded in length from one to three and four reels to fit the needs of the emerging "Palace" theatres that were steadily replacing the tacky nickelodeons, penny gaffs, and fair grounds as exhibition sites.[49] The movement from nickelodeon to palace resembled the shift from the "public" Globe to the "private" Blackfriars playhouse in Shakespeare's London, though the new movie palaces unlike the Blackfriars, attracted both the classes and the masses. S. R. Rothafel's ("Roxy") opening in 1916 of the Regent movie theatre in New York City at the corner of 116th Street and 7th Avenue signaled an emerging era in New York,[50] and Rothafel in 1927 followed up with his famous $10-million Roxy Theatre, "a cathedral of the motion picture" near Times Square. Among its wonders were "foyers and lobbies of incomparable size and splendor" as well as "a staff of attendants [ushers] thoroughly organized and drilled under the direction of a retired Colonel of the U.S. Marines."[51] Roxy's ostentatious theatres, temples of dreams, enshrined megalomania, monuments of bad taste, were part of an international movement. By 1914 Paris boasted a Pathé Palace (600 seats), and Gaumont-Palace (6,000 seats) with an 80-piece orchestra pit.[52] In England, the Balham Empire had already opened in 1907, and was unique in being "a theatre devoted entirely to the display of living pictures."[53] The grand opening of the Palace Electric in Mansfield, England, sent Alderman Alcock into raptures as he congratulated all involved for having produced such a fine building, with its "marble-floored vestibule . . . brass-mounted beveled glass entrance and electric blue seats."[54] In Croydon, another palace opened with "a beautiful vestibule, carpets, hangings, etc."[55] With theatre names like Odeon, Bijou, Jewel, Picturedrome, Electroscope, movies were clearly acquiring the "classy" cachet the movie people were dying for. As Dennis Sharp has pointed out, the new theatres often functioned "like Roman Catholic churches," resembling "a bulging whale on the outside and a stomach full of whipped cream on the inside," for the function of church and theatre building alike is to keep the faithful focused on the holy mysteries within, not the superstructure without.[56]

A two-reel, 33-minute *Shylock* (1913), one of the last of the Film d'Art attempts to record classical French theatre, might have been suitable for Paris' grand new Gaumont Palace. Directed by Henri Desfontaines, the Globe Film Company trade journal advertisement declared that it "would be impossible to exaggerate the splendour and attractiveness of this beautiful and compelling picture story adapted from Shakespeare's immortal work, 'The Merchant of Venice.'"[57] The distinguished cast included Harry Baur (Shylock) of the Athénée Theatre, Romuald Joubé (Antonio) of the Odeon, and Mlle. Pépa Bonafé (Portia) of the Apollo – all from leading Paris theatres. Harry Baur first appears on screen in a formal cutaway, as if he, like W. Stephen Bush, would lecture on Shakespeare's play, with Jean Hervé (Bassanio) and Mlle. Pépa Bonafé in Elizabethan dress. Title cards confide that this is "Venice on the Rialto" and that in Belmont nearby there is "a lady richly left . . . her name is Portia." The establishing shot of the Rialto with its pathetic cardboard backdrop disappointed a contemporary critic, who noted that "the film producer by not making the greatest possible use of natural outdoors effects, deprives himself of one of the greatest advantages that he possesses over the regular stage."[58] A crowd scene on the Rialto, a flashback of Bassanio spitting on Shylock as he drafts the bond, and crosscutting to compress the space between Portia's carefree Belmont and Shylock's careworn Venice reveal a shift from theatricality toward narrative film making. Title cards bridge the episodes as with an announcement about the loss of Antonio's ships just before the opening of a frenetic trial scene. Harry Baur's Shylock is of the pre-Holocaust vintage, an object of mirth and scorn rather than a victim of bigotry. Ironically the Jewish Harry Baur would himself a few years later fall victim to Adolf Hitler's pathological antiSemitism. In the courtroom, he menacingly whets his knife, and then a minisecond later he is being pursued by a hooting, jeering mob. The deeper point that Belmont, like the golden casket, remains only superficially attractive and that Shylock, like the leaden casket, yet conceals stern virtues, remains unexplored.

To the south, during this pre-war period, the Neapolitan flair for grand opera infiltrated Italian Shakespeare movies, which also in the Film d'Arte Italiana mode displayed the same anxiety as the French to please only the elitist cadres from the theatrical world. While partial toward the Roman history plays, the Italians also drew on *Hamlet, King Lear, Merchant of Venice, Midsummer Night's Dream, Othello, Romeo and Juliet, Taming of the Shrew*, and *Winter's Tale*.[59] A Film d'Arte Italiana *King Lear* (1910) followed the French model of Film d'Art by putting famous actors and great plays into movies. Directed by Gerolamo Lo Savio, the celebrated tragedian Ermete Novelli played the title role with Francesca Bertini as Cordelia. An 11-minute one-reeler, *King Lear* omits the Gloucester plot and focuses on the king, his three daughters and faithful Kent. Even with the Gloucester plot eliminated, the story line still requires heavy use of title cards for coherence. Having the wind actually ruffle the actors' hair and garments shows another step in the movement away from theatricality toward realism.

Francesca Bertini (Portia) and Ermete Novelli (Shylock) appear again in Lo Savio's color-tinted *Il Mercante di Venezia* (1910). The very first title card by proclaiming that "Lorenzo who is in love with Jessica, the daughter of Shylock the Jew, arranges to come for her" privileges Jessica's rebellion against Shylock over the bond, ring, and casket plots. Novelli's interpretation of Shylock as a man primarily distraught over his wayward daughter turns the Jew into a King Lear figure: "How sharper than a serpent's tooth it is / To have a thankless child!" (*Lear* 1.4.288). The ingrate Jessica's betrayal exacerbates Shylock's anguish over the loss of Leah, the wife whose "turkis" ring he would not have sold "for a wilderness of monkeys" (3.1.122). An inter-title announces that "Antonio's ships have been wrecked, and he is ruined . . . He is taken before a court of justice," after which in a familiar stage tradition Shylock whets his knife. A title card prints out Portia's reading to Shylock of the law that plainly outlines the penalties for shedding Christian blood. Sadly as Shylock bitterly laments his predicament, the surviving print (from the NFTVA) abruptly ends.

Lo Savio's 25-minute *Romeo and Juliet* (1911) gave the lovely Francesca Bertini, who by 1915 became one of Italy's greatest stars, a chance to display her talents as a silent film actress with Gustavo Serena as her Romeo. Like Lillian Gish, Bertini could convey almost any mood with only a slight change in expression, showing radiance when with her Romeo, and sullenness when told by Father Capulet to marry Paris. Lo Savio's editing included deletions, transpositions, and additions to adapt the play script to the needs of an audience unfamiliar with the play, and to make the verbal visual. In place of the opening brawl, which comes after the Capulet ball, a mounted Romeo dismounts to retrieve Juliet's glove, which Romeo will later rhapsodize over ("O that I were a glove upon that hand, / That I might touch that cheek!" – 2.2.24). The Italian love for operatic spectacle, which survives in Zeffirelli's Shakespeare movies, brightens the *mise-en-scène* for the Capulet garden, which is filled with statuary, handy for concealing eavesdroppers like the Nurse. The ballroom gleams with shimmering candelabra, a vaulted ceiling and elegantly costumed dancers.

A clichéd establishing shot of William Shakespeare reading the play aloud to a circle of friends frames Baldassare Negroni's *Una Tragedia alla Corte di Sicilia* (1913). With its lavish costumes, realistic settings, and relatively sophisticated editing, a movie that begins in bondage to the library escapes into a filmic world. In rewriting for the screen, Negroni keeps major sections of the play intact but combines them with traces from Shakespeare's own source, Robert Greene's *Pandosto, The Triumph of Time*. The Italian flair for the spectacle of grand opera and the nineteenth-century taste for extravagant stagings of *The Winter's Tale*, like the revivals of Mary Anderson (1887) and Beerbohm Tree (1906), are reflected in the opulence of the banquet at Leontes' palace, as well as with the crowds of extras for the trial of Hermione. The fluid camera work embraces a variety of shots from mid to long, and then some tight framing to show Leontes' inner torment over Hermione's friendliness with Polixenes. If there were sound he would be muttering, "Too hot, too hot! / To mingle friendship far is mingling bloods" (1.2.108). The ostensive acting style of silents, carried over from theatre, allows the sharptongued Paulina, whose nagging tongue almost comes alive even in the silence of the screen, to plead eloquently for her mistress, until interrupted by the arrival of the oracles. A title card relays the news that "The two messengers return with the oracle," and we are told that the queen remains distraught. Paulina administers a sleeping potion to Hermione, tells Leontes that the queen is dead, and excoriates him again for his cruelty. Antigonus arriving with little Perdita at Bohemia, for inexplicable reasons is not pursued and eaten by a bear (thus throwing away Shakespeare's most memorable stage direction, *Exit pursued by a bear* – 3.3.58). He is instead captured by thieves and thrown alive into a volcano crater, reminiscent of Vesuvius or Etna. The statue scene goes in a whole new direction when Paulina displays a supine Hermione, who shows no signs of awakening, not even a twinge, despite the title card's contrary "the wakening of Hermione." The film ends with a return to the framing device of Shakespeare and his friends, who like the Hermione of his play have been miraculously revived.

Another Italian film, Paulo Azzuri's *Midsummer Night's Dream* (1913), shows a film rhetoric so highly developed that some historians have challenged the accuracy of its release date. The iris-outs, the dissolves, the cross-cutting, the story-telling powers, clearly go far beyond the Vitagraph *Midsummer Night's Dream* (1909). While starring Socrate Tommasi (Lysander), and Bianca Hübner (Helena), an adorable Puck's flagrant scene-stealing validates the proverbial warning against acting with dogs or children. Chiaroscuro lighting makes the wood at night intensely plausible, and the excessive use of inter-titles notwithstanding, this unpretentious movie leaves the audience as cheerful as the fairies happily skipping down the road in the closing fade. The day of Jan Kott and the dark wood had not yet arrived.

The scope and grandeur of Shakespeare's Roman plays make fine scenarios for lush Italian epics like Enrico Guazzoni's *Quo Vadis* (1912), and Giovanni Pastrone's *Cabiria* (1914), which paved the way for D. W. Griffith's colossal *Intolerance* (1916),[60] and ultimately the Cecil B. De Mille Hollywood extravaganza "with a cast of thousands in living Technicolor." Enrico Guazzoni's eight-minute *Brutus* (1910) drew on Shakespeare's sources in Plutarch but without much reference to the way that Shakespeare imagined them. More realistic than the Vitagraph *Julius Caesar*, it shows a triumphal march through Rome with hundreds of gawking and cheering extras, double exposures of the dream "recounted" to Calphurnia, Calphurnia begging Caesar not to go to the senate, and Caesar's ghost appearing magically in Brutus' tent at Philippi. After his triumph with *Quo Vadis*, Guazzoni's ambitious multi-reel Cines *Marcantonio e Cleopatra (1913)*[61] and *Giulio Cesare* (1914) inevitably privileged spectacle over Shakespeare and showcased leading Italian actors Gianna Terribili-Gonzales and Amleto Novelli as Cleopatra and Caesar. Marching Roman legions, unruly mobs, sea fights, catapults, and arrows provide the spectacle of a real movie in contrast with the British Will Barker *Julius Caesar* (1911) that uneventfully recorded a stage production at the Stratford Memorial Theatre. Vestiges of Shakespeare's play survive in *Giulo Cesare* in the plot against Caesar with title cards proclaiming "Beware O Caesar of the Ides of March," "And thou too, Brutus," and "Friends, Romans, countrymen." Guazzoni's energies did not go unappreciated. Eight years later in 1922, the film was brought to New York for a showing at Bim's Standard Theatre in "revised and re-edited" form, possibly with spliced-in clips of mob scenes from the very similar *Marcantonio e Cleopatra*. One critic thought it of "relatively ancient manufacture" with "its harsh, ungraded lighting... episodic rather than continuous story and its dependence upon mass as opposed to individual action." The audience of teenagers "accorded Antony [*sic*] Novelli (as Caesar) the same honor they customarily give to Tom Mix, Harry Carey and William S. Hart."[62]

In England, just before the outbreak of the war, at London's New Gallery Kinema in Regent St., Gaumont premiered an important feature-length *Hamlet* (1913) in E. Hay Plumb's film produced by Cecil Hepworth using the Drury Lane stage company. This most complete (59-minute) film of *Hamlet* yet then made allows a glimpse into late Victorian theatrical codes as interpreted by an actor many considered the greatest Hamlet of the century, Sir Johnston Forbes-Robertson. With the help of supporting players like Gertrude Elliott (Ophelia), Percy Rhodes (Ghost), and Robert Atkins (First Player), Forbes-Robertson, though at sixty in one sense hopelessly miscast, with his cadaverous and melancholy face nevertheless embodied the establishment's image of a lofty and unendurably sensitive Hamlet, an English variation on a Jules Laforgue's Franco-romantic idea of "Hamletism." Modern audiences, sated on post-Freudian readings, will find such restraint as Hamlet *not* putting his head on Ophelia's lap at the play scene refreshing. Just as if he were at Drury Lane, Sir Johnston actually recites his lines while on camera. At the same time, there is an unmistakable escalation in cinematic adeptness, Hepworth having insisted on translating "the words of the play into action in the film"[63] as shown with the exterior shots at Lulworth Cove in Dorset, with the Méliès-like dissolve in the Ghost scene, and with the intercutting between Ophelia walking by a stream and of Claudius and Laertes conspiring to poison Hamlet.[64] Hepworth and Plumb's attention to cinema art challenges the dogma that London's West End theatre always suffocated the British film industry's initiative.

With war clouds gathering over Europe, four feature-length Shakespeare movies appeared in the United States between 1912 and 1916 ("feature" being defined as a film lasting at least 40 minutes). M. B. Dudley's "lost" five-reel *Richard III* (1912) besides being one of America's earliest feature-length movies also went beyond merely recording Shakespeare's play and moved toward

2   The versatile Frederick B. Warde, the Yorkist duke of Gloucester in M. B.
Dudley's recently discovered *The Life and Death of King Richard III* (USA 1912),
exults over the demise of his victim, King Henry VI of the House of Lancaster.

an independent cinematic art. In 1996, it miraculously surfaced in the Oregon
basement of William Buffum, a former projectionist and amateur collector,
who had carefully preserved the highly flammable and wickedly unstable
old-fashioned nitrate print. The title role of the malevolent Richard duke of
Gloucester belonged to an itinerant British-born actor, Frederick B. Warde
(1851–1935), whose stage career took him into every backwater in America,
as well as to the major cities, where he played an amazing variety of characters, everything from Brutus to Hamlet to King Lear.[65] Directed in part at least
by James Keane, the 61-year-old Warde eagerly adapted to the new medium,
speaking of what "a great thing moving pictures had become," and how the

French Film d'Art had embraced "the services of real artists."[66] As a practical man of the theatre, Warde, a regular on the prestigious North American Chautauqua Assembly lecture circuit and the recipient of an honorary doctorate of letters from the University of Southern California, discovered that he could tour with a film more economically than with an entire acting company, especially if he single-handedly furnished the commentary and the recitations during the reel changes, as advocated by the industrious W. Stephen Bush. Like a Japanese *benshi*, he could explain to his fans what they had already seen to make the silent movie's inscrutability scrutable.

Despite Warde's stage background, the filmed *Richard III* is not a stagy movie, unlike F. R. Benson's contemporaneous British *Richard III* (1911) whose firm attachment to the Stratford Memorial Theatre moved film historian Rachel Low to pronounce anathema on it as typical of "pre-1914 stage adaptations at their worst."[67] Playing the prototypical medieval vice figure and serio-comical villain, Richard duke of Gloucester, Warde's homicidal antics prefigured Hollywood's enormously popular gangster film genre of the 1930s. Marching armies and mounted knights, and bevies of lavishly dressed ladies-in-waiting fill the *mise-en-scène* in various locales of Westchester, New York. A real two-masted warship arrives at "Milford-Haven" (actually City Island on Long Island Sound) with the rebellious Lancastrian forces of Henry earl of Richmond, the future King Henry VII. James Keane, who is thought to have composed the screenplay, was caught up in a whirl of adding, deleting, and switching seventy-seven separate scenes around to make the play into a movie. He followed in the Colley Cibber stage tradition going back to at least 1700 by opening with Richard's vicious murders in *King Henry VI, Part Three* of the Lancastrian Prince Edward and King Henry VI to whip the audience into a froth of indignation over the abominations of Richard, this "bottled spider," this "boar," this "toad." There are scenes added: Edward signing the death warrant for Clarence, Richard wooing Princess Elizabeth, and Richard's hapless Anne drinking poison. Characters are deleted: the acid-tongued Queen Margaret, "she-wolf of France," and the Woodville faction of Rivers, Dorset, and Grey. Events are transposed to explain the strange death of Clarence in the Tower. Visual metonymy translates Shakespeare's words into sharp visual equivalents, as when Machiavellian Richard, following Colley Cibber's famed Drury Lane alterations. ("See how my sword weeps for the poor king's death"), wipes the blood off his sword after the assassination of King Henry, or thrusts his ring at the helpless Lady Anne in the first wooing scene, or fawns before the two little princes. These illusions then turn back into reality as the film ends by showing Frederick Warde himself, now in the mufti of a tweed jacket, as he appeared long ago live in the theatre, bowing and smiling graciously to his adoring fans. The film falls short of the contemporary Italian epics like

Guazzoni's *Quo Vadis* but compares favorably with the techniques of most American movies of the period.

In a Warde Shakespeare movie, the page and stage always hover in the background. The opening of Edwin Thanhouser's ambitious art film of *King Lear* (1916) looks back nostalgically to the library. Again the star is Frederick B. Warde, this time with cigar smoke curling around him, and perusing a volume of Shakespeare. Suddenly he dissolves from a Victorian gentleman actor/scholar, the "Irving of America," into a hirsute King Lear. Page, stage and screen, the triad of Shakespearean incarnations, have momentarily interfaced, but book and stage must literally be dissolved to make way for the movie. As a special effect, the dissolve seems tame by comparison with today's John Woo, Hong Kong exploding action movies but for Edwardian audiences it may have stirred up a sense of "wonder" like that which Jacobean audiences at the Whitehall court masques felt after the sudden and abrupt disclosure of masked figures in grottos and caves.

Ernest Warde, the director and Frederick's son as well as the Fool in the movie, employs a film rhetoric of long and close shots, as well as sporadic close-ups. Nevertheless a 30-second framing card outlines the plot, and more title cards list names with images of the leading actors, as, for example, "Goneril, eldest daughter of King (Ina Hammer)," and "Her husband duke of Albany (Wayne Arey)." A contemptuous Goneril and Regan with headbands around their brunette hair and glowering expressions embody pure malignancy, while Cordelia (Lorraine Huling) in white radiates schoolgirl innocence. In mid-shot the entire assemblage, some ten persons in the crowded *mise-en-scène*, cluster around the royal throne for the division of the kingdom. Additional intercut title cards thread the narrative together with comments such as "Which of you doth love us most?" though cards do not always literally reflect the Shakespearean text, as when Kent says "Check this hideous rashness, O king, thy youngest daughter does not love thee least." Warde energetically exploits the ostensive acting techniques of the nineteenth-century stage with semaphore-like arm waving, much stalking about, considerable writhing, shaking of the head, finger wagging, and grimacing at the camera. Perhaps as Robert Ball has said, so much has been crammed into the movie, that the directors only succeeded in confusing matters.[68] On the other hand, the visual story-telling devices of a silent movie manage this archetypal conflict between father and daughters fairly well. Extraordinary horn wine goblets convey the primitive life style at the court, and a great battle scene shot somewhere in New Rochelle, New York, contains almost as much cavalry as D. W. Griffith's *The Birth of a Nation* (1915). Given the heavy, immobile cameras, the results are impressive as dozens of extras in costume armor carry out a cavalry charge while foot soldiers murder one another with wicked-looking swords, or throw rocks at the helpless wounded. Reaction shots record Regan and Goneril's gloating over this dreadful carnage while an angelic Cordelia recoils in horror. The very end of the movie, whether through accident or design, leaves an indelible memory of the heartbroken, dying king gradually sliding out of the frame, as if the world were too small to contain his massive anguish. It's a trope that is revived in Peter Brook's *King Lear* (1971), where it becomes a metaphor for post-modernist alienation.

The American Shakespeare boom continued in 1916 with two competing feature-length productions of *Romeo and Juliet*, a Metro release with matinee idol Francis X. Bushman opposite Beverly Bayne, and a Fox studio version with Theda Bara, celebrated as "The Vamp," opposite Harry Hilliard. Intended to celebrate Shakespeare's 400th birthday' except for a few surviving stills, both have been lost, but there is always the bright hope of their being rediscovered, like the 1912 *Richard III*, in some secluded archive.

Growing out of the rich decadence of the "golden age" in German film making's post-war Weimar period, Svend Gade's *Hamlet: The Drama of Vengeance* (1920), starring Danish film actress Asta Nielsen, struck a great blow in liberating the Shakespeare movie from theatrical and textual dependency and moving toward the filmic. As Dudley Andrew succinctly puts it, "during the cinema's first twenty-five years of existence, art was conceived of not as something cinematic, but as something one put into a film: famous actors, a serious drama."[69] In the Weimar phase, a paramount motif was the expressionism that derived from the anti-naturalistic stagings of Max Reinhardt,[70] who in turn had been influenced by the British director Gordon Craig. Max Reinhardt's influence on Shakespeare film had already occurred before the war with Hanns Heinz Ewers' eccentric adaptation of *A Midsummer Night's Dream* (1913),[71] and it was to continue straight through to the Hollywood career of German emigré director F. W. Murnau, whose prodigious indoor urban sets for *Sunrise* (1927) nearly bankrupted Fox studios, and most importantly to the Reinhardt/Dieterle Hollywood film of *A Midsummer Night's Dream* (1935).

Unlike her Hamlet predecessors, Bernhardt and Forbes-Robertson, Nielsen spent more of her career in film than on stage, which may account for her avoidance of an ostensive acting style, such as Emil Jannings' in a silent *Othello* (1922). Even though she was the greatest screen actress of Europe, celebrated for her Hedda Gabler and Miss Julie, and often compared with Greta Garbo, with whom she actually appeared, along with Marlene Dietrich, in *The Street of Sorrow* (*Die Freudlose Gasse*) (1925), her sex made her Hamlet's claim to reputability shaky. Unlike Bernhardt, however, she played Hamlet as a hybrid somewhere between a *travesti* and a "breeches" part; a *travesti* in the Comédie Française mold totally conceals his/her gender in usurping the guise of the opposite sex, while the English "breeches" part like Viola or

Rosalind integrates cross-dressing directly into the role. Later, Judith Anderson (1970), Diane Venora (1982), Marnie Penning (1998) and others, out of "Hamlet-envy," have challenged the monopoly of male actors on the greatest role in theatre. They could legitimately ask if Shakespeare's Hamlet does not have a "feminine" sensibility that can best be captured by a woman.[72] Moreover as Bernhardt argued, "A boy of twenty cannot understand the philosophy of *Hamlet* . . . without understanding there is no delineation of character. . . . the woman more readily looks the part, yet has the maturity of mind to grasp it."[73] As Lawrence Danson has said, however, "a critic who seriously proposes that *Hamlet* is a woman will seem either mad or, with the right theory behind him, very modern."[74] On the other hand, the nineteenth-century concept of "Hamletism" allowed for a considerable streak of femininity in the character of the prince. Hostile to the *travesti* code, Edward Weitzel thought it was "a sacrilege to couple it [the movie] with the name of Shakespeare,"[75] which did not deter *The New York Times* from listing it as one of the "Ten Best Films of the Year," along with *The Cabinet of Dr. Caligari*.

Even more than the Warde *Richard III* and *King Lear*, Nielsen's *Hamlet* draws for its artistry as much on filmic as on literary models. Its record number of iris fades encircling Asta Nielsen's ethereal face alone would qualify it as the ultimate "Iris-out *Hamlet*," though it also abounds in other cinematic tropes after the style of the D. W. Griffith silents. Principally, it becomes unabashedly cinematic in its spatializing of the text through allowing the camera freedom to record not only the text but the subtext, paratext, prototext, crypto-text, and meta-text of Quarto, Folio, and even narrative legends from Saxo Grammaticus. Being silent, what it lacks in sound it does not make up for in sense, but in its surreal redeployment of the *Hamlet* story. Its scenario mines, however, an obscure 1881 monograph by "Dr. Edward P. Vining (Yale-Hon. M.A.)," a reliance on fanciful scholarship matching Roman Polanski's dependency on M. F. Libby's equally recherché "Some New Notes on *Macbeth*" (1893) for his privileging of Rosse in that remarkable 1971 movie.[76] The opening title of Gade's film draws heavily on Vining's theory in notifying the audience that

> This screen version of *Hamlet* is based upon the ancient legends from which Shakespeare drew his first conception for his immortal tragedy . . . It also reveals the contention of the eminent American Shakespearian scholar, Dr. Edward P. Vining . . . that Hamlet was a woman, who for reasons of state, was compelled to assume the guise of a man.

For "reasons of state" the daughter born to Gertrude while the king is absent fighting the war against Norway must be raised as a boy to protect the queen from the wrath of the people. She lied to them about the infant's sex because she mistakenly assumed her husband had been killed in battle. A title card amplifies: "The Nurse's crafty scheme. 'Tell the people it is a son. You can save the crown and still be queen'." An iris fade as the queen exults. When the king unexpectedly returns home alive, he will not admit to the people that their queen has fibbed and so the deception continues. From this white lie a whole array of flaccid watches and curious juxtapositions emerges that in a bizarre way represents Prince Hamlet more effectively than *Hamlet* itself. It is *Hamlet* in a bad dream, a step away from a Dada-suffused Buñuel film. The worst and best kind of the character criticism so roundly excoriated after Bradley also surfaces in the shameless but fascinating exploration of Hamlet's student days at Wittenberg, where he/she falls in love with Horatio to set up a titillating homoerotic agenda. The cross-dressed prince embodies all the ambiguity in the play's leitmotif of the interplay between illusion and reality ("Seems, madam? nay, it is, I know not 'seems'." (1.2.76)), and a Hamlet who is inwardly "female" and outwardly "male" plays a variation on the play's obsession with delay, hesitations, and indecisiveness.

Not the least of the perversities is the anxiety brought on at Wittenberg University when Hamlet feels a strong tug of attraction to fellow student, Horatio, in what looks like an exhumation and legitimization of latent homosexuality. When Horatio then disastrously falls in love with Ophelia, Hamlet has even better reasons for putting on an "antic disposition." Using source material from Saxo Grammaticus, when Hamlet returns alone to Elsinore to discover Ophelia's death, he witnesses first-hand a drunken orgy presided over by Claudius, locks the doors, and sets the house afire. Gertrude is left widowed to preside alone at the duel scene and to drink from the poisoned cup. At the close when Hamlet lies dying in Horatio's arms, Horatio in groping to locate his friend's chest wound makes a startling discovery, which had hitherto gone unnoticed. He brushes against Hamlet's bosom and a look of wonder comes over his face. Then in what Danson wittily calls "the greatest scene of *anagnorisis* Shakespeare never wrote,"[77] he cries out (on the title card) "Death reveals thy tragic secret. Now I understand what bound me to that matchless form." It is the measure of the film's artistry that for many viewers the line comes across as more poignant than hilarious.

The movie's split vision of a human being divided between an inner female and outer male persona, the *Doppelgänger* effect as it has been called,[78] which is heavily exploited also in the Celestino Coronado film society *Hamlet* (1976), finds support in Gade's array of expressionistic devices – lengthy hallways and corridors, vast assembly rooms, steep flights of stairs, sloping surfaces, chiaroscuro effects of contrasting light and shadows, energetic camera work, a brooding film noir type atmosphere, and ostensive acting styles taken from the stage. After Fortinbras' final entry, much footage is given over to a solemn procession with Hamlet's body borne aloft down the vast hall, past rows of

3   The internationally celebrated silent movie star,
Asta Nielsen, as a cross-dressed prince in Svend
Gade's imaginative *Hamlet: The Drama of Vengeance*
(1920).

standing soldiers, and out into a thoroughfare, which, though arguably overdone, in its generous spatializing reveals new potentials for elegizing *Hamlet*.
John Milton's *Lycidas* comes to mind.

Current interest in "queer theory," with its resistance to dogmatic catego-
rizations of gender and sex, has brought the movie into the spotlight again as
the homoerotic flavor of a feminized *Hamlet* carries Goethe's idea of Hamlet as
an unbearably sensitive hero to its ultimate polarity. Textual scholars like Ann
Thompson have recently delved into Vining's theory that the three texts for
Hamlet show a gradual evolution from Hamlet's "pangs of despised love" to
"dispriz'd love," the latter suggesting the kind of love that has no name. Vining
further goes on to characterize Hamlet's apparent love for men and contempt
for women as "inverted," which could be taken as code for homosexuality.
It is a clever and enticing argument that requires more consideration than I
have room for here, but Thompson's interest in the film,[79] as well as that of
J. Lawrence Guntner, Lawrence Danson and others, suggests how after nearly
eighty years the movie has renewed the idea of Hamlet in an entirely fresh context. Whether *travesti*, "breeches," or simply cross-dressed, this bizarre *Hamlet*
moves directly to the play's concern with revenge, with delay, with metaphysical probing, with deep-seated mysteries of the mind and heart. It did not hurt
either that Asta Nielsen was a marvelous actress, who "does not just pose before

the camera, nor does she rant and tear around violently . . . Her mouth . . . is an organ to express the thoughts and feelings of the woman within."[80] Gade's movie may not have been *Hamlet* but in many ways it not only deconstructed Goethe's Hamlet but also in re-imagining the *Hamlet* text foreshadowed new paradigms for the Shakespeare movie. This paradoxical bondage to and liberation from nineteenth-century "Hamletism," as well as the Quarto and Folio texts, paved the way for more probing treatments in the *Hamlet* films of Wirth, Lyth, Kline, Richardson, Zeffirelli, Kozintsev, and Branagh. Above all else, the movie casts a spell ensnaring the viewer in its web of flickering black-and-white images.

After Nielsen's performance, the Dmitri Buchowetski *Othello* (1922) comes as an anticlimax, even though it stars the formidable Emil Jannings, winner of a 1927 Academy Award for *The Way of All Flesh*, but best known today as Professor Rath, the pathetic schoolmaster enslaved by the sultry Marlene Dietrich in Josef von Sternberg's *The Blue Angel* (1930). Its mammoth sets, exotic lighting, milling crowds, and flamboyant acting identify it with major patterns of expressionism but its streak of realism makes it too literal-minded for greatness. The more grandeur and pomposity the less believable the behavior of the three principals, Othello, Desdemona (Ika von Lenceffy), and Iago (Werner Krauss). As the Moor of Venice, Jannings seems more concerned with self-indulgently playing the role of the great actor than with locating the soul of Othello. His stage technique burdens his acting style, but as a museum display of the lost art of scenery chewing, the movie is superb, a kind of magnificent wreck. A dubbed-in organ accompaniment on the commercially available video version sonically supports the highs and lows of emotion, as Jannings mimes Othello's growing paranoia. He is goaded on by a demonic Iago, played by the famous Werner Krauss, who appeared in dozens of silent movies, the best known being his title role in the classic, *The Cabinet of Dr. Caligari* (1921). Krauss lurks behind every pillar and post of the gingerbread palace, his pasty white face and tiny moustache turning him into an allegory for Adolf Hitler. He plays Othello like a musical instrument until in the movie's benchmark scene, his crafty insinuations drive Othello to madness. The berserk Othello, his eyes popping, beats himself on the head with his fists, twists and folds Desdemona's handkerchief, and then, in the ultimate act of frustration, literally chews on it in a textbook example of the use of an inanimate "expressive object" to convey emotion.[81] If the handkerchief, as has been suggested by psychoanalytical critics, also represents the wedding sheets, then Jannings is externalizing Othello's innermost resentments.[82] Iago tenderly, affectionately cradles Othello while the Moor cries out (on title cards) "Suspicion, doubt, devil!" and then again "Proof. Proof." With the sonic punctuation provided by the organist, Jannings and Krauss bring out the strange chemistry that makes this implausible story plausible. The smothering of Desdemona is orchestrated as a terrible rite of sacrifice in which the Moor acts as a satanic Abraham sacrificing his Isaac at the behest of the devilish Iago. The valiant film ends in the city square with hundreds of extras waving their arms and screaming "O perfidy!" Never have so many extras done so much to accomplish so little, but the bravura performances of Jannings and Krauss make it worthwhile.

The following year, Werner Krauss emerged again in a loose adaptation of a Shakespeare movie playing Shylock opposite Henny Porten's Portia in *Der Kaufmann von Venedig* (1923), released in North America as *The Jew of Mestri.* As much or more in debt to Shakespeare's own source tale, *Il Pecorone,* than to the *Merchant* itself, it focuses more on the woes of Jessica (Rachela) than on Portia, the "Lady of Belmont." This refocusing underscores the shared affliction of Jessica and Portia in being the daughters of overbearing and demanding fathers. Henny Porten, a superstar until the advent of Adolf Hitler, captures Portia's grace and elegance by parading her Russian wolfhounds across the screen. Ambitious attempts at realism include location shots of Venice with analytical close-ups of feeding pigeons, city clocks, market stalls, and canals. The great hall at Belmont and the trial scene offer opportunities for complicated sets and bizarre lighting schemes in the Weimar tradition, and sophisticated intercutting between the extravagance of Belmont and the sterile world of Shylock. The trial scene features the cliché of a sadistic Shylock whetting his knife but an unusual twist has Gianetti (Antonio) fainting in fright. The Freudian ring plot remains as Portia and Nerissa wrangle their rings away from the bewildered Bassanio and Gratiano: "Sweet Portia, / If you did know to whom I gave the ring, / And how unwillingly I left the ring" (5.1.192). The horror just under the surface of *The Merchant of Venice* is summed up in Shylock's anguished expression as the movie cuts away from him and returns to the carefree young people at Belmont, who are the same rich crowd displaced in time from F. Scott Fitzgerald's *The Great Gatsby.*

Hollywood's four seasons of Shakespeare

As early as 1914 a letter writer to *Bioscope* was railing against the "arty" types who would ignore the plain fact that the business of motion pictures is business – profit, the bottom line, "tickling commodity," commodification, not art.[1] Given this Gradgrindian reality, to no one's surprise out of hundreds of Hollywood talking pictures only four have been full-scale studio feature-length treatments of a Shakespearean text, a fifth – Welles's *Macbeth* (1948) – being a special low budget "poverty row" aberration. Coincidentally, though, Hollywood fell over backwards into Northrop Frye's seasonal classifications by providing a springtime comedy (the rollicking *Taming of the Shrew*); summery idyll (a romantic *Midsummer Night's Dream*); autumnal tragedy (a reverential *Romeo and Juliet*); and wintry tragic irony (a remarkable *Julius Caesar*). For a total investment of about $6 million, the four movies' producers tested the iron law of capitalism that art cannot be divorced from entertainment if it is to survive in the free market. They also replaced the problems of making silent Shakespeare films with a new set of problems in producing sound films. Sometimes actors' voices were not nearly so attractive as their silent images, and the need to speak a specific language automatically destroyed the wonderful internationalism of the silent movie era when a Lillian Gish or Mary Pickford was understood everywhere in the world through gesture rather than language.

Taylor's *The Taming of the Shrew*

By 1929 the audience for the American movie industry had safely progressed, as Steven J. Ross has put it, "from working class to middle class,"[2] a sea change either encouraged by, or resulting in, the replacement of the nickelodeons with the new palace theatres that allowed even the poorest folk to be surrounded for just a few hours by unimagined opulence. When Mary Pickford, "America's Sweetheart," and her independent company decided to make *The Taming of the Shrew* (1929), the queen of silent film actresses was only following Al Jolson's famous advice in the pioneering sound picture, *The Jazz Singer* (1927). "You ain't heard nothin' yet," he rasped, and she gave audiences much more to hear with her talking picture *Coquette* (1929). In it, she abandoned her persona as a golden-haired, sweet, dear little innocent thing for an Academy Award best-actress role as a brunette roaring-twenties flapper. Her success with *Coquette* encouraged Miss Pickford to accept Sam Taylor's proposal for doing William Shakespeare's *The Taming of the Shrew*[3] with her husband, Douglas Fairbanks, devil-may-care hero of *The Thief of Bagdad* (1924), as a swashbuckling Petruchio. By casting themselves in the lead roles, the fabulously popular Fairbanks also guaranteed a huge audience as an antidote to the "box-office poison" of a highbrow movie. The "poison," however, was administered not at the box office – the movie budgeted at $504,000 grossed $1.1 million – but at the hands of a myth. Sam Taylor's credit line, "Written by William Shakespeare with additional dialogue by Sam Taylor," shocked the "purists,"[4] and "the film [was] immediately discounted."[5] Ironically Taylor's infamous and endlessly repeated credit line may never have existed[6] and at its release the film was for the most part favorably received. Professor Ball, who knew Taylor, found "no evidence whatsoever that the credit ever appeared in the film."[7] Even if the line existed on one lost print, the witty and astute Taylor probably meant the whole thing as a joke. After all, Shakespeare's *Shrew* is a farce, not a tragedy. A studio worker provided the *reductio ad absurdum* when he said, "Sure, we're making *The Taming of the Shrew*, but we're turning it into a cah-medy."[8] Perhaps he meant to say, "we're turning it into a movie, whose artistry will depend more on its filmic values than on its literary origins."

Still another misconception is that Pickford's movie was the first Shakespeare talking picture, a myth perpetuated in the explanatory cards for the 1966 re-release. Not so. It is, however, the first *feature-length* talking Shakespeare movie. The first Shakespeare movie that successfully synchonized sound and image came from England, a ten-minute extract from the trial scene probably in an experimental De Forest Phonofilms' *The Merchant of Venice* (1927).[9] With sound slowly evolving, movie theatres in many smaller towns lacked sound equipment so *Taming of the Shrew* was filmed in both a silent and talking version, though another option in 1929 was to have movies combine sound with title cards. In an ultimate irony, Mary Pickford herself believed the movie an abysmal failure: "I was talked into doing *The Taming of the Shrew* against my better judgment . . . [it was] my finish. My confidence was completely shattered, and I was never again at ease before the camera or microphone."[10] She banished the offending print to the archives but after the success of the Zeffirelli *Taming of the Shrew* (1966), she relented and commissioned Matty Kemp to restore the movie at a cost of $100,000 for wide screen exhibition. A *Variety* reviewer said that the reissue proved that the Fairbanks "richly deserved their long held positions as top artists."[11]

The world premiere in London's Pavilion Theatre should have alleviated Miss Pickford's despair. Even allowing for his being a hired publicist, James Agate's commentary in the gala printed program demonstrated that movies at last had attracted the "best class of people," which was another way of saying that pictures empathetic to working-class consciousness were being safely shunted aside. Agate combs performance history to show how the abridged film stems more from David Garrick's shortened version of *Shrew*, presented at Drury Lane on March 18, 1754, as *Catherine and Petruchio*, than from the tomfoolery of Sam Taylor's notorious gag writers: "It is Garrick's version upon which the present film is based. Hollywood has taken nothing from Shakespeare's play, which Garrick did not take." The film, in his view, had "nothing of Hollywood about it, except the superb lighting."[12] An equally successful November opening at New York's Rivoli led to the film being included in *The New York Times* list of the "Ten Best Films of the Year." A. M. Sherwood, Jr. called it a "grand talking picture" comparable to "the best Shakespearean productions of all time."[13] Mordaunt Hall of *The New York Times* thought Miss Pickford "delightful" in "her fits of fury and also in those moments when she . . . trembles at Petruchio's wrath."[14]

Slapstick rules. With Fairbanks and Pickford brandishing whips like lion tamers, the movie is more whippy than witty, a reminder that *Shrew* ranks with *Comedy of Errors* as one of Shakespeare's least cerebral comedies. Fairbanks and Pickford make Petruchio's servants hop and skip, and the audience jump. Pickford's movie replaces the traces of profundity on the Italianate motif of "supposings" in the Induction, which Shakespeare borrowed from Ludovico Ariosto's *I Suppositi* (1509), with a crude Punch-and-Judy show. "Kiss me, kiss me," says Punch. "I'll kiss you," Judy says and whacks him. After several whacks, he goes off to get his fool's cap, returns, and conks her three times on the head with his fool's staff. "I'll tame you," he says. "Oh, you're wonderful," she says and throws her arms around him in surrender. Stressing the primal battle of the sexes, the impudent film downplays the massive "supposings" that have Tranio pretending to be Lucentio; Lucentio, Cambio; and Hortensio, Litio. The Lord's concern for the proper care of his hunting dogs is gone, with its anticipation of the "taming school" for Kate, when Petruchio discourses on ways to "man [his] haggard" (4.1.193), Shakespeare at some point having forgotten that Kate is a shrew not an adult hawk.

When the camera pulls back from the Punch-and-Judy show, a realistic street scene from Renaissance Padua fills the *mise-en-scène*, designed by William Cameron Menzies, who did the spectacular sets for *The Thief of Bagdad* (1924), and *Gone with the Wind* (1939), and who learned the "Warner look" from German expressionist Anton Grot,[15] even though the happy glare of California sunshine exposes the expensive studio set as another movie mirage. The ambient music by strolling musicians supports the bustling street scene of stalls, sidewalk cafés, peddlers, and stone archways but the extras look just a little bit too well-scrubbed to be Italian street people.

Marble and hangings and a sweeping staircase adorn Kate's sumptuous domicile, which is presided over by Baptista Minola (Edwin Maxwell). Shakespeare's text suffers ruthless deletions not only from the tyranny of time but also from the movie's having been intended originally as a silent, especially in the case of the pruned Bianca subplot, but the story line survives, at least for those who know it, with a clever exploitation of visual metonymy. There's a quick glimpse of an embracing Hortensio and Bianca framed in a doorway, just before they are caught *in flagrante delicto* by the harried Baptista Minola, who declares that his eldest daughter must marry before the younger. Multiple analytical close-ups and reaction shots spliced in from several different camera set-ups clinically document the Minola family's dysfunctionality. There is a great clatter above, a smashed window, people and objects hurtling down the staircase, a shattered mirror, a dog scrambling for cover underneath a chest, a picture falling off the wall, a man with his head sticking through the picture frame, a cat running up on a chest, and a woman cowering in a closet. The camera moves up the stairs to reveal mayhem – furniture, clothing, objets d'art, everything, smashed and tossed about in disarray, and then the camera pans left to reveal the vixen herself, Katherina Minola (Mary Pickford), smoldering with anger and holding the cruel whip, an instrument of oppression. Verily, the woman is a shrew. Not a large shrew, only five feet tall, but shrewish enough, even off camera, to have once bitten the great D. W. Griffith for raising his voice to her. Her scratchy voice aside, she makes a splendid Katherina Minola.

Douglas Fairbanks, not having a great voice for the talkies either, relies on his trademark expression of maddening insolence. His face fixed in a default mode of mockery, he calmly endures Kate's initial assault, even to the point of stoically ignoring vicious whip lashes across his back, which only exacerbates her fury. Fairbanks' supreme moment, however, comes in the wedding scene. As always, Kate is seen fuming on the church steps with her distraught father, both wondering what has become of the tardy bridegroom. In the packed church, spectators buzz with curiosity. In long shot, Petruchio approaches mounted on a sorry-looking nag, and wearing his ridiculous jackboot of a hat. Insolently munching on an apple and demonstrating an "attitude," he saunters up to his enraged bride. The events at the altar, which are merely reported by Gremio in Shakespeare's play, give director Taylor a loophole for indulging in a series of silent film gags. The oafish Petruchio hands the core of his apple to the wretched Grumio, who then spends the next few minutes trying to figure out how to dispose of it surreptitiously, even under the baleful stare of a nearby monk. When a thoroughly disgusted Kate shows signs of not responding positively to the

4   In the midst of William Cameron Menzies'
opulent set, Mary Pickford and Douglas Fairbanks
rest between rounds in the battle of the sexes in *The
Taming of the Shrew* (USA 1929), directed by Sam
Taylor.

priest's query, "Do you take this man for a husband?" the boorish Petruchio
stomps on her foot so hard that she cries out "I do."

The physical abuse of little Kate continues after the wedding feast, when
Petruchio drags her off to his place in the country, carrying her like a sack
of wheat on his horse, and dumping her into the mud, as called for in the
play (4.1.57). As she sits inside by the roaring fire, Kate's expression registers
exhaustion, cold, hunger, wetness, and an aching desire for warmth, while
above on a balcony Petruchio appears dry and warm in a splendid dressing
gown, his expression revealing tenderness for Kate. To burnish his image of
cruelty, however, he cracks the terrifying whip at the scrambling servants. The
charade continues with Kate's attempts to eat being continually thwarted by
Petruchio's loutish antics – knocking over a water basin, and roundly cuff-
ing the servants, while Kate enduring the torture of Tantalus must watch
the food forever receding away from her. When she picks up the meat, he

[31]

declares it "burnt," has it thrown away, and then begins hurling objects. A tightly framed shot of a servant's knees knocking together gives a micro-picture of the macro-terror at the Petruchio household. The two squabble until Kate finally hurls one of the whips into the fire. The sequence ends in an embrace. Fade out.

For Kate's admirers, the crux of the play comes at the banquet scene when Kate wins Petruchio's wager with her infamous speech of submission. Rather than seeing it as an abject surrender, most Elizabethans would have interpreted her sentiments as entirely decorous and proper, an act of faith. If Kate can willingly acknowledge that the moon is the sun and the sun the moon, she can also pay fealty to her lord and master, who in return will care for her or earn the parish's opprobrium, or so the doctrine of passive obedience, which seems so repulsive to modernists, was theoretically intended. The pace of the editing neatly builds up toward Kate's "surrender," and also provides for the surprise twist by which she will both yield and not yield. About a dozen different camera set-ups mostly in long shot of the entire banquet table at Minola's mansion, are then followed by a close-up of Petruchio, still clinging to his beloved whip, though with a bandaged head from colliding with Kate's stool. As a dignified Kate utters the words "sea and land" (5.2.149), she's shown in close-up, before a cut to mid-long shot where the guests at the table are arranged clockwise from the left with Bianca, Gremio, Petruchio, Kate (standing), and Baptista Minola, all awaiting Kate's climactic declaration that "Such duty as the subject owes the prince, /Even such a woman oweth to her husband" (5.2.155). That makes Bianca very uncomfortable but Petruchio wears his patented cocksure grin. At line 164, Kate utters the word "obey" and then subverts her own declaration by broadly winking in the direction of Bianca in such a way as to suggest their sisterly bond in the "female subculture,"[16] leaving men out of it. Kate has shown her ability to manage Petruchio, while Mary Pickford has self-reflexively demonstrated for the world how to be the first speaking Shakespearean heroine on screen. She has taken the Shakespeare movie beyond the actualities, the silents, the proscenium stage, and positioned it for a new role among "spirits of a different sort."

The Reinhardt/Dieterle *A Midsummer Night's Dream* (1935)

In the next (and the best) major Hollywood Shakespeare movie, the Teutonic romanticism of Max Reinhardt and William Dieterle's *A Midsummer Night's Dream* (1935) replaced the rollicking farce of *Taming of the Shrew*. After the success of émigré Max Reinhardt's spectacular live production at the Hollywood Bowl, movie mogul Jack Warner courageously gambled on making it into a movie. It became not only Shakespeare filtered through the Hollywood studio system but also the *Dream* as re-imagined after Gothic films like F. W. Murnau's *Nosferatu* (1921), adapted from Bram Stoker's *Dracula*. That is to say, at one level *Dream* is a classic comedy of the green world triumphing over the wintry as young lovers push aside the blocking parental figures of authority and establish their own hegemony; at another, it is a dark vision of disorder and chaos with nature gone awry and the rule of reason threatened by unchained forces. Its four separate but contiguous plots swirl around, and in between, and among one another. There are the putative ruler, Duke Theseus of Athens, with his weird bride, the captured Amazon queen, Hippolyta; the half mad and thoroughly confused young lovers, Lysander and Hermia and Demetrius and Helena; the powerful underworld of fairyland presided over by the quarreling fairy king and queen, Oberon and Titania; and the socially marginalized "crew of patches, rude mechanicals" (3.2.9), comprised of Bottom, Quince, Snug, Flute, Snout, and Starveling. Reinhardt and Dieterle incarnated this fantasy world of mirror and reverse-mirror effects into a swirling electronic Masque of Light and Dark on the theme of the search for certainty in uncertainty. The casting of Hollywood's effervescent stars by filtering Shakespeare through popular culture made mass audiences comfortable, but the uncomfortable side, the darkness, as subsequently underscored by Jan Kott,[17] remains secreted in the Gothic recesses of Reinhardt's enchanted forest.

Director Max Reinhardt's deep interest in *Midsummer Night's Dream* began with a 1905 production at Berlin's Neues Theatre, and continued at places like Salzburg, Oxford, and finally in 1934 the Hollywood Bowl.[18] The Warner Brothers poured $1^1/$_2$ million into the production, orchestrating myriad details and filming on a huge sound stage of over 38,000 square feet. Erich Wolfgang Korngold arranged the musical setting based on Mendelssohn's thrilling *Overture to a Midsummer Night's Dream*, as well as later incidental music, and Max Reinhardt ordered a special machine called an "Akron Spider" to manufacture sufficient cobwebs for the set; the donkey's head for Bottom's scene (James Cagney) with Titania (Anita Louise) was constructed at considerable trouble and expense; central casting called on all available dwarves in Los Angeles county to fill up the gnomes in the elfin orchestra. Art director Anton Grot, who had also worked on the seminal *Thief of Bagdad,* designed the sets for the ballet sequences in the dark wood. The fabled Nijinsky's ballerina sister, Bronislawa, choreographed the dances.[19] The cast included rising stars like Olivia de Havilland (Hermia) and fourteen-year-old Mickey Rooney (Puck), who earlier had worked with Reinhardt in the Hollywood Bowl outdoor production, as well as household names among the rude mechanicals – Joe E. Brown (Flute), James Cagney (Bottom), Frank McHugh (Quince), Hugh

Herbert (Snout), Arthur Treacher (Ninny's Tomb). Dick Powell (Lysander), Jean Muir (Helena), and the incredibly beautiful starlet Anita Louise (Titania) opposite a menacing Victor Jory (Oberon) all epitomized the charisma of Hollywood in the Golden Years before World War II.

The movie begins as a Masque of Night, which is a visual meditation on a surreal forest in charcoal hues like something out of a set for *Nosferatu*. A luminous quarter moon, intermittent clouds, and bright stars echo the play's iterative images of moonlight, and Titania's ominous diagnosis of disturbed nature, "Therefore the moon (the governess of floods), / Pale in her anger, washes all the air" (2.1.103). Generally thought of as sprightly, Mendelssohn's score contains a darker gothic subtext, embodying in its varied strings and horns the contradictory motifs to come – nuptials and feasting, and high hopes, yet poised on the edge of a dark wood harboring acts of unspeakable bestiality. The chiaroscuro lighting after a seventeenth-century Dutch painting of domestic life colors the mechanicals' rehearsal scenes for *Pyramus and Thisby*, where James Cagney's bouncy gait, Frank McHugh's earnestness, Hugh Herbert's silly giggle, and Joe E. Brown's deadpan face bring the full animal vitality of Hollywood creativity to the redeployment of the Shakespearean text. Indeed the play's imagery translates into a feast for the camera's eye, its swirling non-linear patterns of movement made to order for what Lorne Buchman has described as "the multiple perspectives" in "the spatial field of cinema" for "a world of infinite relationships, of images, sounds, textures, and colors in constant motion," resulting in "a spectacle of multiplicity."[20]

After a title card announcing the duke's desire for "masques and plays to be readied against the nuptial day," the spectacular but overblown baroque establishing shot of the Athenian court, which follows well-entrenched Victorian stage traditions, becomes a dumb show for identifying the key characters and hinting at the future complications. Shielded by an ornate canopy and beatified with the ambient music of trumpets and a mass chorale by loyal subjects, Theseus the duke of Athens (Ian Hunter) and his Amazon fiancée Hippolyta (Verree Teasdale) ascend the steps of a pseudo-Greek temple toward their rightful thrones. A variety of splicing and cutting and editing of close-ups and mid-shots reveals Lysander (Dick Powell) singing and mugging and frantically waving to Olivia de Havilland (Hermia), as Hermia's irascible father, Egeus (Grant Mitchell), pounds his staff to remind the distracted girl of her obligation to join in the vocalizing. In a flurry of cross-cutting, Demetrius (Ross Alexander) competes with Lysander in a singing contest to see who can project more loudly, while there is a reaction shot of Helena looking quite lonely and hurt when Demetrius cuts her dead. The choristers fit into discrete clusters: charming young ladies fresh from the daisy chain, a geriatric male choir, a Hollywoodized Vienna boys' choir, and representatives of the deserving poor embodied in Peter Quince's delegation of rude mechanicals. Despite competition from Hollywood's funniest people, Joe E. Brown manages to steal the show with an expression of matchless stupidity as he chews on and spits out litchi seeds while half-heartedly singing, much to Peter Quince's disgust.

The strains of Mendelssohn's Wedding March underscore the play's original role as a celebration for a wedding reception, yet many dusky currents run just beneath the bright surface. Philip C. McGuire has noted that the "opening moments . . . include a silence – Hippolyta's – that has reverberations" throughout the text.[21] Hippolyta's sullen resentment toward Theseus for his rape of the Amazons, which the Coronado *Midsummer Night's Dream* (1984) makes far more explicit, suggests a covert feminist agenda. Her repellent Max Ree snake costume foreshadows Oberon's, "And there the snake throws her enamell'd skin, / Weed wide enough to wrap a fairy in" (2.1.255), and Hermia's nightmare about the "crawling serpent" (2.2.146). For haughty Hippolyta, it would hardly be a calamity if Theseus' longed-for nuptial night never came.

The movie turns most filmic in the orchestration of camera work, editing, and theme music for the dazzling ballet sequence. There are glimpses of owl, deer, frogs, tiny creepy things, and waterfalls. A spunky little Puck rises out of a damp bed of leaves; fairies in gossamer white emerge from the mist; the disputed Indian boy rides a fabulous unicorn through the forest; and an orchestra of gnarled little gnomes with bizarre masks frantically tootle and saw away. Dozens of shots angled in different ways and spliced into a rhythmical pattern correlate with Mendelssohn's theme music and with glimpses of the Athenian lovers scooting through the forest. Mounted on an ominous black horse, Oberon peremptorily orders Puck to fetch the magic flower "love-in-idleness," and like his forebears in the old Vitagraph *Midsummer Night's Dream*, Puck soars through the air, while Oberon, crowned with a magnificent headpiece, is ensconced in a tree staring down at the lovers. The lighting is a miracle, wringing subtleties out of stark black-and-white, and turning the screen to silver. Even the most enthusiastic cinéphile may turn sullen purist, though, when the theme music drowns out Oberon's "I know a bank where the wild thyme blows" (2.1.249), Keatsian in its lyric sublimity. The subsequent Triumph of the Night ballet has Oberon re-entering on a black horse with a huge black cape billowing behind him and gradually enfolding all the white-costumed attendants of Titania, who has been distracted by her affair with Bottom. The squat dwarves resembling Martians, who adumbrate Dieterle's grotesque Quasimodo in his *The Hunchback of Notre Dame* (1939) fiddle away. Meanwhile the prima ballerina (Nini Theilade) ascends toward the stars with her arms and hands gracefully writhing, twining and intertwining until all that can be seen are the exquisite white hands before they slowly dissolve into the blackness.

5   In the dark wood near Athens, Mickey Rooney's Puck and
Olivia De Havilland's Hermia show how "quick bright things"
do indeed "come to confusion" in this episode from *A
Midsummer Night's Dream* (USA 1935), directed by Max
Reinhardt and William Dieterle.

Poignant in the way that it manifests the play's precarious equilibrium teeter-
ing between the forces of light and dark, the scene would qualify as another
talisman of wonder in the Inigo Jones/Ben Jonson masques at the court of
James I.

   With time, the movie's critical reputation has recuperated from the prere-
lease grumblings about Hollywood's impudence in meddling with a classic,
which even fomented "indignation meetings" in London over the casting of
"vulgar" actors like Brown and Cagney in a Shakespeare production. Following its release, critics better tolerated the "switching of codes" that involved
the wrenching of well-known actors out of their stereotypical roles into unexpected new ones, e.g., having gangster James Cagney play Shakespeare's Bottom. One American critic wrote that "*Midsummer Night's Dream* is by no means
as bad as it might have been," followed by a candid admission that it compared
favorably with any stage production.[22] John Russell Taylor got about half way
there when he wrote, "Not, clearly, a 'serious' approach to Shakespeare at
all, and yet, strange to relate, a remarkably successful film."[23] The way that
the enthusiasm of Taylor's subordinate clauses subverts the clamminess of
the main clauses suggests deep ambivalence. Graham Greene disapproved of
Reinhardt's directing in general but admired the acting for the very reason

that it lacked "proper Shakespearian diction and bearing."[24] A maelstrom of opinions, they reflect the anxieties of confronting not only the transition from stage to screen but the new technology that gave voices to previously silent film actors.

The Thalberg/Cukor *Romeo and Juliet* (1936)

With their $2-million *Romeo and Juliet*, Irving Thalberg and George Cukor revered Shakespeare so much that they suffocated his play. A British film critic seemed to think so in noting that "the cinema is not yet at ease with Shakespeare; it approaches him with an anxious sense of occasion, not venturing to make a friend of him but determined to do him proud."[25] The timing was good, however. *A Midsummer Night's Dream* and *Romeo and Juliet*, both sonnet plays written at the same stage of the poet's career, ricochet off each other. As everyone knows, the *Pyramus and Thisby* play not only self referentially spoofs the four young lovers in *Midsummer Night's Dream* but also burlesques the lugubrious tale of *Romeo and Juliet*.

In casting expatriate British actors, the producers made a preemptive strike against more "indignation meetings" over the *lèse-majesté* of American actors in Shakespearean roles. A veritable wax works of British upper class snobbery filled the screen: Leslie Howard (Romeo), Basil Rathbone (Tybalt), Ralph Forbes (Paris), Violet Kemble Cooper (Lady Capulet), and C. Aubrey Smith (Capulet). Somehow 35-year-old American Norma Shearer was allowed to play Juliet, not just because her husband, Irving Thalberg, had status at MGM, but because she was a recognized star of considerable thespian talent. As a business man constantly exposed to "tickling commodity," Thalberg, the youthful genius at Metro Goldwyn Mayer, would never have risked a $2 million investment by indulging in an act of uxorious nepotism. He also still nurtured the old Vitagraph ambition to make movies with "class" for "classier" audiences, and saw the "picturization" of a Shakespeare play "as the fulfillment of a long-cherished dream," since Shakespeare was a playwright whose "dramatic form is practically that of a scenario."[26] His 35-year-old wife was only following a long stage tradition of mature actors playing Juliet and Romeo, the most recent precedent then being Katherine Cornell as a 36-year-old Juliet on Broadway in 1934. Despite the problem that studio lights are harsher than footlights on older actors, Norma Shearer's Juliet and Leslie Howard's 43-year-old Romeo exactly fit the middle-brow stereotype of "sublime" Shakespearean actors, still closer to a lofty Forbes-Robertson than to a cantankerous Nicol Williamson. To add even more "class," the great John Barrymore as a scenery-chewing, over-aged but nevertheless charming Mercutio aroused faint echoes of past glories on the

New York stage. Barrymore had already done screened Shakespeare with his solo appearance as a soliloquizing Richard duke of Gloucester in *The Show of Shows* (1929), a cinematic vaudeville show, where his sweeping declamation from *Henry VI Part III* further endorsed the supremacy of Warner Brothers Vitaphone process.[27] As if terrified that youthful actors might desecrate the worshipful rite, they let 44-year-old competent but icy Basil Rathbone try to be a fiery Tybalt.

The dialectical structure of *Romeo and Juliet* with its deeply embedded antitheses between light and dark, womb and tomb, youth and age, love and death lent itself admirably to the cinematic style of George Cukor and the classical Hollywood film. Romeo hints at this rhetorical strategy when listing his oxymorons of "bright smoke," "cold fire," "sick health" (1.1.180), and the "ancient grudge" between Montagues and Capulets sets thesis against antithesis in a clash of opposites. The visual equivalents emerge on screen through parallel editing and montage that reflect the alternate surges of subversion and containment wrenching Verona apart. The geometrical symmetries of parallel shots correlate with a Verona ruled by reason, and the montage and random cuts become metaphors for overwhelming passion. "They stumble that run fast," the Friar reminds us (2.3.94). Echoing Edmund Spenser's *Mutabilitie Cantos*, which strove to make all things irreconcilable reconcilable, the Panglossian Friar Lawrence would have Romeo's misfortunes magically become fortunate: "thy Juliet is alive ... / There art thou happy" (3.3.135).

The studio spared no expense in the quest for authenticity and realism. Since a plan to film on location in Italy for "real" realism was ruled out,[28] the producers settled for the *faux* realism of Prospero's "insubstantial pageant" by spending $1 million on a back lot Verona in Hollywood, modeled after Hogenberg's *Civitates Orbis Terrarum*. Two underlings had been dispatched to Italy to make 2,769 pictures for conversion into 54 scale models. Carpenters had then constructed on eight acres of the MGM lot, a Disneyland conflation of buildings from Verona. Professor William Strunk, Jr. of Cornell University, the rhetorician who teamed up with E. B. White to inflict the *New Yorker* style on America, dispensed academic reputability like holy water by declaring the grandiose set to be "an ideal Veronese public square ... such as Shakespeare himself might have imagined from the accounts of returned travelers."[29] Oliver Messel's original costume sketches for the household liveries, the canopies, the drummers, trumpeters, and guards show Juliet in a blue gown, and a "Negro" page to Paris in pink, red, and white livery. Altogether the costumes required hundreds of sketches, and some 38,000 yards of material, which would have been a triumph in Technicolor but muted in black-and-white.[30] Herbert Stothart's musical themes from Tchaikovsky's *Romeo and Juliet* (1871) enhanced the funereal atmosphere, but Stothart until countermanded by Thalberg had originally planned carefully researched fifteenth and sixteenth-century modes. Agnes De Mille, choreographer of the $100,000 Capulet ballroom scene, tells the story that Thalberg suddenly heard Tchaikovsky's music on the radio for the first time and called Stothart, crying out, "Why did no one ever tell me of this?"[31] Instinctively Thalberg wanted something like the incomparable fusion of sight and sound in Bo Widerberg's *Elvira Madigan* (1967) when the slow movement in F major from Mozart Piano Concerto no. 21 in C major (K 467) punctuates the progress of a young woman running in slow motion across a lush meadow. According to Herbert Coursen, Jr., in the late 30s spinoffs from Tchaikovsky cloyed the airwaves with sentimental hits like "Our Love" and "The Night Is Young and You're so Beautiful,"[32] which inevitably infiltrated this conception of *Romeo and Juliet*.

The Thalberg/Cukor movie works symbiotically with Shakespeare's text by taking its cues and camera angles from the thematic implications and rhythms of the play itself. After old-fashioned credits showing the actors in cameo frames, and after a lookalike John Barrymore as prologue appears on a proscenium stage, there is a cut to Verona's cathedral square. The stylized, geometrical, movements of the opposing houses of Montague and Capulet as they cross the main square of Verona provide fodder for multiple reaction shots among the gawking citizenry of extras. As Cedric Gibbons, the film's designer, explained, "with the movement of the camera, the audience is permitted to look at the settings from the same angle as the people who are actually in them."[33]

The first 36 of the movie's 262 set-ups must suffice to illustrate Cukor's method. Three men and a woman, all muttering apprehensively, stare at the Capulet and Montague retinues, who in a motif inspired by Gozolli's "Procession of the Magi" fresco from Florence,[34] have just entered the piazza from opposite sides and are converging on a collision course toward the cathedral steps. In medium shot, others cry out, "The Capulets!" which provides the visual metonymy for the reactions of the hundreds of other pseudo- Veronese extras. Rich alike in dignity, Lord Capulet (C. Aubrey Smith) and Lady Capulet (Violet Kemble Cooper) lead the way, attended by servants in light livery and black badges. Then from an over-the-shoulder angle, the stately column continues to march toward its inevitable collision with the rival house. The entrance of the Montagues precisely mirrors the Capulet procession, even down to and including the murmured "It's the Montagues" in more reaction shots. Cross-cutting continues with the Montagues glowering in the direction of the Capulets, and vice versa. A cutaway to the Capulets reveals a sneering Basil Rathbone, who had raised sneering to a high art, as a vexed Tybalt, who is whispering into Lord Capulet's ear: "The house of Montague, our foe," while C. Aubrey Smith, for once not the colonel of the Queen's Own Royal Regiment of Imperial Horse Dragoons at the Khyber Pass, warns the impetuous lad, "Soft, keep the peace."

As the editing tempo increases, it echoes the escalating anger of the warring houses. There are two seconds (48 frames perhaps) of Tybalt under a canopy glaring at the Montagues; three seconds (72 frames) of Benvolio responding with a match cut in kind. A Montague retainer grabs for the hilt of his sword; and a parallel shot follows of Tybalt reaching for his sword but being restrained by Father Capulet. The fine-tuned match-cutting between Capulets and Montagues culminates in a full-scale riot in the streets. This is highly skilled, technically proficient movie making whose shifting camera angles, splicing and dubbing of bits and pieces of action and sound create a photographic mosaic that mimics actuality. Cukor's classical style offers a polar opposite to the filmic expressionism in Reinhardt's *Midsummer Night's Dream.* The danger is that patently faked realism like a mockup Verona may turn out looking less real than the blatant falsifications of expressionism. Anthony Davies puts the matter this way: "The cinema aims at spatial realism. Nonetheless our collusion with the medium is such that we will tolerate . . . photographic tricks so long as they are wholly convincing; so long as we are given at the visual level what appears to be spatially real, and so long as we can believe in a spatial reality beyond the boundaries of the frame."[35]

For all the movie's high gloss, at some point rigor mortis sets in. To anyone today grown accustomed to the kind of shock editing used in Oliver Stone's *Natural Born Killers* (1994), the pace borders on the tedious. Even the slapstick antics of Andy Devine as Peter biting his thumb at the Montagues comes across as a dutiful interruption for comic relief, of which Mr. Thalberg wrote that "four of the five acts are lightened with comedy and gags, all aiming at the diversion of the audience."[36] The indomitable Nurse (Edna May Oliver) waggles her finger at the blubbery Peter to the joy of the Montagues, who revel in Peter's humiliation.

Orderly patterns of parallel editing yield to chaotic montage when fullscale street fighting breaks out. *"They Fight"* licenses directors to use the camera unflinchingly. A wild mêlée follows that in forty or so shots from a variety of camera angles shows Capulets rushing toward Montagues; Peter comically struggling to remove his dagger from a scabbard; a man under flower pots being brutally clubbed; duelists in single combat; a terrified woman with a baby (in a quotation from Eisenstein); a man being throttled; two other combatants rolling down the church steps; a Capulet skewered by a sword. With the entrance of the prince to restore order, the wild montage gives way to a full framed *mise-en-scène* filled with the chastened and subdued crowd.

The Cukor *Romeo and Juliet* defines the play this way in the context of broadly sketched dialectical tensions through symmetry and asymmetry in framing

6   Super stars Norma Shearer and Leslie Howard meet
and dance at the Capulet ball in this multi-million dollar
motion picture of *Romeo and Juliet* (USA 1936), directed by
George Cukor.

and editing. The metronome-like cutting shows again with the balcony scene
where the approach of Leslie Howard through sepulchral gardens to Juliet's
fairy-tale balcony proceeds at the stately pace of 90 shots for 205 lines of dialogue, more attuned to forty-year-old actors than to the teenagers of Zeffirelli
and Luhrmann. Howard and Shearer speak their lines well, with clarity and
conviction but not with the transcendent fire that makes the words burn in
the heart. The overly predictable and mechanical editing straitjackets the film
in the way that the sonnet imprisons Juliet's language at the Capulet ball,
until she breaks out of its rigidities and speaks alone in her own unfettered
blank verse (3.2.1). A mild rebellion against textual purity does occur in the

omission of the Friar's prolix speech of exculpation, "I will be brief" (5.3.229), which though to a modern audience is unbearably anticlimactic after the tomb scene, yet retains vital components of Elizabethan moralizing. For one thing, it somewhat exculpates Romeo and Juliet's defiance of parental authority. Little of this means anything today with society's moral roots eroding under modernist relativism, and George Cukor was not to be alone in jettisoning this problematic scene from a movie of *Romeo and Juliet*. He would be joined by Zeffirelli and Luhrmann in 1968 and 1996. Even with this deletion, however, the film remains a reverential but not warm and vibrant *Romeo and Juliet*, received respectfully but not lovingly by the critics, and ultimately too wrapped up in a high mimetic bardolatry for either Shakespeare's or Hollywood's own good. Besides, "tickling commodity" proved too much for it, and its malaise at the box office encouraged Hollywood's moratorium on major Shakespeare films for nearly two decades.

The Mankiewicz/Houseman *Julius Caesar* (1953)

Seventeen years after the studio's *Romeo and Juliet*, MGM's vice-president Dore Schary, with the enthusiastic help of Joseph L. Mankiewicz and John Houseman, again ventured into the perilous waters of Shakespeare movies, this time with a remarkable $2-million *Julius Caesar* (1953),[37] packed full with renowned actors. By 1953 the emerging television industry, the impending collapse of the studio monopoly on distribution, and the new practice of allowing stars a percentage of the gross profits was already chipping away at the Golden Age of the major Hollywood studios. *Julius Caesar* barely squeaked in under the wire before the old centralized system gave way to decentralized, individual producers. It borrowed, though, from television's knack for presenting history as a current newsreel event in a "you are there" mode. It was a gambit that Orson Welles stole from "The March of Time" for *Citizen Kane*, though Mankiewicz's picture for all its stark realism lacks the grainy texture of an actual newsreel. While not so extravagant as Giovanni Pastrone's *Cabiria* (1914), or Cecil B. De Mille's *Ten Commandments* (1956) with a cast of thousands, Mankiewicz's Rome shows an array of crowded streets, steep staircases, elevated pulpits, pillars, balconies, statuary, and 1200 toga-clad extras milling around before a painted backdrop of the entire ancient city. Technical adviser P. M. Pasinetti also wanted an authentic "lived-in" look, a Rome not just of the Forum but one that "was also a city of narrow streets, slums, dirty little taverns, peddlars [sic], small squares with people yelling across at each other, etc."[38] Rejecting the modern dress approach of Worthington Miner's Studio One television production (1949), John Houseman put the cast in togas and on heroic theatrical sets like Gordon Craig's but of course free of the proscenium arch. He remained sanguine that "the magic power of lens and microphone"[39] would prevent the sheer size of the sets from overwhelming the actors.

To avoid confusion, William Shakespeare should have called his play *The Tragedy of Marcus Brutus* instead of *The Tragedy of Julius Caesar*, for this most rhetorical of his plays mainly focuses on the tragic irony of Brutus' incapacity for self-scrutiny. After Caesar's assassination in the third act, Brutus (James Mason) takes center stage and must deal with Antony (Marlon Brando), Octavius Caesar (Douglas Watson), and Cassius (John Gielgud). First, Caesar (Louis Calhern) experiences the tragedy of a great fall – Caesar suffers from "the falling sickness" (1.2.254), "great Caesar fell" (3.2.189) – but then after Antony's brilliant eulogy he is raised up again as the mob shouts, "Most noble Caesar!" (3.2.243). When he is as yet unfallen, at the apex of his power and arrogance, Caesar remains framed at the center of the film, whether progressing through the crowded streets preceded by Roman legionnaires, or pressed in on the sides by cheering riffraff. As Robert Hapgood has pointed out,[40] the film supports these spatial arrangements with photography and a set design of steep inclines, platforms, and balconies that serve as metaphors for the ups and downs of power in Rome itself and at Philippi, where Cassius stupidly marches straight into an ambush set up by the triumvirate on both flanks of a narrow defile. Brutus thereby discovers that actually there is no "tide in the affairs of men, / Which taken at the flood, leads on to fortune" (4.3.218), a passage often quoted out of context. Too often insufficiently noticed, Miklos Rozsa's musical score aurally supports the visual codes in the elaborate thematic counterpointing between the rising and falling fortunes of Caesar and Brutus.[41]

This *Julius Caesar* above all remains an actors' film, an unusual decision having been made to give priority to actors over technicians by filming the virtually uncut play[42] in its original sequence and by eliminating distracting reaction shots. The actors even resemble the many busts and statues of important Romans on the vast sets, not only in physiognomy but even in the folds and drapes of the togas. The movie opens with a tight shot of a bust of Caesar before focusing on the two tribunes, puritanical prigs, scolding the crowd for acclaiming Caesar: "Wherefore rejoice? What conquest brings he home?" (1.1.32), and protesting against the city's excessive quantity of statues of Caesar: "Disrobe the images, / If you do find them deck'd with ceremonies," says Flavius (1.1.64). The busts of noble citizens with their hair brushed well forward in the high Roman style represent the lost world that is now embodied in a living world of the movie's beautiful actors, whom Houseman wanted to look like "men wearing clothes, not characters wearing costumes."[43]

As a man whose lofty idealism ironically makes him into a terrorist, James Mason's Brutus strikes exactly the right note. A complex character, Brutus combines Macbeth's ruthlessness with Hamlet's introspection, and convinces himself that what happens to Caesar underneath Pompey's statue is not so much "a savage spectacle" (3.1.223) as a kind of blood sacrifice: "Let's be sacrificers, but not butchers, Caius / . . . Let's carve him as a dish fit for the gods" (2.1.166). Made all the more imperious by a low angle shot, Caesar at the Capitol, surrounded by the conspirators, spurns Metellus Cimber's (Tom Powers) petition asking a pardon for his brother, Publius: "I am constant as the northern star" (3.1.60). Behind him a dark-browed, scowling Casca (Edmond O'Brien) is maneuvering to deliver the initial blow. After Casca plunges the first knife into Caesar's back and after Caesar has been cruelly stabbed by the other conspirators, and as a bloodied and suddenly pitiful Caesar lurches toward him, Brutus draws back, retreats, sickened by the spectacle of what he has engineered, but then resolves to honor his oath and stabs Caesar, notoriously, in the groin, though it's been said (even in Plutarch) that Brutus was Caesar's illegitimate son. Louis Calhern speaks Caesar's immortal "*Et tu, Brute*? – Then fall Caesar!" (3.1.77) as the camera probes his unspeakable anguish.

Other high points include a disingenuous Cassius (John Gielgud), who persuades Brutus of Caesar's untrustworthiness even as he stands in the shadow of yet another statue of Caesar: "Why, man, he doth bestride the narrow world / Like a Colossus" (1.2.135). At the gathering of the conspirators in Brutus' garden, Casca's pedantic correction of Decius Brutus (John Hoyt) and Cinna's (William Cottrell) bickering over where the sun rises make a little more sense when Casca points his sword at the approaching Marcus Brutus, who then metaphorically becomes the rising sun: "Here, as I point my sword, the sun arises" (2.1.106). Brutus' vast capacity for *hamartia*, or "the missing of the mark," emerges when he spares Antony's life: "Our course will seem too bloody, Caius Cassius, / To cut the head off, and then hack the limbs" (2.1.162). As Cassius, Gielgud predictably and characteristically stresses verse over sense, tending to "sing" the lines[44] as he mellifluously but futilely protests against Brutus' decision, leaving unanswered the question of how a man who once so dominated Brutus could now be dominated by him. Deborah Kerr (Portia) and Greer Garson (Calphurnia), portray aristocratic Roman women with steel backbones, Portia after all being "Cato's daughter," who could swallow fire. They glitter with jewelry, necklaces and earrings, upswept hairdos, and wear elegant gowns of miraculously intricate tucks, folds, and pleats. Kerr's eloquence and beauty stay unruffled even when defeated by Brutus' obstinacy. In the parallel "mirror" scene between Caesar and Calphurnia, Greer Garson, for all of her power, also loses out to Decius Brutus, who scoffs at her interpretation of the dream ("This dream is all amiss interpreted" – 2.2.83) and flatters her husband into going to his death at the senate. She is last seen standing alone, the doors shut behind her, as Caesar marches off to the Capitol with a claque of his false friends, her private sufferings, as well as those of Portia, offering fertile ground for essays exposing systems of patriarchal subjugation. Another political subtext also lurks just below the surface with covert parallels to the rise and fall of Mussolini and Hitler in World War II, while the terrible fate of Cinna the poet comes close to echoing the feverish witch hunt hysteria of the McCarthy red scare era: "I am not Cinna the conspirator . . . It is no matter, his name's Cinna" (3.3.32).

Marlon Brando's Broadway role as Stanley Kowalski, the Polish redneck with slurred speech in a *Streetcar Named Desire,* had so stereotyped him that there was a visceral denial of his right or ability to play a Shakespearean role. As a method actor, Brando carried his stage persona of a "tough guy," Hells Angels type into his private life.[45] Despite his charismatic Antony, the critics competed to see who could administer the most unkindest cuts of all: "[he is] so far from Shakespeare's image that the lines cannot be made to stretch"; "he needs a bit of speech training"; and "[he is] oddly muscle-bound and speaks as though a wad of gum lurked in his jaws."[46] A few, however, defied the "switched code" taboo and confessed that Brando brilliantly handled Shakespeare's blank verse and that his silences could be even more eloquent.[47] Elocution aside, Brando radiates power with or without words, his splendid physique then not yet ravaged by time and sloth. Grieving over Caesar's bleeding corpse, he builds up to his bloodthirsty call for revenge in the wildness of, "Cry 'Havoc!' and let slip the dogs of war" (3.1.273).

In the great eulogy over Caesar's body in the public arena, Brando energizes Shakespeare's words from deep reservoirs of strength. The Godfather has no need to shout in order to have others listen. He stands like a Roman statue on steeply rising steps with a backdrop of mighty vertical columns.

Fortunately for Brando, Mankiewicz insisted on the actors' completing their lengthy speeches while the cameras were rolling, even if it meant paying the crew overtime. He feared that "looping," or having actors dub in speeches in a post-filming session, could maim Shakespeare's blank verse, as it notoriously did for Orson Welles's patchwork *Macbeth* (1948). In the film's typically realistic way, Antony actually uses the opening lines of the speech, "Friends, Romans, countrymen, lend me your ears!" (3.2.72) to quiet down an unruly mob who are perched on a rude wooden scaffolding in the public square. In contrast with the rabble, whom Shakespeare himself seemed to despise, Antony from a low camera-angle and over the shoulders of the assembled crowd stands high above, gowned in a graceful toga with the Roman eagle icon on a shoulder clasp. As he moves his arms, the drapery of the toga ripples gracefully in rhythm with his speech. In the crisply blocked crowd scenes, the hoi polloi look alternately brutal, mean, stupid, and occasionally intelligent. Now and then in the foreground, three or four men and women turn and glare at the theatre audience warning them (us) to be silent that Antony may be heard. Brando's Antony validates again Cassius' famous prediction that "this our lofty scene [shall] be acted over / In [states] unborn and accents yet unknown!" (3.1.112). The likes of this remarkable performance will rarely be seen again.

- 3 -

Laurence Olivier directs Shakespeare

As talented an *auteur* of Shakespeare film as ever existed, Laurence Olivier at mid-century reclaimed the British role as guardian of its national poet. Merging art with entertainment, he compromised with "tickling commodity" – one might venture to say he tickled commodity rather than allowing it to tickle him – by producing a "commodified" Shakespeare designed to fit the by then well established Palace theatres that attracted both the classes and some of the masses. A virtuoso actor with a thousand faces, he could banter with Rosalind in the Forest of Arden, rally the troops at Agincourt, scold Gertrude at Elsinore, send the little princes to the Tower, smother Desdemona (in blackface), demand the bond from Antonio, and reject Cordelia. On stage and film, he also managed, among other roles, to be Oedipus Rex, a Nazi dentist, a pathetic music hall entertainer, the cantor father of the Jazz Singer, Emily Brontë's Heathcliff, and Jane Austen's Fitzwilliam Darcy. By age twenty-nine he had already established Shakespearean and Shavian credentials with London's Old Vic playing Romeo, and with West End appearances as Captain Stanhope in *Journey's End*. With the exception of a rare brickbat hurled at him by Russell Davies on the 1992 British Channel Four television program "J'accuse/Without Walls," which painted him as performing with more show than substance, he has been universally acclaimed.[1]

Secretly his inner being may have tugged him toward Austen's Fitzwilliam Darcy, who is thinly concealed in the sullen and diffident Orlando of Hungarian-born director Paul Czinner's $1-million *As You Like It* (1936). Olivier looks all the more gloomy and morose, better suited as Oliver than as Orlando, for being paired opposite the effervescent Polish-born actress, Elisabeth Bergner, wife of director Paul Czinner, whose sprightly Rosalind saves the picture from utter ruin.[2] Thirty-six-year-old Elisabeth Bergner's special knack for Peter-Pan giggling and wriggling may have charmed the film's advisory-scenarist, J. M. Barrie, but it irritated some estimable critics, like the late Roger Manvell, who thought her "kittenish" attitude reflected a "self-destructive femininity," and deplored her "habit of turning somersaults."[3] Olivier and Bergner both faced, like Christine Edzard's recent film-festival *As You Like It* (1992), the uphill challenge of making one of Shakespeare's talkiest plays move. Its sparkling language subordinates plot to a labyrinth of mirror effects through which various deceptions and usurpations devolve on Orlando and the disguised and cross-dressed Rosalind, whose exiled father, "Duke Senior" (Henry Ainley), presides over a band of "merry men," who live "like the old Robin Hood of England . . . and fleet the time carelessly" (1.1.115). As denizens of the forest of Arden, where "sweet are the uses of adversity" (2.1.12), Duke Senior's honest followers in the tradition of pastoral myth implicitly rebuke the depraved courtiers at Duke Frederick's palace.

Rightly described as too stagy, the film remains firmly rooted in London's West End theatre. By contrast, having left the theatre thousands of miles behind in New York, Hollywood's new sound films like *Taming of the Shrew* evolved directly from the silent into the talking pictures. Typically one critic wrote that "it remains more a photographed version of a stringently cut stage presentation than a comic classic shaped to the cinema."[4] Even the break with expressionism in francophile Lazare Meerson's "poetic realism" of black-and-white fake woodlands, bubbling brooks, and peasant scenes, some inspired by the Flemish painter Pieter Brueghel, disappointed cinéphiles. The stylized *faux* medievalism, however, anticipated the famous scenes based on the 1490 manuscript of *Les très riches heures du Jean, duc de Berri* in Olivier's subsequent *Henry V*. Meerson's sudden release of genuine sheep, rabbits, and squirrels into the *mise-en-scène* shattered the fragile world of his imaginary barnyards and woods.

Despite the staginess, however, Czinner's resourceful camera work and David Lean's editing transform the text into a plausible film narrative. Intimate as two teenagers with a schoolgirl crush, Rosalind and Celia (Sophie Stewart) in the same brief scene are viewed from every angle on the compass, whether in two-shot, close-up, or over-the-shoulder and in a half-dozen camera set-ups. As Rosalind, Elisabeth Bergner with her charmingly accented English, whirls, turns, sparkles, dazzles, giggles, crosses her arms and offers unconditional love to her best friend, Celia, now cross-dressed as Aliena. At the phrase, the "bay of Portugal" (4.1.208), Rosalind executes her famous somersault as a final desperate measure for energizing words with her body. Adding piquancy, she brandishes a scroll of paper for swatting Touchstone, or for playfully tapping Orlando with, indexing her hidden need to dominate. She punctuates the classic line directed at Phebe for not wanting to marry Silvius with an ominous flourish of her switch fetish: "For I must tell you friendly in your ear, / Sell when you can, you are not for all markets" (3.5.59). Even so, contemporary reviewer James Agate thought her "tenderness and gaiety" insufficient to make up for a lack of "wit," which he attributed to her Teutonic sensibility.[5] By contrast, her Orlando (Olivier) seems wooden. His praise for old Adam ("O good old man, how well in thee appears / The constant service of the antique world" (2.3.56)) sounds singsong and uninflected, like a sullen pupil called on to read aloud in class. It is not just that he is playing Orlando, who is not nearly so witty as Rosalind, indeed is quite dull, it is that he is not playing anyone in particular at all, unless it's Fitzwilliam Darcy.

The supporting cast includes Leon Quartermaine (Jaques) listed in the credits as "dialogue supervisor," who again demonstrates the old adage that "those who can, do; those who can't, teach." His big moment with "All the world's a stage, / And all the men and women merely players" (2.7.139) looks and sounds too theatrical while trying not to be theatrical. Orlando's wrestling match before a jeering mob with the flabby Charles, the wrestler (Lionel Braham), consumes myriad shots from different angles to record the tossing and thumping in the ring. Abundant reaction shots catch the dismayed faces of Celia and Rosalind, the leering countenance of the wicked duke (Felix Aylmer), the absorbed faces of the peasants crammed behind the palace gate, and an ongoing blow-by-blow account as Touchstone (Mackenzie Ward) pantomimes and viscerally reacts to the wrestlers' crunches and grunts. The London Philharmonic Orchestra's arrangement of Walton's score for the wrestling match between Charles and Orlando foreshadows the quickened tempo during the French cavalry charge at Agincourt in *Henry V*. Incongruously dressed as a bunny rabbit, Touchstone's courtship of Audrey (Dorice Fordred) becomes even more unbelievable, though it's only a mirror to the affairs of Orlando-Rosalind and Celia-Oliver (Sophie Stewart and John Laurie). Touchstone's threat to the scapegoated William, "I will kill thee a hundred and fifty ways: therefore tremble and depart" (5.1.56), comes across as more grotesque than funny, in fact downright cruel.

With a running time of only 97 minutes some key moments have vanished: Oliver Martext's mock wedding scene; and Touchstone's set-piece description of seven types of quarrels. The big wedding scene at the end has been squeezed, compressed, truncated, or filleted out of existence, with Hymen's lines being turned over to Rosalind. Jaques de Boys suddenly arrives with news of the totally implausible conversion of Duke Frederick ("meeting with an old religious man, / After some question with him was converted" (5.4.160)), and of the decision to restore all the lands "to his banish'd brother" and "that were with him exil'd" (5.4.164). When Jaques, the melancholy one, is deprived of the gloomy announcement of his intention to join the duke as a "convertite," the dark subtext, the *memento mori*, so typical of every Shakespearean comedy vanishes. The general rejoicing remains unshadowed by encroaching darkness until Elisabeth Bergner steps in, oozing charm, to steal the show with a wonderful epilogue in which, cross-dressed as a man, she brandishes her favorite switch while admonishing the women, and then magically dissolves into a white virginal gown as she flatters the men. Bergner's Rosalind and Laurence

Olivier's Orlando may not be exactly as you like it, but in the realm of filmed Shakespeare no one has yet succeeded in being more likeable.

Henry V (1944)

Eight years later the sobriety and high seriousness that had made Olivier look miscast in a Shakespearean comedy proved exactly right for the role of an enigmatic 28-year-old soldier-king in the landmark *King Henry V* (1944). The movie not only launched, indeed invented, the modern Shakespeare film, but also showed that the Shakespeare movie could survive in the Palace theatre as well as in the rarified art houses. Olivier created a cinematic equivalent to the tantalizing ambiguities that reside in the Shakespearean vision of *King Henry V*.[6] The movie in recapitulating the most primal dichotomy in film making between the realism of the Lumière brothers and the fantasy of Georges Méliès simultaneously interrogates the quagmire of doubts in Shakespeare's play about the nature of governance, of kingship, and of the hero, young King Hal.

The ingeniously contrived film echoes the structure and themes of *Henry IV Parts One and Two* as through cross-cutting it moves back and forth between the holiday tavern world of Falstaff and the workaday courtly world of the usurping Lancastrian King Henry. It explores the nature of reality in assessing the gap between the authentic vs. the "counterfeit," the usurping King Henry being after all something of a counterfeit monarch – "Counterfeit? I lie, I am no counterfeit," says Falstaff (*1 Henry IV* 5.4.114) –, and draws attention to the "guilt" over the death of King Richard II concealed beneath the "gilt" of the crown: "England shall double gild his treble guilt" (*2 Henry IV* 4.5.128). As a result, the young king who appears on the screen has an emotional pedigree rich enough for several psychoanalysts, and neither Falstaff's tavern people nor the king's courtiers own a monopoly on morality or counterfeiting.

The film's existence on multiple levels renders it liable to exegesis like some medieval text. Simply as an entertainment the movie belongs, as Harry Geduld has said, to the heroic/action genre in which "a thorough-going extrovert, an almost entirely externalized image of a hero"[7] overcomes evil against all odds. Anthony Davies then further identifies *Henry V* with the western genre, citing André Bazin's definition that calls, among other things, for "simplicity of narrative concentration on archetypes rather than on complexity of character."[8] Bazin's displacing of Hal into the type of a strong, silent western hero endorses the traditional view of many critics that *Henry V* lacks nuance, qualifying splendidly as epic but weakly as drama.

There is much more to the story, however. With battle scenes shot on location in Ireland and interiors at Denham studios in England, the movie has been widely viewed as a propaganda film, mostly because of its dedication to the "Commandos and airborne troops of Great Britain." For that to happen, as John Collick shrewdly has pointed out, there needed to be a "mythical ideal of a wholly integrated British literary culture" in which Shakespeare was as meaningful to the masses as "the songs of Vera Lynn." For Tommies and GIs, it seems safe to say, Will Shakespeare took a back seat to Vera Lynn and Betty Grable. To work as good jingoism, the king had to be sanitized by deleting his "war crimes," such as the obscene threats before the French city of Harfleur: "Your naked infants spitted upon pikes, / Whiles the mad mothers with their howls confus'd / Do break the clouds" (*Henry V* 3.3.38), and the notorious order to put the French prisoners to the sword: "Then every soldier kill his prisoners, / Give the word through" (4.6.37). Michael Manheim has also discussed the movie's ideological parallels to E. M. W. Tillyard's celebrated *The Elizabethan World Picture* that reinforced "the order, system, hierarchy, and the demonstrated superiority of Anglo-Saxon values in the Europe of World War II."[9] Far more than a documentary like Leni Riefenstahl's beatification of the Nazi mystique, *The Triumph of the Will* (1935), *Henry V*, if it is propaganda, veers toward what Walter Benjamin called "the aestheticization of politics," as opposed to the "politicization of art."[10] Obviously, Olivier does not "eroticize"[11] Henry V in quite the way that Riefenstahl makes Hitler an object of desire among the masses, but in many isolated shots, as when the king unsheathes his great speech in the tradition of Armada rhetoric before Agincourt – "we few, we happy few, we band of brothers" (4.3.60) –, the camera gazes adoringly on the hero figure. A closer German parallel to *Henry V* lies in a wartime costume drama of nationalistic propaganda, Veit Harlan's *Der Grosse König* (1944), a celebration of the victories of Frederick the Great in the Seven Years War.[12] Despite these political tasks, the movie still finds some room, however tangentially and tentatively, for the young king's ethical quandaries. Although he is on the surface a carefree young man, a Jack Kennedy style leader, prone to tossing his crown on a post, all the censorship in the world cannot erase the Hamlet-like burden imposed on the king (and his audience) by his having "two bodies," one of an ordinary mortal and another of an incarnate divine sovereign, "the mirror of all Christian kings"(Chorus, 2.6).[13]

Quite rightly, however, Ace G. Pilkington and others feel that the movie's enduring value arises out of its consummate artistry as a film.[14] It consciously bridges the gap between theatre and film, and in the act of interrogating the idea of making a Shakespeare play into a film through a virtuoso display of cinematic codes self-reflexively valorizes it. Shakespeare movies, as Laurence Guntner has stressed, need to be studied not just in the context of their texts but in the realm of film codes, the visual tropes and conceits such as camera angles, movement, focus, lighting, montage, music, etc. that film

makers have contrived for communicating meaning to audiences.[15] Film critic
Dudley Andrew's astute analysis of the interplay between artifice and realism
in Olivier's film of *Henry V* reveals a cunning structure of nested episodes. Borrowing from André Bazin, Andrew calls this pattern a *hyperbola*, whose outer
and inner limits converge in a progression toward both Henry's meditation on
the eve of battle and the Battle of Agincourt itself.[16] Essentially a play-within-a-
play, or movie-within-a-movie with the Globe playhouse as a framing device,
the film critiques the differences between stage and screen. When the limitations of the Globe stage become apparent, the camera steps in to make possible
the chorus' advice to take the audience across the channel to France: "Work,
work your thoughts, and therein see a siege" (Chorus, 3.25).

The initial bracketing of the film begins, however, with a fluttering handbill proclaiming that today's (1 May 1600) performance at the Globe is "The
Chronicle History of King Henry the Fift." Resembling a quarto title page, the
handbill's realism supports the subsequent "actualities" of an aerial survey
(accompanied by a solemn chorale) tracking southwesterly over Elizabethan
London, passing over London Bridge, over St. Mary Overy (now Southwark
cathedral), hesitating before seeking out the Globe after snubbing the Bear
Gardens,[17] showing the house flag ascending the pole on the roof of the Globe
and a trumpet call announcing the show, an ensemble entering the music
gallery and starting up a lively overture with flutes and soft recorders, the
arriving audience, the circulating orange women, the gallants and ladies, the
raucous catcalls, the better sort of persons in the galleries, the book-holder taking his place,[18] the boy with a placard announcing the play's title, the sweeping
arrival on stage of the chorus (Leslie Banks), the soul-stirring prologue ("O for a
Muse of fire, that would ascend / The brightest heaven of invention!"), the boy
actors cross-dressing backstage as Mistress Quickly and Katherine of France,
the entrance above of the clownish Canterbury (Felix Aylmer) and Ely (Robert
Helpman), and the beginning of the play. Canterbury and Ely turn their scene
into a comic *shtick* that makes a mockery of the corrupt trade-off by which
they will bless Henry's war against France in exchange for church lands, the
legalisms behind Canterbury's brain-numbing, 85-line explanation being anything but "as clear as is the summer's day" (1.2.8). The truculent audience lives
up to its reputation by loudly hissing and booing and jeering at the unfortunate Bishop of Ely. On the other hand, it's also possible to see their antics as
stemming from their incompetence as actors rather than from their putative
roles as bishops. After all this realism, though, Olivier's clearing of his throat
as he prepares to enter from backstage reminds us that he is an actor not a king,
just as the Globe is a playhouse not the vasty fields of France.

These actualities inside the playhouse yield to the stage-set theatricality of
the Boar's Head tavern showing Falstaff's demise in melancholy circumstances

punctuated by William Walton's dirge-like *passacaglia*, a musical commentary in bass on the inevitability of death. Theatrical reality then yields to a greater but paradoxically non-alienating fantasy when King Henry boards a warship at Southampton that displays the blatant stylization of a medieval tapestry. Then the camera moves to the pure fantasy world in France that designer Roger Furse modeled on *Les très riches heures du Jean, duc de Berri*, a 14th-century illuminated calendar,[19] its creator the Duke Berri himself (Ernest Thesiger) actually appearing as a character at the French court. The Technicolor parade through "realism" to "neo-illusionism" to "illusionism" to "fantastic," ends at Agincourt, the film's epicenter.

The king's secret anxieties about the state of his soul lie here encrypted under the outer wrappings of the film's illusion and fantasy. The soil of Agincourt is Henry's Garden of Gethsemane: "What infinite heart's ease / Must kings neglect, that private men enjoy!" (4.1.236). In the crucible of the following battle, the king begins the spiral upward again toward reconciliation with the world of reality. Called by Harry M. Geduld, "the most glorious display of pageantry ever to grace a motion picture screen,"[20] the 17-minute Agincourt sequence used hundreds of extras recruited from the Irish Home Guard, cost £80,000 out of the film's projected budget of £300,000 (which escalated to a final cost of £475,708), needed a half-mile railway track for the French cavalry charge, survived a whole series of minor delays from weather and technical glitches, and consumed 39 days of shooting time. According to Dallas Bower, the veteran director who played a crucial role in making the film, the Agincourt scenes shot at Powerscourt near Dublin could not have been made without the help of poet John Betjeman, who as press attaché to the British High Commissioner gained Lord Powerscourt's permission to film on the estate.[21] A crowning glory of the battle scene was the integration of movement with William Walton's inspired music, which in turn followed the example of Sergei Prokofiev's collaboration with Sergei Eisenstein in the battle scenes for *Alexander Nevsky* (1938).[22] Eisenstein is said to have re-edited to make the visuals more compatible with Prokofiev's score. The close tolerance between word and image nowhere shows better than in the analytical close-up when the camera echoes the prologue by showing the horses "printing their proud hoofs I' th' receiving earth" (Chorus, 1.27).

After the battle, like a film run backwards, the same transitions from realism to fantasy and then back to realism occur in reverse order. Back at the French court, Burgundy delivers a panegyric about "our fertile France" that is "the best garden in the world" (5.2.36) while the camera scans a dioramalike landscape beyond the tracery windows of the set. Burgundy's prelapsarian world and the postlapsarian world of Agincourt's battlefield parallel the contrast between the world of the film's "actualities" on the stage of the Globe and the fantastical

Europe upon which the chorus has urged the audience to "let [their] imaginary forces work." The contrast between what seems and what is emerges again in the wooing scene when King Henry proposes to Katherine of France (Reneé Asherton), France's most precious ornament. The king passes himself off to Katherine as a rough, crude sort of fellow, the character of a "plain dealer," a kind of John Wayne figure: "thou wouldst find me such a plain king that thou wouldst think I had sold my farm to buy my crown" (5.2.124). The actuality is that he is not a plain farmer at all but king of England and a world-class Machiavel. Olivier and Asherson survive only briefly as the fairy tale king and princess in the Paris Louvre before, almost imperceptibly, they are again back in the Globe, like Cinderella figures, having been dissolved into a mere player king and princess, Reneé Asherson transmogrified into the crudely cross-dressed boy player who was earlier glimpsed backstage at the Globe stuffing oranges into his shirt for décolletage. The fantasy world ends but the journeymen actors now playing the roles are in themselves also fantasies, though less polished ones. The fluttering handbill returns to list the credits and the revels are ended. Those credits include besides Dallas Bower, wonderfully talented assistants for design (Paul Sheriff), costuming (Roger and Margaret Furse), photography (Robert Krasker), and film music (William Walton), plus the inestimable help of Italian producer Filippo Del Giudice.[23] Olivier did more than make the Shakespeare movie suitable for "the better classes" of people. He created a great film. Dudley Andrew writes almost sacerdotally of it as having joined "the fragile momentary inner life of every viewer to the continuity of cultural life in history . . . Seldom has cinema participated in a more massive ideological undertaking. Seldom has it seemed . . . more worthwhile."[24]

Hamlet (1948)

After the heady success of *Henry V*, producer Filippo Del Giudice of Two Cities Films gave Olivier a free rein and a budget of £475,000 to do *Hamlet* (1948) as he wished. To dull the sharp edges of purists' tongues, Olivier let it be known that his film should be regarded "as an 'Essay in *Hamlet*,' and not as a film version of a necessarily abridged classic."[25] From the realistic/fantasy dichotomies of *Henry V* in Technicolor, he turned to a spartan black-and-white, the inspiration for the *mise-en-scène* no longer the Duke of Berri's colorful Calendar but instead Daniel MacLise's nineteenth-century black-and-white engraving of "The Play Scene in *Hamlet*." Olivier informed his staff that "to me Hamlet is an engraving, not an oil painting,"[26] though his biographer has suggested that the use of black-and-white stock grew more out of expediency than artistic goals when Technicolor film proved unavailable.[27] In any case, black-and-white enhances the deep-focus photography, and better suits the atmosphere of a dark and forbidding tragedy. His sets also remain sparse, abstract, and ultimately timeless. Except for the murals and frescoes of warriors, knights, priests, and saints from twelfth-century European and Byzantine works of art painted on the walls and alcoves, the bareness and emptiness – there is a nearly total lack of furniture – make the castle a metaphor for the protagonist's isolation and loneliness. The result is film noir for highbrows, with chiaroscuro effects reminiscent of Rembrandt's *The Night Watch*, as in the opening scene when Marcellus, Barnardo, and Horatio cluster together in unholy terror of the ghost.

Critics have engaged in quasi-theological disputes about whether the film is primarily "theatrical" or "filmic." Shifting from a movie about the "mirror of all Christian kings" to the tale of a prince who bears "the trappings and the suits of woe" inevitably meant a movement away from a centrifugal to a centripetal kind of space. Epic requires space; tragedy, intimacy. Just as *Henry V* was sweeping and open in response to the chorus' plea for "a muse of fire," *Hamlet* is introspective, at times almost claustrophobic, a constant reminder of Hamlet's observation to Rosencrantz and Guildenstern that "Denmark's a prison" (2.2.243). The empty, virtually unfurnished sets are in one sense theatrical but in another filmic in that their size and scope defy the spatial limitations of a proscenium stage. Certainly this is in many ways a stagy film, all forty of the sets but three having been filmed in the studio at Denham. The sole outdoor shot is apparently of Ophelia's drowning and is modeled on Sir John Millais' famous nineteenth-century painting. Bernice Kliman has observed, however, that "Olivier . . . created a hybrid form, not a filmed play, not precisely a film but a film-infused play."[28] In a later study, Dr. Kliman concluded that this *Hamlet* both "suggests and transcends" the stage as Olivier sought through film "to expand theater" and "[open] up space and [move] the audience without losing the theatrical essence of nonrealistic space."[29] Anthony Davies saw the production as ultimately one of filmic design: "the film is radiant with its essential cinematic conception."[30] Olivier's art director, Carmen Dillon, anticipated this academic debate when she observed that the *Hamlet* sets at Alexander Korda's Denham studio "defy outright classification into [the] cinematic or theatrical." On the one hand, they are filmic in that they have been envisioned for photography not as stage sets, and on the other they are theatrical in that they neither support a roof nor have "any geographical relationship with one another."[31]

The film's credits appear against an establishing shot of the angry sea that besieges Elsinore, the very "sea of troubles" (3.1.58) from Hamlet's flagship "To be or not to be" soliloquy. Desmond Dickinson's cinematography remains a masterpiece of consistent texture, nearly always in control of the pictorial

7   An example of Desmond Dickinson's
deep-focus cinematography in *Hamlet* (UK
1948), as Hamlet (Laurence Olivier) observes
Ophelia (Jean Simmons) framed in an arch of the
castle at Elsinore.

design. A rare discontinuity occurs when Hamlet, facing a foggy storm-tossed
sea, begins his soliloquy from atop the battlements. In a tracking shot from
behind, the camera seems literally to move inside his skull and show not only
his actual brain but also, as N. L. Alkire has argued, subliminal representations
of the masks of comedy and tragedy.[32] A reversal then shows the prince facing
the camera in mid-shot and suddenly posed as if for a studio photograph with
not a trace of foul weather in the clear skies behind him. Meantime his soliloquy
is heard in voice-over.

Olivier liked to bracket his films, this time the framing device being the
windswept battlements of Elsinore, where the movie begins and where it will
end with four captains bearing Hamlet's body aloft. The castle's dizzy height at
the apex imposes the spatial boundary for the multiple levels and planes of the
sets as well as serving as the point of departure and arrival for the roving camera on a crane that peers everywhere into the huge sets. As a part of the establishing sequence, the camera begins at the turret and then obligingly guides
the audience down the circular stone stairway, passes Ophelia's bedchamber
with its window looking out at the sea, peeks into Claudius' "closet," pauses
for a brief inspection of the chamber that contains the polluted "royal bed of
Denmark," moves down into the king's great hall, and lingers on Hamlet's special armchair. For critics like Peter S. Donaldson, the staircase has subliminal

Freudian overtones in echoing a harrowing incident on a stairwell in Olivier's school days.[33]

Olivier's movie is not just film-infused and play-infused but sex-infused. Elsinore holds no greater horror for Hamlet than the recurring icon of the king-sized "enseamed" bed where his mother slept with her own brother-in-law, the "bloat king" Claudius, in "rank sweat . . . / Stew'd in corruption, honeying and making love / Over the nasty sty" (3.4.93). Sexuality, or oldfashioned lust, one of the seven deadly sins, precipitates the "disasters in the sun" at Elsinore. The visual and the aural work against each other. Visually with the symbolic bed Olivier places Hamlet's horror of sexuality, of women, of penetration into the female body, at the core of the action. Aurally, the opening of the film signals quite a different intention with the recital in voiceover of Hamlet's musings on the "stamp of one defect" that may cause a man to "take corruption / From that particular fault" (1.4.31–38). When Olivier's voice then gratuitously announces that this is the tale "of a man who could not make up his mind," he invites assault by Peter Alexander, whose book interrogates this painfully reductive statement.[34] Ironically the movie is not about a man who couldn't make up his mind but about a man who couldn't relate to women, since the political aspect has been shut out by the banishment of Fortinbras. Hamlet's ruin stems from his Oedipal complex and corollary total inadequacy for dealing with Ophelia. "Frailty, thy name is woman!" (1.2.146) he says, but ironically that very frailty carries a deadly capacity for destroying unwary males, as perhaps Olivier's own recent stage appearance as Oedipus had warned him. Prince Hamlet as misogynist is but one of the prince's multiple masks that include avenger, wit, actor, manager, director, philosopher, murderer, duelist, soldier, courtier, "glass of fashion," and almost every other imaginable human trait. Hamlet is to an amazing degree Everyman and Everywoman, as Asta Nielsen and Sarah Bernhardt so aptly demonstrated, yet in this movie a good deal of Fitzwilliam Darcy's misogyny lurks behind the Hamlet mask.

Of course everything about Hamlet is enigmatic, Mona-Lisa like, as T. S. Eliot said, and the camera's endless peering and probing implies a restless desire to pluck out the heart of the mystery. Like Orson Welles who famously used deep-focus photography in *Citizen Kane* (1941), Olivier employed an identical technique in *Hamlet*, though his immediate inspiration may well have been a pioneering BBC production of *Hamlet* (1947) transmitted from Alexandra Palace. Michael Barry claims that George More O'Ferrall's ambitious television drama (he cast some 70 persons) inspired the tracking shots in Olivier's movie.[35] And tracking shots there are. A labyrinth of hallways, stairways, chambers, inner chambers. Hamlet climbs up the stairway toward the ghost of his father, an analytical close-up showing only his feet. The father's ghost emerges from a mist. At "Alas, poor ghost!" (1.5.4), there's an interpolated flashback to the actual poisoning in the garden, though unlike in the Branagh *Hamlet* (1996) the perpetrator remains appropriately unidentified. In one interchange made possible by deep focus, Hamlet is seated in a chair and watches Ophelia approaching him through a long series of archways blocking his view of Polonius, who is hiding behind a pillar and in a position to warn Ophelia away. When she turns away from him, Hamlet mistakenly concludes that it is of Ophelia's own free will.[36] The castle is filled with balconies, stairwells, ledges, so that high and low angle shots can be employed for empowering and disempowering characters, as when Hamlet looms on a ledge above Polonius to lecture him on the sad state of old men's "most weak hams" (2.2.200), or when in long shot the entourage arriving for the play of the "Murther of Gonzago" grandly progresses down the sweeping staircase. Indeed the horizontal and vertical spatial arrangements unify the entire movie, as Anthony Davies has so effectively pointed out.[37] William Walton's music functions as an integral part of the film's emotional texture. For the players, a consort performs a period piece with violins, cello, oboe, cor anglais, bassoon, and harpsichord, which is immediately followed again by the full symphonic orchestra of some 50 players on the soundtrack. When "the King can stand it no longer, the full power of the big orchestra rises up . . . and [ends] in a tremendous 'crash chord' as the King roars, 'Give me some light. Away!'" (3.2.269).[38]

Deletions from Quarto and Folio eliminate Rosencrantz and Guildenstern and Fortinbras' world beyond Denmark, which makes the movie seem all the more centripetal and claustrophobic. "The Murther of Gonzago" has been combined with the preceding dumb show, and scenarist Alan Dent liberally transposed episodes to clarify the narrative, so that the "To be or not to be" soliloquy comes after rather than before Hamlet's quarrel with Ophelia. The acting is superb. In Gertrude's chamber, the mistaken slaughter of Polonius and the visibly erotic bond between son and mother grotesquely restate the primal love and death motif so pervasive in Elizabethan verse, but played on a different key from the thematic treatment in *Romeo and Juliet*, or in *Antony and Cleopatra*. On the heinous bed, a distraught Gertrude (Eileen Herlie) recoils from her ranting self-righteous son who threatens her with a wicked looking phallic knife. Felix Aylmer again shows his versatility, having been Duke Frederick in *As You Like It*, Canterbury in *Henry V*, and now a garrulous Polonius. Stanley Holloway, later famous as Eliza Doolittle's father in *My Fair Lady*, makes a superb gravedigger. Jean Simmons in her blonde wig looks too sweet and virginal to even think about copulating with Hamlet. Once again the specter of Fitzwilliam Darcy looms as Hamlet shows only coldness without a trace of tenderness for the poor, beleaguered young woman, who remains the ultimate female victim.

At the close of a sequence that actually took several days to film, after the wild duel between Hamlet and Laertes, after the fearful moment when Gertrude stares as if hypnotized at the poisoned cup, after Hamlet's famous fifteen-foot leap on Claudius, Hamlet stands bolt upright in a theatrical pose to deliver his last words, omitting any reference to the missing Fortinbras: "Horatio, I am dead, / Thou livest. Report me and my cause aright / To the unsatisfied" (5.2.338). The soldiers shoot and the framing device that began the movie repeats as if someone had hit the reverse button on a VCR. The camera pulls back from the great hall, takes us up the stairs, the four captains bearing Hamlet's body aloft, up and up, past the chapel where Claudius prayed, past the bed chamber of the king and queen where the camera briefly pauses, glances in at the "nasty sty," and then moves on until Hamlet's body has been borne to the castle's turret and the pallbearers with their burden are etched against the gloomy and melancholy sky. Olivier, like many others, has done his best with a camera to report Hamlet's "cause aright," though like the prince himself no stage production, no scholar, no critic will ever plumb the mystery of how best to tell that story "aright."

Richard III (1955)

With *Richard III* (1955), Olivier returned to the Technicolor that he had employed so effectively in *Henry V*, this time supplemented with a spectacular widescreen process known as VistaVision. In a pioneering film and television crossover, the movie was transmitted on North American television on the afternoon of March 11, 1956 by 146 NBC stations in 45 states on the same day that it was released in movie theatres. Estimates put the television audience at 25 million, though most saw it in black-and-white and a handful, perhaps 25,000, in color. Even if inflated, these statistics imply that more people saw a Shakespeare play on that winter afternoon than in all the previous centuries of Shakespeare performances combined. The producers pocketed a $500,000 fee to offset their multi-million investment but the experiment was never repeated because the television exposure ate drastically into later box office receipts.[39]

Olivier, the actor of a thousand faces, after portraying King Henry V, "the mirror of Christian princes," as a kind of Eagle Scout, yearned to play the villain. When plans for *Macbeth* disintegrated, he settled on the most outrageous usurper of all, Richard duke of Gloucester, the anti-Christ himself. Anthony Davies has also pointed out how *Henry V* and *Richard III* act as reverse mirrors by enacting first the culmination of medieval values, and then their collapse in emerging amoral capitalism. Hamlet, for whom "the time is out of joint," is caught indecisively between these two world views, the old emblemized by the father figure King Hamlet and the new by the corrupt stepfather Claudius.[40] In this sense, *Richard III* completes a master design.

This remarkable movie, which lacks the cinematic complexity of *Henry V* but deserves a separate trophy for sustained acting brilliance, won Olivier an Oscar nomination. Olivier assembled an outstanding cast to include such perennials in his retinue as text advisor Alan Dent, designer Roger Furse, art director Carmen Dillon, editor Helga Cranston, and actors Norman Wooland (Catesby), Esmond Knight (Ratcliffe), John Laurie (Lovel). New on board were notables like Sir John Gielgud (Clarence), Ralph Richardson (Buckingham), Claire Bloom (Lady Anne), and the femme fatale figure, Pamela Brown (Jane Shore). Returning also was composer William Walton, whose score provided stirring descriptive music as the little princes ride toward London, the reinforcing sound of a lute just as Richard in his opening monologue speaks of "the lascivious pleasing of a lute" (1.1.13), or the recurring themes that sonically characterize the despair of Lady Anne.

As a film maker and hostage to "tickling commodity," Olivier also again had the problem of making sense for an unschooled audience out of a segment from a longer saga. As is well known, *Richard III* is the last of the four plays of the "minor tetralogy" that depict the feuding baronial houses of York (the white rose) and Lancaster (the red rose) during the ugly fifteenth-century Wars of the Roses. Shakespeare's *Three Parts of Henry VI* ends with the Yorkist victory over the Lancastrians at the 1471 Battle of Tewkesbury, following which the Yorkist Richard duke of Gloucester allegedly murdered both the Lancastrian King Henry VI, the feeble-minded son of King Henry V, and his son, Edward Prince of Wales. When Shakespeare's *Richard III* begins, the Yorkist King Edward has already ascended the throne and his younger brother, the misshapen Richard duke of Gloucester – "Then since the heavens have shap'd my body so, / Let hell make crook'd my mind to answer it" (3 *Henry VI* 5.6.78) – is scheming to usurp his brother's crown. To make these machinations plain to the audience, Olivier, like Frederick B. Warde in the 1912 version and other directors, adapted Colley Cibber's eighteenth-century strategy of grafting lines from *Henry VI Part Three* onto *Richard III*. That way at once the most dastardly side of Richard's character emerges as he confides to the audience that he can "murther" while he smiles and set "the murtherous Machevil to school" (3 *Henry VI* 3.2.180, 193). Acting as his own chorus, Richard then revels in his plans for destroying all who stand between him and the crown, including his brother Clarence, as well as Hastings, his two little nephews, and ultimately even his former ally, Buckingham. They all parade before him in ghastly retribution during the nightmare in the tent on the eve of battle at Bosworth: "O coward conscience, how dost thou afflict me!" (*Richard III* 5.3.179).

The royal crown of England functions this time as Olivier's framing device, appearing in the beginning and then at key stages during the movie, when Richard is himself crowned as king of England and again when at Bosworth Field he has lost his horse and his army and the crown, which falls off his head, and rolls berserkly through the field. It is picked up from a bramble bush by Lord Stanley. In a great moment, supported by Walton's stirring music on the soundtrack, Stanley triumphantly bears the crown aloft as he ceremonially approaches Henry Tudor earl of Richmond, about to be King Henry VII. The expressionistic imaging of the crown as dreamlike obsession reifies Richard's soliloquy in *Henry VI Part Three* when he says "I'll make my heaven to dream upon the crown" (*3 Henry VI* 3.2.168). After the silent-screen cards explaining English history, the crown appears as a large coronet suspended directly over the throne of Edward of York who is about to be ceremonially crowned king of England. Simultaneously with his older brother's coronation, Richard duke of Gloucester in black velvet with his back to the camera has a coronet emplaced on his head. He turns and stares at the camera as if ready to address the theatre audience (us) in an aside but then, as Dale Silviria points out, "the camera cuts to the full figure of Buckingham, then pans to Clarence, then on to a tight knot of figures – the Queen, the princes, the old Duchess of York, the Queen's relatives."[41] In one sweep the camera tracks Richard's future victims like so many skittles waiting to be bowled over.

As emblematic as the crown, iterative shadows providing visible evidence of Richard's poisonous miasma fall on the walls, on the floors, and even on the Lady Anne's white gown. It's as if the "glorious son" of York, Richard's brother Edward, must inevitably be eclipsed by this younger "sun/son" of York. A crucifix on the wall of Clarence's cell in the Tower, after he has been sequestered there partly through Richard's lies and insinuations, identifies Clarence (John Gielgud) as a sacrificial figure. There is no hint here of Clarence's prior treasonous activities, summed up in Shakespeare's text with the inculpatory words, "thou, perjur'd George" (*3 Henry VI* 5.5.34). Gielgud's mellifluous voice elevates Clarence to sainthood in contrast to his demonized younger brother, who blasphemously thirsts for the blood of his victims as an unholy sacrament for a black mass. After Hastings' execution, Richard snappily says "I will not dine until I see the same [Hastings' head]" (*Richard III* 3.4.77). At the end of the play the proto-angelic Richmond with rapt and holy prayer – "O Thou whose captain I account myself, / Look on my forces with a gracious eye" (5.3.108) – makes England safe again for the true decencies of the Holy Eucharist. Old Queen Margaret, the she-wolf of France, widow of Henry VI, has been banished from the movie, most unfortunately because she, Queen Elizabeth, and the Duchess of York constitute a doleful Senecan chorus for ritually excoriating Richard as "that bottled spider, that foul bunch-back'd toad!" (4.4.81). Among those not banished, however, is Jane Shore (Pamela Brown), the mistress of King Edward, a non-character merely alluded to in Shakespeare's play. Appropriately she remains beautiful, mysterious, ubiquitous but usually mute, and often appears silently framed in doorways or inscrutably smiling in the background, a classic object for the camera's "male gaze." After his coronation, King Edward, known as "lascivious Edward," ogles her in public while his queen resolutely ignores her husband's wandering eye.

In Shakespeare's second longest play, and arguably the most sprawling, the character of Richard duke of Gloucester must hold center stage. Without his dynamism, the audience would soon be coughing, shuffling, and wriggling. Olivier plays the role brilliantly, almost as if he had abandoned Fitzwilliam Darcy in favor of a far darker incarnation. A cartoon figure, with his humped back, false oversized nose, beetle brows, lurching limp, and withered arm he resembles a Halloween or Guy Fawkes prankster. The pendent sleeves on his tunic make him look spidery, and his tone of voice hints of unimaginable malice. Olivier's impression seems to have come straight out of Edward Hall's *Union of the Two Noble Famelies of Lancastre and Yorke* (1548), which says of Richard, that

> he was litle of stature, eivill featured of limnes, croke backed, the left shulder muche higher than the righte, harde favoured of visage ... malicious, wrothfull and envious, and ... he came into the world the fete forwarde ... not untothed ... He was close and secrete, a depe dissimuler, ... outwardely familier where he inwardely hated ... despiteous and cruell ... he spared no mannes deathe whose life withstode his purpose. He slewe in the towre kynge Henry the sixte, saiynge now is there no heire male of kynge Edward the thirde, but wee of the house of Yorke.[42]

Vocally, Olivier's magical cadences and rhythms also capture the serio-comical villainy that allows Richard to say the vilest things with a touch of wit, and that in asides to the audience may make him seem downright likeable, scoundrel that he is. Except for the fringe "Friends of Richard III" society, who claim that his reputation was sullied by the House of Tudor official propagandists, Richard is invariably thought of not just as a deep-dyed villain, a Machiavellian, or even a vestige of the medieval Vice like Iago, but as the embodiment of that dread figure, the anti-Christ. In Shakespeare's time, the Protestant reformer, Bishop Jewel, warned that the "anti-Christ shall procure himself credit under the name of Christ" and that "the devil hath devised a new kind of policy, under the very name of Christ to deceive the simple ... Christ [we are warned] is the truth itself; anti-Christ is the truth counterfeit."[43] Olivier out-demonizes the demonizers of Richard III, like the anti-Christ capable of

8   Laurence Olivier's cartoon-like Richard duke of
Gloucester in *King Richard III* (UK 1955), directed
by Olivier, makes it impossible to forget that
Shakespeare's villain is not only "serio" but
"comic."

seeming genial, friendly, persuasive, in order to deceive the simple. Buckingham's spin-doctor advice to Richard could have come out of a handbook
on the anti-Christ: "Look you get a prayer-book in your hand, / And stand
between two churchmen" (3.7.46), who then before the assembled multitude
will become "two props of virtue for a Christian prince" (3.7.96). In the first
wooing scene, the way that he overwhelms the Lady Anne (Claire Bloom),
widow of the man he has murdered, shows his fatal sexual attraction despite
his twisted body. Some differences have arisen over whether this gifted villain qualifies as a modern tyrant, along the lines of Adolf Hitler,[44] or whether
his engaging charm does not exempt him from this kind of calumny.[45] As the
anti-Christ he embodies all these elements, tyrant and charmer, and other gifts
for mischief as well. Richard has a dazzling way, like so many complex Shakespeare characters, of evading all the handy labels – Vice figure, Machiavellian,
and in modern psycho-babble, a sociopath. Deeper more diabolical energies
drive the twisted body and soul that Olivier portrays so stunningly.

   If the overall impression left by Olivier's *Henry V* is one of grandeur, and
by *Hamlet* one of waste, this *Richard III* shocks the audience into seeing not so
much the banality as the grandeur of evil. From the outset, the insolent Richard
radiates more poison than Chernobyl, embodying the Marlovian overreacher
and aspiring to the *Übermensch*. The editing further energizes Richard's swift

judgments with segues and quick cuts such as when the beheading block for Hastings jump cuts to a washerwoman with a sopping cloth; the way that Olivier's camera tracks the gliding movements of the mute but enigmatic Jane Shore; or the cut from the bright palace to the dark horror of Clarence's Tower cell. The parade of ghosts on the eve of Bosworth precedes the final act of retributive justice as Richard lies dying orgasmically on the battlefield, twitching and jerking like an impaled boar, ringed by spears. At the close the morality play message is there for everyone to see, "Crime does not pay," and yet, even knowing he is the anti-Christ, there is a sneaking admiration for the scoundrel, a subversive tug, a shameful desire to be a member of that old Miltonic circle called "the devil's party." Without Elizabeth Bennet, Fitzwilliam Darcy himself might have fallen to this low estate.

Othello (1965)

Olivier bid farewell to the Shakespeare movie, as distinguished from television, with his title role in Stuart Burge's recording of John Dexter's National Theatre production of *Othello* (1965). F. R. Leavis' famous anti-Bradleyian essay that toppled Othello from his lofty perch and painted him as filled with "an insane and self-deceiving passion" powerfully influenced the original stage production. Olivier's Othello rather than being a dupe to Iago was, in Dexter's words, "a pompous, word-spinning, arrogant, black general," while Olivier himself conceived of Iago (Frank Finlay) not as a "witty, Machiavellian" but rather as a "solid, honest-to-God NCO."[46] Despite this theoretical bias, Olivier's innate dignity transcends any attempts to make him look "word-spinning" and "arrogant" and Finlay's insinuating lower-class accent endows him with an animal cunning more sinister than Machiavellian intrigue. A recording of a stage play more than a full-scale movie, the hasty filming at Shepperton studios took less time than the battle scenes for *Henry V* or *Richard III*, to the distress of director Burge.[47] Stagy it may have been but this *Othello* was still a masterpiece of its own kind – the record essentially of a great theatre experience that would otherwise have been forever lost. The term "theatrical" should be thought of as merely descriptive, not prescriptive, not in any way prima facie evidence of inferiority. The acting makes or breaks the experience.

True, *Othello* lacks outdoor scenes, pitched battles, massive sets, but it shows assorted filmic resources that set it apart from a stage production. Filmed with three Panavision cameras,[48] the various takes have been edited to allow for multiple reaction shots and analytical close-ups. For some scenes, as when Othello debarks at Cyprus (2.1), the *mise-en-scène* is so patently theatrical that, as someone once said, the actors might as well have been talking to an empty auditorium. Elsewhere the multiple cameras and editing permit cutaways from one character to another that would be impossible on stage. Frank Finlay's rugged "honest NCO" profile benefits the most, when, for example, he is foregrounded in profile observing Cassio (Derek Jacobi) and Desdemona (Maggie Smith) on the waterfront at Cyprus as they await Othello's arrival from Venice (2.1.103). A crane shot of Iago's demonic seduction of Othello as the dialogue peaks with Othello's Faustian "Now art thou my lieutenant," and Iago's fervid "I am your own for ever" (3.3.479) qualifies as the most "cinematic" shot in the film.

Olivier, the most versatile of actors, eagerly embraced the challenge of playing a black man, which even before the age of political correctness stirred up a tempest. He is said to even have lowered his voice an octave to qualify for the role. Bosley Crowther complained that Olivier looked "like Rastus or an end man in an American minstrel show";[49] Judith Crist, that Olivier played Othello as "a manic depressive skirting the edges of paranoia";[50] and Brendan Gill, that Olivier's reading of the title role was "utterly daft."[51] A more general condemnation of the production as being insufficiently "cinematic" came from Nathan Kallet: "[the] film is dragged by bloat" because the director "did not seek a cinematic equivalent to Shakespeare's play."[52] Only a unique performance could draw such scathing fire and Olivier's Othello achieves not just technical perfection but genuine passion. From his first appearance at the Venetian court, languidly sniffing a long-stemmed red rose and speaking in a low-pitched West Indian accent, Olivier's Moor radiates primal energy. He taps Iago on the chest with the rose as if to warn him that softer measures will be needed in the weeks to come. The same love of disguise that turned him into a menacing anti-Christ in *Richard III* serves to make him an imposing black warrior.

Wicked, evil, malicious Iago (Frank Finlay) always threatens to upstage Othello and without the formidable presence of Olivier, Frank Finlay may well have succeeded. He conjures up whole new reservoirs of malice and obscenity as he plays the voyeur, "He takes her by the palm; ay, well said, whisper . . . Yet again, your fingers to your lips? Would they were clysterpipes for your sake!" (2.1.167 ff). Finlay's Iago is a sinister, leering, foulminded, lower-class East London type, whose drive to control and manipulate is underscored by this camera work that consistently foregrounds him in profile to give the impression of the master puppeteer manipulating a creature ripe for exploitation. From all accounts, he came through more powerfully on camera than on stage in the National Theatre production.

Other cast members turn in equally striking performances. As Michael Cassio, Derek Jacobi, addled with drink by perfidious Iago, foreshadows his future brilliance in major screen and television Shakespeare productions. As

Desdemona, Maggie Smith radiates a clear-eyed decency and innocence rooted in an innate strength and dignity worthy of the daughter of Brabantio, a pillar of the Venetian establishment. Her white skin against the coal-black flesh of Olivier points to the play's pervasive subtext of miscegenation. Burge's *Othello* then remains an actor-centered rather than a director-centered production, primarily preserving a record of a first-rate stage performance. A major share of Shakespeare's text remains. With more time to rehearse and a larger budget, Stuart Burge might have made his recorded stage play into a great movie as well. The world would be richer now if, for example, someone had recorded the *Othello* (1959) starring Paul Robeson as Othello with Sam Wanamaker as his Iago.

The Merchant of Venice (1973) and *King Lear* (1983): TV Appearances

Olivier's entry into Shakespeare on television began as early as 1937 when he acted with Judith Anderson in a 30-minute BBC excerpt from the Old Vic *Macbeth*.[53] Many years later, he appeared in two wonderfully skillful televised Shakespeare plays as first Shylock and then in his old age, appropriately, as King Lear. In Jonathan Miller's and John Sichel's 1973 Precision Video adaptation of the National Theatre Edwardian dress production of *The Merchant of Venice* (1970), he re-invented Shylock with the help of director Jonathan Miller as a Baron Rothschild figure,[54] elegantly turned out in a frock coat, with only a skullcap to identify him as an outsider. The Edwardian milieu is urbane, polished, Miller having even thought of Bassanio and Antonio as mirroring the love between Oscar Wilde and his Bosie. The sleek and well coifed youthful friends of Antonio and Bassanio indolently lounge in waterside cafés. Their infuriating insouciance and glossy façades subvert their own self-images by exposing an intrinsic shallowness of spirit. If the Belmont crowd had lived in Nazi Germany they "would not have known about Hitler's concentration camps," nor would they have cared to know. Although the usual cries of "anti-Semitism" swirled around the show,[55] Miller presented a sympathetic Shylock, more victim than villain.

As a supremely self-confident Portia, Joan Plowright, comfortably tucked away in suburban Belmont with Nerissa (Anna Carteret), gets the first glimpse of her suitors by means of a period-piece stereo-opticon. In an astonishing *tour de force*, a perfect Miller touch, two spinsterish looking ladies (Clare Walmesley and Laura Sarti) suddenly appear on screen and erupt into the wildest but most compelling rendition in history of "Tell me where is fancy bred [?]" (3.2.63). The singing sardonically reflects on the patriarchal tyranny that has enmeshed Portia in the absurd casket scheme. Their obvious prompting of Bassanio toward the lead casket, however, somewhat justifies June Schlueter's objection to the "trivializing" of the casket plot into a "sideshow."[56] After the harsh disposal of Shylock in the trial scene and after the sadistic teasing about the lost rings of Bassanio and Gratiano by Portia and Nerissa, Jessica, Shylock's ingrate of a daughter, is left standing alone, while the Jewish requiem, the "Kaddish" (sung by Heinz Danziger), reverberates on the soundtrack. In Miller's hands and with Laurence Olivier's miraculous contributions, *The Merchant of Venice* surely becomes the woefullest but most complicated comedy ever written.

When nearly twenty years later, Olivier agreed to play the title role in *King Lear* (1983), he was not in good health and at 75 nearly a match for the age of Shakespeare's irascible old king, whom he had played on stage at the Old Vic with Alec Guinness as Fool in 1946. Taped in three weeks at the Manchester TV Centre studios on a set with a polystyrene mock-up of Salisbury Plain's mysterious Stonehenge, the $2-million Granada TV production featured an Olivier not only playing King Lear but also his aged self, a real life embodiment of Shakespeare's geriatric hero. To spare Olivier from excessive strain and to save time, the original idea of a taped stage play was jettisoned in favor of television.[57] Director Michael Elliott could the more easily then edit the action from an elevated central vantage point.

As television host Peter Ustinov said with little hyperbole, it "featured the best Shakespearean cast ever assembled." Not exactly "stunt casting," as Kenneth Branagh's Shakespeare movies have been uncharitably charged with, the director did recruit prominent BBC and RSC regulars, though no Hollywood superstars: Leo McKern (Gloucester), Dorothy Tutin (Goneril), Diana Rigg (Regan), Anna Calder-Marshall (Cordelia), Jeremy Kemp (Cornwall), Colin Blakely (Kent), and John Hurt (Fool). As is often true of televised Shakespeare (see chapter 5), the performance is actor-centered, but Elliott encoded visual signposts expressive of the spiritual turmoil in this epic clash between a father and his three daughters. Stonehenge itself, mysterious druid relic from Britain's ancient times, frames the teleplay. At the beginning to the sound of primitive horns, Lear enters with Cordelia, laughing and chatting and agreeably at ease with himself and his daughters. The decision to tape in color instead of in black-and-white, as is usually the case with screen versions of *King Lear*, makes the sequence almost lighthearted, until the king's initial outburst of choleric rage when Cordelia snubs him. Olivier's prodigious acting skills remain intact, as shown, for example, in the uncanny gift for rolling vowels, and in the body language with his hands when reacting to Cordelia's blunt "Nothing, my lord" (1.1.87).[58] The approach to the play favors the old king over his daughters as the wronged one, disprivileging any post-modernist victimization scenarios of patriarchal oppression. In the last frames, the return to Stonehenge allows Lear and Cordelia to be seen as sacrificial victims stretched out on the temple's slaughtering stone.

A gigantic, rug-sized map, unfolded before Lear to calibrate the division of the kingdom, then becomes the site of the hypocritical obeisance of Regan and Goneril and the arena for the king's petulance when he hurls the crown away. To counterpoint the harshness of stone, the greenery of an oak tree[59] suggests harmony and reconciliation when the chastened old king meets with the blinded Gloucester. The king returns to the basics of nature with his crown of wild flowers and in one very potent episode consumes a freshly slaughtered rabbit, raw and uncooked. With these talismans, he renews his pact with himself in the loneliness of the heath, where in the exposure of his pathetically withered, aged body, he embodies the loathsome appearance of a Swiftian Struldbrug. Except in the notorious Tate eighteenth-century version, the play brooks no happy ending, yet in the last moments when Olivier appears in full color, close-shaven, pink-cheeked, cherubic, robed in white, in his new cleanliness ready to be reborn, he takes the Lear figure close to heavenly enthronement. This is anthropology's sacrificial king, about to be slaughtered that the crops may be renewed, with Anna Calder-Marshall's ethereal Cordelia thrown in for good measure. "Is this the promis'd end?" (5.3.264) asks Kent as the old king dies. A wrenching denouement for Shakespeare's king, no doubt, but for Olivier a noble and dignified exit from the theatre for the man of a thousand faces. The pleasure he has brought to millions might even make Fitzwilliam Darcy smile. Certainly some critics smiled. On a 1998 British Film Institute list of 360 film classics released prior to 1981, only two Shakespeare movies were included and these were both directed by Olivier – *Henry V* and *Richard III*.[60]

- 4 -

Orson Welles: Shakespeare for the art houses

One of Orson Welles's many, many biographers recently argued that after the legendary film maker's first and greatest success, *Citizen Kane* (1941), "the remaining forty-five years of Welles's life are a sort of sustained falling apart . . . he came increasingly . . . [to be] the legend of the self-destroyed artist."[1] That period when he was "falling apart," however, ironically marks the years when Welles produced the three Shakespeare movies, *Macbeth* (1948), *Othello* (1952), and *Chimes at Midnight* (1966), that showed an admirable resolve not to fall apart. Not that Welles should be beatified as a kind of plaster saint who at all costs put art above "tickling commodity," but his Shakespeare movies were by box office guidelines demonstrably "uncommodified." Scholars and journalists have struggled without great success to pluck out the heart of Orson Welles's mystery.[2] As James Russell Lowell said in *A Fable for Critics* (1848) of another American genius, Edgar Allan Poe, Welles too was perhaps "three-fifths . . . genius and two-fifths sheer fudge." If Laurence Olivier's work is Apollonian, reasonable, comfortably mainstream, and commodified, Welles's is Dionysian and passionate, rough-hewn and unpredictable, and uncommodified. Put reductively, Olivier's work remains theatrical and English; Welles's, cinematic and American.

Orson Welles loved magic. There is a photograph of him on the set of *The Magnificent Ambersons* (1942) gleefully pulling a rabbit out of a hat to the amazement of Joseph Cotten and Dolores Costello;[3] an unfinished movie, *The Magic Show* (1969–85) in which "some of his best acts of prestidigitation [were] done without camera tricks";[4] Suzanne Cloutier's casual remark about how on the *Othello* set in Morocco "he created a magical world for us;"[5] Keith Baxter's saying "Orson was a conjuror, you know," as he described the trick shots for Prince Hal in *Chimes at Midnight*;[6] and Gregg Toland's influence in teaching Welles about wide angle lenses for his trademark deep focus shots.[7] The fascination with magic also extended beyond theatrics into his whole world view. As a child prodigy, he apparently enjoyed playing tricks, in pulling the wool over people's eyes, so to speak.

One of his last films, *F for Fake* (1973), revels in the charms of the art forger, Elmyr de Hory, who could dash off a passable Matisse quicker than Matisse himself. De Hory exemplified to Welles the aphorism attributed to Picasso that "Art is a lie that makes us realize the truth."[8] With Orson Welles blandly announcing that he is himself a "charlatan," the riddle becomes one of figuring out whether Welles really is a charlatan, or is only pretending to be a charlatan. The bewildering search for reality disintegrates into shards like the multiple mirror scene in Welles's *The Lady from Shanghai* (1946). In the ultimate provocation, Welles hints that "profound" symbols, such as the enigmatic "Rosebud" in *Citizen Kane*, may have absolutely no meaning at all. It stands only for a child's sled, like Freud's cigar that only stands for a cigar. The mystery in the movie, or in its ironical director, may be that there is no mystery.

Orson Welles's troubles in Hollywood began when he arrived under contract to RKO at age twenty-three, already heralded as a "boy wonder," and thus inevitably bringing down on his head the wrath of everyone older and less successful than he was. Years later Welles said that all he knew about movies had been learned from viewing John Ford's *Stagecoach* forty-five times and from his cameraman, Gregg Toland, who offered to teach Welles everything about movie making in three hours. Welles was quick to add, however, that "Everything else is if you're any good or not."[9] And as a film maker he was not just "good," he was superb. Whiffs of this youthful condescension toward movie making wafting out into the California sunshine may very well have enraged the unfriendly local cinéastes. His reputation rested on the WPA *Macbeth* (1936) and Mercury Theatre *Julius Caesar* (1937) stage productions in New York, his CBS radio role as the sepulchral voice in "The Shadow" series, and the sensational hoax radio show based on H. G. Wells's "War of the Worlds" (1939) that sent thousands of panicked New Jersey citizens screaming into the streets. Soon, though, after an aborted fling at making Joseph Conrad's *Heart of Darkness*, Welles produced with Herman J. Mankiewicz and John Houseman *Citizen Kane* (1941), which may be America's greatest film but it earned the youthful *auteur* a powerful foe in the William Randolph Hearst publishing empire. After the controversial *Citizen Kane* and production turmoil with *The Magnificent Ambersons* (1942), his situation in Hollywood was precarious. In a *felix culpa*, though, his inability "to eat lunch in that town again," was what eventually made the Shakespeare movies possible.

Macbeth (1948)

Orson Welles's *Macbeth* could have been the first feature-length talking picture of Shakespeare's Scottish play had it not been for David Bradley who, with some help from Charlton Heston, made the first feature-length talkie *Macbeth* at Northwestern University in 1947 on a budget of $5,000.[10] With even a low

B-movie budget from Republic Pictures, Welles tapped resources far beyond those available to Bradley and his undergraduate crew. Still, the movie sometimes functions at the amateurish level of provincial theatre, which is where it began when Welles directed the play for the Utah Centennial Festival.[11] The costumes seem tacky, especially the series of ridiculous headgears worn by Macbeth, the first resembling a "beanie"; the second, the crown on the Statue of Liberty; and the third, an inverted kitchen stool. Welles himself complained about the Statue of Liberty crown and explained that it was because the Western Costume company had nothing else to offer. He insulated himself against future critics by describing the hastily made film – the shooting schedule was twenty-three days – as a "violently sketched charcoal drawing of a great play."[12] The hasty filming had been preceded, though, with rehearsals in Utah, four days of performances in May 1947, and Welles's earlier experience at age twenty as director of the famous "Voodoo" *Macbeth* (1936) with an all-black cast at Harlem's Lafayette Theatre. His interest in Shakespeare went back into childhood and continued with an adolescent portrayal of Richard III at the progressive Todd School.[13]

His *Macbeth* then explores the tortured soul of the protagonist through the Wellesian world of skewed camera angles and brilliant découpage. The movie's reception has been almost as fragmented as the film, ranging from Bosley Crowther's denigration of the characters as "half-mad zealots in a Black Mass"[14] to Jean Cocteau's admiring comment that "not a single shot is left to chance."[15] With his hypnotic voice and overwhelming presence, Welles almost literally drowns out all the other characters, his Lady Macbeth, Jeanette Nolan, a competent radio actress, being so upstaged as to be virtually non-existent. The bombast leaves very little room for embodying the nuances and subtleties of a character so complex as Macbeth, who is both gangster and poet. Welles's Macbeth fears evil but he roars about it more than he contemplates it. The great speech in which he ruminates about the murder of Duncan, "If it were done, when 'tis done, then 'twere well / It were done quickly" (1.7.1), sounds more declamatory than meditative.

The scenario includes inspired additions, deletions, and transpositions of all sorts and varieties. With the help of a dialogue overlap, Macbeth is dictating the first part of the letter to Lady Macbeth, who then suddenly is seen at the castle reading the last half aloud (1.5.1); some kind of high priest looking like a character out of *Alexander Nevsky* stands in as a surrogate for Rosse; a Voodoo doll with Macbeth's head sprinkles in pagan elements that are at war with the Christian symbolism so pervasive everywhere else; the Porter loses virtually all of his comic shtick except "Knock, knock, knock!" (2.3.3); Macbeth shows up first-hand for the murder of Lady MacDuff; and Lady Macbeth speaks some of Rosse's lines, and so forth.[16] A remnant from the "Voodoo" stage *Macbeth*

9   Orson Welles as Macbeth and Jeanette
Nolan as his Lady filmed in one of
Welles's characteristically bizarre camera
angles that suggests the growing schism
between the ambitious couple. *Macbeth*
(USA 1948).

lingers on in the execution of Cawdor, who is lugged around like a sack of flour,
until to the eerie thudding of Haitian tom-toms a giant axe descends on his
neck. In the psychomachia between cinéastes and bardolaters, Welles had no
trouble choosing sides. Shakespeare's play was there to be made into a movie,
not the other way around.

The director's inability to merge his considerable talents for both radio and
film remained a problem. He loved images but he seemed at times to love
voice more, especially his own. Actually in *Macbeth* he was experimenting
with the favoring of sound over sight in a style that would be perfected by
the time he directed *Othello*. That is to say, in films like Olivier's *Henry V*,
William Walton's music supports the cavalry charge at Agincourt, while in
Welles's *Macbeth* the execution of Cawdor supports the hypnotic drumbeat of
tom-toms. Curiously this reversal of sight/sound for sound/sight replicates
Thomas Edison's original goal, which was to develop pictures to support his
phonograph, not the other way around.

Even inhibited by the speed of production, Welles's genius peeks through
the makeshift papier-mâché sets and the diminutive budget. One of the reasons that the movie, like Welles himself, oscillates between the sublime and
the ridiculous lies in the complicated maneuvers in both the pre- and post-
production phases. To economize and to show Hollywood how movies "of
this importance [could] be made on such a schedule and such a budget,"[17]

Welles had the actors pre-record their lines in a Scots burr to slow down their rapid speech and to approximate the sound of Elizabethan actors at the Globe. During the actual shooting of the film, the actors on the set in Hollywood mimed their lines in synch with the speeches that had been prerecorded in Utah.[18] After the initial release, however, the unhappy producers disliked the soundtrack enough, particularly the Scots burr, to withdraw the print and ask for pruning and relooping (re-recording). They became highly exercised when Welles went abroad, leaving the brunt of the editing to his assistant, Richard Wilson. To the Republic executives, the situation threatened a replay of an earlier fiasco when Welles was filming in South America during the editing phase of *The Magnificent Ambersons*, and RKO's Robert Wise added an unauthorized upbeat ending. The 1950 re-release of *Macbeth* engendered more problems when the original Scots burrs got totally confused with the new unaccented and often unsynched voices. A third restoration in 1979 by the UCLA film archives and Folger Library brought the movie back close to its original form. The Scots burr comes across loud and clear when Macbeth says things like "my soul is too much charrrrged" (5.8.5).

In shot after shot, Welles's radio background results in disembodied dialogue that never really gets into synch with the actors' bodies. The pre-recording created a disjunction between words and images, so that the actors may be speaking off camera, or at times their lips are simply out of synch, or again the words come through in voice-over while lips remain sealed. Jeanette Nolan gives a curiously epicene performance even with "Come, you spirits / That tend on mortal thoughts, unsex me here" (1.5.40),[19] in which the words come mostly in voice-over while she lies first inertly on a bed and then stares out the window at the clouds. She seizes on none of the obvious cues (i.e., "Come to my woman's breasts, / And take my milk for gall" (1.5.47)) for energizing her speech with a writhing body as Jane Lapotaire does so spectacularly in an otherwise pedestrian BBC television version (1983). Similarly with Macbeth's "Out, out, brief candle! / Life's but a walking shadow, a poor player" (5.5.23) there is no Macbeth, only a screen full of ominous clouds. Now and again Welles's dialogue overlaps, which makes one speech slur into another and creates more confusion than artistry. Symbolism oscillates between Christian and pagan with glimpses of a kilt or the skirl of a bagpipe pasted on a weird, Druid background.[20]

On the other hand, the images on screen, while often divorced from the dialogue, show how Welles benefited from his tutoring by cameraman Gregg Toland on *Citizen Kane*. The stylization, surreal effects, and chiaroscuro lighting of German expressionism, along with debts to compositional strategies in Eisenstein's *Alexander Nevsky*, may also have contributed to Welles's filmic grammar. Many low-angle and deep-focus shots resemble the "bravura" effects in *Citizen Kane*. A conversation between Macbeth and Lady Macbeth with the king ensconced high on a throne and Lady Macbeth yards away quotes a blocking of Charles Kane and Susan Alexander in the great hall at Xanadu. The wide-angle lens by distorting the connection between the man and woman underscores their spiritual isolation. Macbeth like Kane is often photographed from a low angle to give him the image of overpowering authority. Instead of the oppressive low ceilings of the *Kane* film, the theatrically inspired sets are vast units that allow the camera to remain stationary while recording the action in the spacious papier-mâché halls, left over from a Republic picture B western. When Lady Macbeth leaps off a precipice, there is a $53.36 special effect[21] in which she falls endlessly, her twisting body gradually receding from view as she hurtles into a bottomless gorge. The banquet scene allows for another deep-focus shot as Banquo's ghost, seen only by a terrified Macbeth, emerges and disappears and reemerges at the end of an elongated dining table.

His strong theatrical background gave Welles a special interest in lighting effects, especially in the blacking out of one part of the set to shift audience attention to another part of the stage. To the consternation of the studio crew, he tried to take over the lighting on the *Citizen Kane* set from his veteran camera man. The Megahey television interview shows how the lighting for his staged *Julius Caesar* influenced the filmed *Macbeth*. In its expressionistic style, *Macbeth* echoes Robert Wiene's *The Cabinet of Dr. Caligari* (1919) for like other geniuses, William Shakespeare for instance, Welles was fully capable of making inventive use of the work of others. Despite the hostility of many critics, the sheer nerve and energy of the movie in probing for the devildriven horror at the soul of its tragic hero makes it impossible to ignore. Welles biographer Joseph McBride completely reversed his negative attitude toward the 1950 release when he saw the 1980 restored version and declared it to be an event of "hypnotic intensity."[22] Like the probing camera that slips past the No Trespassing sign at the opening of *Citizen Kane*, Welles persisted in his epic quest to lift any veil that obscured the truth about others and even about himself.

Othello (1952)

With *Othello*, Welles invented the MTV style decades before it was invented. He abandoned the *mise-en-scène* doctrines that he had learned from Gregg Toland in favor of the opposite school of Sergei Eisenstein's bias toward *découpage*. That is to say, in place of the long take (the classic in the Wellesian *oeuvre* being the kitchen scene between Tim Holt's George and Agnes Moorhead's Aunt Fanny in *Ambersons*), he turned toward montage, which involves the juxtaposition of short scenes. Toland thought that the wide angle lens could permit viewers to select for themselves what to observe on the screen and thus put motion pictures a step closer to reality itself. Instead Welles assembled bits and pieces from Shakespeare's most domestic tragedy, brought together fragments from all corners of the play, reworked them into a mosaic and then shattered them as a talisman to Othello's chaotic search for beauty and love. He played a variation on the jigsaw puzzle trope that he obsessively repeated in *Kane*, and magically in *Othello* it coalesced into a film worthy of a *Palme d'Or*.

The movie of *Othello* opened to a hostile reception. A headline for a London newspaper review sets the tone: "Mr. Welles Murders Shakespeare in the Dark," and the reviewer went on waspishly to note of Welles that "the play-wright who has him for a friend does not need any enemies."[23] Another British critic further lambasted the film "made by that big prankish schoolboy Orson Welles" and pontificated that out of this "Wellesian fun fair of angelic, disembodied voices, dizzy camera angles, and shadowy sepulchral scenery [there might be] some small unexpected suggestion which may, one day, help a real director to make *Othello* into a worthy film."[24] Critics back home were no friendlier. Robert Hatch in *Nation* sarcastically observed that "Orson Welles has proved by now that he is too good for Shakespeare; I wish he would start reviving Dion Boucicault."[25] The commentator for *Time* did finally admit, though, after sneering at Welles for several paragraphs, that the work "moves forward with a pulse-quickening stir and bustle."[26] The ultimate insult came with the movie's 1955 release in the United States when box-office receipts amounted to a pathetic $40,000.

With the 1992 re-release, however, a sea change occurred. Some critics saw genius where previously there had only been fudge. After four decades in exile, the film was elevated to "the class of *Citizen Kane*,"[27] and became "a wind-blown, turbulent, bravura movie."[28] Of course the movie hadn't changed, the times had, though some critics protested that the 1992 release damaged the original soundtrack by electronically altering dialogue so that the film's "restoration" became "a shameful travesty of film history."[29] As Samuel Crowl has suggested, European post-structuralist literary theory paved the way for tolerating narrative discontinuities unfathomable to the rigid mindset of the Fifties.[30] Although not a strident ideologue, Welles was enough of a man of the left to know the penalties for non-conformity in the Eisenhower years when McCarthyism, or Hooverism, turned the American dream into a nightmare for dissident intellectuals. The expectations that made Olivier's *Henry V* acceptable to the critics at mid-century suddenly shifted into the taste for fragmentation that makes Welles's rough-hewn *Othello* the poster child for the chaotic Nineties. In 1952 no one had heard of Roland Barthes' *S/Z* with its painstaking and often tedious explication of the *lexia* or segments that make up a completed narrative.[31] The isolation and decoding of segments in a narrative become an exercise involving the paradox of the hermeneutical circle – the whole cannot be understood without understanding the part, nor the part without under-standing the whole.[32] Welles's *Othello* is an exercise in hermeneutics in the way that it takes segments of *Othello* and reconstitutes them spatially to throw fresh light on the machinations of Iago. The segments, like Susan Alexander's jigsaw puzzle in *Citizen Kane*, must be reassembled in the mind of the viewer, preferably with the technical help of a laser disk recording and a Pioneer disk player.

It took Welles three weeks to film *Macbeth*, nearly three years to complete *Othello*. Micheál MacLiammóir's amusing and informative journal[33] chronicles the serio-comic disasters that have made the film's production woes the stuff of folk tales. In June 1949 Welles found himself stranded in Morocco on the Atlantic coast at Mogador, with neither money nor costumes when his Italian backers declared bankruptcy. In the next two years, one financial crisis after another interrupted filming. Actors were "stranded" in remote places and whole scenes had to be re-shot in entirely different locations when the original cast members disappeared. Welles denied that the actors were "marooned" but were left in luxury hotels at Welles's own expense while he undertook an heroic search for money to keep the show alive. He acted in other people's films, playing Harry Lime in *The Third Man* (1949), General Bayan in *The Black Rose* (1950), and himself in *Return to Glennascaul* (1951), borrowed money, ran up huge bills. There were brilliant expedients. When shooting began in French Morocco with no costumes on hand, he hit on staging the murder of Roderigo in a Turkish bath so that bath towels would suffice as costumes. Since actors were forced to abandon the unfinished project to find other work, the move toward montage and away from *mise-en-scène* stemmed not only from artistic design but from the need to cover up defects brought on by the many breaks in the production schedule. Actors who appeared to be in the same scene had actually been photographed in different times and places, perhaps not in Morocco but in Italy, or vice versa. Miraculously, a film eventually emerged from this nervewracking ordeal.

Whatever outsiders thought, people who worked with him swore eternal allegiance to Welles. Suzanne Cloutier (Desdemona) testified to the director's enormous powers of invention. "He created all the time," she said, and he left the cast and crew constantly wondering what novel idea he would come up with next. Camera man Obadan Troiano said of Welles's photographic sensi-bility that "his shots had a language of their own," and facetiously added that working with Welles had "ruined" his career, for ever afterwards if directors "didn't live up to Welles, I couldn't work for them." Composer Francesco Lavagnino was impressed by Welles's musical abilities. He and Welles together conceived of evoking a middle-eastern sound with the mandolin and percussion effects that replaced the original idea for themes from Verdi's *Otello*. Welles liked Lavagnino's work so much that, in an extraordinary reversal of normal expectations, he persuaded him not to cut down on his music but to compose an additional three minutes. Welles then set about to shoot extra footage to go with the music, in yet another demonstration of how his background in radio could make him regard sound as equal to sight. Lavagnino trenchantly said of Welles that "he invented you."[34] Just, one might add, as Welles often invented himself.

According to Welles's own account, the movie's design stemmed from Iago's delight in schemes of entrapment: "With as little a web as this will I ensnare as great a fly as Cassio" (2.1.168), or "And out of her own goodness make the net / That shall enmesh them all" (2.3.361). The resulting foray into entrapment and fear carries the movie into the realm of film noir, the Hollywood B movies that reflected the dark, paranoid side of America obscured by the genial fatuousness of the Eisenhower years. Welles's own film noir masterpiece was *A Touch of Evil* (1958) starring Charlton Heston as a Mexican attorney and Welles as the corrupt and gross police captain with a cameo appearance by *femme fatale* Marlene Dietrich. As Robert Sklar has said, "the hallmark of the film noir is its sense of people trapped . . . trapped in webs of paranoia and fear,"[35] a formula made to order for *Othello*, where there is ample "magic in the web" (3.4.69).

In post-modernist rejection of seamless narrative, *Othello* begins where it should end, with the funeral procession for Othello and Desdemona. In the opening shot, Othello is already not only dead but also upside down as if to stress the unnatural reversal of the moral order in the life of Venice. The funeral procession is cliché Eisenstein, its shadowy black figures silhouetted against the stark unrelieved whiteness of the sky over the roaring sea, with a dirge-like wailing and chanting on the soundtrack. The cortège winds its way along the ramparts of the eighteenth-century Mogador fortress. There are glimpses of the biers of Othello and of Desdemona sometimes seen through the long pikes and spears of armored soldiers, other times in long shot. Then suddenly viewed from a crane shot, there is a wretched man, a rope around his neck, being dragged through the crowd toward a cruel and savage looking cage. He is roughly thrust into it and by the means of a creaking iron wheel and pulley the cage is hoisted skyward to dangle in front of the high stone wall. Framed by the bars of the cage is the bleak, enigmatic face of the arch villain, Iago himself. "I am not what I am," he has said (1.1.65), but now he will have "daws to peck at" him, while his lips remain forever sealed: "Demand me nothing; what you know, you know: / From this time forth I never will speak word" (5.2.303). He stares down at the human wreckage caused by his malice.

Since Welles disliked, or pretended to dislike, ponderous theories, Iago is the ideal Wellesian villain. There is really nothing for him to explain about himself, or others to explain about him. He is simply motivated by pure evil, "unmotivated malignancy," nothing more, or so it is generally believed except by those who take seriously his whining about being passed over for promotion, or his lust for Desdemona. A born actor with a truly magnificent voice, who began listening to Shakespeare read aloud at age three or four, Welles thought formal acting lessons superfluous. Still, Welles apparently allowed Stanislavsky a foot in the door by toying with the idea of Iago being driven by his impotence, as somehow hinted in his remark that Cassio "hath a daily beauty in his life / That makes me ugly" (5.1.19). The skewed camera angles showing people and settings in Venice and Cyprus from every conceivable perspective aid and abet in imagining a dysfunctional world tailored for a sociopath like Iago.

Iago's cage then becomes the *locus classicus* for the rest of the movie. The iron bars that signify entrapment surface everywhere. Othello as he listens to Iago stands under the crisscross of a lattice; Othello overhears Cassio's apparent bantering with Iago about Desdemona from a concealed niche; Desdemona's bedroom contains a leaded glass window through which she is seen as virtually penned in; the sewer in Mogador that serves so usefully for corridors and as a bathhouse is full of cul-de-sacs, arches, corridors, barriers that evoke fantasies of dungeons and torment. When Roderigo is slain by Iago he is entrapped under a barrier of duckboards through which Iago's sword flashes mercilessly. At the very end of the movie, after Othello has smothered Desdemona, he himself stands alone, piteously forlorn, imprisoned behind the bars of an enormous iron door that soars to a lofty ceiling. Like Mister Kurtz in Conrad's *The Heart of Darkness*, which Welles once spent considerable time planning to film, Othello has discovered his own horror. The iron bars imprison him in a private hell exiled from Venice's comfortable bourgeois society. Respectable citizens peer down on him through an open dome as if he were an ape in a cage. As he portrays Othello's remorse and spiritual agony, "Then must you speak / Of one that lov'd not wisely but too well" (5.2.343), Welles does not merely rely on the God-given gift of his hypnotic voice but reaches deep down within himself for the tragic emotion to arouse pity and fear for Othello's unbearable suffering. Iago's net has finally ensnared not only Iago but everyone else as well.

The integration of sight, sound, and music in a baroque scheme of complicated point and counterpoint makes Welles's *Othello* a work of art. No single component stands in isolation from any other but every event on screen counts. The Venetian artist, Vittore Carpaccio (c.1465–1523), inspired Alexandre Trauner's artistic design for the film. The little white dog that follows Roderigo around derives from Carpaccio's painting of St. Jerome in his study, but the mirror that Othello examines himself in, attributed by Welles to Carpaccio, has not been so easily traced.[36] The setting remains stark and bare rather than crammed with objets d'art as in a Zeffirelli film, an important exception being

Desdemona's jumbo-sized bed. When Michael Cassio (Michael Lawrence) reels around during the drinking bout with Iago, walls and crude benches seem to be the only physical details apparent in the kaleidoscopic blur of editing.

Welles's editing at the movieola finally defines the production's value. He immensely enjoyed film editing as shown in his *F for Fake* and again in the television documentary, *Filming Othello* (1978), where he sits at a movieola as he reminisces about *Othello* and how much better it would have been if he could have made it again. Welles matches sound with sight in ingeniously complicated ways as when we see Othello smothering Desdemona with the white handkerchief that then turns into a death mask starkly outlining her features. There is a sighing on the soundtrack, a gong, a beeper, the thud of heartbeats, and then a chilling silence, as Othello says "Cold, cold, my girl?" (5.2.275). Off camera he begins "Blow me about in winds! Roast me in sulphur!" (5.2.279) almost simultaneously with Emilia's transposed "My lord, my lord! / What ho! my lord, my lord!" (5.2.84), accompanied by more pounding and wailing.

Despite Welles's refusal to commodify his work, to make a Faustian bargain by putting commerce above art, *Othello* weathered incredible difficulties. A major difference between it and *Macbeth* is that Welles preserved artistic control of the editing until the film's release date, not wanting to repeat the post-production fiascos with *Macbeth*. After the modest but assured financial underwriting by Republic Pictures for *Macbeth*, he never again had the support of major backers with bundles of cash as Olivier did with producers Filippo Del Giudice and Alexander Korda. In Hollywood he had been virtually blacklisted as an unreliable genius. Yet *Othello*, after receiving a hostile reception, and languishing for decades in the archives of the Library of Congress, phoenix-like, emerged in a controversial resurrection in 1992, which had the effect of renewing interest in his earlier work. Like other great artists, Welles suffered the fate of having his masterworks appreciated only after his death. The suffering, however, contained its own seeds of inspiration for by 1966 he was ready to give his greatest performance as another larger-than-life but vulnerable anti-hero, Sir John Falstaff.

Before that happened, however, Welles enjoyed an opportunity in 1953 to play King Lear on American television. In a rearguard action to rescue the commercial airwaves from the advertising industry, the Sunday afternoon TV Radio-Workshop of the Ford Foundation, known as Omnibus, sponsored *King Lear* in a truncated production directed by Peter Brook that foreshadowed elements of Brook's feature-length *King Lear* (1971) starring Paul Scofield. The tyranny of time demanded the sacrifice of optimistic elements in the Gloucester subplot to compress the performance into 73 minutes, which was framed between commercials for Greyhound buses and bath tissues and embellished with a commentary by a baby-faced Alistair Cooke. An enormous paper map of England inscribed on a theatrical curtain is suddenly ripped open, shredded, and Orson Welles as King Lear steps through, growling and roaring, and bellowing "Give me the map there" (1.1.37), ready to begin the division of the kingdom. When Lear destroys his map, he loses his way, breaking his bond with Cordelia, and falling into a nightmare world of domination and subjugation. This is a "bondage" *King Lear*. Besides the Brechtian and Kottian intellectualization of despair, there is a trace of the obsession with human degradation in Alfred Hitchcock's spy thrillers. It's a sado-masochistic world of iron gates, steel bars, and hempen ropes. As Tony Howard says, "This is the *Marat/Sade* in embryo," as well as a transgressive attack on the smug world of Sunday afternoon cultural television programming.[37] In the windmill where Lear and his party (including longtime Wellesian collaborator Micheál MacLiammóir as poor Tom) take refuge from the storm are hooks, grinding wheels, chains – icons for "the rack of this tough world" (5.3.315) upon which the old king will be figuratively tormented. In the terrible windmill, Gloucester is seized, bound, and has his eyes gouged out with the thumbs, not the spurs, of the venomous Cornwall (Scott Forbes). A wooden-faced Regan (Margaret Phillips) looks on without pity.

The striking camera angles and choreographing of the characters' movements take the production away from naive literalism toward expressionism. In a memorable closing moment, the old king's howls over the death of Cordelia originate in the darkness and dwindle as he moves into the light. Shockingly the rag doll he seems to be dragging turns out to be Cordelia, a bit of business imitated from the Italian tragedian, Tommaso Salvini.[38] The loyal daughter has become a bauble in the hands of a man who has himself reverted to childlike innocence. The primitive studio lighting, probably the "three-point technique" with one key light in front, one back light, and a floodlight in front opposite the key light,[39] correlated darkness with chaos, light with harmony. As might be expected, Welles overacted but with power, verve, and ultimate authenticity. Predictably, critics savaged him, the unkindest cut of all declaring that Welles resembled "a man who had been hauled off a park bench and hastily pressed into service as Macy's Santa Claus."[40] Unhappily Welles never got the opportunity, as we shall see, to make a second attempt at a role that in so many ways intrigued him and suited his volcanic talents.

Chimes at Midnight (1966): The tragedy of Sir John Falstaff (and Orson Welles)

If Orson Welles could not satisfy every actor's ambition of doing Hamlet, in Falstaff he found a role almost as challenging. Using Falstaff as the protagonist,

Welles's *Chimes at Midnight* shows the dark side of the youthful monarch whom Laurence Olivier sanctified in *Henry V* as "the mirror of all Christian kings," and "the star of England." In Olivier's movie, King Henry V is the paragon who has defeated Henry Percy (Hotspur) at Shrewsbury, ascended to the throne of England after the death of his father King Henry IV, destroyed the French army at Agincourt, and wooed and won the beautiful princess, Katherine of France. Olivier's movie censors out anything in *Henry V* potentially damaging to the king's candidacy for sainthood. On the other hand, as portrayed by Shakespeare, King Henry V oscillates between heroism as an anointed king and deceit as a mere mortal. What Olivier chose to disregard about the king, Welles chose to regard, but there is something in Shakespeare's sweeping panorama for both those who adore and those who loathe either Falstaff or Hal. A minor character in *All's Well that Ends Well* sums up Shakespeare's gift for articulating the tangled skein of human experience, its daily grubbiness: "The web of our life is of a mingled yarn, good and ill together: our virtues would be proud, if our faults whipt them not, and our crimes would despair, if they were not cherish'd by our virtues" (4.3.71).

For *Chimes*, Orson Welles has ransacked the subtext of the Henriad (*Richard II, 1 Henry IV, 2 Henry IV, Henry V*), as well as shards from *The Merry Wives of Windsor* to show the unintended consequences of Hal's rise to power. The story of Falstaff as victim has been assembled from bits and pieces and scraps scattered throughout the Henriad. His sad tale, which is The Tragedy of Falstaff, has not been fabricated but has been nestling all along within the sprawling historical saga like the core of a Russian doll. Shakespeare's democratic admission into the play of the ordinarily marginalized lower-class tavern characters clustering around Falstaff inspired Welles's foray. While *Richard II* excluded all but the high and mighty, kings and barons, the remaining three plays of the tetralogy beginning with *1 Henry IV* admit the meaner sorts of persons such as Hostess Quickly, Pistol, Nym, Bardolph, hostlers, and tapsters, who might have stepped out of a seventeenth-century Flemish painting of mundane domestic life.

Although Falstaff stands out among the tavern *Lumpen* as socially superior, having been a page to Sir Thomas Mowbray, a student at the Inns of Court, and a knight and officer in the armies of England, he shares in the misery of his forlorn cronies. On the surface only a comic foil to the ambitious young prince, at a deeper level Falstaff becomes the catalyst for exposing society's inner mechanisms of power, greed, and ambition. Falstaff, like one of today's "welfare cheats" in the post-Reagan, post-Thatcher era, is scapegoated as the "disease" infecting all of England, thus distracting from the entrenched hegemony's role in creating the national malaise. As a whipping boy for the diseases of his betters, he plays the role of mock king offered up in sacrifice to propitiate the gods. The tragedy lies in the way that he and Hal alike have been entrapped in the necessity of their own roles as monarch and jester. The king's betrayal of Falstaff ironically rebounds off the king's smug belief on the eve of Agincourt that "the King is not bound to answer the particular endings of his soldiers" (*Henry V* 4.1.155). *Chimes* is about the "particular ending" of one of those soldiers, Falstaff.

It has often been said that *2 Henry IV* repeats the same story as *1 Henry IV* in showing the young prince struggling to come to grips with his frightening responsibilities. In both plays, the young prince serves two fathers: the authentic one, Henry Bolingbroke; and the surrogate one, Falstaff. As has been observed, Hal shows the valour of the lion in arms at Shrewsbury by slaying Hotspur at the close of *Part One*, and the cunning of a fox in statecraft at Westminster by rejecting the destabilizing Falstaff at the close of *Part Two*.[41] In the Henriad, warning signals about the inevitable schism between Hal and Falstaff appear from the beginning of *Part One*, but in *Part Two* Falstaff's talents as bon vivant and life force noticeably wane. Becoming shriller and meaner, he degenerates from an engaging rogue into a stock *miles gloriosus*, a mere braggart warrior. Welles's adaptation plays up the second Falstaff, the shrunken one of *Part Two* who betrays Mistress Quickly, and becomes the designated buffoon of *The Merry Wives of Windsor*, but just underneath there is the earlier, rollicking jester of *Part One*, the victim of unkind fate and his own bad judgment.

In struggling to pare down Shakespeare's sprawling chronicle of English history, Welles self-referentially identified with the king's rejection of Falstaff, seeing it as a mirror to Hollywood's rejection of him. Jack Jorgens observed that perhaps Welles "saw too much of himself in Falstaff."[42] Keith Baxter from his vantage point of having worked directly with Welles on *Chimes* said much the same thing: "It was his life's ambition to make this film and also to play Falstaff . . . You felt that there was a great deal of him in Falstaff – this sort of trimming one's sails, always short of money, having to lie, perhaps, and to cheat."[43] Behind Falstaff's comic mask, Welles saw the inner desperation. As he said, "the more I studied the part, the less funny he [Falstaff] seemed to be."[44] Ironically as Welles grew older his own "waist" grew in proportion to the apparent "waste" of his career and it was all too easy for people who confuse solemnity with seriousness to misconstrue his irony as a lack of high seriousness. Like Falstaff, a man large of spirit and imagination, Welles forgot he was living among Lilliputians. Given this background, *Chimes*, like *Othello*, had to end up as film noir.

Chimes at Midnight also drew heavily on Welles's theatrical experience, going back to the vast epic of a play called *Five Kings* that opened in Boston in 1939, the script being constructed from about half the major tetralogy. A plan to do the minor tetralogy (*The Three Parts of Henry VI and Richard III*) in tandem

10   Orson Welles as Falstaff and Keith Baxter as
Prince Hal prepare for one of the ubiquitous
partings in *Chimes at Midnight* (*Falstaff*), directed
by Welles (Spain/Switzerland 1966).

was never realized, though the title of *Five Kings* (Richard II, Henry IV, Henry
V, Richard III, and Henry VI) vestigially remained. The huge cast included
Robert Speaight (Chorus), Burgess Meredith (Prince Hal) and Orson Welles
as Falstaff. With Welles interpreting Falstaff as a tragic figure, the play got to
Washington, D.C, and then faltered in Philadelphia. Critics complained that it
lacked unity and was only a series of "random stage pictures."[45] Welles then
subsequently staged a successful *Chimes at Midnight* in Dublin, which put even
greater emphasis on Falstaff.[46]

Benefiting from this incubation, the film script for *Chimes* goes beyond mere
tinkering with Shakespeare's scenes; it massively reworks, transposes, revises
and deletes, indeed deconstructs them. The radical textual surgery that worked
so well for *Othello* operates in *Chimes* at an even more intense level. Was Welles
on an ego trip bent on destroying Shakespeare's work? Not at all. He told Peter
Bogdanovich "no movie that will ever be made is worthy of being discussed
in the same breath [with Shakespeare]."[47] He simply intended to re-inscribe
a Shakespearean play in the spatial and temporal grammar of cinema, rather
than literally inscribing the play itself.

In an exhaustive analysis, Robert Hapgood has located five "hallmarks"
in *Chimes* for Welles's style in making complicated textual deletions,
transpositions, and additions: (1) expansion/contraction, (2) dynamism,

(3) pointing/counterpointing, (4) knitting, and (5) narrative coherence.[48] Sometimes the textual plundering defies neat categories, though it always testifies to Welles's ingenuity and scholarship. For example, a conversation between Shallow and Falstaff at the film's opening plunges deep into the Henriad to hijack twenty-five lines from *2 Henry IV* (3.2.194–219). The language is Shakespeare's but so drastically altered from the original sequence as to be almost a new scenario: "Jesus the days that we have seen. / Ha, Sir John? Said I well?" to which Falstaff replies with the haunting line, "We have heard the chimes at midnight, Master Robert Shallow."[49] "Chimes at midnight" resurfaces in its proper place at Justice Shallow's Cotswolds farm much later in the film (shot 1206, Lyons). One of Welles's most ingenious conflations occurs when Falstaff is substituted for the drunken soldier whom the king orders to be released from the brig just before the fleet sails from Southampton for France: "Uncle of Exeter, / Enlarge the man committed yesterday / That rail'd against our person" (2.2.39). Not only is there a neat pun on "enlarg'd" (which means of course "to set free") in connection with Falstaff's "largeness," but Falstaff has notoriously "railed against [the king's] person." Welles was sparing with additions, only occasionally introducing a word or phrase to clarify the narrative, as in something like Falstaff's "Zounds, this confounded Percy!" (shot 93, Lyons) at the sight of Hotspur's body on the Shrewsbury battlefield.

The movie transcends The Tragedy of Sir John Falstaff,[50] being also as its director thought an elegiac lament for the loss of an older world, "Merrie England," which was "a season of innocence, a dew-bright morning of the world ... Falstaff ... its perfect embodiment." As a tavern wit, "he [Falstaff] sings for his supper" but that "isn't really what he's all about."[51] In this nostalgia for a lost world, *Chimes* follows *The Magnificent Ambersons*, which dealt in a Chekhovian kind of way with the demise and decay of an old American family doomed by a new industrialism embodied in the automobile.[52] For the Ambersons, the automobile spelled ruin; for Falstaff, the demise of chivalry deprived him of a life style. When Hal slew Hotspur at Shrewsbury, he also slew Falstaff. On the other hand, Hal's faults are balanced off against Falstaff's, who egregiously cheats poor Hostess Quickly of her tavern receipts and weasels on a £1000 debt to Shallow. As early as *Citizen Kane*, Welles was preoccupied with this theme of loss, of nostalgia for some lost idyll, even when it is symbolized by something so banal as Charles Kane's yearning for the childhood sled, "Rosebud." An instinctive aristocrat, Welles knew as well as Falstaff the sting of impecuniousness among one's inferiors. Worse yet, his art of cinema demanded enormous sums of money to stay alive. Had he been a nineteenth-century painter, he would not have been so enslaved to commodity.

The alternation between court and tavern in the Henriad provides the basis for a textbook scenario with cross-cutting between the two venues, the court

being generally identified with austere stone and the tavern with more congenial wood.[53] In making *Chimes*, Welles had the actors on the set for decent
periods of time, so that the subsequent editing was not dictated, as was the
case with *Othello*, by the need to cover up gaps and inconsistencies brought on
by the absence of actors. Sir John Gielgud as the king actually spent two weeks
at Madrid and Cardona, Spain, being filmed, among other sites, in a gothic
church, while Margaret Rutherford who is shown in a reaction shot as Hostess
Quickly laughing at the play scene in the tavern actually never saw it. She
was simply told to laugh at the camera, and the illusion of her spectatorship
was edited in later. Keith Baxter as the Prince counted fourteen appearances in
the film where he was not playing Hal but was filling in as an extra.[54] Welles
wanted this to be an actor's film and the wide-angle lenses and closeups allow
actors to use the camera instead of permitting the camera to use them.

The continuing décor of stone and wood for the settings of court and tavern
reflect the character of Hal's real and surrogate fathers. Hal oscillates between
the two poles, moving back and forth between the worlds of stone and wood,
between workaday duty and holiday festivity, between the restraint of time
and the timelessness of festivity, but inevitably he will choose authentic over
surrogate father, containment over subversion, and become the chilly monarch
his father had been before him. The King is associated with the stone walls
of Cardona cathedral, with vertical planes of light streaming through high
windows, with austerity, with loneliness and pitilessness. As Anthony Davies
says, "the expansive uncluttered spaces allow the King a slow, majestic fluidity
of action . . . The sense of high, open, vertical space above the King affords these
shots uninterrupted power, for there is no ceiling to suggest that the King is
any way 'contained' or diminished by the world."[55] The King is not contained
but he contains others who would challenge his hegemony. The expressionistic
lighting streaming through great vertical windows in the vast empty interior
of the church, frames him in low-angle shot. Gielgud speaks sepulchrally in his
musical but stagy voice, which in giving sound priority over sense perfectly
embodies the ethical dilemma of Henry IV. King Henry IV is after all the
ultimate hollow man, having usurped the throne from his weak first cousin,
Richard Plantagenet. The low-angle perspective stresses the king's enormous
power, as well as his isolation and sickness of spirit, the "gilt" that crowns his
head being only a cover-up for the "guilt" growing out of his usurpation of the
throne from Richard II. His austerity contrasts with Falstaffian cheer, making
the "fat guts" all the more attractive.

Falstaff, on the other hand, is associated with horizontal planes of light,
squatness, frivolity, and subversion. Falstaff's festive world thrives on wooden
structures, either the Boar's Head tavern or the country estate of Master Shallow. Just as the king's stony court remains the barren site of the workaday

world, Falstaff's holiday world teems with humanity, with throngs of attractive young women clattering up and down the wooden stairs of the ramshackle inn. If wood is supposed to represent a more organic and softer world than that of stone, then this seedy inn exposes Falstaff's vision of total freedom and generosity as a mirage. Total freedom from restraint only leads to a new kind of bondage. Hal's "fool-born" jester, like all mock kings will be sacrificed on the altar of state and authority. Welles identified with Falstaff's status as a mock king, remarking how as an actor he himself was a "royal bum" with a crown of "tin," and how the biggest sin in the world to him was "betrayal," as "you know from *Chimes at Midnight*."[56]

Close-ups probe for clues about the inner lives of the characters. In what Hapgood might see as "dynamism," Welles has transposed 100 lines to highlight the abyss between Hal and Falstaff. With Falstaff in the background, just outside the tavern entrance, viewed over the Prince's shoulder, Hal utters his cold-blooded intention to betray his tavern cronies: "I know you all, and will a while uphold / The unyok'd humor of your idleness" and ending with "I'll so offend, to make offense a skill, / Redeeming time when men think least I will" (1.2.195ff). As he speaks, he turns away from Falstaff, faces the camera, and seems to be talking to himself. Falstaff who in Shakespeare's Henriad admits to suffering from "the disease of not list'ning, the malady of not marking" (2 *Henry IV* 1.2.120) misses the mark again in trying to turn the somber mood into jocularity by asking, "But I prithee, sweet wag, shall there be gallows standing in England when thou art king?" (1 *Henry IV* 1.2.57). The grim expression on the prince's face makes plain that in his reign gallows will grow like weeds but Falstaff doesn't see that.

The climactic scene in 1 *Henry IV* when Falstaff petitions Hal for understanding calls for close-ups: "but for sweet Jack Falstaff, kind Jack Falstaff, true Jack Falstaff, valiant Jack Falstaff." As Falstaff in low angle begs for exculpation, reaction shots show the women on the balcony waving and derisively laughing: "banish not him thy Harry's company, banish not him thy Harry's company – banish plump Jack, and banish all the world!" (1 *Henry IV* 2.4.476). Oblivious to his inevitable doom from the disease of "not listening," Falstaff's harsh fate as buffoon and scapegoat at the hands of the house wives in the *Merry Wives of Windsor* has been sealed. Then Hal jumps into the frame, pushes Falstaff into the background, and intones the four words "I do, I will." Devastating, they mean death for Falstaff, and for all he stands for – "Merrie England" and the feudal way of life.

As in any other war movie, farewell scenes in *Chimes* accentuate the idea of loss and departure. After his soliloquy about "redeeming time" (shot 81, Lyons), Hal departs from the tavern and Falstaff watches him slowly walking toward the distant stony castle. Hal's sudden break from a walk into a run symbolically increases the gap between him and Falstaff. Falstaff indulgently chuckles and waves, as yet mercifully oblivious to a prince's Machiavellian capacity for jettisoning inconvenient friends. In another farewell, as the sheriff's men pound on the tavern door, the Prince's hiding of Falstaff under a trap-door foreshadows Falstaff's rejection at Westminster. When Falstaff emerges from hiding (shot 409) mumbling "we must all to the wars," an angry Hostess Quickly exposes him as a deadbeat, sternly saying "You owe me money, Sir John." Doll Tearsheet's (Jeanne Moreau) farewell to Falstaff as he leaves for the wars temporarily restores the old man to grace. Welles patches the dialogue together from lines scattered through act two, scene four of *2 Henry IV*. "[You] whoreson little tidy Bartholomew boarpig"(2.4.231), says Doll and then holding him close, "Come, I'll be friends with thee, Jack. Thou art going to the wars, and whether I shall ever see thee again or no, there is nobody cares" (shots 411–12; 2.4.63). Welles transposes the most poignant words to a later shot:

> *Doll.*   By my troth, I kiss thee with a most constant heart.
> *Fal.*   I am old, I am old.
> *Doll.*   I love thee better than I love e'er a scurvy young boy of them all (shot 1124).

When Falstaff admits to his age and failing strength, he confirms the phallic pun on his name ("Fall-staff"), which the eavesdropping Poins has already observed. "Is it not strange that desire should so many years outlive performance?" (2.4.260).

The farewells over, Falstaff emerges as malingerer, misfit, and outright fraud in the great battle scene at Shrewsbury from *1 Henry IV*, which echoes a similar struggle in *Alexander Nevsky*, as well as contrasting with Olivier's prettified Battle of Agincourt in *Henry V*. Welles once said of Olivier's cavalry charge in *Henry V* that "you see the people riding out of the castle, and suddenly they are on a golf course somewhere charging each other."[57] There is nothing remotely resembling a golf course in Welles's searing Brueghel-like battle that strips "glorious" war of its claim to "pomp and circumstance." And while Eisenstein drew on a cast of thousands for the enormous battle on the ice in *Nevsky*, Welles conjured up the entire battle by magically expanding 200 or so skillfully deployed Spaniards into thousands.

The reliance on *mise-en-scène* so successfully employed in most of the movie for close delineation of character yields in the battle scenes to montage, a tribute to Orson Welles's skill as a film editor, the Battle of Shrewsbury being a collage made up of over 200 separate shots cut from his long takes.[58] This remarkable panorama of the horrors of medieval warfare was recorded in long takes to allow the troops to build up to a plausible rage, and then subsequently cut and spliced and edited. The spectacle becomes a slow death dance for the rites of feudalism. It opens with Hotspur's mindless enthusiasm for violence, "Harry to Harry, shall hot horse to horse, / Meet and ne'er part till one drop down a corse" (4.1.122), though ironically it is Harry Percy, not Harry prince of Wales, who is "to drop down a corse." There is nothing here like the elegant knights in the Olivier film. The soldiers lowering Falstaff from a scaffold to his horse lose their grip on the rope and drop him to the ground like a stone. He lies there encased in his huge armor unable to move. Later, Falstaff appears as a tubby man puffing along well to the rear of the central action, or hiding behind a bush, though in response to Hal's "Why, thou owest God a death" (5.1.126), he is allowed his great commentary on honor (5.1.127), which makes him something more than a mere wastrel and turns him into an existentialist hero. From the brilliant speech on counter-feiting (5.4.111), only the catch phrase, "The better part of valor is discretion" remains. As infantry and cavalry charge toward one another there are the rallying cries of "Percy!" and "St. George for England," with flashes of Falstaff waving his troops forward. Gradually, however, as the fighting becomes increasingly deadly, the martial élan fades. The gallant soldiers are transmogrified into muddy wretches too exhausted even to clobber one another with their axes, clubs, spears, and chains. Against this holocaust backdrop, Hal conquers Hotspur in single combat, copes with Falstaff's ridiculous claim to having slain Hotspur, and then turns Falstaff over to the command of his priggish brother, John.

Like a juggernaut, the movie inexorably rolls toward the newly crowned king's crushing public rejection of Falstaff at Westminster. Falstaff's fatal disease of *hamartia*, or "missing of the mark," nudges him into a calamitous miscalculation when he blunders into the coronation processional to speak to the newly crowned king, thereby setting himself up for scathing public rebuke. Falstaff has trespassed from his own sphere into the forbidden world of stone. In extreme low angle, the king, now entirely his father's man with the vertical light streaming on him, coldly stares down at the expectant Falstaff, who cries out "Speak to me, my heart." The response falls on Falstaff's ears like stones: "I know thee not, old man, fall to thy prayers" and the prince adds the chilling *coup de grâce* of "How ill white hairs becomes a fool and jester!" (*2 Henry IV* 5.5.47). After Falstaff's destruction, the movie quickly moves toward a close, as if to draw a curtain over events too embarrassing to view. Despite Hal's intention to save the old man from poverty, Falstaff finds being humiliated in front of his cronies unendurable. The old insouciance momentarily flares up as he assures them that "he will be sent for [by the king] in private," but that gesture is undercut by Shallow's bluntly demanding that the delinquent Falstaff come up with at least one half of the £1-thousand debt. This time Falstaff's blustering fails to convince Shallow that "[Falstaff] will be as good as [his] word."

The game is up, Falstaff's ignominious bankruptcy crystal clear to everyone. Falstaff is last seen in a deep-focus shot, walking toward a backlit arch, alone, and mumbling to himself that "I shall be sent for soon . . . at night." He is sent for, true enough, though not by Hal but by his Creator. Hostess Quickly in yet another farewell, leaning against the wall of the tavern, speaks the haunting eulogy from *Henry V*: "He's in Arthur's bosom, if ever a man went to Arthur's bosom" (2.3.9).

The bitterest irony comes at the end, when as Falstaff's enormous casket is trundled across the bleak winter landscape, the voice of Ralph Richardson praises the young king with encomiums from Holinshed's *Chronicles*:

> This Henry was a captain of such prudence and such policy that he never enterprised anything before it forecast the main chances that it might happen. So humane withal, he left no offense unpunished nor friendship unrewarded. For conclusion, a majesty was he that both lived and died a pattern in prince-hood, a lodestar in honor, and famous to the world alway. [A drum beats a processional rhythm on the soundtrack.][59]

Falstaff, the holy fool, one of those men Paul spoke of who are foolish in the eyes of men but wise in the eyes of God, is betrayed by his best friend, who is then in turn eulogized as a national hero and a kind of saint. Welles understood this.

Like Falstaff, Welles still hoped to "be sent for," yet fresh betrayals and disappointments lay ahead as he dickered to make more Shakespeare movies. He undertook ambitious plans for feature movies based on two of Shakespeare's other suffering human beings, Shylock and King Lear, but neither project was completed. He was also called to play Brutus in the Burge/Snell *Julius Caesar* (1970), but for obscure reasons had to be replaced at the eleventh hour by Jason Robards, Jr.[60] His film of *The Merchant of Venice*, in which Welles played Shylock and Charles Gray played Antonio, is said to have been completed in 1969. Since then it has been as elusive as Hawthorne's Giant Transcendental-ism, various accounts claiming that it never saw the light of day because two reels were stolen from the Rome production office, that a 40-minute segment may be stored in a Hollywood vault, and that excerpts have appeared in a television documentary. In a bold stroke, when Welles's good friend, Oja Kodar, refused to play Portia, the role was eliminated.[61] Footage from the lost *Merchant* is also reported to be contained in Kodar's feature-length movie *Jaded* (1989).[62] Welles's other plans for a major film of *King Lear* were also dashed when much to his disgust the French backers withdrew their support, causing him, he said, more humiliation than "even in the worst days of the old Hollywood." Planning to cast Kodar as Cordelia and Ab Dickson, his magician friend, as the

Fool, he envisioned a Shakespeare movie that was to be "not only a new kind of Shakespeare but a new kind of film."[63]

So until 1985 when he died quite unexpectedly, Welles remained the embattled artist besieged by "tickling commodity." In his struggle to find the best available means for putting Shakespeare on screen, he never quite made the transition from art house to mall house. His detractors pursued him relentlessly, mercilessly: "Has he [Falstaff/Welles], deep down, a spirit of rebellion against stuffy authority? Or is he merely what he looks like – a dissolute, bumbling, street-corner Santa Claus?" one reviewer asked of his acting in *Chimes*.[64] Significantly the journalist didn't declare, he interrogated. The element of mystery, of magic, was always there. What Marlene Dietrich as the smoky Tanya memorably said in *A Touch of Evil* about Hank Quinlan, the police captain played by Welles, remains Orson Welles's best epitaph: "He was some kind of a man."

- 5 -

Electronic Shakespeare: from television to the web

Electronic Shakespeare unobtrusively began on Friday afternoon, February 5, 1937, at 3:55 pm, with an 11-minute scene from *As You Like It* transmitted from the BBC's elegantly named "Alexandra Palace," perched on a 400-foot hill in north London. More base than aristocratic in origin, the BBC station was actually "a derelict resort,"[1] a relic constructed from remnants of London's 1851 Great Exhibition and had once seated 1,000 holiday makers in a great hall for luncheon. The scene from *As You Like It*, directed by Robert Atkins, included RADA-trained Margaretta Scott as Rosalind, a West End stage actress who had played Ophelia in a radio *Hamlet*, and Ion Swinlay (or Swinley) as Orlando.[2]

Thanks to pioneers like John Logie Baird,[3] who had by 1930 managed to broadcast Pirandello's *The Man with a Flower in His Mouth* from primitive London laboratories, television, which had been gradually developing over a period of several decades, was beginning to fulfill its multiple inventors' dream of "seeing over the horizon."[4] Some early viewers complained that the image on the screen gave one "the feeling of looking through a cabin keyhole on a rather rough day at sea."[5] No matter that viewers were threatened with seasickness, the march of Shakespeare on television was inevitable, especially when in August 1936 according to Barbara Freedman, the BBC had even earlier transmitted a clip of Elisabeth Bergner in *As You Like It*.

As was the case with Sir Herbert Tree's 1899 *King John* movie and the Vitagraph silents, the fledgling television industry instinctively exploited Shakespeare's cultural capital to its own ends. Ironically Shakespeare on television arrived on the British scene at exactly the time when the London critics had been happily bashing Hollywood's *Midsummer Night's Dream* (1935) and *Romeo and Juliet* (1936) for the *lèse majesté* of putting Shakespeare in moving images. There remained until late in this century the unshakable conviction of traditionalists that any Shakespeare on screen was bound to be a vulgarization, and of the *avant-garde* that it was indubitably *kitsch*. A flurry of articles in *The Listener*, a BBC house organ, by such luminaries as J. Dover Wilson,[6] G. B. Harrison,[7] and Tyrone Guthrie,[8] demonstrated how Shakespeare on page and stage retained unassailable authority over Shakespeare on screen, whether on film or television. An occasional seer might object: "It is wholly unreasonable to demand that all productions of Shakespeare should be Elizabethan. The surest proof of the greatness of his plays is their adaptability."[9] Whatever the protests, Shakespeare was bound to be swept up in the "mass distribution and mass consumption of television programs for huge profits."[10] Shakespeare's insight in *King John* about "tickling commodity" again anticipated everyone. Not Britannia but the bottom line would rule the airwaves.

With television's roots in radio, not movies, cinema was by no means the dominant model for its pioneers. As with the early silent films, stage actors from the West End were imported to parade before the pioneering transmission systems in Alexandra Palace. On the same day in February that saw the *As You Like It* segment, a snippet was transmitted from *Henry V*, with actress and pianist Yvonne Arnaud[11] as Katherine of France. It was directed by George More O'Ferrall, who would later play a major role in the BBC's expanded Shakespeare programming. From 1937 to 1939, the BBC scheduled nearly two dozen Shakespeare programs, translating the studio performances into electrical impulses that could then be scanned and reassembled in home receivers. As with early silent film, television favored Lumière-like "actualities" of such news events as the coronation of King George VI, but soon the technology was in place for live transmissions from London's West End playhouses. Through spring 1939, the 11,000 or so owners of London television receivers within a 25-mile vicinity[12] had the opportunity to watch Shakespeare programs based on some fifteen different plays, with three repeats of *A Midsummer Night's Dream*, and *Twelfth Night*, and one repeat of *Julius Caesar* and *Macbeth*. A televised 30-minute segment from the Old Vic *Macbeth*, produced by George More O'Ferrall, with Laurence Olivier and Judith Anderson, on December 3, 1937, moved the *Times* television critic to remark that Olivier and Anderson, were "effective" but they failed "to moderate their voices to television scale, and still spoke to the utmost recesses of an imaginary theatre." In the new medium, the lighting designer held the key to success: "the weird sisters were seen in a series of close-ups, which were rather too brightly lit, so that they appeared grotesque rather than macabre."[13]

Producer/director Dallas Bower's ambitious 141-minute modern dress *Julius Caesar* on July 24, 1938, included a cast of thirty, many of whom doubled in minor roles as Third or Fourth Citizens. Inspired by Orson Welles's Mercury Theatre production, there were special scenic effects by Malcolm Baker-Smith, incidental music by James Hartley, background film of "Riots" from British Movietone, "Gunfire" from the Film Library, an "Explosion Sequence" and "Aeroplanes" from British Movietone. Special disks provided the noise of "Angry Crowds," "Cheering Crowd," "Gunfire," "Thunder," the "Internationale," and the Halle Orchestra conducted by Sir Hamilton Harty doing Berlioz's "The Royal Hunt and Storm."[14] A critic praised the

11 Iago (Stephen Murray), Desdemona (Joan Hopkins), and Emilia (Margaretta Scott) in a tense moment during a "live" BBC transmission of *Othello* from Alexandra Palace in 1950.

"penumbrascope," which added space and depth to the small studio and enhanced the quick change of scenes from "close-up to mid-shot," but he also wondered why "Mr. Bower did not raise one of his cameras to a higher angle after the fashion that the newsreel camera oversees a procession."[15] Another critic expressed surprise that "Ernest Milton as Caesar (dressed like General Franco) was magnificent, but then it is a strange thing that his performance was also good Shakespeare,"[16] while the old bugaboo of Shakespeare in modern dress put a third critic off when "the wife of the modern gangster-politician Brutus smokes cigarettes."[17]

Other major productions included George More O'Ferrall's abridged (67-minute) studio *Othello* (Dec. 15, 1937) with Baliol Holloway in the title role, Celia Johnson as Desdemona and Anthony Quayle as Cassio, initial attempts to cast Ralph Richardson and Jessica Tandy having fizzled. The production's budget at about £300[18] contrasts with the £2,376 cost a decade later for George More O'Ferrall's *Hamlet*, or the £7,000 price tag for a single episode of the 1964 *Spread of the Eagle* series. Although unhappy with the "microscopic screen," the *Times* critic wrote that "Miss Celia Johnson [as] Desdemona . . . made one forget the marvels of science and remember only the beauty of the English language as it should be spoken."[19] Shakespeare's birthday on April 23, 1937, called for a "Mask" arranged from the fairy scenes of *A Midsummer Night's Dream*, which leaned heavily on Felix Mendelssohn for theme music.

The first phase of televised Shakespeare began winding down with Dallas Bower's 100-minute *The Tempest* (1939), with incidental music and dance by Sibelius and the London Ballet. Various BBC internal memos circulated after the performance reveal the perils of live television broadcast with complaints about a lack of rehearsal time resulting in a "prompter standing in the foreground of a long shot," "an actor walking behind the penumbrascope," and "property men entering [a] superimposed shot."[20] Approving of Peggy Ashcroft as Miranda, Grace Wyndham Goldie, the *Listener* critic, reflected on television's increasing maturity declaring that "plays are staggeringly successful on the television screen," and "getting better and better every minute."[21] Things were not always fated to "get better and better," though. On September 1, 1939, at the end of a Mickey Mouse cartoon, with "the lights going out all over Europe," the BBC television also switched off its lights. Its ultra-short waves of seven meters would otherwise have offered handy navigation aids for the Luftwaffe.

When the lights finally came on again all over Europe, the BBC energetically continued to transmit uncommodified Shakespeare, protected from commercialism by the state subsidy but equally protected from any far-out directors. Veteran producer/directors Ian and Robert Atkins and George More O'Ferrall along with Michael Barry, among others, for three decades from 1947 faithfully served the Shakespeare industry with over sixty performances of individual plays in whole or in part, and a complete run of the English and Roman history plays as mini-series. Only such notoriously unpopular titles as *Henry VIII*, *Titus Andronicus*, and *Pericles* got neglected. Until 1978, when the great geyser of the BBC Shakespeare Plays series saturated the market with six plays a year, *Julius Caesar* appeared most frequently with seven productions, followed by *A Midsummer Night's Dream* and *Macbeth* with six each, not including the Roman history saga, *The Spread of the Eagle*.

Prior to that, however, the BBC and independent television, even with competition from boxing and football matches, managed to squeeze out of stingy budgets George More O'Ferrall's full-length, two-part, meticulously planned BBC *Hamlet* (1947) with John Byron as Hamlet and Sebastian Shaw as Claudius, for which the British Television Society awarded O'Ferrall its Silver Medal. Around seventy persons were approached to fill forty-eight roles, with some doubling. Special recordings had to be made for Ophelia's songs and the noise of the ghost. Fittings for costumes at Foxe's ate up considerable time, and Hamlet's customary suits of solemn black had to be made dark green because of lighting problems. The detailed planning included five weeks of rehearsals, all the stage props and scenery of a major theatrical production (a locket for Hamlet, wild flowers for Ophelia, wine goblets for Claudius, etc.), elaborate lighting plots, and the pre-arrangement of angles for cameras one and two and the ubiquitous microphone boom, which hovered menacingly over the whole set.[22] If as Michael Barry has suggested, O'Ferrall's tracking camera inspired the deep-focus cinematography for the filmed Olivier *Hamlet* (1948),[23] then this forgotten 1947 *Hamlet* deserves not to be forgotten. Journalist Drew Middleton became the first American to review a televised Shakespeare play when he reported back to *The New York Times* that John Byron "played the prince for all that it was worth" in a production full of "blood and thunder elements [that gripped the audience] without interruption."[24] The era's lack of kinescope recording makes any reappraisal of these critics' insights impossible.[25]

A cluster of three major mini-series in the 1960s based on the English and Roman history plays resulted in some of Great Britain's most distinguished Shakespeare on television. The first and most ambitious, *An Age of Kings* (including *Richard II*, *Two Parts of Henry IV*, *Henry V*, *Three Parts of Henry VI, and Richard III*) compressed the minor and major tetralogies of the English history plays into a fifteen-week cycle of eight 60-to-90 minute segments. Beginning with "The Hollow Crown" (*Richard II*) on April 28, 1960, and ending with "The Boar Hunt" (*Richard III*) on November 17, 1960, all of them were broadcast nationally on educational television in the United States beginning in October 1961 and were repeated again in 1962. Producer Peter Dews carried out the Herculean casting of some 600 parts for the sprawling, epical dramas, which required thirty weeks of rehearsals, and cost as much as £4,000 an episode. For clarity, the plays were shown in their historical sequence, which meant that the apprentice work of the minor tetralogy covering the years 1422 to 1485 followed the mature artistry of the major tetralogy spanning the years 1399 to 1422. Milton Crane aptly remarked that it was a little bit "like seeing *Titus* after *Hamlet*."[26]

Even on blurry kinescope, the performances hold up extremely well. David William as the feckless King Richard II walks a fine line between vanity and brutality as he exiles Henry Bolingbroke (Tom Fleming) and Mowbray (Noel Johnson) and then heartlessly mocks the dying Gaunt (Edgar Wreford). Gaunt still manages to convey the correct fervor in his set-piece aria of Armada rhetoric: "This blessed plot, this earth, this realm, this England" (2.1.50). As Henry Bolingbroke, Tom Fleming sternly lectures the fettered and cowed "caterpillars of the commonwealth," Bushy and Green, who grovel, weep, and moan before being led away, shrieking, completely terrorized by Boling-broke's chilling: "See them delivered over / To execution and the hand of death" (3.1.29). You hear off camera the mumbling prayers of a priest, and then the thud of an axe. Silence. Very effective television drama. In another master stroke, a passing courtier's interruption of Northumberland's tangled, and much parodied, order of battle speech makes an unconvincing moment convincing: "receiv'd intelligence / That Harry Duke of Herford, Rainold, Lord Cobham,/ [Thomas, son and heir to th' Earl of Arundel,] / That late broke from the Duke of Exeter" etc., etc. (2.1.278). A "forceful" Sean Connery as Hotspur, en route to being James Bond, and the RSC's Frank Pettingell as Falstaff also convert the bare set into a convincingly mobile territory for the sprawling action. Except for a few disclaimers, the reception was positive, one critic fearing that Falstaff had been buried alive under the relentless pageantry, and that the sense of the "diseased" kingdom (so trenchantly represented a few years later by Orson Welles in *Chimes*) had gotten lost.[27]

Three years later in the nine-part *Spread of the Eagle* (1963), director Peter Dews tried the same formulas, but with somewhat less success, in a mini-series based on *Coriolanus, Julius Caesar*, and *Antony and Cleopatra.* Budgeted at as much as £7,000 per program, the series swallowed up a huge cast of some seventy-six actors. According to Dews, the common denominator was Plutarch's account of three personal tragedies set against a violent political background. In *Coriolanus* there is a fearless soldier (Robert Hardy), out of his depth in politics; in *Julius Caesar*, a cabal of political moderates out of their depth as terrorists (Barry Jones as Caesar and Keith Michell as Antony); and in *Antony and Cleopatra*, a fabled couple (Keith Michell and Mary Morris) out of control in a middle-aged love affair. A recurring theme echoes a sim-ilar concern in *An Age of Kings* – the Tudor obsession with degree and order in government.[28] This Tillyardian view comfortably meshed with the bland bourgeois values of the mid-Sixties in the pre-Vietnam era. To achieve continuity, Dews used the same cast throughout the nine parts, including several veterans from *An Age of Kings.* Robert Hardy traded Prince Hal for the role of Coriolanus, and Frank Pettingell abandoned Falstaff for Junius Brutus. The critic for the *Times* thought that the lack of continuity worked against it since *Antony* is the only character who appears in more than one sequence.[29] In 1965, Michael Barry, BBC's Head of Plays, televised the 1963 RSC Stratford Memorial Theatre production of the *Three Parts of Henry VI* and *Richard III*, which came to be known as *The Wars of the Roses.* Directed principally by Peter Hall and scripted by John Barton, the production rearranged Shakespeare's four plays into three for television – *Henry VI, Edward IV*, and *Richard III.* Twelve cameras taped the resulting pageant of English kings and queens, with a cast of seventy-six, which resourcefully recreated "a theatre production in television terms."[30] The Stratford theatre was converted into a huge television studio by boarding over orchestra seats to extend the stage forty feet outward for a sense of space lacking in the original stage productions, featuring John Bury's influentially realistic metallic settings.[31] Glowing performances offer imaginative visual equivalents to Shakespeare's language, as when, for example, the opening of *Henry VI* seizes on Bedford's lugubrious "Hung be the heavens with black, yield day to night!" (*1 Henry VI* 1.1.1) as a leitmotif by focusing on the corpse of Henry V. When in the Temple Garden the Lancastrians and Yorkists pluck their symbolic red and white roses, tight head shots and rapid cutting, along with banners and music support this most aesthetic of warrior rituals. Still another cut to a close framing of a white rose adumbrates the ascendancy of the Yorkist hegemony. A quicksilver Joan of Arc, Janet Suzman anticipates her later triumphs on television as Lady Macbeth and Cleopatra, by infusing the doggerel verse with fire and beauty. Even the dramatically hopeless scene when Mortimer responds with a prolix narrative of Lancastrian outrages to Richard Plantagenet's disingenuous, "Discover more at large what cause that was, / For I am ignorant and cannot guess" (2.5.59), captures the imagination. The wretched Mortimer, who looks terrible, with lumps all over his face, as if he vaguely understood that his creator, Shakespeare, had confused him with another Mortimer, parses the bewilderingly complicated family tree of the descendants of King Edward III: "Henry the Fourth, grandfather to this king, / Depos'd his nephew Richard, Edward's son," etc. In the critical raves, special praise went to David Warner for his King Henry VI, Ian Holm for Gloucester, Peggy Ashcroft for Margaret, and Donald Sinden for York.[32] Professor Alice Griffin, America's reigning authority on screened Shakespeare, even thought that "these are the best television productions of Shakespeare's plays in the history of television."[33]

In the United States, where major corporations like RCA cautiously studied the possibilities of this strange new creature,[34] the television industry prior to World War II lagged far behind Great Britain's, offering little more than blurry ice hockey games from Madison Square Garden on tiny tavern screens within greater New York City. After World War II, however, US television led the world in quantity with ten million receivers by 1951. As early as 1948 North America's first Shakespeare "event" on television was a transmission of Verdi's *Otello* live from New York's dignified old Metropolitan opera house. During the next decade, Shakespeare indirectly benefited from the Golden Years of pioneering television when commercial networks and sponsors underwrote live drama on Philco Playhouse, Studio One, Kraft Theatre, Omnibus, and the Hallmark Hall of Fame. Quality programming was soon doomed, though, when the working people's perverse willingness to squander hard-earned wages on television sets redirected programming from the classes to the masses. Unlike the films, which started in squalor and yearned for "quality," television began with "quality" and ended with trash. The Madison Avenue advertising industry and its corporate clients now had a clear license for lobotomizing the American mind. "Quality" programming, which publicists for commercial broadcasting cleverly stigmatized as "elitist," suffered another blow when the industry began to "package" programs out to Hollywood producers like Columbia Pictures' teleplay subsidiary, Screen Gems.[35] Uncommodified Shakespeare and drama in general were in serious jeopardy.

Somewhat against the prevailing winds, from 1953 to 1970 Kansas City's Hallmark Greeting Card company underwrote eight televised Shakespeare plays, *Hamlet* (twice), *Macbeth* (twice), *Richard II*, *Taming of the Shrew, Tempest*, and *Twelfth Night* – nine if you include *Kiss Me Kate* (1958). Principal director was George Schaefer, a television veteran, who really enjoyed the excitement of the early live transmissions, which carried with them "the hysteria of an opening night performance."[36] A traditionalist, Schaefer fit the greeting card company's profile for a director interested in such "higher forms of entertainment" as Shakespeare. He also as a sergeant in the US Army's troop entertainment program collaborated with Major Maurice Evans in producing wartime Shakespeare for troops overseas.

In the initial Hallmark Shakespeare play, Schaefer directed Maurice Evans, with Sarah Churchill as Ophelia, in *Hamlet* (1953), most memorable for the really stunning Gertrude played by Ruth Chatterton. The $185,000 budget, even allowing for inflation, by today's standards for hit shows like *Seinfeld* is ridiculously low. Maurice Evans' voice resonated exactly the right way for Americans who thought Shakespearean stage diction must inevitably be "RP" British. Moreover his wartime "GI" *Hamlet* had given Evans the requisite "regular guy" image to offset any Shakespearean taint. His admirers mostly failed to notice that the voice, a kind of perpetual quaver, remained pretty much unvaried in every role. Neither did anyone have the poor taste to point out that American soldiers in overseas backwaters made up a world-class captive audience for anything, even a church service, to relieve the boredom. Given her father's record in World War II, Sarah Churchill was well insulated against carping critics.

Evans appeared in the leading role in a 1954 *Richard II* that again featured Sarah Churchill, this time as the unhappy little queen, and then in a pioneering color transmission of *Macbeth* (1954) with Judith Anderson as Lady Macbeth. Professor Alice Griffin caught on to Evans' trick in both *Macbeth* and *Richard II* of "recit[ing] rather than act[ing]."[37] The *Time* critic praised the four cameras for the fluid way they moved "into and out of the scene during each long sequence."[38] In 1956 there was a *Taming of the Shrew* with the very proper Evans badly miscast as Petruchio and Lilli Palmer as Katherine Minola; in 1957, a *Twelfth Night* with Evans as Malvolio and Rosemary Harris as Viola; and in 1960, Hallmark achieved its greatest success in a relaxed *Tempest* with Evans plausibly cast as Prospero, an incredibly beautiful Lee Remick as Miranda, and the gifted Richard Burton as a gruff Caliban. Virginia M. Vaughan compared it to Peter Brook and Derek Jarman's darker visions of *The Tempest*, and said even though it was as "light as a souffle," its lack of pomposity qualified it for a "main course."[39]

With partial funding from Hallmark, Evans and Anderson's second *Macbeth* (1960) was filmed in color on location in Scotland for crossover theatrical and television release, in a collaboration of the arch-rivals: "TV helping the cinema, and the cinema helping TV."[40] Thousands of school children exposed to the 16mm rental version grew up thinking of the Macbeths as looking like Maurice Evans and Judith Anderson, just as in their imaginations Raymond Massey was Abraham Lincoln and Gregory Peck, Captain Ahab. The company sponsored a British *Hamlet* (1970), directed by Peter Wood, with a cluster of well-known actors, including Richard Chamberlain as the Prince, John Gielgud as the Ghost, and Michael Redgrave as Polonius. In turning to England, however, for theatrical talent, Hallmark followed a trend begun as early as 1959 with the Dupont Show of the Month *Hamlet*, which gradually eliminated home-brewed serious drama on American television. Commercial programming increasingly was targeted at the plain folk of Middle America, while the cultural elite choked on a diet of public television's British-made Masterpiece Theatre. And "public television" slowly came under the control of major sponsoring corporations to guarantee a blackout of any counter-culture tendencies.

Hallmark Greeting Cards, however, did not entirely monopolize American televised Shakespeare. In the thirty years between 1949 and 1979 (when the BBC Shakespeare Plays series saturated the market), nearly fifty major televised

12   Richard Chamberlain as the prince and
Ciaran Madden as Ophelia in Regency
costumes have Raby Castle as a background
in this scene from a Hallmark Hall of Fame
Hamlet that was imported from Great Britain
for transmission on North America's NBC-TV
in November 1970.

Shakespeare programs appeared in the United States. As early as 1949, NBC
made a pilot scene from *Henry V* featuring the late Sam Wanamaker, founder
of the Globe replica in London. An amateurish Players Club *Macbeth* (1949)
survives on a blurry kinescope with Walter Hampden, described by one critic
as looking "uneasy."[41] At CBS, Worthington Miner produced for Studio One
a modern dress *Julius Caesar* (1949) starring Robert Keith with the actors
costumed in the period's ugly, wide-lapel, padded business suits. A youthful Charlton Heston, who importantly contributed to movie Shakespeare in
the years ahead, played Cinna.[42] Television critic Jack Gould praised Miner
because he didn't just "take" a picture but "made" one in "the most exciting
television yet seen on the home screen."[43] In a pre-feminist, modern dress
Taming of the Shrew (1950), Charlton Heston manhandled Lisa Kirk's thoroughly subjugated Kate. Starred again in a 1951 *Macbeth*, Charlton Heston's
speeches were condemned as "lifeless and meaningless" and the production
itself denounced for "too obtrusive" camera work, whatever that time-honored
brickbat may mean. In another program that year, Richard Greene played the
title role in a *Coriolanus* in the modern dress that Worthington Miner faithfully believed would appeal to a mass audience, optimistically estimated at
ten million.

The miracle was not that Shakespeare was done timidly on television but that he was done at all. Producers like Miner fought a rear-guard action against stultifying political conformity and the Madison Avenue ad-agency hegemony. Shakespeare indirectly even became hostage to the holy war against godless communism when at mid-century McCarthyism thoroughly intimidated the moguls of mass entertainment. The rantings of Walter Winchell on national radio, in complicity with his crony, J. Edgar Hoover, and the HUAC Grand Inquisition, effectively silenced politically suspect "reds" and "traitors,"[44] who were blacklisted, jailed, exiled, exposed to the wrath of vigilantes, or bullied by HUAC into ratting on fellow actors. One positive note was that the Hollywood studios' refusal to allow their contracted actors to appear on the feared rival medium of television offered an unparalleled opportunity for younger, unknown actors like George C. Scott, Jack Lemmon, and Charlton Heston (then twenty-three) to win instant reputations.[45]

In a 1956 innovative "crossover," which preceded the Schaefer/Evans *Macbeth* experiment, an audience estimated, perhaps with some exaggeration, at twenty-five million watched a televised Olivier *Richard III* on the same afternoon that the movie was being theatrically released. Imported Shakespeare from Great Britain on television increasingly became a national habit, as, for example, with a 1959 CBS DuPont Show of the Month Old Vic *Hamlet*, starring John Neville as a thin, anxiety-ridden but very effective prince in the "Hamletism" tradition. A handsome illustrated souvenir television script on expensive rag paper testifies to CBS's serious commitment.[46] Three made-in-the-USA Shakespeare productions, all of them simply recordings of stage performances, surfaced on the national scene. Two came out of the workshops of Joseph Papp's New York Shakespeare Festival: a *King Lear* (1973) and a *Much Ado about Nothing* (1973). James Earl Jones's performance as King Lear when finally televised on public television in 1977 allowed thousands to see a famous black actor cross a color line by impersonating an English king. With his powerful physique, Jones managed to make the old king not so much old and fragile as newly conscious of senescence. Director A. J. Antoon's *Much Ado* with Sam Waterston as Benedick and Kathleen Widdoes as Beatrice, "Americanized" the play by shifting the period from a vaguely medieval Messina to the America of Col. Teddy Roosevelt's Spanish–American War Rough Riders, and by borrowing from film such tropes as slow and accelerated motion and Keystone Kop antics. Regrettably, the exposure on television while the play was still live on Broadway resulted shortly thereafter in the show's demise when box office receipts dried up. In the American Conservatory Theatre's *Taming of the Shrew* (1976), William Ball's San Francisco company displaced *Commedia* tropes into slapstick routines and the Mickey Mouse sound effects of Walt Disney. The presentation, was, however, frankly theatrical, not telegenic, in the sense that even the offstage audience was made a part of the *mise-en-scène*. By the close of the Seventies, then, there was less studio televising than off-site recording of theatrical productions.

Using the technology of "Electronovision," or alternatively "Theatrofilm," a simultaneously released recording of *Hamlet* (1964), directed by John Gielgud and starring Richard Burton, went out from Broadway's Lunt-Fontanne theatre to 976 American movie theatres in the hinterlands. The idea was to lure provincial folk in Dubuque to the local Bijou at $2.50 a head to enjoy the ritual and glory of a "live" performance on the New York stage. The concept was doomed by alternative, more home-centered, methods of entertainment, which rendered "electronovision" almost immediately obsolete. The "live" performance was actually pieced together from two performances.[47] Nevertheless this experiment managed to gross over £1 million but like Beerbohm Tree's silent movie of *Macbeth* (1916) was to be destroyed after its brief exhibition, particularly because of Richard Burton's dissatisfaction with it, though in fact it has miraculously resurfaced in recent years on voice recordings and widely available videocassettes in the English PAL format.

Richard Burton as the melancholy Dane gives acting lessons to everyone else in the cast, many of whom seem wooden, nervous and uncertain. Even if he was "tired," and "lacked lustre," and the show was "no more than a curiosity," or worse yet, "really dreadful," as various critics remarked after a 1972 revival in London,[48] an actor so richly talented as Burton, with his "animal" vitality, can never be entirely bad, only wonderfully charismatic. Burton's natural gifts included a sturdy Welsh voice, a magnificent head on strong shoulders, and the creativity to energize Shakespeare's language deeply within himself. Perhaps his genius depended in part on the accident that his mellifluous Welsh dialect coincided in mysterious ways with the spoken English heard on the stage of Shakespeare's Globe. At Shakespeare's Globe, the actors' diction would have sounded to modern ears less like a speech by Margaret Thatcher and more like a lilting brogue, perhaps resembling "Ohhh thet thisss tew tew soil-èd flaish would mellt,/ Thawww, and reeesollve itself into a dewww!" (1.2.129). More of the secret of Burton's genius, which he himself apparently understood no more than anyone else,[49] lay in an uncanny knack for perfect timing, pacing, and enunciation – the daring to turn a vowel into a screech. When he says "seems, madam? nay, it is" (1.2.76) to Eileen Herlie as Gertrude (an encore from her same role in the Olivier film), the "seems" crackles throughout the theatre. When he speaks of how "the funeral-bak'd meats / Did coldly furnish forth the marriage tables" (1.2.179), he chuckles at his own witticism and pauses for the audience to share in the joke. When he sends Ophelia to a "nunnery," his last verb, "go" (3.1.149), emerges muted, almost a whisper, magnificently anti-climactic to the way he has just excoriated the poor girl while spinning, whirling, and circling around her in a towering rage. His gifts bring out a side of Hamlet deeply buried in the subtext – the irascible, wilful, petulant, yes, even dangerous, Hamlet, that too easily eludes the grasp of lesser actors. The scene between Hamlet and the Ghost brings Burton together with a shadowy Gielgud as Ghost whose dreadful tale of perfidy and poison emerges in Gielgud's unvaried speaking voice, little different from the voice for King Henry IV in *Chimes at Midnight*, John of Gaunt in the BBC *Richard II* (1979), or Prospero in Greenaway's *Prospero's Books* (1991). Hamlet listens to the voice, interjects, and reacts. Unlike Gielgud's singing voice, Burton as Hamlet rasps and roars.

Except for the visiting players come to Elsinore, it is all done in ordinary street clothes, on a bare stage, pretty much like a first rehearsal off book. Partly because of the poor lighting and partly because of the inept camera work (despite fifteen concealed cameras), Burton's supporting players add very little. Hume Cronyn's Polonius seems bloodless, perhaps miscast; Ophelia (Linda Marsh) is anxious and tentative; and Alfred Drake (Claudius) was better employed on Broadway as Fred Graham (Petruchio) in *Kiss Me Kate* (1958). Without Burton in the cast, no one would have had the consummate gall to offer so little to the trusting folk in the provinces. The off-stage audience in the theatre collaborated by applauding wildly at the slightest sign of life from the actors. Is there maybe just a touch of self- referentiality when Burton utters Hamlet's last words to Horatio: "O God, Horatio, what a wounded name" (5.2.344)? Burton felt that preserving the record of this performance could have "wounded" his name, but to make the "rest . . . silence" would have robbed posterity of a rare snapshot of a real actor in action.[50]

Prior to the 1978 inauguration of the mammoth BBC Shakespeare series, much truly first-rate televised Shakespeare came out of England from networks other than the BBC. Several of these appeared within a few years on various alternative television outlets in the United States like Classic Theatre produced by Station WGBN in Boston, PBS offerings from WNET/Thirteen in New York City, or the Bravo Channel. An important rival to the Burton *Hamlet* was the Philip Saville *Hamlet at Elsinore* (1964), which in contrast to the bare-stage Burton *Hamlet* was taped on location in Kronborg Castle at Elsinore in Denmark, where the actual historical events in the play may or may not have taken place. Dr. Bernice Kliman remarks that the result was like Henry James's *The Real Thing*, where the bogus aristocrats look more like aristocrats than the authentic aristocrats. She prefers Kozintsev's madeup sets.[51] A stellar cast and imaginative camera work on the outdoors sets make for a crossover type of production that edges toward the resources of film. Christopher Plummer's Hamlet has been described as "the Hamlet of Goethe and Coleridge, the gentle spirit broken by a burden too heavy for him to bear,"[52] but he can also be cited as a most ingenious and resourceful Hamlet who excels as much with body language as with the spoken word. Michael Caine (Horatio), Robert Shaw (Claudius), Donald Sutherland (Fortinbras), Alec Clunes (Polonius), mime Lindsay Kemp (Player Queen), and Jo Maxwell Muller as a "nastily" crazy Ophelia give him first-rate support.[53]

One of the great successes on Rediffusion Network Television production was Joan Kemp-Welch's 1964 *Midsummer Night's Dream*, which featured England's immensely popular comedian, Benny Hill, as Bottom, though Hill was then virtually unknown to mass North American audiences. The expressionistic influences of the Reinhardt school show just beneath the surface, with Mendelssohn's sprightly incidental music on the soundtrack, risking the condescension of those who prefer to dwell on the play's "darker elements." The woodland *mise-en-scène* showcases shrieking animals, an ubiquitous Puck (Tony Tanner) and a formidable Oberon (Peter Wyngarde) with a pre-punk haircut. The actors' short hair puts Shakespeare's world in the mirror of current fashions.

John Dexter's ATV *Twelfth Night* (1970) can be pleasurably recollected years later, partially because the cast was the best ever for a televised Shakespeare comedy. As Malvolio, the protean Alec Guinness is a marvel of subtle restraint, a fussy, ridiculous but nevertheless forlorn creature, the embodiment of one of Shakespeare's roster of lost souls. Ralph Richardson's Sir Toby comes across as more sinister than farcical, which makes sense because when all is said and done Sir Toby is really quite a mean fellow, while casting pop star Tommy Steele as Feste turned Shakespeare's clown into a boy with a guitar. Joan Plowright's Viola captures the oscillations between femininity and androgyny accounting for that young woman's confused relationships with both Olivia and Count Orsino. The shifting camera angles embellish the dramatic irony of the letter scene in Olivia's garden when the pathetic, bemused Malvolio discovers the forged letter but cannot overhear his tormentors' cruel japes.

A recording of Trevor Nunn's RSC *Comedy of Errors* (1976) takes imaginative liberties with the Shakespearean original by turning it into a musical comedy, though not quite so wildly divorced from the original source as *The Boys from Syracuse* (1940). Duke Solinus is burlesqued as a kind of Mussolini dictator while Griffith Jones as old Egeon remains wonderfully lost, addlebrained, and unbearably dense. The Antipholus and Dromio pairs of twins function like lab rats in a Skinnerian box blindly responding to rewards and punishments. The most poignant moments come when Judi Dench as Adriana and Francesca Annis as Luciana exchange confidences about their "relationships" with men. Having Barbara Shelley's Courtesan as a flagrant hussy underscores the womens' resentment. Nunn's probing treatment, as with Miller's *Merchant* (1973) and Dexter's *Twelfth Night* (1970) discussed above, shows again how the lightheartedness in Shakespearean drama may conceal monsters from the deep.

Shakespearean comedy and tragedy intertwine the carnivalesque and lenten in ways that defy neoclassical yearnings for pure genre.

Surely only by coincidence, *Macbeth* had a minor vogue in the United States after the Kennedy assassination, coming to an apex with the irreverent stage travesty, *MacBird*. A British *Macbeth* (1970), produced by Cedric Messina and directed by John Gorrie for BBC One with US funding, helped to satisfy the unspeakable craving for news about regicides and/or prexicides. A pilot project, as it turned out, for the subsequent BBC Shakespeare Plays series in which Messina and Gorrie were major figures, it features Janet Suzman opposite Eric Porter. Suzman's outward beauty and inner corruption as Lady Macbeth encompasses the play's major theme of the foulness of the fair and the fairness of the foul. That equivocal condition, deeply embedded in the play's language, gets visual support from camera angles forcing the audience to look down, at these two handsome but treacherous creatures. Unfortunately the *faux* realism of the stony castle walls works at cross purposes with the obvious fakery of the crowd scenes. Having Macbeth walk on foot rather than ride into the castle suggests either a low budget or a paralysis of the imagination. Janet Suzman's dynamic readings against Porter's stolid presence show how acting remains the one crucial variable determining success on stage or screen. When she says "We fail? / But screw your courage to the sticking place, / And we'll not fail" (*Macbeth* 1.7.59), she almost manages to break through the glass prison of the television screen and enter alive into our living rooms. Suzman herself felt that the play had special possibilities for television because of its "conspiratorial" nature with the action confined largely "to two or three people."[54] Television expert H. R. Coursen found Suzman's acting "superbly articulated,"[55] but some saw the rest of the cast as just "passing through."[56]

Trevor Nunn's 1972 "Roman Plays season" at Stratford resulted ultimately in a televised production of *Antony and Cleopatra*, this time with the help of ATV network director Jon Scoffield. Despite some lukewarm reviews of her Stratford stage performance,[57] Janet Suzman and Richard Johnson's televised version won such accolades as "the finest Shakespearean production on television up to 1975."[58] After the establishing shot of a richly colored Egyptian frieze with superimposed credits and movie composer Guy Woolfenden's music on the soundtrack, the charismatic Janet Suzman made the legendary queen into a divinity but one sparkling with human wit. In a nod to filmic values, an opening sequence in black-and-white dovetails Philo's description of Antony as "the triple pillar of the world" with a montage symbolic of the Roman empire of orgies, soldiers, faces. Another cut localizes this sweeping panorama to Antony and Cleopatra themselves, who embody Rome and Egypt. Like Orson Welles, the directors were inspired by radio's sonic techniques and introduced a wonderful galaxy of sound for gulls, waves, and so forth; while Patrick Stewart's voice carried the description of Cleopatra's barge by truly describing what he saw, rather than just mechanically grinding out words. Few will forget Suzman's Cleopatra when she utters the words, "I have / Immortal longings in me" and "I am fire and air" (5.2.280, 289). At the end, imperiously erect even at death's door, she becomes an Egyptian icon, who has entered not only into history but into the lives of the audience. Robert Speaight in reviewing the earlier Stratford stage production understandably thought that she had "succeeded [in the role] where Peggy Ashcroft and Edith Evans had both failed."[59]

Arguably one of the greatest successes in the history of televised Shakespeare, Trevor Nunn's *Macbeth* (1976) at Stratford's The Other Place was adapted to television in 1979 without loss to either theatrical or telegenic values. As Michael Mullin observed, "instead of re-conceiving the production for television, the television director Philip Casson seems to have set himself the task of finding ways in which television could re-create the experience of the theatre."[60] With Judi Dench and Ian McKellen, and the rest of the cast in a circle so that they are themselves both actors and audience, the minimalist, starkly bare *mise-en-scène* in a meta-theatrical way virtually puts the audience in the same circle with the actors. Adroit camera angles and tight framing enhance the illusion that the screen is a mirror for ourselves rather than a frame for defining the actors.

Ritual replaces realism. The bizarrely eclectic costumes range from a prissy Rosse in a business suit to Scottish lairds in turtle-neck sweaters, to Macbeth in a black leather-and-boots Nazi outfit, to Lady Macbeth in some kind of black, tent-like garment and black headscarf. Ian McKellen's punk-like hairdo, slicked down and greased, demonizes a face that is egregiously at odds with A. C. Bradley's concept of a romantic/tragic hero, as conceived, for example, by Maurice Evans. Judi Dench, despite the vast folds of her curious garment, exudes a sensuality that makes Macbeth's infatuation with his lady believable. In one close-up, she and Macbeth virtually melt into each other as fervor overwhelms decorum. Ian McKellen makes the tragedy of Macbeth over into the unmasking of Macbeth, the exposure of the man's essential sordidness. Brilliantly, the same actor (Ian McDiarmid) who plays Rosse then turns around and doubles as an astonishing Porter wearing braces over a bare, hairy chest. Unbearable tension grows from such vignettes as Lady Macbeth's sleepwalking when she still wears that horrible black headpiece, and from Ian McKellen's terse spitting out of his "To-morrow, and to-morrow, and to-morrow / Creeps in this petty pace" (5.5.19). The spoken word sustains the chilling atmosphere. Despite many encomiums, a dissenting Richard Ingrams found it strange that the play was "greeted with rapture" by all the critics, thought the costumes, "ridiculous," and lamented that "poor Judi Dench...had to wear a duster around her head like a char lady."[61]

More pure video than television, Paul Bosner's plan to record live Shakespeare in performance at London's St. George's theatre produced a *Romeo and Juliet* (1976) starring Sarah Badel and Peter McEnery. In Sarah Badel, Bosner offered "a dreamy-eyed, enchanting Juliet." Nevertheless a stage play recorded on film remains one of the trickier equations to deal with, especially with the fierce competition from the then emerging BBC Shakespeare series.

In 1978 BBC's Cedric Messina, with Dr. John Wilders as literary consultant, began putting all thirty-six plays from the 1623 Folio plus *Pericles* into a six-year series called "The Shakespeare Plays," an epic task that marked a watershed in the history of Shakespeare on screen. The logistics of recruiting actors, designing sets and costumes, and finding creative directors, all within the constraints of a six-year timetable, approached megalomania and inevitably put the BBC production staff under fearful pressure. An unfortunate decision by British Equity to cast only British actors revived the ancient American inferiority complex over things British. Even worse, the decision to ignore American actors meant that American schools and colleges had less interest in spending money on the series. Since the project was heavily funded by US banks and corporations, this protectionism, which has often been reciprocated just as narrowly by Actors Equity on Broadway, sent prominent American theatre people like New York City's Shakespeare impresario, Joseph Papp, into a rage. On the other hand, the series revolutionized the teaching of Shakespeare in the schools. Great numbers of skeptical classroom teachers, taking a leaf from art history lecturers, began exploring the dynamics of screening scenes on the classroom television monitor as a supplement to amateurish readings by teachers and students.

The series got off to a slow start with a lackluster *Julius Caesar*, whose papier-mâché Rome, bedsheet costuming, and rhetorical paralysis signaled a decision to play it safe at all costs, even with estimable acting in Richard Pasco's Brutus, Keith Michell's Antony and especially Elizabeth Spriggs's Calphurnia. An outdoorsy *As You Like It*, filmed on location in May and June at Glamis Castle, Scotland, with Helen Mirren as a somewhat sullen Rosalind, unfortunately clashed with the "icy fang" of winter's wind associated with the Forest of Arden.[62] After that came a dismal *Romeo and Juliet* that was a shadowy replica of the dazzling Zeffirelli film; a king-centered *Richard II* that became a rostrum for the sinewy talents of Derek Jacobi as the narcissistic monarch; a highly successful *Measure for Measure*; and a surprisingly appealing *Henry VIII*. Director Desmond Davis' *Measure for Measure* was the season's hit. Kate Nelligan's Isabella and Tim Pigott-Smith's Angelo with strong support from John McEnery's Lucio (Mercutio in the Zeffirelli *Romeo and Juliet*) and Kenneth Colley's godlike Duke Vincentio, offered a familiar tale of sexual harassment well suited to a medium so congenial to soap opera. The casting of actors familiar to the British on popular programs, e.g., Kenneth Colley who played the blind beggar in *Pennies from Heaven*, was unfortunately lost on American audiences. John Stride, who was the ubiquitous Rosse in the Polanski film version of *Macbeth*, breathed new life into the infrequently performed *King Henry VIII*.

The second season began with John Gorrie's *Twelfth Night*, in which Trevor Peacock played a remarkably "manly and substantial" Feste and Alec McCowen a "deliciously obnoxious" Malvolio.[63] While the sets could not match the extravagant 1955 LenFilm version directed by Y. Fried, sensitive performances by Sinead Cusack as Olivia and Felicity Kendal as Viola conjured up some of the Illyrian magic. A repeat performance of *Richard II* then served as a prologue to the *First and Second Parts of Henry IV and Henry V*. The season ended with an inert *Tempest*, starring Michael Hordern and directed by John Gorrie again, whose gestures toward realism backfired when the plastic island remained dead even to the cry of sea gulls.

The subsequent televising of the major tetralogy of the English history plays allowed viewers a rare opportunity, as with *An Age of Kings*, to see the four plays virtually uncut. As Bolingbroke, Jon Finch suffers from a mysterious skin disease that serves as a metaphor for the diseased body of king and state, but unfortunately begins to make the audience homeopathically itch right along with him. As the "guilt" beneath the "gilt" of the crown surfaces, tension between father and son (Prince Hal is played by David Gwillim) escalates, until catharsis arrives in the great reconciliation scene in *Henry IV Part Two* (4.5.88–240). In the rejection scene during the coronation procession, Anthony Quayle (Falstaff) divulges the inner pathos of Shakespeare's "plump Jack," whose banishment spells the end of the whole world, with at least as much cogency as in Orson Welles's reading (5.5.47). As a Shakespearean actor, Quayle's screen appearances included Cassio in *Othello* (1937) and Marcellus in the Olivier *Hamlet* (1948), while in a lengthy stage career he once even directed at the Stratford Memorial Theatre. The tavern scenes, which as in *Chimes* also suggest the influence of the seventeenth-century Dutch painters, introduce a garrulous Mrs. Quickly (Brenda Bruce) and a sleazy Doll Tearsheet (Frances Cuka), whose middle-aged seediness contrasts with the youthful glow of Jeanne Moreau in Welles's *Chimes*. The earlier plays of the BBC series mostly fell into the trap of assuming that television needed to be realistic even when a milieu such as the lists in Coventry made realism unrealistic. The battle scenes, especially with the gory close-up of Hotspur vomiting blood in his death throes at Shrewsbury, only succeeded in alienating the audience. The tiny television screen shrunk the epical Henriad down in scale so that David Gwillim as King Henry V, the "mirror of Christian princes," seemed to be wearing the borrowed robes of Laurence Olivier.

Nothing revolutionary happened at the beginning of the third season in 1980 with a *Hamlet* starring Derek Jacobi, which suffered from the recurring indecisiveness about whether to be theatrical or telegenic, and succeeding in being neither. The minimalist *mise-en-scène* with a small ramp and a cycloramic curtain looked in its bareness more like a budgetary than an artistic decision, but it did move away from realism toward expressionism. Derek Jacobi delivered his usual brilliant readings, but for those who had recently seen his *Richard II*, it was sometimes hard to tell whether he was Hamlet or a self-pitying "Landlord of England" (*Richard II* 2.1.113).The characters acted but did not interact. It was a Hamlet without *Hamlet*, so to speak, but Claire Bloom was a memorable Gertrude and Emrys James a fine First Player. In a meta-theatrical touch, Hamlet directly enters into the performance of the Mouse Trap as a foil to Lucianus, the nephew of the player king.

In the third year, the versatile and imaginative Dr. Jonathan Miller, sometime member of the satirical Edinburgh Festival group, *Beyond the Fringe*,[64] replaced Cedric Messina, the veteran BBC producer of the project's first perilous years. Miller had the advantage of profiting from his predecessor's mistakes. Most notably he changed the design codes by looking to contemporaneous paintings and architecture as models for costuming and *mise-en- scène*. This same concept had already been explored in the first season with Desmond Davis' intriguing *Measure for Measure*, when designer Odette Barrow built costumes modeled on the clothing of people in seventeenth-century Dutch paintings. By broadening the scope of "Elizabethan" to include all European painting, Miller opened up fresh possibilities for his designers. Shakespeare's own players ignored historical consistency, as illustrated by the famous Longleat sketch of *Titus Andronicus*, in which, except for the principals, all the actors wear Elizabethan attire.

In *Antony and Cleopatra*, Paolo Veronese's paintings inspired the costumes and sets, while Colin Blakely (Antony) and Jane Lapotaire (Cleopatra) compressed the sprawling drama to the size of a geriatric love duet for the television screen. Indeed Richard David feared that "the necessary miniaturization for TV must be more damaging to *Antony and Cleopatra* than to any other play in the canon."[65] In *All's Well that Ends Well*, when Helena is seated at the clavichord with a mirror on the wall above her, she echoes the lady in Emanuel de Witte's "Interior with a Woman at a Clavichord." Beyond that, aided by designer John Summers, Elijah Moshinsky, a television *auteur* equal in talent to Jane Howell and Jonathan Miller, figured out how to enrich Angela Down's eerie Helena with a clever lighting plan. An acerbic Ian Charleson as a grumpy Bertram and the ubiquitous Michael Hordern, who surfaced in so many BBC plays, made the production from a technical point of view as unproblematic as the first season's play, *Measure for Measure*, was problematic. Director Jack

Gold's *Merchant of Venice* drew on Tiziano Titian as a backdrop for the stony-faced Portia (Gemma Jones), who in true poststructuralist style subverts her own speech on mercy at the trial of Shylock (Warren Mitchell). Gold's camera also nicely pinpoints the spiritual desolation of both Jessica and Antonio, who at the end are left apart from the other far happier, more integrated, citizens of a waspish society. Despite the ethnic background of the production's director and star, some Jewish groups predictably objected to *Merchant* as anti-Semitic.

While Miller's design policies in drawing on high art drastically improved the series' visual attractiveness, considerable leeway yet remained for the genius of individual directors like Jane Howell, whose *Winter's Tale* experimented with minimalist, expressionistic sets and symbolic costumes (a bearskin hat and cloak for Leontes in prefiguration of the famous bear in the third act). And Miller himself truly ran against the grain of *The Taming of the Shrew* when he reinvented *Fawlty Towers'* comic innkeeper John Cleese as a puritanical and deadly solemn Petruchio. Cleese's prune-faced Petruchio contrasts so vividly with Richard Burton's oafish portrayal in the Zeffirelli movie (1966) as to make them seem altogether different characters. Miller ferreted out a subtext in Petruchio's scorn for the outward trappings of success, and turned him into the dour moralist implicit in his admonishment to Kate that "our purses shall be proud, our garments poor, / For 'tis the mind that makes the body rich" (4.3.171).

The pace slowed somewhat in the fourth season (1981–82) with only four plays: *Othello, Timon of Athens, A Midsummer Night's Dream,* and *Troilus and Cressida.* The two satirical plays, *Timon* and *Troilus,* brought Elizabethan esoterica within the range of mass audiences. Jonathan Pryce as the curmudgeonly and indubitably crazy Timon progressed from the excesses of generosity to the deficiencies of misanthropy. In *Troilus,* director Miller's design theories transported the play about ancient Troy to a world somewhere "between the medieval Gothic of Chaucer and Henryson and the Renaissance of Shakespeare." Theorizing that the Troy story was essentially a medieval legend anyway, Miller looked to woodcuts by Cranach, Dürer, and Altdorfer. Cranach, for example, made Paris over into a Gothic knight in his Judgment of Paris, but Miller also eclectically borrowed from the American television hit MASH for the dreary camp scenes. Charles Gray, a workhorse BBC actor, who in 1979 had played the title role in *Julius Caesar* and the Duke of York in *Richard II,* did Pandarus, while Jack Birkett (The Incredible Orlando [sic]) of the Lindsay Kemp company, a blind dancer and mime, whom Miller had seen as Caliban in the Derek Jarman *Tempest* (1980), was the spiteful and "bitchy" Thersites.[66] Director Elijah Moshinsky continued his career as a video *auteur* with a *Midsummer Night's Dream* that followed his earlier *All's Well* in its visual borrowings from the Dutch masters. A shot of the "rude mechanicals" posed on a bench outside a tavern mirrored Hans Bols's "Members of the Wine Merchants Guild," while a touch of whimsy made Cherith Mellor as Helena with her granny glasses and stick figure into an icon for adolescent misery.

The season's most ambitious but not most rewarding production was *Othello*. With Anthony Hopkins as the Moor, Bob Hoskins as Iago and Penelope Wilton as Desdemona, Director Miller's work "represents a noteworthy instance of transferring/transforming Shakespeare to video."[67] Unfazed by the controversy that erupted when British Equity refused permission for black American actor James Earl Jones to accept the role, Miller blithely declared that the play really had little to do with race after all but was focused on the question of jealousy.[68] He then cast Anthony Hopkins as a light-skinned Moor, a decision that was anathema in North America where political correctness makes a white actor playing Othello taboo. Low-keyed, almost humdrum at the beginning, Hopkins' Moor erupts into a manic fit when Hoskins' demonic, insinuating, cackling Iago finally unhinges him in the third act. Even if a mere coincidence, the linkage of the names, "Ho*p*kins," and "Ho*s*kins," hints at the production's stress on the *Doppelgänger* relationship between hero and villain. Like Kenneth Colley in *Measure*, Hoskins also represented for the British audience an unusual casting decision since he had played the pathetic music salesman and accused rapist in Dennis Potter's wonderful *Pennies from Heaven*, again a code switching that was lost in North America. No one questioned, however, the great power and authority of Hopkins' astounding performance. Costumes and sets showed the influence of a veritable art gallery of Renaissance painters to include Titian, De La Tour, Tintoretto, Brueghel, El Greco, Joos van Wassenhove, and Velasquez! Cyprian settings were modeled on a Renaissance palace in Urbino, Italy.[69]

The frenetic pace continued in the fifth period (1982–83) with six more plays captured on tape. An understated *King Lear* marked the third time, no less, that director Jonathan Miller, and actors Michael Hordern (King Lear) and Frank Middlemass (Fool) had collaborated on Shakespeare's supreme tragedy. Miller and Hordern de-mythologized King Lear by showing how his wicked daughters, with entire logic, might indeed have found the grizzled, somewhat dyspeptic, old king a royal pain in the neck. Instead of the flamboyant, ranting King Lear of a Frederick B. Warde or an Albert Finney as "Sir" in Peter Yates's *The Dresser* (1983), this king looked more like almost anybody's granddad on the verge of Alzheimer's. Through this subversion of the conventional image of the king as Jove-figure, the father–daughter bond became notably more poignant. Since Hordern appeared as King Lear at virtually the same time as the Granada TV Elliott/Olivier *King Lear* (1983), the two visual treatments invite close comparison. Competing with Lord Olivier was hardly anyone's desire, but Hordern's rather cynical old man in dark tones compares favorably

13   In a later televised version of *Othello* (1981), Bob
Hoskins as Iago works Anthony Hopkins' Moor into a
jealous rage over the alleged infidelity of Desdemona.

with the more romantic image projected by Olivier in bright color. Both actors
were self-referentially playing an aged star at the end of lengthy stage and film
careers. They chose to interpret King Lear in the same way that they had lived
out their professional lives – Hordern as a skilled and reliable journeyman
actor, and Olivier as a mercurial and spectacular superstar.

Elijah Moshinsky's *Cymbeline* allowed him to put Claire Bloom back on the
screen as the malevolent queen, while a perfidious Iachimo (Robert Lindsay)
schemes against an innocent Imogen (Helen Mirren). The following month saw
Ben Kingsley as a paranoid Mr. Ford and Richard Griffiths as the scapegoated
Falstaff in *The Merry Wives of Windsor*. The season's greatest achievement, however, was the sleeper of the entire series – Jane Howell's imaginative production
of the minor tetralogy of the English history plays, *1–3 Henry VI* and *Richard
III*. The BBC plays ripened as the directors began to discover the best means

available for presenting them. Thus, Jane Howell junked the stodgy realism that had left audiences yawning in favor of a visually exciting expressionism. With mirrors and with the unlikely help of a children's "adventure playground" in Fulham, Howell's illusory battles became gorier than the real thing. Ron Cook as Richard duke of Gloucester and Julia Foster as Queen Margaret, the "she-wolf of France," portrayed impressively nasty royalty. As the Lady Anne, Zoë Wanamaker deepened and enhanced the role of this tortured but opaque young widow. At the same time, as a person of the twentieth century, Howell condemned war fare while sensationalizing this saga of division and rebellion, as indeed Shakespeare did himself. Howell turns Julia Foster as Queen Margaret into a "kind of death-goddess" as "she sits atop the mound of corpses which have been steadily building up at the end of each play."[70]

The sixth season (1983–84) of *Coriolanus, The Comedy of Errors, Two Gentlemen of Verona, Pericles*, and *Macbeth* was to have brought closure, but in fact four plays had yet not been released. Shaun Sutton had by then replaced Jonathan Miller as producer, and each year the insoluble problems of putting Shakespeare on the small screen seemed more soluble. The way that Alan Howard played Coriolanus opposite Mike Gwilym's Aufidius hinted at a homo-erotic link, while veteran Shakespearean actress, Irene Worth, was Volumnia, exalted mother of the "boy of tears." Both *Comedy of Errors* and *Two Gentlemen of Verona* generated the requisite farce and romance, though the sets for *Errors* with a crane shot of a gigantic map of the Mediterranean right out of Ortelius' atlas, seemed the more cleverly adapted to the medium. Pop singer Roger Daltrey, doubling as the Dromios in *Errors*, went over smashingly with American students, who could identify with him more readily than with actors from the Royal Shakespeare Company. Starring Mike Gwilym in the title role, Director David Jones's *Pericles* with its visual codes of soft Mediterranean lighting caught the flavor of Greek romances like the anonymous *Apollonius of Tyre*. In the brothel scenes, Trevor Peacock as Boult and Amanda Redman as Marina lent credibility to the faraway and exotic mood, while a high frequency of dissolves for Gower's narrative commentary visually corresponded to the rapid reversals of fortune in romance narrative. The season's nominees for best acting, however, were Nicol Williamson and Jane Lapotaire as Macbeth and his Lady, who ransacked the subtext for imaginative readings. Lapotaire's soliloquy, "Come, you spirits / That tend on mortal thoughts, unsex me here" (1.5.40) will surely go down in acting history as anything but unsexed in its steamy nonverbal gestures. Nicol Williamson, as in the Tony Richardson filmed "Roundhouse" *Hamlet* (1969), again brutally assaulted the text until it confessed its innermost secrets. Williamson and Richard Burton, between the two of them, virtually patented a whole new aggressive style for approaching Shakespeare's language, hitherto hostage to the elocution of genteel versifiers.

The years 1984 and 1985 saw the release of Elijah Moshinsky's *Love's Labor's Lost*; Stuart Burge's *Much Ado about Nothing*; David Giles's *King John*, and Jane Howell's *Titus Andronicus*. The first, *Love's Labor's Lost*, broke with the BBC house style when director Moshinsky put his actors in eighteenth-century instead of Elizabethan or Jacobean dress. Burge's rather inhibited *Much Ado* featured a somber Beatrice and Benedick but Susan McCloskey nevertheless praised Burge's spatial sense in arranging the *mise-en-scène* to fit the play's alternating moods of light and dark.[71] David Giles switched codes in *King John* by putting British comic actor Leonard Rossiter in the title role of the unhappy monarch, yet once more the mischief was lost on American audiences ignorant of the funny roles generally associated with Rossiter. By rediscovering the possibilities for Gothic thrills in Shakespeare's strange Senecan tragedy, *Titus Andronicus*, Jane Howell spawned a Rocky Horror Picture Show in minimalist guise. Gripping performances by Trevor Peacock in the title role and Anna Calder-Marshall as the ravished Lavinia make credible the incredibility of the Ovidian/Senecan rhetoric in Shakespeare's grotesque but compelling Roman history play.

Even while the BBC series was unfolding its magisterial design, other notable treatments of Shakespeare on television and/or video were either appearing or waiting in the wings. In New York City, Joseph Papp's *Midsummer Night's Dream* (1982) at the Delacorte Theatre in Central Park cleverly decoded Shakespeare into an idiom understandable to a contemporary audience. The rude mechanicals, for example, are reinvented as hardhat New York construction workers. Marcel Rosenblatt's antic Puck also confirms the post-modernist understanding of the dream as always on the edge of a nightmare. Far away from Central Park in Johannesburg, South Africa, former RSC actress Janet Suzman, herself a stellar Cleopatra and Joan of Arc, daringly recorded the *Othello* (1988) performed at the Market Place Theatre. "Daringly" because in the context then of South Africa's apartheid policies, the close juxtaposition of a black man and white woman on stage invited brutal reprisals. Barbara Hodgdon reports that some white South Africans walked out of the theatre at the first embrace between Desdemona and Othello.[72] John Kani as a black actor playing Othello stirs memories of electrifying performances by Paul Robeson and James Earl Jones. Richard Haddon Haines's Iago seems less compelling, but he shows an incomparable gift for mistreating Emilia, while Joanna Weinberg as Desdemona adds to her shimmering whiteness the extra touch of wearing a green gown in anticipation of Othello's jealous fit. The reception was enthusiastic, both in South Africa and after a 1989 telecast from London's Channel Four. Hugh Herbert of *The Guardian* wrote that "John Kani's is a fine and masterful performance that should make every white actor think twice before blacking up for the Moor."[73]

Michael Bogdanov's brilliant seven-part *Wars of the Roses* (1988–89) glitters with bright ideas, but never attracted all the attention and praise that it deserves. The apparent inconsistency of having the characters in the first installment, *King Richard II*, appear in Edwardian costumes and the characters in *Richard III* in modern dress quietly reflects the historical fact that nearly a century elapsed between Bolingbroke's usurpation of Richard II in 1399 and the victory of Lancastrian Henry Tudor at Bosworth Field in 1485. Bogdanov, and his colleague Michael Pennington, supported the recorded performances by the English Shakespeare Company at the Grand Theatre, Swansea, with a clever mixture of theatre, television, and cinema, and used montages of key figures and events for linking episodes. The haunting, hallucinatory, watery transitions hint at the deadly secrets and horrors that Queen Margaret, the "she-wolf of France," never tires of reciting.

Ever since Colley Cibber's eighteenth-century production, directors have ransacked their ingenuity to clarify the complicated politics behind the opening events of *Richard III.* Here the witty gimmick, in what seems to prefigure the opening scene of the Ian McKellen and Richard Loncraine *Richard III* (1995), lies in having a "Prologue," Barry Stanton, introduce the assembled cast, who have gathered in modern dress for a cocktail party. The tuxedoclad Chorus, who wears a red-and-white rose boutonniere in sign of the houses of Lancaster and York, genially sorts out the complicated relationships among the characters, introducing each in turn. The doomed Clarence, Rivers, Grey, and Dorset register wonderfully pained facial expressions when they hear Stanton telling the audience that they will die during the play. When Stanton finishes his labyrinthine plot summary, a masterpiece of black humor, he turns to the audience and in a flash of ironic understatement says, "Simple!"

Most unforgettable, however, is Andrew Jarvis' Richard duke of Gloucester. In a drape suit three sizes too big for him, showing a slight hump at the left shoulder, wearing a black glove and heavy orthopedic shoe, his shirt collar unbuttoned, tie askew, and stomping around with an exaggerated limp, Jarvis oozes pure, unadulterated evil. When he woos the Lady Anne over the corpse of her murdered father-in-law, and allows her an opportunity to stab him – "Take up the sword again, or take up me" (1.2.183) – he yanks out a pair of wicked-looking switch-blade knives that give him the look of an Edward Scissorhands. His absolutely bald skull adds yet another repellent feature to this variant on the Beauty and the Beast fable. To rescue him from being a mere caricature of the anti-Christ, though, Richard's response to being spat at by the Lady Anne is an unexpected look of deep hurt and anguish, as if he were truly wounded. Or again, is this just another example of Richard as the "murtherous Machevil," who can "frame [his] face to all occasions" (*3 Henry VI* 3.2.185)? Jarvis plays it too cleverly for anyone to be sure.

There was more happening than just on television, though. Shakespeare in moving images has proliferated with the new technology of cheaper, more user-friendly, magnetic taping, hand-held cameras, and portable recording and sound equipment. The residual rights for the sale of home videocassettes transformed the economics of the industry, where theatrical release recoups the cost of a movie and overseas and video sales turn the profit. The commercial exploitation of the entire BBC Shakespeare series on videocassettes by Time Life Inc. opened up a fresh market in the schools with state funds underwriting audio/visual equipment. In addition the possibilities for cheap magnetic recording of Shakespeare on stage, even with camcorders, began to be explored increasingly, as organizations such as the New York City Lincoln Center Library TOFT (Theatre on Film and Tape) collection, the Folger Library, and the embryonic Globe Bankside Centre in London began collecting archival videotapes for study purposes only. Most notably the Royal Shakespeare Company in Stratford-upon-Avon also taped its theatrical productions for storage in the Stratford Shakespeare Centre Library, where one can now view rare footage of Charles Laughton as Bottom in a Peter Hall production from the 50s, and the Royal National Theatre established a performance archive at the British Theatre Museum in Covent Garden. The Canadian Stratford Shakespeare Festival markets videotaped segments of plays like *The Taming of the Shrew* (1981) starring Len Cariou and Sharry Flett, with added commentary for the educational sector. If the Actors' Equity and musicians' unions relax copyright restrictions, future theatre historians will study late twentieth-century Shakespeare performances at video archives.

The growing bifurcation between video as a publication like a book and video for terrestrial transmission has encouraged the recordings of Shakespeare plays on stage primarily for home VCR use rather than for television. With success directly related to the quality of the actors, some notable examples have been R. Thad Taylor's videotaping of a lively *Merry Wives of Windsor* (1979) starring Gloria Grahame as Mistress Page at the Los Angeles Globe Playhouse. Bard Productions, Ltd., with the specific goal of allowing American students to see Shakespeare performed by well-known American daytime soap opera actors, has marketed a *Macbeth, Richard II, Antony and Cleopatra*, and *The Tempest*. The Bard *Macbeth* has received a mixed reception, one critic declaring it "absolutely awful...a deed without a name,"[74] but the *Richard II*, starring well-known daytime television star David Birney, is impressive. When Bolingbroke interrogates Bushy and Green, the "caterpillars of the commonwealth," he behaves less like the stern English headmaster, as played by Jon Finch in the BBC version, than like a tough cop in a B movie giving a perp the "third degree." Quite a hair-raising scene.

Director Sarah Caldwell's *Macbeth* (1981), a stage production at New York's Lincoln Center available on videocassette, was also televised on a cable channel in 1982. A zany slapstick *Comedy of Errors* (1987) with The Flying Karamazov Brothers circus act and a Kamikaze Ground Crew shown over PBS stations has videotaped a performance from New York's Vivian Beaumont Theatre. An actor costumed as Will Shakespeare occasionally appears to shake his head sadly over what is happening on stage. One of the best of what might be called this video genre is the Cambridgeshire postmodernist *Hamlet* (1987) that, with only four actors, deconstructs and then reconstructs Shakespeare's text in the idiom of a psychedelic rock video. "This is *Hamlet* with an antic disposition,"[75] its re-envisioning of the text springing from an honest drive to use the camera not just for recording a play but for artistry in its own right. Another important televised *Hamlet* was the recording of Kevin Kline's 1990 performance at New York's Public Theatre for WNET/Thirteen's "Great Performances" series. A strong, powerful prince with excellent diction, Kline was helped by a steamy Dana Ivey as Gertrude and a waifish Diane Venora as Ophelia. Meanwhile in Great Britain, the nearly unbroken chain of televised Shakespeare continues, most recently with a *Merchant of Venice* (1995) directed by Alan Horrox for the government-subsidized "schools" programs. With a first-rate professional cast including Bob Peck as Shylock and Haydn Gwynne as Portia, the program examines such contemporary issues as capitalism, feminism, and anti-Semitism.

Yet another thriving sub-species of Shakespeare on television derives from the hijacking of bits and pieces and segments of Shakespeare by scenarists hungry for material. Often not separately listed in *TV Guide*, they are difficult to track down. For example, viewers of ABC's *Moonlighting* enjoyed a radically altered *Taming of the Shrew* (1986) starring Bruce Willis and Cybill Shepherd. Both a broad parody and a feminist revision, the production shrewdly revealed that Kate and Petruchio are "much alike, both shrewish and full of high spirits."[76] British television audiences were regaled with the inspired and sometimes not so inspired nonsense of Rowan Atkinson as Edmund duke of Edinburgh and Brian Blessed as "good King Richard IV" in the BBC sitcom, *The Black Adder* (1983), which sent up costume dramas like Olivier's films of the English history plays. The fabled *Star Trek* in an episode called "The Conscience of the King" has "Riley visit the theater area where the Karidian Players are performing *Hamlet* for the crew,"[77] and the subtitle for *Star Trek VI*, "The Undiscovered Country," does little to conceal its origins. These many, many flash appearances validate how deeply Shakespeare is embedded in popular culture throughout the English-speaking world, the *Star Trek* vein having alone stimulated its own sub-specialty of scholarly commentary.[78] Additionally, keeping track of the myriad videos that come and go in the Shakespeare educational market requires the services of a full-time central archivist like the British Universities Film & Video Council.[79] Instructional videos include everything from "Shakespeare of Stratford and London," to "The Staging of Shakespeare," "Shakespeare's Country," "Reconstructing the Bankside Theatre," "Teaching Shakespeare," and the eleven-part "Playing Shakespeare" series, presided over by John Barton, originally televised in England on the South Bank Show. Even the splendid documentary of the New York Shakespeare Festival *Taming of the Shrew* (1981) with Meryl Streep and Raul Julia falls into some hybrid form of educational program. Several movie versions of the plays (e.g., the Olivier *Hamlet*, the Pickford/Fairbanks *Taming of the Shrew*), and Kenneth Branagh's televised Renaissance Theatre *Twelfth Night* (1988) have found their way into the laser disk market that provides new and highly sophisticated methods for close scanning of the plays with the aid of a Pioneer Disk Player. Shakespeare has emerged on the cutting-edge CD-ROM market with a Voyager Company *Macbeth* (1994), edited by A. R. Braunmuller with commentary by David Rodes, which is a veritable electronic library combining the resources of a variorum with those of a concordance, a map and picture gallery, spoken and screened performances, and even a Karaoke, where a student can play a role in tandem with professional actors. And Shakespeare has entered into the World Wide Web of the computer age where a library of textual and scholarly information can be tapped through Terry Gray's "Mr William Shakespeare & the Internet" at <http://www.palomar.edu/Library/shake.htm>. Most recently the *Encyclopaedia Britannica* has compiled a Web site to celebrate the first season of London's new Globe Theatre (1997) at <http://shakespeare.eb.com/>.

Thus televised Shakespeare that began as a hybrid genre wandering somewhere among the realms of theatre, radio, television studio, and cinema, by the end of the century has evolved into a matrix of crossover potentials. As the century winds down, the differences among television, video, and movies will increasingly narrow with the emergence of high-definition transmission, and the coming digital revolution will also connect in unpredictable ways with personal computers. The need to write a separate chapter on televised Shakespeare may be made obsolete as cutting-edge technology makes Shakespeare on television and film increasingly synergetic. But that is futurist speculation about electronic Shakespeare for the next century to validate.

- 6 -

Spectacle and song in Castellani and Zeffirelli

There is a kind of poetic justice in the way that Shakespeare who filtered Renaissance Italy through the lens of English experience should in the twentieth century have been refiltered through the lens of Italian cinema. A playwright with a European vision, Shakespeare set his plays in all sorts of exotic places, from Verona in Italy to Messina in Sicily to Ephesus in Asia Minor, though it seems likely that he never traveled to any of them. The Italian scholar Mario Praz thought that the quick-witted Shakespeare could have faked his foreign expertise simply by conversing with London's expatriate Italians at the Bankside Elephant Inn.[1] Two Italian directors, Renato Castellani and Franco Zeffirelli, reclaimed the franchise of Italian cinéastes from the silent days of Guazzoni and Lo Savio to resituate Shakespeare's Romeo and Juliet in an ambiance that their creator could only have imagined. A complicated combination of lighter camera equipment, the post-war influence of *cinema verité*, the waning of the once powerful Hollywood studio system, and currency and tax laws affecting American money in European banks made possible the abandonment of the sound stages for the realism of European streets.

Castellani's *Romeo and Juliet*

Renato Castellani's Technicolor *Romeo and Juliet* (1954) inaugurated the vogue for "authentic" Renaissance settings in Shakespeare movies and teleplays. Castellani "recreated works of pictorial art for the camera,"[2] before the idea was discovered by Jonathan Miller and made into a house style for the BBC Shakespeare plays. New portable camera and lighting equipment eliminated the need for a fake Verona on a back lot in Hollywood. Italy itself became the backdrop for *Romeo and Juliet* with filming variously in Siena, Venice, Verona, and Montagana. In a country that remains an outdoor museum immune to bulldozers, Robert Krasker, the cameraman responsible for Olivier's *Henry V*, inscribed Castellani's movie in a world of cobblestone streets, piazzas, and the clustered and shuttered structures of uniquely Italian architecture. Only a few querulous people objected that city streets in Shakespeare's time would have looked less worn than they appear today in the film.

Bardophiles despised Castellani's *Romeo and Juliet* because it put movie making ahead of the text, while the cinéphiles saw it as a work of art independent of its literary source. Outraged "purists" went into the usual feeding frenzy. Castellani's movie was "ineluctably, unforgivably prosaic" for "visual distinction makes a poor substitute for poetry," observed one;[3] another wrote that "never, I imagine, since *Lear* received a happy ending, has any Shakespeare text been so hacked, patched, and insensitively thrown away";[4] and to yet another, the "tragedy collapses and is swept away in a visual flood."[5] Even the detractors, however, confessed that the movie was spectacularly beautiful but, unlike the cinéphiles, they overlooked the nexus between this visual beauty and Shakespeare's lyrical language. Bosley Crowther, on the other hand, saw that Castellani was more interested in making a movie out of the play than in literally reproducing the text on screen: "The lyrical language of Shakespeare ... was plainly secondary to his concept of a vivid visual build-up of his theme."[6]

Castellani's visual lyricism stands in for Shakespeare's verbal lyricism. The opening prologue ceremonially recited by John Gielgud, costumed rather ridiculously to look like William Shakespeare, identifies the film with the grandest Shakespearean stage traditions. This obligatory concession to Shakespeare's language having been made, Castellani never apologizes for privileging *opsis* over *lexis*, but at the same time he notably strives to transfer Shakespearean themes into vivid images. A medium shot of the city gate of Verona shows the town's name inscribed above it, as people casually stroll in and out past a lone sentry. The highlighting of the city's name in the establishing shot signals that it will not only rival the young lovers for prime billing, but also imprison them within its walls, its alleys, its confused masses of people, its feuds and its anxieties. The city gate exemplifies Romeo's belief that, "There is no world without Verona walls, / But purgatory, torture, hell itself" (3.3.17). All other citizens can pass easily through these walls, but Romeo's misfortune is to be banished, set outside from both the city and his beloved: "The orchard walls are high and hard to climb, / And the place death," says Juliet in the balcony scene, to which Romeo ironically replies "With love's light wings did I o'erperch these walls, / For stony limits cannot hold love out" (2.2.63). His frantic running through the narrow claustrophobic streets also emblemizes Friar Lawrence's warning against Romeo's weakness for "sudden haste": "Wisely and slow, they stumble that run fast" (2.3.94).

Graphic images of confinement, separation, and suffocation replace the emotional content lost by textual deletions. Castellani's wedding scene (not Shakespeare's, where it takes place off stage) underscores the irony of the

14   Romeo (Laurence Harvey) and Juliet (Susan
Shentall) in Renato Castellani's spectacular color
movie set in sunny Italy (Italy/UK 1954).

forlorn marriage by putting an iron grille between the lovers during the
exchange of their wedding vows. In medium shot, Juliet looks through the
network of bars, while in low angle Romeo stares down at her from the opposite side of the barrier. A medium shot of Juliet receiving a flower through
the bars follows a two-shot of Romeo and the Friar. Off camera, there is the
hypnotic sound of Friars' chanting, and then a cut to the Nurse kneeling in
medium shot on the stone floor. Romeo and Juliet's sealing of the matrimonial
vows with a kiss through the barriers of iron faintly echoes the *Pyramus and
Thisby* play in *Midsummer Night's Dream*. Friar Lawrence's, "So smile the heavens upon this holy act" (2.6.1), which is of course transposed from its place
before the wedding, tinges this pathetic marriage sanctified behind bars with
even more irony.

   In a tight framing, the "cords," or rope ladder that the Nurse provides for
Juliet flop down from the balcony near a stone urn in another trope for impris-
onment. As Nurse, Flora Robson brings admirable competence to the role but
fails to capture the creature's coarseness of soul. Dread of confinement in the

[121]

tomb haunts the isolated Juliet: "Shall I not then be stifled in the vault, / To whose foul mouth no healthsome air breathes in [?]" she asks (4.3.33). In her bedchamber, the gold brocaded bridal gown (copied from Botticelli's Flora) draped over a dressmaker's frame ominously prefigures the darkness ahead. Before drinking off the potion, she puts on the wedding dress, which she will wear not for Romeo but for the other bridegroom, Death. In the morning, after a dissolve from the Capulet courtyard to the sleeping Juliet, the camera pulls back to reveal the dress frame tumbled over sideways. Later, Romeo's heroic efforts to crack the seal on Juliet's tomb using a huge metal candlestick for a crowbar encapsulates the tension between the incarcerative city and the ardor of the young lovers. The great door sealing the Church of San Zeno al Maggiore dwarfs the lone figure of Romeo, the star-crossed victim of fate.

Renaissance painting and sculpture, as well as architecture, support the movie's visual splendor. Among the fifteenth-century artists who provided ideas for costumes and props Meredith Lillich catalogs such names as Uccello, Piero della Francesca, Fra Filippo Lippi, Filippino Lippi, and Carpaccio. The Empress Helena in Piero's fresco of the Holy Rood in Arezzo inspired Lady Capulet's hairstyle; the Luca della Robbia sculptured singing gallery in Florence, the five boys singing at the Capulet ball; Raphael's portrait of the Pope, Capulet in his study, and so forth.[7] Among the supporting players, Sebastian Cabot as Capulet wins a lifetime claim to being the best ever Capulet with his ferocious scolding, or scalding, of Juliet for refusing to marry Paris. Juliet remains foregrounded in a hallway while backgrounded in deep focus her father stomps back and forth, appearing and disappearing in an open doorway, raging at her. His adventitiousness supports the discontinuity of his language, and the camera responds rhythmically to the frenetic tempo of his anger. He rants, raves, and roars, indeed "out-Herods Herod," in a temper tantrum only rivaled by Orson Welles's denunciation of his mistress in *Citizen Kane*. Cabot's talent for choleric wrath also adds weight to the ballroom scene when Tybalt's threat to challenge the intruding Romeo stirs Capulet into a froth of alternating geniality and anger. Susan Shentall (Juliet) and Laurence Harvey (Romeo) flourish in these exotic settings that highlight their status as beautiful but fragile young lovers trapped by a star-crossed fate. Several critics noted a certain listlessness or languor in Laurence Harvey's performance but the root cause may actually have been Castellani's intent to make Romeo over into a sacrificial offering, like Juliet. As Paul Jorgenson has said, the chief aim of Castellani was to highlight the "youthfulness and helplessness"[8] of Romeo and Juliet by deliberately imprisoning them in the stony walls of Verona. In both images and words, the film skews the lovers' plight more toward pity than fear to create a "comitragedy," from a play whose comic potential invariably works at cross purposes with the tragic denouement.

Zeffirelli's *Taming of the Shrew*

The Italianate expropriation continued with Franco Zeffirelli's exuberant *Taming of the Shrew* (1966) also filmed in Italy but in Dino de Laurentiis' new studio rather than on location. Zeffirelli said that shooting the film in the studio "gave it an air of unreality which matched the remoteness of the language."[9] A major *auteur* of Shakespeare movies, Zeffirelli was to go on from *Shrew* with a sensational *Romeo and Juliet* (1968), a dazzling Verdi's *Otello* (1986), and a thoughtful *Hamlet* (1990). Bringing his background in opera to the Old Vic, Zeffirelli enjoyed considerable success with his stage *Romeo and Juliet* (1960), starring John Stride and Judi Dench, which wrung from notoriously hard-to-please critic Kenneth Tynan the verdict of a "masterly production." Peter Hall's subsequent invitation to direct *Othello* (1961) at Stratford with John Gielgud as the Moor led, however, in Zeffirelli's own words to an opening night that "must have been one of the most disastrous and ill-fated in the history of the English – and possibly the world – stage."[10] With extensive operatic background, Zeffirelli brought special expertise to a scintillating *Otello* (1987) starring Placido Domingo, which as filmed opera remains outside the scope of this book.

Just as in Castellani's movie, the casting for Zeffirelli's *Taming of the Shrew* favored British and American actors despite the Italian milieu, the stars being Richard Burton and Elizabeth Taylor, then reigning king and queen of the movies. As an assistant to and designer for stage director and film artist Luchino Visconti, Zeffirelli early in his career developed a trademark passion for meticulous authenticity in costumes and settings. Zeffirelli's vision of *Shrew* nearly matched in splendor Douglas Fairbanks and Mary Pickford's 1929 black-and-white picture, which was designed by William Cameron Menzies, creator of the mammoth sets for *The Thief of Bagdad*. As a serious Shakespearean, Richard Burton wanted to do the film badly enough to underwrite part of its costs, though Elizabeth Taylor, while a brilliant actress as well as a movie star, regarded it as simply another movie.[11] During this same period, she played a devastating Helen of Troy, the ultimate femme fatale, against Burton's Faustus in a film society movie of Christopher Marlowe's *Dr. Faustus* (1968).

Too much has been written about what Zeffirelli's *Shrew* loses from Shakespeare's play and not enough about what it adds. One reviewer began by admonishing his readers: "Don't bother to brush up on your Shakespeare when you go see Elizabeth Taylor and Richard Burton ... in this totally wild abstraction of the Bard."[12] In fact the movie makes more sense, a lot more sense, if you do bother to "brush up on your Shakespeare." Franco Zeffirelli's movie is by no means a literal-minded adaptation of Shakespeare's text but rather an imaginative filmic reconstruction of the play's essential concerns, which have to do with the ongoing battle of the sexes starting with Adam and Eve and continuing, it would seem, from the medieval Mystery plays about Noah and his wife down to today's feminist animadversions. As with the farcical *Comedy of Errors, Taming of the Shrew* addresses serious concerns behind a façade of absurdity, badinage, and slapstick.

With the help of script writers Paul Dehn and Suso Cecchi d'Amico, as well as genius composer Nino Rota, who had also worked with Visconti, and photographers Oswald Morris and Luciano Trasatti, Zeffirelli happily ignored the play's darker side and turned its sexual warfare into a springtime rite free from any hint of approaching autumn. Much of Shakespeare's text has been slyly (no pun intended) embedded in the movie. Motifs from the Induction scene, centering on the "tinker" Christopher Sly, which sets up the play's major theme of "supposings," the ways in which illusion can distort reality, have been transposed and sprinkled throughout the film. Shakespeare's Induction keeps reappearing almost subliminally throughout the movie as with the arrival in Padua of Lucentio (Michael York) and servant Tranio (Alfred Lynch): they pass under a cage labeled "Drunkard" imprisoning an unhappy wretch, which is a wry reminder of Christopher Sly. Elements of the oafish Sly surface in Burton's boorish portrayal of Petruchio. Of course Petruchio may only be pretending, "supposing," to be a boor just as Sly wonders about his own identity: "Am I a lord, and have I such a lady? / Or do I dream? Or have I dream'd till now?" (Ind. 2.68). "Supposings" also emerge in the multiple disguisings of Hortensio as Litio, Lucentio as Cambio, Tranio as Lucentio, as well as the "suppos'd Vincentio," the pedant who tries to pass himself off as Lucentio's father.

Behind this overt disguising, or "supposing," though, is the psychological "supposing" within the minds of Petruchio and Kate as they engage in a duel of wits and egos to discover ways to reach out to, or to reject, or come to terms with, the impossible person that fate has saddled them with. The studio ambiance of the painted backdrop of Padua already implies a "supposing" that this is not really Padua but only a celluloid fantasy. Michael Pursell has carried the idea a step further in showing how the use of an "ochre or sepia-tinted filter" on the camera lens has altered color values to embed the play's theme of "supposings" in the movie's cinematic infra-structure.[13]

A ribald festival of misrule, subversive of hierarchy, in the shape of carnivalesque street revelry after a university semester opening ceremony replaces Shakespeare's Induction in the opening scene. Graham Holderness describes how Zeffirelli (sometimes nicknamed "Shakespirelli") hired eager local *capelloni* ("long-haired ones") as extras.[14] The street festival also cleverly embeds the Bianca/Lucentio subplot into the film's opening. Rota's musical score supports the carnal excitement of the processional, which is reminiscent

of a scene in Marcel Carné's *Les Enfants du Paradis* (1944), with a varia-
tion at a faster tempo on Petruchio's recurring theme of "What Is a Life?"
As a worshipful Lucentio (Michael York) gazes on a lovely blonde Bianca
(Natasha Pyne), a prankster with a fish hook on a line raises the veil covering her face, and a cluster of university singers fill the soundtrack with
Nino Rota's dulcet ballad "Let me tell, gentle maiden, let me tell." Rota's
"Bianca theme" that so eloquently celebrates the outward beauty of Bianca,
as if she were Petrarch's Laura, then re-emerges when Kate "surrenders"
to Petruchio. The music supports Shakespeare's "chiasmus" motif in which
Bianca and Kate gradually exchange roles – Bianca revealing her innate
shrewishness; and Kate, her innate generosity. The festive processional with
an immense, blowzy blonde framed in the window, a *memento mori* figure carried on a mock bier, masked mummers, and rich costumes, shows Zeffirelli's
famous talent for crowd scenes and opulent costumes and sets. Estimating
Kate's dowry, Petruchio examines the rich furnishings of Baptista Minola's
mansion with all the devotion of a Sotheby's appraiser. As he says, "I
come to wive it wealthily in Padua; / If wealthily, then happily in Padua"
(1.2.75).

Zeffirelli himself (or was it Dehn's idea?) executes one of the greatest "supposings" of all when he conflates the drunken, lower-class Sly with Petruchio.
The real Sly remains the sodden wretch fettered in a cage at the entrance to
the city, but the sensuous symbols and images from the Induction, the scented
bedchamber and the rose-watered bath, for example, are linked with Petruchio. Unfortunately, Zeffirelli's "supposing" turns Petruchio into a lout rather
than the impoverished scion of country gentry, as he is in Shakespeare's play.
On the other hand, the idea does not violate the play's mysterious way of casting doubt on people's true identities. Even Petruchio, who might be thought
of as the play's "norm" figure, completely reverses himself by turning from
a fortune hunter into a true lover. The egregious rough-and-tumble slapstick
in the hayloft semiotically matches the indecent exchange about "tales" and
"tongues" between Kate and Petruchio ending with Petruchio's outrageous
"What, with my tongue in your tail?" (2.1.217).

Petruchio's raucous arrival at the wedding in an "in-your-face" costume
seems perverse but actually has the moralizing purpose of teaching Kate (as in
Jonathan Miller's 1981 BBC television version) that "Our purses shall be proud,
our garments poor, / For 'tis the mind that makes the body rich" (4.3.171). The
added farcical scene based on Gremio's (Alan Webb) narrative of the "mad
marriage" (3.2.182), which quotes from the 1929 Pickford/Fairbanks movie,
achieves its height of sublime impudence when Petruchio drinks off the com-
munion wine, crying out "gogs-wouns" (3.2.160), and stifles Kate's "I will not"
in response to the vicar's question by kissing her with "a clamorous smack"

(3.2.178). The vicar (Giancaro Cobelli) first steps back in horror from the mad-cap couple at his altar but then his face is suffused with relief as he hastily pronounces them man and wife. The close-ups of Michael Hordern as Baptista Minola capture his fluttery helplessness over this cranky daughter, as he plays out a father–daughter relationship on a drastically different key from his experience with Cordelia in the 1982 BBC *King Lear.*

Actually the greatest "supposing" or "wonder" of all comes at the end of the film: "Here is a wonder, if you talk of a wonder," says Lucentio (5.2.106). Throughout, Zeffirelli's movie closely follows Shakespeare's play in setting up patterns of wooing and wedding against a backdrop of alternating harmony and discord. Expecting to end on a note of discord rather than harmony, director Zeffirelli was amazed, and apparently so was Richard Burton,[15] when Elizabeth Taylor, hardly a submissive type, delivered Kate's famous speech of surrender in the wager scene without a trace of irony. There was no Mary Pickford wink to her sister Bianca, instead only an eloquent and beautifully spoken tribute to the Elizabethan doctrine of passive obedience, which comes straight out of the Church of England Book of Homilies: "Such duty as the subject owes the prince / Even such a woman oweth to her husband" (5.2.155). So when Burton says, "Why, there's a wench! Come on, and kiss me, Kate" (5.2.179), his words are heartfelt, yet Kate's gesture of suddenly running away from her bewildered bridegroom problematizes the event. Burton and Taylor's Petruchio and Kate are doomed to grow older and turn into the George and Martha of *Who's Afraid of Virginia Woolf* (1966), whom they so brilliantly portray in Mike Nichols' film of Albee's play, but until those shadows encroach they remain in the memory as the irrepressible couple of this sprightly movie.

Zeffirelli's *Romeo and Juliet*

Franco Zeffirelli's *Romeo and Juliet* (1968) showed how "Shakespeare" with some help from a clever movie director can generate an immense profit at the box office. A masterpiece of intricately choreographed music, poetry, and photography, the movie shamelessly plays on the emotions of all but the most stony-hearted critics. From an Anglo-American perspective, the Italian willingness to expose emotions, something that Zeffirelli also saw in Visconti's neo-realist films, turns Shakespeare's play into a "weepy," too low mimetic in sensibility for tragedy. One of its heirs has been the Romeo and Juliet subtext deployed in James Cameron's wildly successful *Titanic* (1998), which packs in teenagers eager to blubber over the fate of Jack (Leonardo DiCaprio) and Rose (Kate Winslet). Inevitably the textual "purists" railed against Zeffirelli's deletions, which were needed to cram the action into two hours and nineteen minutes. The consort in the fifth act has disappeared; the Nurse's neo-Senecan mourning for Juliet, gone; the apothecary scene, jettisoned; Juliet's potion speech, obliterated; and, with some justice, the friar's last-act plot summary, even though it eliminates Shakespeare's important warning against youthful transgressive behavior. Every deletion, however, has been replaced with an addition to show that Shakespeare may legitimately belong to the screen as well as to the stage. Overly sentimentalized or not, the film moves audiences however indirectly toward Aristotle's cryptic notion of "catharsis" through a purging away of emotions. At the fatal climax in the tomb scene, few can resist feeling pity and fear.

To conclude that Zeffirelli sacrificed art on the altar of "tickling commodity" assumes that he might have wanted to handle his movie differently. As one critic wrote, "Zefirelli's [sic] aesthetic, in fact, seems funded on a principle of excess for its own sake."[16] Jack J. Jorgens found much to admire but gagged on the "sticky sweet" neo-Petrarchan song, "What Is a Youth?"[17] Yet Zeffirelli, an unabashed populist in art, the prize architect of low mimetic representation, despite his political conservatism, paradoxically thinks that art should be approachable rather than unapproachable, and that elitist cadres, who patronize simple folk, like the Sicilian fishermen in Visconti's *La Terra Trema* (1948), for example, often stray from the primal roots of human experience. Robert Hapgood makes a nice distinction between Olivier's English way "of sharing a family heirloom with outsiders," and Zeffirelli as an outsider, "escorting the uninitiated on the same journey of discovery [of Shakespeare] he himself had made as a youth."[18]

Despite the immense success at the box office of *The Taming of the Shrew*, Zeffirelli's plan to proceed at once with a *Romeo and Juliet* was funded only grudgingly by Paramount Pictures with what he describes as "the derisory sum of $800,000,"[19] though later it was to gross $48 million. Besides the risk of bankrolling a Shakespeare movie, the studio executives were dismayed that Zeffirelli had no plans for big-name stars like Taylor and Burton as box office magnets. Generations of directors had acknowledged the impossibility of finding adolescent actors with the dramatic talent to play Romeo and Juliet and had fallen back, as did George Cukor and Irving Thalberg, on aging matinee idols like Norma Shearer and Leslie Howard. Zeffirelli boldly rejected the superstar route and cast unknown teenagers, Leonard Whiting and Olivia Hussey. As Albert R. Cirillo has observed, "these actors [Hussey and Whiting] have no existence until the film begins, when they *are* simply Romeo and Juliet."[20]

At exhausting auditions, three sets of the company's casting people screened Hussey and some 350 other eager young girls.[21] Hussey won out. Zeffirelli described her as "classically beautiful, with mesmerizing eyes, a certain coarse strength."[22] Even in hiring the extras, Zeffirelli took thousands of photographs for close study and then, as Devlin has noted, made all his extras *do* something – wash, carry, scrub, peddle, or whatever, so that the screen bustles with activity.[23] For locations like Tuscania, Pienza, and Gubbio,[24] he showed the same meticulousness, believing that in these storied old Italian towns, "the whole thing begins to spin, to get nearer to the truth."[25] Finally, even more so than in *The Taming of the Shrew*, Zeffirelli's movie domiciles the neo-realism of his hand-held cameras, professional and non-professional actors, domestic detail, and the splendors of upper-class Renaissance Italy, in the context of lush Renaissance masterworks. He combined the neo-realism of Italian cinema with the unabashed sentimentality of a Puccini opera.[26]

"I want this to be a young people's *Romeo and Juliet*," Zeffirelli said.[27] It has always been a tale *about* but not necessarily *for* young people. Shakespeare's immediate source was Arthur Brooke's moralizing narrative poem, *The Tragicall Historye of Romeus and Juliet* (1562), which loads guilt on the young people rather than on the parents, but the pedigree of the potion motif extends far back in history. Moreover Zeffirelli's admiration of Leonard Bernstein's Broadway musical, *West Side Story* (1961) shows up in his resolve to make the movie palatable to the rebellious university students of the late sixties, who never doubted for a moment that the guilt was all on the parents.

Like the play, the movie neatly divides into two parts: the comic and the tragic. Except for unfortunate misadventures, particularly Friar John's failure to deliver Friar Lawrence's letter to Romeo in Mantua, it could have ended happily in festivity, like any other respectable comedy, the old people having been shunted aside in favor of the new generation. In London movie theatres, this division was clearly shown with an intermission between the wedding scene and the dueling on the piazza. Part two opens with an establishing shot of Mercutio's white handkerchief ominously covering the screen like a shroud, which plainly defines the division between comedy and tragedy, and their associated imagery of light and dark, and love and death.

In filmic conceits of sight, sound, and music, disparate elements are yoked together to visualize Shakespeare's verbalizations, Shakespeare's fourteen references to the sun being a prime example. In the establishing long shot, the burning sun over Verona, half hidden in a haze, joins with Laurence Olivier's voice-over of the Chorus' sonnet ("Two households, both alike in dignity, / In fair Verona where we lay our scene") and Nino Rota's film music to adumbrate Romeo's "my mind misgives / Some consequence yet hanging in the stars" (1.4.106). While credits roll over, the shrouded sun serves as an emblem of a "fair Verona" that is really not so fair; of a Juliet who according to Romeo is the "sun" (2.2.2) but one he does not yet know will be eclipsed; of lovers whose fate hangs in the "stars"; and of a city that finally must endure in "glooming peace" when "the sun, for sorrow, will not show his head" (5.3.304).

Zeffirelli sets up numerous visual tropes based on Shakespeare's imagery and sometimes on his own inventions. A low medium shot of their codpieces as the Capulet servants swagger down the street in the heat of the day puts a visual spin on the lewd puns, which permeate Shakespeare's bawdiest play: "Draw thy tool, here comes [two] of the house of Montagues" (1.1.31). The frequency of hands in tight framings, for example, reflects a Shakespearean pattern that begins with the prologue's "civil *hands* unclean," and continues at the Capulet ball with Juliet's "For saints have *hands* that pilgrims' *hands* do touch" (1.5.99).[28] Zeffirelli punctuates Juliet's "Parting is such sweet sorrow" (2.2.184) at the close of the balcony scene with a close-up of the lovers' hands clasping and unclasping. At the wedding, the Friar must break up the intense hand holding. In the tomb scene, Romeo grasps Juliet's hand just before he drinks off the poison, and the faint stirrings of her own hand signal her awakening.

Zeffirelli's equivalent to Laurence Olivier's William Walton, composer Nino Rota, who also did the score for *The Taming of the Shrew,* works multiple variations on themes from festival and liturgical sequences. The leitmotif derives from Glen Weston's on-screen vocalization of "What Is a Youth?" at the Capulet ball. Later a popular hit, the lyrics of this neo-Elizabethan ballad by Eugene Walter mimic the overall two-part design of the film. That most common of Elizabethan devices, a question, "What is a youth?" opens a ten-line statement on the *carpe diem* theme, complete with a fading rose. The closing verses anticipating death in their sobriety and bitter-sweetness speak to the fate of the star-cross'd lovers. Variations of these melodies support the first appearance of Romeo ambling up a street toying with a sprig of blossom, and later at a slower tempo lugubriously comment on the deaths of Tybalt and Mercutio.

A second melody, derived from the Latin hymn *Ave maris stella* ("Hail, star of the sea . . . , / Gabriel's word believest / Change to peace and gladness / Eva's name of sadness") defines the mood of both wedding and funeral, [29] love and death, which is implicit in Juliet's "Come, cords, come, nurse, I'll to my wedding-bed, / And death, not Romeo, take my maidenhead!" (3.2.136). The traditional *Magnificat* ("My soul doth magnify the Lord, / And my spirit hath rejoiced in God my Saviour") fills the nave of the Romanesque church during the rendezvous between Romeo and the Nurse.

For the brilliant dance sequence at the Capulet ball, Pasqualino de Santis' subjective camera approaches virtual reality in giving viewers the illusion of their actually participating in choreographer Alberto Testa's "wild Morisco," a dance of Moorish origin mentioned in *Henry VI Part II* (3.1.365) reshaped here to modern taste but cunningly plausible. It immediately follows a *"sinistra tempo giusto* played by a quartet of soprano recorders and a trio of transposed flageolets."[30] The dizzy whirling of two concentric rings of dancers moving in opposite directions restates Zeffirelli's iterative images of circles, Juliet's desire to be enfolded in them, and Mercutio's bawdy innuendo to Romeo about circles: "'twould anger him / To raise a spirit in his mistress' circle" (2.1.24). A circle on the ballroom floor corresponds to the dancers who exclude Romeo and Juliet from their territory where Juliet wistfully hovers on the fringe, peering in. Mosaics in circular patterns decorate the church floor where Romeo and Juliet kneel for the marriage. Dances and duels spin into rituals of love and hate, acted out in circular motions, suggesting that the headlong love affair has no possibility of doing anything but circling back against itself. During the fight between Tybalt and Mercutio, which is the dance of death, Romeo, like Juliet at the Capulet ball, is barred from the inner circle. The raucous crowds encircling the Nurse and Mercutio in the piazza enact a ritualized fertility dance, and the Duke Escalus joins in the geometrical conceit by speaking from the center of a ring of mounted retainers. Besides quasi-operatic strategies, the film employs more conventional sound effects. The cueing of music to speech, for example, may now and then hint at recitative (e.g., Romeo's sobs in the crypt scene), and a paralanguage of grunts, groans, and gasps lends realism to the duel between the desperate and exhausted Romeo and Tybalt. Then, too, the soundtrack includes a variety of real noises belonging to the diegesis: horses' hooves, church bells, echoes, crickets, clanging swords, barking dogs, and a category that can be summed up as "tumult, confusion, cries, questions." Crowd scenes invite additions: "Did he hurt you?" when John McEnery's Mercutio strikes a bystander while dueling with Michael York's Tybalt. Disguising his voice, Laurence Olivier generously contributed many bits and pieces of random speeches.[31]

John McEnery's powerful manic-depressive Queen Mab speech stands alone, free from musical punctuation. The teenage Romeo and Juliet speak the verse for the balcony scene without major sonic backup, though the short takes probably allowed for editing out imperfections. A zoom shot punctuated with discordant music conveys an unspoken thought when a sourlooking Lady Capulet shuts a window just as Lord Capulet remarks to Paris "and too soon marr'd are those so early made" (1.2.13). Lady Capulet, it would seem, has herself been subjected too soon to a forced marriage. The funeral cortege for Romeo and Juliet needs only eloquent silence, with a tolling bell and murmuring wind for sonic punctuation. Laurence Olivier comes back on the soundtrack to steal the epilogue from the Prince and make even doggerel sound magnificent: "For never was a story of more woe / Than this of Juliet and her Romeo" (5.3.309). The credits roll and in a rite of reconciliation the houses of Montague and Capulet file up the church steps. Albert Cirillo eloquently observes that Zeffirelli "gave us the *Romeo and Juliet* Shakespeare wrote and felt," even more so than the man "who did the definitive edition, or the man who corrected that

15   Silent screen idol Francis X. Bushman and Beverly Bayne in the lost Metro Studio feature-length movie (80 mins.) of *Romeo and Juliet* (1916).

edition," and thereby he made the play "meaningful here and now," in "a new medium."[32] It is hard to disagree.

Zeffirelli's *Hamlet*

With the exception of the filmed *Otello*, over two decades went by before Zeffirelli undertook another Shakespeare movie, this time not one of the Italian-based plays but the thoroughly English and thoroughly difficult and impenetrable *Hamlet* (1990). By the 1990s, which saw an unprecedented release of big-budget Shakespeare movies, every new film had the specter of a prior huge success peering over its shoulder. By the time that Zeffirelli got around to *Hamlet*, Laurence Olivier's *Hamlet* (1948) and Tony Richardson's "Roundhouse" *Hamlet* (1969) were like two more ghosts at Macbeth's banquet, endlessly scowling and defying him to do any better. With a multi-million dollar budget and a cast of famous actors, Franco Zeffirelli's *Hamlet* competed with Hollywood blockbusters in the cineplexes that became the sites of cultural disbursement in late twentieth-century suburban shopping malls. Zeffirelli "switched codes" by daring to reinvent Australian superstar and action hero "Mad Max" Mel Gibson as the melancholy prince. Zeffirelli knew that

Gibson's diploma from Australia's NIDA (National Institute of Dramatic Arts) gave him impeccable acting credentials, and that as a wildly popular actor Gibson could also restore Shakespeare's Hamlet to the masses. Besides, there is nothing inherently un-Shakespearean about a Hamlet with a strong masculine presence, for Hamlet as a Renaissance man out of Baldassare Castiglione's *Book of the Courtier* needed to be as skilled with swords, wrestling, and horses as with a fast quip, always with *sprezzatura*, or nonchalance, no matter how daunting the challenge. As mentioned previously, Zeffirelli, an unabashed low mimeticist, unlike JeanLuc Godard or Peter Greenaway, believes strongly in the popularization of great art. "It irritates me that some people want art to be as 'difficult' as possible, an elitist kind of thing."[33]

The fifth-act duel with broadswords instead of thin epées epitomizes Zeffirelli's conception of a macho Hamlet, equipped to survive in the world of Rambo and the Evil Empire. If Gibson's Hamlet ever delays, it is only momentarily, for much of the text showing indecisiveness has been deleted. The movie's most irresolute character is not Hamlet but Claudius (Alan Bates), who is often caught on camera in moments of hesitation. Hamlet slams poor little Ophelia (Helena Bonham Carter) against a stone wall, assaults Rosencrantz (Michael Maloney) and Guildenstern (Sean Murray) with a recorder, and mocks Laertes (Nathaniel Parker) with a broadsword. Gibson's prince is not weighed down by "conscience," which means in Elizabethan usage "thoughtfulness" rather than moral scruples ("Thus conscience does make cowards [of us all]" – 3.1.82); or what today might be called "guilt." This Hamlet is more the avenger than the thinker, though not merely a brainless gun-toting prince out of Arnold Schwarzenegger's sly meta-cinematic commentary on *Hamlet*, *Last Action Hero* (1993).

Gibson's prince lives in the universe of Foucault's panopticon, a society about spying, about surveillance. Gibson speaks with his cold blue porcelain eyes, as do other talented movie actors, stars of the caliber of Lillian Gish, Buster Keaton, and Robert Mitchum. He can project the demons of a terrifying mad man with a maniacal look as well as play a thoughtful speaker in the "To be or not to be" soliloquy, set in the *memento mori* atmosphere of the crypt where his father is entombed. The eyes of the entire court are more often than not fixed on Hamlet, just as he in turn watches everyone else, something that Gibson was intensely aware of. "Everyone spied on Hamlet, and Hamlet spied on everyone else," he said in an interview.[34] High above on a balcony he is examining Gertrude (Glenn Close) or his stepfather, or he is eavesdropping on Polonius (Ian Holm) lecturing to Laertes and Ophelia, or he is looking down on Claudius engaged in "heavy-headed revel" (1.4.17) at an extravagant feast, or searching on a parapet in the mist from behind the hilt of his sword for a glimpse of his father's spirit (Paul Scofield). He is truly "th'observ'd of all observers" (3.1.154).

This is also a movie that uses Shakespeare's language as a blueprint for the dynamics of motion. The opening scene in the crypt, which is entirely invented by Zeffirelli, establishes the action by triangulating in close-up the film's major characters – Claudius, Gertrude, and Hamlet. To that end fragments from the second scene of act two have been transposed so that in the crypt by his father's body Claudius immediately reassures Hamlet of his rights to succession: "You are the most immediate to our throne" (1.2.109), though the legal claims to succession by "election" in Hamlet's tenth-century Denmark remain murky. Bits and pieces of scene two also drift into the great hall of the castle where Claudius in his oily public-man voice announces the marriage to Gertrude, "With mirth in funeral, and with dirge in marriage" (1.2.12). Still other lines are transposed to Hamlet's library for the king's instructions to Laertes, "What wouldst thou beg, Laertes[?]" (1.2.45), while a fourth setting in Hamlet's study makes a backdrop for the crucial exchange between Hamlet and Gertrude with Hamlet's, "Seems, madam? nay, it is, I know not 'seems'." (1.2.76). Zeffirelli and script collaborator Dyson Lovell have rearranged the text to fit the require-ments of a *moving* picture, where spatial barriers can be easily transgressed. To do otherwise is to risk having the static arrangements of, for example, the Kevin Kline televised *Hamlet* where there is virtually no movement as the actors simply stand and rather woodenly deliver their speeches like school-room recitations. This is not to say that there are not in Kline's *Hamlet* fine individual performances, Peter James's Horatio being one of the best ever, but they are carried out within the limitations of a television studio set. Limited to two hours by budgetary constraints, Zeffirelli sacrifices Fortinbras, who makes an important mirror foil to both Hamlet and Laertes. This textual loss repre-sents a filmic gain in the way that the opening scene establishes the sense of activity, of motion, characteristic of the entire film. Like Polanski's castle in *Macbeth*, Zeffirelli's is also the locus of a life force, of people moving in and out, people serving on tables, people weaving, cooking, serving, reading, handling horses. There is nothing here of the school of John Cassavetes' counter-cinema *A Woman Under the Influence* (1974) where the characters talk but rarely move.

Claudius' "Give me some light" (3.2.269) after the play-within-the-play points toward the movie's lighting design, which makes extraordinary use of baroque contrasts between light and dark. Designer Dante Ferretti and Zef-firelli copy the rich tones of painters like Vermeer, who provides a model for the library in the castle. Zeffirelli's love for detail, as with the overflowing *objets d'art* in Baptista Minola's villa in *Taming of the Shrew*, has no place in a film set in feudal northern Europe, so David Watkin's lighting and camera work attempts to compensate for that loss. Zeffirelli's style might be called "enhanced realism," which is a variation on Michael Skovmand's preferred description of "picturesque naturalism."[35] The drafty, cold stone walls of Elsinore could not be more "real" than this castle patched together from autochthonous British ruins at Dover, Blackness, and Dunnottar. Deprived of his lush Italian settings, Zeffirelli struggles to make this cold surface appealing by keying the movie to "mostly grays and ash colors, a 'medievalprimitive' look" so that when rich colors do come out "the effect is even more vivid."[36] David Impastato sees the "baroque" influence of the late Renaissance as an encouragement to the obvious fluidity of the actors' movements in and around the castle.[37] He goes a step further, however, in finding metaphorical significance in the interplay between light and dark. In the opening crypt scene, for example, a shaft of light from a window plays over a tightly framed hand holding dirt that is to be scattered over the King's body, after which the camera shows that it is the hand of a deeply hooded Prince Hamlet, whose penetrating eyes glow in the shadows. Again in "O that this too too sallied [solid] flesh would melt" (1.2.129), Hamlet moves in and out of the light until backlit against an enormous window as the soliloquy ends. In the crane shot of the death scene that ends the movie, Hamlet's head recedes into shadows directly after Horatio's "Good night, sweet prince." Michael Skovmand asks if the shadows and light constitute deeply embedded metaphors, like the portentous ones in the Olivier *Richard III*, or if they simply highlight particular moments.[38] Zeffirelli himself describes how the duel scene was deliberately heightened by placing huge white sheets on the walls to bounce the light back on the scene, but says nothing about a symbolical significance.[39]

The musical enhancement (Ennio Morricone) offers a minimalist backdrop score that avoids drawing attention to itself and a flurry of horns and drums for diegetic moments such as toasting during banquets. Film star Glenn Close's sensuous Gertrude turns the modern tradition of a Freudian subtext into hypertext by rarely missing opportunities to kiss fervently both her husband and son full on the mouth. As Edward Quinn has said "you never accept for one moment the notion that Glenn Close's Gertrude and Mel Gibson's Hamlet are mother and son…there's nothing Oedipal in their straightforward sexuality."[40] On the other hand, Gertrude must be young and attractive enough to justify Claudius' interest in her as a trophy wife. A difficult tightrope. Ian Holm makes a somewhat fatuous but not entirely silly Polonius, who in any event never deserves the harsh fate behind the arras handed to him by Hamlet. As might be expected, Paul Scofield, Peter Brook's King Lear, makes a formidable presence as the ghost, and Helena Bonham Carter scraps the Millais-like romanticism of Jean Simmons' golden-tressed Ophelia in the Olivier version to resituate the role squarely in the context of contemporary feminist militancy. Despite her tiny stature, this Ophelia remains feisty even when driven mad by her men. Framing Gertrude's poignant description of Ophelia's drowning between flashbacks of the actual scene ingeniously preserves both the visual and verbal splendor: "There is a willow grows askaunt the brook / That shows his hoary leaves in the glassy stream" (4.7.166). An aging but familiar face materializes in John McEnery as Osric, the unforgettably manic-depressive Mercutio in Zeffirelli's *Romeo and Juliet* of three decades previously. Emerging personalities include Michael Maloney (Rosencrantz) who also played the Dauphin in the Branagh *Henry V* (1989) and Roderigo in the Parker *Othello* (1995). Pete Postlethwaite (Player King) will turn up as the hip priest in the Luhrmann *Romeo & Juliet* (1996). Ace Pilkington observes that Zeffirelli has produced "a body of work that is always interesting and sometimes splendid, that cuts but does not shirk, rewrites but does not abandon,"[41] and Robert Hapgood thinks that Zeffirelli's work has withstood the test of time even better than Olivier's.[42] High praise, but single-handedly Zeffirelli has probably done more than the entire educational establishment to keep Shakespeare's language alive in an age when images have eclipsed words.

- 7 -

Shakespeare movies in the age of angst

After 1960, the increasing pessimism stemming from the Vietnam war and other deleterious world events inevitably spun off on the Shakespeare movie. The conflict in Southeast Asia had plunged the United States into a cultural revolution pitting youth against age, and in France, Great Britain, and elsewhere university students also rebelled against threadbare conventions. Residual Victorian social codes withered and died as this "youthquake" overturned the restrictive norms of the older generation in favor of an emerging demand for personal liberation. As much as any other book, Jan Kott's unsettling *Shakespeare Our Contemporary* (1964) encapsulated the era's nihilistic, despairing, anti-melioristic ethos, which in literature and art emerged as bitter and dark irony. The genteel aspirations for Shakespeare movies of the innocent Vitagraph and Thalberg/Cukor days likewise went up in smoke as the disintegrative political movements and outright anger in the streets escalated.

Two British Shakespeare movies illustrate this ironic drift, which had already surfaced as film noir in mainstream movies: Tony Richardson's *Hamlet* (1969), and Peter Hall's *A Midsummer Night's Dream* (1969). More in the art-house category than in the heavy-hitting commercial world of Zeffirelli's *Romeo and Juliet*, each in its own way enjoyed a critical but not a box-office success. Modestly budgeted (*Hamlet* at only $350,000), today they would be labeled "Indies" or independents to set them apart from the major studio's $40 million plus action blockbusters. By the same token, their limited filmic values and tight framing identified them as crossover films made for television as much as for theatrical release. Richardson's introspective *Hamlet* stretches the limits of interior filming, while Hall's extrovert *Dream* goes outside, and shows what can be done with hand-held cameras and sound looping.

Richardson's *Hamlet*

Richardson's claustrophobic movie was actually filmed at London's Roundhouse Theatre, a recycled railway locomotive shed, in fewer than ten days.[1] The damp stone walls, flickering candles and dark ambience evoke the spirit

[136]

of gloomy Elsinore. The production had been successfully staged in London, New York, and smaller cities, where the star, Nicol Williamson, developed a reputation for an "attitude," having in Boston actually stalked off in the middle of the play scene, leaving the whole company with "egg on their faces."[2] Nevertheless Williamson's powerful presence, or "being," as an "angry-young-man" Hamlet, recklessly broke with the genteel elocutionary tradition of, say, a John Gielgud. Williamson doesn't just recite but energizes Shakespeare's words with every nerve, fiber, and bone in his body so strenuously that one fears he will self-destruct. He similarly erupts in his BBC *Macbeth* with Jane Lapotaire as Lady Macbeth. Hoping perhaps to capture some of this raw power, Richardson wrote that he wanted "to make a movie of *Hamlet* in which . . . you would *devalue* the power of the image and let the text and performance speak uninterruptedly, scaling the production down and staging it for cameras."[3]

In many ways, Richardson's movie reifies Sir Philip Sidney's definition in *The Defence of Poesie* (1595) of mimesis as "representing, counterfeiting, or figuring forth – to speak metaphorically, a speaking picture." Its system of portraiture – single portraits, double portraits, triple and group portraits – makes it a montage of speaking pictures, or "talking heads." The film so closely depends on close and medium shots that many critics assumed that it was made for the small screen of television rather than for theatrical release.[4] The tight framing inevitably invited comments about its "explosiveness" – a kind of visual tautness. As Bernice Kliman says, "by making the frame a keyhole" there was even a suggestion of a larger world beyond the frame.[5] A *Time* critic saw Williamson as a Hamlet "lit by inner fire" and carrying with him "the smell of smoldering cordite."[6] Louis D. Gianetti thought the Olivier *Hamlet* was "essentially an epic," made up of long shots, while Richardson's offers a psychological study in close-ups in which Hamlet seems to be bursting the confines of the frames, nearly spilling out into "oblivion."[7] The film choreographs not bodies but faces, sometimes singly, sometimes doubly, sometimes triply, like some infinite variation on the figures in Rembrandt's *Night Watch*. The most interesting face is Williamson's, which Alan Brien caricatured as having "eyes like poached eggs, hair like treacle toffee, and a truculent lower lip protruding like a pink front step from the long pale doorway of his face."[8] A deliberate speeding up of the dialogue, breathless at times, enhances the visual tautness. To accelerate the impetuousness, Richardson filleted long speeches or deleted short exchanges to fit into the jumpy montage.[9] Williamson's "rasping, nasal tones . . . liberate him from all the fancy echoes of previous performances," we are told.[10] This madcap behavior creates a Hamlet closer to Kate's Petruchio than to Ophelia's melancholy prince, not at all indecisive but rather outrageously decisive, equipped to handle a torrent of events that would paralyze a lesser mortal. He cannot "delay" because he lacks the time to delay.

Still, as Brendan Gill acknowledged, Williamson masters the soliloquy.[11] A quick cut from the gloomy ramparts of Elsinore to the brightly lit great hall establishes the gap between the dark world of a murdered king and the superficial world of courtly badinage, where suddenly Hamlet appears lower left in the frame. Now in close-up, a speaking picture, Williamson begins the first soliloquy, his head moving as if "it were thrust from the mouth of a jug."[12] He speaks in staccato bursts, making myriad, small gestures, repeatedly thumping knuckles against his forehead. Toward the end, at "O most wicked speed: to post / With such dexterity to incestious sheets" (1.2.156), the film indulges in one of its rare long shots with the arrival of Horatio (Gordon Jackson), Barnardo (John Trenaman), and Marcellus (John Carney).

The "To be, or not to be" sequence begins with a supine Hamlet, profile facing upward on the frame, to mark his isolation. Part way through, he moves to a posture of resting on his elbow, and then at "fardels bear" (3.1.75) sits straight up, looking back over his shoulder at the camera. He pops up, laughs out loud, and spots Ophelia (Marianne Faithfull) who appears to the right. With Claudius (Anthony Hopkins) and Polonius (Mark Dignam) blatantly eavesdropping, Hamlet and Ophelia are viewed through a hammock netting, their faces crisscrossed, cut up, as if in a Sunday supplement illustration of the ravages of schizophrenia. When the obliging camera, now more of a participant in than a mere recorder of the action, pulls back we observe Hamlet and Ophelia over the shoulders of the eavesdroppers and see the sudden flash of suspicion on Hamlet's face. His mood turns dark as he flies into a tantrum. "Where's your father?" he asks Ophelia (3.1.129), and from then on "nunnery" takes on the bawdy "brothel" insinuation. The motif of the divided self continues as when Ophelia says "O, what a noble mind is here o'erthrown!" (3.1.150), her face is fragmented and cut up by the ham-mock ropes.

Two-shots handle the hints of incestuousness hovering around Laertes (Michael Pennington) and Ophelia as they bid each other farewell with an intimacy that mirrors the emotional bond between Hamlet and Gertrude (Judy Parfitt). In another two-shot, now in the bed chamber, a looming Hamlet in the upper right corner of the frame dominates his upset mother. Reverse shots capture the wounded looks on the faces of the distraught mother and son – "O Hamlet, speak no more! / Thou turns't [my eyes into my very] soul" (3.4.88). When the ghost reappears, heralded by anguished wailing on the soundtrack, a splash of intense light falls on Hamlet's face – "Look where he goes, even now, out at the portal!" (3.4.136). Mother and son collapse into each other's arms, weeping and sobbing.

Multiples of three work as well. The faces of Hamlet, Horatio, and Marcellus on the ramparts perpetually change positions, being grouped, separated, exchanged, switched, synchronized, and syncopated. Cinematized portraiture occurs when Hamlet is hemmed in on either side by the king's two spies, Rosencrantz (Ben Aris) and Guildenstern (Clive Graham). "Were you not sent for? is it your own inclining?"(2.2.274), he asks the guilty pair, and then like Edmund Kean before him throws his arms around them, symbolically blocking the two conspirators from uniting against him. By contrast, with the arrival of the players, Hamlet moves freely in and out and among them, more at ease in the world of motley and grease paint than in the prison house of Elsinore. In act one, scene two, the meanness and imbecility in the faces of the sycophantic courtiers at Elsinore achieve toxic levels as they show their eagerness to laugh heartily at any of Claudius' slightest witticisms.

Not that every shot in the film is a close-up. There are some medium shots, but the impression of being in an amputee ward remains powerful. A voyeuristic peek at the royal bed of Denmark shows a depraved Gertrude and Claudius swinishly eating sticky things in bed while dogs snuggle up to them. When Polonius shows up to report on "the very cause of Hamlet's lunacy" (2.2.49), the wanton, bestial behavior of king and queen robs him of any dignity and Gertrude's "more matter with less art" (2.2.95) seems curt, even cruel. The editing and mixing work variations on the basic blocking of one, two, and three, throwing in, as it were, a few sharps and flats, a chord here and there, to transform a simple melody into a complex polyphonic arrangement.

As First Player and Gravedigger, Roger Livesey's hoarse and yet compelling voice, as if he had damaged vocal chords, sears into the memory. In a *tour de force*, Richardson manages to film the complicated duel scene between Hamlet and Laertes without a significant long shot. Richardson's *mise-en-scène* remains sparse and shadowy, in contrast to the elaborate unit sets of Olivier's *Hamlet* with the spacious stairway sweeping down into the throne room. The editing moves backward and forward between the contestants and the queen, whose demise brings about a mini-tragedy with her dying recognition, *anagnorisis*, that "the King's to blame" (5.2.320). Claudius dies horribly, shrieking, vomiting up the wine that Hamlet has forced down his throat. Horatio and Hamlet revert to the two-shot phase, with Hamlet now firmly planted in the dominant position on the right, not on the less assertive left as he had been at the film's outset. In these final moments Williamson's histrionics translate into a sincerity appropriate to the prince. There is no Fortinbras to carry on, that whole external political angle having been deleted by the exigencies of time. Ultimately, however, Richardson achieved what he set out to do in producing a two-hour *Hamlet* with a major actor in the title role. The synecdoche for the greater whole emerges in turmoil, madness, energy, frenzy, despair, frustration, bitterness, irrationality, and the unadorned nobility of a Danish prince. The rest of the tragedy remains for the audience to piece out for themselves. Richardson's "speaking pictures" suggest but do not flesh out completely "the ripeness [that] is all."

Hall's *Midsummer Night's Dream*

The seeds of Peter Hall's and producer Michael Birkett's film of *Midsummer Night's Dream* were planted at the Stratford Memorial Theatre in 1959 when Hall's cast included Charles Laughton as Bottom, Vanessa Redgrave as Helena, Mary Ure as Titania, and Albert Finney as Lysander. NBC announced that it would eventually televise the stage production in the United States,[13] though the film actually came more directly out of the 1962 Stratford revival, in which the casting had undergone radical changes, and finally was transmitted in 1969 "coast to coast" for some 25 million viewers in North America.[14] Like Richardson's *Hamlet* it emerges straight out of the *Zeitgeist* of the 1960s when a whole phalanx of "angry young men" felt that society had cheated and deprived them of their proper place in the world. Nicol Williamson's raw, hostile, nervous style made him the perfect Hamlet for the times, and in a comic variation on the angry young man, David Warner's Lysander in a Nehru jacket stamps him as a grumpy young man, unlikely to trust anyone over thirty. A crossover film made for both television in the USA and theatrical release in England, it combines the expressionism of the Reinhardt Weimar school with the neo-realism of the post-war Italian school. Like Peter Brook's famous idiosyncratic staged *Midsummer Night's Dream* (1970),[15] it too rejects the Regent's Park style of cute elves and cuddly animals to please the children and their nannies, and stabs at the darker side of the dream, the dream that turns into nightmare in a dark wood. Guy Woolfenden's low-key musical score, which is used very sparingly, replaces the romanticized idyll of Mendelssohn's *Incidental Music* in the Reinhardt version, and a hand-held camera suggests a rawness of experience.

The establishing shot shows an English country house (Compton-Verney in Warwickshire) with the single word "Athens" inscribed over it. The alienating conceit pokes ironic fun at Shakespeare's own whimsy of putting the "duke" of Athens, Hippolyta the Amazon Queen, and a cluster of honest English workingmen like Quince and Bottom all in one time and place in ancient Greece. The English country house setting emphasizes, in Hall's own words, that the play's action takes place during "an English summer in which the seasons have gone wrong ... everywhere is wet and muddy."[16] Judi Dench as Titania, while wearing virtually nothing to shield her nubile body, recites the 40-line speech about the inclement weather. "Therefore the winds, piping to us in vain, / As in revenge, have suck'd up from the sea / Contagious fogs"(2.1.88), she says in medium and close shots from slightly different angles. The English summer that has gone wrong stands for the contemporary England that has "gone wrong," in the eyes of the young, who are busy looking back in anger or anticipating the despair in Derek Jarman's *The Last of England* (1988).

Hall treats the predicament of the four young lovers with disarming wit. The silly infatuations of the young lovers, Helena (Diana Rigg) and Demetrius (Michael Jayston), Hermia (Helen Mirren) and Lysander, take place "on the dank and dirty ground" (2.2.75), their faces even being daubed with mud. At the same time, however, this documentary realism is counterpointed with an expressionistic, or even surrealistic, vision suggested by the peculiar color of the terrain, the lead-green texture of Puck's face (Ian Holm), the array of bright lights in the dark wood, and the weird nature of the fairy world. The wood is both actuality and fantasy, Lumière and Méliès.

For those who like their Shakespeare well spoken, Hall gathered together an ensemble of brilliant actors from a Royal Shakespeare Company then at the peak of its prestige. Jay Halio, who commented favorably on the film's keeping Shakespeare's text virtually intact, unlike the free adapting in the Reinhardt version, thinks also that "this is probably the best spoken of any Shakespeare film that has been made."[17] To insure that outcome, Hall "postsynched" the dialogue to give the actors a friendlier environment for speaking the lines. There has never been a more magnanimous Duke Theseus (Derek Godfrey), who radiates a generosity of spirit toward persons inferior to himself without flipping over into condescension. "If we imagine no worse of them than they of themselves, they may pass for excellent men" (5.1.215). His Hippolyta (Barbara Jefford) abandons the Reinhardt snake costume for a slightly kinky look of boots and a skin tight mini-skirt, but retains the fiery menace of an Amazon queen underneath the icy exterior. The four young lovers embody the "quick bright things [who] come to confusion" (1.1.148), David Warner's Lysander as a headstrong, truculent young man, and Helen Mirren (Hermia) and Diana Rigg (Helena) as wonderfully befuddled ingenues. At the court during the Pyramus and Thisby play, the two couples expose their own youthful arrogance as rich spoiled darlings by condescending to the earnest but inept actors. The girls' costumes incongruously reflect the swinging London of the late Sixties when Carnaby Street became a household word signifying mini-skirts, rock and roll, and mind-altering drugs. As Michael Mullin has said, the result is to suggest that "Hall has assembled a house party of brilliant people and said 'Let's make a movie'."[18] It is also a house party where they serve Electric Kool-Aid. The fairy world matches the courtly world with a rather sinister Oberon (Ian Richardson), and a hyperactive Puck, whose tongue never stops darting in and out. Judi Dench's voluptuousness stirs up the whiff of bestiality in the nocturnal union between Titania and Bottom (Paul Rogers) with its latent eroticism. As always, the rude mechanicals, led by veteran Shakespearean actor Sebastian Shaw (Quince), steal the show with their Pyramus and Thisby *shtick*. At the very end, the diabolical-looking Puck and Oberon return to cast their spell of magical finality on an English country house, whose "constancy" still remains in doubt.

These virtues notwithstanding, the film received mixed reviews, one of the chief protests centering around the alleged amateur photography: "The hand-held camera constantly joggles the image, wearying eyes already repelled by the sheer ugliness of the huge warts-and-all close-ups . . . His [Hall's] film is leaden."[19] At times it looks that way, as when Helena laments about Demetrius' preference for Hermia, moving about, or popping and hopping about, some-times standing behind a tree, or again emerging from behind the tree to address the camera directly again. "For ere Demetrius look'd on Hermia's eyne, / He hail'd down oaths that he was only mine" (1.1.242). But rather than being inadequate camera work, the gap between the continuity in the flow of the words and the discontinuity of the images suggests a major theme of the play as articulated by Hippolyta: "But all the story of the night told over, / And all their minds transfigur'd so together, / More witnesseth than fancy's images, / And grows to something of great constancy; / But howsoever, strange and admirable" (5.1.23). The jumpy camera reflects the Elizabethan concern with the interplay between change and constancy, or as Edmund Spenser called it, "mutability" (*Two Cantos of Mutabilitie*, 1596). "New philosophy" had put all in doubt and there was unease about the nature of the universe – what of it was changeable and what unchangeable, what in flow and what in flux. ("Proud Change [not pleasd in mortall things, / Beneath the Moone, to raigne] / Pre-tends, as well of Gods, as Men, / To be the Soueraine.") In Hippolyta's words it can be had both ways. Things can be changeable but also unchangeable, and Hall's visual trope for this paradox that Frank Occhiogrosso has labeled "cinematic oxymoron"[20] involves continuous and discontinuous employment of picture and word, ringing variations on interchangeability in the relation-ships of the characters to themselves and to nature.

The Brook/Birkett *King Lear*

Peter Brook's and Michael Lord Birkett's *King Lear* (1971) inflected Shakespeare into a dark and relentlessly ironic vision of the human condition. This uncom-fortable tale of an aged and irascible old king who foolishly gives his property away to his ungrateful daughters turned out to be an allegory for the times. Everywhere in the West parents were caught up in daily combat with their children over life-style issues running the gamut from hair styles to pot. They, like Lear, wanted to cry out, "How sharper than a serpent's tooth it is / To have a thankless child!" (1.4.288). Jan Kott was again a powerful influence, his essay, "*King Lear* or *Endgame*,"[21] having identified the analogies between the grotesque elements in Beckett's Theatre of the Absurd and Shakespeare's tragedy. This malaise was already apparent in Brook's earlier "bondage" *King*

Lear (1953) with Orson Welles on North American television. Despite protests to the contrary, Brook did not so much drain *King Lear* of its "Christian" elements (if it ever had any) as displace seventeenth-century Christian stoicism into the contemporary idiom of the Theatre of Cruelty, in which Good Friday overwhelms Easter Sunday and the Book of Job replaces the New Testament. A key difference of course is that Christian stoicism was rooted in absolute notions of divine order, and Theatre of Cruelty reflects the existentialist view of the world as absurdity, "absurdity" in Ionesco's terms meaning simply "life without purpose." While the Medieval schoolmen shadowed forth Christian values in pagan terms (*prisca theologia*), Brook embodied Christian stoicism in absurdist symbols. The redemptive elements in Shakespeare's scorching tragedy having been erased in the Birkett/Brook *King Lear*, the movie reflects the ironic, fractured universe poised on the edge of apocalypse after Hiroshima.

Such a dark view inevitably brought the full wrath of the critics down on Brook's head. Even though he had originally staged *King Lear* at Stratford (1962), and producer Birkett had thought the actors in the stage version were far too valuable not to use again in the movie,[22] these fine credentials did not spare Brook from the venting of spleen. The movie was "depoeticized";[23] inept "in handling the film medium . . . a travesty";[24] "an image, not of regeneration, but of moribundity and sad decay";[25] "look[ed] like an overexposed 8mm home movie which [had] been smuggled out of a disaster area";[26] and "murder[ed] [the play] altogether," making it resemble "a telecast of moon landings . . . an electronic blizzard," which is "impossible to follow . . . a pogrom on poetry."[27] A rival player, Orson Welles, was reported as "wildly furious" over Scofield's playing the part as if he were still doing Sir Thomas More in *A Man for All Seasons*.[28] Reigning American film critic Pauline Kael summed it all up. She did not just "dislike" it; she "hated it."[29] On the other hand, a few understood that the camera was *deliberately* out of focus, and acknowledged that though the film may have been "flawed," it also possessed a "wonderful" quality of imagination.[30] Some even found that it "made big demands on the audience, but [that it] is very impressive."[31] The late Lillian Wilds saw the film's defects as artistic triumphs,[32] and Frank Kermode declared, though with some qualifications, that Brook had made "the best of all Shakespeare movies."[33]

Yet Brook's movie is more than a movie about *King Lear*, it is a movie about making movies, deeply post-modernist in its meta-cinematic posture. State-of-the-art technology – hand-held cameras, lighter sound equipment, and superior film stock – liberated the director to re-envision Shakespeare's play spatially. Its grainy texture and deliberately out-of-focus frames shot in black-and-white show a winter world in North Jutland of unrelieved grimness. Aggressively cinematic, it discards Hollywood seamlessness in favor of deliberate strategies of alienation. It is not designed to make audiences comfortable but uncomfortable. Like Jean-Luc Godard, Brook employs discontinuities, zoom-fades, accelerated motion, freeze frames, shock editing, complex reverse-angle and over-the-shoulder shots, montage, jump cuts, overhead shots, silent-screen titles, eyes-only close-ups, and hand-held as well as immobile cameras. His camera redirects the Lear story into its own filmic idiom, just as it had once been hoped that Ted Hughes could "translate" Shakespeare's words into his own personal style,[34] though that scheme fell apart when it became apparent that even a poet so gifted as Hughes could hardly improve on Shakespeare's language. Shakespeare's words burn on the page, but smolder on the screen in charcoal grays and blacks.

A few examples of the ironist agenda must suffice. Shakespeare's play is framed by a map – "Give me the map there"(1.1.37) – and a mirror – "Lend me a looking glass"(5.3.262) – emblems for the geriatric king's futile journey and search for identity. In Brook's movie, however, the mirror seems to have been forgotten but the map plays a pivotal role as an expressive object in the division of the kingdom. Before that, however, an establishing shot, which may be a quotation from Fritz Lang's *M* (1931) starring Peter Lorre, pans over the faces of Lear's notorious 100 knights, who so sorely try his daughters' domestic tranquillity. A study in heads, they remain frozen in position, staring into nothingness, silent and enigmatic. They remain outside, barred from access to the presence chamber by an absurdly tiny door, not to be seen again until the old king angrily exits after Cordelia's impudence. From a reverse angle there is a shot of the claustrophobic throne, in which Paul Scofield is ensconced, a talking head that emerges, slowly but powerfully. Speaking oracularly like some kind of *deus absconditus* from deep within the recesses of his phallic-shaped retreat, his gravelly "No" prefigures the play's existentialist fetish, a leitmotif of "nothingness" ("Nothing, my lord"(1.1.87)). Scofield's king never calls directly for the map ("Give me the map, there" (1.1.37)), but it appears in time for distributing Goneril's one third of the kingdom. Holding aloft the symbol of royal power and justice, an orb surmounted by a cross, Goneril (Irene Worth) attests to her loyalty. Her sycophancy done, the king unfolds a fuzzy, blurry map, so shabby it looks as if it had been stored in a fruit cellar. Cords radiating from a small stake at its center indicate boundaries, as Lear himself says, comprised of natural barriers such as "shadowy forests ... with champains rich'd, / With plenteous rivers and wide-skirted meads" (1.1.64). Tightly framed, wizened scribes record Lear's decrees on parchment.

A smirking Regan (Susan Engel) then sacramentally elevates the ceremonial orb, recites her hymn of adulation and earns her share of the kingdom. The two outwardly compliant but inwardly recalcitrant daughters have triumphed over the outwardly recalcitrant but inwardly compliant Cordelia

(Annelise Gabold), though Brook's movie hints at possible excuses for Regan's and Goneril's impatience with the cantankerous old king. Meanwhile Cordelia remains backgrounded, isolated, alone, in medium long shot, awaiting her turn to speak the fatal three words, "Nothing, my lord." The cinematic rhetoric of shot/reverse shot visually punctuates the dialectical cross-purposes of king and daughter, the virtuous daughter resisting the power of the patriarchal oppressor. Cordelia banished, the king fades back into his vast, enclosed seat of power. When he exits, it is through the little door that separates him and his 100 knights from the cheer and company of his daughters. He has no clear map for his future.

The exterior shots emblemize the king's spiritual agony. Even when filmed out of doors, with horses thundering across frozen turf, tumbling and pitching wagons lurching over the landscape, hard-bitten knights moving en masse, pitched battles on bleak terrain, the movie still retains a sense of the claustrophobic. In the strobe-lit scene on the heath near Gloucester's (Alan Webb) castle, the "poor naked wretches," Lear, the Fool (Jack McGowran) and Edgar (Robert Lloyd), play out intricate variations on the theme of Lear's "Thou art the thing itself: unaccommodated man is no more but such a poor, bare, fork'd animal" (3.4.106). Flashes of lightning illuminate Shakespeare's apocalyptic language with glimpses of Edgar as mad Tom, a Christ figure with a crown of thorns, shivering, twitching, and trembling under torrents of icy rain water. The camera rudely surveys the bare chest, nude abdomen, thinly clad groin, of this "bare, fork'd animal." Drowned rodents fill the screen. The Fool's Erastian taunting of Lear, which penetrates into the old king's deepest reservoirs of denial, adds wormwood to the sufferings on the heath: "Fathers that wear rags / Do make their children blind / But fathers that bear bags / Shall see their children kind" (2.3.47). No character than the Fool better explores the paradoxes of Pauline Christianity: foolishness in wisdom, wisdom in foolishness; sight in blindness, blindness in sight; life in death, death in life; and victory in defeat, defeat in victory. Lear like God's lowliest handmaiden of the Magnificat falls in the eyes of men and rises in the eyes of God. The Fool guides him in a Dantesque kind of way through the inferno of the wild storm scenes, his aphorisms of cynical prudence always near the surface. Everywhere malignant nature rules in a space closed off to benevolence.

King Lear's crisis of knowledge about the human experience needs more than the services of a holy fool. The transcendent catalyst emerges in the absurdist, Beckett-like play-within-a-play starring the mad old king and the blinded Gloucester. Viewed from a crane shot, they are tiny figures on a bleak landscape, emblems of the dispossessed state of man. They raise insoluble questions about cause-and-effect, good and evil, which ricochet off texts as ancient as the

Book of Job, as recent as Friedrich Nietzsche's *Thus Spoke Zarathustra*, and as contemporary as Derrida's *Of Grammatology*. "Hark in thine ear: change places, and handy-dandy, which is the justice, which is the thief?" (4.6.151), says the old king in a typical reversal of cause and effect.

At the close, the images of horror proliferate. The charcoal texture becomes darker and grayer, more gothic. The old king in a bit of tricky editing speaks first on the left and then on the right side of the frame to explore his innermost being within himself. Looking bedraggled and exhausted, Goneril and Regan smolder in two-shot as they wrangle over their sordid claims to Edmund. As if in agony from strychnine poisoning, Goneril writhes and thrashes about, her body spastic with pain, and then in a supremely perverse act of will bashes her own head against a boulder. A mini-second later, Cordelia appears for a fleeting moment (perhaps four or five frames) just exactly as her neck audibly snaps inside the hangman's noose. The king staggers across the barren land-scape holding Cordelia in his arms and howling like a trapped animal. He hallucinates, thinking that he sees Cordelia alive. Does this last mirage signify that only mad men can live happily in this fallen world? Is the world finally a place where the sighted remain sightless and the sightless sighted? A place where only a blind man, a beggar and a fool really come to grips with the true horror of man's fate? Brook's movie interrogates but doesn't answer the questions. Instead the ravaged king gradually and inexorably simply falls out of the frame and out of the world, very much like Frederick B. Warde in the old silent Thanhouser *King Lear* (1916). Only a blank screen remains, an exercise in white on white. Despite the map, despite Edgar's faith that the gods are just, despite Kent's (Tom Fleming) loyalty ("I have a journey, sir, shortly to go" (5.3.322)), there is after all out there in nature – nothing. God is dead.

Polanski's *Macbeth*

Roman Polanski's blood-soaked vision of *Macbeth* (1971) moved into even darker waters than Brook's *King Lear* in its unsparing journey into the heart of darkness.[35] While "purists" were still agitated over the "mistreatment" of Shakespeare by directors like Peter Hall and Peter Brook, Polanski's sensation-ally publicized film had a sufficient level of violence to make them apoplectic. Yet another of the plays had been taken by a movie director and resituated in the frantic, disoriented world of the early 70s, when youthful war protesters were shot dead by the Ohio National Guard and when Charles Manson's crazed drug addicts murdered Sharon Tate, Polanski's pregnant wife. Lady Macbeth was everybody's favorite paradigm for the scheming wife of a power exec-utive, and having the film bankrolled by Hugh Hefner's outrageous *Playboy* magazine on a budget of $2,400,000 made it all the more scandalous.[36] For Polanski, though, the movie was a dream come true for he had long been hoping to do a Shakespeare movie but could not because of "the money." He said in his own wry commentary on "tickling commodity," that "the money people are always afraid of Shakespeare. Shakespeare is never a good – how do you say it? – product."[37] Filming began in North Wales in November 1970.

With modern mass communications blurring the line between fact and fiction, Polanski's checkout-counter, tabloid-style personal life inevitably got confused with his film. Audiences arrived at the theatre expecting to see a link between the stabbings of Duncan and of Sharon Tate; the witches, and Polanski's earlier blockbuster movie of Ira Levin's *Rosemary's Baby*; and a nude Lady Macbeth (Francesca Annis), and *Playboy* centerfold soft porn. Yet this "expectational text"[38] was already lodged in Shakespeare's tragedy: the multiple recurring images of blood in *Macbeth* were there before Charles Manson cruelly murdered Sharon Tate; the *Macbeth* witches have always exhausted the ingenuity of directors and make-up artists; and Lady Macbeth's *déshabillé* in the sleepwalking scene is almost virginal, an emblem of her pathetic vulnerability more than anything like *Playboy* eroticism. As Bernice Kliman has pointed out, the play's violence has always been there, though a surprising amount of it has been mitigated even in Polanski's grim portrayal. She gives as an example the restraint shown in the bear baiting sequence, and in the off-camera rape of Lady MacDuff.[39] Squeamish directors for genteel audiences have averted their eyes from what Rosse implies as the despoliation of Lady MacDuff, who was "savagely slaughter'd" (4.3.205). The man who wrote *Titus Andronicus* might not himself have been quite so squeamish.

With some exceptions, Polanski's critics spared him the deluge of hostility that greeted Peter Brook's efforts, perhaps a sign that critics had grown more tolerant of filmed Shakespeare. Of course many complained about the film's egregious violence that brought too much attention to itself;[40] another more complicated argument, assuming film is always naturalistic, concluded that "*Macbeth* fails as a film [because] Polanski's appropriation is incomplete or half-hearted, leaving, for instance, an artistically unbridgeable gap between Shakespeare's supernaturalism and the modern director's naturalism";[41] and Frank Kermode liked it but did not like it, equivocating like Macbeth himself in his quandary over prophecies that "cannot be ill; cannot be good" (1.3.131).[42] Kermode's equivocation is understandable. Violence as art invites culture shock.

The Columbia Pictures release script uses only about forty percent of Shakespeare's text but it substitutes for deleted text a glittering array of visual and aural images. As cameraman Gil Taylor remarked, "nothing is ever static."[43] Polanski, like Zeffirelli and the seventeenth-century Flemish painters, crams his *mise-en-scène* with realistic furniture, hangings, goblets, etc., but he is even more resourceful than Zeffirelli at subtly embedding them into the thematic design, being obsessed with promulgating his agenda down to the last tiny detail. In Polanski's conception of Macbeth's castle, things and people are forever moving. Extras push carts, carry pigs, sweep stairs, feed chickens. Animals fill the courtyard – geese, dogs, chained bears, falcons, and so forth. And his sonic punctuation matches Orson Welles's – horses' hooves, wheels squeaking, chains clanking, seagulls squawking, geese honking, bells ringing, cocks crowing, hens clucking, water splashing, soldiers grunting, warriors gasping, dogs barking, doors groaning, etc., etc. The soundtrack penetrates into the heart of the diegesis.

The pre-credit, spectacular long take subliminally gives portents of the events to follow,[44] and predicts what it means for Macbeth to "have supp'd full with horrors" (5.5.13) before he suffers death by beheading at the hands of MacDuff. First, there is a hazy sunrise and seascape of a lonely beach, and then a crooked stick enters the frame from the right followed by two withered crones and a young woman, whose fairness contrasts with the foulness of the older women: "Fair is foul, and foul is fair" (1.1.11). From a squeaky, dilapidated cart, these less than supernatural hags remove an assortment of macabre objects, among them a hangman's noose and a severed arm, into the hand of which they insert a dagger (is that a sufficient portent?). In closeup, the cackling trio bury the arm in the sand and pour a vial of blood over it. A gull squawks, a talisman of a galaxy of birds' cries to follow, all of which echo Shakespeare's own ornithological obsession in *Macbeth*: "Light thickens, and the crow / Makes wing to th' rooky wood" (3.2.50). Fog and mist roll in with superimposed titles fading in and out, while the Third Ear Band provides discordant violin and bagpipe music for the departure of the witches' rickety cart. The soundtrack reverberates with horses' hooves, shouting and screaming, clashing of swords, the whinnying of horses, human wailing, coughing, and moaning, while the superimposed credits continue to roll on the now completely fog-bound screen. After the fog dissipates, dead and wounded litter the battlefield at Forres. In mid-shot a soldier stops by an injured man lying face down on the ground, pulls at his boot, and the man stirs. The injured man feebly lifts his head and the soldier shatters his spine with two or three sickening whacks with an iron ball on a chain. The camera moves on to the bleeding sergeant's battle report and then to a bloodied Thane of Cawdor (Vic Abbott) bound and stretched out on a horse-drawn litter.

Polanski husbands his aural and visual images the way a good writer squeezes words. The mist and fog again suggest the play's leitmotif – the equivocal nature of reality – "Is this a dagger which I see before me [?]" (2.1.33). The beauty of nature contrasts with the ugliness of battle. The medallion and ceremonial chain that Duncan (Nicholas Selby) lifts from the defeated Thane of Cawdor foreshadows more chain images, to include the iron collar and chain around the neck of Cawdor at his grisly execution, an episode only reported in the play. A defiant endomorph, Cawdor oozes contempt for his captors, especially the double-dealing Rosse, and leaps off a castle parapet to die brutally at the end of a chain fastened to an iron collar around his size twenty-two neck, "Nothing in his life / Became him like the leaving it" (1.4.7), reports Malcolm (Stephan Chase) to Duncan. Chains hold the bear to the stone column in the baiting scene before the disastrous banquet. Later, Macbeth awards Lennox's medallion and chain to Seyton (Noel Davis) as a payoff for his corrupt services. The chain motif also stands for Macbeth's self-enchainment, who, as has rightly been said, murdered himself when he murdered Duncan.

Hanged men dangle, slowly twisting in the wind, from a crudely constructed gallows, while below several more of the condemned are queued up awaiting their turns. Those uncooperative with their hangmen are pummeled into submission. A twitching and jerking wretch is hoisted up high by a rope around his neck. Muffled cries, grunts, groans. Off in the distance, a mounted Macbeth (Jon Finch) and Banquo (Martin Shaw) impassively watch the chamber of horrors, a Brueghel-like nightmare. In the words of the bleeding sergeant, "another Golgotha"(1.1.40), the place of the skull. In Kottian terms, it is the world as the inexorable Grand Mechanism, a crunching power struggle. This is Theatre of Cruelty – a demonic universe of whips, gibbets, and scaffolds. The violence, as Polanski himself would argue, is not gratuitous but necessary: "if you don't show violence the way it is, I think that's immoral and harmful."[45] The suffering is the outward and visible sign for Macbeth's inner agony. In Jack Jorgens' apt phrase, Polanski makes the "inner outer."[46]

Pictures cling to the memory. In a scatological moment, the Porter (Sydney Bromley), after the terrible knocking at the gate, noisily urinates against the castle wall. He obscenely thrusts out his dagger in a show-and-tell for his thesis that drinking both "provokes, and unprovokes: it provokes the desire, but it takes away the performance" (2.3.29). In the light of dawn, the castle is revealed for what it is, a barnyard, where cocks crow and flea-bitten hounds hop in and out of the straw mattresses on the crude beds.

Spirited *découpage* enhances the horror. The murdered Banquo falls into a stream, an axe protruding from his back, and floats on the water, face-down. This time there is no hope of water washing away "the deed without a name" (4.1.49). A split second later, a chained bear materializes, the same bear that had previously been seen being dragged into the castle. Savage dogs snap at the animal, which is fettered to a ring in a stone column. A strange look of half revulsion and half gloating crosses Lady Macbeth's (Francesca Annis) face as if the spectacle of cruelty erotically stimulated her. Once again, "foul is fair, and fair is foul." The bear-baiting becomes associated with another complex of images. As the mangled bear carcass is dragged through the corridors, attendants sprinkle the fouled floor with rushes to make it fair again. After Macbeth has been traumatized by the sight of Banquo's ghost, he drops his wine goblet and Lennox in a tight frame wipes up the foul stain to restore the floor to fairness. This obsession with wiping things clean resonates off Lady Macbeth's vain hope that "a little water clears us of this deed" (2.2.64), which comes full circle in the sleep-walking scene when she discovers that "All the perfumes of Arabia will not sweeten this little hand. O, O, O!" (5.1.50). She herself is of course outwardly fair and inwardly foul, especially in a film that makes her over from the traditional nag/shrew into a fashionable young woman with the style of a super model. As already mentioned, the chain around the neck of Cawdor resonates against the metal collar around the bear's neck, and then at the very end of the film, Macbeth himself falls near the same iron ring in the stone column that had chained the bear. He indeed "bear-like ... must fight the course" (5.7.2). These complex mirror relationships and visual associations deserve enough close exegesis to qualify Roman Polanski as a James Joyce with a camera.

Another Polanski tactic is summed up in his remark that he likes "a realistic situation where things don't quite fit in."[47] Nowhere does this mining of an incongruity for an artistic congruity better show than in the famous banquet scene when Macbeth is confronted by Banquo's ghost. Macbeth enters the dining hall the soul of geniality, like some Mafia godfather. With consummate hypocrisy, concealing the foul with the fair, he remarks on how much happier he would be if "the grac'd person of our Banquo [were] present" (3.4.40). Lennox (Andrew Laurence) and Rosse (John Stride) urge him to be seated at the banquet table, assuring him that a place has been reserved. A quick cut to the table does show a vacant place, but a few seconds later Macbeth glances at the table and says "the table's full" (3.4.45). And indeed it seems so. The camera pans back to reveal an unbroken row of human backs. For a second we are as convinced as Macbeth that all the chairs at the table are occupied but Lennox insists, "Here is a place reserv'd, sir." Again Macbeth peers, looks puzzled. Again he sees only a solid phalanx of human backs. Obviously, though, there is something going on that "doesn't quite fit in." "Where?" says a perplexed Macbeth, echoing the thoughts of the audience as well, who have shared his vision, not Lennox's. Then in a masterstroke of editing, one of the guests turns around, the one at the center, raising his hand to his face, and stares at the king. It is the butchered Banquo (Martin Shaw). Terrified, the king drops his wine goblet and cries out, "Which of you have done this?" and then "never shake / Thy gory locks at me" (3.4.49). The barriers between the king and the off-screen audience evaporate. There is a magical convergence so that Macbeth's and the audience's consciousnesses merge. The thing that "doesn't quite fit in" has been fitted into an artistic coup.

A great oddity is that this hyper-trendy film actually drew for its scenario, which was co-authored by the brilliant but astringent Kenneth Tynan, on M. F. Libby's obscure Victorian essay, "Some New Notes on *Macbeth*" (1893). In it, Libby imaginatively fictionalized that Rosse to curry favor with Macbeth had Cawdor "framed" and executed on the hasty command of the king. Rosse then busily went on to serve Macbeth, grew jealous over Macbeth's intimacy with Banquo, took on the job of the elusive Third Murderer of Banquo, assisted in covering up for Macbeth at the banquet, and became a key agent in the murder of Lady Macduff and her children. After deserting to Malcolm, he finally "as a reward of endless treachery [was] made an earl."[48] Played by John Stride as a smirking sociopath, Rosse's complicity with Macbeth is insinuated by almost every camera angle from his early assistance in Cawdor's destruction, to his iterative, almost subliminal appearances, when he hovers in the background. A murderers' murderer he pushes Banquo's two inept assassins down a castle well with a makeshift crutch that resembles the witches' ragged bough at the beginning of the movie. His fortunes rise further when he orchestrates the heartless slaughter of Macduff's family, which begins with Ian Hogg contemptuously sweeping trinkets off the fireplace mantle in a terrified Lady MacDuff's private quarters. (A Nazi bully apparently once subjected Polanski to a similar treatment when he was a child.) At the end of the film, Rosse, the tireless opportunist, picks up the crown and proffers it to Malcolm, crying "Hail, King of Scotland!" (5.9.25). Off camera, almost lost, Macduff utters his traditional line "The time is free" (5.9.21). The silent movie about Rosse remains nested within the framework of the talking movie about Macbeth.

The last thing that Macbeth sees in his life is a subjective whirl of jeering and catcalling soldiers as his head is swished about on a pole. Only later do we realize that Polanski's subjective camera has positioned us, the audience, *inside* the severed head, so that we too are experiencing the terminal spasms of sensory apprehension, the death throes, *after* the beheading. The time may be "free" in Shakespeare's play but the limping Donalbain's return to the witches' cave suggests the "time" is not free in this movie. The cyclical pattern of evil has begun again and presumably usurper will replace usurper in an infinite regression of existential despair as the Grand Mechanism works out its inexorable design. Polanski's vision echoes Macbeth's, but not necessarily Shakespeare's, view of life as "a tale / Told by an idiot, full of sound and fury, / Signifying nothing" (5.5.26), which runs against the tradition in Shakespearean tragedy for a "wraparound" ending with assurances of a return to order and decency. Yet Polanski never pretended to be Shakespeare. He is a gifted film maker with a genius for pointing a camera. He makes magic out of filming rather

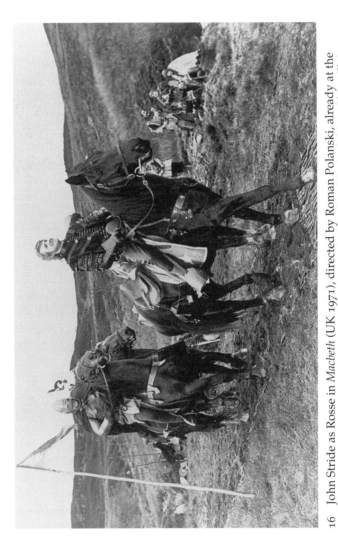

16 John Stride as Rosse in *Macbeth* (UK 1971), directed by Roman Polanski, already at the beginning of the film contemplates his dark scenario for rivaling Macbeth himself in villainy.

than filming to make magic. He didn't need to borrow Shakespeare's robes when he had so many of his own.

The Burge/Snell *Julius Caesar*

In roughly the same time frame when Polanski was making *Macbeth*, Peter Snell was working on his *Julius Caesar* (1970) and Charlton Heston on *Antony and Cleopatra* (1972). Neither film was sealed of the tribe of Kott, being "straight Shakespeare" innocent of any transgressive impulses. Peter Snell, a youthful Canadian producer working for Great Britain's Commonwealth United, was joined by Stuart Burge, an experienced television director, who had directed a BBC *Julius Caesar* (1959) that cost over £8,000 with ninety-nine in the cast. Snell's Anglo-American cast almost matched the distinction of the actors in Mankiewicz's 1953 film. They included John Gielgud, Jason Robards, Jr., and Charlton Heston. Heston's willingness to play Antony for a modest $100,000 plus fifteen percent of the world gross was precisely the leverage that a hard-pressed Peter Snell needed to entice financial backers.[49]

Heston's passion for Antony had begun in a 1950 *Julius Caesar* filmed in and around the environs of Northwestern University, which cleverly exploited the abandoned University of Chicago football stadium as a Roman setting. Made on a tiny budget of $15,000 and directed by David Bradley, the film, though amateurish in many ways, still won good press notices. Critics like Bosley Crowther were sympathetic to *Julius Caesar* but not dazzled, acknowledging the ambitiousness of a 16mm film produced by undergraduates but that ultimately betrayed "its amateur origins and its 'little theatre' bounds."[50] David Bradley, who had also directed a *Macbeth* (1947), that time on a budget of $5,000 at the University of Chicago, played Brutus himself, but never achieved the enormous success in film making of his friend, Heston.

The Burge/Snell *Julius Caesar* remains one of the great mysteries in the history of filmed Shakespeare. Presumably it had everything going for it – professional direction, an excellent cast, intelligent script, and yet somehow it remained dead in the water. As *Variety* said, "it is difficult to pinpoint just what is lacking in Commonwealth's *Julius Caesar*. It has most of its "i's" dotted and its "t's" crossed, but its fire seems manufactured rather than inspired."[51] Other critics were downright hostile: "The new picture is as flat and juiceless as a dead haddock," wrote Howard Thompson;[52] "Robards appears to be receiving his lines by concealed radio transmitter, and delivering them as part of the responsive reading in a Sunday sermon," said Tom Castner.[53]

Filmed in Technicolor instead of black-and-white like the Mankiewicz version, Burge's movie achieves plausibility but not inspiration. With a limited budget of $1,600,000, which needed to cover major battle scenes in Spain, its cast included one star from the Mankiewicz film, John Gielgud, now Caesar not Cassius. Gielgud as Julius Caesar is Gielgud as Gielgud all over again, the singer's voice disconnecting from the character's innermost being. Insufficiently grubby-looking for backdoor politics, Gielgud seems less made-to-order for Caesar than Mankiewicz's phlegmatic Louis Calhern, who fit the stereotype of the ambitious public man so perfectly. With his virile physique and voice, Charlton Heston once again turns Antony into one of the triple pillars of the world. The director hit on the happy idea of having him deliver part of the soliloquy over Caesar's body at the base of Pompey's statue in voice-over, which toned down Heston's histrionics: "O, pardon me, thou bleeding piece of earth, / That I am meek and gentle" (3.1.254).

Where Brando's eulogy at the Forum over Caesar's body reflects the inner writhing of the Stanislavsky school of acting, then a dominant trend in New York theatre circles, Heston speaks with the big voice and authoritative manner of an old-fashioned Shakespearean actor of the Frederick B. Warde school. Richard Johnson makes a more satisfactory Cassius than Gielgud's effete young man in the Mankiewicz movie. With a dark moustache and smoldering expression, he has the Iago-like sneakiness that can justify Caesar's fears: "Yond Cassius has a lean and hungry look, / He thinks too much; such men are dangerous" (1.2.194). Unlike Gielgud, Johnson can plausibly manipulate Brutus to his will, though neither actor's performance sheds light on how by the end of the play the two reverse roles, Brutus being empowered and Cassius disempowered. Both Diana Rigg (Portia) and Jill Bennett (Calphurnia) had the misfortune to repeat the roles played so expertly by Deborah Kerr and Greer Garson. Rigg shows a charming, almost cuddly, appeal but it works against the concept of a high Roman aristocrat who is "Cato's daughter" with the capability to "swallow fire." Bennett, hard put to it to match Greer Garson's formidable earlier cool portrayal of Caesar's wronged wife, is beautiful and appealing, almost a "trophy wife" to the aging Caesar, but lacks the requisite imperial bearing for the spouse of Rome's greatest man. There are grand montage effects in splashy color of swirling crowds, processions, battles, with Michael Lewis' stirring music to enliven the action. Not least are the battle scenes made in Spain with hundreds of extras costumed as Roman soldiers at Philippi. As the horses rear up and fall to the dust and the soldiers hammer away at one another, the battle increasingly quotes from the fighting on the ice in Eisenstein's *Alexander Nevsky*, or even its derivative in Welles's *Chimes at Midnight*. Man against man, horse against horse, hacking away in blind rage.

Sharmini Tiruchelvam's film diary of the daily activities in Spain throws some light on why this otherwise promising venture somehow fell short of expectations. Apparently Jason Robards' low-key performance stemmed from his interpretation of Brutus as an intellectual suppressing his emotions after being traumatized by his entanglement in a political assassination. When James Mason played Brutus in the Mankiewicz film, he spoke Brutus' Hamlet-like soliloquy in a meditative, thoughtful, introspective way: "Th' abuse of greatness is when it disjoins / Remorse from power; and to speak truth of Caesar, / I have not known when his affections sway'd / More than his reason" (2.1.18). By contrast, Robards speaks the lines as if he "lacked affect" (in the psychological sense), totally flat and uninflected. Besides covering up any sign of emotion, Robards also conceived in some high-minded way that "rehearsing in movies should be done just before takes. Then those small spontaneous things can be retained." He grew "restive" on the set, even disappeared, so that "there was talk of recasting."[54] If this is so, in an ironically self-referential way, Robards' lofty scruples about how to interpret Brutus and his idealistic view that rehearsing violated artistic fidelity, sabotaged the film in much the same way that Brutus' lofty idealism virtually destroyed Rome.

Heston's *Antony and Cleopatra*

Charlton Heston's ambitious *Antony and Cleopatra* (1972) reconfirmed his selfless devotion to Shakespeare, particularly for the role of Antony, whom, as we have seen, he had twice previously done on screen. In the 1950s when still a recently discharged Army Air Corps veteran from the Aleutian campaign, he had played Petruchio and Macbeth on television, Macbeth and Proculeius (with Katherine Cornell as Cleopatra) on stage, and most recently he has been a powerful First Player in the Kenneth Branagh *Hamlet* (1996). No two Shakespeare film directors could be more opposite in temperament than Heston and Polanski, the former a sturdy Midwesterner,[55] and the other a decidedly hippy Polish Jew. Heston approaches Shakespeare deferentially, taking the high road, without a jot of Brook's or Polanski's bitter irony. His commitment to the National Rifle Association agenda has made him *persona non grata* to the politically correct in Hollywood. In his commitment to Shakespeare, however, Heston defies stereotypes. He invested time and money to film *Antony and Cleopatra* with its understated but evocative language because he thought it had been neglected, which is hardly indicative of a man with a shriveled soul. Like Plutarch's Antony, perhaps Heston had also been caught up in Cleopatra's "strong toil of grace."[56]

After Orson Welles's warning that without a Cleopatra there was no play,[57] Heston at considerable travail found Hildegard Neil, a stunningly beautiful South African, who possessed the "infinite variety" to survive three weeks of rehearsals in dingy quarters near Covent Garden. Once filming began on location in Spain, Heston's careful preparation allowed him to shoot the scenes in almost any order.[58] As Moses in Cecil B. De Mille's *Ten Commandments* (1956), he had learned first-hand about the logistics of a super-extravaganza in Technicolor with a cast of thousands. Unfortunately his budget pointed him in another direction and he had to cut corners by, for example, intercutting outtakes from MGM's war-galley scenes in *Ben Hur* (1959) for his sea battle of Actium. Borrowed or not, they still capture the horror of ancient naval warfare. In tight frames, battering rams penetrate deep into an enemy ship's hull. Galley slaves chained to their oars shriek in terror as sea water pours in. Images of Octavius (John Castle) and Antony appear superimposed on the screen against the backdrop of battle. The land warfare, though not at the level of Olivier's French cavalry charge at Agincourt in *Henry V*, pieces out the imperfections of stage presentation with an Egyptian army uniformed as Muslims perfidiously stepping aside to allow Octavius' cavalry charge to fall heavily on Antony's infantry.

As Heston himself said, by reason of its wide-ranging geographical scope, *Antony and Cleopatra* cries out for a camera. From the establishing helicopter shot of a trireme at sea to the closing when the camera pulls up and back to show Cleopatra's monument gradually diminishing, the movie shifts venues from Rome to Egypt and from Egypt to Rome. Unlike the battered lovers in Jonathan Miller's television version, Heston's Antony and Cleopatra project the mythical aura of godlike creatures. Heston smoothly shifts from the soldierly Antony in *Julius Caesar* to the lover in midlife crisis of *Antony and Cleopatra*, who makes an attractive bauble for the sensuous and dangerous Cleopatra. From the beginning while symbolically tearing away at an encircling necklace of pearls and proclaiming, "Let Rome in Tiber melt, and the wide arch / Of the rang'd empire fall! Here is my space" (1.1.33), Antony has unconsciously set himself up to be seduced, betrayed, and ruined by Cleopatra. Hildegard Neil as Cleopatra, though less smoldering than Janet Suzman in the Nunn television version, embodies the wildness of the "Egyptian dish," as Enobarbus (Eric Porter) calls her. A striking brunette with ivory skin and dark eyes, her hair piled high and carefully coifed, she is the femme fatale, or *la belle dame sans merci*, the beautiful woman without pity, seductive enough to make any man throw away an empire. She appears in a variety of sybaritic poses, lounging on a luxurious bed, painting her own or Antony's face, calling for her claque of "women" to wait on her, or displaying total petulance toward anyone unlucky enough to interrupt her crowded agenda of self-indulgence. The hapless messenger who brings the news that Antony has married Octavia feels the full brunt: "I'll spurn thine eyes / Like balls before me; I'll unhair thy head / [*She hales him up and down*] Thou shalt be whipt with wire, and stew'd in brine, / Smarting in ling'ring pickle" (2.5.62). Her delight in inflicting pain rivals that of Antony when he catches Octavius' messenger Thidias kissing Cleopatra's hand: "Whip him, fellows, / Till like a boy you see him cringe his face, / And whine aloud for mercy" (3.13.99). Still, what would seem sordid and cruel in others, somehow with Antony and Cleopatra acquires a measure of grace.

Cleopatra includes in her "strong toil of grace" not only the enchanted Antony but also her faithful retinue of Charmian (Jane Lapotaire), Iras (Monica Peterson), and the eunuch, Mardian (Emiliano Redondo). As Charmian, Jane Lapotaire understudies Neil's Cleopatra, a role that she finally won for herself with Colin Blakely as her Antony in the Jonathan Miller 1981 BBC version. Lapotaire and Peterson make up a pathetic little feminist phalanx protecting Cleopatra from the disastrous consequences of her meddling in Antony's military campaigns. When she blunders into the naval battle and seals her own doom, a soldier protests "trust not to rotten planks" (3.7.62) and Canidius despairs for Antony's cause, "We are women's men" (3.7.69).

In Rome, Antony appears at Octavius' box at the arena, where gladiators train to fight to the death. The chilling spectacle of two exhausted men fighting in the arena for their lives with swords and tridents and shields (2.2) is intercut with Antony's negotiations with Octavius for marriage to Octavius' sister. As if to epitomize Roman cruelty, Octavius Caesar heartlessly ignores the gladiators while he bargains with Antony for power. As Enobarbus, Eric Porter colorfully describes Cleopatra's barge, which may have been inspired by the royal vessel of Queen Elizabeth, depicted on the Thames in Visscher's 1616 engraving of London: "The poop was beaten gold, / Purple the sails, and so perfumed that / The winds were love-sick with them; the oars were silver" (2.2.192), and he also pays the greatest tribute of all to Cleopatra: "Age cannot wither her, nor custom stale / Her infinite variety" (2.2.234). After Enobarbus' appalling desertion of Antony for Octavius, the meanspirited Octavius places Enobarbus in the vanguard of his attacking troops: "Go charge Agrippa / Plant those that have revolted in the vant" (4.6.7), while Antony fills him with guilt and self-loathing by generously returning his personal property to him. The spiritually desolate Enobarbus laments that "I am alone the villain of the earth, / And feel I am so most" (4.6.28), and vows to "seek / Some ditch wherein to die" (4.6.36). Heston ratchets the "ditch" up several notches into a cliff from which the fallen and wretched Enobarbus hurls himself into the sea.

The crucial death scenes of Antony and Cleopatra have rarely been done any better. Critics tended to be rather harsh, one declaring Heston's Antony to be lacking in "sensual drive,"[59] while another opining of Neil's Egyptian queen that she was "disastrous" with neither "presence ... nor sexuality."[60] On the other hand, a *Variety* reviewer said that the "film is a neat balance of close-up portraiture and panoramic action" and that "Hildegard Neil proves one of Cleo's more convincing screen incarnations."[61] In the monument, betrayed

17   Paul Scofield in an unforgettable performance as the tyrannical old king in Peter Brook's bleak vision of *King Lear* (UK 1971).

by Cleopatra, but nevertheless bound to her in a common passion, Antony, for the first time perhaps, shows a sense of loss and humility: "I am dying, Egypt, dying. / Give me some wine" (4.15.41). With Antony's body in front of her, Cleopatra courageously chooses death over certain dishonor in Rome. She shrewdly sees through the sham offers of Octavius and his messenger Proculeius (Julian Glover). Her unbearable fate would be to be shown to "the shouting varlotry / Of censuring Rome" (5.2.55), or to see "some squeaking Cleopatra boy [her] greatness" (5.2.220) in a public playhouse. Cleopatra accepts the notorious basket of asps "I wish you joy o' th' worm" (5.2.279) from a ubiquitous soothsayer who thriftily doubles for Shakespeare's grotesque little clown. Plutarch says that she experimented on prisoners to determine what the least painful mode of death would be: "She hath pursu'd conclusions infinite / Of easy ways to die" (5.2.355). Her faithful ladies-in-waiting, Charmian and Iras, respond to her last request: "Give me my robe, put on my crown, I have / Immortal longings in me" (5.2.280). She then says the ineffable, "I am fire and air" (5.2.289), and manages in her last gestures to perfume the air with sensuous imagery: "Now no more / The juice of Egypt's grape shall moist this lip" (5.2.281); and death itself becomes erotic: "the stroke of death is as a lover's pinch, / Which hurts, and is desir'd" (5.2.295). When Octavius enters and says that "she looks like sleep, / As she would catch another Antony / In her strong toil of grace" (5.2.346), the movie matches the play's largeness of soul. In another costly helicopter shot, the camera pulls back and up and away from the monument, leaving Antony and Cleopatra in another time and place but somehow appropriating their lost world into our own as well.

- 8 -

Other Shakespeares: translation and expropriation

Movie makers from non-Anglophone countries all over the world have resituated Shakespeare's plays in the idiom of their own language and film culture. Not needing to record in English on the soundtrack, they enjoyed the luxury of reinventing the plays in purely cinematic terms, as if they were silent movies. Sometimes the results have met with wide acclaim, as with Akira Kurosawa's famous 1957 *Macbeth* adaptation, *Throne of Blood* (*Kumonosu-Jo*), sometimes with hostility, as with an Indian *Hamlet* (1955), but in all instances these non-Anglophone films show the universal appeal of Shakespeare as a cultural trophy. Few other English writers, if any, have attracted admirers in places so remote as, say, sub-Saharan or East Asian nations. Once removed from the original Anglophone context, the plays have often been converted into "other Shakespeares, Shakespeares not dependent on English and often at odds with it,"[1] so that the shadow of cultural imperialism gradually diminishes.

The vast Indian film industry, which in North Africa, the Middle and Far East has rivaled Hollywood in productivity and influence, in 1979 alone produced more than 700 feature-length movies.[2] The Indian upper middle classes have traditionally been nurtured on Shakespeare in the school curriculum, and, significantly, scholars in New Delhi edit an important English language Shakespeare journal, *Hamlet Studies*. The Merchant/Ivory film *Shakespeare Wallah* (1965) captures the flavor of Anglo/Indian culture with scenarist Ruth Prawer Jhabvala's loose adaptation of actor Geoffrey Kendal's real-life diary of a Shakespeare troupe touring India in 1947. Jhabvala's treatment turns the story of the strolling Anglo players, led by a fictional Mr. and Mrs. Buckingham, into a "metaphor for the end of the British Raj."[3] The talented actors superbly perform scenes from *Antony and Cleopatra, Othello, Hamlet,* and *Twelfth Night* in settings ranging from a Maharajah's palace to a boys' school, the smothering scene from *Othello* being particularly exemplary. British cultural as well as economic imperialism is waning, however, and the audiences' growing impatience with the vestiges of the Raj evoke a compelling, almost Chekhovian, nostalgia for a lost Anglo/Indian culture that might rightly be entitled "A Passage *from* India." A sterner critic has said "Good riddance" to the poor Buckinghams, whom she views as agents of oppressive colonialism, and "slightly ridiculous" at that.[4] Chekhov's people are, it is true, often also "slightly ridiculous" but also touchingly and ineffably glorious in sensibility. Banish them and, as with Falstaff, banish the whole world. As Lizzie Buckingham, popular British television actress Felicity Kendal (Viola in the BBC *Twelfth Night*) plays the daughter of the troupe's director (Geoffrey Kendal), a man forced to watch the demise of a lifetime's work. Although in love with a young Indian suitor of means, Lizzie sails off to England, a country that she has in fact never known. With its soft-textured black-and-white photography and deep sensitivity to the nuances of the Anglo-Indian love/hate affair, the low-budget film is a treasure. And it helps to explain why Shakespeare movies were made in the native dialects of India as well.

In India there have been at least two films of *Hamlet* in native languages, probably more. Peter Morris reports on a *Khoon ka Khoon* (1935) directed by Sohrab Modi as a recording of a stage production. If so, this is one of the earliest Shakespeare talkies ever made anywhere.[5] More is known in the West about the earnest 1955 *Hamlet* produced and directed by Kishore Sahu, who for his pains was rewarded after a gala premiere at the Metro Bombay Theatre with unparalleled vituperation by a hostile review in *Filmindia*, "Sahu's *Hamlet* Flops at the Met." Not only does the film "slander" Shakespeare's memory but also "Hiralel who plays the king was made a drunken clown," and Laertes, we are told, had "a callow and silly face." The picture itself is "stupid" and displays "stinking selfishness." An accompanying photograph shows Dame Sybil Thorndike on the opening night posing with a proud and beaming theatre manager, Mr. Butani.[6] In unpublished comments, film archivist Luke McKernan agrees that Sahu's Hamlet left much to be desired, for "a Hamlet who has no idea of what he is doing is not the same as one who simply cannot make up his mind." McKernan was also troubled by some textual changes involving the play-within-the-play and the duel scene; on the other hand, Ophelia was about "as good as you will ever see," being "perky, impassioned, human." Gertrude too was fine, and the film worked hard at imitating the *mise-en-scène* for the Olivier *Hamlet* with castle battlements, poses (Hamlet in his chair), and stair imagery. The two gravediggers unforgettably dance while singing a bizarre comic song. The film's "lack of Indian-ness" disappointed McKernan but he thought its technical side far better than the *Filmindia* reviewer's assessment.[7]

In Ghana, where Anglo influence remains powerful, there was another version of *Hamlet* released in 1964, *Hamile: The Tongo Hamlet*, in which the play's action had been transferred to Tongo, the home of the Frafra people in northern Ghana. The strongest cinema in sub-Saharan Africa has emerged from Francophone rather than Anglophone zones of influence mainly because the French were more inclined than the British to encourage native cinema production. Even so the students at the University of Ghana School of Music and Drama managed to produce this adaptation based on their stage production,[8] which was entered in the 1965 London Commonwealth Film Festival. A few years later, Brazilian Director Ozualdo R. Candeias released an 87-minute Portuguese-language *Hamlet, a Heranca* (1970), which was "based on Shakespeare's play."[9]

The universality of *Romeo and Juliet* with its young lovers frustrated by the older generation cuts so easily across national boundaries that it may be safe from trendy theories of social construction. Thus Peter Morris reports an Egyptian version, *Shuhaddaa El Gharam* (1942) and a Hindi language film *Anjuman* (1948), both with debts to *Romeo and Juliet*.[10] Out of the mideast comes word of a fairly recent variant in *Torn Apart* (1990), the melancholy tale of an Israeli Romeo (Adrian Pasdar) and Arab Juliet (Cecilia Peck), though the soundtrack seems to be in English, not Hebrew.[11] The Indian film industry delved into Shakespeare again with a hit film *Henna* (1992) that retold the story of the star-crossed lovers in both Hindi (the language of India) and Urdu (the Pakistani language), with Zeba Bakhtiar (Juliet) as a Pakistani Muslim and Rishi Kapoor (Romeo) as an Indian Hindu playing the title roles.[12]

A Portuguese-language *Romeu e Julieta* (1980), directed by Paulo Afonso Grisolli for Brazil's Globo TV, and starring Fabio Junior and Lucelia Santos, though strictly speaking a television production, has the "crossover" potential for theatrical release. Freely adapted from Shakespeare's tragedy, it has been removed, according to the narrator, to Ouro Preto, "like Verona . . . a perfect setting for a tragedy of love," a mining town in Brazil reminiscent with its slanted hillsides, red tile rooftops, and cobbled streets of the fragile beauty of the Italian Riviera. It combines the spectacle of Renato Castellani's *Romeo and Juliet*, the operatic flavor of Zeffirelli's, and the topicality of Leonard Bernstein's *West Side Story*. It recontextualizes the play in a Brazilian Portuguese culture, vibrant, topical, and yet, as with all good non-English screen treatments of Shakespeare, paradoxically faithful to its source.

The family Christopher, who are the Capulets, worship at a private chapel along with Juliet's future groom, Paul Rogerto, known in his fraternity as "Skull." Heavy moralizing about the dire consequences of young people disobeying parental authority bypasses Shakespeare and reverts to Arthur Brooke's long-winded narrative poem. The camera travels across the city to a university cafeteria where Romeo studies pharmacy, when not at wild fraternity parties so notorious that Juliet's father has forbidden her to attend them. During a raucous street processional, Juliet falls in love with Romeo and rescues him from the scorn of the entire community as he does a parody of a bull fighter not ritually arraying but disarraying himself for work in the arena. A police commissioner (Prince Escalus) admonishes the boys for their rowdy behavior. Masquerading in drag, the fraternity brothers crash a sorority party that stands in for the Capulet ball, which vibrates to disco rather than to the stately Morisco of the Zeffirelli movie. At the ball, Juliet and Romeo exchange vows, though in English subtitles remote from Shakespeare: "*J*.:'I'm ignorant, retarded and boring';*R*.: 'Me, too, I'm neurotic, conceited, ungrateful'." After that, however, the language turns lyrical again and closer to its source with Juliet's impassioned declaration that her love is as "boundless as the sea" (2.2.133). While in Latinate style, baroque funeral rites for Tybalt (Tides) celebrate the cult of death, and Juliet's Nurse becomes a black woman, the potion scene remains, though in displaced form, as does the mourning at the mock death of Juliet. In the altered tomb scene Juliet whispers "O sinister divine peace," as haunting guitar music fills the soundtrack and a high-angle shot reveals the still bodies of the lovers artfully posed in the cellar of a ruin. The production exhibits a clarity and sharpness rarely seen on North American television. A good example of "other Shakespeare," it is unpretentious but serious drama, well done.

Another Portuguese-language production, Grisolli's *Otelo De Oliveira* (1984), re-appropriates *Othello* for the tale of Otelo and Denise, residents in a shanty town in Rio de Janeiro. Otelo leads a sambo band that is rife with jealousies, somewhat like the jazz band in the British *All Night Long* (1962) with Johnny Dankworth and Dave Brubeck (see chapter 9). A charismatically forceful black man plays a Iago with a deceptively soft face that twists on demand into terrifying malevolence. The rich soundtrack provides such special effects as the whirr of a rattlesnake to punctuate Iago's dialogue, while radical alterations accommodate the text to the *mise-en-scène* of a poverty-stricken Rio neighborhood. Otelo is a convincingly graceful and handsome, light-skinned man, married to a very fair Desdemona, who manages to be both virtuous and sexy, a tricky feat. Both Emilia, an agreeable black woman, and Cassio, a white man and a guitar player, make excellent quarry for the predatory Iago. A mysterious ring, which Otelo is of course inordinately fond of, replaces the most celebrated stage prop in history, the handkerchief. Like *Romeu e Julieta*, the movie has been thoroughly Latinized, as, for example, in its fascination with voodoo. A mysterious woman in white periodically appears to sacrifice tiny animals in front of a spooky altar ringed with leering, devilish creatures. As a pagan outsider obsessed with the "magic in the web" of his mother's handkerchief, Otelo seems to fit nicely into this ambiance. Like Shakespeare's formula at the Globe, the film offers complexity in the guise of simplicity.

Wirth's *Hamlet*

Germany and Sweden have also invested in major television Hamlets, whose scale has given them a crossover potential for theatrical release. Among these was *Der Rest Ist Schweigen* (1959), a modernized *Hamlet* directed by Helmut Käutner. Of greater interest internationally is Franz Wirth's *Hamlet* (1960), which was originally made for German television but which achieved such success that Hollywood director Edward Dmytryk bought it and arranged to dub in English dialogue, which sometimes created an egregious gap between the aural and the visual. The forthright star, Maximilian Schell, could easily have been cast in a Hollywood wartime propaganda movie as the "good" Wehrmacht officer, secretly opposed to the Nazi regime, who spares little French orphans, while Claudius (Hans Caninenberg) would qualify as the central-casting U-Boat commander especially keen on torpedoing Red Cross hospital ships. From all accounts, the producers rejected Maximilian Schell's request for subtitles, and instead went for the rather awkward dubbing.

Despite this technical problem, the movie contributes a fresh chapter to the history of filmed *Hamlet*s in presenting, if nothing else, a thoroughly unneurotic, emotionally stable, prince, who indeed can be envisioned as Ophelia's "glass of fashion and the mould of form" (3.1.153). On the surface, Schell's prince shows none of the emotional problems of Nicol Williamson's troubled, edgy Hamlet. Where Williamson parades his inner anxieties in outer histrionics, Schell conceals the inner turmoil with a controlled façade. Also original is Franz Schafheitlin's foolish Polonius who must consult a notebook to finish his famous advice to Laertes: "This above all: to thine own self be true, / And it must follow, as the night the day, / Thou canst not then be false to any man" (1.3.78).

The establishing shot showing two vacant thrones immediately underscores the director's concept of Hamlet as a play about politics, about the Grand Mechanism of power and struggle, an allegory easily connected to the post-war hostility between East and West Germany. As the camera pans around two vacant thrones set against a dark background, Rosencrantz's sycophantic speech to Claudius from the third act can be heard in voiceover: "The cess of majesty / Dies not alone, but like a gulf doth draw / What's near it with it" (3.3.15). According to Bernice Kliman, this speech on the Fall of Kings juxtaposed to the two thrones underscores the vulnerability of both Claudius and Hamlet, who will each fall victim to Elsinore's internal power struggle.[13] The camera will return to them again and again as symbols of political turmoil, until in the film's closing moments the dying Claudius strains unsuccessfully to remount the throne. A minimalist *mise-en-scène*, spartan in understatement, employs a symbolist style that Jane Howell used admirably in her BBC *The Winter's Tale* (1980). The late Lillian Wilds thought that the set becomes "unremittingly claustrophobic" and "there is perhaps no daylight, no world outside. Hamlet's world is completely circumscribed by blackness."[14] On the other hand, the set equally liberates by projecting oceans of implications beyond the narrow confines of its catwalks, stairs, and blocks. With superb lighting, the tightly framed faces of the characters in one and two and three shot endow the movie with the patina of a fine lithograph, virtually an exercise in portrait photography.

Director Wirth wrings miracles out of this unadorned set with Rolf Unkel's harsh, discordant musical score, and with such deft strategies as having Hamlet do the "To be or not to be" soliloquy with a close-up of his face cramped under a stairwell, as if confined behind bars: "Denmark's a prison" (2.2.243). At "Ay, there's the rub," Schell leaps up, symbolically unleashed from his bondage and prepared for action. The arrival of the players at Elsinore, when Hamlet openly admires the First Player (Adolf Gerstung), remains a memorable vignette in the film. When later, seated quietly, Hamlet speaks his "O, what a rogue and peasant slave am I!" (2.2.550), the contrast between his lack of a "cue for passion" and the player's passion born of trivia has never been better explicated. The tight framing has the effect of speeding up the action to diminish the sense of Hamlet's delaying in his quest for revenge. A "decisive prince" is a kind of oxymoron but Schell's Hamlet comes close to it, even in his callous treatment of a terrified Ophelia (Dunja Movar). Of course Schell's very certainty leaves the audience in uncertainty over whether he has missed out on the complicated emotional agenda locked away in Hamlet, or simply allowed it to simmer just below the surface. To answer that question, however, would be to demand the impossible, which is to pluck out the heart of Hamlet's mystery.

Lyth's *Hamlet*

Although made for Swedish television and shown with subtitles in North America on Station WYNC-TV, the Ragnar Lyth *Den tragiska historien om Hamlet, prinz av Danmark* (1984) also qualifies as a "crossover" film not only because it was originally made on 16mm but because, as Bernice Kliman says, "it aspires to the more varied life of a moving image on the large screen."[15] It is a truly bizarre *Hamlet*, not quite like any other and yet too close to the essence of Shakespeare's play for summary dismissal, throwing out an aura of being but not being *Hamlet*, as if all the characters had been filtered through some kind of a gauzy lens and emerged only partially recognizable but nevertheless certifiably themselves. By restating *Hamlet* in visual rather than aural terms, Lyth sets up a paradigm for the paradoxical destruction and reconstruction of a Shakespearean work in a foreign language and uncovers subtexts that might be lost to an Anglophone director.

For his filmic strategy, Lyth adroitly combines *mise-en-scène*, montage, and eccentric characterization. Instead of an establishing shot of a remote castle, the film opens with an elaborate montage showing routine domestic life at Elsinore. It is a shadowy, subdued world of labyrinthine corridors, flaring torches, and tolling bells, with intercutting between the watchmen and chefs who are preparing a feast for the wedding celebration of Gertrude and Claudius: "Thrift, thrift, Horatio, the funeral bak'd meats / Did coldly furnish forth the marriage tables" (1.2.179). To a sighing of wind and clanking of iron wheels, the shadowy, barely glimpsed, ghost terrifies Horatio, Marcellus and Barnardo on the battlements. A moon-faced Horatio rightly shivers at this dreadful spectacle, and three scenes before its proper place Marcellus utters the seminal line, "Something is rotten in the state of Denmark" (1.4.89), which is a verbal surrogate for the skipped establishing shot.

The opening montage quickly yields to the *mise-en-scène* of a great but decaying hall, an abandoned warehouse that once belonged to the Nobel dynamite factory.[16] Only unlike the emptiness of Tony Richardson's Roundhouse *Hamlet* or Franz Wirth's minimalist version, this set pulses with activity. A great fire flickers cheerfully at one end of the hall to enhance the convivial, house-party atmosphere. Claudius' courtiers dance, bowl, play chess, fence, or energetically chatter, perhaps exchanging court gossip. Children run happily about and a genial Claudius picks up one child and hugs him. Throughout the film, children serve as innocent foils to the corruption around them and rays of hope against a dark Kottian vision of despair. Claudius himself perpetually grins and smiles and chuckles, almost idiotically, as if Lyth had decided to build his whole character around Hamlet's observation that "one may smile, and smile, and be a villain!" (1.5.108). In this way, Frej Lindquist's Claudius projects the image of a man desperately reaching out to ingratiate himself with other human beings because he harbors deep within a searing guilt. He embodies Hamlet's original "guilty creature[s] sitting at a play" (2.2.589).

Way off by a window with his back turned to the camera lurks a painfully grumpy young man, who, of course, turns out to be Hamlet (Stellan Skarsgård). His costume and demeanor are pure grunge – a soiled white shirt, baggy black breeches, a woeful expression on his face and a shock of very long, unkempt hair badly in need of a shampoo. If Richardson's Hamlet is the angry young man of the Sixties, Lyth's is the heir apparent to the age of punk and grunge and crack. He only lacks a pierced nose. Cleverly, though, this is not the real Hamlet but the Hamlet of the antic disposition who is only masquerading as a lunatic to confound his mother and step-father. He is a Hamlet who is capable of extreme violence, a "crazy" young man not to be trifled with. Meanwhile Claudius briefs Voltemand (Tomas Laustiola) and Laertes (Dan Ekborg) for their mission, while the courtiers, silenced by the tinkling of a little bell, momentarily pause from their entertainments to listen. In a portent of imminent disaster, a little boy knocks over his chess set. A plump, buttoned-up Gertrude (Mona Malm) moves toward Hamlet to console him, while Claudius lectures his nephew on the foolishness of excessively grieving over his father's death: "'tis unmanly grief, / It shows a will most incorrect to heaven" (1.2.94). A sweet demure Ophelia (Pernilla Wallgren) hastens toward Hamlet's side and hands him a letter decorated with her trademark, a flower, transient in beauty and easily crushed by a cruel world. Later, she plays a flute while reclining on her bed in a plain unadorned room in the style of a Vermeer. Among all the bric-à-brac, a caged raven ominously reinforces the image of Denmark as a prison. By the end of the movie, Hamlet and Laertes thrust and parry in this same cavernous, all-purpose room, where the raven still presides, its hovering cage a reminder of man's fate.

Like any film maker into shock editing, Lyth makes bizarre juxtapositions. The virginal Ophelia accidentally opens a door to catch a sinful priest and servant *in flagrante delicto*; Ophelia's sacrificial drowning is intercut by panning over stacks of meats, breads, fruits, and stoups of wine set out for Laertes and Claudius' festive banquet, while a singer entertains with snatches of old lays; and a guileless little boy in pointing out the murderer in the play-within-the-play exposes the king's guilt. Other motifs range from the disgusting to the grotesque. When Claudius grasps the point of the play-within-a-play, he abruptly vomits all over everybody in sight, while shrill atonal wind instruments and percussion effects punctuate the panic and disorder in the court. A tight close-up of a swaying shred of clothing turns out to be the remnant of a garment worn by the drowned Ophelia, which Gertrude is bringing in to show to a stunned Laertes. Yorick's skull is no smoothly polished stage prop but a muddy horror that Hamlet spears through the eye socket with a twig. Ophelia's funeral drives home the full meaning of "maimed rites" (5.1.219), when Lyth unsparingly shows the dreadful outcome of the feud between Hamlet and Laertes. Ophelia's plain wooden coffin, followed by hooded, black-robed figures, out of some macabre *Totentanz*, is trundled on an ugly cart and dumped beside the open grave. The removal of the coffin lid exposes the corpse's eerily still body and bluish face. The priest and all mourners quickly turn away to flee when Laertes cries out "Must there no more be done?" Enraged by the priest's response that to do more would "profane the service of the dead," Laertes spits at the cleric. When Hamlet emerges and begins fighting with Laertes, they upset the open coffin and send Ophelia's body lurching out of it and gruesomely sprawling in the grave.

Lyth makes a major point over the change in Hamlet's personality after his return from the aborted trip to England. As everyone knows, the Hamlet of this last part of the play is 30 years old in contrast to the student prince of the earlier scenes, a puzzle that has never really been resolved. Back in Elsinore, the prince has discarded the long, stringy hair of a squalid hippie and reinvented himself as a crew-cut nordic avenger. The crazy Hamlet has metamorphosed into the killer Hamlet. Like the funeral scene, the duel scene again displays Lyth's gifts for imaginative staging. A grotesque mix of brutality and farce terminating in horror replaces the stately grandeur of the duel scene in Olivier's or Branagh's *Hamlet*. Gertrude voluntarily drinks from the poisoned cup to save her son from what she suspects is a murderous plot. Hamlet "moons" Laertes by turning his [clothed] bottom up at him and suggesting that he attack him there. The insulted Laertes lashes Hamlet across the buttocks with the poisoned sword and inflicts the fatal wound. Aware of his approaching death, Hamlet then slowly wriggles his sword through Claudius' neck until in close-up the point emerges on the other side. Blood spatters from the dying Claudius but his silly giggling never stops. Even knowing that he is a dead man, the king pathetically continues his childish efforts to charm people into loving him and implores his stony-faced courtiers for help. The expiring Hamlet ruthlessly pours the poisoned wine over the king's corpse and dies. In the background, the caged raven implacably observes all these lamentable events. When Horatio reads a letter implicating the king, the stony-faced courtiers walk away, having lost interest in the whole affair. It remains, one suspects, for men like Lyth to try to tell the tale "aright" and in doing so conjure up myriad fascinating details that the rest of us, who think we know the play, might never have thought of.

France: Cayette and Chabrol

The French film industry, which once led the world in film making until Hollywood usurped its hegemony, has never made a feature length "conventional" Shakespeare movie. Notwithstanding, in the silent era the French were among the very first, as we have seen, to film Shakespeare, and two French movies from the 1950s and 1960s, which are movies about making Shakespeare movies, interrogate with Gallic wit the unanswerable question, "But is it Shakespeare?" *Les amants de Verone* [*The Lovers of Verona*] (1949) was made in the Paris Studios-Cinema at Brillancourt and in the glass factory of Pauly & Co. in Venice. Directed by André Cayatte, the movie places *Romeo and Juliet* under a French gaze, while at the same time it creates one of those ironic structures where a "real" story unfolds within the "fictional" story. Like *West Side Story* essentially a modernization, it begins at a Venetian glass factory where location scouts from a company about to film *Romeo and Juliet* inspect the premises. Angelo, a handsome young glassblower, impudently makes a heart-shaped piece of glass for the voluptuous actress, Bettina. A foreshadowing mirror shot frames Bettina and Angelo in the same glass. The director explains to a friend,

Maglia, that he will film only interior shots in Venice; the rest of the film will be made in Verona on location. "Poor Shakespeare," says Maglia.

Increasingly then the movie self-referentially deals with movie making and the aesthetics of Shakespeare adaptation. On the movie set, the sissy actor cast as Romeo is too "giddy" to climb the balcony. Angelo (Serge Reggiani), hired as an extra, comes out of the ranks to stand in for the pusillanimous thespian, while the stand-in for Juliet is Georgia Maglia (Anouk Aimée), a daughter of the proud and haughty Maglia family, quite disdainful of simple glassblowers. From then on the plot thickens and curdles, as the head of the Maglia family is exposed as an ex-fascist judge with underworld connections, and in a wild shootout, Angelo is fatally wounded. The real-life dying lovers act out their tomb scene in the artificial world of a movie set, while Shakespeare's lines are spoken in voice-over and a stagehand closes the door to leave the set in darkness. Despite the inane plot, *Les amants* has powerful redeeming episodes in its *film noir* brooding, atmospheric representation of Venice and Verona. Romeo and Juliet have been displaced to a movie set, as if their myth could only be inscribed on the celluloid frames of film. There are splendid close-ups, one thinks of Carl Dreyer's *Passion of Joan of Arc* (1928), which reinforce the commentary on the destruction of youthful love and innocence in a corrupt and decaying European city.

New Wave film maker and *auteur,* Claude Chabrol, acclaimed in *Cahiers du Cinema*, directed yet another meta-cinematic French Shakespeare film, *Ophelia* (1962). Chabrol's admiration for Alfred Hitchcock once led him away from the film d'art movement and into making suspense movies, which may account for the frisson in *Ophelia*. Like Cayatte's *Les amants*, Chabrol's postmodernist, film-society movie critiques our unexamined assumptions about reality. The protagonist, Yvan, whose mother has recently remarried with his uncle, sees a poster for the Olivier *Hamlet* in a theatre lobby that undermines his ability to distinguish between Shakespeare's prince and Olivier's portrayal. The journalistic critics of the Sixties had little sympathy for this quirky film that gave no quarter to philistines. Surveying at least three planes of reality – the world of the village, the world of Yvan, and the world of a fabled Hamlet – there are multiple perspectives within each category. *Ophelia* therefore, while not itself literally Shakespeare's *Hamlet*, explores how versions of the play intersect with reality and resist clarification. The LeSurfs (Claudius and Gertrude) and LaGrange all inscribe their understanding of the village of "Erneeles" (Elsinore) into their own subtexts in protean and impenetrable ways. As a disciple of Jacques Derrida might say, "there is no outside" to their texts. Karen Newman has pointed out how *Ophelia* is primarily an exercise in perception, "a whimsical and half-heartedly frightening parody of the entire enterprise of adaptation, for Shakespeare himself repeated his *Hamlet* from some unknown ur-*Hamlet*."[17] Chabrol's movie not only explores the complicated patterns of intertextuality that lie behind the making of any Shakespeare movie but also reconfirms the elusiveness of the Shakespearean text.

The Soviet Union: Fried, Yutkevich, and Kozintsev

The most important European Shakespeare movies came, however, from the former USSR. Under socialism the Russian film industry flourished with the VGIK (All-Union State Institute of Film Making) training cadres of technicians, scenarists, and directors, who churned out hundreds of feature-length movies for the state-owned theatres. The downside was a demand for ideological conformity to doctrines of "socialist realism" (which film makers often subverted), but the upside was the liberation of the artists from "tickling commodity's" obsession with "the bottom line." An unrealistic and puritanical goal of "socialist realism" was to entertain the masses without resorting to the sex and violence of western film and television. For these films, the state apparently never sent a bill. One expert has even suggested that "reform" (i.e., counter-revolution) with its return to "tickling commodity," has done more than the old state-controlled apparatus to damage the film industry.[18] Shakespeare had always appealed to Russians on stage because of some innate need in the Russian soul for romanticism and depth of feeling. In the golden era for post-World-War Soviet film known as the "Thaw" after the death of Stalin, four major Shakespeare movies spoke to this need: Yakov Fried's *Twelfth Night* (1955), Sergei Yutkevitch's *Othello* (1955), Grigori Kozintsev's *Hamlet* (1964), and Kozintsev's *King Lear* (1969). There was also Yuli Raizman's *And What If It's Love?* (1962), which spun off from *Romeo and Juliet* as a film subversive of socialist realism.

Whatever its defects, Yakov Fried's rather stodgy *Twelfth Night* (1955) triumphs as spectacle with its vigor, enthusiasm, bounce, and extravagance. The sweeping vistas of the coast line, the elaborate interiors for Olivia's palace, the hunting scenes, the sumptuous costumes, the glittering cast, all recorded in lavish Sovcolor reflect the generosity of the old Soviet studio system. In the first indication of culture shock to come, as the credits roll, a troubadour jauntily perched in a window frame energetically sings a thoroughly Slavicized Elizabethan ballad. Throughout, singers like Feste and Sir Toby resolutely bellow away in Russian while stand-in English actors speak the dialogue in RP accents. The tolerably authentic storm at sea that strands Viola and Sebastian in Illyria erupts in a studio tank, but cinematically surpasses the Vitagraph silent that had Viola demurely wading ashore from the placid waters of Long Island's Great South Bay. This is a fantasy Illyria of great

18 A powerful Sergei Bondarchuk and elegant
Irina Skobtseva in Sergei Yutkevich's
"slavicized" version of *Othello* (USSR 1955).

white marble palaces, sweeping lawns, colorful hunting scenes, with actors
of a quintessentially Russian temperament notable for openness and generosity of spirit. The costumes remain conventionally Elizabethan and the outdoor settings make room for a noticeable equestrian influence, with Orsino (V.
Medvediev) mounted like some statue of a condottiere in an Italian renaissance
piazza.

If English-speaking audiences find the cultural codes embedded in Elizabethan comedy perplexing, there is no reason to expect less difficulty for
non-English speaking cadres. Esoteric puns are edited out, such as Feste's on
"hanging" and "colors": "He that is well hang'd in this world needs to fear
no colors" (1.5.5); or Maria's reference to "the new map, with the augmenta-
tion of the Indies" (3.2.79); or Sir Toby's "passy-measures" (5.1.200). Malvolio's
"cross-garters" have no more contemporary relevance than arcane tavern jokes
about "we three" (2.3.17). Doubly afflicted because he is dealing with a foreign
language, Fried understandably elected to glide along the surface of the text
and focus on familiar scenes that come across to audiences visually rather
than linguistically. Thus his charming Viola (Katya Luchko), who doubles as
Sebastian, eloquently pleads to a gorgeous blonde Olivia (Anna Larionova),
"Make me a willow cabin at your gate . . . / Write loyal cantons of contemned
love" (1.5.268). A robust Sir Toby (M. Yanshin) with a fierce guardsman's moustache thoroughly manipulates the ectomorphic Sir Andrew (G.Vipin) who is an
imbecile of spectacular dimensions; Malvolio (V. Merkuriev) makes a complete

ass of himself wooing Olivia in his cross-garters and yellow stockings; and a plump Maria (A. Lisyanskava) presides over her little entourage of Fabian, Sir Toby, and Sir Andrew. All these sketches follow in the play's stage tradition, especially since roguish Sir Toby, a diminished Falstaff who is the type of one of Lear's one hundred knights, shows traces of the underlying streak of meanness in a professional sponge and free-loader. As one reviewer remarked, however, despite the challenges of translation, "it is surprising how much of the spirit of the piece has survived."[19] To which it might be added that while the festive side, "What You Will," is undeniably present, the pre-Lenten side, the hidden liturgical codes for "Twelfth Night," which Feste sums up in his closing ballad of "With hey ho, the wind and the rain" (5.1.390), have been obscured in translation.

Sergei Yutkevich, the director of *Othello* (1955), possessed an extraordinary knowledge of Shakespeare film that ultimately led in 1973 to his scholarly *Shekspir I Kino* (*Shakespeare on Film*), which includes in-depth studies of work by Olivier, Welles, and Kozintsev. As reviewer Mark Pomar wrote, Yutkevich rejects the argument of "purists" that Shakespeare belongs entirely to the theatre and instead maintained that "Shakespeare's drama reveals its artistic richness when presented in different media: theatre, film, television," and insisted that "film is an heir to the Elizabethan theater."[20] With a score by Aram Khachaturian and translation by Boris Pasternak, the opulence of this romantic, virtually operatic, *Othello*, a sweeping costume drama, originally in SovColor but released in the west in Technicolor, reflects again the abundant budgets of the post-war VGIK era. The actor playing Othello (Sergei Bondarchuk), a stern-looking young man whose hair turns white after the smothering scene, had been designated an artist of the Soviet Union, and his Desdemona (Irina Skobtseva) had studied at Moscow's Art Theatre. Regrettably the dubbed-in, and badly out of synch, voices of English actors deprive western audiences of the rich Slavic timbre except for the songs that remain anachronistically but delightfully in Russian.[21] As A. H. Weiler wrote of the movie's virtues and defects: "Although it is beautifully housed and caparisoned, this Russian *Othello* is embarrassed by the gifts [*sic*] of tongues."[22]

Anthony Davies felt that Yutkevich gives us an *Othello* of "blue skies, open sea and spaciousness,"[23] far removed from the play's innate claustrophobia. Before the credits even roll, an establishing montage shows the beautiful Desdemona day dreaming. Standing beside a globe, she imagines Othello's "battles," "sieges," "moving accidents by flood and field," and life as a galley slave (1.3.130). Sea fights, land battles, and wretched galley slaves chained to their benches fill the screen. Reminiscent at times of the Orson Welles seainfused *Othello* at Mogador, long shots of clouds, sunsets, and crashing seas act as metaphors for the turmoil within the hearts of Othello and Desdemona, and reminders that in *Othello* the sea is always present, beginning with the tension when the Turkish fleet indulges in feinting tactics to confuse the Venetians, and continuing with the 1,400-mile voyage from Venice to Cyprus: "Tempests themselves, high seas, and howling winds" (2.1.68). The sense of space persists when Cassio takes on the entire watch in the drunken brawl scene with a swashbuckling sword fight on sweeping stone staircases: "Why, very well then; you must not think then that I am drunk" (2.3.118), or when the camera tracks Othello debarking at Cyprus and trotting up a dizzy flight of stairs to the top parapet, where he breathlessly cries out to Desdemona, "O my fair warrior!" (2.1.182).

For all this virtuoso skill with macro effects, Yutkevich shows equal competence with the micro shot. Tightly framed close-ups during Othello's defense against Brabantio's charges at the palace inspect the sculptured faces of the Duke of Venice, Brabantio, Lodovico, and Iago (Andrei Popov), as well as the blonde Slavic beauty of Desdemona. The editing includes rhythmical cross-cutting and reaction shots, like one of wide-eyed Venetian children staring up at the charismatic Moor in awe. A well with a reflecting pool of water becomes a focal point when Iago plots his diabolical schemes: "I'll have our Michael Cassio on the hip" (2.1.305). First clearly reflected in the still water, his face suddenly dissipates in a swirl of ripples. At a decisive moment for Othello, the same pool of well water mirrors his face until the moment of extreme distress when the rippling water disrupts his image "Confess? Handkerchief? O devil!" (4.1.43). Along the sea shore, Iago tempts Othello in the midst of a tangle of fishing nets, metaphors for the villainous scheme to ensnare Othello in his web. As a micro-study, the handkerchief scene excels in ingenuity with the right side of the frame showing only Desdemona's fair white profile and the empty space on the left being occupied by the Moor's contrasting black hand. The black hand punctuates his terse demands for "The handkerchief!" (3.4.92), while his bewildered wife unwittingly fuels the fire by blithering on about the virtues of Michael Cassio. Feminists will object to Yutkevich's omission of Emilia's low opinion of men: "They eat us hungerly, and when they are full / They belch us" (3.4.165), though with a Iago for a husband she must have often seen the darker side. Again, in the smothering scene, in an over-the-shoulder shot showing only Othello's broad back, Desdemona lies terrified on the bed framed between Othello's two black hands while he menacingly advances on her.

As a film made in the shadow of "socialist realism," the play's sub-textual elements rarely surface in this reworking in a tragic key of the old commedia scenario about a January–May marriage. In both appearance and ideology, the production might have qualified for a grand nineteenth-century staging at the Moscow Art Theatre. As with Fried's *Twelfth Night*, there are no hidden agendas, no Freudian innuendoes, no leering hints of homoeroticism between Iago and Othello. In the three-way triangle of Othello, Iago, and Desdemona, Popov's nondescript Iago suffers from comparison with the charismatic Sergei Bondarchuk's Othello, who in low angle towers over his crafty lieutenant, until his perfidious underling in turn emotionally subjugates him. Desdemona remains as Shakespeare envisioned her, pure as the driven snow, innocent and unspotted, free from any kind of nasty suspicions about her relationship with Cassio. Leavisite arguments about whether Othello was destroyed by his own weakness or by Iago's fiendish scheming resemble the old riddle about the distinction between the dancer and the dance, but the vivid portrayals of Othello's epileptic fits suggest that Othello's handicap helped Iago along.

At the end, after Othello utters the hypnotic, "Put out the light, and then put out the light" (5.2.7), and after he smothers the sacrificial Desdemona, Bondarchuk achieves heights of ostensive acting equalled perhaps only by Emil Jannings in the 1922 silent *Othello*. As he approaches the great curtained bed, the lighting further accentuates the fury in his eyes until he seems literally to be flashing fire, his eyeballs electrified. In a compelling interpretation of the "tragic loading of this bed" (5.2.363), Othello then carries Desdemona's limp body in his arms, like King Lear with Cordelia, up winding stone stairs to the castle's battlement. Atop the parapet overlooking the sea and a craggy promontory, he confronts Lodovico and the other Venetians, before ending his life with all the majesty and dignity of a great opera star projecting a glorious aria, like Placido Domingo in Zeffirelli's film of *Otello* (1986). "Then must you speak / Of one that lov'd not wisely but too well" (5.2.343). In a budget-breaking exterior shot, Lodovico sails back to Venice with the enshrined bodies of the two lovers, and with the wretched Iago pinioned to the mast high aloft. The sumptuous *mise-en-scène* of Yutkevich's *Othello* underscores the magnificence of the Othello story but muffles the squalid underside that Orson Welles caught so well with his schizophrenic camera angles. Heroically amplified, this *Othello* aspires to reach some past idealized peak of high mimetic western tragedy.

While Fried and Yutkevich's *Twelfth Night* and *Othello* occupy important niches in the history of Russian Shakespeare movies, Grigori Kozintsev's *Hamlet* (1964) and *King Lear* (1969) have been widely nominated, along with Akira Kurosawa's Japanese adaptations, as the most effective translations of Shakespeare into a foreign language. Preparation for his Shakespeare movies, which were both supplied with Russian translations by Boris Pasternak and epic musical scores by Dmitri Shostakovich, started in 1941 when Kozintsev directed a stage version of *Hamlet* at the Pushkin Academic Theatre in Leningrad, and of *King Lear* at the city's Bolshoi Drama Theatre. Kozintsev has also published two book-length meditations on his Shakespeare movies,[24] in one of which he discusses "Hamletism," the phenomenon by which a whole conglomerate of legends, expectations, myths, conventions accrue to the popular image of Prince Hamlet like barnacles to a ship's hull. Such a "phantom text" emerged in the nineteenth century when Jules Laforgue popularized Goethe's romantic portrait of Hamlet as a delicate, tender prince, "an oak tree planted in an exquisite vase."[25] The image of this "black plume" Hamlet, so-called because it became a stage convention for Hamlet to wear a black plume on his headpiece,[26] created an "expectational text"[27] for audiences who imagined Hamlet should always look that way. Kozintsev rejected this stereotype of a fragile Danish prince filled with "doubt, vacillation, split personality, and the predominance of reflection over will to action."[28]

Kozintsev's Hamlet (Innokenti Smoktunovsky) consequently emerges as anything but a "black plume" prince; instead he is a throwback to a presumably more activist Elizabethan *Gestalt.* He is so virile and decisive that his struggle against Claudius and Polonius has been allegorized as an Aesopian attack on Stalin,[29] whose death in 1953 had brought about a "thaw" in the film industry. When this Hamlet dies, Fortinbras' celebration of his soldierly qualities is privileged over Horatio's christening of him as "a sweet prince." Kozintsev's interpretation of Hamlet is neither Freudian, like Olivier's; nor absurdist, like Lyth's; nor embittered, like Richardson's, but is rather an existentialist engagement with the world around it. In the dialectic of "to be" or "not to be," Kozintsev's prince chooses the former. Kozintsev's sharply etched black-and-white sets alternate between a subdued expressionism and a dynamic realism. Images of stone, fire, and water provide recurring tropes. The obsession with stone, which is a Kozintsev hallmark derived from his passion for Japanese formal gardens, signifies the obdurate forces arrayed against Hamlet; fire stands for the volatile passions in the court at Elsinore; and the sea figures forth the timeless ebb and flow of the natural order of things. These cosmic images then enclose the puny human action within the prison of the castle. Vistas of the sea, castle walls, black flags of mourning, galloping horses, a huge portcullis with iron teeth, and a tolling bell replace the traditional opening on the battlements. On a realistic note, scene two begins with a herald reading announcements from a scroll to the assembled people outside the castle wall. His words have been transposed from Claudius' speech: "Therefore our sometime sister, now our queen" (1.2.8). It is as if Claudius had hired a public relations agent to mediate between himself and the common people, who play a vital role as silent spectators in Kozintsev's Shakespeare movies. Shakespeare himself shows Claudius' sensitivity to, and fear of, public opinion when he mentions to Laertes how much love "the general gender bear him [Hamlet]" (4.7.18). And this Hamlet is surrounded by prying and snooping courtiers, while poor Ophelia (Anastasia Vertinskaya) can never escape from the surveillance of her clutch of shriveled duennas.

The film's kinetic flow comes out of the rhythmical cutting back and forth between the expressionistic castle exteriors and the relative light and warmth of the realistic interiors. For example, when Hamlet in the blackness encounters the ghost of his father, the ghost remains an ominous, hovering figure with an enormous black cape that swirls and flutters in the darkness against a backdrop of stone and crashing seas. When the stocky, forty-ish Smoktunovsky as Hamlet insists on obeying the ghost's summons despite the frantic protests of his retainers, he breaks away from them saying "My fate cries out . . . I say away" (1.4.81). The actors internalize the words and then energize them by writhing and twisting and turning and gesticulating in their efforts to hold back a Hamlet who is about to be symbolically separated forever from ordinary men. In a terrifying mini-second, Hamlet shows how desperate he is to know his fate, at all costs, and the rhythm of the scene like a flash of lightning illuminates the metaphysics of Hamlet's damnable but wonderful election as the agent of both "heaven and hell" (2.2.584). Kozintsev resists the temptation to illustrate the ghost's narrative by showing the poisoning but later he interpolates a lengthy sequence about Hamlet's sea voyage to England and his hoisting of Rosencrantz and Guildenstern on their own petards. Somewhere in the midst of all this perturbation, the Grim Reaper appears as a carved figure on an elaborate mechanical clock. A quick cut follows to the raucous festivity inside the castle as Claudius and Gertrude in high spirits celebrate their nuptials, surrounded by candle light and sycophants clad in the ornate finery of the Elizabethan era. The *memento mori* haunts the festivity.

Shostakovich's exalted musical score punctuates Hamlet's second encounter with his father's ghost in the bed chamber, which resists a descent into sexual horseplay. In yet another episode, Hamlet begins his "O, what a rogue and peasant slave am I! / Is it not monstrous that this player here" (2.2.550), while the First Player (A. Chekaerskii) is still passionately reciting his passage from Aeneas' tale to Dido about the fall of Troy ("Now is he total gules, horridly trick'd / With blood of fathers, mothers" (2.2.457)). In the very loftiest traditions of the mysterious First Player role, Chekaerskii sets a standard for all the other actors in the play. If there is such a thing as a Russian soul, he embodies it with his flair for expressing the inexpressible sorrows of the human condition. It's a style completely beyond the range of earnest American MFA theatre graduates, and maybe even RSC actors as well. After the king cries out for light, the mouse trap scene ends in catastrophe with a great commotion and swirling of the entire court, which literally falls apart, courtiers rushing this way and that way. At the peak of the hubbub, the symphonic score reinforces the action with a bravura crashing and thudding of strings, horns, and drums. And there is the innovation of having Gertrude (Elza Radzin-Szolkonis) arrive

19   Innokenti Smoktunovsky as Hamlet in Grigori Kozintsev's 1964 film ponders over Yorick's skull in a macabre but nostalgic moment in the famous graveyard scene.

late for the duel so that she can in no way be privy to her husband's nefarious plot with Laertes to poison Hamlet.

The film's most strikingly original contribution to the Hamlet legend, though, may be the probing portrait of Ophelia as an innocent and pathetic victim of both her father and Hamlet. She is first seen dancing like a mechanical doll to the tune of a tinkling child's music box. Later, when being prepared by her swarm of attendants to attend her father's funeral, she is ceremonially encased in an iron corset and farthingale like a bullfighter being prepared to go into the ring, and then draped over like a dressmaker's dummy with a gauzy black gown, both body and soul being symbolically imprisoned. Always elegantly turned out in the tyranically stiff costumes of the Elizabethan era, she wears a pendant with an eastern orthodox cross. A recurring shot of a lone gull flying over the sea sums up the estrangement that she ironically shares with Hamlet. At her burial in the cemetery, silhouetted in the background is a broken cross that parodies the unbroken cross she wore in life. The giggling idiot of a gravedigger (V. Kolpakor) achieves sublimity as a surly lout, his banter with Hamlet sounding gruff and compelling even in the terse subtitles of the American release. As a final insult, the knave insolently hammers nails into the flimsy lid of Ophelia's cheap wooden coffin. Ironically the wronged Ophelia's debasement in death, her "maimed rites," as it were, contrasts with Hamlet's ennoblement as Fortinbras' four captains bear his body aloft up the sweeping stone stairways. This is the man who has helped to destroy Ophelia and whose ineptness as an avenger has caused multiple deaths. Such a bleak interpretation, however, remains unexplored in this movie for it would subvert Kozintsev's central goal, which is to make a film of *Hamlet* that enlarges rather than diminishes the human spirit.

After *Hamlet*, Kozintsev plunged into his exhaustive work on *King Lear* (1969), this despite his sense that as a play with no "ultimate interpretation"[30] it was a text to be wrestled with, like Jacob with the river god. With origins in Marxist meliorism rather than in Kottian pessimism, the movie looks more optimistically on the human condition than its western rival, Peter Brook's *King Lear*, which was made at almost the same time. It rejects political dogma in favor of a generalized humanitarianism (not humanism). Quite reasonably a Soviet critic concluded that it went no further ideologically than denying that "cruelty, violence, and callousness are innate qualities of man" and simply expresses "anger at anything that tramples upon human decency."[31] Like Kozintsev's *Hamlet*, however, it profoundly "Russianizes" Shakespeare's script. By that I mean plot, characters, and *mise-en-scène* are saturated in a Slavic sensibility made up of Boris Pasternak's translation of Shakespeare's language into the sonorities of Russian, Dmitri Shostakovich's powerful musical score, and the cherished acting traditions of the Russian theatre. The huge screen allows the action to flow out into infinity.

Kozintsev thought *Hamlet* almost cheerful by contrast with *King Lear*. He wrote of the latter play that "suffering passes over the whole world like a spasm and even the rocks have split and fallen in ruins . . . It is an unfriendly, ruined and distorted world: there is nothing to eat, nowhere to sit and nowhere to shelter; a mean, cruel and heartless nature."[32] Nevertheless Kozintsev squeezes some hope out of hopelessness by identifying his mad king with the struggles of humanity in general. The cryptic establishing shot wallows in suffering as in close-up hundreds of poorly shod peasant feet clump up a bleak, stark, rock-strewn hillside. The people wear rags. There is a low chanting, more like a moaning, on the soundtrack. Some trundle pathetic belongings on a crude wooden cart. A scrawny child and a legless man on a home-made go-cart appear. The people struggle painfully uphill, and others join them, until a throng of suffering humanity covers the hillside. In long shot is a castle. On a steep staircase leading up to the stone walls of the castle stand Gloucester, Kent, and Edmund, surveying the masses beneath them. The subtitles tell us that the Russian voices are saying, "I thought the king had more affected the Duke of Albany than Cornwall" (1.1.1). The empowered noblemen stand high above the disempowered masses, who stare up at them awe-struck.

The hillside was no accident. Kozintsev painstakingly searched and searched for just the right location, finally discovering it on the Kazantip promontory bordering the Azov Sea, which connects with the larger Black Sea and the Crimean archipelago. "A film landscape," Kozintsev wrote "is concealed, hidden under another sort of covering . . . you do not so much see it as feel it." The landscape that he chose was "the world after the catastrophe."[33] In his remarkable book on the making of *King Lear*, Kozintsev meditates on the mystical experience of contemplating a stone one hot August day in an exquisite Kyoto temple garden. He tells of feelings at the Hiroshima museum, of Noh drama, of the influence of Meyerhold, of Brecht, of Zen, of his own association in the early Twenties with Sergei Yutkevich in FEKS ("The Factory of the Eccentric Actor"), and remarks on the grotesqueries of Gogol and probings of Dostoyevsky.[34] His Shakespeare movies grow out of all these influences, as well as the rich cultural lode nurtured by Russia's temporal and spatial vastness.

The depressing beggars at the beginning of his movie, who replace the surly faces of the 100 knights in the Brook film, embody the wretched of the earth, the "Internationale's" "prisoners of starvation." The landscape, in John Collick's view, becomes "a blank page that can reflect a person's state of consciousness."[35] Brook's movie ignored the disempowered; Kozintsev's serves notice that lowly feet may challenge the hegemony of the arrogant head, which comes very close to the Christian belief that the meek will inherit the earth. As in *Hamlet*, fire is a recurring motif. There is the fireplace near the king during the division of the kingdom scene; the flaming torches in the king's train of carts; the army campfires; the searing tar catapulted at the fort; and a gutted city that resembles Hiroshima. A scribe intones the royal decree, the family enters a cavernous room with light and shadows flickering from the roaring flames in the stone hearth, the women's heels click and pound on the floor. The fire is associated with warfare just as Cordelia is associated with water. As Jack J. Jorgens observes, the fire "seen first in the domestic hearth . . . is soon blazing from the castle walls and in the end destroying the whole kingdom."[36]

The daughters and the courtiers move decisively, rapidly. Heralded by the tinkling of the Fool's tiny bell, the frail old king (Yuri Yarvet) comes through the door light-heartedly, laughing over a joke, and he removes a Noh-like mask from his face before warming his hands over the fire. The mask, a talisman of Kozintsev's interest in Japanese drama, foreshadows the unmasking of the king's pretensions to power and authority, as he progresses in Aristotelian terms from a self-deceived *alazon* to a painfully aware *eiron*. He initially stands high on the castle parapet denouncing his own daughter before the assembled populace, and at the end he returns to the same pinnacle, only this time heartbroken, grieving over the loss of his daughter and appealing forlornly to his subjects for support: "O, [you] are men of stones!" (5.3.258). A harrowing wail satisfies Shakespeare's, "Howl, howl, howl!," a line Marvin Rosenberg describes as a projection of "suffering too fierce for verbalizing" that has been interpreted by various actors as "an anguished cry," "a quiet sobbing," "a deep baying," "the wail of a wolf," a "mourning dog, and even an indignant demand for response from the men of stone."[37]

Not even a native speaker of Russian, Estonian Yuri Yarvet's casting as King Lear came about almost by accident when he was originally auditioned for the role of Fool. A most unlikely looking King Lear, grizzled and withered, not at all a majestic Frederick B. Warde type, Yarvet's repressed power boils over when it is finally released. The opening scene records the intensity and anxiety in the faces of Regan, Goneril, Albany, over the impending division of Lear's kingdom. The old king remains near the fire, warming his aged bones, and Goneril (E. Radzins) speaks first, flattering the king: "Sir, I love you more than [words] can wield the matter" (1.1.54). Next comes Regan (G. Volchek) her head muffled, for her ritual speech of obeisance. Only Cordelia's (Valentina Shendrikova) face is serene, untroubled. Her aside is on the soundtrack, "What shall Cordelia speak? Love and be silent" (1.1.62). She stands alone, a figure in white surrounded by black. Nothing prepares anybody for the king's sudden explosion of rage. "Thy truth then be thy dow'r!" he says (1.1.108), which somehow sounds more menacing for having emerged from the mouth of such

20   Yuri Yarvet as her remorseful and
devastated father cradles the hanged Cordelia
in his arms in *King Lear*, directed by Grigori
Kozintsev (USSR 1969).

a gaunt human being. The helpless map becomes the target of the king's wrath.
He snatches it up, rends it, twists it this way and that way, moves it back and
forth, shakes it and rattles it so fiercely that it sounds like distant thunder. He
tosses it away, a spoiled and shriveled symbol of his lost hopes. Crying out,
"Call France. Who stirs? / Call Burgundy" (1.1.126), he aims yet another kick
at it. Ironically the map disorients rather than orientates the king. To ward
off the disaster, Kent (V. Emelyanov) clings to the map but the king spits at
him. In Russian, his scolding sounds especially ferocious: "Hear me, recreant"
(1.1.165). The very earth trembles.

The aural dissonance upsets the imperturbability of the human figures, who
have until now looked like the subjects in an engraving, faces chiseled from
stone. The rapid movement begins again. The king vigorously marches off. A
complicated tracking shot follows him through the palace, into the stables, his
retinue skipping along behind him, past magnificent horses, beautiful hounds,
setters, greyhounds, and falcons. He ascends stairs, shows himself to the people, who look up. The people kneel in low angle. Lear stands above on the
parapet. Music comes up and achieves a crescendo. This king having achieved
the apex of his power stands at the edge of a precipice for the inevitable fall.
The editing reinforces the severing of the bond between father and daughter
with a cut to Cordelia and France being blessed by a priest before setting off
for the continent with their retinue of cavalry and carriages.

There are startling vignettes. Regan in a white heat to possess Edmund tears
off his clothing, only shortly later to plant an erotic kiss full on the lips of
Cornwall's corpse. Kozintsev's *découpage*, the quick cuts, display the hanged

Cordelia dangling obscenely high above the castle walls. Murky pools of fetid water suggest both everything and nothing. Kozintsev's Fool does not disappear at the end of the third act ("And I'll go to bed at noon" (3.6.85)) but reappears to help comment on the desperate condition of humanity. A funeral cortège bears the bodies of the fallen while the Fool (now transformed into a Russian village idiot) sits amidst the rubble grieving over the loss of his master and of his own identity. And just as the film begins with the sense of a social order, of people relating to a king, it ends with the old king not isolated and alone, not falling out of the frame with a blank nothingness behind him, as in the Frederick Warde and Peter Brook *King Lears*, but rather with the king surrounded by friends. He calls out *"Nyet! Nyet! Nyet!"* over and over again. A man douses a fire. The camera tracks back to reveal that the forlorn weeping comes from the Fool, who plays his flute among the ashes, the same shrill flute featured at the beginning. The cortège winds through the ruined villages, where there are signs of restoration as a man attempts to raise the joist on a ruined house. Edgar (L. Merzin) moves forward but there is silence. A fertile field is superimposed on the carnage. A sign of hope? Images have conveyed meanings that words cannot express. Kozintsev has shared with Shakespeare "the image of that horror." Years ago a reviewer hit the mark when he wrote that the film "reconstructs [a] hellish vision not in the easy, fashionably austere styles of today but in visual terms one imagines would have been acceptable to the author. Is there any higher praise?"[38]

Japan: Akira Kurosawa

Among makers of "foreign" Shakespeare movies, Japan's late Akira Kurosawa has been as much acclaimed as Russia's Grigori Kozintsev, particularly for *Throne of Blood* (or *The Castle of the Spider's Web*) (1957), and *Ran* (1985). *Throne of Blood* has been aptly described as a transformation rather than an adaptation of *Macbeth*; and *Ran*, though it draws less directly than *Throne of Blood* on its Shakespearean prototype, clearly adapts motifs and situations from *King Lear*. Since the 1853 arrival of Commodore Perry, the Japanese, despite the inherent difficulties of translation, have experimented with a variety of Shakespearean productions ranging from Kabuki and Noh-style adaptations to *shingeki*, "translations of European plays staged in western style."[39] Director Yukio Ninagawa's recent Japanese language *Hamlet* (1998), staged at London's Barbican Centre, exhibited a verve and boldness that made most western productions of the tragedy seem pale and timid by comparison. A third Kurosawa movie, less well known in the West, *The Bad Sleep Well* (1960), a modernized *Hamlet*, very loosely adapts the Hamlet story but nevertheless usefully serves as a springboard for looking at the synergy joining Shakespeare and Kurosawa. As James Goodwin has shown, Kurosawa's "intertextual cinema"[40] ransacks Western and Japanese culture for its music and art, as well as for the existentialism and absurdism of Dostoevsky and Gorki, all of which affects his Shakespearean adaptations. Kurosawa, while intensely Japanese, is therefore paradoxically not solely a Japanese film maker. On the other hand important Japanese scholars like Professor Yoshio Arai see all three of Kurosawa's Shakespeare films as having been "entirely acceptable and comprehensible to the Japanese audience as Japanese films."[41]

The Bad Sleep Well turns out to be a *film noir* thriller about big business and corruption in postwar Japan in the tradition of *gendai-mono* ("modernstory films")[42] with overtones from *Hamlet,* though Kurosawa has himself denied any particular influence from Shakespeare. The intricate plot is of less importance here than the thematic parallels to Shakespeare, but, briefly, what happens is that a young business man, Nishi (Toshiro Mifune), sets out to avenge the death of his father, Furuya, who was forced into a staged suicide. To achieve his goal by craft, Nishi plays a variation on Hamlet's "antic disposition" by assuming the identity of a friend, Itakura (who loosely corresponds to Horatio). The scenario veers wildly away from *Hamlet* when Nishi marries Kieko (Ophelia), the daughter of Vice-President Iwabuchi (Claudius/ Polonius). Kieko's brother, Tatsuo, resembles Laertes; Wada and Shirai, subordinate executives who come between the "mighty opposites" of Nishi and Iwabuchi, correspond to Rosencrantz and Guildenstern; and the obliging Moriyama, always available to spy for his boss, resembles Reynaldo. In a space as claustrophobic as Elsinore, they are constantly under surveillance or lost in a maze of deceptions or foundering in a sea of self-doubt. The nexus between Kurosawa's and Shakespeare's artistry lies in a common vision of reality as a fugue-like interplay between conflicting and inexorable forces.

A case could be made that even if Akira Kurosawa had never heard of *Hamlet, Macbeth,* or *King Lear,* he would still have made movies that seemed to echo them in their indeterminacy, their tantalizing interplay between illusion and reality, their focus on usurped authority. From *Rashomon* (1950) to *Throne of Blood* (1957), *The Bad Sleep Well* (1960), *The Shadow Warrior* (*Kagemusha*) (1980), and the more recent *Dreams* (1990), Kurosawa plays variations on the theme of the equivocal nature of reality, the gap between the seen and unseen, between the false and the real. "Seems, madam? nay, it is, I know not 'seems' " (1.2.76), says Hamlet to Gertrude in the quintessential assertion of what is not just Hamlet's but his creator's *modus operandi.* Kurosawa, as Donald Richie notes,[43] is more of a social observer than an activist. Shakespeare likewise, as John Keats realized, is by his temperament blessed, or afflicted, with *Negative Capability,* which allowed him to live with "uncertainties, mysteries, doubts without any irritable reaching after fact and reason."[44] This willingness to describe rather than prescribe the way of the world links the two men even over centuries.

The Japanese are second to none in their willingness to spend a fortune on a wedding. The elaborate wedding reception in a luxury hotel for Nishi and Kieko (Kyoko Kagawa) at the opening has been cited as a triumph of cinematic narration. In twenty-three minutes of screen time, it compresses Nishi's relationship with his new father-in-law, the deep corruption in the business community, and the strange death of Nishi's father. Every frame reflects motifs of confinement, surveillance, and claustrophobia, all reminiscent of the "prison," which is Hamlet's Denmark. Characters are framed between, or through, the configurations of right angles in windows, doorways, shop display-windows, stairwells. In an instance of Kurosawa's frequent use of western music, the powerful wedding march from *Lohengrin* heralds the arrival of Nishi's bride, who is hemmed in by the formally attired guests. An intrusive tight framing exposes how the bride's *zori* (slipper) is raised to compensate for her lameness. The bride's stumble foreshadows disasters to come, yet ironically the non-diegetic theme music abruptly shifts to the light-hearted Strauss piece, "The Voices of Spring." A gaggle of newspaper reporters peering at the wedding reception through the frame of the wide entrance hall can hardly wait to sensationalize a scandal involving a corporation executive who will soon be arrested and dragged out of the party in disgrace. They constitute an "onstage" audience watching another audience, the wedding guests, who are about to be treated to a play-within-a-play, a "dumb show" as Marion Perret has called it.[45] The "dumb show," it develops, is a wedding cake molded in the shape of the building from which Nishi's father was forced through a window. The reporters also vestigially act as the Japanese *benshi*, an all-purpose narrator who explained events onstage to any in the audience fearful of missing out on details.[46]

As Nishi, the ubiquitous Toshiro Mifune, Kurosawa's favorite actor, wears spectacles and western morning attire in contrast to his usual action-hero roles in costume dramas, such as the bandit Tajomaru in *Rashomon* (1950), the gruff Kikuchiyo in *The Seven Samurai* (1954), the beleaguered Washizu in *Throne of Blood* (1957), and the samurai bodyguard in *Yojimbo* (1961). The eyeglasses serve the double function of converting the samurai-like Mifune into a corporate bureaucrat and underscoring the underlying motif of surveillance. Richie comments on Kurosawa's iteration of this bias toward glasses, mirrors, etc., in *Ikuru* (1952): "Enormous use is made of mirrors, reflecting surfaces, the shiny tops of automobiles, prisms – all those things which reflect (distort) reality."[47] Fog and mist mask reality in *Throne of Blood*; the Noh-like mask of Kaede's face in *Ran* conceals her fiendish desire for revenge on her husband's Ichimonji clan. Cigarettes often swathe the characters in smoke, all of whom seem hopelessly addicted. Nishi smokes, Nonaka smokes, Iwabuchi smokes, Itakura smokes. Smoke turns to fog and mist when Wada attempts suicide at the crater of a live volcano. The clouds and mist suggest the battlements at Elsinore when Nishi appears, ghost-like, out of the fog to implicate Wada in the revenge plot.

In a trope echoing Hamlet's confrontation with Gertrude, Nishi forces Shirai to examine a picture of his late father as a way of clarifying the enormity of his crime. Nishi like Hamlet then discovers that "conscience [i.e., "reflection"] does make cowards [of us all]" (3.1.82). As a "thoughtful avenger," Nishi turns into a walking oxymoron. His father-in-law Iwabuchi reacts to Nishi's non-action by murdering him in a staged automobile accident. Itakura's hysterical description of how Nishi was set up for the faked car wreck by being injected with alcohol corresponds to Horatio's last words about Hamlet. To complicate things, Nishi's friend, Itakura, turns out to be the real Nishi. The labyrinthine plot keeps returning, though, to the epistemological issue of the equivocal nature of truth. At the end the bad, the wicked, still flourish, for in a world of smoke and mirrors few can see through pretense into the world's inherent evil. The rest of us may squirm and turn at night, but the bad still sleep well.

Identical motifs to those found in *The Bad Sleep Well* also surface in the far better known *Throne of Blood*. Forty years ago, J. Blumenthal declared that "Akira Kurosawa's *Throne of Blood* (1957) is the only work…that has ever completely succeeded in transforming a play of Shakespeare's into a film."[48] Blumenthal's bold thesis has been a mantra ever since for eminent persons like Roger Manvell,[49] Peter Brook,[50] Peter Hall,[51] and Robert Hapgood.[52] Without in any way denigrating Kurosawa's achievement, the anti- Anglophone bias here should be warily inspected. It's like the snobbish preference for foreign imports over domestic cars, or it smacks of an Ahab-like search for the white whale of the pure film, the invention of sound having in some Luddite way been declared a disaster for movies. Yet movie makers, as we have seen, have always yearned for spoken dialogue, have struggled for it, and Edison only dabbled with films to find an accompaniment for his phonograph invention, not the other way around. As dissident John Gerlach has asserted, the problem of graphically expressing Shakespeare's language actually eludes *Throne of Blood*. It ignores the iterative images of blood in *Macbeth*, and diminishes Macbeth's stature (Washizu) because of his over-dependency on Lady Macbeth (Asaji).[53]

In *Throne of Blood*, as in *The Seven Samurai*, Kurosawa not only draws on the same unique perspectives that informed *The Bad Sleep Well* but also nests traces of the classic western movie inside the cultural codes of Japan's Noh drama. Unlike *The Bad Sleep Well, Throne of Blood* as a costume drama belongs to the genre of *jidai-geki* ("period pictures"). As Anthony Davies has said, the graphics of the movie oscillate between the vertical lines of the forest and the horizontal lines of the rooms within the castle.[54] Geometrical patterns of circles and angles function metaphorically for the ways in which the worlds of man and nature interact to destroy the overreaching Washizu. Kurosawa frames his film with the forest at the beginning and ending. The film opens in the fogbound forest with a lugubrious off-camera Noh-style chanting about the folly of ambition, which translates as: "men are vain and death is long." A wounded soldier (Bleeding Sergeant) reports to Kuniharu (Duncan) on the heroism of Washizu (Macbeth) and Miki (Banquo) in defeating the rebels. Kuniharu orders the execution of the rebel leader (Thane of Cawdor). The action moves to the deep forest where in a famous scene, thoroughly analyzed by Jack J. Jorgens,[55] Washizu and Miki have become hopelessly lost in the tangled undergrowth and mist. An occasional shaft of sunlight illuminates how what is fair can also be foul. Their frenetic galloping back and forth from left to right and then from right to left illustrates what Stephen Prince sees as an example of another Kurosawa signature, fascination with "the dynamics of motion," in this instance embodied in "lateral motion across the frame."[56] Marsha Kinder further points out how motion is then set off intermittently against its opposite, stasis, in such immobile figures as Asaji (Lady Macbeth), who in Noh style barely breathes.[57] The two samurai encounter a ghostly white figure hunched over a spinning wheel (the Witches) inside a ramshackle hut. Some kind of arbiter of fate, like the Greek Clotho, the old crone equivocally predicts both success and failure, namely that Washizu will rule the Forest Castle but that one day Miki's son, Yoshiteru (Fleance), not Washizu's, will inherit the dominion. The witch's makeshift hut ironically counterpoints the brazen strength of the fortress that Washizu will rule over. In a further irony, it is the forest that will finally win out over the fortress when Birnan wood comes to Dunsinane.

After Kuniharu installs Washizu as Master of the Fort, events unfold very much along the lines of Shakespeare's play, though they have been displaced from tenth-century Scotland to Japan's "Sengoku period of civil wars (1467–1568) when there were frequent incidents of *gekokujo*, the overthrow of a superior by his own retainers."[58] No Scots noblewoman like Lady Macbeth, Asaji (Isuzu Yamada) has been thoroughly made over by the Noh mask of *Shamkumi*, which in representing a beautiful young woman about to go mad was eminently suitable for Lady Macbeth. Because in the Noh tradition, actors study the mask and then adapt themselves to its attributes, Kurosawa exposed Toshiro Mifune (Washizu/Macbeth) to a warrior mask named *Heida*.

When Asaji urges Washizu to assassinate Kuniharu, she rebukes him for his cowardice, takes the bloody spear from his hands, and displays no more emotion than a robot, but she is after all nursing a ferocious grudge. Unlike Macbeth, Washizu actually plans to proclaim Miki's son (Fleance) as heir but Asaji stops him by announcing her own pregnancy. As Miki (Banquo) prepares for the fatal ride through the forest, his horse panics, an ominous prophecy that he unwisely ignores, but that gives Kurosawa, a horse lover, an excuse for alluding to the equine imagery in *Macbeth*: "And Duncan's horses (a thing most strange and certain), / Beauteous and swift, the minions of their race, / Turn'd wild in nature, broke their stalls, flung out" (2.4.14). In the legendary banquet scene that follows, Asaji as a loyal but perplexed hostess explains away her husband's embarrassing behavior. Washizu hallucinates that he is seeing Miki's ghost, panics, silences an innocent entertainer, and lashes out at the specter with a sword. Unlike the Macbeth in the Polanski version, who has Rosse push the assassins down a well, Washizu handles his own bloody work. When a soldier brings Miki's head wrapped in a cloth, Washizu is so shocked over the news of Miki's son still being alive, that he instantly puts the man to death. Like Macbeth, he has then become "in blood / Stepp'd in so far" (3.4.135) that there is no turning back.

As calamities multiply for Washizu, including a report that Asaji's child has been "stillborn," he distills the apocalyptic "to-morrow, and to-morrow" (5.5.19) lamentation into a single word, "Fool!" The film's "materiality," its relentless quest for images as powerful as Shakespeare's language, renders "all our yesterdays have lighted fools / The way to dusty death" (5.5.22) partially redundant. Washizu becomes increasingly restless, moving back and forth and around with a rapidity that contrasts with Asaji's stillness.

In another Kurosawa trademark, characters are given unique behavior traits like Washizu's scornful, nearly hysterical, laughter. In *The Bad Sleep Well*, for example, Nishi is constantly adjusting his eyeglasses on the bridge of his nose, or flicking away cigarette ashes. Asaji's eerie stillness continues even in the hand-washing scene, which finds her crazily trying to purge the blood stains. With enemy forces of Noriyasu approaching the castle, Washizu's defiance escalates. He irrationally boasts of the castle's impregnability: "I bear a charmed life, which must not yield / To one of woman born" (5.8.12), and insists that an ominous flock of birds (inspired by Shakespeare's ornithological imagery) means nothing. "Light thickens, and the crow / Makes wing to th' rooky wood" (3.2.50). The birds also herald the ultimate triumph of the forest over the fortress. Next he is seen peering through the castle's parapets anxiously observing the moving wood, and then maniacally appealing to his sullen troops for support. They respond with a hail of arrows that turn him into a veritable porcupine, as arrow after arrow skewers him, leaving him staggering wildly, crying out in pain, and horribly suffering. A final arrow pierces the side of his neck and he reels toward his troops, the tip and butt of the arrow grotesquely protruding from each side of his neck, eyes glazed, still living and breathing, until after a moment of piquant stasis, he abruptly drops dead. The mist returns, the Noh chanting about a warrior murdered by his own ambition comes up on the soundtrack, but there is no redemptive movement, no

Malcolm, for example, to restore order to the gored state. The forest has won out over the fortress. Only remaining are fog, mystery, and the pitiful condition of humanity, always unequivocally doomed by an equivocal fate.

Serge Silberman, a generous patron of the art movie and producer of Luis Buñuel's films, made possible Kurosawa's *Ran* (*Chaos*), a bold re-appropriation of the King Lear tale. With a $10.5-million budget, *Ran* stands as that rare thing, a reasonably well-funded art movie. Still, thrift was required. Instead of expensive studio sets, two of Japan's historical castles, Himeji and Kumamoto, were requisitioned for the First and Second Forts, while the Third Fort, the one belonging to Saburo that is burned to the ground in the middle of the movie, was constructed out of plywood on the slopes of Mount Fuji. The extras needed 1,400 suits of armor, and the samurai's fifty-two horses were flown in from Colorado.[59] The spectacular torching of the castle during the assault by the forces of Taro and Jiro required a risky and nerve-wracking but nevertheless successful single take with all cameras running. A single glitch would have meant financial ruin.

For *Ran*, Kurosawa synthesizes the cultural codes of East and West to unify a marvelous grab-bag of bits and pieces from *King Lear*. Like *Throne of Blood*, *Ran* is a period-piece costume drama, not in fog-shrouded black-and-white, but in bold and vibrant color reflecting sunshine that even at the cataclysmic end tinges the image of the Buddhist Amithab with a golden sheen. The sumptuous costumes of the ancient samurai set against the green hills make for a visual feast at odds with the grim realities of Lear's fate, though the greenery underscores the ironic gap between the glory of nature and the wretchedness of man. The multiple alterations in plot and character mainly stem from a desire to blend Japanese with western cultural codes. The characterization of seventy-year-old Hidetora (King Lear) aligns him more with sadistic Cornwall than with doddering Lear, a version of the old king who is plainly not "More sinn'd against than sinning" (3.2.59). His atrocities include sacking the castles of the families of future daughters-in-law, Sué and Kaede, and gouging out the eyes of Sué's brother, Tsurumaru. In rebuke, Tsurumaru's plaintive Noh flute haunts the old man. The patriarchal biases of Japanese society dictate having the kingdom divided among three sons, Taro, Jiro, and Saburo, rather than to three daughters. In fact, Kurosawa originally planned a movie about the legendary Motonari Mori, a sixteenth-century warlord whose three sons in a reversal of the Lear story were admired as models of virtue. Kurosawa rewrote that script so he could speculate about what would happen if the sons turned out to be wicked rather than virtuous![60]

Ran also reflects Kurosawa's fascination with the samurai warrior codes and their swashbuckling love affair with cavalry and swordplay, which survived well into World War II when Japanese soldiers committed mass suicide with hand grenades on remote north Pacific islands like Attu rather than dishonorably surrender to US Seventh Division infantry, and when American soldiers prized more than anything else an officer's samurai sword as booty. The deep-rooted Japanese conception of *giri,* which deals with the duty owed by a child to his parents, a wife to a husband, sounds remarkably like the Elizabethan doctrine of passive obedience. The unspoken "bond" sets up a tension between apparent presence and actual absence of a moral order that lends itself to philosophical exploration. In a famous mixed metaphor, Samuel Goldwyn summed up litigious American attitudes toward the unspoken "bond," or covenant, if indeed he ever said that "an oral contract isn't worth the paper it's written on."

The boar hunt at the opening of the film at once establishes the grandeur of nature and the pettiness of man. Against the big sky and green hills, Hidetora draws his bow and aims at the prey, his "hawkish eyes [shining] in his tan face."[61] As he pulls the arrow back, the image dissolves into the blood red title, *Ran,* and suddenly it becomes apparent that Kurosawa has materialized King Lear's "The bow is bent and drawn, make from the shaft" (1.1.143).[62] At the family camp of Ichimonji, the patriarchal Hidetora sits cross-legged in stiff formality with his three sons, Taro, Jiro, and Saburo, who are respectively costumed in dazzling yellow, red, and blue kimonos so that it is possible for westerners to keep them all sorted out. Hidetora explains his plan for retirement and the division of the fiefdom. The eldest son, Taro, will receive the First Fort; Jiro, the Second; and Saburo, the Third. As is to be expected, Taro and Jiro outrageously flatter their father but faithful Saburo (Cordelia) bluntly tells him that he is either senile or mad to propose such a scheme. Loyal retainer Tango (Kent), who would never consider violating the "bond," agrees with Saburo, his honesty earning him a curt dismissal. Meanwhile another loyalist, the effeminate Kyoami (Fool), who was played by "Peitah," a famous Japanese transvestite, dances and sings satirical songs and as "an all-licensed fool" is the only person in the frame with the freedom to violate the rigid protocols for sitting and standing. Instead of the map found in *King Lear,* Hidetora uses an arrow to point out the forts that will be given away. When he also moralizes to the sons that a single arrow can be easily broken but three together cannot, he is stunned when Saburo symbolically breaks three arrows apart at once, in sign of the forthcoming divisiveness in the kingdom. Jiro's deep resentment of his older brother's ascendancy combines elements of the Edmund/Edgar plot and Regan/Goneril rivalry.

Predictably, when Hidetora sets out with a retinue of thirty retainers to visit his son's castles, he sets himself up for disrespect. Taro's wife, Lady Kaede, humiliates her father-in-law by occupying the seat nearest the wall traditionally reserved for the senior person in the room. When second son, Jiro, insultingly notifies Hidetora that he has no need for retainers, the father's retort that only the birds and beasts can live by themselves echoes "O, reason not the need! our basest beggars / Are in the poorest thing superfluous" (2.4.264). Old Hidetora undergoes his darkest moment when Taro forces him to sign in blood a contract acknowledging that he no longer heads the house of Ichimonji. In a magnified displacement of Kent's striking of Oswald, Hidetora kills one of his son's impudent retainers at the Castle of Taro with a well aimed arrow. After the terrible battle at Third Fort in a wild storm, the Fool shouts that "in this mad world it is the sane who are mad!" paraphrasing Lear's "What, art mad? A man may see how this world goes with no eyes . . . change places, and handy-dandy, which is the justice, which is the thief?" (4.6.150). Again when Kyaomo cries out "All human beings cry when they are born," he borrows from Lear's "When we are born, we cry that we are come" (4.6.182). During the battle at the Third Fort, which occupies the middle of the film, the apocalyptic scenes of warfare peak in the torching of the castle. The brightly uniformed cavalry and infantry advance in a blood bath that is conceived as the "terrible scroll of hell," the only sound being "the wailing of countless Buddhas" as horror piles on horror. There are bodies hurled into the air by explosions, horses galloping madly, a forest of spears, a man pierced with arrows, a stream of blood with "islands" of severed arms and legs, soldiers raping chambermaids, and so forth. When a single shot rings out and kills Taro at the instigation of his younger brother, Jiro, authentic battle sounds of screams, roaring of fire, hoofbeats, shouting, and gunfire replace the low chanting on the soundtrack. Hidetora trapped high in the burning tower frantically searches for his dagger to commit the honorable act of harakiri. Ignominiously, with his aides committing suicide, the women taking one another's lives to avoid a fate worse than death, he cannot find the dagger and instead must endure the insolent stares of enemy soldiers. After that he goes quite mad in the open fields, his face having deteriorated from the mask of a high-born patrician to a desperate and lonely old man.

Lady Kaede (Mieko Harada) is first Taro's wife, then Jiro's. A lady of exquisite sensibility with a cold-blooded talent for manipulating men, she strongly resembles Asaji, the Lady Macbeth of *The Throne of Blood*. Virtually immobile in the ritualized style of Noh, Lady Kaede, expressionless, stonefaced, inscrutable, barely moves her lips, but she projects a miasma of evil prodigious enough to suffocate the entire castle. After the melée at Saburo's Third Fort, where Jiro dispatches Taro, the widowed Kaede accepts Jiro as a husband but for a price. She demands the head of Jiro's first wife, the gentle Sué. The intoxicating leap from absolute stillness to unchecked ferocity, from subjugation to domination, unleashes a disturbingly erotic scene. With Jiro's own sword, dressed in her widow's white mourning robes, and showing the physical agility of a gymnast, she throws Jiro to the floor, holds the point of his own sword against his throat until the blood runs, and terrorizes him into revealing the identity of Taro's murderers. Jiro, at her nagging, then agrees to the assassination of Sué, his first wife, so that Kaede's relationship with him can be legitimized. Kaede displays her fastidiousness and concern for others by ordering the designated assassin, Kurogane, to wrap Sué's severed head in salt to prevent decomposition in the heat, which she thinks would be a shame. Kurogane instead infuriates the dangerous Kaede by returning with the head of a fox and hinting that the fox's cunning traits are like Kaede's. Kaede's main motive all along has been not to marry into the Ichimonji clan but to avenge the death of her father, slain by Hidetora.

Sué is then saved momentarily for a subsequent meeting with her blind brother, Tsurumaru, also a victim of Hidetora, though by the end of the film she will suffer death by order of Kaede anyway. The faithful son, Saburo, dies in his father's arms, victim of enemy fire, and Hidetora grieves inconsolably over him, like Lear over Cordelia. Kyoami, the Fool, spits toward heaven and cries out against an indifferent Buddha and God. Tango retorts that it is not God or Buddha at fault but the evil of human beings. The blind man, Tsurumaru, still playing his reedy Noh flute, taps with his stick toward the edge of an abyss. It has been a journey through hell, an allegory of the hopeless condition of man. The apostle of existentialist despair, Jan Kott, saw the ending of the film as an expression of complete emptiness: "The blind man feels his way to the edge of the abyss. The parchment falls from his hands . . . The blue sky is completely empty."[63] As Lear himself said, "Nothing will come of nothing." Kurosawa's *tour de force* has been to use Shakespeare's Anglophone texts as blueprints for performance and imagine his words recycled in the cultural iconology of Japan. What he has created is truly in the category of "other Shakespeares."

- 9 -

Shakespeare in the cinema of transgression, and beyond

While prior to the 1960s irony and *film noir* provided the main conduit for covert resentment of the social order, by the Sixties the underlying tensions among the new generation erupted into an overt cinema of transgression. As confrontation replaced irony, progressive cadres rebelled against the policing of art, and broke the stranglehold of the Catholic Legion of Decency and the House Committee on Un-American Activities. England's angry young men and America's hippies beatified avant-garde directors like Italy's Pier Paolo Pasolini who flouted Vatican values with the blasphemous *La ricotta* (1962) that parodied the Deposition from the Cross. In the United States, Andy Warhol's underground *Blowjob* (1964) and *Blue Movie/Fuck* (1968) were roundly denounced as pornographic but were actually too boring to be erotic. In the political arena, Stanley Kubrick's *Dr. Strangelove, or How I Learned to Stop Worrying and Love the Bomb* (1963) exposed the stupidity of HUAC's persecution of the anti-nuclear movement. Commercial movies had already begun to change. Film historian Linda Williams cites Alfred Hitchcock's *Psycho* (1960) as the first film to bring sex and violence into mainstream cinema,[1] where it has been firmly entrenched ever since. More recently the gay rights movement has created a climate for what has been labeled "Shakesqueer" movies, like *My Own Private Idaho* (1991), which even a decade ago would have been taboo.[2]

Celestino Coronado

Celestino Coronado's transgressive *Hamlet* (1976) and *Midsummer Night's Dream* (1984) in their insouciance embody the sort of underground or film society "Shakespeare" movie that makes many critics very uneasy. Coronado's dedication of his misogynist *Hamlet* to Pasolini, *auteur* of *The 120 Days of Sodom* (1975), reflects his artistic and intellectual proclivities. Made on video by the Royal College of Art at North London Polytechnic on a tiny budget of £2,500, but then transferred to 16mm film for screening at the 1976 London Film Festival, this highly experimental student production has enough "crossover" potential to justify its being designated a Shakespeare film.

Beginning students of *Hamlet* looking for a handy visual aid should not consult Coronado's post-modernist movie. It demands a sophisticated audience to appreciate how using a methodology like Roland Barthes' in *S/Z*, Coronado has both de-segmented and then re-segmented the play to privilege Hamlet's dysfunctional connections with Gertrude and Ophelia. Graham Holderness believes it to be "a film treatment attuned to the intellectual sophistication and imaginative complexity of the post-structuralist, post-modern Shakespeare text."[3] The surrealism of "expressionistic, garishly- colored images"[4] includes tightly framed eyeballs belonging to Polonius, a frontally nude ghost of Hamlet's father, twin Hamlets, a Gertrude who also doubles as Ophelia (Helen Mirren), a monocled Polonius (Quentin Crisp), a Laertes and Hamlet "duel" as a wrestling match with the antagonists wearing only athletic supporters, and a soundtrack filled with whistles, bells, flutes, and chimes. These destabilizations coalesce around a central theme of Hamlet's misogyny as the driving force behind his dysfunctionality at Elsinore.

The framing device of a dream/nightmare, punctuated with thunder and lightning, depicts a sleeping Hamlet tormented by the soliloquies, beginning with "To be or not to be." Two Hamlets, played by Anthony and David Meyer, who also both double as the Ghost, represent his split personality. Piercing screams, a howling wind, and gongs accompany close-ups of Hamlet's restless slumber with his head grotesquely distorted by being photographed upside down. A frontally nude ghost, who is also Hamlet's *Doppelgänger*, materializes in a titillating spectacle for patrons who enjoy viewing male bodies, but it is more likely intended as shorthand for the play's labyrinthine but mostly occult sexual politics. The speaking of the verse, however, is wonderfully well done, and the rearrangement and redistribution of segments of the play to get at the mystery of Hamlet stays honest and often witty. David Meyer, who played Hamlet and designed the sets, recently spoke of how the whole project grew out of the youthful exuberance of the times more than from any solemn artistic goal,[5] which apparently went unnoticed by a stern *Time Out* critic who denounced the movie as "at worst, offensive; at best, joyless."[6] Coronado was employing a new paradigm for interrogating the play's mysteries, which have kept themselves inviolate for centuries. A very young Helen Mirren, who doubles as Ophelia and Gertrude, speaks her lines with the conviction and élan that later assured her international success, and Vladek Sheybal invents a uniquely villainous look for the First Player and Lucianus. The movie ends as it begins in thunder and lightning with Hamlet stretched out on a white pallet, his face a death mask. In the struggle against evil, the passive inner Hamlet, the old "black plume" prince of the romantic era, becomes a tor-tured and tormented reverse mirror to the aggressive, New Age outer Hamlet. In a favorable review, Tim Pulleine rightly points out that Coronado was interested not so much in holding a mirror up to nature as in holding "a mirror up to artifice."[7] Viewed that way the jumble of images, the phal- lic *Hamlet*, emerges not irrelevantly but imaginatively from the maelstrom of the play's linguistic entanglements.

A few years later, Coronado teamed up with Lindsay Kemp's counter- culture theatrical company to film *A Midsummer Night's Dream* (1984). The play has been variously envisioned on screen as romance (Reinhardt-Dieterle, 1935), as Carnaby Street (Hall, 1968), as fantasy (Moshinsky, BBC-TV, 1981), as pop (Noble, 1996), and in the hands of Coronado and Kemp's "in-your-face" company as "gay." Coronado's film combined "the disparate elements of high camp and low burlesque, aesthetic courtliness and bawdy vaudeville... interlaced with snatches from Shakespeare's text and bound together by Carlos Miranda's haunting original musical score."[8] Opera, ballet, and pantomime replace Shakespeare's text in this near travesty, which began as a Sadler's Wells stage production in Islington, then was filmed in Spain for television as *Sueno de Noche de Veran*, and shown in 1984 at the London Film Festival, where a reviewer described it as having "plenty of uninhibited nudity" and "a fairy king and queen [who] are splendidly campy characters."[9] It is indisputably joyful in the zany spirit of its progenitor, Lindsay Kemp, a self-described "ancient Jewish fairy," who is also a "Negro and homosexual."[10] The cast includes not only David Meyer as Lysander, who played one of the two Hamlets in the Coronado *Hamlet*, but also The Incredible Orlando (Jack Birkett), a blind drag queen, as Titania; François Testory as the Indian Boy, of whom much is made by a prurient Oberon; Lindsay Kemp as a sinister voyeur of a Puck with a greenish pallor, who engorges on grapes and approaches orgasm as he spies on young lovers; and a *Pyramus and Thisby* play that turns into a version of *Romeo and Juliet* on stilts. It all adds up to completely irreverent "nose-thumbing" but exuberant entertainment. As Kemp himself said, "What I want to do with the theatre is to restore the glamour of the Folies Bergères, the danger of the circus, the eroticism of Rock 'n' Roll, and the shiver of death."[11] Shakespeare's store-house of verbal images sorely tempted Kemp to whip up a feast of visual images, and to explore any subterranean homoeroticism.

A ballet prologue shows Theseus' soldiers raping the Amazons against a backdrop of an enormous moon, a talisman of the play's status as "moon-drenched." There then follow the blindfolded four young lovers, snatches of mechanical music, a Helena who moves like a dancing doll, and raucous wood sprites who mock the romantic creatures of more decorous productions. Watery visions fabricate a dreamy rain forest of Freudian displacements, substitutions, fusions, and overlaps. For example, the crossed lovers awaken under the spell of Oberon's enchanted "love-in-idleness" (2.1.168) not to fall in love as Hermia with Lysander or Helena with Demetrius but as Hermia with Helena and Lysander with Demetrius, though all show versatility by sorting out their "queerness" in time to return to safe heterosexuality. At this point, Puck is amply entitled to his famous line, "Lord, what fools these mortals be!" (3.2.115). When Bottom awakens from his "dream" with Titania, the obscene grin on his face signals that he remembers very well what events have transpired during the night. Love in this *Dream* transcends gender to include all creatures willy nilly and to validate Hippolyta's observation that "This is the silliest stuff that ever I heard" (5.1.210). What saves the day, though, is recollection of Theseus' urbane warning against rushing to judgment: "If we imagine no worse of them than they of themselves, they may pass for excellent men" (5.1.215).

Derek Jarman

The late Derek Jarman's disdain for the cultural norms of a "repressive" British society suffused his prolific work, which heroically but forlornly ran against the grain of commercial movie making. He never allowed establishment standards of good taste to stand in the way of the search for the holy grail of "a new cinema," while bringing an activist gay/punk sensibility to subversive films like *Sebastiane* (1975), *Jubilee* (1978), and *The Tempest* (1980), which sometimes were underwritten by grants from the British Film Institute. Early in his career a set designer for Ken Russell's *The Devils*, among Jarman's other artistic idols were Italian renaissance painter Michelangelo Caravaggio (1573–1610) and film director Pier Paolo Pasolini, both patron saints of the gay movement. Caravaggio's stormy life inspired Jarman to film the semi-documentary *Caravaggio* (1986),[12] and of Pasolini, he wrote "had Caravaggio been reincarnated in this century it would have been as a filmmaker, Pasolini."[13] Throughout his short but energetic lifetime, Jarman struggled like a displaced Oscar Wilde to defang "heterosoc" prejudice against "queers" that he saw as the lynchpin for ideological, racist, and gender policing.[14] Like Wilde, he was a pure aesthete, and except for an occasional political foray with left-leaning fellow actors, did not seem to have much interest in the plight of exploited workers under capitalism.

His transgressive *Tempest* was an art-house movie first screened at the 1979 Edinburgh Festival. Much to Jarman's distress,[15] who had hoped for mainstream acceptance, at the New York Film Festival it was torpedoed and sunk without a trace by *New York Times* critic Vincent Canby,[16] but it did invade new turf by imposing a gay/camp vision on a Shakespearean play. Budgeted at £150,000, it was filmed in seven weeks on location mostly at Stoneleigh Abbey, an eighteenth-century Italianate mansion built around the remains of a fourteenth-century monastery in Warwickshire near Coventry. After Jarman's even naughtier *Sebastiane* and *Jubilee*, his *Tempest* seems understated, but insufficiently so to prevent some critics from pronouncing anathema with adjectives like "perverse," or "ugly." Most recently, though, Diana Harris and MacDonald Jackson have energetically defended it: "Jarman's movie, though often bizarre, engages the feelings; it is genuinely moving, and the emotions it arouses are essentially those aroused by Shakespeare's play."[17] In an early draft of his plans, Jarman himself anticipated that "stylistically the film will take great freedom" and it will be "in black-and-white, shot like a German expressionist horror film (*Nosferatu*)," but at the end it "will burst into radiant color," though he must have changed his mind because the final cut emerged in color throughout.[18] The exterior scenes with a blue filtered lighting may possibly have been inspired by Caravaggio's hallmark *tenebrism*, that is to say, muted contrasts between white and black. Jarman saw the enigmatic Prospero as more smug than tyrannical, perhaps a Colonel Blimp figure, "unable to see his exploitation of Caliban and Ariel," while Ariel is essentially "a projection of Prospero's mind which [is struggling] to free itself and escape." As for Caliban, Jarman followed modernist critics in thinking that he is "the exploited servant of Sycorax [who] was beautiful before Prospero introduced the language that enabled Caliban to curse him and exploit his innocence." A benevolent despot, Prospero always suffers from the impossibility of reasonably governing the unreasonable. In Ferdinand, however, he has a subject that Jarman thinks is the embodiment of "youth and innocence," and Stephano and Trinculo remain "simple and ordinary people,"[19] in fact filmed as characters from *The Wizard of Oz* happily skipping along a beach.

Predictably, the establishing shot is a tempest. Alonso's (Peter Bull) ship, a modern vessel, labors through a wild storm with angry waves crashing over the bow, and a gasping and panting on the soundtrack. The panting seems to emit both from the imperiled mariners and from Prospero (Heathcote Williams) restlessly turning and tossing in bed, tormented in his dream by Gonzalo's (Ken Campbell) cries of "We split, we split!" (1.1.62). The "split" acts as metaphor for Prospero's own desperate struggle against the alienation of self from self and society, as well as self-referentially Jarman's own split from conventional movie making. "We are such stuff / As dreams are made on" (4.1.156), says Prospero but his dream becomes a nightmare, after the style of Jan Kott's *Shakespeare Our Contemporary*, which redefined *The Tempest* as a play about power rather than forgiveness. This is a major "split" from the light and airy "soufflé"[20] of George Schaefer's Hallmark *Tempest* (1960) with Richard Burton as Caliban, or the BBC-TV soporific version (1980) with Michael Hordern as Prospero. Prospero cruelly grinding his foot on Caliban's fingers works as visual metonymy for this dark vision. His study in tumbledown Stoneleigh Abbey bursts at the seams with the exotic bric-à-brac of a magus – astrological charts, a model of the zodiac, *The Occult Philosophy* of Agrippa, crystal balls, and so forth. The dialogue is transposed, pushed around, pruned, and yet idiosyncratically intact. What remains is delivered in decidedly non-transgressive establishment RP accents, while the plot follows Shakespeare's with considerable fidelity.

The characters have been audaciously displaced into a contemporary mold, the boldest stroke being the re-invention of Miranda (Toyah Willcox) as a voluptuous tart, a "nymphomaniac" to use Jarman's own label. Caliban, played by the perennial favorite of the Lindsay Kemp clique, The Incredible Orlando (Jack Birkett) of Titania fame, is a giggling obnoxious satyr who resembles Lindsay Kemp's Puck in the Coronado *Midsummer Night's Dream*. Unlike Kemp's Puck, he is no passive voyeur but a lecher intent on pawing the nubile and intermittently topless Toyah Willcox, who was also a major player in Jarman's decadent *Jubilee*. Frontal nudity designed to *épater le bourgeois* is a well-worn trope in the films of transgressive cinema; here David Meyer as Ferdinand (Hamlet and Lysander in the Coronado films) emerges shivering, stark naked, from an icy sea but in a modestly remote long shot. Elements of bondage and aggression in Prospero's mistreatment of Ferdinand conveniently merge with Jarman's sado-masochistic fantasies of the martyrdom of St. Sebastian, who is often portrayed looking almost as pierced with arrows as Washizu at the end of *Throne of Blood*.

Campy sequences abound. Miranda playing dress-up in a tattered gown stands on the stairs, while Caliban, "this thing of darkness" (5.1.275), the hidden side of Prospero, grinds away on a hurdy-gurdy, adding diegetic music to the strange off-camera non-melodies of the film's music makers, *Wavemaker*. Almost everyone has agreed that the flashback of a gross, flabby Sycorax nursing a grown-up Caliban is at best "intrusive" and at worst "disgusting," but even that revolting episode has been rationalized as artistically valid. Caliban's portrayal as a "giant baby" makes having him nursed at his dam's breast "strangely appropriate."[21] Despite the boldness of interpretation, the actual filming is confined to conventional masters, mid-shots, and close-ups with very little use of a wandering camera. Jarman, in a rare fit of conservatism, felt that experimental camera work with unconventional subject-matter could easily "push a film over into incoherence."[22]

A cast of fifteen actors and a chorus of singers and dancers support soloist Elisabeth Welch, a black blues singer who as "Goddess" combines the roles of Iris, Ceres, and Juno, in the closing "Stormy Weather" dance sequence. Perhaps intended as a mild spoof on a Busby Berkeley production number, it rescues the film from any tendency to fall into a solemn apocalyptic mode like Jarman's *The Last of England* (1987). In what may have been a gay injoke,[23] several dozen men in white sailor suits along with Welch as soloist do a ragged song-and-dance routine of "Stormy Weather." As Samuel Crowl has pointed out, the refrain of "Keeps rainin' all the time," provides a modern equivalent

21   Jack Birkett (The Incredible Orlando) as an
incredible Caliban in Derek Jarman's
post-modernist vision of *The Tempest* (UK 1979).

to Feste's "for the rain it raineth every day" in *Twelfth Night* (5.1.392).[24] Jarman
transposes "Our revels now are ended" (4.1.148) from act four to the end of
the movie, where it works better as a coda anyway, much more compelling
than "Now my charms are all o'erthrown" (Epilogue). Behind all the gaiety
and frivolity, the brave front, is the dark agenda in Jarman's life, an endless
struggle to locate funding for his films, a vision of a western civilization on the
edge of apocalypse, and the ultimate calamity of AIDS, which is the subject
of his last film, *Blue* (1993). In this nightmare world, Prospero's name might
better be changed to Impecunero, a conclusion covert in Shakespeare's play but
made overt here. One thing can be said. No one will ever fall asleep watching
Jarman's *Tempest*, which has been so rudely wrenched out of the context of any
solemn classroom discussion.

Peter Greenaway

Peter Greenaway's *Prospero's Books* (1991), a post-post-modernist adaptation of
The Tempest, ratchets Jarman's quest for a new cinema up a notch by combining

conventional 35 mm film with television post-production techniques using high-definition television processes (HDTV). The result moves beyond Walter Benjamin's concept of the mechanical reproduction of art to the post-mechanical workings of digital cinema, or even the electronic reproduction of art.[25] By his own admission, Jarman was hopeless with machinery and could never have utilized so effectively Greenaway's array of electronic gadgetry. Indeed the master magician Georges Méliès himself, stuck with his hand-cranked camera, would have eaten his heart out with envy to have beheld such technological wizardry. Greenaway's own widely acclaimed visual imagination as shown in enigmatic films like *The Draughtsman's Contract* (1982), and *The Belly of an Architect* (1987), made this marriage with new-age technology all the more promising. His transgressive *The Cook, the Thief, his Wife and her Lover* (1990), which survived briefly in the multiplex market, also vaguely echoes the Thyestean feast in *Titus Andronicus* when a freshly roasted human being serves as the center-piece of a restaurant table. Like Shakespeare, Greenaway also understands the magician's trick for making what may be only an accident of juxtapositions, as in *Hamlet*, seem enormously profound. Yet Prince Hamlet warns us that what "seems" "is," and what "is" may "seem," and who is so wise as to tell the difference? For that reason, *Prospero's Books* contains the ingredients for three doctoral dissertations in film studies.

In *Prospero's Books*, Greenaway comes very close to achieving his ideal of making a movie that is, like Alan Resnais' *Last Year at Marienbad* (1961), a "film-film" that cannot be anything else, neither text, painting nor play. He believes that even after a century "we probably haven't seen any cinema yet, only ... a multi-hybrid that has been slow to develop an autonomous character." Greenaway admired the structure of Resnais' film in the way that it could "manipulate chronology ... repeat and reprise ... take multiple views of the same phenomena, and ... do it with elegant and witty self-reflexion."[26] Resnais' co-scenarist, avant-garde writer Alain Robbe-Grillet, insists that what we see on screen, as compared with written fictional narrative, is always in the present tense, "*in the act of happening,*" the audience receiving the "gesture itself, not an account of it."[27] This anti-linear agenda infiltrates *Prospero's Books*, where John Gielgud as Prospero, Peter Greenaway and William Shakespeare all rolled into one is self-reflexively writing *The Tempest* as we watch him in his writing room modeled on the cell in Da Messina's St. Jerome.[28] The grammar of *Prospero's Books* also resembles Resnais' more accessible *Mon Oncle d'Amérique* with its flow of discontinuous images connected by a voice-over commentary. In *Mon Oncle*, the medical researcher's clinical observations on the behavior of laboratory rats establishes a parallel to the lives of the characters in the movie, just as in Greenaway's film Prospero comments on the action of *The Tempest*. Despite these cinematic biases, Greenaway paradoxically shows great "respect for the literality of Shakespeare's text . . . [his film] being as it were a literal rewriting of *The Tempest*."[29]

Few will deny that Greenaway makes intimidating movies. The easy way out is to announce, like Vincent Canby, that *Prospero's Books* will probably make "some people run boldly for the exits,"[30] which it doubtlessly will, my own daughter among them. Yet as Canby also implies, there is a numinous sense of being in the presence of a masterpiece that makes glib dismissals egregiously philistine. Like Jarman, Godard, and other avant-gardists, Greenaway takes no prisoners when it comes to mediating between his art and his audience. Not just a superb technician, he is also a scholar and an artist who uses film to present a modern version of a dazzling Jacobean court masque. The whole of it is too mannerist, too rich, too impossible, for consumption by any but the most dedicated specialists, but there is much pleasure in dissecting and examining the parts. Greenaway's work is a *Finnegans Wake* of visual art.

Greenaway reconstructs the library of fourteen books that old Gonzalo presumably loaded into Prospero's "rotten carcass of a butt" (1.2.146) when he was exiled from Milan with little Miranda. Even if the movie had never been made, Greenaway's talent for capturing the essence of the "Elizabethan lumber room," as Virginia Woolf called it, would deserve a separate museum exhibit. His *Flying Out of this World* (University of Chicago Press, 1992), which traces the history of flight through images, demonstrates his skill as a collector and editor of, and commentator on, exotic sketches and paintings. For *Prospero's Books*, Greenaway imagines and creates a series of majestically illustrated volumes with titles such as "The Book of Water" (1), "A Book of Mirrors" (2), "A Book of Mythologies" (3), "A Harsh Book of Geometry" (6), "The Vesalius Anatomy of Birth" (8), "The Ninety-Two Conceits of the Minotaur" (13), "The Book of Languages" (14), and finally "Thirty Six Plays" (24). The last book is Shakespeare's 1623 First Folio but with the first nineteen pages left blank for Gielgud as Prospero to insert *The Tempest* into them at the end of the movie when he has finished writing it. In a supreme irony, this play, *The Tempest*, thought to be Shakespeare's "last," was printed first in the Folio. Greenaway works with the imagination of a painter, the meticulousness of a draughtsman, and the eye of a master film maker. In the present context, it is impossible to do justice to even a single one of the books, which have been prepared with the help of a "digital, electronic Graphic Paintbox" that Greenaway sees as the "newest Gutenberg technology."[31]

As Prospero, the magus and creator of the characters, inscribes the words of the play in elegant Elizabethan secretary hand (calligraphy by Brody Neuenschwander), he eventually draws on all of the books, which are stored in compartments around his study. As Donaldson points out, Prospero becomes a magus for our time who gives a "technological inflection" to the white magic of the Renaissance.[32] For example, as Prospero/Greenaway conceives of *The Tempest* and its opening storm, "The Book of Water" lies on his desk along with a model of a galleon. "The Book of Mythology" helps in the first twenty minutes or so of screen time to flesh out the story of his exile from Milan as told to Miranda, with allusions to Hades, Vulcan, Juno, Venus, Hercules, and Ariadne, and attendant nymphs. In the "Bath-house," where water flows so copiously that the audience can easily grasp why Gonzalo would "fain die a dry death" (1.1.67), nude nymphs swim like phantoms underwater. A young boy (Ariel) with a bladder the size of a dirigible holds his "small penis like an ornamental water-spout" and pees torrents into the pool, which drollery may have been inspired by a similar fountain statue in Brussels. It has also aroused murmurs of "kiddy-porn" in some circles. The book of a "Primer of the Small Stars" shows maps for the voyager, constellations, meteors, night skies, while "The Book of the Mirror" includes mirror images for a three-year-old Miranda surrounded by her doting attendants. There are glimpses, for example, of Prospero proceeding through arcades modeled on Bernini's in St. Peter's Square. In Prospero's study, a brisk west wind scatters his papers around, which is yet another quotation, this time from Botticelli's "Birth of Venus." Later, when Antonio gathers his conspirators around him, the visual quotation is from Veronese, though the participants are in Dutch costumes. "Vesalius' Anatomy of Birth" contributes a horrifying cutaway in full color of a woman's womb, in which psychoanalytical critics have mined a rich lode for speculation about Prospero's terror of the female body and his efforts to exert control over its reproductive powers.[33] Colors play a key role in exposing the animal nature of Caliban, who as the paradigm for the ultimate redneck reinforces Alexander Hamilton's belief that "Your people, sir, is a great beast." As prologue to Caliban's entrance, and as totem for his illiteracy, close-ups of dripping urine and glops of vomit stain the pages of books. The rich mosaic of Greenaway's varied images defies description and makes writing about them an exercise in describing the indescribable, which valorizes Greenaway's belief that images should not be surrogates for words but independent of them. To put it another way, the film is a "cultural caprice" that forces the viewer/auditor "to move around among [its] sights, sounds, and accidentals ... assembling and disassembling meanings as they fleetingly present themselves."[34]

Drawbacks appear, despite the profound reworking of Shakespeare's images and Greenaway's acknowledged genius at film making. For one thing, the choreography often seems disconnected from everything else, as an inordinate number of young, and not so young, men and women prance around nude, seemingly for the sake of prancing around nude, to the rhythms of Michael Nyman's band. A telling point, however, rests in the costuming of Antonio, Alonso, and others in an outlandish travesty of Jacobean clothing with prodigious Milanese ruffs as if to acknowledge the superiority of man's natural to his unnaturally clothed state. Allowed to play every male role in the play, Sir John Gielgud outdoes himself as a singer of verse, his already mellifluous but stagy voice being unnaturally amplified and resonated through the sophisticated electronic recording equipment. Finally, the last word may be that of a reviewer who thought that "by presenting too much to take in at a glance, Greenaway tests to the limits his ideal of a painterly cinema."[35] Notably humorless, the movie leaves you intellectually gorged but emotionally starved.

Jean-Luc Godard

With Jean-Luc Godard's "twisted fairy tale" of a *King Lear* (1987), the cinema of transgression vents its anti-establishment spleen less in the private realm of sexual identity than in the public arena of politics. It was conceived in a legendary way on a table napkin at the Cannes Film Festival with the promise of big name stars, Orson Welles even, and with a $1.4 million budget from Cannon Films. The deal somehow went awry and resulted in the film being partly about how the director was allegedly "stabbed in the back" by his colleagues' breaking of a bond.[36] Godard was playing Cordelia to Cannon Films' King Lear, as it were. As a post-modernist, Godard does not so much give the audience a movie as invite the audience to make a movie out of a kaleidoscope of segments. Peter Donaldson's extended analysis demonstrates that the film is more of a "dissemination," or even a deconstruction in the Derridean sense, than a representation of *King Lear*.[37] By the time he made *King Lear*, Godard had turned his back on the Hollywood movies he once admired in his earlier "bourgeois" films like *Breathless* (1960), and devoted himself entirely to working for the revolution. His *King Lear* takes the spectator on a journey (maybe "three journeys" as one alienating inter-title suggests). His movie is an anti-movie that meta-cinematically shows the impossibility of making movies, of finding visual equivalents for any verbal structures. It is, as a persistent inter-title insists, about "No-thing." Since *Two or Three Things I Know about Her* (1967) Godard has spurned filmic grammar that promotes viewer passivity. He scorns the seamless Hollywood narrative as an instrument of oppression for suppressing independent thought in a mindless consumerist society. Like television, mainstream film lobotomizes the masses and neutralizes them politically. David Impastato puts it succinctly when he says, "Godard himself dispenses with all the basic courtesies of story-telling."[38] Philosopher Gilles Deleuze thinks that Godard's films raise "questions which silence answers."[39] In short, it is up to the viewer not only to look but to see, "See better, Lear" (1.1.157), and, as with Greenaway's work, to construct a personal narratology out of the galaxy of images.

Most critics despised it. Brickbats flew. "Tedious convolutions." "[Shake-speare] doubtless rotating in his grave." "A massively perverse farrago." "A vulgar contrivance." David Nokes thought that "not the least of the priva-tions of a nuclear winter would be the threat that its culture might be com-prised of films like this."[40] Others saw things differently. Sheila Johnston found "integrity and conviction,"[41] and J. Hoberman thought it was "deft, funny, and intermittently exhilarating . . . as stylized a reading as Kurosawa's *Ran*."[42] There is little point, however, in looking for linearity in a deliberately non-linear work that turns what is fragmented, segmented, and disjointed into a celebra-tion of apocalypse. Syntax crumbles like Mad Tom's gibberish about the "foul fiend." This thing of shreds and patches struggles with the insane condition of man after Chernobyl, after the Death of God, after the old king's calamitous fall into misery. Artful segmentations, however, often give more truth than inept full-scale dramatizations. Like a metaphysical poem that yokes together disparate images, Godard's *King Lear* offers an academic feast for explication of the way it juxtaposes apparently irrelevant images.

Godard sets his cryptic movie in the Hotel Beau-Rivage at Nyon, Switzer-land, on the shores of Lake Léman, though there are vague references to its being also located in America. The casting includes Norman Mailer as The Great Writer and his daughter Kate. After one day's shooting, Mailer departed in a rage for the States ("first class for himself and daughter, economy for his daughter's boy friend," we are snidely told), his role as Don Learo being taken over by Burgess Meredith, a versatile and skillful actor. Mailer's disaffection becomes a leitmotif in the movie as Godard explores the alleged breach of trust between him and the film's backers, and the recurring inter-title, "Stabbed in the Back," raises connotations of perfidy, treachery, and villainy, if not para-noia. The opening scene, however, remains The Great Writer's, who declares that "the Mafia's the only way to do *King Lear*." His perplexed daughter anx-iously asks "Why are you so interested in the Mafia?" Later, we find out why. Burgess Meredith, by now cast as Don Learo, reads from Albert Fried's book on Jewish gangsters about how Bugsy Siegel's efforts ultimately "Las Vega-sized" the entire United States. In a passage lifted verbatim from Fried, we hear Don Learo quoting Meyer Lansky sounding like Michael Cassio: "When you lose your money you lose nothing; when you lose your character, you lose everything."[43] The nexus is suddenly clear. This moralizing gangster fits into Lear's own vision of a world as morally bankrupt, a predatory jungle:

> What, art mad? A man may see how this world goes with no eyes. Look with thine ears; see how yond justice rails upon yond simple thief. Hark in thine ear: change places, and handy-dandy, which is the justice, which is the thief? (4.6.150ff)

Molly Ringwald as Cordelia contributes a pretty but petulant face that reflects the thinly disguised impatience of an adolescent girl with a tiresome father. When she stands alone in a white dress on the hotel balcony while her father reads letters from her sisters, "Gloria," and "Regina," she embodies the recurring Godardian image of women entrapped by language and customs. Only her disjunctive voice on the soundtrack reciting sonnet 47 ("Betwixt mine eye and heart a league is took") tips off the audience to her inner estimate of herself. Like all Cordelias a holy mystery, she is an object to gaze at while she is gazing at herself, in a role that takes her back to her equally appealing Miranda in Paul Mazursky's *The Tempest* (1981).

As William Shakespeare, Jr. The Fifth, Peter Sellars plays the role of an editor in search of the unrecoverable text of his ancestor. At first he is struggling for the title of *As You Like It*, which initially emerges as *As You Wish It*. Later he begins transcribing passages from *King Lear* that gradually are transferred over to Don Learo himself, who pathetically becomes dependent on young William for his lines. The search for the text becomes an icon for the artist's impotence in a post-modernist world, "after Chernobyl," when art is dead.

In a paroxysm of self-referentiality, Godard plays himself playfully in a ridiculous get-up with dreadlocks and dogtags streaming from his head, his redeeming ability not to take himself too seriously having even led to his casting the inimitable Woody Allen in the movie. As Professor Pluggy, Godard affects some kind of a speech defect, talking out of the corner of his mouth in a maddeningly garbled way, again to show the inadequacy of language for expressing ideas. As well as being Lear's Fool, Professor Pluggy conveniently serves as the philosopher-commentator, a stock figure in many of Godard's movies who discourses learnedly on the action. Questions directed at Professor Pluggy, "Just what are you aiming at, Professor?" really sum up the audience's collective resentment over being so thoroughly bamboozled. There are no answers, only alienating title cards with enigmatic messages like "No-thing," "Power and Virtue," "An Approach to Lear," and "Fear and Loathing."

All the clutter from the family attic crops up in the movie. There is Albert Fried's *The Rise and Fall of the Jewish Gangster in America* with its mythmaking about Meyer Lansky and Bugsy Siegel; a page out of the technical history of film making; iterative images of the Angel Raphael, who may have been "shot in the back" (see this identical motif at the close of *Breathless*); photo albums with tributes to great film directors like Welles and Renoir; frequent disjunctions of sound and image; many squawking gulls; and now and then Burgess Meredith's great voice enunciating majestic passages from *King Lear*. Standard Godardian tropes, like the covers of books being incorporated into the narrative and outdoor advertising billboards, show up in close-ups of a copy of Virginia Woolf's *The Waves* washed up on the beach, and the neon-lit sign of the Hotel Beau-Rivage at night. Other memorable images include a galloping white horse from the stirring last paragraph of Virginia Woolf's novel; Godard as the Professor striving for closure in untangling his hopelessly snarled film; a beautiful Cordelia in white robes lying as a sacrifice on a large boulder.

All of this chaotic material might be suspected of being mere gibberish – or clinically speaking, "image salad," the cinematic equivalent to the pathology of "word salad," which is defined as the brilliant images in muddled syntax characteristic of schizophrenia[44] – if it were not for the movie's denseness of texture. It all adds up to a radiant nothingness of the variety that threatens to turn back into a something too profound to capture in any known language. In these ways, Godard "spectates" the sight of his own film's impossibility for closure to illustrate, as he puts it, that "cinema plays with itself." At the end of the movie, Alien (Woody Allen), perhaps in a quote from Orson Welles's *F for Fake*, sits at a Movieola ineptly trying to splice together the flawed film with needle and thread. In voice over, he recites Shakespeare's sonnet 60 ("Like as the waves make towards the pebbled shore / So do our minutes hasten to their end").

Contrary to what has often been claimed, Godard's alienating images – aggressive *découpage*, rapid editing, discontinuities, fractured images – do not detract from the language of *King Lear* but frame it. The raucous, mocking cries of the gulls over the lake sonically underscore Shakespeare's exposure of the horror of the human condition. Cordelia is displaced into the teenage surliness of Molly Ringwald. Burgess Meredith's splendid American voice turns sacerdotal with the devastating, "She's gone forever! / I know when one is dead" (5.3.260). The pale white horse moves like a phantom across the screen, and the waves beat on the shore. The images dazzle but even in this strange new world of pure images, Shakespeare's language still holds center stage, as the work of an Academy Award nominee for scenarist should.

Independent film makers

Perhaps less "transgressive" than "quixotic" are the independent Shakespeare movies that emerge as a labor of love without any hope of financial reward in the cruel world of "tickling commodity." Of three that appeared in the late 80s and early 90s, two versions of *Othello* came from minority American film makers, and one of *As You Like It* from British film maker Christine Edzard. For the same reasons that Janet Suzman chose it as her Market Theatre statement against South African apartheid, minority film makers have shown special interest in *Othello*. On a tiny budget of $200,000 she financed herself, Liz

White's all-black *Othello* (1980) with Yaphet Kotto in the lead and Audrey Dixon as Desdemona added a heroic marker to the history of filmed Shakespeare. The challenges faced by independent film makers entitle them to their own modern singer of epic tales of the hero/artist in formidable combat against the tyranny of the distribution system. The artist manqué descends into the Hades of Heartbreak House but unlike Odysseus never re-ascends. Originally a 1966 summer theatre production at Martha's Vineyard, where the director's family had long been established in the island's elite black summer resort community, the 16 mm movie had award-winning Charles Dorkins as cinematographer and Jonas Gwangwa as composer of the Afro-American jazz score. Peter Donaldson has praised it not just for White's ethnically subtle casting of a black actor to play the role of Othello among lighter-skinned blacks, but also for how "the social context of the production becomes part of the meaning of the film."[45] Director White had apparently disliked seeing Caucasian actors like Olivier and Sergei Bondarchuk playing Othello in blackface. She interprets Iago's malice toward Othello as stemming from the psychological damage caused by his subconscious displacement of himself into the role of a rejected son. Regrettably the film remains sequestered in archives, having never been distributed commercially, as it deserves comparison with the recently released Oliver Parker *Othello* (1996), starring Laurence Fishburne and Irene Jacob.

Yet another example of minority film making is Ted Lange's Rockbottom Productions *Othello* (1989), which began as a stage production at the Inner City Cultural Center in Los Angeles. Aimed at American audiences in an MTV and "Miami Vice" style with generous use of music and shock editing, Lange, an experienced commercial television director, cast a black Othello (Ted Lange) and Iago (Hawthorne James) against a white, blonde Desdemona (Mary Otis). The result privileged Iago's envy over Othello's jealousy with a subsequent diminishment of the other characters.[46] One mainstream reviewer praised the movie, especially for Hawthorne James's performance as Iago and thought its "novelty elements . . . could generate theatrical and video interest."[47]

So far mostly exhibited only at film festivals, Christine Edzard's *As You Like It* (1992) has created quite a stir among academics. Edzard, director of the award-winning *Little Dorrit* (1988), has also worked with Franco Zeffirelli and has played a key role in establishing the independent Sands Film Studio in London. Her film's low budget, technical glitches, and impenetrable British diction, however, condemned it to a short life even though the cast includes some well-known British actors. Because its displacement of the Forest of Arden into a starkly realistic urban jungle runs against the grain of Shakespeare's festive language and was widely misunderstood, most viewers would agree with Derek Elley's judgment that it "sacrifices sylvan whimsy for social edge."[48] Her *As You Like It* takes exactly the opposite approach from the 1936 film with

Laurence Olivier and Elisabeth Bergner. Instead of studio opulence designed by the prestigious Lazare Meerson, the movie's sets look as if they had been thriftily recycled from Derek Jarman's *The Last of England* (1987), which wallows in urban grime. The Forest of Arden has been transmogrified into a vacant lot on the East London waterfront, and Duke Senior and his merry crew are making sweet the uses of adversity by living out of packing cases. The pastoral myth at the core of Shakespeare's play that contrasts the edenic countryside with the fallen world of the city and court has been stood on its head. Now it is the wretched of the earth within the city itself that implicitly condemn the callous Thatcherites. Appropriately for this reading, the court of the bad Duke Frederick seems to have been constructed out of an abandoned bank lobby, and he and his friends cavort in splendid clothing vastly superior to the rags of his good brother's cohorts. A shivering Duke Senior and the melancholy Jaques huddle around an oil drum brazier, and Orlando dwells in a polyurethane shack.

An imaginative decision to use Jaques' Seven Ages of Man speech as a prologue to the movie goes astray when in his subdued reading James Fox, dressed in a shabby black hat and overcoat, confuses somnambulism with understatement. Some clever doubling reinforces the split between city and urban pastoral by having Andrew Tiernan play both Orlando and Oliver, Don Henderson both of the dukes, and Roger Hammond both LeBeau and Corin. In an apparent bid for the youth market, Edzard cast the very young Emma Croft as Rosalind against Tiernan's youthful Orlando. The contrast between Tiernan as Orlando and the aged Cyril Cusack, who did Aegeon in the BBC *Comedy of Errors*, as old Adam almost self-reflexively underscores the past and present in British theatre. Emma Croft brings energy, youth, bounce to the demanding role but there is so much bounce as she leaps and swirls and cavorts that it distracts from the bouncy language. "Wherein went he? What makes he here? Did he ask for me? Where remains he? How parted he with thee? And when shalt thou see him again? Answer me in one word." (3.2.221). This interrogative torrent pours out of a Rosalind costumed in jeans, a work jacket and watch cap which to the literal-minded makes the references to her "doublet and hose" seem odd, but on the other hand the modern unisex style blends nicely with the play's androgynous politics.[49] Orlando's love poems that normally get tacked up on trees turn up as graffiti on the fence around the vacant lot. For American audiences ignorant of Griff Rhys Jones's work as a British television comic, his thick dialect as Touchstone raises formidable barriers. No one nowadays expects RP (BBC Received Pronunciation) but for overseas English-speaking audiences Jones's character might as well be speaking in Swahili. As snobbish and painful as RP may be, it has the virtue of being easily understood by speakers of any other English dialect. The surface and air traffic noises on the uneven soundtrack suggest that filming took place directly under the main flight path to Heathrow. This unfiltered rumble either enhances the urban atmosphere, as Samuel Crowl thinks,[50] or is intrusive and points to the need for better technical work in the sound department. Sonic support in an interesting avantgarde Godardian kind of way is one thing, but faulty recording is something else. Two actresses nicely catch the spirit of the production: Celia [*sic*] Bannerman as a pert Celia, and Valerie Gogan as a mini-skirted, punk-style Phebe, with a sassy attitude. The closing Masque of Hymen successfully integrates the mystery of the past with the ugly realities of the present by having a mist roll in from the river just as the wedding preparations begin. "Pray you no more of this, 'tis like the howling of Irish wolves against the moon [*To Silvius.*] I will help you if I can. [*To Phebe.*] I would love you if I could" (5.2.109), though the singing of "It was a lover and his lass" might have worked better if it had been entrusted to some passing street urchins rather than to the two elderly actors who are allowed to make spectacles of themselves cavorting around the "palace" of Duke Frederick. Edzard's movie is certainly fresher and livelier, if less polished, than the wooden 1936 version with Laurence Olivier but the first truly successful film of this challenging play has yet to be seen.

Shakespeare derivatives of seven kinds: beyond the fringe

The Shakespeare movie that drifts far away from "Shakespeare" raises uncomfortable questions about taxonomy. Roger Manvell's system of six stages of adaptation, which categorizes films by their distance from stage productions, has not really been improved upon very much.[51] Jack J. Jorgens' scheme complements it, however, through sorting out Shakespeare movies in three-step pigeonholes such as "theatrical, realist, and filmic," or by criteria of "presentation, interpretation, and adaptation."[52] The drawback is that the six categories sometimes overlap and cross one another like Polonius' infamous "tragedy, comedy, history, pastoral, pastoral-comical, historical-pastoral, [tragical-historical, tragical-comical-historical-pastoral,] scene individable, or poem unlimited" (*Ham.* 2.2.396). For example, the Stuart Burge *Othello* is "theatrical-presentational-interpretative" but probably not very "realistic" or "adaptational," while the RADA *Romeo and Juliet* (1966) as a plain record of a stage performance remains purely theatrical and perhaps only mildly interpretative – in short, embalmed theatre. It should be understood that these labels are not to be construed as either pejorative or honorific, but simply descriptive and in no way prescriptive. In its own way, a "theatrical" *Romeo and Juliet* may equal in merit a "realist" Mankiewicz *Julius Caesar*, or a "filmic" Kurosawa's *Throne of Blood*. Ultimately all Shakespeare movies, like stage productions, are adaptations in that they mediate between Shakespeare and the director, but they take so many forms as to make rigorous taxonomy elusive.[53] As Orson Welles said, sooner or later "we all betray Shakespeare."[54]

If there were an imaginary scale from one to ten, then a movie faithful to stage tradition or textual authority (e.g., the Burge *Othello*) could be labeled "conservative" or "closed," and rated a "one"; another more realistic as cinema but conservative with textual changes (e.g., the Mankiewicz *Julius Caesar*), would be a "five"; while a film that massively rearranges the text and embellishes the *mise-en-scène* could be called "radical" or "open," and rated as a "ten" (e.g., Greenaway's *Prospero's Books*). Mainline Shakespeare movies mostly fit into this scale of one to ten, as they go up and down the scale from "closed" to "open," "conservative" to "radical," "presentational" to "filmic," or "theatrical" to "adaptational," but others as yet unconsidered elude these categories. Sometimes bizarre or eccentric, these films do not so much *adapt* as *derive* from Shakespeare. The major difference between the adaptation and the derivative is that adaptations in English (foreign adaptations represent another issue: see chapter 8) rely heavily on Shakespeare's actual words, and derivatives abandon his language altogether. For textual scholars, the remoteness of derivatives from Folio and Quarto relegates them to the fringe, but for cultural historians they may offer a gold mine for speculation about mass consciousness. Like unwanted illegitimate children, no matter how emphatic the protests that they are "not Shakespeare," they have the impudence to lurk on the fringe of the family circle.

There are seven kinds of Shakespeare derivatives, which take protean shapes in plot, theme, language, design, purpose, and camera work. Those of the first kind (recontextualizations) will keep the plot but move Shakespeare's play into a wholly new era and jettison the Elizabethan language (*Joe Macbeth*); the second kind (mirror movies) will meta-cinematically make the movie's backstage plot about the troubled lives of actors run parallel to the plot of the Shakespearean play that the actors are appearing in (*A Double Life*); the third kind (music/dance) will turn the plays into musicals (*West Side Story*), or ballets and operas such as Zeffirelli's *Otello* (1986), the latter of which lie outside the range of this book; the fourth kind (revues) will use the excuse of a biography (*Prince of Players*), or of a documentary (*Looking for Richard*), or even a horror show (*Theater of Blood*) to showcase scenes from Shakespeare's plays; the fifth (parasitical) will exploit Shakespeare for embellishment, and/or graft brief visual or verbal quotations onto an otherwise unrelated scenario (Katharine Hepburn in *Morning Glory*); the sixth kind (animations) – at this point the scheme does begin sounding like Polonius' – will put Shakespeare into cartoon images (*The Lion King*); and finally the seventh kind (documentaries and educational films) will make a variety of pedagogical films that in turn may overlap with any of the permutations and combinations in the previous categories. Howsoever labeled, this catalog of hundreds of titles, not so much "Shakespeare" as "Shakespearean," testifies to Shakespeare's prodigious cultural capital.

Briefly, examples of the first kind of derivatives include the American *Strange Illusion* (1945), which retells the Hamlet legend in modern guise. Starring James Lydon, who later made a career out of playing Henry Aldrich, and directed by Edgar G. Ulmer who began as a director of European Yiddish films, the movie is a prime specimen of the *film noir* B movie, whose trademark dark lighting may have come more from the accident of stingy budgets than from any artistic genius. The movie begins with Paul Cartwight's nightmare about the problematic death of his father, and resentment of his widowed mother's infatuation with Brett Curtis (Claudius). A sullen young man with a taste for wide-lapel suits, Paul mopes about in the baronial family mansion and occasionally shows interest in Lydia (Ophelia). His experiments with real and pretended madness in an effort to block his mother's marriage to Curtis especially link this strangely disturbing film to *Hamlet*.

Like other derivatives of its type, *Joe Macbeth* (1955) makes no pretensions to representing Shakespeare's text on screen but instead recontextualizes the play, again in *film noir*, by moving the Scottish tragedy into the underworld of Chicago's gangland. The parallels are pervasive. Joe Macbeth (Paul Douglas) after rubbing out the Mob Boss's Lieutenant (Cawdor), learns from Rosie, a fortune teller (the witches), that he is destined to be Lord of Lakeview Drive, and ultimately King of the City. A hackneyed cops-and-robbers chase yields to a quick shot of a bawling baby, "And pity, like a naked new-born babe" (1.7.21), and Joe's wife, Lili (Ruth Roman), to advance her husband's career, invites the Duke (Duncan) to be an overnight guest at her home, where he is terminated, or rubbed out. The moment when Lili hands the knife to Joe becomes prime *film noir* as the somber lighting and *mise-en-scène* reflect the anguish in Joe's eyes over his coming act of betrayal. The metaphysics of the witches' prophecies in *Macbeth* are summed up in a single remark to Joe: "Maybe it didn't happen because Rosie said it would but because you did what she said."

Men of Respect (1990), directed by William Reilly and starring John Turturro and Rod Steiger, plays a variation on *Joe Macbeth* in modernizing the play as a gangster movie but the title itself suggests the further influence of Francis Ford Coppola's trilogy based on Mario Puzo's Mafia novels. *Godfather III* (1990) also fits into the category Shakespeare derivative of the fifth kind with a plot that vaguely echoes *King Lear* as well as a direct quotation from it. No Shakespearean playing King Lear has ever surpassed Al Pacino as Don Corleone when on the steps of the opera house he cradles the body of his beloved daughter, a Cordelia figure, and lets loose with a heart-rending "Howl, howl, howl!" (5.3.258). Director Fred Wilcox's *Forbidden Planet* (1956) takes the Shakespeare movie into the realm of science fiction with the story of the mad scientist Dr. Morbius (Walter Pidgeon). Dwelling with Dr. Morbius (Prospero) on Planet Alain-4 is Altaira (Miranda), whose equanimity is upset by the arrival of a space ship with a Ferdinand figure aboard. There is a robot who vaguely corresponds to Ariel and enlisted crew members who are surrogates for Trinculo and Stephano. A great scary, amorphous creature dredged up from Dr. Morbius' Id (Calibaen?) terrifies everyone. A reviewer called "the Freudian monster from the Id . . . a finely outrageous conception, a King Kong of space."[55]

Another farfetched derivative is Peter Ustinov's *Romanoff and Juliet* (1961), which uses Shakespeare's plot and themes but displaces the Capulet / Montague feud into Cold War politics. Igor Romanoff of Concordia, an imaginary obscure East European country, falls in love with Juliet Moulsworth (Sandra Dee), the daughter of the US ambassador. Her parents, surrogates of course for the Capulets, prefer her ex-boy friend, the vapid Freddie (Paris) as a suitor. Tybalt appears in the guise of a KGB agent, and the president of Concordia (Escalus, the prince of Verona) mediates between the warring factions. In the midst of this star-crossed love affair a little boy with a 98-cent chemistry set manages to build an A-bomb, throwing the movie right back in the maw of Cold War hysteria. Unlike Shakespeare's tragedy, the springtime world of youth triumphs over the winter world of the elderly with the marriage of Lt. and Mrs. Igor Romanoff. Behind its surface frivolity, the movie subverts McCarthyism by condemning the stupidity of the Cold War era.

Hollywood director Paul Mazursky, an associate of maverick film maker John Cassavetes, has been responsible for two first-kind derivatives in *Harry and Tonto* (1974), in which a retired New York school teacher reenacts the agony of *King Lear*,[56] and *Tempest* (1982). Filmed on a budget of $13 million at several locations from New York to Atlantic City to Rome and Greece,[57] this modernized *Tempest*, starring John Cassavetes as a New York architect in mid-life crisis, shows again how Shakespeare's play covers the entire history of humanity. Mazursky's cast of Gena Rowlands (Antonia), Susan Sarandon (Aretha/Ariel), Molly Ringwald (Miranda), Raul Julia (Caliban), and Cassavetes (Philip/Prospero), play out variations on Shakespeare's themes as the troubled Philip summons up tempests as ferocious as his own inner demons. On a desolate island in Greece, Philip recognizes like Prospero the intractability of human relationships. Even though "The rarer action is / In virtue than in vengeance" (5.1.27), there yet remains the problem of equitably distributing forgiveness and power among the Calibans and Antonios of the world. Raul Julia's Caliban rivals Jarman's The Incredible Orlando for leering prurience. Molly Ringwald as an innocent but scarily invulnerable Miranda contrasts with Toyah Willcox's minx-like but appealingly vulnerable characterization.

22   Michael Matou as Oberon and Lindsay
Kemp as Puck suggest some of the wild
charm of this transgressive *A Midsummer
Night's Dream* (Spain/UK 1984), directed by
Celestino Coronado.

Derivatives of the second kind almost invariably involve a meta-cinematic scenario in which a backstage intrigue mirrors the plot of a Shakespearean play. Perhaps because on the surface *Othello* shares in such major motifs of soap opera as jealousy and misunderstanding, it has inspired several mirror-like derivatives, not the least being the real-life O. J. Simpson case. A silent era movie, *Carnival* (1921), serves up the standard plot in which actors playing *Othello* on stage find the Othello story mirrored in their personal lives. Silvio Steno, the great Italian Shakespearean actor, goes mad with jealousy and on stage, egged on by Lelio (Iago), almost strangles his wife, Simonetta, to death while she is playing Desdemona.

Two British movies, *Men Are Not Gods* (1936) and *All Night Long* (1962) mine the same material, again to show how an actor can easily lose his grip on reality. A scene in a pre-war London theatre frames *Men Are Not Gods* when, as was then the custom, the audience rises just before the curtain goes up to sing "God Save the Queen." The wife and leading lady (Gertrude Lawrence) of the actor playing Othello, Edmund Davey (Sebastian Shaw), rescues her egocentric husband from a cruel review of his opening performance by persuading the critic's little secretary, Ann Williams (Miriam Hopkins), to alter it. For her trouble, Ann is fired by her waspish employer (Skeates), but she remains so smitten with Davey that she attends *Othello* night after night to admire the man whom she sacrificed her job for. One night by screaming from the balcony, she just manages to prevent Othello from smothering Desdemona (Gertrude

Lawrence) for real on stage. Meanwhile she is courted by obituary reporter Tommy Stapleton, played by a very young and amiable Rex Harrison. This gem of a movie never falters.

Compelling in a different kind of way is *All Night Long* (1962), which uses a jazz band as the core for the machinations and plots that drive Aurelius Rex (Paul Harris/Othello) nearly to strangle his Delia (Marti Stevens/ Desdemona) because of the nefarious plotting of Johnny Cousin (Patrick McGoohan/Iago). In a flagrant modernization, a cigarette case substitutes for Othello's handkerchief and Iago uses a tape recorder to entrap people. The *mise-en-scène* is a renovated luxury flat in London's East End, or Bankside, maybe the Liberty of the Clink before it was gentrified, filled with famous musicians like Johnny Dankworth and Dave Brubeck, all sartorially qualified to be J. Edgar Hoover FBI agents with their short Fifties-style haircuts, narrow ties, and dark suits. Jazz lovers will find the movie intriguing even when it wanders away from Shakespeare, though I personally find reaction shots of grown people at jam sessions tapping, clapping, and nodding to the beat embarrassing. Still another mirror plot based on *Othello* turns up in the Academy-Award-winning *A Double Life* (1947), directed by George Cukor. Ronald Colman plays John Anthony, a great British matinee idol on Broadway, who with good reason fears taking on the role of Othello. His inability to separate his stage and real-life persona deludes him into strangling a pathetic waitress (Shelley Winters), whom he mistakes for an unfaithful Desdemona. Wonderfully acted snippets from *Othello* occur during the on-stage sequences in a movie about the agonies and doubts of the actor's trade that Shakespeare himself knew so well ("As an unperfect actor on the stage, / Who with his fear is put besides his part," sonnet 23).

A movie that fits this rubric, though farcical rather than serious, is *To Be or Not to Be* (1942), Ernst Lubitsch's clever exploitation of *Hamlet* in which Jack Benny's rendering of Hamlet's soliloquy becomes the signal for a Polish airman in the audience (Robert Stack) to go backstage for an assignation with the actor's wife, who plays Ophelia (Carole Lombard). Unfortunately, as Robert F. Willson, Jr., has pointed out, Ophelia should be on stage at this point with Hamlet for the "nunnery" scene, making the dressing room assignation impossible, but Willson admits that only the most dyspeptic purist would object to this bit of whimsy.[58] Also in the mirror/backstage genre is *The Goodbye Girl* (1977), an amusing tale by Neil Simon about a struggling actor (Richard Dreyfuss) who is cast as Richard duke of Gloucester in an off-off-Broadway *Richard III*. The play's pompous ass of a director insists on a ludicrous interpretation of Richard as a homosexual cripple in lavender, but there are also some parallels between the wooing of Lady Anne by Richard in the play and the pursuit of Marsha Mason by Richard Dreyfuss in the movie.[59]

Most recently Kenneth Branagh's *In the Bleak Midwinter/A Midwinter's Tale* (1995) has depicted impoverished British actors putting on *Hamlet* at Christmas time in the abandoned church of a village ironically called Hope. Although Branagh has said that he was influenced by the old Judy Garland/Mickey Rooney movies when the youngsters decide to put on a show in the barn, his movie stirs up much deeper emotional waters. This backstage serio-comic drama happens to deal with actors who are losers, not glamorous stars, making pathetic efforts to interest the world in their Shakespearean tragedy. Essentially Luddites, the actors' obsolete but precious literary values are threatened by the whole mega-entertainment complex of mass communications, just as the abandoned church represents the triumph of consumerism over Christian values. The enchantment of assuming the identities of fabled persons like Hamlet, Gertrude, and Ophelia casts its spell and their play turns into a Christmas miracle in which wretchedness is transfigured into sublimity. As an aspiring actor says in auditions, *Hamlet* is not just a play but his whole life. One critic has faulted the movie for its "cloying sentiment,"[60] but I see it instead, like the Merchant/Ivory *Shakespeare Wallah*, as a poignant defense of a lost world of the imagination. The presence of sleek Joan Collins as the actor's agent in the midst of all this genteel decay adds further interest.

The film adaptation of Jane Smiley's best-selling novel, *A Thousand Acres* (1997), which in turn reappropriated *King Lear*, brings a third-hand Shakespearean derivative to the screen. Smiley's, or perhaps more accurately, director Moorhouse's King Lear (Jason Robards, Jr.) has been updated into a mean-spirited midwestern farmer and child-molester whose daughters rightly despise him. Even the best efforts of talented actresses like Jessica Lange and Michelle Pfeiffer cannot save the movie from degenerating into a weepy. Another derivative, whose special status springs from a gay orientation, is Gus Van Sant's art-house/mainstream *My Own Private Idaho* (1991), starring the late River Phoenix and Keanu Reeves. With overt textual appropriations from the Henriad and the redeployment of the Prince Hal prodigal-son story in Scott Favor's (Keanu Reeves) role as a street hustler and the ne'er-do-well son of Portland's mayor, the movie makes heavy Shakespeare claims. Scott's surrogate father is a beery Falstaff figure, who guzzles from bottles of Falstaff beer, and his friend Mike Waters' (River Phoenix) forlorn search for home in Idaho implicitly comments on American family values. The big question, raised by the film's leading critic, is where in all this is Shakespeare?[61] If Shakespeare is only window dressing, the movie belongs more to Shakespeare movies of the fifth kind (parasitical) than to those of the second kind, where I have tentatively assigned it.

A third kind, the musical, is also doubly derivative in that it usually arrives on screen as the filming of a successful theatrical event rather than as direct inspiration from Shakespeare. Examples include *The Boys from Syracuse* (1940), *Kiss Me Kate* (1953), *West Side Story* (1961), and *Catch My Soul: Santa Fe Satan* (1973). In *The Boys from Syracuse,* based on the Abbott/Rodgers/Hart Broadway musical, director A. Edward Sutherland never hesitates to turn a farce into a travesty as *Comedy of Errors* becomes grist for campy jokes and absurd sight gags. The taxi taking one of the Antipholuses to the "Wooden Horse Inn" is a metered chariot, and the Hollywood star system provided a cast of stereotyped comics like Joe ("Wanna buy a duck?") Penner and Martha ("Big Mouth") Ray. Singer Allan Jones warbles away as Antipholus of Ephesus. Newspapers in Ephesus blare out headlines with faded allusions in need of glossing for today's audiences: "Ephesus Blitzkriegs Syracuse." Only the terminally stuffy will be offended by this good-natured hilarity.

The celebrated Cole Porter *Kiss Me Kate*, which remains a perennial stage hit famous for such witty lyrics as "Brush up your Shakespeare," represents another backstage story. Except for its being a musical, it could as logically be classified with derivatives of the second kind. Squabbling actors Fred Graham (Howard Keel) and Lilli Vanessa (Kathryn Grayson) mirror the stormy behavior of Kate and Petruchio in *The Taming of the Shrew*. Similarly the movie of *West Side Story* evolves from previous stage incarnations. With music and lyrics by Leonard Bernstein and Stephen Sondheim, and extensive choreography by Jerome Robbins, it transforms Romeo Montague and Juliet Capulet into Tony and Maria, pawns in a struggle between warring street gangs in a New York City slum. Compared to today's hip-hop street thugs and punks, the gang members in *West Side Story* look like choir boys, but the movie's powerful linkage of Shakespeare's play with modern youth culture has been copied since then in Franco Zeffirelli's *Romeo and Juliet* and Baz Luhrmann's recent *Romeo & Juliet* (1996). Yet another musical treatment of Shakespeare that came to film via the stage is *Catch My Soul: Santa Fe Satan* (1973), a musical of *Othello* that first played in London as a rock opera in the voguish style of *Jesus Christ Superstar* and *Hair*. Later, Patrick McGoohan, who also appeared in *All Night Long*, made it into a movie, which is set a long way from Piccadilly in the New Mexico desert. In this derivative, Othello is a black cult leader (Richie Havens), while Desdemona (Season Hubley) is a round-faced white girl with granny glasses. Emilia turns into a raffish looking hippie, and Iago fits all negative stereotypes for dropouts with his scruffy beard and unwashed look. The plot follows Shakespeare's quite closely with the scene when the church burns down standing in for Cassio's drunken brawl, and Iago tormenting Othello with innuendoes about Desdemona's interest in Cassio (Tony Joe White). Iago's immortal ploy for generating paranoia, "Hah? I like not that" (3.3.35), remains intact. As the evil Santa Fe Satan, Iago manipulates Othello into smothering Desdemona while the Moor's

"Put out the light, and then put out the light" (5.2.7) pulsates in electronic rock rhythms.

The fourth kind uses a biography or a documentary as the rationale for doing scenes from the plays. *The Royal Box* (1930), where Alexander Moissi as Edmund Kean plays a scene from Hamlet with Camilla Horn as Ophelia, furnishes an early example. As Edwin Booth in *Prince of Players* (1954), Richard Burton performs as Romeo, Hamlet, and Richard duke of Gloucester. His strong personality, especially as Richard III, reminds everyone that in Shakespeare movies all the talk about technical problems, camera angles, *découpage*, and so forth, is so much rubbish without a gifted actor of Burton's caliber. An all-time favorite must be Vincent Price's *Theater of Blood* (1973), which ingeniously mines the canon for horrible murders. An aging Shakespeare actor, Edward Lionheart (Vincent Price), embittered by hostile reviews, sets out with the help of his balmy daughter (Diana Rigg) to avenge himself on the critics who have made his life miserable. He chooses to murder them with the methods used in Shakespeare's plays, which turns the movie into a veritable quiz show as the audience guesses which Shakespearean play is being quoted. One arrogant critic is stabbed like Julius Caesar; another, drowned in wine like Clarence in *Richard III*; yet another finds himself eating his pet poodles in a baked pie like Tamora in *Titus Andronicus*, and so forth. Sometimes this category may take the shape of a documentary such as Al Pacino's imaginative *Looking for Richard* (1996) in which Pacino constructs a documentary about Shakespeare's Richard duke of Gloucester and unifies the different interviews with actors, with scholars, and people on the street by means of powerfully acted segments from the play. As an actor who has played Richard twice on stage and who, as noted above, clearly quoted from *King Lear* at the ending of *Godfather III*, Pacino wants to share his bardolatry with others. His purity of motive in rendering a votive offering to Shakespeare suffuses the whole film and makes it utterly delightful. Never talking down to the audience, Pacino adopts a Socratic pose of ignorance to win it over. His street interviews with surprised New Yorkers "stand as an engaging documentary about the relevance of Shakespeare to 90s culture."[62] As the actors sit around a table rehearsing in a Manhattan office, the casual situation develops its own dynamic, with glorious moments when one actress gives an extraordinary reading of Queen Elizabeth's lines. Pacino shows his own skills in the first wooing scene as he pursues Lady Anne (Winona Ryder) over the corpse of her deceased father-in-law at New York City's The Cloisters. Janet Maslin rightly thought that no major Shakespeare film could match this low-budget endeavor for "irresistible zeal."[63]

As for the fifth kind, derivatives that use only fragments of Shakespeare that are not deeply embedded in the film's main plot, the canon is lengthy and overwhelming. In the silent era, for example, Buster Keaton in *Day*

Dreams (1922) imagined himself in Walter Mitty style as an actor playing Hamlet.[64] Two early revue-type talkies used Shakespeare. A charismatic John Barrymore performed Gloucester's soliloquy from *King Henry Sixth Part Three* in the early talkie revue, *Show of Shows* (1929), which critics felt was the stand-out performance from among "76 stars, a chorus of 500, 18 songs and fifteen specialty acts";[65] John Gilbert and Norma Shearer played the balcony scene from *Romeo and Juliet* in *The Hollywood Revue of 1929*. Later, Katharine Hepburn as a tipsy ingénue recited the "To be or not to be" soliloquy and fragments of Juliet's balcony speech at a stuffy party in *Morning Glory* (1933);[66] the drunken actor (Alan Mowbray) in an Arizona saloon attempted a soliloquy from *Hamlet* under duress by the Clanton gang in the John Ford western *My Darling Clementine* (1946); Karidian Players do *Hamlet* for the crew in an episode of *Star Trek*, called *The Conscience of the King* (1966); tryouts for a show in *Fame* (1980) feature Shakespeare recitations; Robin Williams directs the school play of *Midsummer Night's Dream* for his entranced pupils in *The Dead Poets Society* (1989); Steve Martin wittily spoofs the *Hamlet* graveyard scene in *L.A. Story* (1991); and Danny DeVito teaches an unlikely class of army recruits about the glories of *Hamlet* in *Renaissance Man* (1994). A thorough treatment of the unwieldy subject would need a book far lengthier than this one.[67]

The derivative of the sixth kind appears in the animations of Shakespeare's plays, which began as early as 1920 with Anson Dyer's black-and-white cartoon of *Othello* for Cecil Hepworth. In what is for the times a technical *tour de force*, a black-faced Minstrel falls in love with Mona, the daughter of a bath house proprietor. Richard Burton and Alec McCowen supplied voices for Czech animator Jir' Trnka's feature-length *Midsummer Night's Dream* (*Sen noci svatojánské*, 1959). The recent Disney *The Lion King* (1994) with its over-tones from *Hamlet* took in millions at the box office despite fears that its "sexist, racist, [and] homophobic" overtones might upset the very young.[68] A recent series, aimed at schools, "Shakespeare: The Animated Tales," scripted in Wales and animated in Moscow, with scenarios by Leon Garfield and the advice of Shakespeare scholar Stanley Wells, offer brilliantly executed thirty-minute versions of the plays with voices by well-known British actors. Laurie Osborne's definitive essay likens their cultural impact today to the *Tales from Shakespeare* (1807) by Charles and Mary Lamb that gripped the imaginations of Victorian children. Osborne explores in depth the technical challenges underlying the creation of the cartoons, cites their allusions to more conventional Shakespeare movies, and comments on how animations of Shakespeare's plays "can and should be culturally positioned."[69]

The derivative of the seventh kind, mainly educational and documentary and more often than not made for television, again represents too vast a landscape for consideration here, ranging everywhere from *Discovering Hamlet*

(1990) with Derek Jacobi directing Branagh in rehearsal as the prince, to John Barton's *Playing Shakespeare* series (1984) on acting the plays.[70] Needless to say, they often egregiously overlap with all of the above categories, particularly the fifth, the "revue" picture. They also satisfy "tickling commodity" by generating considerable income from the insatiable demand of schools and universities for the products of the Shakespeare industry.

Beyond all classifications, way beyond the fringe, lie Shakespeare movies of no kind, which are a sub-class of hard-core pornography. To say they are beyond the pale is only to risk offending marginalized deviants, or looking priggish twenty years from now when western civilization may have completely collapsed. The borderline between the cinema of transgression (art) and pornography (smut) has eluded definition even by the United States Supreme Court. A few Shakespeare movies dwell in the suburbs. *Playboy* magazine produced a soft-core *Twelfth Night* (1972), directed by Ron Wertheim for its television program, "Playboy at Night." There have also been a "hard-core" *Romeo and Juliet* (1987), directed by Paul Thomas, in which Juliet and Romeo "end up having sex on stage," as well as a sequel, *Romeo and Juliet 2.* Other risqué titles include *Hamlet: For the Love of Ophelia* (1996) featuring porn star Sarah Young as the object of Hamlet's lust, *A Mid-Slumber Night's Dream* and reportedly a *Much Ado about Humping.*[71] Most recently commercial theatres in London saw a widely released *Tromeo and Juliet* (1996) made by Troma Pictures, which specializes in not just transgressive but outrageously transgressive films. Kim Newman has acidly observed that "Lloyd Kaufman's Troma pictures (essentially a one-man outfit) works so hard at degeneracy and self-delighted crassness that it's a miracle they have never made a good film."[72] Supposedly a redeeming element is that Shakespeare's dialogue is firmly separated from its grossest episodes, but even that hope is blasted with such inanities as "What light from yonder plexiglass shines?" At this point the distance from the Shakespearean vision is so vast that the label must be something like Shakespeare movies of no kind whatsoever. And yet no kind may turn out to be some kind, after all.

10

The renaissance of Shakespeare
in moving images

Towards the end of the century, beginning with Kenneth Branagh's *Henry V* (1989), the multi-million-dollar Shakespeare movie underwent a powerful resurgence. The 1990s renaissance had deeper roots of course than in the commendable energies of Kenneth Branagh alone. He and others benefited from the movie industry's rising fortunes, whose shrinking box-office receipts were reversed by the development of the multiplex. Theatre owners followed the customers out of the cities and into the suburbs with multi-screen theatres in shopping malls, sometimes on the same acreage that had once been taken up with drive-in movies. Unlike the old single-screen picture palaces, the multi-screened cineplex offered a wide variety of choices congenial to both highbrow and lowbrow tastes, and it also made movie going almost as easy as sitting at home slumped in front of the VCR. The dress protocols and uniformed ushers of the old Palace theatres no longer existed, and in North America T-shirts, jeans and baseball caps became the fashion statement for movie going. A Shakespeare film stood a better chance of securing a niche in this open market, especially if it was packaged with big-name stars and state-of-the-art sight and sound.

The Loncraine/McKellen *Richard III*

Investors were courageous enough to put up $8.5 million for Ian McKellen's brilliant modernization of *Richard III* (1996). Like Zeffirelli, McKellen was determined to make Shakespeare entertaining without concessions to either *hoi polloi* or the elite.[1] His Richard does not quite capture the sly wit in the serio-comic medieval vice figure, which Olivier mastered in the 1955 version, but McKellen is otherwise in a reptilian kind of way as certifiably diabolic. Like Olivier's movie a costume drama, its milieu has been reset from the corrupt, late medieval world of the Yorkists and Lancastrians into the age of the Duke of Windsor and Wallace Warfield Simpson. British upper middle-class 1930s society with its mannequin women, opulent surroundings, and ruthless politics have been recreated in a style that McKellen described as "heightened reality."[2] It might also be thought of as "enhanced but ironic realism." As James N. Loehlin suggests, the irony seeps through in a self-mockery nested away in the standard visual codes for upper-class "Englishness,"[3] often labeled the "heritage" look. While the gap between England as it is and as it is represented in this romanticized view may induce cognitive dissonance in British intellectuals, Americans who watch Sunday night mini-series like *The Jewel in the Crown* on public television see it as the fulfillment of all their cherished stereotypes about the English upper classes, whom they secretly admire. While the ballroom scene is quintessentially "heritage," the movie also quotes from the John Woo action movie, documentary newsreels, traces of the gangster movie, tropes from Dennis Potter's television scripts, and in some sequences, a destabilizing mix of realism and surrealism reminiscent of a Luis Buñuel movie like *The Discreet Charm of the Bourgeoisie* (1972). That is to say, there are elements of nightmare and the grotesque, as in the dream when Richard sees himself with a boar's head, or the parade of ghosts on the eve of Bosworth. Most macabre, though, is a low-angle shot of Hastings' body as it hurtles down from the gallows, the sickening jerk as the rope catches his neck, his body spinning and twisting just above the audience's heads. The Dennis Potter trick from *The Singing Detective* of backing up Michael Gambon's serious moments with contrapuntal popular music surfaces in the grim mortuary after the battle, where Richard skips and hops to a jazzy off-camera tune. At the end of the movie when the satanic Richard tumbles downward into the fiery pit, and Al Jolson's voice is overlaid singing "I'm sitting on top of the world," the enhanced realism turns bitterly ironic.

McKellen and director Richard Loncraine, forced to economize on settings, ingeniously made a virtue out of necessity with brilliant use of ready-made locations in Greater London, though Samuel Crowl preferred the symbolic and suggestive settings of the 1990 National Theatre stage play to Loncraine's "relentlessly realistic" film.[4] The exterior of Bankside Power Station near the site of the New Globe Theatre becomes a convincing Tower of London, redesignated as simply "The Tower"; the vast decaying Victorian railway hotel at St. Pancras station on Euston Road, Buckingham Palace; the basement of a vacant insurance building in Holborn, a mortuary for the body of Prince Edward; the Long Gallery at Brighton Pavilion, a drawing room; the abandoned Battersea Power station, the battlefield at Bosworth, and so forth. Happily sound mixer David Stephenson[5] managed to filter out the traffic noises that plagued the Edzard *As You Like It* on its urban wasteland.

To displace Shakespeare's controversial King Richard into a twentieth-century social and political context, McKellen hit on the year 1936 as being neither too remote from, nor too close to, contemporary concerns. McKellen's

23   Kenneth Branagh as the beleaguered young
warrior/monarch in *King Henry V* (UK 1989),
directed by Kenneth Branagh.

duke of Gloucester combines the ferocity of Adolf Hitler with the suaveness of
Juan Peron, as imagined in *Evita.* He sports smartly tailored uniforms with the
boar's head insignia and addresses the hypnotized masses from a lofty podium
festooned with banners. The deep circles under his eyes and the pencil-thin
moustache emblemize his dual persona of a great lover like Clark Gable in fantasy and a loathsome creep in reality. McKellen explains Lady Anne's abrupt
capitulation to Richard in the first wooing scene as purely mercenary, a necessary step to shore up her income, analogous to the widowed Jacqueline
Kennedy's marriage to Aristotle Onassis.[6]

No Shakespearean play has a more confusing story line than *Richard III*
and only one (*Hamlet*) is lengthier. Few but specialists can readily untangle
the tangle of relationships among the warring factions in the play. Like many
other directors, McKellen has generally followed Colley Cibber's formula of
employing bridging materials from *The Third Part of Henry VI* to sort out the
power struggle among the unpleasant descendants of King Edward III (1312–
77). Because the play is impossibly lengthy, Queen Margaret, the Lancastrian
"she-wolf of France," mother of the murdered Henry VI, had to be cut to
keep the audience on the edge of their seats. With Margaret went the choric
diatribes against Richard, though McKellen gives some of them to the Duchess
of York (Maggie Smith), who closely resembles Queen Mary in scratchy 1930s
newsreels.

[221]

In the opening scene, a Yorkist tank smashes into the headquarters of Edward Prince of Wales's Lancastrian army. Richard duke of Gloucester, disguised by a gas mask, calmly executes the young prince, who wears the well-tailored uniform of a British army officer, and then cold-bloodedly shoots King Henry VI in his bedroom. Soon after, Richard triumphantly returns to London to a glittering ballroom filled with kings and queens, princes and princesses, and lesser aristocracy, where he delivers the famous opening soliloquy, "Now is the winter of our discontent / Made glorious summer by this son of York" (1.1.1). After the harrowing gangster-style executions of the Lancastrians, the sumptuous Victory Ball comes as a culture shock and furnishes the "gilt" to cover up the "guilt" of what is now Yorkist, but once had been Lancastrian, villainy: "England shall double gild his treble guilt" (2 *Henry IV* 4.5.128). A twenty-piece band led by a Glenn Miller lookalike plays on the dais behind music stands emblazoned with the letters "WS." A female vocalist (Stacey Kent) warbles Trevor Jones's "Come live with me and be my love" so slickly arranged that the anachronism of the Christopher Marlowe lyrics set to a catchy 30s tune goes unnoticed. On the ballroom floor, the king (John Wood) and his American queen (Annette Bening) foxtrot to the applause and admiration of the exquisitely gowned ladies and their white-tie-and-tails, or baroquely uniformed, escorts. This sophisticated, worldly, elegant but heartless society would not be unhappy with a monarch, or an Adolf Hitler, who kept the labor unions and undeserving poor in their places.

Subliminal references to Shakespeare's play flash across the screen. Preparing for the ball, the notoriously lecherous but now sickly King Edward gropes at the thigh of the nurse attending on him. ("Lascivious Edward, and thou perjur'd George, / And thou misshapen Dick" says Prince Edward of Lancaster just before being stabbed by Edward, George [Clarence], and Dick [Richard] (3 *Henry VI* 5.5.37).) The Princess Elizabeth (Kate Steavenson-Payne), who is a non-speaking character in Shakespeare's play, shows her pleasure in being introduced to her future husband, Henry Richmond (Dominic West), a young naval officer and future Tudor King Henry VII. McKellen's clue for the concept of Richmond as a naval officer came from Lord Stanley's unsettling news that "Richmond is on the seas" (4.4.462).[7] In another astute move, Queen Elizabeth's Woodville brother, Earl Rivers (Robert Downey, Jr.), is imagined as an American playboy, who appears at the ball after arriving on PanAm from New York. Later Tyrell (Adrian Dunbar) stabs him with a phallic knife while he is performing an X-rated sex scene in bed with the airline hostess (Tres Hanley). In Shakespeare's play the outsider Woodville relatives of the widowed queen, by supporting the succession to the crown of her son, the older of the two little princes, earn the hostility of wily Richard, who schemes for the crown himself. As an American, McKellen's Queen Elizabeth shows what might have happened in England if Wallis Warfield Simpson, perish the thought, had become King Edward's queen, and brought her relatives to the court.

To keep things moving (as Zeffirelli did with Claudius' first speech in his *Hamlet*), McKellen divides the opening soliloquy up and resituates the segments. He announces from the bandstand that this is "Now ... the winter of our discontent," to the applause of the champagne-sipping audience, and he continues in the men's room, where he admires himself in the mirror on the wall near the urinals. The face in the mirror is a triumph of make-up artistry with enormous circles under the eyes, a thin moustache, and a slightly puffy cheek. He walks with a limp and has a noticeable hump on his shoulder in the stage tradition of a Richard "crook-back" (3 *Henry VI* 2.2.96), a "foul misshapen stigmatic" (2.2.136), whose physical deformity outwardly and visibly indexes a malignant soul. Then he addresses both himself in the mirror and the theatre audience with the chilling words transposed from *Henry VI Part Three*, "Why, I can smile, and murther whiles I smile" (3.2.182), before returning to the glitzy ballroom, which is now exposed as an elaborate stage set for Richard's power trip.

To further capture the flavor of the 1930s, Ian McKellen chainsmokes "Abdullas" in a virtuoso performance that adds yet another chapter to movie "cigarette semiology,"[8] almost at the level of world-class nicotine addicts like Bette Davis and Humphrey Bogart. His cigarettes become expressive objects, surrogates to his need for human affection, as he caresses, pats, taps, and puffs on them. When, after Hastings' execution, he gloats over obscene pictures of the hanging he is also mimicking one of Adolf Hitler's less agreeable pastimes, except that *der Führer*, the better to enjoy his victims' writhings from slow strangulation, preferred motion to still pictures. In a tell-tale moment, Lady Anne in the privacy of her limousine injects a needle into her thigh, which signals her own addiction, brought on by her fatal relationship with Richard. She dies horribly with a spider crossing her motionless face, presumably the victim of some dastardly intervention by Richard, though Shakespeare never clarifies this point.

Loncraine's *Richard III* met with the wildly varied reception that seems to be the fate of most Shakespeare films, Shakespeare purists having been joined by film purists, who are equally elitist and impossible to please. Two intelligent and knowledgeable critics writing in the same newspaper concluded that the film was (a) "a pathetic pastiche of transplantations," and (b) "opulent and hypnotic."[9] The *New Yorker* critic put the film down with clever sound bites about a "time-travel experiment gone wrong."[10] Most reactions, however, were more like that of Brian Gilbey, who even after complaining that the film is "more concerned with visuals than with verse" also confessed that not "any of this really matters."[11] As James Cameron-Wilson put it, "The film's terrific... McKellen has taken us by the scruff of the neck and shaken it into a cinematic context,"[12] and David Gritten thought it was "a piece of cinema in its own right, emphatically not a filmed version of a stage play."[13] Critics heaped scorn on Richard's uttering "A horse, a horse! My kingdom for a horse!" (5.4.13) while anachronistically riding in a jeep. Yet omitting the best-known line in the play would have stirred up even more of a tempest. In truth, old army types, World War II cavalrymen like General George Patton, an avid polo player, often nostalgically yearned for a horse while seated in a jeep. If, as has been argued, McKellen and Loncraine have done nothing original with the play, they have most certainly made an original *movie* out of it, one of the best of its kind.

Parker's *Othello*

While critics accused the Loncraine/McKellen *Richard III* of being too cine-matic and insufficiently Shakespearean, the Oliver Parker *Othello* of the same year (1995) was indicted for the opposite crime. It was too theatrical and insuf-ficiently cinematic.[14] Although not so "filmic" as Orson Welles's *Othello*, only a step away from theatre actually, it nevertheless goes beyond the merely pre-sentational. While Parker's lighting and camera angles, his *mise-en-scène*, seem cautiously theatrical, his editing shows a talent for telling a story visually. The opening montage clarifies the vague pronoun reference, "this," in the first line of *Othello*, when Roderigo says to Iago "[Tush,] never tell me! I take it much unkindly / That thou Iago, who hast had my purse / As if the strings were thine, shouldst know of *this*" [italics mine] (1.1.1). This what? Parker replies in pictures. The clichéd establishing shot of a gondola in Venice actually shows Desdemona en route to her elopement with Othello. Then, in another invented scene, Desdemona steps out of the gondola and runs down a long piazza, while in the foreground a concealed Iago and Roderigo peer at her. She stops wide-eyed in a doorway greeting someone, who later turns out to be Othello.

The film jumps ahead to scene three at the palace where the duke and his counselors are evaluating the threat from the Turkish fleet and examining a map of the Mediterranean showing the enemy fleet deployment: "The Turkish preparation makes for Rhodes" (1.3.14), and it is decided that Othello must lead the Venetians against the enemy. In tight framing, two hands clasp, one black and one white, and one hand places a ring on the other, after which the camera pulls back to show a priest officiating over the marriage of Othello and Desdemona. The camera pulls even further back to reveal Roderigo peer-ing through the window and spying on the marriage between Desdemona and Othello. A cut back to Shakespeare's opening lines has Iago (Kenneth

Branagh) and Roderigo (Michael Maloney) reviling Othello with racist epithets ("the thick-lips," "lascivious moor"), and tormenting Brabantio with the news that "an old black ram / Is tupping your white ewe" (1.1.98). A glimpse of Cassio (Nathaniel Parker), throws kerosene on Iago's fiery contempt for "One Michael Cassio a Florentine" (1.1.20).[15] Next, there is Desdemona's irate father, Brabantio, leading a posse of angry citizens toward the ducal palace to lodge a complaint against the Moor. This intricate montage has explained much of what is behind the single pronoun, "this." Desdemona has eloped with Othello; Iago is a hate-filled malcontent; Roderigo is Iago's puppet; Brabantio is outraged by his daughter's marriage; Venice is at risk from an approaching Turkish fleet; and Othello's services as a *condottiero* are needed in Cyprus.

Not untidy like *Richard III*, *Othello* has the focused plot and characters of a classical tragedy. Parker's aim was to foreground the love affair of Othello (Laurence Fishburne) and Desdemona (Irène Jacob) and to downplay Iago (Kenneth Branagh). Critics nevertheless found the movie "Iago-centric," as if the talented Branagh had totally stolen the show, even though Fishburne[16] contributes a massive dignity and physical presence. Egg bald and covered with bracelets and earrings, he most resembles Sergei Bondarchuk in the Yutkevich *Othello*. His Desdemona projects a wonderful innocence and sweetness, which her slight Swiss accent makes all the more endearing. In the movie's boldest stroke, it pries into the connubial activities of Othello and Desdemona, a topic that Shakespeare avoids and that scholars have mostly averted their eyes from. When, if ever, the literal-minded have asked, did the happy pair consummate their marriage? There was little time for dalliance since they were abruptly dispatched to Cyprus on separate vessels, and Cassio's drunken brawl egregiously interrupted their first night together. Steamy boudoir footage of Othello and Desdemona resolves the mystery when in close-up Othello removes the leather belt from around his waist, and in a long shot Desdemona opposite him provocatively disrobes. Elements of "heteroc," as Derek Jarman might call them, include a paranoid Othello's porn fantasies about Desdemona and Cassio frolicking in bed; and a Iago discoursing to Roderigo on the subject of "Lechery, by this hand; an index and obscure prologue to the history of lust and foul thoughts" (2.1.257), while they sit under a wagon occupied by two copulating Cyprians. A very nice touch has Iago observing Cassio through the reflected image from a knife blade as "He takes her by the palm" (2.1.167) immediately after disembarkation in Cyprus.

Fishburne's and Jacob's success by no means detracts from Branagh's skillful Iago that demands an actor capable of simultaneously projecting overt bonhomie and covert malice. Olivier's Iago, Frank Finlay, mastered the difficult trick, but most actors tend to be too genial for serious villainy. Kenneth Branagh juggles this Janus-like stance mainly by a knack for timing that suggests he is speaking very reluctantly even when he is actually falling all over himself to slander Cassio and Desdemona. He adds to that a gift for facial expressions, often in collusion with the audience, that clearly signal his innate vileness. Parker's tight shots and deft camera movements support the acting talents of the principals by, for example, zooming in on Iago's moving lips as they telegraph his perfidious intentions. More interested in interpreting Shakespeare's play than in indulging in cinematic rhetoric, Parker pays no attention to the fashionable vogue for a homoerotic attraction between Iago and Othello. On the other hand, the camera dutifully records the progress of the play's most famous expressive object, the handkerchief, as it is passed along from Emilia to Iago to Bianca. Covered with the strawberry marks that also appear on Desdemona's wedding sheets, the fetish handkerchief floats aloft as a surrealistic image of its terrible powers. Michael Maloney, who even threatens Iago with a knife, plays Roderigo as surprisingly truculent, not at all the gullible wimp. After his particularly nasty murder, blood spills out of his mouth just before a jump cut to Othello extinguishing a row of candles firmly connects the two masques of death. All the more dreadful in its cold-blooded moralizing, Othello's self-righteous "It is the cause, it is the cause, my soul" (5.2.1) initiates the ritual of Desdemona's demise. Surprisingly, the angelic Desdemona does not go quietly into the night, but fiercely resists the bullying Othello, and fights desperately for her life. Once exposed by Emilia, Iago invokes his obstinate silence: "Demand me nothing; what you know, you know: / From this time forth I never will speak word" (5.2.303). The bodies of Iago's victims, Emilia, Othello, and Desdemona, lie side by side on display, bathed in sunlight from an opened window, literally illustrating "the tragic loading of [the] bed" (5.2.363). A somber burial at sea replaces the grand funeral cortège in the Welles *Othello,* or the mob scene in the piazza in the silent Emil Jannings *Othello*. Perhaps Lodovico who has gone "straight aboard" to return to Venice, has arranged for this consummation of a marriage in death even if not in life. Parker has used his license as a movie maker to embellish the Othello story with one more vignette.

Nunn's *Twelfth Night*

Trevor Nunn's $5-million *Twelfth Night* (1996) added yet another mainstream Shakespeare movie to the glittering array of late twentieth-century offerings. By far the best screen treatment since the John Sichel 1970 British television version starring Alec Guinness (Malvolio), Joan Plowright (Viola), and Ralph Richardson (Sir Toby Belch), in its world-weariness and rather fashionable despair it ironically replicates the *fin-de-siècle* mood of the late nineteenth century. Kenneth Branagh's description of his own Renaissance Theatre *Twelfth Night* as "close[r] to Chekhov"[17] applies equally well to Trevor Nunn's, which shares a bitter-sweet melancholy and nostalgia with *Uncle Vanya* and *The Cherry Orchard*. Just as *Twelfth Night, or What You Will*, first performed around 1600, probably either at the court or at one of the Inns of Court, marks the end of Shakespeare's festive comedies and the beginning of the darker period of city comedies and tragedies, so the Christian feast day of "Twelfth Night" (January 6) terminates the Twelve Days of Christmas, and shadows forth Lent.

Nunn does not allow any of the potentially serious subtext to spoil the fun of a good movie, which is about "what you will," though as a veteran stage director he admits to having expected an "imminent thunderbolt" as he "tampered" with Shakespeare's language to convert it into a film scenario.[18] The fashionably melancholy Illyrians in their desire for love, and frustration in not being loved, reflect various stages of order and disorder, with little Viola / Cesario at the still center of a whirligig of emotions. Nunn fleshes out Shakespeare's plot with two major additions. The first, a *Titanic* trope, imagines Viola (Imogen Stubbs) and Sebastian (Stephen Mackintosh) in the dining salon of a nineteenth-century passenger vessel on the edge of doom. It is the last night out and at the captain's party the brother and sister, costumed as Moslem women with yashmaks, are entertaining the first-class passengers with a duet of "O mistress mine." When they remove their veils, Viola is sporting a moustache like Sebastian's. The full implications of this cross-dressing are suspended when the ship founders in a wild storm, and pandemonium erupts. Convincing special effects spill Viola into the briny sea and show her struggling for survival under water. The second addition occurs when she comes out of the ocean to crawl ashore on the seacoast of Illyria, and asks "And what should I do in Illyria?" (1.2.3). The answer must be that she should keep a very low profile, for Nunn has added the twist that her native Messaline and Illyria have long been at war, a motif copied from contentious ancient cities of Syracuse and Ephesus in *The Comedy of Errors*. Unfortunately this added plot element also robs Viola of some of the mystery that Shakespeare surrounded her with, and turns Illyria into a police state. Much later, in a touch of whimsy when Sebastian comes ashore in this now hostile territory, he carries a copy of the *Baedeker Guidebook to Illyria*.

Nunn's cross-cutting supports the cross-dressing that is so much a part of the play, and undercuts beliefs that the movie favors the theatrical over the filmic. Viola and Olivia (Helena Bonham Carter) mirror each other in their grief for lost brothers and in their quest to find substitute males. The camera explores the gender anxieties brought on by Orsino's falling in love with a boy, and Olivia's infatuation with the same man / woman. As Nunn has said, this is "the most fundamental Shakespearean play about sexuality and gender,"[19] featuring as it does identical twins of opposite gender. As the cross-dressed Viola/Cesario, Imogen Stubbs interrogates the feminist fantasy that being male can resolve all female problems. Under the watchful eye of the sea captain, she wraps herself like a mummy to flatten her bosom, and stuffs cloth into her trousers to conceal how much she "lack[s] of a man" (3.4.303). Putting on a brave front for Orsino, as the newly invented Cesario she takes up horseback riding, billiards, fencing, learns to walk like a man with hands in pockets, and, hilariously, to puff on a cigar in a macho kind of way, though the latter rite almost finishes her off. The fencing lessons pay off when, for possibly the first time in the play's performance history, she manages a respectable sword fight against the terrified Sir Andrew Aguecheek. When Viola delivers the poignant set-piece to Olivia beginning, "Make me a willow cabin at your gate" (1.5.268), she really does make Olivia's name "reverberate [into the] hills." Helena Bonham Carter in her regal black Victorian mourning dress, and then later when she swoons over Cesario, in a preRaphaelite turquoise gown, brings high fashion to the P. G. Wodehouse country-house setting. Meanwhile little Viola must be content with a pert but unadorned military tunic. The sea is never far away. As Samuel Crowl has pointed out,[20] Nunn integrates the play's water imagery by having the worldweary Orsino (Toby Stephens) compare the capacity of love with the sea (1.1.10), by placing Orsino's home directly at the sea, in Cornwall actually, and then by having Viola miraculously come out of the sea. Later on Viola says cryptically, "Tempests are kind and salt waves fresh in love" (3.4.384).

Like Falstaff in *The Merry Wives of Windsor*, the merry pranksters, Sir Toby Belch (Mel Smith), Maria (Imelda Staunton), Fabian (Peter Gunn), and Sir Andrew Aguecheek (Richard E. Grant), end up looking somewhat more boorish than funny. When the grumpy Malvolio (Nigel Hawthorne) attempts to break up the midnight revelry, Sir Toby scathingly puts him down with his famous one-liner, "Art any more than a steward? Dost thou think because thou art virtuous there shall be no more cakes and ale?" (2.3.114). Wholesale deletions of the badinage, punning, quibbling, and bawdry from this linguistically rich play work against Sir Toby, but no modern audience could possibly decode, for example, the labyrinthine puns on "hang," "colors," and "none" in act one, scene five. A tight frame of Maria's yellow stockings during Malvolio's row with Sir Toby hints at a major element in Malvolio's future martyrdom.

Nigel Hawthorne masterfully plays the scapegoated Malvolio with an air of "injured majesty,"[21] reminiscent of his film role as King George III. At the end of the play, having escaped the dark house, but having been further rejected and humiliated in front of the entire household staff, Feste maliciously baits him, "And thus the whirligig of time brings in his revenges" (5.1.376). Olivia says that Malvolio has been "most notoriously abus'd" but he remains unmollified and stomps out of the house carrying a pathetic suitcase. Hawthorne energetically ferrets out the hidden speck of humanity in Malvolio's shriveled soul, yet the film leaves little doubt that Malvolio will one day have his revenge "on the whole pack" of them. While some critics have deplored his sobriety, Feste (Ben Kingsley) frames the film with his "hey ho, the wind and the rain" (5.1.389), whose haunting words, which also become the Fool's in *King Lear* (3.2.74), warn against the consequences of folly, indeed, of doing "what you will." At the height of the fraternity house roistering with Sir Toby and Maria, an aloof Feste renders a heartfelt solo of "O mistress mine, where are you roaming?" (2.3.39), which is all the more compelling for its rugged amateurism. When he reaches "Then come kiss me, sweet and twenty; / Youth's a stuff will not endure," Maria senses the deep pathos and her face crumbles almost into tears. Kingsley's somber tone reflects a major streak of sobriety in *Twelfth Night*, which the late Harry Levin once encapsulated in the remark that "the cakes and ale of Illyria are consumed in a house of mourning."[22] In *Twelfth Night*, Shakespeare created a verbal structure that probes the sadness and sweetness in the mystery of life, and Nunn has gracefully and wittily put that daunting challenge into moving images.

Luhrmann's *Romeo + Juliet*

Baz Luhrmann's Generation-X *William Shakespeare's Romeo + Juliet* (1996) makes Franco Zeffirelli's *Romeo and Juliet* (1968) look stodgy by comparison. The film rhetoric in Luhrmann's screenplay introduces terms undreamt of thirty years ago, like "Whip Pan," "Super Macro Slam Zoom," "Chopper P. O.V.," "Window Cam," "Distorted Out-of-Control Close-up," and even a "Slow Motion: Washing Machine Tumble Shot."[23] This is watching Shakespeare's *Romeo and Juliet* under strobe lights. It has been filtered through John Woo's Hong Kong action movies, and the hiphop and gangsta rap of MTV, yet the characters speak in Elizabethan English. The verbal runs against the grain of the visual semiotics. Yes, it is odd to hear Romeo say "O me! what fray was here?" (1.1.173) after a violent explosion in a gasoline station, but once the ear adjusts, it becomes a probable improbability. The flat American voices lack the stagy sonorities of John Gielgud but carry fierce conviction. There is absolutely nothing new about putting Shakespeare in modern dress but dressing him in the jeans and T-shirts and pierced bodies of the MTV generation ratchets the transgressiveness up a notch. It was Luhrmann's intention "to make this movie rambunctious, sexy, violent, and entertaining the way Shakespeare might have if he had been a filmmaker."[24] Janet Maslin summed up a general critical attitude of dismay combined with admiration: "This is headache Shakespeare, but there's method to its madness."[25]

For music, Luhrmann scraps Zeffirelli's variations on a single theme from Nino Rota's "What Is a Youth?" in favor of a mélange of pop singers and bands to include Garbage, Everclear, One Inch Punch, Butthole Surfers, The Wannadies, almost everybody, one might say, except the Screaming Headless Torsos. And yet the soundtrack can no more be stereotyped than the scenario for at pivotal intervals when Romeo is first introduced, or in the tomb scene, a graceful passage from Mozart or Wagner's *Liebestod* captures the mood. Luhrmann's movie also eschews Zeffirelli's heightened realism in an Italian hill town for the constructed world of a never-never land of Verona, partly filmed in Mexico City but as placeless in many ways as the set for a sci-fi movie. The great statue of Jesus looms over the action, a rebuke to the city's warring factions and a surrogate for the golden statue that in a variation on the Midas myth one day will memorialize the martyred Juliet.

In a major conceit, Luhrmann inserts the sonnet prologue within the frame of a television screen, giving the speech to the anchorwoman on the evening news. The anchorwoman's formulaic reading of the evening news replaces the formal three-quatrains-and-a-couplet Elizabethan sonnet as a symbol of oppression. When Romeo says "O me, what fray was here?" he is actually witnessing a derivative replay of the rioting between Capulets and Montagues on a television monitor. The new challenge for the young is not to break out of the formal restraints of the sonnet into blank verse as Juliet does with "Gallop apace, you fiery-footed steeds" (3.2.1), and her equally compelling but horrifying potion speech, "What if it be poison which the friar / Subtilly hath minist'red to have me dead [?]" (4.3.24), but to escape from television's straitjacket of mass conformity. Like nothing else in history, the tube has the power to manipulate ordinary people into confusing reality with fantasy to the extent of having them emotionally identify with celebrities that they have never laid eyes on, nor ever will. The film's blurring together of the multiple planes of perception in the world of the audience, the world of the movie, of the illusory television newscast, which is so easily confused with an actual newscast, gets as bewildering as Shakespeare's own meta-dramatic taste for putting plays within plays within plays.

The interplay between the crude actualities of television newscasts and MTV fantasies generates the film's *raison d'être*, which is the displacement into contemporary idiom of the oxymorons of Shakespeare's oppositions of womb and tomb, love and death, youth and age, and so forth. The gap between profane and sacred love is everywhere. The Verona sea shore, as littered as a Sicilian beach, is a showcase of tawdriness, a hangout for prostitutes, where a decaying theatrical stage with a Globe theatre marquee underscores the gap between the majesty of the sea and the tackiness of the polluted beach. The machine has invaded the garden in the shape of sleek automobiles, beatup jalopies, and roaring motorcycles.

The sacred love of the teenagers, Leonardo DiCaprio and Claire Danes, counterpoints this profane disease and corruption. Like all youthful Romeos and Juliets, they are accused of not being up to the challenge. Rex Reed thought that neither "has a clue to what they are saying, or what Shakespeare is all about," moreover DiCaprio has "raw talent, no discipline or training, and a spectacular stupidity."[26] The young stars of the Zeffirelli movie, Olivia Hussey and Leonard Whiting, in their day were maligned no less vitriolically. The course of their true love unfolds from the episode when to the strains of Mozart, Romeo is first seen musing alone by Benvolio, to the arrival at the Capulet ball when Romeo must douse his head in a basin to shake off the mind-altering effects of Mercutio's pill, to the strangely displaced balcony scene that immerses Romeo and Juliet in the Capulet swimming pool (presumably to emerge reborn from the sacred waters), to the violent duel with Tybalt using "Sword 9mm series S" pistols to slide around an awkward anachronism, to the candle-lit tomb scene (following a cops-and-robbers chase sequence) when Juliet awakens before Romeo dies and each is made aware of the terrible irony in the way their "stars" have cheated them. Actually Luhrmann did not invent this searing piece of business, its origins having been traced back at the least to eighteenth-century staging, though a more recent film precedent is the Theda Bara and Harry Hilliard silent *Romeo and Juliet* (1916). Wagner's *Liebestod* rather than Rota's sentimental score more appropriately colors Luhrmann's anti-romantic dénouement.

The lovers use almost all of Shakespeare's sonnet sequence in the Capulet ballroom, and some of the verse from the truncated aubade scene. When Father [sic] Laurence instructs Juliet on how to take the sleeping potion, realism gives way to filmic tactics as in the background the screen fills with an envelope addressed to Romeo in Mantua. The "Post Post Haste" delivery van misses Romeo in Mantua when the headphones of his Walkman radio deafen him to the knocking on the door of his grungy house trailer. A "We Called" card is shoved under his door, just before the dissolve to Juliet's bed chamber where she is about to imbibe the sleeping potion.

The movie tears off the façade of bourgeois respectability from Juliet's parents and turns [Lady] Gloria Capulet (Diane Venora) into a shallow, pillpopping fashion plate and Father Fulgencio Capulet (Paul Sorvino) into a monstrous tyrant. Sorvino's scolding of Juliet for her unwillingness to marry Paris nearly matches the volcanic eruption of Sebastian Cabot in the Castellani *Romeo and Juliet*. In the service of diversity and multi-culturalism, the film includes a black actor, Harold Perrineau, as a splendid Mercutio, who performs a virtuoso Queen Mab speech and whose friendship with Romeo hints at a streak of homoeroticism. For the Capulet ball, Mercutio cross-dresses in a mini-skirt, Romeo wears the armor of a young King Arthur, Gregory and Sampson are Vikings, and Benvolio wears a monk's habit. Perrineau's "A plague a' both your houses!" (3.1.106), after the disastrous duel with Tybalt, takes on a special edge in view of the lily-white status of both Montagues and Capulets. The English actress, Miriam Margolyes, also adds to political correctness by becoming a Hispanic Nurse, though she is denied her great monologue about Susan, "Well, Susan is with God, / She was too good for me" (1.3.19), and her betrayal of Juliet, "Romeo's a dishclout to him" (3.5.219), is weakly orchestrated.

As "Father," not "Friar," Laurence, Pete Postlethwaite, who also turns up as the Player King in the Zeffirelli *Hamlet*, incarnates the contemporary type of the troubled clergyman, close to a public scandal over charges of pedophilia, or worse. With a kinky look, a Runic cross emblazoned on his back like a tattoo, or the back of a Gianni Versace dress, he is not the sort to be entrusted with choir boys. A victim as much as anyone else of the media tyranny, he is shown fantasizing, like Walter Mitty, about newspaper headlines that will proclaim his genius in mediating the feud between Montagues and Capulets. His tiresome fifth-act plot summary telling the fidgety audience what it already knows, though admittedly the on-stage persons may not know it, suffers an unkind cut, but his craven desertion in the tomb of Juliet, "the watch is coming / Come go, good Juliet [*noise again*], I dare no longer stay" (5.3.158) partly survives.

The candle-lit, acid-trip atmosphere of the ornate tomb-scene then yields to footage on the evening news of the young lovers' bodies being hauled off in an ambulance. The confident tones of the oracular anchorwoman reporting terrible events in the tomb redefine reality as sound bites and isolated segments. From actualities to fantasies to actualities, the lines separating the one from the other recede into the electronic time warp. Romance has given way to actuality. And to make the question of reality all the more elusive, the television screen gradually fades away into a pinpoint of blackness. All may be "punished," as Captain Prince (Vondie Curtis-Hall) proclaims, but all will most certainly end by disappearing into the black hole of the television screen. Romeo and Juliet are lost like the rest of us in the empty spaces of electronic media, but not before this perversely beautiful movie employs Shakespeare's text as a kind of surrogate to "inspect the place of Shakespeare ... in contemporary culture."[27] In a stunning reversal of the normal stage to screen formula, a 1998 touring RSC production of *Hamlet* directed by Matthew Warchus and starring Alex Jennings has "clearly been inspired by Baz Luhrmann's inventive 1996 film version of *Romeo and Juliet*."[28]

Another of the ambitious films of the 1990s was Adrian Noble's made-for-television *Midsummer Night's Dream* (1996), which was theatrically released

24   Ian McKellen as the villainous Richard duke of
Gloucester in the 1990 Richard Eyre stage production at
the National Theatre, which preceded the making of
Richard Loncraine's 1996 movie, also starring McKellen.

in England. It makes all the right gestures but never quite comes up with a
protocol believable enough to attract the widespread interest generated by
competing productions. The idea of having the audience experience the action
through the eyes of a small boy (Osheen Jones), who dreams the events in
the play, comes close to Jane Howell's use of a similar point of view in her
successful BBC *Titus Andronicus*. The boy/spectator entering and re-entering
the computerized *mise-en-scène* possibly is designed to enchant the children
in the audience, along with the quotations from Mary Poppins, Beatrix Potter,

Victorian cut-out theatres, and country music for the rude mechanicals. Today's over-stimulated children, however, may find all of this just a bit too much department-store Christmas decorations for acceptance. At the other end of the spectrum, the movie contains adult material involving sexual innuendoes that almost qualify the film as a chapter nine event in this book alongside the Coronado gay/punk *Dream*. For instance, a languid Puck kisses a limp-wristed Oberon full on the mouth, and Hippolyta is shown supine on a pink couch resembling the "medlar" fruit that Mercutio bawdily describes to Romeo (2.1.36). The actors vary in quality, the men sometimes veering toward the prissy, particularly Theseus/Oberon (Alex Jennings), the women sometimes first-rate as in the happy case of Hippolyta/Titania (Lindsay Duncan). The impeccable RSC diction carries more polish than feeling. The choreography and costumes are like a box of overly rich cream-filled chocolates, so sweet as to be slightly nauseating. Putting the rude mechanicals on a motorcycle is a good idea but somehow out of synch with the decadent style of the rest of the production. Critic Mark Sinker put it well when he wrote that it is "fitfully engaging at best, [but] ends up implicating no one.[29]

The age of Kenneth Branagh

By a shrewd merger of art and commerce, Kenneth Branagh magically resuscitated the Shakespeare movie just when everyone was announcing its death at the hands of television. He was a young man of working-class origins from Belfast and Reading, who attended the Royal Academy of Dramatic Art and who against all odds swiftly rose to the pinnacle of the acting profession.[30] At twenty-six, he founded his own repertory company, the Renaissance Theatre Company, and talked major stars like Judi Dench and Derek Jacobi into being directors. He directed the RTC version of *Twelfth Night* (1987), which was subsequently taped for video release,[31] played the lead in Adrian Noble's *Henry V* at Stratford (1984), did *Hamlet* with the Renaissance Theatre Company (1988), and again for Adrian Noble at the RSC's Barbican (1992), and took the leading role in *Coriolanus* at the Chichester Festival Theatre (1992). So by 1989 when he produced his film of *Henry V*, which heralded a fresh parade of Shakespeare movies in the 1990s, his career was already in fast forward. Besides supervising three large-screen Shakespeare movies, he has, as we have seen, also played Iago in the Oliver Parker *Othello* (1996), and produced his *Hamlet* derivative, *A Midwinter's Tale* (1995). Most recently he has even successfully impersonated Woody Allen's voice and manner in *Celebrity* (1998), and he has been planning a film of *Love's Labor's Lost*. With his $9-million *Henry V*, he boldly moved from stage to screen to create what has been widely acclaimed as "an audacious, resonant, passionate film,[32] "a Henry for a decade,"[33] and one "masterfully adapted,"[34] especially in North America where the politics of British theatre lose velocity. For many of his countrymen, however, Branagh had not only sold out to the Thatcherites and the feel-good Shakespeareans[35] but also committed the unpardonable sin of being too successful too young. Branagh's movie was self-reflexively the equivalent of Hal's invasion of France. When this novice director's work then turned a handsome profit for its plucky backers, his success became unbearable.

While his King Henry inevitably triggered comparisons with Laurence Olivier's performance in the famous 1944 movie, as well as suggestions of influence, it was Branagh's stage experience in Adrian Noble's RSC *Henry V* (1984) that mainly inspired the movie.[36] He kept saying that he did not want to be the "new Olivier" but to create a film that was special and unique in its own right.[37] Olivier's film reflected the wartime ideologies of 1944, while Branagh's grew out of the late-80s post-Falkland era, though there were efforts to transcend any particular topicality. Olivier's king was an invulnerable matinee idol; Branagh's king, vulnerable and plain-spoken, outwardly a warrior king but inwardly a Hamlet figure, torn between duty and compassion. Branagh speaks of trying "to realise the qualities of introspection, fear, doubt and anger"[38] which he saw in the character and which dictated more close-ups than long shots. With some justification, critic Jill Forbes, besides disliking the soundtrack, thought that Branagh's down-home monarch sacrificed "the notion of ceremony" among kings which Olivier's anti-naturalistic acting reinforced.[39] And where Olivier censored out images damaging to the "mirror of all Christian kings," like ordering the deaths of the Cambridge conspirators, Branagh not only arrests but assaults Cambridge, Gray, and Scroop, though he also scraps the notorious order for genocide at Agincourt: "Then every soldier kill his prisoners, / Give the word through" (4.6.37). Olivier's camera tended to pull back and up so that the actors' voices grew and flourished in rhetorical splendor as the bodies diminished; Branagh's movie often begins a sequence in mid-shot and then moves in tighter and tighter to peer more and more closely at faces. When Hostess Quickly (Judi Dench) poignantly eulogizes Falstaff, the camera bores in on her stricken countenance as if it would wrest the truth out of her innermost secret being.

Branagh's gift is in knowing how to combine the theatrical with the filmic. He brought with him to film making none of the prejudices of stage against screen, nor does he particularly worry about the opposite dilemma of privileging screen over theatre. What is mostly a realistic film ironically begins with a touch of Brechtian alienation in its meta-cinematic concern with the mechanics of making the movie. The Chorus (Derek Jacobi), who dresses as and acts the role of a CNN war correspondent in the midst of Elizabethan warfare, recites the prologue in a deserted Shepperton sound stage, strewn about with the props for the filming of *Henry V*. When he lights a match to locate the giant studio switchboard, the sudden spluttering and flare gives "Muse of fire" a clever spin. And the glare of the studio arc lights suggests "the brightest heaven of invention!" The Olivier Globe has given way to the motion picture studio. Jacobi continues the Chorus' lines, until, shouting as he reaches the last word in "kindly to judge our *play*," he flings open gigantic wooden doors to enter the world of the film. The avant-garde film making ends here as Canterbury and Ely loom out of the darkness and, with the exception of the Chorus' occasional appearances, some flashbacks to the Boar's head tavern, and decelerated motion in the battle sequences, the picture settles back into the realism of a seamless narrative.[40] A pragmatic Branagh uses whatever film grammar works to his advantage.

Like the play, the film carries a heavy freightage of ambiguity about the true nature of the young king. As often said, King Henry embodies the type of the "king's two bodies," one human, the other virtually divine. Shakespeare often leaves unresolved the question of when his hero is plain old Prince Hal and when God's deputy on earth. Critics of Branagh's film, like Donald K. Hedrick and Dympna Callaghan, have cogently argued that the movie is even more ambiguous than its Shakespearean source in its ability to appear anti-war while employing pro-war codes. As Hedrick says, if "war has a necessary dark or muddy side," then the king's character is "exonerated"; if the king has a "dark side" then war is "exonerated."[41] This "knotted ambiguity" also crops up in Callaghan's noting of the interplay between "resistance and recuperation"[42] by which the king can be all things to all men. To put it reductively, and not do full justice to Hedrick's and Callaghan's subtle analyses, Branagh has the ability to have his cake and eat it too. He can make an anti-war movie that also glorifies war.

The Archbishop's Rube Goldberg explanation of the Law Salique – "No woman shall succeed in Salique land" (1.2.39) – is only one of many ambiguous cruxes. Hooded and muffled, a proto-conspirator against man and the commonwealth, the archbishop (Charles Kay) takes a brain-numbingly boring passage on the legitimacy of the French monarchy and actually makes it engrossing, without resorting to the clowning of the two clergymen in the Olivier movie. The panning camera tracks the faces of his auditors during his labyrinthine recitation, a masterpiece of legalese, of learned double talk, which justifies an immoral invasion of France. When he ends by saying that all this is "as clear as is the summer's sun" (1.2.86), the nervous barons catch the irony and relax into sniggers. Meanwhile Exeter and Westmoreland exchange meaningful glances, hinting at some kind of collusion between them to manipulate their sovereign into the invasion.[43] Young Henry, however, is apparently not fooled. Sensing furtiveness in the archbishop's demeanor, he yet ignores his doubts and embarks for France. The son now carries the guilt of genocide just as his father before him endured the guilt of regicide for the slaying of his cousin Richard II. Heavy is the "guilt" behind the "gilt" of the crown.

In his dissolute youth, King Henry has also accumulated his own inventory of guilt. To survive as king, he has needed to reject his tavern crony, Falstaff, at his Westminster coronation, which is shown in flashback: "I know thee not, old man, fall to thy prayers. / How ill white hairs becomes a fool and jester!"(*2 Henry IV*, 5.5.47). The gruesome hanging of Bardolph for the theft of a "pax" (*Henry V* 3.6.40) also calls for a flashback to the cronyism of the good-old-boy Boar's Head tavern days. As a leader, the king cannot afford the self indulgence of compassion, but must hang his friend in order to remain credible to an army that has been put on notice that looters and rapists will be put to death. Another poignant reminder of Hal's wild youth occurs at the end of the battle of Agincourt when Pistol, in language transposed from act five, contemplates a bleak future in England after the wars: "Doth fortune play the huswife with me now? / News have I that my Doll is dead i' th' spittle" (5.2.80). Both play and movie are haunted by the Faustian question of "What shall it profit a man to gain the whole world and lose his own immortal soul?" When in an interpolated flashback, Falstaff turns to the king and says, "We have heard the chimes at midnight, / [Master Harry]" (3.2.214), a line actually addressed to Master Shallow in *Henry IV Part Two*, even those unfamiliar with the entire tetralogy can sense the king's spiritual torment. Somehow he is made to look good even when he is betraying the companions of his youth.

Minor characters like Nym, Pistol, Bardolph, and Hostess Quickly have tired, worn, defeated faces. When they go off to war they slouch and crawl rather than move in quick step to fife and drum. Perpetual tavern cronies, they have never managed to sort out workaday from holiday, so time wastes them as they waste time. Paul Scofield as the French king is sober and thoughtful unlike his scatter-brained predecessor in the Olivier film, though his son the Dauphin (Michael Maloney) remains mindless. The French Princess Katherine (Emma Thompson) offers a counterweight to her lightheaded brother, appearing especially delightful in the dazzling English lesson episode with the lady-in-waiting, Alice (Geraldine McEwan). Gallic fastidiousness and Anglo bluffness are contrasted when squat, burly Exeter (Brian Blessed), the king's chief aide, shows up as an envoy at the French court looking like a cement mixer in a rose garden.

Olivier's picture-book romanticizing of Agincourt on a sunny green field is replaced with a surrealistic tapestry of slow-motion medieval horror reminiscent of the butchery in the battle scenes of Welles's *Chimes at Midnight*. Olivier's English archers with the devastating long bows that destroyed the overly armored mounted French knights do reappear, but the magnificent French cavalry charge with prancing steeds "printing their proud hoofs I' th' receiving earth" (Pro. 27) and with royal pennants are replaced with hacking and groaning and thieving and wretched deaths in a muddy field. When it is all over, a mammoth tracking shot, filmed in Shepperton, follows the king, cradling the body of a slain page boy, as he wearily traverses the battlefield carnage. Thieves plunder bodies and angry French women scream at the man responsible for their new widowhood, this spectacle all having been managed with "150 extras, thirty horses, numerous carts, actors, and stuntmen," even while coping with the "the sonic horrors of the Heathrow flight path."[44] Patrick Doyle's stirring vocal and orchestral "Non Nobis" swells and builds to a crescendo, so climactic that some in the New York audience thought it was the end of the movie and began to put on their coats. Well worth waiting for, Henry's wooing of Princess Katherine is carried out charmingly enough to suggest it is more than just a dynastic marriage. Even the cultural materialists who loathe Branagh's politics might concede that this *Henry V*, while not so breathtaking as Olivier's film, far overshadows any televised version, including the recent transmission of *Henry V* for the inaugural program at the new Globe Bankside.

While Kenneth Branagh's next Shakespeare film, *Much Ado about Nothing* (1993), offers striking cinematic moments, especially in the opening quotation from *The Magnificent Seven*, its strength lies in the style and elocution of Emma Thompson as the petulant but brilliant Beatrice, who was born to play the role. When Don Pedro (Denzel Washington) says "You were born in a merry hour," and she replies, "No, sure, my lord, my mother cried, but then there was a star danc'd, and under that was I born" (2.1.332), Thompson's eloquent eyes certify that Beatrice is vulnerable after all, an *eiron* aware of her own limitations. Outwardly "merry," engaged in a "merry war" and "skirmish of wit" (1.1.62) with Benedick, she is yet like other mortals inwardly subject to doubt, and ultimately "star-cross'd" in some arcane way. After she exits, Denzel Washington in a tightly framed shot, his face aglow with admiration, reacts to her presence with "By my troth, a pleasant-spirited lady" (2.1.341). Alternating camera angles and close shots, of course, involve filmic as well as theatrical resources but the effect comes mainly from the power of Shakespeare's language and the charisma of the actors. While the bravura but irrelevant opening shot of the horsemen grabs the attention of the audience, Thompson's studied readings traverse back to the essence of Shakespeare's play about the serio-farcical battle of the sexes.

Despite Thompson's extraordinary performance, which correctly privileges the play's wit over its sentimentality, British critics uncovered flaws where Americans were more likely to find virtues.[45] Vincent Canby called it a "ravishing entertainment ";[46] Stuart Klawans said that it "neatly balanc[ed] the demands of the box office with those of the script";[47] and Todd McCarthy called it a "spirited, winningly acted rendition."[48] A critic in an American magazine under British editorship, however, could hardly contain his scorn: "Rarely has the title [*Much Ado about Nothing*] rung so true."[49] There were other non-believers as well, again British, such as Leslie Felperin Sharman, whose complaint about Branagh's "imaginative banality" and "cinematic bardology" echoes the mantra of British cultural materialists that Kenneth Branagh is some-how darkly complicit with agents of capitalist imperialism. Shaman while deploring this side of Branagh also acknowledges that it is his "biggest asset as a purveyor of lucrative filmic commodities for a specialized middle-brow market with upwardly mobile tastes."[50] Branagh's concern for pleasing the suburban cineplexes may have led to his shrewd casting of American film stars, Keanu Reeves and Michael Keaton, as well as acknowledging multi-culturalism by casting Denzel Washington as Don Pedro.

Cinematic rather than theatrical elements dominate three parts of the movie – the establishing shots, the garden scene, and the grand finale – while elsewhere the movie lapses into theatricality. The production opens almost clandestinely like a prelude to a silent film with the words from Balthasar's song, "Sigh no more, ladies, sigh no more / Men were deceivers ever" (2.3.62), inscribed in white against a dark screen, but instead of a bouncing ball inviting an old-fashioned sing-along, the words are spoken in impeccable "RP" by Beatrice. Then there is a dissolve to a full frame of an impressionistic watercolor of the fourteenth-century Villa Vignamaggio in Tuscany's Chianti wine region, where Branagh elected to film for better light instead of in Messina, Sicily, the locale for Shakespeare's play.[51] Soon the camera pulls back to reveal the ancient villa itself where Mona Lisa once resided, a verdant hillside, the painter Leonato (Richard Briers), the fashionable picnickers, and finally red-haired Beatrice herself perched in a tree reading the poem aloud to her doting friends. There is a glimpse of Brian Blessed, once the formidable Exeter in *Henry V*, now transformed into Antonio, Leonato's brother, and a presence, though mainly silent, throughout the film. This is the green world of comedy that always ends in the victory of the young over the old, and in feasting and matrimony.

The stasis of the watercolor gives way to a kinetic screen alive with motion as a messenger brings news of the approach of Don Pedro, prince of Arragon with a retinue that includes Benedick (Kenneth Branagh), Don John bastard brother of Don Pedro (Keanu Reeves), and Claudio (Robert Sean Leonard). A stirring proto-symphonic score by Patrick Doyle fills the soundtrack as in a mix of real time and slow motion the women scurry to the showers to prepare for the men's arrival, the horsemen hoot and holler and gallop over the hill in a quotation from *The Magnificent Seven*, a steadicam pursues the women into the shower for a melée of scrubbing, washing, shrieking, and titillating split-second exposures of bare bosoms and backs, the men gallop into the villa grounds and tumble and splash into an outdoor wash area for their own ritual of cleansing and scrubbing, the women climb into nearly identical flowing white dresses of which there seem to be an endless supply, and the men emerge from their cleansing uniformed in breeches and white tunics. The camera lifts up high for a crane shot and far down below through an opened gate, the gentlemen in a V-shaped formation spearheaded by Don Pedro approach the ladies, and the ladies in turn approach the men, as if this were a ritual prelude to the Battle of the Sexes.

The camera next most actively participates in the garden scene with the release of Benedick and Beatrice from the thralldom of their own wit by means of what Northrop Frye calls a "benevolent practical joke."[52] The business in the garden that makes Benedick into a bumbler as he struggles in Robert Benchley fashion with a recalcitrant lawn chair and eavesdrops on the staged conversation about Beatrice's feelings, momentarily tips the balance of power toward Beatrice. She herself would not be caught dead in so awkward a performance. Benedick's ridiculous Cary Grant imitation by the fountain as she approaches further exposes his deep-seated insecurity. In rapid intercutting, alternating between real time and slow motion, Beatrice ecstatically soars through the air on her swing, and Benedick dances and sloshes around the fountain, but the intercutting segues into a double exposure that superimposes the one overjoyed person on the other. The non-diegetic music reprises "Sigh no more, ladies," and the moving images of soaring and splashing manifest the spiritual rebirth of two previously self-repressed people. As Frye also points out, the parallel practical joke, this time malevolent not benevolent, is carried out by Don John in tricking the gullible, and very young, Claudio into thinking that his Hero is a strumpet.

To remain accessible and popular, Branagh resists any transgressive temptation to deconstruct the psychology of the Benedick–Beatrice relationship, which unravels under the cloud of an egregious Elizabethan pun involving "no-thing," bawdry for a lack of sexual parts. Is the wit of Beatrice and Benedick really a cover-up for closeted lesbianism and homosexuality? "Middlebrow" film goers with "upwardly mobile tastes" out for popcorn and a good time at the mall do not want to hear about such destabilizing matters, which are best left to the seminar room. Nor does Branagh exploit the parallel between Claudio/Hero/Don John and Othello/Desdemona/Iago. Hero (Kate Beckinsale) and her Claudio, though principals in the main plot, pretty much remain marionettes as the sentimental lovers who play off against the usurping witty pair of Beatrice and Benedick in the minor plot. The third major cinematic moment involves the steadicam shots of the dancing and singing at the end of the movie, and the crane shots high above filming the entire ensemble skipping and hopping and laughing and dancing through the lush courtyards of the villa grounds. The theme of "Sigh no more" swells on the soundtrack again and off in one corner is the figure of Don Pedro, alone, made doubly compelling by Washington's status as the sole black actor in the cast.

Keanu Reeves as Don John and Michael Keaton as Dogberry bore the brunt of critical disapproval, again for unfathomable reasons. The complaint that Reeves did little but scowl ignores the fact that Shakespeare gave his Don John very little to do but scowl, he not being a full-fledged Shakespearean villain or vice in the tradition of Aaron the Moor, Richard Crookback, or Iago. While the other Shakespeare villains are serio-comic, Reeves was stuck with being merely serious. In short, Reeves was doing what the script called for. Purist rage against movie Shakespeare rose to a crescendo, however, in the attacks on Michael Keaton's lunatic Dogberry. Keaton became the movie's designated scapegoat, yet his bizarre mugging, staring, grimacing, and clenched teeth delivery, his zany entrances and exits on a non-existent horse, his sadistic tormenting of the "opinion'd" Conrade and Borachio, and his Three Stooges routine with Verges (Ben Elton) derive, it can be said, not from sheer perversity but from both textual and cinematic considerations. In Dogberry, Shakespeare created another minor character, like Hostess Quickly, whose mysterious past is hinted at in the wistful remark that he is "a fellow that hath had losses, and one that hath two gowns" (4.2.84). Keaton's Dogberry recreates the type of the frustrated, minor bureaucrat, in a role of petty authority, an incipient Adolf Hitler as adept at making life miserable for his inferiors as he is at toadying to his superiors. Ironically he lacks control over what he most prizes, which is his language, and has a repertory of malapropisms rivaling Hostess Quickly's or even Mrs. Malaprop's: "O villain! Thou wilt be condemn'd into everlasting redemption for this" (4.2.56). Branagh reified the malapropisms by making Dogberry both physically and verbally inept.[53] When granny-glassed Ben Elton peers closely into Dogberry's face, and when they prance off on imaginary horses, mirroring the *Magnificent Seven* quotation at the beginning of the film, the approach becomes hilariously funny. Yet when he asks the unrepentant Conrade (who has called him an "ass"), "Dost thou not suspect my place?" (4.2.74), Dogberry's primal despair peeps through. Thousands and thousands in the multiplexes, who would otherwise have yawned through Dogberry's mostly obscure homonyms and quibbles, must have been touched by the "switching of codes" in Keaton's "whacko-manic conception," as Samuel Crowl characterizes it. Crowl also wittily concludes of Branagh's "screwball comedy" that he "gives us the most successful translation we have of a Shakespearean comedy onto film and converts all our potential critical sounds of woe 'Into Hey nonny nonny'."[54]

Kenneth Branagh next accomplished what everyone had always said couldn't be accomplished – a four-hour, uncut *Hamlet* (1996) on widescreen in full color, based on the First Folio and Second Quarto texts, whose scenario by Shakespeare, in a great irony, was thought well enough of to be nominated for an Academy Award. Despite its 240-minute duration, many ordinary citizens said that they had found it anything but unendurable. Quite the contrary: it was gripping. Branagh's precedent for the uncut version was of course Adrian Noble's RSC production that ran fifteen minutes over four hours. Praise and condemnation for Branagh's work were this time distributed more or less evenly on both sides of the Atlantic. Few if any denied the movie's visual splendor, its Masterpiece Theatre lushness of sets, costumes and good-looking people. Critics variously thought it "relentless and overpowering and devastating";[55] praiseworthy for "the quality and elegance of its treatment of Shakespeare's verse";[56] and "often inspired, bringing new life to scenes that were regularly drawing unintentional laughter."[57] Others found the very Masterpiece Theatre look too conservative, too middlebrow, and Branagh unconvincing as the prince. Stuart Klawans dismissed it as "a certifiable mess,"[58] and John Mullan while still reserving high praise for Derek Jacobi's Claudius labeled it a *folie de grandeur*.[59] The dread v-word, "vulgar," popped up at least once.[60]

Again as in *Much Ado*, Branagh had continued his astute policies of casting internationally, of using a realistic speaking style, of choosing a setting consistent with the heightened language, and above all of making the work "accessible... to modern life."[61] The same perspicacity by the producers of the BBC Shakespeare series in reaching out worldwide for actors would have made their work instantly more popular. As Marcellus, veteran movie star Jack Lemmon, like Michael Keaton in *Much Ado*, became the designated scapegoat, feeling the sting of "age-ism" from critics, who thought him "too old" for the role. Actually except for throwing away the gem, "Something is rotten in the state of Denmark" (1.4.89), Lemmon performed tolerably well and even that lapse may have been more an editing fumble than his. Imperturbable French superstar Gerard Depardieu as Reynaldo made a foxy spy for a hypocritical old Polonius (Richard Briers), who after moralizing to his own children conceals a prostitute (Melanie Ramsey) in his chambers. Although made to order for the role, right out of central casting, Robin Williams to his credit understates the role of Osric, an inept and insecure dandy. As Player King, Charlton Heston cannot help sounding like Moses in a meticulous recitation of Aeneas' tale to Dido, while Rosemary Harris' Player Queen supports him in the "mouse trap." Stand-up comic Billy Crystal as the impudent First Gravedigger knew exactly how to bandy with Hamlet about Yorick's skull, and Richard Attenborough lends a special dignity to the tiny role of English Ambassador. In tribute to their honorific status, during the Player King's speech Judi Dench and John

25 In two-shot, a cross-dressed Imogen
Stubbs as Viola/Cesario attracts the
attention of a bemused Olivia, played by
Helena Bonham Carter in the 1996 film of
Twelfth Night, directed by Trevor Nunn.

Gielgud mime Hecuba and Priam. For all these pains in signing up unsignable
actors, Branagh was immediately attacked for "stunt casting." Famous faces, it
was said, distracted the audience from the text. No one would admit that these
big stars also woke the audience up and breathed new life into obscure roles.
Who ever paid any attention to Marcellus until Jack Lemmon came along?
Branagh's plight illustrates again the wisdom of Machiavelli's famous dictum
that a man is more obliged for those favors he confers than those he accepts.

As for the principals he did as well. Derek Jacobi turned out to be one of the
greatest ever players of Claudius with a real knack for being a charming cad
and bounder. If Zeffirelli's *Hamlet* was Gertrude-centered then this *Hamlet* is
Claudius-centered. When first viewed in the opulent interior set at Shepperton
with sensuous Julie Christie in her bridal gown, happily skipping by Claudius'
side, the couple take on the aura of a fun-loving Scott and Zelda Fitzgerald.
Their effervescence squashes any thought that Claudius could commit a dastardly deed like kill a king and then marry his widowed sister-in-law. The
handsome king with a trim beard and athletic figure speaks confidently, intel-
ligently, in measured tones, savoring the antithetical clauses in his opening
speech and demonstrating his superb self-confidence by ripping up the insolent letter about the disputed lands from a scowling young Fortinbras (Rufus
Sewell). The camera, which is restlessly peering, circling (often dizzyingly),
probing, zooming in and out, and analyzing, then moves right to reveal Hamlet
in the customary suits of solemn black sulking under the bleachers. The effect

of seeing this petulant young man after witnessing the polished and urbane uncle is to undermine confidence in Hamlet. How can anyone be so sullen in such jovial surroundings? When shown later, the monarch-sized royal bed of Denmark that is "a couch for luxury and damned incest" (1.5.83) resembles a lush advertisement for Laura Ashley sheets, at times suggestively rumpled from marital activity. Kate Winslet brought a fresh-faced vulnerability to her Ophelia, who in her madness is cruelly incarcerated in a padded cell and hosed down. Horatio (Nicholas Farrell) handles the jargon-riddled legalistic speech about the covenant between Norway and Denmark with the help of flashbacks to workers in a gun factory, making in Marcellus' words "the night joint-laborer with the day" (1.1.78).

The large and reliable Brian Blessed turns up again, this time not as Exeter nor Antonio, but as the Ghost of Hamlet's father. To Hamlet, he oozes contempt for his younger brother, Claudius, "that incestuous, that adulterate beast" (1.5.41), while a tight framing shows his beautiful teeth and serpent's eyes. The flashback showing dear little Prince Hamlet playing with his father helps to explain Hamlet's Electra complex but the flashback to the poisoning in the garden makes Claudius' culpability as the sneaky bearer of "juice of cursed hebona in a vial" (1.5.62) far more obvious than it was probably intended. Despite jeers about "sensationalism" and imitating Stephen Spielberg, the special effects of exploding ground in the cellarage scene derive from Hamlet's expletive, "a worthy pioner!" (1.5.163). Hamlet is referring to the military's "pioneer," or "sapper," a kind of glorified ditch-digger, now called "engineers," who tunnel under enemy lines to implant explosives for blowing the enemy to smithereens as in *Henry V* (3.2.87). These same base fellows, "pioners," were the knaves that the paranoid Othello feared had tasted of Desdemona's "sweet body" (3.3.346). Helping out with *memento mori* motifs is Ken Dodd, British stand-up comic little known in the United States, who in flashback displays teeth identical to those in the skull tossed up by the Gravedigger. Finally, versatile Richard Briers, Malvolio in the Branagh *Twelfth Night*, Leonato in the Branagh *Much Ado*, plays Polonius as crafty, lecherous, dangerous, cruel, doting, and even inept. He delivers his farewell advice to Laertes, however, sincerely and poignantly, as if subconsciously aware of the dramatic irony – the whole family is doomed, like the Tsarist Romanoffs, Polonius to be stabbed behind the arras, Ophelia drowned, and eventually Laertes slain in a duel.

Naturally all eyes are on "th' observ'd of all observers" (3.1.154), Prince Hamlet. Many years ago, S. F. Johnson argued that the Hamlet of the first act is "the student prince," while the Hamlet of the fifth act is "the ordained minister of providence."[62] In Kenneth Branagh's hands, Hamlet embodies Johnson's "student prince," who at the end can swing on a rope like Douglas Fairbanks to kill Claudius, but who comes up short as "the ordained minister of providence."

The lavish Shepperton studio set for Elsinore could be thriftily recycled for Sigmund Romberg's *The Student Prince* (1924). Its grand chandeliers and balconies and mirrored walls serve as backdrop for bevies of elegant women in flattering hour-glass gowns, and platoons of handsome men in comic opera uniforms. The ladies look as if they will momentarily join their dashing men for a Strauss waltz on the checkered ballroom floor, if the men have not gone off for a rousing songfest at the beer garden, or maybe a little gentlemanly fencing at the dueling society. These Technicolor fantasies, a far cry from the ominous unit set of Laurence Olivier, the brick basement of Tony Richardson, or the clammy stone walls of Franco Zeffirelli, correlate with a Hamlet who turns into one of the more affable princes in performance history, not stern like Smoktunovsky, solemn like Olivier, nor neurotic like Williamson but plain spoken and direct, almost pleasant. The long rows of gnostic mirrors on the walls of the throne room into which Hamlet addresses his "To be or not to be" warn, though, that all that glisters may not be gold. Behind the outward festivity of this glittering Elsinore lurks inwardly the corrupt and dissolute court in which that which "seems" conceals that which "is." The mirrors also signify how every character in this most baroque of verbal structures mirrors every other, like infinite reflections in the contiguous mirrors of an old-fashioned barber shop. This is particularly so with Hamlet, Laertes, and Fortinbras, all sons of wronged fathers. Hamlet has returned from Wittenberg University to a "prison" of spying, corruption, scheming, and incest. Fortinbras sums it up pithily when he says, "For he was likely, had he been put on, / To have prov'd most royal" (5.2.397). Hamlet never gets a chance to prove himself "most royal" but instead shows a potential for performing in a circus high-wire act.

It is not what Branagh omitted (very little) but what he added that further reinforced this image of an undergraduate Hamlet. In the extraordinary flashbacks, for example, of an angry, surly Fortinbras haranguing his officers and viciously stabbing at military maps, the Norwegian plays Adolf Hitler invading Poland to Hamlet's Neville Chamberlain. None of Fortinbras' ravings fits very well with Hamlet's subsequent description of him as a "delicate and tender prince" (4.4.48). Branagh's Hamlet, not Sewell's Fortinbras, turns out to be the "delicate and tender" one, a description Goethe might have endorsed. Branagh's tendency to shout out the soliloquies, as if he were still on the Stratford stage instead of in a movie annoyed some reviewers. An egregious example occurs at the climactic end of Part One, just before the interval, when Fortinbras' army is passing through a valley in the remote background and Branagh is shrieking at the top of his lungs to drown out Patrick Doyle's theme music, "My thoughts be bloody, or be nothing worth!" (4.4.65). Not only an unfortunate reprise of a Julie Andrews' *shtick* in *The Sound of Music*, it also makes Hamlet seem less antic than hysterical. In short, a Student Prince.

As a consequence, when Fortinbras' menacing gray wool army crashes into the palace, even wounding the harmless "water-fly" Osric, no one, least of all Fortinbras, seems terribly interested in what Hamlet's views are on his successor, "I do prophesy th' election lights / On Fortinbras, he has my dying voice" (5.2.355). The steamy sex between Hamlet and Ophelia reaffirms Hamlet's heterosexuality but compromises the priest at Ophelia's burial who, despite her "doubtful" death, will "yet here [allow] her virgin crants, / Her maiden strewments" (5.1.232). Since "virgin crants" and "maiden strewments" were reserved for virtuous young maids, the good doctor must have been ignorant of Ophelia's dalliance with Hamlet.

For too many in the audience, majestic Blenheim Palace, ancestral home of the Duke of Marlborough (who appears fleetingly in the film) and birthplace of Winston Churchill, looked less like Elsinore and more like a mecca for tourist buses. Branagh's company filmed in the winter, however, and the snowy grounds lend credibility to Francisco's "'Tis bitter cold" (1.1.8), but make incredible King Hamlet's afternoon naps outdoors in the snow-covered garden with a charcoal brazier fire to keep him warm. The winter set also causes the literal-minded to fret that Ophelia's drowning in mid-winter might wreck her plans for assembling "fantastic garlands" of "crow flowers, nettles, daisies, and long purples" (4.7.169). Maybe because of this inconsistency, Branagh scraps the conventional movie flashback to Ophelia's drowning, and instead has Gertrude deliver her famous aria-like description without visual aides, which Julie Christie admirably accomplishes. The movie ends as it begins with a framing shot of the statue of old King Hamlet, except that at the end it has been toppled over like some forlorn bust of Lenin in the former Soviet Union. With his epic film, Kenneth Branagh also toppled over the taboo against making movies of an uncut *Hamlet*. For this heroic effort, he deserves much thanks.

In conclusion, I would add that despite the great variety of successful screen adaptations, there remain pockets of resistance to Shakespeare movies among bardolaters who see them as endangering the word, and among cinéastes who find them unsuitable for images.[63] The ongoing revolution in communications technology makes speculation about the shape of twenty-first-century Shakespeare movies idle. The eye of man cannot see nor the ear of man hear what is to come, but Peter Geenaway's belief that film is still in its infancy applies with special force to the Shakespeare movie. Whatever new paradigms the future holds for Shakespeare cinema, Shakespeare will remain on the page for the bibliophile, on stage for the theatre lover, and on the screen for the cinéphile. These are not gated communities, though; they remain eminently synergetic. To echo Paul, "there is one glory of the page [the sun]; and another glory of the stage [the moon]; and another glory of the screen [the stars]; for one star differeth from another star in glory" (1 Cor. 15:41). True, the unanswerable questions will never stop. "Is it Shakespeare?" "What is the best available means for putting Shakespeare on screen?" "How best to imagine his words in moving images?" "How to attract the 'best class of people'?" Nor should they. As has been wisely said, art is never completed, only interrupted.

11

Shakespeare in love, in love with Shakespeare: the adoration after the millennium

Shakespeare in Love

At the outset of the twenty-first century, Shakespeare's "great feast of languages" spawned a "great feast of moving images" for which director John Madden's crowd pleaser, the $25 million *Shakespeare in Love* (1999), served as prologue. For a time it seemed that the whole world was as much in love with Shakespearean cinema as Madden's "Will Shakespeare" was in love with Viola de Lesseps. Will Shakespeare (Joseph Fiennes) is desacralized into a starving hack with a bad case of writer's block, struggling to write a ridiculous play called *Romeo and Ethel, the Pirate's Daughter*. The awkward fact of Will's having a family back in Stratford is conveniently forgotten, while a star-crossed romance between Will and heiress Viola De Lesseps (Gwyneth Paltrow) both mirrors and intertwines with *Romeo and Juliet*. Employing Stoppard's trademark epistemological riddles and meta-dramatic forays, scenarists Marc Norman and Tom Stoppard, bootlegged episodes from *Romeo and Juliet* into a pseudo-biography of Shakespeare's life. By focusing on the so-called "lost years" (1585–92), which are a mystery to even the greatest scholars, they shrewdly preempted any pedantic carping about historical accuracy. Recherché allusions to John Webster (Joe Roberts) as a vicious adolescent, to Kit Marlowe's (Rupert Everett) violent death in the Deptford tavern, to impresario Philip Henslowe (Geoffrey Rush), and painstaking replicas of the Rose and Curtain playhouses, allowed the better informed in the audience to share in-jokes denied to *hoi polloi*, who were lobotomized with romantic fluff involving the attractive stars, Paltrow and Fiennes. Even more pleasing to the better sort was Viola's eloquent audition piece at the Rose theatre, using Valentine's speech from *Two Gentlemen of Verona* ("What light is light, if Silvia be not seen?"), which decisively reaffirmed the superiority of words to images.

Given these charming diversions, highbrows, who knew about the influence of Arthur Brooke's narrative poem, perhaps took less umbrage at the fiction that an infatuation with a young woman could alone have inspired *Romeo and Juliet*. An unlikely event becomes likely when a feminist Queen Elizabeth (Judi Dench) rises in all her majesty from the audience to stop Tilney, Master of the

Revels (Simon Callow), from shutting down the Curtain theatre. "That woman is a woman!" a shocked Tilney unforgettably declares, having discovered that Viola, not a boy actor, is playing Juliet.

Viola's enforced marriage to the obnoxious Lord Wessex (Colin Firth) separates her from Will but they remain forever inseparable through the wonder of the Sonnet (no.18) that Will has handily composed just for her: "So long as men can breathe or eyes can see, / So long lives this, and this gives life to thee." Viola magically then is transformed into another Viola, the heroine of *Twelfth Night*, on a beach in Illyria. "It's a mystery," says Viola. And so it is. As Courtney Lehmann has pointed out, among other things, the film itself hints at an even greater mystery, which is the figurative and literal disappearance of the body of William Shakespeare.[1] And in its independence from academic orthodoxy, *Shakespeare in Love* reflected the dialectic between high and low culture typical of post-modernism. Increasingly Shakespeare's text was to become the springboard rather than the anchor of screen adaptations.

Love's Labour's Lost

It was highly appropriate to have Kenneth Branagh's whimsical re-imagining of *Love's Labour's Lost* (2000) as a 1930s musical comedy usher in the new century, given his major film contributions in the *fin de siècle* of the prior century. The Hollywood-musical ambiance broke with Branagh's earlier "doublet and hose" *Henry V* (1989) and *Much Ado About Nothing* (1993), though ample precedents for making a Shakespeare play over into a musical already existed, for example, in *The Boys From Syracuse* (1940) and *West Side Story* (1961 – q.v., 215). The white-tie-and-tails and flowing tea gowns of Fred Astaire and Ginger Rogers, and the music of Cole Porter, George Gershwin, and Irving Berlin, embellished Shakespeare's verbally challenging text. Branagh put the wobbly flirtations of the eccentric King of Navarre and his three quirky pals at the center of his script, jettisoning the opening ten lines, which advocate the conquest of "devouring Time" by winning fame through achievements in arts or letters.[2] Browne's eloquent fourth-act tribute to women is then transposed to a more strategic position near the end of the movie ("For where is any author in the world / Teaches such beauty as a woman's eye?" (4.3.308)). The surrender of the narcissistic vow fellows to the "tongues of mocking wenches" turns the phallocentricity of *The Taming of the Shrew* inside out and shows the play's "labors" as fodder for a gynocentric subtitle, *The Taming of the Machos*.

In the fugue-like main plot, Ferdinand the King of Navarre (Alessandro Nivola), Browne (Kenneth Branagh), Longaville (Matthew Lillard) and

Dumaine (Adrian Lester), vow to spend three ascetic years in high minded study, despite Berowne's healthy skepticism. When four exquisitely gowned young women – the Princess of France (Alicia Silverstone), Rosaline (Natascha McElhone), Maria (Carmen Ejogo) and Katherine (Emily Mortimer), accompanied by the princess' attendant lord, the sycophantic Boyet (Richard Clifford) – arrive by water in exotic punts on a moonlit canal, their coeducational influence quickly sabotages the men's cloistered world. Silverstone as a princess of France has soared high above her role as the adorable nitwit Cher Horowitz of *Clueless* (1995).

The play, as Moth (Tony O'Donnell) says, is "a great feast of languages," whose banter and badinage add up to a whole warehouse of Elizabethan trivia, everything from the Euphuistic style of court playwright John Lyly, to Shakespeare's dark lady, to Elizabethan sonnet cycles.[3] The heavy topical satire has dampened enthusiasm for both stage and film productions, though, as Miriam Gilbert has shown,[4] Michael Kahn's 1968 American Shakespeare Festival production discovered the trick of satirizing 1960s instead of 1590s affectations. His four vow fellows were filtered through the Beatles, who were busy satisfying the "reigning chic" of the day by journeying to India for meditation. Robert C. Fulton also found a template in the Marx Brothers' *A Night at the Opera*, which both "...make [s] and mar[s] silliness, thereby providing an antidote to the overdone style of the age."[5]

Grainy newsreel clips show the playboy King of Navarre, a glamorous Prince of Wales figure, en route home from military maneuvers. A voice-over commentator (who seems to be Branagh) intones the latest gossip, while a montage narrates the story with newspaper headlines, a misogynist proclamation declaring "No women," and a mound of discarded uniforms. In the king's elegant library, the young men suddenly erupt into "I'd Rather Charleston," the first of several song-and-dance acts, which they perform with notable alacrity, though many of the film's critics, who were unable to willingly suspend their severity, grumbled about the choreography's amateurishness, calling it "mediocre popularization,"[6] or even worse "this misguided mess [which is] ...mostly a yawn."[7]

The musical numbers that mock Hollywood tropes like the Esther Williams water ballets and Busby Berkeley dance extravaganzas do not merely replace word with image, *lexis* with *opsis*, but domicile Shakespeare in a fun house of trick mirrors. A sensuous, quasi-pornographic dance number set to Irving Berlin's "Let's Face the Music and Dance" replaces "The Masque of the Muscovites" which the DVD version shows as outtake. Men and women cling as if glued together, while the voyeur camera ogles at net stockings stretched over lush white thighs. Not really gratuitous sex for the sake of sex, the soft porn restates the way that *Love's Labour's Lost* conceals behind its innocent façade a cesspool of bawdy puns about male and female genitalia. Harmless words like "thorn" and "gate" take on phallic and vaginal significance; "prick," and "pricket" set off an avalanche of smutty associations. Maria chides Costard (Nathan Lane) for talking "greasily," but he is not the sole offender.

In place of Shakespeare's "Play of the Nine Worthies," Broadway superstar Nathan Lane leads the entire company in a fervent chorus of Irving Berlin's "There's No Business Like Show Business." The show-stopping line about going on with the show no matter how "low" you feel echoes the frolics at Navarre, which also have been but a "show," an elaborate diversion, awaiting the arrival of the messenger of death, Marcade (Mercury), an agent of the *memento mori*, forever iconicized in Yorick's skull. The movie drowns the audience in nostalgia when the farewell scene quotes from the Bogart / Bergman tableau at the Casablanca airport (1942). The women in their tiny but elegant 1930s-style felt hats one by one gamely smile through the cabin windows of the DC-3 as it fights to get off the runway; the men are left on the canopy also in alternate close ups, awkwardly crooning, or croaking, "Oh no they can't take that away from me." Branagh's movie forges an alliance with Shakespeare's text to create something new and charmingly strange.

A Midsummer Night's Dream

Film makers generally avoided Shakespeare's comedies in favor of the tragedies and history plays, largely because of the archaic and user unfriendly language that reaches an apotheosis in *Love's Labour's Lost*. An exception has been the highly visual and spectacular *Midsummer Night's Dream*, which was a part of the Vitagraph repertory as early as 1909 and inspired the artistically successful 1935 Warner Brothers film. Michael Hoffman's 1999 *A Midsummer Night's Dream* ("Based on the play by William Shakespeare") displaces the time to the Victorian era and the locale to Monte Athena in Tuscany, Italy, a fabulous hilltop town but not exactly the Athens of Shakespeare's play. The *mise-en-scène* for the festive establishing shot on the veranda of Villa Athena, the Duke Theseus' (David Strathairn) palace, echoes the northern Italian effulgence of Branagh's *Much Ado About Nothing* (1993). A battalion of butlers, footmen, and kitchen wenches, are adorning sturdy wooden tables with gleaming crystal and starched linen for an *al fresco* wedding feast that is sure to include, as Hoffman says in his script, "whole roast pigs, pollo, tachinno, bistecca Florentina ... huge vats of pasta,"[8] accompanied perhaps by a robust *Chianti* from Duke Theseus' own grapes. Predictably Felix Mendelssohn's sprightly "Incidental Music" washes over the sound track, but when the scene shifts to the exhibitionistic hour of the promenade on the main piazza of Athena,

26   Kevin Kline stars as Bottom and Michelle Pfeiffer as Titania in Michael
Hoffman's *A Midsummer Night's Dream.* Photo: Mario Tursi (USA 1999).

Mendelssohn yields to the lilting ball room music from Verdi's *La Traviata*,
more suited to the festive mood of the carefree citizenry.

Visually the film is a masterpiece, so exquisitely conceived by Hoffman and
designer Luciana Arrighi that it upstages even the pomp and glitter of the BBC
corset dramas. Titania (Michelle Pfeiffer) wears unbearably exquisite gowns
inspired by the pre-Raphaelites, while Hippolyta (Sophie Marceau), a woman
of ineffable dignity with her parasol and flowing habiliments, and Hermia
(Anna Friel) crowned with epic millinery, echo John Singer Sargent's regal
portraits. Less regal is Calista Flockhart, famous in North America for her
television role as the lawyer, Ally McBeal, forlorn victim of male chauvinism.
She is type cast by playing the equally forlorn Helena, whose ubiquitous bicycle
becomes an expressionistic object signaling the bid for the Victorian women's
emancipation from patriarchal tyranny.[9]

On a darker note, during the prologue a gnarled little boy and a dwarfish
woman purloin from the duke's bustling kitchen a gramophone and a cache
of 78 rpm Red Seal Victor *bel canto* recordings of Italian operas. They reappear
in the bizarre fairy world, where in an ironic turnabout mythical fairies are as
much enchanted by a ravishing "Casta Diva" from Bellini's *Norma* played on
a scratchy gramophone, as mortals in the new age of mechanical reproduction are intrigued by the very unmechanical fairy world. Filmed indoors at

Rome's vast Cinecittà studios, Hoffman's fairy world, inspired by the tombs of the lost Etruscans, their labyrinthine caves, dancing and feasting, satyrs, griffins, Janus figures and dwarves, wallows in a luxurious excess reminiscent of Edmund Spenser's Bower of Bliss. Hoffman's Fairy Queen dwells in a magical realm of lithe beauty, while her Oberon (Rupert Everett) manages to look simultaneously both raffish and heroic.

Unintimidated by text-centered advocates, Hoffman breezily commits the academic heresy of "character criticism" by giving the movie to Nick Bottom (Kevin Kline). In other words he speculates, hypothesizes, and fictionalizes a Bottom who never existed in Shakespeare's play. Everyone else in the play – the young lovers, the Athenian rulers, the fairy denizens, takes a back seat to Bottom, who emerges as a kind of Walter Mitty figure imagining himself a dashing man about town. In reality he is the henpecked husband of a nagging wife (Heather Parish), who of course also does not exist in Shakespeare's play.[10] At first, Bottom is a dandy flirting in the market place, a would-be actor whose beautiful (and only) white suit is doused in red wine (though the printed text says it is "donkey manure") by twelve-year-old hoodlums. At the end of the film, though, Bottom transcends his role as a foolish *alazon* and evolves into a Pauline "holy fool," an unlikely saint who is foolish in the eyes of men but wise in the eyes of God. A shower of lights hints at a sliver of hope in his "bottom-less dream." As Nicholas Jones has pointed out, the "rich, generous" operatic arias on the sound track, rather than being irrelevant or anachronistic, help to give Bottom "the sonic space" that compensates for his wizened marriage.[11] Sentimental, yes, but the poignancy in Bottom's newly discovered interior life resonates with modernist weakness for victimology.

The Children's Midsummer Night's Dream

Quite different from Hoffman's sophisticated "adult" film is Christine Edzard's Sands Film *The Children's Midsummer Night's Dream* (2001). The very thought of a Shakespeare play acted by primary-school children from inner London is enough to unsettle even the most devout believers in school drama clubs. To compensate for the childish treble, incoherent speeches, and singsong voices, there are yet memorable moments: little Daniel Rouse as Peter Quince issuing orders in a squeaky voice to the rude mechanicals, and petite Anglo-Indian Rajouana Zalal reciting from memory Titania's prolix speech beginning, "These are the forgeries of jealousy" (2.1.81). Counterpointing the children's high-pitched voices are the sonorities of the mannequin-sized adult actors. It all has the innocence of a *Midsummer Night's Dream* in Regent's Park, being in David Jays' apt phrase "a decorous whimsy."[12] After all, Edzard gives her audience an opportunity to see what Rosencrantz was talking about when he warned Hamlet about "an aery of children, little eyases who have taken over the London stage" (2.2.339).

10 *Things I Hate About You*

If Shakespeare was box office poison fed "straight" to the masses, he proved a money maker when commodification inevitably enforced accommodation to popular culture. Director Gil Yunger embeds shards of Shakespeare like fossil remains into 10 *Things I Hate About You* (1999), a teen movie based on *The Taming of the Shrew* but filtered through Amy Heckerling's cult film *Fast Times at Ridgemont High* (1982). As Kat, Julia Stiles, later to become a disturbing Ophelia in the Almereyda *Hamlet*, emerges as an angry, witty little feminist, who is untamable even by the school's chief rebel, Pat Verona (Heath Ledger), a variant on the Sean Penn role in *Fast Times*. There are at least ten things about the movie that will horrify persons opposed to "dumbing down" Shakespeare, which means the scandalous subordination of text to performance-centered values. David Rumholz plays an engaging Tranio figure busily running about and toadying up to everyone in the classic style of the Roman *dolosus servus* (tricky slave). Joseph Gordon-Levitt as Cameron (Lucentio) even manages to speak words directly from the text when on first glimpsing Bianca (Larisa Oleynik) he says "I burn, I pine, I perish." Ms. Perky (Allison Janney) adds brio as the guidance counselor more interested in writing porn love stories than in advising students, and gynecologist Dr. Walter Stratford is the Jonsonian humor figure obsessed with the fear that daughters Kat and Bianca may be impregnated. At the end Kat recites her poem, assigned by the martyred English teacher, a born loser, Mr. Morgan (Daryl Mitchell), "I hate the way you talk to me" which of course corresponds to but, as Deborah Cartmell[13] points out because of contemporary sexual politics, does not recreate Kate Minola's notorious surrender speech.

The Tempest

The Tempest is large and contains multitudes having been saddled in the Sixties by Polish critic Jan Kott with the burden of being an allegory of western imperialism. Therefore it can likely survive scenarist James Henerson's brain storm of transforming, or transmogrifying (?), it into an NBC television movie, with an American Civil War setting. This lavish costume drama starring Peter Fonda as Gideon Prosper focuses on Gideon's southern plantation before his exile with daughter Miranda Prosper (Katherine Heigl). Gideon Prosper falls victim to an usurpation by his younger brother Anthony (John Glover) when the study of black magic with slave woman Azaleigh (Donzaleigh Abernathy) distracts him from the daily business of the plantation. He is banished to a swampy mosquito-infested island in the deep recesses of the Louisiana bayou country with Miranda, Ariel (Harold Perrineau, Jr.), and the Caliban-like brute, Gator Man (John Pyper-Ferguson). *The Tempest* plot expands so that the men of evil who come to the island turn into Confederate cronies of Anthony Prosper, who as a perfidious double agent spies for both North and South.

A plethora of occult bonfires and bubbly ponds litter the landscape in sign of Prosper's magical powers, which he invokes with complicated weaving and waving of hands. The same incantatory skills empower Ariel, a black slave, to fly as a bird into any corner or crevice of the swamp or the Union encampments. Miranda's brave new world arrives in the person of Captain Frederick Allen (Eddie Mills), a dashing young Union Army officer, an aide de camp to legendary figures like Generals Grant and Sherman. In the denouement, General U. S. Grant rounds up Anthony Prosper, Willy (Dennis Redfield), who resembles Shakespeare's Gonzalo, and Gator Man, for Gideon Prosper's judgment, who behaves, even though he never utters the words, as if "The rarer action is / In virtue than in vengeance" (5.1.27). He frees Ariel to fight for the liberation of his people, forgives Willy as one who formerly helped in the cause of righteousness, dispatches Gator Man back to work as a laborer at the Plantation, and resisting the desire to kill him, turns perfidious Anthony over to the Union army for court martial as a spy. None of this resolves the quandary raised by Shakespeare, which is the timeless riddle of how to rule rationally over irrational persons. Even in a Shakespeare television movie that wraps the text in layers of Civil War costume drama, director Jack Bender cannot sidestep that darkest mystery of political theory.

Hamlet on film and television

Of all the tragedies, *Hamlet* attracts the most attention from film makers, whether as a text-centered adaptation (Branagh's version), a liminal derivative (Coronado's split image of the prince), or a "paratext"[14] (*Let the Devil Wear Black*). An endless challenge, *Hamlet* is the Sunday crossword puzzle from Hell whose blank squares never quite get filled in. In Michael Almereyda's noirish, fast-forwarded, post-modernist "attempt" (Almereyda's word) at *Hamlet*, electronic "images, images, images" replace the prince's bookish "words, words, words." The sullen and brooding prince (Ethan Hawke) has been displaced to New York City, where his mother and uncle live in the Hotel Elsinore and the Denmark Corporation exercises its worldwide capitalist hegemony from a skyscraper. "Meta-electronicity," if there be such a thing, replaces the meta-theatricality of Shakespeare's play. That is to say, alienating electronic or photographic images surrogate for the widely employed "Idea of the Theater" embedded in the play (i.e., Hamlet's play-within-a-play, or Polonius's eaves-dropping on Hamlet and Gertrude). Soulless technology suffocates the prince, whose grouchiness and grungy sartorial style, echoing James Dean, has no existence independent of his array of gadgetry: cell telephones, TV monitors, fax machines, camcorders, cameras, laptops, mirrors, intercoms, answering machines, speakerphones, surveillance cameras, snapshots, and video stores chock full of DVDs and cassettes. Lurking behind an arras or peering over a balcony seem egregiously obsolete as surveillance technologies compared to hi-tech electronic eyes and swipe cards.

Never has a Shakespeare movie cast so many high-priced stars with so few dollars ($2 million). Almereyda's powers of persuasion plus Shakespeare's cultural capital attracted, "at scale," Bill Murray (Polonius), Diane Venora (Gertrude), Kyle MacLachlin (Claudius), Sam Shepard (Ghost), and Julia Stiles (Ophelia). When Murray as a curiously flat, even laconic, Polonius wires up Ophelia for her rendezvous with Hamlet, the bizarre scene, as the director says, has been inspired by Linda Tripp's betrayal of Monica Lewinsky.[15] Diane Venora's Gertrude, poised, cool, and meticulously groomed, one of Manhat-tan's upper east side "ladies who lunch," finds Hamlet's ranting, against the "rank sweat of an enseamed bed" (3.4.93), not just horrifying but, worse yet, in poor taste. Playwright Sam Shepard as a very palpable Ghost but nevertheless the incarnation of the "Other," lurks near a Pepsi machine in the hallway and delivers his lengthy speech to Hamlet while pacing around the living room. His burning eyes and gaunt face project an air of unfathomable mystery, like some-thing out of the *The Twilight Zone*, even in the very fathomable *mise-en-scène* of a minimalist New York co-op. Whiffs of corporate corruption waft from Kyle MacLachlin's Claudius, who is a central casting C.E.O., with $1500 suits, sleek limousines, and an air of command – "Something *is* rotten in the state of Den-mark." For his Ophelia, Almereyda snared Julia Stiles, the petulantly cute teen Shakespearean actress from the MTV generation who plays Desi in *O* (2001) and Kat in *10 Things I Hate About You* (2000). Well known critic Herbert Coursen, who has otherwise pronounced anathema on the movie, spares Julia Stiles from excommunication, because her "pouty" Ophelia is so "potent."[16] Stiles makes her supreme bid for fame as Ophelia when she goes quite loudly mad on a ramp in the Guggenheim Museum on Fifth Avenue, far removed in style from the quavering histrionics of Laurence Olivier's ethereal Jean Simmons. Hora-tio's (Liev Schreiber) interest in a girl friend, Marcella (Paula Malcomson), a

27   Julia Stiles with Ethan Hawke in Michael Almereyda's *Hamlet* (USA 2000).

transgendered Marcellus, liberates Hamlet for a robust, heterosexual interest in Ophelia.

An obsessed video freak, Hamlet narcissistically records a visual autobiography. Oddly enough, his video recorder is a low-tech Pixelvision, or PLX-2000 video camera, originally designed as a children's toy, but now endowed with cult status.[17] In his earlier *Naja* (1996) Almeryeda employed a Pixelvision "to show the world from the point of view of Dracula's daughter."[18] Hamlet's video masterpiece becomes "The Mousetrap / A Tragedy / By Hamlet / Prince of Denmark." As an increasingly distraught Claudius watches from the rear of the screening room, Hamlet's montage flashes images of a blooming rose and an idyllic happy family, suggesting that all is well with the world. Then abuptly there is the "image of an ear as poison is poured into it . . ."[19] Soon, Claudius as the guilty creature at the movie leaps up and cries out "Give me some light. Away!"

As a modern dress version reminiscent of Edgar Ulmer's *Strange Illusion* (1945, q,v., 210), and Akira Kurosawa's *The Bad Sleep Well* (1960, q.v., 182–84),[20] Almereyda's movie also shows traces of Orson Welles's signature cinematography, turning it into what Samuel Crowl describes as "a great Wellesian collage of image and idea."[21] Mark Thornton Burnett sees it as a creature of "the globally reproductive disciplines of the post modern movement," in which a high tech cultural agenda intervenes between the Shakespeare text and its performance.[22] Yet the heart of the play's mystery, the haunting sense of grappling, groping, toward some elusive epiphany, somehow permeates even this impermeable city of glass and steel. Barnardo's famous interrogation in the play's first line, "Who's there?", need only be amended to "Is there any there, there?"

Campbell Scott *Hamlet*

Modestly designed for television and video stores rather than for theatrical release, Eric Simonson and Campbell Scott's stagy, text-centered *Hamlet* (2000) achieves the intimacy of a small playing space but lacks almost all of the visual excitement found in a kinetic movie. Campbell directed, co-produced and acted in this under-funded production, which was filmed in twenty-nine days. Made for the small screen of television, it requires a different critical perspective from a film, like Almereyda's, though in fact a good deal of the latter was also shot with video equipment. Given the powerful father/son dynamic in *Hamlet*, nothing could be more apposite than to have the prince played by an actor, Campbell Scott, who also self-referentially lives in the shadow of his father. The father, George C. Scott, will be forever known as the loony General Buck Turgidson in Stanley Kubrick's *Dr. Strangelove* (1963), and as General George Patton in the bio/pic he was possibly more the general than the manic warrior himself. Campbell Scott's resemblance to his father keeps flashing through the face of Hamlet, though the sensitivity of the son's approach to Hamlet betrays none of the father's gruffness. At age thirty-nine, nicely calibrated between youth and middle age, Scott is not a rebellious adolescent after the style of Ethan Hawke, but rather a likeable young man made vulnerable by his own good nature.

The vaguely provincial atmosphere suggests the American South sometime immediately following the Civil War. Its defiantly American cast ignores British stage codes. To ratchet up the nationalism, African-American actors Roscoe Lee Brown and Lisa Gay Hamilton play Polonius and Ophelia, whose presence, as has been said, ". . . only lends a new depth and meaning to their roles."[23] Their skillful acting cannot thrive in the unblinking realism of the photography in Hamlet's death scene, which runs against the grain of the highly expressive language. All the underwalks of persons stand like mutes in a stiff tableau encircling Hamlet and Horatio. In a fine camera moment, however, when the dying Hamlet stares at the ring of courtiers, we too gaze at them, as if through a subjective camera. Uncannily we see the other inmates in the prison of Denmark through the gauzy haze of death just as Hamlet sees them, looking stolid, implacable, invulnerable, still surveilling him, even as Hamlet in his eternal loneliness continues as always to surveil them.

Let the Devil Wear Black

Let the Devil Wear Black (1999) bears at best a paratextual relationship to *Hamlet*, or might even be gazetted for Richard Burt's apt label of "Schlockspeare,"[24] those "Shakespeare" films that have fallen entirely into the hands of mass culture. The dead hand of an undergraduate professor reaches out from the grave to admonish against shameful pleasures such as movies that may cause brain damage. Yet like all forbidden fruit, the movie tempts us anyway. The need to stage or film *Hamlet* wrenches at directors with the urgency of King Hamlet's ghost goading his son into action. Having apparently heard the call, Jonathan Penner, once a nominee for an Academy Award, and famous for his *The Last Supper* (1995), has created a tangled but compellingly noirish vision with southern California as background. The title comes from Hamlet's moody speech to Ophelia: "Nay then let the dev'l wear black, for I'll have a suit of sables" (3.2.129). The scenario inspires *déjà vu*, as Jack Lyne (Jonathan Penner), a neurotic graduate student adrift in a nihilistic universe, returns home, to find his mother romantically involved with the brother of his recently deceased father, once a powerful underworld figure. A flurry of bizarre camera angles, jump cuts, and modish sound effects bring Jack, after labyrinthine intrigues, to his inevitable end when he is shot to death and his mother Helen Lyne (Jacqueline Bissett) is accidentally poisoned by his uncle Carl Lyne (Jamey Sheridan). Penner seriously grapples with the twisted metaphysics of Hamlet's universe even as the movie teeters on the edge of being a slasher.

O

Although Laurence Fishburne's and Kenneth Branagh's commanding presences as Othello and Iago in the 1995 Oliver Parker movie adaptation (*q.v.*, 224–26) have since gone unmatched, the publicity surrounding O. J. Simpson's real life reenactment of the Othello story probably encouraged two other ambitious re-incarnations on screen. Tim Blake Nelson's movie, *O* (2001), an unapologetic modernization of *Othello*, continues the fad for inserting teen/pic topoi between Shakespeare's text and the filmic site, even including Julia Stiles again, this time as Desi. With surgical precision Nelson implants his preppy codes precisely in the spaces vacated by Shakespeare's text. The *divertissement* for Shakespeareans lies in ferreting out the plot analogies; the misery comes from discovering their inadequacies. Desi, a student at an elite co-ed boarding school, along with her black boy friend, Odin (Mekhi Phifer), an exotic outsider and basketball scholarship player, becomes the target of Hugo's (Josh Hartnett) spiteful jealousy. Hugo feels that his father, Duke Goulding, a hyperactive basketball coach played by Martin Sheen, has slighted him in favor of Odin. Hugo, a would-be Iago, yearns to soar like a hawk over the heads of friends and rivals, a metaphor liberally reinforced with images of graceful hawks and cooing doves. Odin's prized scarf stands in for Othello's fetishized handkerchief, which helps Hugo's girl friend Emily (Rain Phoenix) to expose Hugo's duplicity. Hugo as the alienated loner so closely resembles the perpetrators of the real life 1998 Columbine High School massacre that the producers delayed the movie's release. On the other hand, the Columbine horror lends plausibility to the film's implausibility, especially to the scene of roadside gunfire when Hugo destroys Michael Cassio (Andrew Keegan) and Roger Rodriguez (Elden Henson). A non-diegetic aria from Verdi's *Otello* tinges these sordid events with tragic sublimity, but not enough to compensate for the characters' hip hop, in-your-face, attitudes and the relentless iteration of the "F" word. The film got high marks, however, from critic Ben Walters for its superior "cinematic tone."[25]

Othello

Even though not a film but a television movie, Geoffrey Sax's CBC *Othello* (2001) is good enough to deserve theatrical release. All stage and screen productions of *Othello* wrestle with the devilish triangle involving Othello, Desdemona and Iago. In Sax's retelling, a cop show, about the struggle for racial diversity in London's Metropolitan Police, where John Othello (Eamonn Walker) has risen to be commissioner despite racist detractors, intervenes between the Shakespeare text and the film. Acrobatic camera work reinforces the movie's Iago-centeredness with numerous tight close ups of Ben Jago (Christopher Eccleston) branding him as a sneaky, insinuating, treacherous villain. Typically in an over-the-shoulder shot, the camera closes in on Jago's lean, diabolical face, while he is hypocritically embracing and reassuring John Othello (Eamonn Walker) of eternal friendship. Ben Jago's malignant envy has been triggered by the appointment of John Othello, as the Commissioner of police, a post that he had himself craved. Like a serio-comic Vice figure, Jago vents his ugly feelings in a masterly aside that makes crystal clear to the audience but not to the on-screen characters how bitterly he resents Othello's good fortune. As a coda, he saucily exhorts the audience to "Cheer up." When Othello catches Michael Cass (Richard Coyle), the innocent body guard of Dessie Brabant Othello, wearing his precious gold dressing gown, he erupts into a frenzy of jealousy. It is act three, scene four of Shakespeare's play all over again, only this time the expressive object of the handkerchief, the "magic in the web," is not a scarf, as in the teen movie *O*, but instead a dressing gown.

Rapid editing pushes the narrative at a fast-forward pace. A line of word-processor typing fonts that interrupts a steamy frame showing a passionate Othello and Dessie turns out to be the work of Jago, who is spewing out slander on the internet about the mixed marriage of Othello and Dessie to his favorite racist chat room. Inevitably, a crazed Othello smothers Dessie with a pillow, while a sacerdotal non-diegetic chorale by composer Debbie Wiseman ironically dominates the sound track. The final despairing embrace between Othello and Jago lets a homoerotic bond out of the closet as Jago protests that all these dire events happened because of "love." Jago's escape from punishment, however, perhaps stems from today's "episteme," as Herbert Coursen says,[26] when a moral order shattered by nihilism cannot handle the punishment of evil. Instead Jago winds up being promoted to Othello's position as commissioner; the last scene shows him triumphantly reveling in his magnificent full dress uniform.

Scotland PA

Shakespearean "burlesque," "travesty," "parody," or "spoof," however labeled, has been well entrenched in stage history, ever since Shakespeare himself allowed his rude mechanicals in *Midsummer Night's Dream* to parody *Pyramus and Thisby*, or his merry men in *Love's Labour's Lost* to present the "Play of the Nine Worthies." As Richard W. Schoch has shown, the appetite for spoofs on Shakespeare flourished throughout the nineteenth century and ironically served "... not only to criticize contemporary Shakespeare performances but to *correct* them."[27] While overtly aimed at winning cheap laughs, a covert purpose of the burlesque was to rescue Shakespeare from the very people who thought of themselves as Shakespeare's Praetorian Guard, the elitists who would deny *hoi polloi* access to the inner sanctum. A modern instance is *Scotland PA* (2001), which in the act of poking fun at modernized Shakespeare movies also echoes darker moments from the Scottish play.

The nuances and subtleties of *Scotland PA* (2001) qualify it as one of the most fully imagined of the recent derivatives, which borrow the plot but abandon the language. Although at one level it can compete as a *Mad Magazine* spoof, at another this underrated black comedy uses *Macbeth* as a template for its own Pat McBeth (Maura Tierney) and Joe "Mac" McBeth (James LeGros), the

28   Lt. Ernie McDuff (Christopher Walken) stands in front of McBeth's (James LeGros) hamburger stand, which Mac has usurped from Norm Duncan (James Rebhorn) in Billy Morrissette's *Scotland, PA* (USA 2001).

embittered employees of Norm Duncan's (James Rebhorn) hamburger stand. In a bold sortie, director Billy Morrissette demolished the barrier between the exalted kings and queens of the Shakespearean canon and the world's working poor, such as the legions of globalized hamburger flippers. In a masterpiece of "dumbing down," Pat famously says to her pusillanimous husband, whose courage is not sticking enough to kill Duncan and gain control of the lunch counter: "We're not bad people, Mac. We're just underachievers who have to make up for lost time."

Pat McBeth suffers a burned wrist while loyally assisting Mac in the inept and grisly murder of nerdy Duncan, who, after being clubbed, accidentally falls into a vat of boiling oil. The festering sore on her wrist, just "a little burn," becomes the surrogate for the blood on Lady Macbeth's hands that a "little water" can never wash away. After Duncan's nauseating demise, Pat, echoing the cadences from the the Book of Common Prayer confessional that liminally haunt *Macbeth*, says to Mac "You did it, Mac. You did it. It's done. It can't be undone." From a small town young woman steeped in bourgeois false consciousness, she tumbles into depression, suddenly aware that no amount of striving can dig her out of the morass of lower-class despair. Like Titus, she chops off her own hand in an act of tragic gravity that elevates the film far above the niche of "black comedy." Academy nominee Christopher Walken as police Lieutenant Ernie McDuff, a role, according to Courtney Lehmann,[28] modeled on the McCloud of the TV series, can suddenly doff his mask of geniality and reveal the menace underneath while playing a cat-and-mouse game with the wretched suspects, Pat and Mac. Duncan's two ne'er-do-well sons, Malcolm and Donald, a would-be musician and a closeted homosexual, classic ingrates, get even with their father by casually giving away the hamburger "empire" to Mac and Pat. The recurring prefixes of "Mc" and "Mac" constantly jab at the connection with MacDonald's hamburgers as well as slyly commenting on humankind's spiritual degradation at the hands of mass corporate culture. Non-diegetic rock-and-roll aurally pumps up the 1970s ambiance. The blackness becomes momentarily comic when in the closing shot, the triumphant Lieutenant McDuff stands under the sign that now proclaims the hamburger stand to be "McDuff's," it having been first "Duncan's," and then "McBeth's." Besides making a perky, even sassy, recontextualization of the immensely popular Scottish play, the movie's rapid pace and skillful continuity earn it respect as cinema, though it shares with *Let the Devil Wear Black* mass culture's tiresome love affair with the "F" word.

Bogdanov *Macbeth*

From Morrissette's *Macbeth* set in a fast food outlet to *Macbeth* on an urban wasteland in Scotland invites an unwilling suspension of belief. Belief is again suspended nevertheless when Michael Bogdanov returns to Shakespeare with a serious modern dress treatment of *Macbeth* (1998) that is every bit as ingenious as his brilliant 1988 *Wars of the Roses* (q.v., 115). In his TV movie the hags turn into bag ladies inhabiting a junkyard where they have a handy inventory of disgusting objects to dump into their makeshift caldron, which seems to be a rusty boiler. Bogdanov had done a *Macbeth* earlier in Warwick with an English Shakespeare Company stage production that received mixed reviews, being condemned by H. R. Coursen,[29] but finding a warmer reception with critics like *The Guardian's* Robin Thornber who found it "brilliantly effective."[30] Whatever the defects of the earlier stage production this televised but filmic performance with a cast led by Sean Pertwee and Greta Scacchi as an attractive young couple, after the style of Roman Polanski's Jon Finch and Francesca Annis (q.v., 149), achieves considerable panache. Scacchi does her passionate "unsex me here" monologue in what looks like an abandoned warehouse, her face flickering through the smoke and flame from the letter that she is burning; and the sound track vibrant with drum and percussion effects punctuates the hasty comings and goings of a handsome blond Macbeth. Bogdanov builds sexual tension between the Macbeths out of surreal tight shots of mouths or eyes only. This micro-gaze blurs the borders of consciousness to the degree that not only our eyes but the entire nervous system participates in the psyche of the Macbeths themselves. Sharing in the angst and dread of this famously remorseful couple threatens to trigger an attack of Aristotelian pity and fear. Pity for them; fear for us.

Its various *mise-en-scène* draw on the decaying slums of Birmingham, where Bogdanov earlier filmed his *Shakespeare on The Estate* (1994) for British television,[31] which like Al Pacino's 1996 *Looking for Richard* (q.v., 216), explored working-class attitudes toward Shakespeare. Macbeth's castle resembles a vacant warehouse, or at other times an abandoned power plant. The interior shots are intercut with exteriors of a bleak landscape, where the actors sometimes wear not only kilts and tartans but roll out the "rrrrs" of Scots' burrs. Banquo's ghost confronts an unnerved Macbeth not in some crude hall with wooden tables and plank benches, but at an elegant dinner party with gleaming silver, candelabra, and crisp linens of Martha Stewart quality. Macbeth begins to unravel, becomes increasingly unstrung, and then escalates into a towering rage, while a fluttering Lady Macbeth frantically tries to bring him under control. In white-tie-and-tails, he leaps on the exquisitely set table, yanks out a pistol, and fires at the wispy figure of Banquo. Lady Macbeth loses her regal poise, and sounding more like a Marine Corps D.I. than a high society hostess, she blurts out her famous line: "Stand not on the order of your going, but go!" As televised Shakespeare, Bogdanov's show avoids the minimalist look of the Nunn *Macbeth* (q.v., 105) in favor of a baroque setting, more akin to the Lyth *Hamlet* (q.v., 165–68). Although begun modestly as a school project, it rivals both of those imaginative productions in its urgency. At the end, MacDuff and Macbeth, duel with guns, not swords, until the fabled altercation segues into a knockdown fist fight out of a cowboy epic.

King Lear on television and film

Director Richard Eyre appropriates Gloucester's portentous "These late eclipses in the sun and moon portend no good to us" (1.2.103) as a key emblem in his 1998 recording with Ian Holm in the title role of a National Theatre production of *King Lear*. Compared with the performance-based *The King Is Alive* and *King of Texas*, which are discussed immediately below, this fastidious Mobil Masterpiece Theater production clings quite faithfully to the play text. Although stage bound, it nevertheless turns filmic when the probing and peering camera digs deeply into the old king's inner agony. Its sparseness pleases, though, after a steady diet of gourmet postmodernism.

In a cryptic establishing shot, a young man blackens a negative with a candle in order to peer at an eclipse without losing his eyesight, like Gloucester. Through his point of view the audience then sees a blood-red council chamber occupied by Gloucester (Timothy West), Kent (David Burke) and Edmund (Finbar Lynch). The action moves away then from this hellish interior, to the cold gray of harsh exterior shots, made to order as a site for the old king (Ian Holm) to lose his wits and go mad on the heath. With ever so subtle bits of business and vocal pyrotechnics, Ian Holm ekes out fresh ways for embellishing the old king's geriatric petulance. When he cries out "Give me the map, there," there is none of the fatigue in the voice of either a Michael Hordern or a Laurence Olivier, but a raging, ill-tempered tyrant, on the edge of lunacy, choleric over the slightest delay in meeting his demands. When the old king says that he will "unburthen'd crawl toward death," he chuckles as if to enjoy his own black humor. When the courtiers in a collegial kind of way genially share in the jest, he suddenly lashes back in paranoid fury, as if he feared being the object of, rather than the cause of, laughter. The Gloucester subplot segues in with a harrowing torture of Gloucester by a sinister Cornwall (Michael Simkins), which leads to the now predictable Beckett-like dialogue between the ruined Lear and Gloucester, the pair of them wrapped in a blurry white haze like a shroud.

Cordelia's (Victoria Hamilton) inability to honor his mandated proclamation of love brings him perilously close to apoplexy. All the daughters are arrayed in tunic style gowns that seem to put them outside of time, as if they were inside some spaceship, which gains support from the opening sequence about sun, moon and eclipses. Goneril (Barbara Flynn), and Regan (Amanda Redman) fawn on their irascible father not just with words but by showering him with highly effective non-verbal hugs and kisses. By the end of the division scene, Lear has escalated to higher and higher levels of volcanic fury, until he achieves the pinnacle of wrath by leaping on the table and roaring at Kent: "Hear me recreant."

The minimalist set then serves as an antiseptic dining room, like a school refectory, with white tablecloths to accommodate his 100 knights, who are soon charging out of Goneril's establishment after the impudent Oswald commits an act of unspeakable *lèse majesté* to his sovereign. King Lear, it is almost universally acknowledged, is "more sinned against than sinning," but in today's anti-patriarchal climate when he bellows "Detested Kite" at Goneril the tear that rolls down her cheek earns sympathy. The moral swamp of checkout counter tabloids also cohabits with the sleazy love triangle among Edmund, Goneril and Regan, a soap opera in the midst of tragedy. Unfortunately North Americans find the broad dialect spoken by Lear's Fool (Michael Bryant) a barrier to appreciating his witty lines. Rembrandt lighting effects complement Holm's passionate grieving over the hanged Cordelia, which for many will also trigger a poignant memory of Holm as a youthful Puck in the 1969 Peter Hall *Midsummer Night's Dream* (q.v., 141). Caryn James of *The New York Times* got it right when she wrote that this is a "magnificent" *King Lear*.[32]

The King is Alive

More than a crime/thriller, *The King Is Alive* (2001) qualifies for its "Dogme" backers as "an intellectual horror movie" that turns the "promised end" in *King Lear* into a bleak defeat on southwest Africa's Namibian desert. A band of tourists on a safari seek refuge in an abandoned mining camp after their bus runs out of petrol. Henry (David Bradley), a former actor, persuades them to cope with their appalling predicament by rehearsing scenes from *King Lear*, which they more or less agree to do. In post-modernist disconnection, only fragments of *King Lear* emerge, which get attached to the characters in the film, who in their agony and desolation rearticulate Shakespeare's vision of despair and nothingness ("Nothing will get you nothing"). The film is classic "Shake-shard" in the way it exemplifies Helen M. Whall's thesis that shards, that is to say, bits and pieces of Shakespeare from *Bartlett's Familiar Quotations*, have characterized the Shakespearean experience in popular culture.[33] Going a step further, Linda Charnes has extrapolated a bit from *Hamlet* to point out how post-modernism has converted the plea of Hamlet's ghostly father to "remember me" into "dismember me."[34] The Dogme people do their share of dismembering by subjecting the Shakespeare movie to their back-to-basics film making with hand-held cameras, and stern injunctions against extra lights, props, or reshooting. For example, the detached trope resurfaces of patriarchal grieving over the body of a lost child, as, for example, with Al Pacino in *Godfather III*, and here with the perturbing spectacle of Henry's harrowing "Howl, howl" over the body of Gina (Jennifer Jason Leigh).

As a Dogme film, *The King Is Alive* takes on a quasi-theological aura in its dedication to the strict precepts of the Dogme 95 code. As committed to a cause as the fanatical vow fellows in *Love's Labour's Lost*, Danish film makers Lars von Trier, Thomas Vinterberg, and Kristian Levring flout the "decadent illusionism" of classical Hollywood film by confining themselves to a minimalist art and by ignoring the orthodoxy of the seamless narrative. They even include a "Certificate" testifying to the film's dogmatic correctness for having been "entirely shot in Digital Video on location in Kolmanskop (Sperrgebiet), Namibia." The blazing paint box colors of the empty blue skies and the shifting yellow sands of the trackless desert required no artificial lighting.[35]

A depressing array of characters populates the screen. For example, Charles (David Calder), a bluff English fitness freak and a totem for jungle capitalism, preens himself over his conquest of Gina. When Gina lies dying, she denounces Charles so vitriolically it is unbearable to see because of its utter, pitiless destruction of another human being. "When you touch me you want to make me puke," she says, referring back to the way he blubbered and slobbered as he struggled to achieve a middle-aged orgasm. "You're a mean fucking son of a bitch," she adds and then "You look like fucking shit. Get the fuck outta here." Charles, demolished, commits suicide. The cruel windswept sands mirror the vacancy of the characters' inner lives and expose "the promised end" as the bitter knowledge of life's utter meaninglessness. This is a powerful and serious movie about the essence of art and life, which in fact was filmed only ten miles from the sea coast, though its parched landscape reveals not a trace of redemptive moisture. Only a work so cosmic as *King Lear* could have inspired it.

King of Texas

No tale of emotional firestorms between fathers and daughters is more primal than Shakespeare's *King Lear*, so there is little wonder at its being restaged and refilmed in a variety of contexts; in this instance *King of Texas* (2002) made on a ranch by Turner Network Television (TNT). Aimed at a prime-time audience, like the Peter Fonda *Tempest*, it retains Shakespeare's plot but little or none of the language. Irascible old John Lear (Patrick Stewart), having hanged two of his daughter's ranch hands, has enraged the young ladies, Susannah (Goneril/Marcia Gay Harden), Rebecca (Regan/Lauren Holly), and Claudia (Cordelia/Julie Cox). Other grudges fester as well. The daughters despise him, even suggesting that the "gift" of the property comes at the Faustian price of asking them to commit perjury by declaring unconditional love. In an answer to the often raised unanswerable question about what happened to King Lear's missing queen, Susannah says unforgettably, "You're nothin' but an old tyrant. You worked our mother to death." And the cranky, tyrannical, mean-spirited way that Stewart, a Shakespearean actor better known as Jean-Luc Picard of *Star Trek*, enacts the role validates his daughter's opinion.

Emmet Westover (Matt Letscher) corresponding to Edmund and Thomas Westover (Liam Waite) taking the place of Edgar represent the Gloucester plot. Mr. Highsmith, the Cornwall surrogate (Patrick Bergin) tortures their father, Henry Westover (Gloucester/Roy Scheider), and not content to gouge out his eyes, must burn them out with a red hot poker. His wife, Rebecca, cheerfully sears the second eye. At times, the "D" word ("dumbing down") hovers nearby when inarticulate modernizations replace Shakespeare's matchless language. "Ah own the ranch now," says Rebecca pointing a shotgun at the 100 knights. Nevertheless Patrick Stewart's fine credentials as a Shakespearean serve him well in the bravura tableau when he mourns over Cordelia, his bloodcurdling "howl" still steeped in anguish, competing with the best, even Ian Holm and David Bradley. "She's dead as earth," he says falling backwards almost out of the frame, as in the old Warde *King Lear* (1916), and in the Peter Brook version (1971). With so much acting talent on tap, one yearns for more of the "words, words, words" that invigorate the Eyre version.

The Merchant of Venice

Yet another British National Theatre production brilliantly preserved on US public television, Trevor Nunn's *The Merchant of Venice* (2001) wrings out every last drop of the play's complex interplay between menace and magic. Nunn cleverly recycles the same set for the "Cabaret" style Berlin night club, the casket rite at Belmont, and the court room in Venice, though it takes a sharp eye to detect his legerdemain. The decadent young men in dinner jackets like Salanio (Mark Umbers) and Salerio (Peter de Jersey), drunkenly reeling and lurching, if we can presume that "like will unto like," quickly define their friend, Bassanio, as a light weight. The dark and scowling Shylock (Henry Goodman) provides the overt menace. The money lender achieves the nadir of disagreeableness when he raves with a Yiddish accent against the "smell of pork" and admonishes Bassanio that "I will not eat with you [Christians], drink with you, nor pray with you" (*MV* 1.3.36).

In contrast the sleek and imperturbable Derbhle Crotty as Portia remains aloof and well bred in her polite Belmont country club world, safely removed from the sordid Venetian commercialism. Yet the mysterious, magical, contract between Portia and her deceased father hints at a "bond" that may be no less tyrannical than Shylock's with Antonio. When Jessica and Shylock out of their own spiritual malaise sing a duet in Yiddish, they mirror the precarious balance between Portia and her ghostly father. In her clinging gowns, Portia pokes cruel fun at her unlucky suitors as she views them on a movie screen not with a modern VCR but with a flickering 16 mm motion picture projector. Her acolyte Nerissa (Alex Kelly) and her retinue of disciplined house maids in black dresses, stockings, and severe white aprons verify her status as a demi-goddess. The 3,000 ducats required to redeem Antonio's bond strikes the complacent Portia as a paltry sum: "What, no more?" (3.2.298), she asks. Portia's insufferable superiority alone might explain the mysterious depression ("In sooth, I know not why I am so sad") that Antonio (David Bamber), the moon-faced merchant in love with Bassanio, confesses to in the play's opening line. Nunn's wonderfully intricate made-for-TV film, supported by a haunting musical score, leaves that avenue and many others open to exploration.

Titus Andronicus

Out of the swamp of B-grade splasher movies designed for happy evenings at the Sunset Drive-In emerge three televised and one film version of Shakespeare's most violent revenge drama, *Titus Andronicus*, which of course is itself the ur-splasher play. Lorne Richey's *Titus Andronicus: The Movie* (1997), Christopher Dunne's *Titus Andronicus* (1999) and Richard Griffin's *William Shakespeare's Titus Andronicus* (2000) qualify as authentic "Schlockspeare," to use Burt's term. Any Drive-In manager would ache to put them on the same bill with Tobe Hooper's grisly *Texas Chainsaw Massacre* (1974), or even the shocking rape-revenge feminist (*sic*) melodrama, Meir Zarchi's *I Spit on Your Grave* (1978),[36] which uncomfortably resembles *Titus Andronicus*. Occasional glimpses of talent rescue the earnest Richey and Dunne versions from being the worst acted movies in history, Richey's young Lucius (Mark Burson), for example, being quite impressive. For sadistic violence and horror, however, a galaxy of decapitations, dismemberments, rapes, amputations and cannibalism, the Dunne may have an edge. For students of "Schlockspeare," films in the Tromeo tradition (q.v., 218), it will be difficult to find two actors playing Aaron the Moor more adept at sneering, leering, and grimacing than Dunne's Lexton Raleigh, and Richey's Kevin Butler, though Lexton Raleigh should perhaps win the Oscar as the more consummate psychopath. As for Richard Griffin's $16,000 digital-video adaptation, not being able to locate a copy, I can only rely on the public relations blurb proclaiming that Griffin follows the "Kubrick" route and gives us "an almost corporate vision of evil."[37]

In an entirely different *arrondissement* is Julie Taymor's *Titus* (1999) that played a major role in making the disreputable *Titus Andronicus* reputable, after centuries of its being dismissed by critics as either Shakespeare juvenilia, or even non-Shakespearean.[38] In turning shlock into art, Taymor followed celebrated stage productions like Peter Brook's (1955) and Deborah Warner's (1987), which also showed how theatrical can trump literary values. Earlier in her Broadway hit *The Lion King*, and a 1994 Off Broadway *Titus*,[39] Taymor had shown her gift for theatrical expressionism.[40] As she told John Wrathall, "I work cinematically in the theatre and I work theatrically in the cinema."[41]

Shakespeare's *Titus Andronicus* flouts the old classroom rule that tragedy being personal has only a few characters, while comedy being social has many. Like putting the camel through the eye of a needle is the challenge in 71 lines (169–340) of the first act to make coherent the incoherent intrigues of a dozen or so characters. Following Jane Howell in the 1985 BBC version, Taymor elects to filter the action through the eyes of a small boy (Osheen Jones), who when the movie begins is joyfully smashing up toy soldiers on a 1950s style kitchen table. Soon, however, he is transported by a clown back in space and time

29   Anthony Hopkins as the Roman warrior in Julie Taymor's *Titus* (USA 1999).

to the Coliseum of ancient Rome (actually located in Croatia). There, now as Young Lucius, he ceases being a witness and becomes a participant[42] in the bloody affairs of the Andronici clan. In pigheaded bureaucratic devotion to the letter of Roman cultural codes, Titus (Anthony Hopkins) makes an implacable enemy out of the captured Tamora, Queen of the Goths (Jessica Lange), when he orders her son Alarbus (Raz Degan) sacrificed "to appease the groaning shadows" of his own twenty-one sons killed in combat. Like King Lear, Titus continues to make spectacular errors in judgment, displaying *hamartia* (i.e., "missing the mark") over and over again, when in a classic *senex iratus* snit, he orders his daughter Lavinia (Laura Fraser) to marry Saturninus (Alan Cumming), only to discover that she really loves Bassianus (James Frain). Meanwhile dark-skinned, lurking, Aaron the Moor (Harry Lennix), an embryonic Iago, captivates Tamora and becomes her ally in mischief. "Vengeance is in my heart, death in my hand" (2.3.38), he assures her. They conspire to orchestrate the rape and mutilation of Lavinia by Tamora's giggling sociopathic sons, Chiron and Demetrius, devotees of MTV and electronic games.

Part of the genius of Taymor's movie lies in her rediscovery of the nineteenth-century theatrical *tableau vivant*, which was designed to "... punctuate the action, to stress or prolong a dramatic situation, and to give a scene an abstract or quasi-allegorical significance,"[43] and foreshadows its cinematic heir, the freeze frame. Taymor's "Penny Arcade Nightmare" episodes scattered through the movie descend from the turn-of-the-century flipcard Mutoscope and audio/phono Kinetescope peepshows that entertained the masses in shoddy penny arcades. Penny Arcade Nightmare no.2, for example, digs deeper into the ruined Titus' psyche, as he lies weeping in the road, begging for the lives of his condemned sons, Martius and Quintus. An angel materializes over an altar on which lies a sacrificial lamb, whose head suddenly becomes Mutius's just as the knife approaches. Pictorialism flourishes in the Roman bath orgy scene inspired by *Fellini Satyricon* (1969). Deliberate stylization carries over into Tamora's opulent costuming when her metallic golden gown proclaims her new found status among the power elite.

Like shock therapy, realism shatters the stylization. Titus's ritual slitting of the throats of the squeaking and gibbering Chiron and Demetrius, upended and suspended in chains from meat hooks, while an obliging Lavinia brings a white basin to catch the blood, adds a fresh cachet to the theatre of cruelty. A pretence of timelessness, or a-historicity, permeates the narrative: assault vehicles and motorcycles scoot side by side with the chariots of Roman legions; Bassianus and Saturninus campaign for political office from motor cars with loud speakers; and Benito Mussolini's fascist "EUR" office building on the outskirts of Rome suffices for a palace. Quotations from other films pop up unexpectedly: Lavinia on a tree stump holding down her white skirt resembles Marilyn Monroe in *Some Like It Hot*; the cart bearing the heads of Titus's sons and his own severed hand glances at Fellini's *La Strada*; a naked, grayish, perspiring Titus in his bath tub summons up remembrance of Peter Brook's Jean-Paul Marat, and so forth.

As Titus, Anthony Hopkins was born for the role, speaking the hyperbolic language with great flair. Aaron in opposing the racism of his captors ("Zounds, ye whore, is black so base a hue?" – 4.2.71), achieves dizzy heights of Marlovian defiance even while being savagely buried up to his neck in sand: "If one good deed in all my life I did,/ I do repent it from my very soul" (5.3.189). At the end Taymor, being human, apparently could not bear to accept Shakespeare's stark, pitiless, Senecan ending, and spares the infant Aaron, who may one day grow up to be an Othello. Instead she has Young Lucius, whom Lisa Starks has cleverly identified with the Slasher movie survivor figure[44] (e.g., the beleaguered Sally in *Texas Chainsaw Massacre*), pick the baby up and carry it out of the arena toward an arch way where the rising sun beckons. This touch of hope, of redemption, at one level succumbs to the worst Hollywood precedents for feel-good movies but, on the other hand, it follows the recuperative ending in most Shakespearean tragedies. Thereby it relieves not only the director but also her audience from facing the pitiless horrors of a holocaust.[45] One leaves the movie theatre with a sense of relief, where otherwise such calamities might inflict permanent trauma.

Non-Anglophone Shakespeare, documentaries, and a wild spoof

A year after Nunn's televised version, *The Merchant of Venice* appeared on screen again (2002) as a non-Anglophone film in the Maori language with subtitles in modern English. Director and producer, Don C. Selwyn, a prominent player in the New Zealand entertainment industry, had long specialized in mainstreaming Maori culture into New Zealand film and television. Originating in a 1990 stage version at the Auckland Koanga Festival with a script prepared by Dr. Pei Te Hurinui Jones, the film version was shot in and around Auckland with the waterways and buildings selected to suggest a Venetian setting. Traditional Maori codes such as a ceremonial welcome with a conch shell for the Prince of Morocco, and "Karanga" (female cry of welcome) are supplemented by Italian operatic arias. Waihoroi Shortland plays a convincing Shylock; Antonio is Scott Morrison; and Portia, Ngarimu Daniels, a "kapa haka" (traditional Maori dance) tutor. The audience at the 2003 meeting of the Shakespeare Association of America in Victoria, BC, found Shakespeare soaked in the culture of the remote South Pacific novel but ultimately plausible.[46]

Another non-Anglophone movie, also screened in Victoria for the Shakespeare Association, was a charming Japanese takeoff on *Merry Wives of Windsor*. Scenarist Yasunari Takahashi, whose version appeared originally in 1991 at Tokyo's Panasonic Globe Theatre, has liberally borrowed bits and patches from *Hamlet* and *Henry IV Parts One and Two*, the sonnets, and even Nino Rota's theme music from the Zeffirelli *Romeo and Juliet* to round out this merciless lampooning of Sir John Falstaff's pretensions to being a great lover. Falstaff puffs up his own courage with a familiar variation on "honor": "Suppose a samurai goes out to battle for the sake of honour, can honour set to a leg?"[47] The rejected crony of "the young heir of the Shogun," Falstaff has now become a pathetic drunk, a target for cruel farce rather than the cause of wit in others as he once was. Equally clever is *Machigai no Kyogen* (*The Comedy of Errors*), also screened in Victoria, though originally staged in 2001 at Tokyo's Setagaya Public Theatre. Directed by Mansai Nomura, who played Tsurumaru in Kurosawa's *Ran*, the antics of the two Dromios and their masters, the Antipholuses, smoothly translate into the conventions of the Japanese stage. Given the lengthy history of Shakespeare in Japan beginning in 1866, as chronicled in Ryuta Minami's "Chronological Table of Shakespeare

Productions in Japan,"[48] these well wrought performances should come as no surprise.

Also screened in Victoria was *A Dream in Hanoi*, an engrossing film essay about two theatre companies – one Vietnamese and one American creating the first production in Vietnam of *A Midsummer Night's Dream*. Another outstanding documentary, though anathema to Stratfordians for its Marlovian bias, is Michael Rubbo's polemical but cinematically talented documentary, *Much Ado About Something* (2002), which even as its scholarship wobbles adds more amusing anecdotes to the enigma of the disappearing body of Will Shakespeare. Not a documentary but a feature-length bio/pic is Indian director Shekhar Kapur's "historical thriller," *Elizabeth* (1998), which mesmerized audiences with a "Life and Times of William Shakespeare" far gaudier than any introductory essay in an undergraduate textbook. In the UK, ambitious Channel 4 programs provide a deluge of teaching materials, such as the one on *Twelfth Night* at http://www.channel4.com/learning/maininetnotes. Amazon.com.uk has announced the release on August 25, 2003, of Michael Wood's ambitious four-part BBC documentary, "In Search of Shakespeare," which has been favorably previewed by Clive James.[49]

After so long seriousness about the "great feast of moving images," it may seem frivolous to end with the outrageously funny antics of the Reduced Shakespeare Company, advertised as "Three guys, one dead playwright, and 37 plays, all in under two hours."[50] From the opening *schtick* with a condescending academic losing an audience that knows more about Shakespeare than he does, to a rollicking acrobatic performance of *Romeo and Juliet*, to a reinvention of *Titus Andronicus* in the format of a TV cooking program, to a condensed version of the sixteen comedies called "Four Weddings and a Transvestite," to a tasteless joke urging Ophelia to save her dress for the same reasons that Monica Lewinsky saved hers, to a dimwitted belief that Mel Gibson wrote *Hamlet*, and finally to the denouement – the absolute zaniness of doing *Hamlet* backwards, the three actors (Adam Long, Reed Martin, and Austin Tichenor) perform at a level of inspired lunacy. Only a recording of a stage performance in Vancouver, not cinematic at all, yet this is farce as life force, hilarious to all except the living dead. It becomes our Morris Dance for ending on an upbeat note.

At this stage in the new century, it is predictable that Shakespeare in moving images will continue to oscillate between the text-centered and performance-centered, *Lexis* and *Opsis*, the stage-bound and the filmic, Bardolater and Cinephile, and out of that dialectic will grow more extraordinary ventures into the preservation on screen of the spirit, if not the letter, of Shakespeare. Even as I keystroke this last paragraph, the London *Telegraph* reports two rival megaplex-size productions of *The Merchant of Venice* scheduled for release in 2004, starring famous performers like Patrick Stewart, Ian McKellen, Joseph Fiennes, and Al Pacino.[51] As I have previously written, however, Shakespeare remains incarnate in the trinity of page, stage and screen, each offering its own unique insights into his mind and art from the muses of literature, theatre, and mass entertainment. Thrice armed, he is unlikely to go away.

– NOTES –

1 SHAKESPEARE IN SILENCE: FROM STAGE TO SCREEN

1. *King John* was only recently discovered in the Netherlands Film Museum after having been lost for decades, a remarkable story in the annals of film scholarship too lengthy for full discussion here. Years ago Professor Robert Hamilton Ball, the leading expert on Shakespeare silent film, hypothesized from available data that the then lost *King John* was comprised of the "Magna Carta" interpolation in Tree's stage play. See his *Shakespeare on Silent Film: A Strange Eventful History* (London: George Allen & Unwin Ltd., 1968), pp. 21–23; 303–04; and "Tree's *King John* Film: An Addendum," *SQ* 24.4 (1973), 455. Later discoveries by B. A. Kachur pointed to other scenes in the lost film. See her "The First Shakespeare Film: A Reconsideration and Reconstruction of Tree's *King John*," *TS* 32 (May 1991), 43–63. Finally, there was the definitive work establishing the original plan for the filming by Luke McKernan, "Beerbohm Tree's *King John* Rediscovered: The First Shakespeare Film, September 1899," *SB* 11.1 (1993), 35–36; and "Further News on Beerbohm Tree's *King John*," *SB* 11.2 (1993), 49–50.

2. John Wyver, *The Moving Image: An International History of Film, Television and Video* (Oxford and New York: Blackwell/BFI, 1989), p. 17.

3. *NYT* 24 Apr. 1896, 5; 26 Apr. 1896, 10.

4. All Shakespeare quotations are from G. Blakemore Evans, *et al.* (eds.), *The Riverside Shakespeare* (Boston: Houghton Mifflin, 1974).

5. Gerda Taranow, *Sarah Bernhardt: The Art within the Legend* (Princeton University Press, 1972), pp. 265–66. Ball in *Silent Film* (p. 305) raises the possibility of live sound effects, though he then rejects the idea.

6. Sarah Bernhardt, *Memoirs of My Life* (1908, repr. New York: Benjamin Blom, 1968). Among other things, she engaged in balloon ascensions and memorizing her lines in a coffin.

7. Taranow, *Bernhardt: The Art*, pp. 210–11.

8. Gerda Taranow, *The Bernhardt "Hamlet": Culture and Context* (New York: Peter Lang. 1996), p. 129. I am much indebted to Taranow's thorough study of Bernhardt's acting career. See also the thirteen frame enlargements from the Bernhardt *Hamlet* film, pp. 231–34.

9. See Roger Manvell, *Theater and Film: A Comparative Study* (London: Associated University Presses, 1979), p. 36. The late Dr. Manvell's six-step progression from "undisguised recordings of a production" in a theatre (e.g., the Burton *Hamlet*), to complete transformations (e.g., Kurosawa's *Throne of Blood*) remains a starting point for any taxonomy of screened Shakespeare.

10. David A. Cook, *A History of Narrative Film*, 3rd edn (New York: Norton, 1996), p. 5.

11. *MPW* 6 Feb. 1907, 147.

12. *Ibid.*, 2 May 1907, 154.

13. *Ibid.*, 24 Oct. 1908, 317.

14. *Ibid.*, 25 May 1907, 180.

15. "Audience Applauds His Shrieks of Agony," *MPW* 22 Feb. 1908, 138.

16. *MPW* 31 Oct. 1908, 348.

17. Ball, *Silent Film*, p. 108.

18. *Ibid.*, p. 35.

19. Ben M. Hall, *The Best Remaining Seats: The Story of the Golden Age of the Movie Palace* (New York: Clarkson N. Potter, 1961), p. 13.

20. *MPW* 4 May 1907, 140.

21. William Uricchio and Roberta E. Pearson, *Reframing Culture: The Case of the Vitagraph Quality Films* (Princeton University Press, 1993), p. 25.

22. *MPW* 5 Dec. 1908, 444.

23. Uricchio and Pearson, *Reframing Culture*, p. 33.

24. *MPW* 11 May 1907, 153.

25. Robert C. Allen, *Vaudeville and Film 1895–1915: A Study in Media Interaction* (New York: Arno Press, 1980), pp. 220–30.

26. *MPW* 2 Jan. 1909, 3.

27. *Ibid.*, 4 July 1908, 5.

28. See the biography by his daughter, which contains one or two vignettes about his work with Shakespeare, particularly the aging Rose Coghlan's attempt to play a svelte Rosalind in *As You Like It*. Marion Blackton Trimble, *J. Stuart Blackton, A Personal Biography* (Metuchen and London: Scarecrow Press, 1985), pp. 40–41.

29. See Steven J. Ross, *Working-Class Hollywood: Silent Film and the Shaping of Class in America* (Princeton University Press, 1998). Ross's study shows how popular entertainment redefines and reinvents reality for mass audiences. His conclusion is eloquent: "Vision is a gift, a gift held by the best writers, the best orators, and the best film-makers. Committed filmmakers could help replace the current politics of despair with the politics of hope … [cinema] can take a politically blind population and offer them the gift of sight" (p. 257).

30. *MPW* 18 Dec. 1909, 870.

31. Ball, *Silent Film*, p. 314.

32. Kevin Brownlow, *Hollywood: The Pioneers* (New York: Knopf, 1979), p. 28 and *passim*.

33. William K. Everson, *American Silent Film* (Oxford University Press, 1978), p. 36. Everson says that of 525 silents released in 1921 only 50 remained in 1978 (p. 14). Ball indexes over 500 titles of alleged Shakespeare films, of which only a tiny fraction survive. Classics scholars have the same problem in generalizing about Greek drama from a skimpy data base.

34. Brownlow, *Hollywood*, p. 156.

35. Ball, *Silent Film*, p. 43.

36. See Charles Musser, *The Emergence of Cinema: The American Screen to 1907* (New York: Charles Scribner's Sons, 1990), vol. I in *History of American Cinema*, gen. ed. Charles Harpole (New York: Charles Scribner's Sons, 1990–), especially pp. 239–40, 305–06, 540–42.

37. Ball, *Silent Film*, p. 48.

38. Bush, "Our American Letter," *Bioscope* 16 Apr. 1914, 287.

39. *MPW* 4 July 1908, 12. Bush offered to accompany screenings of *Othello* and *Romeo and Juliet* with lectures and recitals as a way of attracting "the best class of people" to the movies.

40. *MPW* 5 Dec. 1908, 446–47.

41. Archival prints of Vitagraph movies often have title cards in languages other than English, e.g., the opening of the NFTVA copy of *King Lear*: "Der Herzog von Kent/Wird Verbannt/Weil er Cordelia/Verteidict." Liberated from spoken language, silent movies ignored national boundaries in favor of a universal system of non-verbal communication. Charlie Chaplin and Lillian Gish worked as well in Berlin as in Peoria. Theatre owners could very cheaply splice in translated cards, or requests for ladies to remove their majestic hats, a practice that may account for the demise of the millinery industry. A trade journal advertisement reads: "Film titles made to order. Five feet for ¢50. No delay. Toledo, Ohio." (*MPW* 9 Jan. 1909, 46).

42. *MPW* 8 Jan. 1910, 101.

43. Everson, *American Silent Film*, p. 102.

44. Bush's remarks do not support the revisionist film scholars who have recently argued that nickelodeon audiences included upper as well as lower-income persons. There is a parallel here in Shakespeare studies with the debates over the make-up of the audiences at the Globe and Blackfriars playhouses. See Sumiko Higashi, "Dialogue; Manhattan's Nickelodeons"; Robert C. Allen, "Manhattan Myopia, or Oh! Iowa!"; and reply by Ben Singer, "New York, Just Like I Pictured It," in *Cinema Journal* 35.3 (1996), 72–128. I personally tend to side with Singer's view of a correlation between neighborhood and audience demography. In Shakespeare's time, the Globe patrons more or less reflected the seediness of Southwark, just as the grander folk at Blackfriars carried with them the whiff of prosperity from their "classier" neighborhood. For details, see my "The Audience for the Blackfriars Playhouse in Shakespeare's London," *The Yearbook of the American Philosophical Society* (Philadelphia, 1969), pp. 649–50.

45. *MPW* 5 Sept. 1908, 234.

46. *Ibid.*, 5 Dec. 1908, 446–47.

47. "Editorial," *Bioscope* 25 June 1914, 1289. The writer was an unrepentant elitist of the pre-politically correct era.

48. Anthony Slide, *The American Film Industry* (New York: Greenwood Press, 1986), p. 372.

49. Richard Abel, *The Cine Goes to Town: French Cinema 1896–1914* (Berkeley: University of California Press, 1994), p. 59.

50. Hall, *Best Remaining Seats*, p. 30.

51. Advertisement, *NYT* 6 March 1927, VIII 9.

52. Richard Abel, *French Cinema: The First Wave 1915–1929* (Princeton University Press, 1984), p. 52.

53. Quoted in Rachel Low, *History of British Film 1906–1914* (London: George Allen & Unwin, 1949), p. 14.

54. *Bioscope* 5 Jan. 1911, 55.

55. "Another Palace Opens," *Bioscope* 12 Jan. 1911, 15; see also David Atwell, *Cathedrals of the Movies: A History of British Cinema and Their Audiences* (London: The Architectural Press, 1980), for descriptions of these early theatres.

56. Quoted in Nathan Silver's review of Dennis Sharp's *The Picture Palace* (London (?): Hugh Evelyn, 1969) in *S&S* 38.3 (Summer 1969), 160 and *passim*.

57. *Bioscope* 12 June 1913, suppl. xxvi.

58. *Ibid.*, p. 835.

59. My database comes from four principal sources: R. H. Ball's *Shakespeare on Silent Film*; K. S. Rothwell and Annabelle Henkin Melzer, *Shakespeare on Screen: An International Filmography and Videography* (New York: Neal-Schuman, 1990), which I have collated with the more recent SIFT database in the British Film Institute Library, and with Luke McKernan and Olwen Terris, *Walking Shadows: Shakespeare in the National Film and Television Archive* (London: BFI, 1994).

60. Brownlow, *Hollywood the Pioneers*, p. 70.

61. The film received a full-page advertisement in *Bioscope* 10 July 1913, 107.

62. *NYT* 12 Feb. 1922, II. 3.

63. "The Filming of *Hamlet*: Interview with Mr. Cecil Hepworth," *Bioscope* 24 July 1913, 275.

64. For detailed analysis, see Bernice W. Kliman, *Hamlet: Film, Television, and Audio Performance* (London and Toronto: Assoc. University Presses, 1988), pp. 247–74.

65. See Frederick B. Warde, *Fifty Years of Make-Believe* (New York: International Press Syndicate, 1920) for a full account.

66. Quoted in American Film Institute Souvenir Program, 29 Oct. 1996.

67. *History of British Film*, p. 224.

68. *Silent Film*, p. 243.

69. *"Broken Blossoms:* The Vulnerable Text and the Marketing of Masochism," in *Film in The Aura of Art* (Princeton University Press, 1984), pp. 16–17.

70. For background, see Siegfried Kracauer, *From Caligari to Hitler: A Psychological History of the German Film* (Princeton University Press, 1947).

71. Ball, *Silent Film*, p. 176.

72. See Ann Thompson, "Asta Nielsen and the Mystery of *Hamlet*," in *Shakespeare, The Movie*, ed. Lynda E. Boose and Richard Burt (London and New York: Routledge, 1997), pp. 215–24.

73. Quoted in Taranow, *Bernhardt: The Art*, pp. 212–13.

74. "Gazing at Hamlet, or the Danish Cabaret," *SS* 45 (1993), 40.

75. *MPW* 19 Nov. 1921, 336.

76. See K. S. Rothwell, "Roman Polanski's *Macbeth*: The 'Privileging' of Ross," *The CEA Critic* 46.1–2 (Fall & Winter 1983–84), 50–55.

77. Danson, "Gazing at Hamlet," p. 48.

78. J. Lawrence Guntner, "Expressionist Shakespeare: The Gade/Nielsen *Hamlet* (1920) and the History of Shakespeare on Film," *Post Script* 17.2 (Winter/Spring 1998), 97. Dr. Guntner is a pioneering student of this film.

79. Ann Thompson, "Asta Nielsen and the Mystery of *Hamlet*," in Boose and Burt (eds.), *Shakespeare, The Movie*, pp. 220–21.

80. *NYT* 9 Nov. 1921, 20.

81. See V. I. Pudovkin, *Film Technique, Film Acting*, trans. Ivor Montagu (1929; repr. Hackensack NJ: Wehman Brothers, 1968), p. 143.

82. Karen Newman, *Fashioning Femininity and English Renaissance Drama* (University of Chicago Press, 1991), p. 91. Newman cites this theory as having been Lynda Boose's.

2 HOLLYWOOD'S FOUR SEASONS OF SHAKESPEARE

1. "Letter," 15 March 1914, quoted in Low, *History of British Film*, p. 29.

2. Ross, *Working-Class Hollywood*, p. 113.

3. Essay on dust jacket, Mirage Corp. laser disk, *The Taming of the Shrew*. The Mary Pickford Co. © 1966; 1990.

4. Russell Jackson points out that the "purists" are essentially bogey men, figments of the imagination of journalists, rarely encountered in real life. See his "Shakespeare's Comedies on Film," in Anthony Davies and Stanley Wells (eds.), *Shakespeare and the Moving Image: The Plays on Film and Television* (Cambridge University Press, 1994).

5. Roger Manvell, *Shakespeare and the Film* (repr. South Brunswick and New York: A. S. Barnes, 1979), p. 23.

6. See, for example, *The Motion Picture Guide, 1927–1983*, ed. Jay Robert Nash and Stanley Ralph Ross (Chicago: Cinebooks, 1987), p. 3274.

7. James M. Welsh, "Shakespeare, With – and Without – Words," *LFQ* 1.1 (Jan. 1973), 88.

8. Manvell, *Shakespeare and the Film*, p. 24.

9. The BFI "SIFT" catalog mentions an excerpt from a 1927 *Merchant* directed by W. R. Newman as a "first" Shakespeare talkie, but rival claimants include excerpts from Gounod's *Roméo et Juliette* (c.1927), cited by McKernan and Terris in *Walking Shadows* (p. 143), and Thomas Edison's unsuccessful scene from *Julius Caesar* reported in *The New York Times* (4 Jan. 1913: 7).

10. Mary Pickford, *Sunshine and Shadow* (New York: Doubleday, 1955), pp. 311–12.

11. *Variety* 2 Nov. 1966.

12. James Agate, "Notes," *The Magazine Programme*, London Pavilion, 14 Nov. 1929.

13. "The Movies," *Outlook* 153 (18 Dec. 1929), 633–34.

14. *NYT* 30 Nov. 1929, 23.

15. John Wyver, *The Moving Image: An International History of Film, Television and Video* (London: Blackwell/BFI, 1989), p. 84.

16. Diana E. Henderson, "A Shrew for the Times," in Boose and Burt, *Shakespeare, The Movie*, p. 154. Henderson's point is well taken since so many have thought the wink was directed at the audience rather than at the sister. She also surveys virtually every screened *Shrew*.

17. "Titania and the Ass's Head," in *Shakespeare Our Contemporary* (New York: Anchor Books, 1966), pp. 213–36.

18. Jay L. Halio, *"A Midsummer Night's Dream": Shakespeare in Performance* (Manchester University Press, 1994), pp. 36–38.

19. Public relations kit, Warner Brothers, at British Film Institute.

20. *Still in Movement: Shakespeare on Screen* (New York: Oxford University Press, 1991), p. 12.

21. *Speechless Dialect: Shakespeare's Open Silences* (Berkeley: University of California Press, 1985), p. 1.

22. *Time* 26 (21 Oct. 1935), 44–45.

23. Quoted in Manvell, *Shakespeare and the Film*, p. 27 from *Shakespeare, A Celebration*, ed. T. J. B. Spencer, pp. 109–10.

24. *The Graham Greene Film Reader: Reviews, Essays, Interviews and Film Stories*, ed. David Parkinson (New York: Applause Theatre Book Publishers, 1993), p. 38.

25. "Films," *The London Mercury* 35 (Nov. 1936), 57.

26. "Picturizing *Romeo and Juliet*," in *"Romeo and Juliet" by William Shakespeare. A Motion Picture Edition* (New York: Random House, 1936), p. 13.

27. A still of Barrymore in this role appears in James Kotsilibas-Davis, *The Barrymores, the Royal Family in Hollywood* (New York: Crown Publishers, 1981), p. 89. (Reference thanks to Craig Toth.)

28. Patrick McGilligan, *George Cukor: A Double Life* (New York: St. Martin's Press, 1991), p. 105.

29. *Motion Picture Edition*, p. 24.

30. Romeo and Juliet. *With Designs by Oliver Messel* (London: B. T. Batsford, 1936).

31. *Dance to the Piper* (Boston: Little, Brown, and Company 1952), pp. 233–34.

32. *Shakespeare in Production. Whose History?* (Athens: Ohio University Press, 1996), p. 49.

33. *Motion Picture Edition*, p. 256.

34. Meredith Lillich, "Shakespeare on the Screen: A Survey of How His Plays Have Been Made into Movies," *FR* (June 1956), 251.

35. *Filming Shakespeare's Plays: The Adaptations of Laurence Olivier, Orson Welles, Peter Brook and Akira Kurosawa* (Cambridge University Press, 1988), p. 7.

36. *A Motion Picture Edition*, p. 14.

37. "M.G.M. Proudly Brings to the Screen," Souvenir Book (n.d.), p. 3.

38. "The Role of the Technical Adviser," from *QFRT* 8.2 (1953), 131–38, as quoted in Eckert, *Focus on Shakespearean Films*, p. 104.

39. John Houseman, "Filming *Julius Caesar*," *S&S* 23.1 (July/Sept. 1953), 25.

40. "Shakespeare and the Included Spectator," in *Reinterpretations of Elizabethan Drama*, ed. Norman Rabkin (New York: Columbia University Press, 1969), p. 123.

41. Miklos Rozsa, "*Julius Caesar*," *Film Music* 13 (Sept./Oct. 1953), 9.

42. See the outline in the film's companion volume, *Julius Caesar and the Life of William Shakespeare*, introduction by Sir John Gielgud (London: The Gawthorn Press, 1953).

43. "Filming *Julius Caesar*," *S&S* 23 (July/Sept. 1953), 25.

44. See Murray Biggs, "'He's Going to His Mother's Closet': Hamlet and Gertrude on Screen," *SS* 45 (1993), 56. Biggs sees 1960 as the year when actors began turning verse into prose, and Gielgud's favoring of song over sense, his "ample vibrato to boot," identifies him with the older era.

45. Linda Costanzo Cahir, "The Artful Rerouting of *A Streetcar Named Desire*," *LFQ* 22.2 (1994), 73.
46. Quoted in Meredith Lillich, "Shakespeare on the Screen," p. 258.
47. Original Film Trailer on MGM/UA Home Video laser disk. Side three.

3 LAURENCE OLIVIER DIRECTS SHAKESPEARE

1. *Walking Shadows*, p. 199.
2. Others do not see it this way. See Donald Spoto, *Laurence Olivier: A Biography* (New York: HarperCollins, 1992), p. 97: "But the direst liability of *As You Like It* was the star [Elisabeth Bergner]."
3. *Shakespeare and the Film*, p. 31. By my count she only turns one somersault, and that not of Olympic gymnastics quality.
4. Howard Barnes, "*As You Like It*," *NYHT* 6 Nov. 1936, n.p.; for similar views, see also W. F., "*As You Like It*," *MFB* 3.33 (Sept. 1936), 147, 519.
5. "Bergner as Rosalind," in *Around Cinemas* (London: Home & Van Thal, 1946; repr. New York: Arno Press, 1972), p. 176.
6. See the frequently cited essay by Norman Rabkin, "Rabbits, Ducks and *Henry V*," *SQ* 28.3 (Summer 1977), 279–96.
7. Harry M. Geduld, *Filmguide to* Henry V (Bloomington: Indiana University Press, 1973), p. 55.
8. *Filming Shakespeare's Plays.* (Cambridge University Press, 1988), p. 36.
9. "Olivier's *Henry V* and the Elizabethan World Picture," *LFQ* 11.3 (1983: Special issue of papers from Seminar 16, World Shakespeare Congress; guest ed. Kenneth S. Rothwell), 179.
10. Quoted in Charles Musser, "Engaging with Reality," in *The Oxford History of World Cinema*, ed. Geoffrey Nowell-Smith (Oxford University Press, 1996), p. 326.
11. *Ibid.*
12. Peter Drexler, "Laurence Olivier's *Henry V* and Veit Harlan's *Der Grosse König:* Two Versions of the National Hero on Film," in *Negotiations with Hal: Multi-Media Perceptions of [Shakespeare's] Henry the Fifth*, ed. Peter Drexler and Lawrence Guntner (Technische Universität Braunschweig: Braunschweiger Anglistische Arbeiten, 1995), p. 129.
13. See Ernest Kantorowicz, *The King's Two Bodies: A Study in Medieval Political Theology* (Princeton University Press, 1957). This well-known concept is touched on by Nicole Weigel and Stefanie Schreiner in "England's Glory, or 'Bildungsroman': A Comparison of Olivier's and Branagh's *Henry V* Films," in Drexler and Guntner, *Negotiations with Hal*, p. 68.
14. *Screening Shakespeare from* Richard II *to* Henry V (Newark: University of Delaware Press, 1991), p. 101.
15. "Recycled Film Codes and 'The Great Tradition of Shakespeare on Film'," in Drexler and Guntner, *Negotiations with Hal*, p. 51.
16. *Film in the Aura*, p. 132. This is the most searching essay on the film that I have found.
17. Robert F. Willson, Jr., "The Opening of *Henry V*: Olivier's Visual Pun," *SFNL* 5.2 (May 1981), 1ff.
18. My colleague R. Thomas Simone in an unpublished paper has made a compelling case that the prompter is actually intended to be William Shakespeare.
19. Spoto, *Olivier,* p. 166. Apparently Olivier himself may have been the one to find the illuminated manuscript.
20. *Filmguide*, p. 42.
21. Brian McFarlane, *An Autobiography of British Cinema* (London: Methuen, 1997), p. 82. I am obliged to Dr. Russell Jackson for drawing this book to my attention.
22. Martin Marks, "The Sound of Music," in *The Oxford History of World Cinema* (Oxford University Press, 1996), p. 257.

23. Manvell, *Shakespeare and the Film*, p. 46.

24. *Film in the Aura*, p. 151.

25. Laurence Olivier, "An Essay in *Hamlet*," in Brenda Cross (ed.), *The Film "Hamlet." A Record of Its Production* (New York: Saturn Press, 1948), p. 12.

26. Souvenir Program, Theatre Guild, n.p.

27. Spoto, *Olivier*, p. 207.

28. "Olivier's *Hamlet*: A Film-Infused Play," in *LFQ* 5.4 (Fall 1977, guest ed. Michael Mullin), 305.

29. *"Hamlet." Film, Television* (London and Toronto: Associated University Presses, 1988), pp. 23–25.

30. Davies, *Filming Shakespeare's Plays*, p. 64.

31. "Building the Sets," in Cross, *The Film* Hamlet, p. 44.

32. "Subliminal Masks in Olivier's *Hamlet*," *SFNL* 16.1 (Dec. 1991), 5.

33. "Olivier, Hamlet, and Freud," in *Shakespearean Films/Shakespearean Directors* (Boston: Unwin Hyman, 1990), p. 39 and *passim*.

34. *Hamlet Father and Son* (Oxford: Clarendon Press, 1955), p. 115 and *passim*. Alexander thinks that *arete* is of greater consequence to the tragic hero than *hamartia*. The stress in the Olivier film on "flaw" distorts Hamlet's character.

35. "Shakespeare on TV," *BBC Quarterly* 9.3 (Autumn 1954), 146.

36. Olivier, "An Essay in *Hamlet*," in Cross, *The Film*, p. 12.

37. *Filming Shakespeare's Plays*, pp. 49, 55. Two stills from *Hamlet* effectively illustrate the vertical and horizontal strategies used in the movie.

38. "Note on *Hamlet*," *FM* 13 (Jan./Feb. 1954), 19.

39. A similar debacle occurred in 1973 when Joseph Papp's Broadway hit version of *Much Ado* was forced to close down only nine days after IBM sponsored its transmission on television.

40. Davies, *Filming Shakespeare's Plays*, p. 66.

41. *Laurence Olivier and the Art of Film Making* (London and Toronto: Associated University Presses, 1985), p. 229.

42. Quoted in Geoffrey Bullough (ed.), *Narrative and Dramatic Sources of Shakespeare*, III (New York: Columbia University Press, 1975), p. 253.

43. "A Defence of the Apologie of the Church of England," in *Works of John Jewel*, III, ed. John Eyre (Cambridge University Press, 1848), p. 152.

44. See Constance A. Brown's unrivalled essay, "Olivier's *Richard III* – A Re-evaluation," *FQ* 20 (1967), 25.

45. Silviria, *Olivier and Film Making*, p. 237.

46. F. R. Leavis, "Diabolic Intellect and the Noble Hero," in *Shakespeare* Othello. *A Casebook*, ed. John Wain (London, 1971), p. 135; Kenneth Tynan, *The Sound of Two Hands Clapping* (London: Jonathan Cape, 1975), pp. 130–31. Tynan's essay offers deep insight into Olivier's approach to this role.

47. Spoto, *Olivier*, p. 334.

48. Jack J. Jorgens, *Shakespeare on Film* (Bloomington: Indiana University Press, 1977), p. 191.

49. "Minstrel Show *Othello*," *NYT* 2 Feb. 1966, 24.

50. "Olivier Paints Othello Ridden by Neuroses," *NYHT* 2 Feb. 1966.

51. "Black and White," *TNY*, 19 Feb. 1966, 145.

52. "Olivier and the Moor," *Holiday*, 26 Apr. 1966, 143 and *passim*.

53. *The Times* 13 Dec. 1937, 18.

54. Jonathan Miller, *Subsequent Performances* (New York: Elisabeth Sifton Books/Viking, 1986), pp. 104–08.

55. John O'Connor, "Olivier as the Controversial Shylock in 1880s," *NYT* 15 March 1974, 67.

[281]

56. "Trivial Pursuit: The Casket Plot in the Miller/Olivier *Merchant of Venice*," *SFNL* 10.1 (Dec. 1985), 7 and *passim*.
57. Peter Cowie, "Olivier at 75 Returns to Lear," *NYT* 1 May 1983, II. 1.
58. Frank Occhiogrosso, "'Give Me Thy Hand': Manual Gesture in the Elliott/Olivier *King Lear*," *SB* 2.9 (May–June 1984), 16–19.
59. Tucker Orbison, "The Stone and the Oak: Olivier's TV Film of *King Lear*," *CEA Critic* 47.1-2 (Fall–Winter 1984), 67–77.
60. *360 Film Classics* (supplement to *Sight and Sound*), ed. Nick James (London: NFTVA and BFI, 1998). Ernst Lubitsch's Shakespeare derivative, *To Be or Not to Be*, also made the list.

4 ORSON WELLES: SHAKESPEARE FOR THE ART HOUSES

1. Simon Callow, *Orson Welles: The Road to Xanadu* (London: Jonathan Cape, 1995), p. 576. Among other biographies consulted for this section are: Frank Brady, *Citizen Welles: A Biography of Orson Welles* (New York: Charles Scribner's Sons, 1989); Barbara Leaming, *Orson Welles* (New York: Viking, 1985); Joseph McBride, *Orson Welles*, rev. ed. (New York: Da Capo, 1996); James Naremore, *The Magic World of Orson Welles* (Dallas: Southern Methodist University Press, 1989); Jonathan Rosenbaum (ed.), *This Is Orson Welles: Orson Welles and Peter Bogdanovich* (New York: HarperCollins, 1992); David Thomson, *Rosebud: The Story of Orson Welles* (New York: Alfred Knopf, 1996).
2. For an overview of this complicated subject, which is beyond the scope of the present study, see Ronald Gottesman (ed.), *Focus on Orson Welles* (Englewood Cliffs: Prentice Hall, 1976).
3. Brady, *Welles*, p. 432.
4. Jonathan Rosenbaum, "The Invisible Orson Welles: A First Inventory," *S&S* 55.3 (Summer 1986), 168.
5. "Interview," from Italian Documentary, *Rosabella*, appendix no. 51, *Othello* [1952] The Voyager Company laser disk, 1995.
6. "Interview with Keith Baxter," in *"Chimes at Midnight"*: *Orson Welles, director*, ed. Bridget Gellert Lyons (New Brunswick and London: Rutgers University Press, 1988), p. 279.
7. See "The Magician," in James Naremore's aptly named *The Magic World of Orson Welles*, pp. 30–51.
8. *Ibid.*, p. 250.
9. "With Orson Welles: Stories from a Life in Film," television interview in 1980 by Leslie Megahey, with Jeanne Moreau, John Huston, Charlton Heston, Anthony Perkins, and Peter Bogdanovich, transmitted on Channel TNT, Monday, 5 Feb. 1990.
10. David Bradley, "Shakespeare on a Shoestring," *Movie Makers* (Apr. 1947), 146ff.
11. Richard Wilson, "*Macbeth* on Film," *TA* 33.5 (June 1949), 53–55.
12. Quoted in Manvell, *Shakespeare and the Film*, p. 59.
13. Richard France (ed.), *Orson Welles on Shakespeare: The W.P.A. and Mercury Theatre Playscripts* (New York: The Greenwood Press, 1990), p. 5 and *passim*.
14. *NYT* 28 Dec. 1950, 22.
15. Quoted in Rosenbaum, *This Is Orson Welles*, p. 203.
16. For analysis of the textual changes, see Michael Mullin, "Orson Welles' *Macbeth*: Script and Screen," in Gottesman (ed.), *Focus on Orson Welles*, pp. 136–45.
17. Harold Leonard, "Hollywood: Notes on *Macbeth*," *S&S* 19.1 (March 1950), 17.
18. Mullin, 136–45. With three different versions in existence, any opinions about the movie are contingent on the incarnation that the critic has screened. Commentary here has been based on re-screenings of the 1979 release available on videocassette from Republic Pictures.
19. The reader is entitled to know that David Thomson sees Lady Macbeth in exactly opposite terms, as "very erotic." *Rosebud*, p. 286.

20. For a superb account of production details, see Bernice W. Kliman, "Welles's *Macbeth*, A Textual Parable," in Michael Skovmand (ed.), *Screen Shakespeare* (Aarhus University Press, 1994), pp. 25–38. See also Kliman's "Orson Welles's 1936 'Voodoo' *Macbeth* and Its Reincarnation on Film," in Macbeth, *Shakespeare in Performance Series* (Manchester University Press, 1992), pp. 86–99.

21. Kliman, "Welles's *Macbeth*," in Skovmand (ed.), *Screen Shakespeare*, p. 28.

22. *Welles*, p. 118.

23. Alan Brien, *The Evening Standard* 23 Feb. 1956.

24. Anon., "The 'Othello' of Mr. Orson Welles," *MG* 25 Feb. 1956.

25. "Films," *TN* 1 Oct. 1955, 81.

26. "The New Pictures," *Time* 6 June 1955, 106.

27. W. J. Weatherby, "Forgotten Heir of *Citizen Kane*," *Guardian* 28 April 1992, 38.

28. J. Hoberman, "Moor Better Blues," *VV* 31 March 1992, 5.

29. McBride, *Welles*, pp. 124–25. McBride points out that a 1995 Criterion Collection laser disk uses the 1955 US release version.

30. *Shakespeare Observed: Studies in Performance on Stage and Screen* (Athens: Ohio University Press, 1992), pp. 51–53.

31. Roland Barthes, *S/Z. An Essay*, trans. Richard Miller (New York: Hill & Wang, 1972).

32. Richard Palmer, *Hermeneutics: Interpretation Theory in Schleiermacher, Dilthey, Heidegger, and Gadamer* (Evanston: Northwestern University Press, 1969), p. 87.

33. *Put Money in Thy Purse: A Diary of the Film of* Othello (London: Methuen, 1952).

34. Interviews from Italian Documentary *Rosabella*, appendices nos. 51, 49, and 50.

35. *Movie Made America* (New York: Vintage, 1975), p. 253; repr. in *The Book of Film Noir*, ed. Ian Cameron (New York: Continuum, 1992), p. 89.

36. Crowl, *Shakespeare Observed*, p. 181, f.n. 9. Crowl failed to find the mirror in any of the reprints of Carpaccio's work that he surveyed but he did find a mirror that is put to a similar reflective purpose in Jan van Eyck's "The Marriage of Arnolfini."

37. "When Peter Met Orson: The 1953 CBS *King Lear*," In Boose and Burt (eds.), *Shakespeare, The Movie*, p. 129. Howard's interesting essay also comments on "how oddly uncomfortable" Welles's films were with "women's sexuality" (p. 131), a provocative point that deserves to be considered at greater length.

38. Marvin Rosenberg, *The Masks of* King Lear (Berkeley: University of California Press, 1972), p. 312.

39. Nikos Metallinos, *Television Aesthetics: Perceptual, Cognitive and Compositional Bases* (Mahwah, N.J.: Earlbaum Associates, 1996), pp. 237–40. A large topic, but Metallinos' chapter on "Applied Rules for Composition of Television Pictures" (pp. 197–283) offers a useful summary.

40. Quoted in Robert A. Hetherington, "The *Lears* of Peter Brook," *SFNL* 6.1 (1982), 7.

41. "Introduction," *King Henry IV Part Two*, *The Arden Shakespeare* (London: Methuen, 1966), p. xxvii.

42. *Shakespeare on Film*, p. 111.

43. "Interview," in Lyons, *Chimes at Midnight*, p. 282.

44. Juan Cobos and Miguel Rubio, "Welles and Falstaff: An Interview by Juan Cobos and Miguel Rubio," *S&S* 35.4 (Autumn 1966), 159.

45. France (ed.), *Orson Welles on Shakespeare*, p. 172.

46. Robert Hapgood, "*Chimes at Midnight* from Stage to Screen: The Art of Adaptation," in *Shakespeare Survey* 39 (1987), p. 40.

47. Rosenbaum, *This Is Orson Welles*, p. 217.

48. Hapgood, "*Chimes at Midnight*," pp. 44–47.

49. See Lyons (ed.), *Chimes at Midnight*, for the film's continuity script. Scene and shot numbers in the text refer to Lyons.

50. Pilkington, *Screening Shakespeare*, p. 137, warns about the "difficulty in identifying Falstaff too closely with Welles." The difficulty granted, there still seem to be many reasons for identifying him with Welles.
51. Quoted in Rosenbaum, *This Is Orson Welles*, p. 100.
52. "The Magnificent Ambersons," in Gottesman (ed.), *Focus on Orson Welles*, p. 123.
53. Davies, *Filming Shakespeare's Plays*, pp. 124–28.
54. Baxter, "Interview," Lyons (ed.), *Chimes at Midnight*, pp. 280–81.
55. Davies, *Filming Shakespeare's Plays*, p. 125.
56. Rosenbaum, *This Is Orson Welles*, pp. 294; 297–98.
57. Cobos and Rubio, "Interview," 158.
58. Lyons (ed.), *Chimes at Midnight*. See "Continuity Script," pp. 142–67.
59. *Ibid.*, p. 254.
60. Sharmini Tiruchelvam, "Encounter on the Field of Philippi," *The Daily Telegraph Magazine*, 6 Feb. 1970, 17.
61. Jonathan Rosenbaum, "The Invisible Orson Welles," pp. 167–68.
62. BFI "SIFT" catalog, entry A02M005.
63. Rosenbaum, "The Invisible Orson Welles," p. 170.
64. Bosley Crowther, "Review," *NYT* 20 March 1967, 26.

5 ELECTRONIC SHAKESPEARE: FROM TELEVISION TO THE WEB

1. Ashley Dukes, "Televised Drama So Far: The English Scene," *TAM* (1939), 259.
2. Transmission data from mimeographed *Television Programme as Broadcast (TPAB)* 1937. BBC WAC, Caversham Park, Reading. Susan Willis, *The BBC Shakespeare Plays: Making the Televised Canon* (Chapel Hill: University of North Carolina Press, 1991) correctly puts the BBC 1937 *As You Like It* as falling on February 5 rather than 6. A blurry mimeographed program caused the incorrect February 6 date in Rothwell & Melzer.
3. Gordon Ross, *Television Jubilee: The Story of 25 Years of BBC Television* (London: W. H. Allen, 1961), p. 13.
4. Albert Abramson, "The Invention of Television," in *Television: An International History*, ed. Anthony Smith (Oxford University Press, 1995), p. 13.
5. Ross, *Television Jubilee*, p. 20. Quotation of a review from *The Guardian*.
6. "Shakespeare: The Scholar's Contribution," *The Listener* 17 March 1937, 498 and *passim*.
7. "Shakespeare in His Theatre," *The Listener* 20 Jan. 1937, 116–18.
8. "Shakespeare on the Modern Stage," *The Listener* 3 Feb. 1937, 207.
9. Allwyn Tibbenham, "Shakespeare Today," in "Points from Letters," *The Listener* 17 March 1937, 521.
10. Nikos Metallinos, *Television Aesthetics*, p. 1.
11. *Radio and TV Who's Who*, 3rd edn, ed. Cyrus Andrews (London: George Young, 1954).
12. Ross, *Television Jubilee*, p. 59.
13. "Review," *The Times* 13 Dec. 1937, 18.
14. BBC, *TPAB* Sunday, 24 July 1938.
15. Anon., "Review," *World Film News* 30 Aug. 1938.
16. "*Julius Caesar* in Modern Dress," *News Chronicle* 25 July 1938.
17. "*Julius Caesar* in Modern Dress: Television Version," *Sunday Times* 24 July 1938.
18. Correspondence about *Othello*, BBC WAC T5/379 *Othello* 1937–50.
19. "Televised Drama," *The Times* 15 Dec. 1937, 14.
20. "Floor Mistakes," internal circulating memo, BBC WAC T5/508, 6 Feb. 1939.
21. "Critic on the Hearth," *The Listener* 29 Dec. 1938, 1428.
22. WAC T5/220, 4 March 1948.
23. "Shakespeare on Television," *BBC Quarterly* 9.3 (Autumn 1954), 146.

24. "Televised *Hamlet*," *NYT* 14 Dec. 1947, X 11.

25. For more production details about televised Shakespeare from 1937 to 1990, see Rothwell and Melzer, *Shakespeare on Screen*. Also useful is the appended checklist in Willis, *The BBC Shakespeare Plays*.

26. "Shakespeare on Television," *SQ* 12.3 (Summer 1961), 323–27.

27. "Uneasy Lies the Head," *The Times* 8 July 1960, 4g.

28. Peter Dews, "The Spread of the Eagle," *Radio Times* 25 Apr. 1963, 49.

29. "Continuity Problem of New B.B.C. Shakespeare Series," *The Times* 4 May 1963, 5d.

30. Elspeth Parker, "*The Wars of the Roses*: Space, Shape, and Flow," *SB* 13.2 (Spring 1995), 40–41.

31. David Addenbrooke, *The Royal Shakespeare Company. The Peter Hall Years* (London: William Kimber, 1974), p. 126.

32. "A Shakespearian Experience on TV," *The Times* 21 April 1965, 13d.

33. "Shakespeare through the Camera's Eye IV," *SQ* 17.4 (Autumn 1966), 385.

34. The ins and outs of this complicated battle for control of the airwaves, and of the consciousness of the masses, are spelled out in William Boddy, "The Beginnings of American Television," in Smith (ed.), *Television: An International History*, pp. 35–61.

35. Boddy, "The Beginnings," p. 48.

36. "An Interview with George Schaefer," *Hallmark Hall of Fame: A Tradition of Excellence* (New York: Museum of Broadcasting, 1984), pp. 29, 30.

37. "Shakespeare through the Camera's Eye: 1953–1954," *SQ* 6.1 (Winter 1955), 65.

38. "*Macbeth* in Color," *Time* 13 Dec. 1954, 36.

39. "The Forgotten Television *Tempest*," *SFNL* 9.1 (Dec. 1984), 3.

40. Clayton Hutton, Macbeth: *The Making of the Film* (London: Max Parrish, n.d.), preface.

41. Jack Gould, *NYT* 22 May 1949, II.9.

42. Charlton Heston, *In the Arena: An Autobiography* (New York: Simon & Schuster, 1995), p. 89.

43. "Worthington Miner's Version [of *Julius Caesar*] in Modern Dress Proves Spectacular TV," *NYT* 13 March 1949, II.11.

44. For a fascinating survey of these political questions, see Neal Gabler, *Winchell: Gossip, Power and the Culture of Celebrity* (New York: Knopf, 1994).

45. Heston, *In the Arena*, p. 87.

46. Ralph Nelson (ed.), Hamlet. *A Television Script* (New York: CBS, 1976).

47. BFI Microjacket Cuttings. Arthur Knight, "Review," *Saturday Review*, 17 Oct. 1964, n.p.

48. BFI Microjacket Cuttings. John Russell Taylor, *The Times* 7 July 1972; David Robinson, *Financial Times* 7 July 1972; and Margaret Hinxman, *Sunday Telegraph* 9 July 1972.

49. See Melvyn Bragg, *Richard Burton, A Life* (Boston: Little, Brown, and Company, 1988), for a remarkable chronicle of Burton's stormy career.

50. For the details surrounding this production, see Richard L. Sterne, *John Gielgud Directs Richard Burton in* Hamlet: *A Journal of Rehearsals* (New York: Random House, 1967).

51. Hamlet: *Film, Television*, p. 154. Kliman's essay covers the production in depth, pp. 154–66.

52. *The Times* 20 Apr. 1964, 16.

53. *Ibid.*

54. "Interview," *Radio Times* 188 (17 Sept. 1970), 6–7.

55. "The Classic Theatre *Macbeth*," *Pulse* (Oct. 1976), repr. in *Shakespeare on Television: An Anthology of Essays and Reviews*, eds. J. C. Bulman and H. R. Coursen (Hanover and London: University Press of New England, 1988), p. 247.

56. McKernan and Terris, *Walking Shadows*, p. 97.

57. Addenbrooke, *Royal Shakespeare Company*, p. 175.

58. H. R. Coursen, *Shakespearean Performance as Interpretation* (Newark: Associated University Presses, 1992), p. 195.

59. "Shakespeare in Britain," *SQ* 23.4 (Fall 1972), repr. in Bulman and Coursen, *Shakespeare on Television*, p. 246.

60. "Stage and Screen: The Trevor Nunn *Macbeth*," *SQ* 38.3 (Autumn 1987), 350–59.

61. *The Standard* 13 Jan. 1979 n.p. [Press cutting, BFI].

62. R. Alan Kimbrough, "The First Season," *SFNL* 3.2 (Apr. 1979), 5.

63. Virginia M. Carr [Vaughan], "The Second Season: *Twelfth Night*," *SFNL* 4.2 (Apr. 1980), 5.

64. Willis, *The BBC Shakespeare Plays*, p. 25.

65. "Shakespeare in Miniature: The BBC *Antony and Cleopatra*," in Bulman and Coursen (eds.), *Shakespeare on Television*, p. 144.

66. Henry Fenwick, "The Production," in *"Troilus and Cressida" The BBC TV Shakespeare* (London: BBC, 1981), pp. 18–24.

67. Lynda E. Boose, "Grossly Gaping Viewers and Jonathan Miller's *Othello*," in Boose and Burt (eds.), *Shakespeare, The Movie*, p. 186.

68. Henry Fenwick, "The Production," in *The BBC-TV Shakespeare "Othello"* (London: BBC, 1981), p. 18.

69. *Ibid.*, pp. 19–21.

70. Michael Manheim, "The Shakespeare Plays on TV," *SFNL* 8.2 (April 1984), 4.

71. Susan McCloskey, "The Shakespeare Plays on TV," *SFNL* 9.2 (April 1985), 5.

72. "Race-ing *Othello*, Re-Engendering White-Out," in Boose and Burt (eds.), *Shakespeare, The Movie*, p. 28.

73. Press kit, *Othello*.

74. H. R. Coursen, "Not Fit to Live," *SFNL* 13.1 (Dec. 1988), 4.

75. Samuel Crowl and Mary Z. Maher, "Cambridgeshire *Hamlet*: Two Views," *SFNL* 13.1 (Dec. 1988), 7.

76. Jack Oruch, "Shakespeare for the Millions: Kiss Me, Petruchio," *SFNL* 11.2 (Apr. 1987), 7.

77. See Bjo Trimble, *Star Trek Concordance*, 1990, n.p. I am obliged to Michael J. Klossner of Little Rock, Arkansas, for useful data on this topic.

78. See the special issue on *Star Trek*: *Extrapolation* 36.1 (Spring 1995), guest editor Susan Hines, published at Kent State University, especially Stephen M. Buhler, "'Who Calls Me Villain?': Blank Verse and the Black Hat," pp. 18–27, which covers Shakespearean allusions in *Star Trek VI*.

79. See *As You Like It: Audio-Visual Shakespeare*, ed. Cathy Grant (London: BUFVC, 1992) for its most recent listings.

6 SPECTACLE AND SONG IN CASTELLANI AND ZEFFIRELLI

1. "Shakespeare's Italy," in *SS* 7 (1954), 104.

2. Willis, *The BBC Shakespeare Plays*, p. 104.

3. "Cinema," *The Spectator* (24 Sept. 1954), 361.

4. William Whitebait, "Romeo and Juliet at the Odeon," *New Statesman and Nation* 48 (2 Oct. 1954), 390.

5. Robert Hatch, "Review," *TN* 8 Jan. 1955, 37.

6. "Review," *NYT* 22 Dec. 1954, 28.

7. "Shakespeare on the Screen," *FR* 7.6 (June/July 1956), 259.

8. "Castellani's *Romeo and Juliet*: Intention and Response," in Eckert (ed.), *Focus on Shakespearean Films*, p. 112.

9. Franco Zeffirelli, *Zeffirelli: The Autobiography of Franco Zeffirelli* (New York: Weidenfeld & Nicolson, 1986), p. 214.

10. *Ibid.*, pp. 164–68.

11. *Ibid.*, p. 212.

12. Bosley Crowther, "Review," *NYT* 9 March 1967, 43.

13. "Zeffirelli's Shakespeare: The Visual Realization of Tone and Theme," *LFQ* 8.4 (1980), 210–18.

14. *The Taming of the Shrew* (Manchester University Press, 1989), pp. 55–58. Holderness' essay offers many interesting insights too numerous to summarize here.

15. Zeffirelli, *Autobiography*, p. 216.

16. Martin S. Dworkin, "'Stay Illusion!' Having Words about Shakespeare on Screen," *The Journal of Aesthetic Education* 11.1 (Jan. 1977), 59.

17. *Shakespeare on Film*, p. 82.

18. "Popularizing Shakespeare: The Artistry of Franco Zeffirelli," in Boose and Burt (eds.), *Shakespeare, The Movie*, p. 85.

19. Zeffirelli, *Autobiography*, p. 225.

20. "The Art of Franco Zeffirelli and Shakespeare's *Romeo and Juliet*," in Fred Marcus (ed.), *Film and Literature: Contrasts in Media* (Scranton: Chandler, 1971), p. 211.

21. Olivia Hussey (as told to Edwin Miller), "Love is the Sweetest Thing," *Seventeen* 27 (Jan. 1968), 104.

22. Anon., "A New *Romeo and Juliet*," *Look* 31 (17 Oct. 1967), 58.

23. *Ibid.*, p. 34.

24. Zeffirelli, *Autobiography,* p. 227.

25. Polly Devlin, "I Know My Romeo and Juliet," *Vogue* 151 (1 Apr. 1968), 52.

26. Michael Pursell, "Artifice and Authenticity in Zeffirelli's *Romeo and Juliet*," *LFQ* 14.4 (1986), 173–78. If I understand him correctly, Pursell makes much the same point in a detailed examination of the film's interplay between realism and artifice.

27. Anon., "A New *Romeo*," p. 55.

28. For close scrutiny of the hand imagery in both film and play, see James H. Lake, "Hands in Zeffirelli's *Romeo*," SAA Abstracts, 1990, in *SFNL* 15.1 (Dec. 1990), 4; and Barbara L. Parker, "Review of George W. Williams' videocassette lecture, 'Feuding and Loving in Shakespeare's *Romeo and Juliet*'," in *SFNL* 16.1 (Dec. 1991), 8.

29. "2nd Vesper Services, Masses for the Virgin Mary," *Penguin Book of Latin Verses*, ed. Frederick Brittain (Baltimore: Peter Smith, 1962), p. 129. I'm obliged to Professor Jane Ambrose of the University of Vermont for tracking down this reference.

30. Page Cook, "The Sound Track," *FR* 19 (Nov. 1968), 571.

31. Zeffirelli, *Autobiography*, p. 229.

32. Cirillo, "Art of Zeffirelli," in Marcus (ed.), *Film and Literature*, p. 227.

33. John Tibbetts, "Breaking the Classical Barrier: Franco Zeffirelli Interviewed by John Tibbetts," *LFQ* 22.2 (1994), 138.

34. Michael P. Jensen, "Mel Gibson on *Hamlet*," *SFNL* 15.2 (Apr. 1991), 1 and *passim*.

35. "Mel's Melodramatic Melancholy: Zeffirelli's *Hamlet*," *Screen Shakespeare*, p. 122.

36. Tibbetts, "Zeffirelli Interviewed," 139.

37. See "Zeffirelli's *Hamlet*: Sunlight Makes Meaning," *SFNL* 16.1 (Dec. 1991), 1 and *passim*; and "Zeffirelli's *Hamlet* and the Baroque," *SFNL* 16.2 (Apr. 1992), 1 and *passim*.

38. *Screen Shakespeare*, p. 126.

39. Tibbetts, "Zeffirelli Interviewed," 139.

40. "Zeffirelli's *Hamlet*," *SFNL* 15.2 (Apr. 1991), 1 and *passim*.

41. "Zeffirelli's Shakespeare," in Davies and Wells (eds.), *Shakespeare and the Moving Image*, p. 176.

42. "Popularizing Shakespeare," in Boose and Burt (eds.), *Shakespeare, The Movie*, p. 85.

7 SHAKESPEARE MOVIES IN THE AGE OF ANGST

1. Tony Richardson, *Long Distance Runner. A Memoir*, intro. by Lindsay Anderson (London: Faber & Faber, 1993), p. 220.
2. *Ibid.*, p. 219.
3. *Ibid.*
4. See Neil Taylor, "The Films of *Hamlet*," in Davies and Wells (eds.), *Shakespeare and the Moving Image*, p. 195. Taylor protests that no evidence has been presented that the film was intended for television; on the other hand, it has never been clear that it was not! Although in his *Memoir* (see above), Richardson throws no light on this question, it would be odd if he and his producers didn't have in mind the profitable residual rights for television that have often underwritten movie production.
5. Kliman, Hamlet: *Film, Television*, p. 169.
6. "Review," *Time* 28 Feb. 1969, 74.
7. *Understanding Movies*, 2nd edn (Englewood Cliffs, NJ: Prentice, Hall, 1976), p. 103.
8. Review in *London Sunday Times* quoted in *Time*, see n. 6, above.
9. Michael Mullin, "Tony Richardson's *Hamlet*: Script and Screen," *LFQ* 4.2 (Spring 1976), 126. Mullin's article exhaustively analyzes Richardson's textual alterations.
10. "Review," *Newsweek* 12 May 1969, 119.
11. "Not Lacking Gall," *TNY* 45, 10 May 1969, 121.
12. Gerald Weales, "I Am Not Prince Hamlet," *Commonweal* 30 May 1969, 319. (Review of stage performance.)
13. Addenbrooke, *The Royal Shakespeare Company*, p. 20.
14. *Ibid.*, p. 282.
15. Crowl, *Shakespeare Observed*, p. 75.
16. Quoted in Manvell, *Shakespeare and the Film*, p. 123.
17. A Midsummer Night's Dream. *Shakespeare in Performance* (Manchester University Press, 1994), p. 93.
18. "Peter Hall's *Midsummer Night's Dream* on Film," *ETJ* 27 (1975), 529–34.
19. Brenda Davies, "Review," *MFB* 36.422 (March 1969), 51.
20. "Cinematic Oxymoron in Peter Hall's *A Midsummer Night's Dream*," *LFQ* 11.3 (1983), 174–78.
21. "*King Lear* or *Endgame*," in *Shakespeare Our Contemporary*, trans. Boleslaw Taborski (New York: Anchor Books, 1966), pp. 127–68.
22. Manvell, *Shakespeare and the Film*, p. 140. Manvell's lengthy interview with Michael Lord Birkett is well worth reading in its entirety.
23. Normand Berlin, "Peter Brook's Interpretation of *King Lear*: 'Nothing Will Come of Nothing'," *LFQ* 5.4 (1977), 303.
24. William Johnson, "*King Lear* and *Macbeth*," *FQ* 25 (1972), 43.
25. Sylvia Millar, "*King Lear*," *MFB* 38 (1971), 183.
26. Jonathan Raban, "Peter Brook's *King Lear*," *New Statesman* 30 July 1971, n.p.
27. John Simon, "Review," *The New Leader* 27 Dec. 1971.
28. Charlton Heston, *In the Arena* p. 302.
29. "Peter Brook's Night of the Living Dead," *TNY* 11 Dec. 1971, 136.
30. Alexander Walker, "Review," *Evening Standard* 22 July 1971.
31. Felix Barker, "Review," *Evening Standard* 23 July 1971.
32. "One *King Lear* for Our Time: A Bleak Film Vision by Peter Brook," *LFQ* 4.2 (1976), 159–64.
33. "Shakespeare in the Movies," *NYRB* 18 (4 May 1972), 19.
34. Manvell, *Shakespeare and the Film*, p. 137.
35. For discussion of Shakespeare movies influenced by Kott, see Samuel Crowl, "Chain Reaction: A Study of Roman Polanski's *Macbeth*," *Soundings* 59.2 (Summer 1976), 226–33.

36. Tynan, *The Sound of Two Hands Clapping*, p. 87.

37. Bernard Weinraub, "Interview with Polanski," *NYT Magazine* 12 Dec. 1971, 36.

38. I owe the phrase to Dr. Barbara Hodgdon's "Two *King Lears*: Uncovering the Filmtext," *LFQ* 11.3 (1983), 143.

39. Macbeth: *Shakespeare in Performance*, p. 121.

40. William P. Shaw, "Violence and Vision in Polanski's *Macbeth* and Brook's *King Lear*," *LFQ* 14.4 (1986), 211.

41. Per Serritslev Petersen, "The 'Bloody Business' of Roman Polanski's *Macbeth*: A Case Study of the Dynamics of Modern Shakespeare [Reception] Appropriation," in Skovmand (ed.), *Screen Shakespeare*, p. 52.

42. "Shakespeare in the Movies," *NYRB* 18 May 1972, 18.

43. Weinraub, "Interview with Polanski," p. 68.

44. The opening "long take" has been much discussed. See Norman Silverstein, "The Opening Shot of Roman Polanski's *Macbeth*," *LFQ* 2.1 (1974), 88–90, which incorrectly corrects my "Roman Polanski's *Macbeth*: Golgotha Triumphant," *LFQ* 1.1 (1973), 71–75, and Jack J. Jorgens' note that correctly corrects everybody, "The Opening Scene of Polanski's *Macbeth*," *LFQ* 3.3 (1975), 277–78.

45. Weinraub, "Interview with Polanski," pp. 36, 64.

46. Jorgens, *Shakespeare on Film*, p. 170.

47. Weinraub, "Interview with Polanski," p. 68.

48. "Some New Notes on *Macbeth*," in *Vindication of the Reading of the Folio of 1623* (Toronto: The Copp, Clark Co., Ltd., 1893), pp. vii–viii. For a detailed analysis of how Libby's theory influenced Polanski's film, see my "Roman Polanski's *Macbeth*: The 'Privileging' of Ross," *The CEA Critic* 46.1&2 (1983–84), 50–55.

49. Manvell, *Shakespeare and the Film*, p. 92.

50. "Review," *NYT* 25 Nov. 1952, 33.

51. "Julius Caesar," *Variety* 10 June 1970.

52. "Jason Robards, *et al.*," *NYT* 4 Feb. 1971, 30.

53. "*Et tu*, Charlton," *VV* 25 Feb. 1971, 57.

54. Tiruchelvam, "Encounter on the Field of Philippi," p. 19.

55. Heston, *In the Arena*, pp. 564–77. These final pages sum up Heston's political and social views, which are difficult to characterize without falling into reductive labels like "libertarian," "conservative," or "liberal."

56. *Ibid.*, p. 445.

57. *Ibid.*, p. 439.

58. Charlton Heston, "Heston Directs Heston," Publicity Booklet, London, 1972, n.p.

59. Sylvia Millar, "Review," *MFB* 39.459 (Apr. 1972), 67.

60. Frank Kermode, "Shakespeare in the Movies," p. 18.

61. "Pit.," *Variety* 8 March 1972.

8 OTHER SHAKESPEARES: TRANSLATION AND EXPROPRIATION

1. Dennis Kennedy (ed.), "Introduction," *Foreign Shakespeare: Contemporary Performance* (Cambridge University Press, 1993), p. 2.

2. See Ashish Rajadhyaksha, "India: Filming the Nation," in *Oxford History of World Cinema*, pp. 678–89.

3. James Ivory, *Savages/Shakespeare Wallah. A Film by James Ivory from a Screenplay by R. Prawer Jhabvala and James Ivory* (New York: Grove Press, 1973), p. 87.

4. Valerie Wayne, "*Shakespeare Wallah* and Colonial Specularity," in Boose and Burt (eds.), *Shakespeare the Movie*, p. 101.

5. Peter Morris, ed., *Shakespeare on Film* (Ottawa: Canadian Film Institute, 1972), p. 8.

6. *Filmindia* (Feb. 1955), 71–75.

7. Luke McKernan, Unpublished private letter, 4 Nov. 1994.

8. See also "Review," *Variety* 20.10 (1965).

9. "Review," *Guia de Filmes* 34 (July / Aug. 1971), 152.

10. Morris, *Shakespeare on Film*, pp. 10, 13. I do not, however, find *Anjuman* listed in the recent *Encyclopedia of Indian Film*, ed. Rajadhyaksha and Willeman (Oxford, 1994).

11. Caryn James, "A Mideast Variation," *NYT* 20 Apr. 1990, C.13.

12. Philip Shenon, "A Hindu Romeo, A Muslim Juliet," *NYT* 5 Sept. 1991, A.4.

13. Kliman, Hamlet: *Film, Television*, p. 139.

14. "On Film: Maximilian Schell's Most Royal *Hamlet*," *LFQ* 4.2 (1976), 139.

15. Kliman, Hamlet: *Film, Television*, p. 206. Kliman's essay is the best close analysis of the film; see pp. 202–24.

16. Bernice W. Kliman, "Swedish *Hamlet* Bursts into View," *SFNL* 11.2 (Apr. 1987), 1 and *passim*.

17. "Chabrol's *Ophelia*," *SFNL* 6.2. (March 1982), 1 and *passim*.

18. Vida Johnson, "Russia after the Thaw," in *Oxford History of World Cinema*, p. 641.

19. J.G., "Review," *MFB* 23.269 (June 1956), 74.

20. "Books in Review," *SFNL* 4.1 (Dec. 1979), 10–11.

21. I have been told by a reliable source that there is an undubbed version available on PAL video in the United Kingdom.

22. "Review," *NYT* 16 May 1960, 39.

23. "Filming *Othello*," in Davies and Wells (eds.), *Shakespeare and the Moving Image*, p. 201.

24. *Shakespeare: Time and Conscience*, trans. Joyce Vining (New York: Hill & Wang, 1966), which deals with *Hamlet*; and King Lear: *The Space of Tragedy: The Diary of a Film Director*, trans. Mary Mackintosh (Berkeley: University of California Press, 1977).

25. Quoted in Taranow, *The Bernhardt "Hamlet"*, p. 10.

26. *Ibid.*, pp. 9–10.

27. See chapter 7, n. 38.

28. Kozintsev, *Shakespeare: Time and Conscience*, pp. 107–8.

29. Bernice W. Kliman, "Kozintsev's *Hamlet*: A Flawed Masterpiece," *Hamlet Studies* 1.2 (Oct. 1979), 127.

30. Kozintsev, *The Space of Tragedy*, p. ix.

31. Alexander Anikst, "Grigori Kozintsev's *King Lear*," *Soviet Literature* 6 (1971), 177.

32. Kozintsev, *The Space of Tragedy*, pp. 130–31.

33. *Ibid.*, pp. 128–29.

34. *Ibid.*, pp. 4, 108, and *passim*.

35. *Shakespeare, Cinema and Society* (Manchester University Press, 1989), p. 145.

36. *Shakespeare on Film*, p. 249. Jorgens' essay is required reading for any student of this film.

37. *The Masks of* King Lear, p. 312.

38. Howard Kissel, "*King Lear*," *Women's Wear Daily*, 4 Aug. 1975, 24.

39. Andrea J. Nouryeh, "Shakespeare and the Japanese Stage," in *Foreign Shakespeare*, pp. 254–55.

40. *Akira Kurosawa and Intertextual Cinema* (Baltimore and London: Johns Hopkins University Press, 1994), p. 233.

41. "Kurosawa's Three Shakespeare Films," in *Journal of the Faculty of Letters, Komazawa University* 55 (March 1977), p. 23.

42. Robert Hapgood, "Kurosawa's Shakespeare Films: *Throne of Blood, The Bad Sleep Well*, and *Ran*," in Davies and Wells (eds.), *Shakespeare and the Moving Image*, p. 235.

43. Donald Richie, *The Films of Akira Kurosawa*, 3rd edn (Berkeley: University of California Press, 1996), pp. 140–46.

44. "Letter 32, To George and Thomas Keats" (21 Dec. 1817), in *The Letters of John Keats*, 2nd edn, ed. Maurice Buxton Forman (Oxford University Press, 1935), p. 72. For a cogent discussion of the Shakespearean ability to live with ambiguities, see Jonathan Bate, "Words in a Quantum World," *TLS* 25 July 1997, 14–15.
45. "Kurosawa's *Hamlet*: Samurai in Business Dress," *SFNL* 15.1 (Fall 1990), 6.
46. During the silent movie era, even in America the house was filled with would-be *benshis*, like my own solicitous father, loudly reading the titles and explaining the movie to wives and children.
47. *Films of Akira Kurosawa*, p. 93.
48. "*Macbeth* into *Throne of Blood*," *S&S* 34.4 (Autumn 1965), 190–95.
49. *Shakespeare and the Film*, p. 106.
50. "Shakespeare and Kurosawa," in James Goodwin (ed.), *Perspectives on Akira Kurosawa* (New York: G. K. Hall & Co., 1994), pp. 31–32.
51. *Ibid.*, p. 33.
52. "Kurosawa's Shakespeare Films," p. 234.
53. "Shakespeare, Kurosawa, and *Macbeth*: A Response to J. Blumenthal," *LFQ* 1.4 (1973), 352–59.
54. *Filming Shakespeare's Plays*, pp. 156–57.
55. "Kurosawa's *Throne of Blood*: Washizu and Miki Meet the Forest Spirit," *LFQ* 11.3 (1983), 167–72.
56. *The Warrior's Camera: The Cinema of Akira Kurosawa* (Princeton University Press, 1991), p. 18.
57. "*Throne of Blood*: A Morality Dance," *LFQ* 5.4 (1977), 340.
58. James Goodwin, *Akira Kurosawa and Intertextual Cinema*, p. 176.
59. See David Kehr, "Samurai *Lear*," *American Film* 10.10 (Sept. 1985), p. 24.
60. Peter Grilli, "Kurosawa Directs a Cinematic 'Lear'," *NYT* 15 Dec. 1985, II. 1 and *passim*.
61. See *Ran*, illus. Akira Kurosawa, screenplay by Akira Kurosawa, Hideo Oguni, and Ide Masato, trans. Tadashi Shishido (Boston and London: Shambhala, 1986), p. 8. Stunningly illustrated by Kurosawa himself, this screenplay is a treasure.
62. Samuel Crowl, "The Bow Is Bent and Drawn: Kurosawa's *Ran* and the Shakespearean Arrow of Desire," *LFQ* 22.2 (1994), 109–16.
63. Jan Kott, "The Edo *Lear*," *NYRB* 32.7 (24 Apr. 1986), 14.

9 SHAKESPEARE IN THE CINEMA OF TRANSGRESSION, AND BEYOND

1. "Sex and Sensation," *Oxford History of World Cinema*, p. 491.
2. See Richard Burt, "The Love that Dare Not Speak Shakespeare's Name: New Shakesqueer Cinema," in Boose and Burt (eds.), *Shakespeare, The Movie*, pp. 240–68. I am obliged to Professor Burt for sharing his unpublished research on this general topic. His recently published book, *Unspeakable ShaXXXspeares: Queer Theory and American Kiddie Culture* (New York: St. Martin's Press, 1998) explores the nuances of "Queer theory," which sees sex and gender as distinct but sometimes overlapping entities.
3. "Shakespeare Rewound," *SS* 45 (1993), 69.
4. "Pit.," "London Fest," *Variety* 1 Dec. 1976.
5. Conversation with David Meyer at London Globe Theatre, October 1996.
6. *Time-Out Film Guide,* ed. Tom Milne, 3rd edn (London: Penguin, 1993), p. 291.
7. "*Hamlet*," *MFB* 45.529 (Feb. 1978), 24.
8. Michael Griffiths, "Review Gay-Music," *Time Out* 1984, in Ritzy-Brixton Cinema Club notes.
9. "Strat.," *Variety* 11 Nov. 1984.
10. Ritzy-Brixton Cinema Club notes, 1984.

11. Quoted in David Haughton, "Program Notes for the Lindsay Kemp Company," Sadler's Wells Theatre, 15 Apr.–11 May, 1985.

12. See Derek Jarman, *Derek Jarman's* Caravaggio, *The Complete Film Script and Commentaries* (London: Thames and Hudson, 1986).

13. Derek Jarman, *Dancing Ledge*, ed. Shaun Allen (London: Quartet Books, 1984), p. 9.

14. Derek Jarman, *At Your Own Risk: A Saint's Testament*, ed. Michael Christie (London: Vintage, 1993). This autobiographical work that sometimes overlaps with *Dancing Ledge* is largely devoted to Jarman's obsession with homosexuality.

15. Jarman, *Dancing Ledge*, pp. 211–12.

16. "Screen: *The Tempest*," *NYT* 22 Sept. 1980, C20. Canby calls the film "very nearly unbearable."

17. "Stormy Weather: Derek Jarman's *Tempest*," *LFQ* 25.2 (1997), 97.

18. Derek Jarman Special Collection, British Film Institute Library, manuscript, item no. 23.

19. *Ibid.*, item no. 17.

20. Alden T. Vaughan and Virginia Mason Vaughan, *Shakespeare's Caliban: A Cultural History* (Cambridge University Press, 1991), p. 206.

21. Harris and Jackson, "Stormy Weather," p. 93.

22. Jarman, *Dancing Ledge*, p. 194.

23. Harris and Jackson, "Stormy Weather," p. 95.

24. "Stormy Weather: A New *Tempest* on Film," *SFNL* 5.1 (Dec. 1980), 1 and *passim*.

25. See Peter S. Donaldson, "Shakespeare in the Age of Post-Mechanical Production: Sexual and Electronic Magic in *Prospero's Books*," in Boose and Burt (eds.), *Shakespeare, The Movie*, pp. 169–85.

26. Peter Greenaway, in "Movie Memories," *S&S* 6.5. n.s. suppl. (May 1996), 15, 16.

27. Alain Robbe-Grillet and Alain Resnais, *Last Year at Marienbad*, trans. Richard Howard (New York: Grove Press, 1962), p. 12.

28. Peter Greenaway, *Prospero's Books: A Film of Shakespeare's* The Tempest (New York: Four Walls Eight Windows, 1991), p. 50. It is hopeless to study this complicated film without the help of Greenaway's lavishly illustrated screenplay.

29. Claus Schatz-Jacobsen, "'Knowing I Lov'd My Books': Shakespeare, Greenaway, and the Prosperous Dialectics of Word and Image," in Skovmand (ed.), *Screen Shakespeare*, p. 133.

30. "Reams on the Renaissance," *NYT* 28 Sept. 1991, 9ff.

31. Greenaway, *Prospero's Books*, p. 28.

32. Donaldson, "Shakespeare in the Age of Post-Mechanical Reproduction," in Boose and Burt (eds.), *Shakespeare, The Movie*, p. 169.

33. *Ibid.*, p. 179.

34. Mariacristina Cavecchi, "Peter Greenaway's *Prospero's Books*: A Tempest Between Word and Image," *LFQ* 25.2 (1997), 87.

35. Jonathan Romney, "*Prospero's Books*," *S&S* 1.5 n.s. (Sept. 1991), 45.

36. David Sterritt, "A *King Lear* Launched over Lunch," *CSM*, 22 Jan. 1988.

37. *Shakespearean Films/Shakespearean Directors*, pp. 189–225.

38. "Godard's *Lear* . . . Why Is It So Bad?" *SB* 12.3 (Summer 1994), 41. The author concludes that the film's so-called "badness" stems only from Godard's "radical faithfulness to his own stance."

39. Colin McCabe, *et al.*, *Godard: Images, Sounds, Politics* (Bloomington: Indiana University Press, 1980), p. 211.

40. "Echoes of Godard," *TLS* 29 Jan. 1988, 112.

41. *Independent* 28 Jan. 1988, 14.

42. *VV* 26 Jan. 1988, 53.

43. Albert Fried, *The Rise and Fall of the Jewish Gangster in America* (New York: Holt, Rinehart and Winston, 1980), p. 80.

44. "Brilliant" but incoherent writing as an index to emotional disturbance is something I explored in "Psychiatry and the Freshman Theme," *College English* 20.7 (Apr. 1959), 338–42.

45. "'Haply for I Am Black': Liz White's *Othello*," *Shakespearean Films/Shakespearean Directors*, p. 130.

46. I'm obliged to Professor Peggy Russo for my information. The film is available on video-tape from Rockbottom Productions, 18653 Ventura Blvd, 131B, Tarzana, CA 91356.

47. "Lor.," *Variety* 31 May 1989.

48. "Review," *Variety* 5 Oct. 1992.

49. For commentary, see Coursen, *Shakespeare in Production*, pp. 98–102.

50. "Review," *SB* 11.3 (Summer 1993), 41.

51. *Theater and Film*, pp. 36–37.

52. See Jorgens' succinct discussion of taxonomy in "Modes and Styles," *Shakespeare on Film*, pp. 7–16.

53. For elaboration on and embellishment of Jorgens' useful taxonomy, see also Peter Holland, "Two-Dimensional Shakespeare: *King Lear* on Film," in Davies and Wells (eds.), *Shakespeare and the Moving Image*, pp. 50–68.

54. Quoted in Tony Howard, "When Peter Met Orson," in Boose and Burt (eds.), *Shakespeare, The Movie*, p. 133.

55. [P.H.] "*Forbidden Planet*," *MFB* 23.269 (June 1956), 71.

56. See S. Schoenbaum, "Looking for Shakespeare," in *Shakespeare's Craft*, ed. Philip Highfill (Carbondale: Southern Illinois University Press, 1982), pp. 156–72.

57. Geoffrey Taylor (ed.), *Paul Mazursky's* Tempest (New York Zoetrope, 1982). This is a wonderful illustrated book about the making of Mazursky's *Tempest*, which is the next best thing to having been there in person.

58. "Lubitsch's *To Be or Not to Be* or Shakespeare Mangled," *SFNL* 1.1 (Dec. 1976), 2 and *passim*.

59. Robert F. Willson, Jr., "Shakespeare in *The Goodbye Girl*," *SFNL* 2.2 (Apr. 1978) 1 and *passim*.

60. David Jays, "Review," *S&S* 5.12 n.s. (Dec. 1995), 47.

61. Susan Wiseman, "The Family Tree Motel: Subliming Shakespeare in *My Own Private Idaho*," in Boose and Burt (eds.), *Shakespeare, The Movie*, pp. 225–39.

62. Geoffrey Macnab, "Looking for Richard," *S&S* 7.2 (Feb. 1997), 49.

63. "Royal Monster, Are You Out There?" *NYT* 11 Oct. 1996, C3.

64. Ball, *Silent Film*, p. 269.

65. Craig Toth, "Letter," personal, n.d.

66. Bernice W. Kliman, "Katharine Hepburn as Hamlet and Juliet," *SFNL* 13.2 (Apr. 1989), 6.

67. An excellent filmography of these elusive moments on screen is the British Film Institute Shakespeare catalog, *Walking Shadows*. A forthcoming study by Robert F. Willson, Jr. will cover much of this ground.

68. See Doug Stenberg, "The Circle of Life and the Chain of Being: Shakespearean Motifs in *The Lion King*," *SB* 14.2 (Spring 1996), 36.

69. "Poetry in Motion. Animating Shakespeare," in Boose and Burt (eds.), *Shakespeare, The Movie*, p. 118.

70. See *As You Like It: Audio Visual Shakespeare*, ed. Cathy Grant (London: British Universities Film & Video Council, 1992) for a good listing of educational films. For older pre-video films, see Andrew M. McLean, *Shakespeare: Annotated Bibliographies and Media Guide for Teachers* (Urbana: NCTE, 1980).

71. Again, I'm obliged to Richard Burt for sharing his unpublished research on transgressive Shakespeare.

72. "Review," *S&S* 6.12 n.s. (Dec. 1996), 54.

10 THE RENAISSANCE OF SHAKESPEARE IN MOVING IMAGES

1. Ian McKellen, *William Shakespeare's* Richard III: *A Screenplay* (New York: The Overlook Press, 1996), pp. 24–27. McKellen's fascinating commentary on the screenplay reveals his tireless concern for making the play relevant to modern audiences.

2. *Ibid.*, p. 44.

3. "'Top of the World, Ma': *Richard III* and Cinematic Convention," Boose and Burt (eds.), *Shakespeare, The Movie,* pp. 67–79. Loehlin's perceptive essay also cites the "Heritage" look and stresses the gangster film codes, which are sometimes hard to sort out from Shakespeare's own patterns of violence.

4. "Changing Colors like the Chameleon: Ian McKellen's *Richard III* from Stage to Film," *Post Script* 17.1 (Fall 1997), 55.

5. McKellen, *Richard III,* p. 244.

6. *Ibid.*, pp. 72, 80.

7. *Ibid.*, p. 258.

8. Gus Parr, "S for Smoking," *S&S* 7.12 n.s. (Dec. 1997), 30–33. A delightful exploration of this neglected topic.

9. Andrew Sarris, "At the Movies," *NYO* 8 Jan. 1996, 17; Rex Reed, "On the Town," *NYO* 8 Jan. 1996, 22.

10. Terence Rafferty, "Time Out of Joint," *TNY* 22 Jan. 1996, 86.

11. "Bard Therapy," *Independent* 2. 25 Apr. 1996, 11.

12. James Cameron-Wilson, "Review," *What's on in London?* 24 Apr. 1996.

13. David Gritten, "Bard with a Vengeance," *Daily Telegraph* 19 Apr. 1996, 21 and *passim*.

14. Geoffrey Macnab, "Review," *S&S* 6.2 (Feb. 1996), 51–52.

15. Parker played Laertes and Maloney, Rosencrantz in the Zeffirelli *Hamlet.*

16. Contrary to some published reports, Fishburne was not the first black actor to play Othello on screen. Although more art house than mall house, Liz White's *Othello* (1980) and Ted Lange's *Othello* (1989) both starred black actors, Yaphet Kotto and Ted Lange. A video/TV version of Janet Suzman's South African *Othello* (1987–89) had a talented black actor, John Kani, as the Moor.

17. "Introduction," *"Much Ado about Nothing" by William Shakespeare* (New York: W. W. Norton & Co., 1993), p. ix.

18. Trevor Nunn (ed.), *"Twelfth Night" by William Shakespeare. A Screenplay* (London: Methuen Drama), 1996, Introduction, n.p.

19. Peter Marks, "So Young, So Fragile . . ." *NYT* 20 Oct. 1996, 13.

20. "Review," *SB* 15.1 (Winter 1997), 37.

21. Geoffrey Macnab, *"Twelfth Night,"* *S&S* 6.11 n.s. (Nov. 1996), 60.

22. "General Introduction," *TRS*, p. 22.

23. See Craig Pearce and Baz Luhrmann, *William Shakespeare's* Romeo & Juliet: *The Contemporary Film, The Classic Play* (New York: Bantam Doubleday Books, 1996). In some publicity materials, the title is given as *Romeo + Juliet.*

24. *Ibid.*, p. i.

25. "Soft! What Light? It's Flash, Romeo," *NYT* 1 Nov. 1996, C.1.

26. "Parting, Like, Sucks! So Does *Romeo,*" *NYO* 11 Nov. 1996, 41.

27. W. B. Worthen, "Drama, Performativity, and Performance," *PMLA* 113.5 (Oct. 1998), 1103.

28. Alan Riding, "The Royal Shakespeare: Renewing Itself under Fire," *NYT* 17 May 1998, II.1.

29. "Review," *S&S* 7.1 n.s. (Jan. 1997), 41.

30. Kenneth Branagh, *Beginning* (New York: W. W. Norton, 1990), pp. 1–53. To write an autobiography at age 28 is also something of an achievement.

31. For commentary, see Peter Holland, *English Shakespeares: Shakespeare on the English Stage in the 1990s* (Cambridge University Press, 1997), pp. 137, 146, 150.

32. Hal Hinson, "The Heart of 'Henry V'," *WP* 15 Dec. 1989, D.1.

33. Richard Corliss, "King Ken Comes to Conquer," *Time* 13 Nov. 1989, 119.

34. Joseph Gelmis, "Shakespeare's *Henry V* in Two Incarnations," *Newsday* 7 Dec. 1990, II.153; see also Jonathan Yardley, "The Metamorphosis of 'Henry'," *WP* 26 Feb. 1990, C.2, for more encomiums.

35. See Michael Skovmand, "Introduction," in *Screen Shakespeare*, pp. 10–11, for discussion of the hostile reaction by several Marxist critics to Branagh's work.

36. Crowl, *Shakespeare Observed*, p. 168.

37. Jack Kroll, "A *Henry V* for Our Time," *Newsweek* 20 Nov. 1989, 78. One of many newspaper and magazine interviews in 1989.

38. Kenneth Branagh, Henry V *by William Shakespeare: A Screen Adaptation by Kenneth Branagh* (London: Chatto & Windus, 1989), p. 9.

39. "Henry," *S&S* 58.4 (Autumn 1989), 259.

40. See Peter S. Donaldson, "Taking on Shakespeare: Kenneth Branagh's *Henry V*," *SQ* 42.1 (Spring 1991), 61.

41. "War Is Mud: Branagh's Dirty Harry V and the Types of Political Ambiguity," in Boose and Burt (eds.), *Shakespeare, The Movie*, p. 47.

42. "Resistance and Recuperation: Branagh's *Henry V*," *SFNL* 15.2 (Apr. 1991), 5.

43. William P. Shaw, "Textual Ambiguities and Cinematic Certainties in *Henry V*," *LFQ* 22.2 (1994), 123. Shaw cites Norman Rabkin's point that *Henry V* is a play about ambiguities, and historical uncertainties. To add to the ambiguity, Shaw disagrees with Donaldson's belief that Exeter, as portrayed in the film, is a surrogate father figure like Falstaff; instead Exeter may be a conspirator against the king! Exeter, it seems to me, behaves like a loyal supporter.

44. Branagh, *Beginning*, p. 234.

45. See Coursen, *Shakespeare in Production*, pp. 102–17, for a detailed survey of the movie's reception.

46. "A House Party of Beatrice, Benedick and Friends," *NYT* 7 May 1993, C.16.

47. "Films," *TN* 256.21 (31 May 1993), 750.

48. "*Much Ado about Nothing*," *Variety* 3 May 1993.

49. Anthony Lane, "Too Much Ado," *TNY* 69.12 (10 May 1993), 99.

50. "*Much Ado about Nothing*," *S&S* 3.9 n.s. (Sept. 1993), 50–51.

51. Kenneth Branagh, Much Ado about Nothing *by William Shakespeare. Screenplay, Introduction and Notes on the Making of the Movie by Kenneth Branagh*. Photographs by Clive Foot (New York: W. W. Norton, 1993), p. 5.

52. *A Natural Perspective: The Development of Shakespearean Comedy and Romance* (New York: Harcourt, Brace & World, 1965), p. 81.

53. Branagh, *Much Ado*, p. xiii.

54. "Review," *SB* 11.3 (Summer 1993), 40.

55. Samuel Crowl, "*Hamlet*," *SB* 15.1 (Winter 1997), 35.

56. Gail Paster, quoted in John F. Andrews, "Kenneth Branagh's *Hamlet* Launched . . . ," *SN* 46.3 no. 230 (Fall 1996), 53.

57. David Parkinson, "Performance of Epic Proportions," *Oxford Times* 2 May 1997, n.p.

58. "Holiday Celluloid Wrap-Up," *TN* 13/20 Jan. 1997, 36.

59. "Ken, Al and Will, too," *TLS* 21 Feb. 1997, 19.

60. Quoted in Nina da Vinci Nichols, "Branagh's *Hamlet* Redux," *SB* 15.3 (Summer 1997), 39. Nichols' excellent reception study surveys a wide range of critical opinion.

61. Kenneth Branagh, Hamlet *by William Shakespeare* (New York: W. W. Norton & Company, 1996), p. xv.

62. "The Regeneration of Hamlet: A Reply to E. M. W. Tillyard . . . ," *SQ* 3.3 (July 1952), 206.

63. Leslie Felperin, *"Hamlet," S&S* 7.2 n.s. (Feb. 1997), 46. Felperin says the Branagh *Hamlet* "like so many of these recent adaptations . . . never convinces us why we still need to keep on adapting Shakespeare for the movies."

11 SHAKESPEARE IN LOVE, IN LOVE WITH SHAKESPEARE

1. *"Shakespeare in Love*: Romancing the Author, Mastering the Body," *Spectacular Shakespeare: Critical Theory and Popular Cinema* (eds.), Courtney Lehmann and Lisa S. Starks (Madison NJ and London: Associated University Presses, 2002), pp. 125–45.

2. Ann Barton's 1953 undergraduate (*sic*) essay, "Love's Labour's Lost," reprinted in *Essays, Mainly Shakespearean* (Cambridge University Press, 1994), pp. 31–50, explains the significance of the omitted lines.

3. For full treatment of these forays into word play, see William C. Carroll's admirable *The Great Feast of Language in* Love's Labour's Lost (Princeton University Press, 1976).

4. *Love's Labour's Lost* (Manchester University Press, 1993), pp. 77–91.

5. *Love's Labour's Lost* and the Marx Brothers," *Upstart Crow* 5 (1984), 125–34.

6. David Jays, "Love's Labours' Lost," *S&S* 10.4 n.s. (Apr. 2000), 54.

7. Rex Reed, "The Bard's Cabaret Act," *NYO* 12 June 2000, 20.

8. Michael Hoffman (adapt.), *William Shakespeare's A Midsummer Night's Dream* (New York: Harper Collins, 1999), p.1.

9. For discussion of the bicycle in the Hoffman film, see Juana Green, "Bicycles, Bustles and Brides in Michael Hoffman's *William Shakespeare's A Midsummer Night's Dream*," Unpub. Paper, "Shakespeare and the Movies" Seminar. Shakespeare Association of America, Victoria BC, Apr. 2003.

10. A wife for Bottom had also been planned but not implemented by the producers of the Warner Brothers 1935 *Midsummer Night's Dream*. See Russell Jackson, "A Shooting Script for the Reinhardt/Dieterle *Dream*," *SB* 16.4 (Fall 1998), 39–41.

11. See Nicholas Jones, "Bottom's Wife: Gender and Voice in Hoffman's [i] *Dream*," Unpub. Paper, "Shakespeare and the Movies" Seminar, Shakespeare Association of America, Victoria, BC, Apr. 2003.

12. "The Children's Midsummer Night's Dream," *S&S* 11.8 n.s. (Aug. 2001), 40.

13. "Franco Zeffirelli and Shakespeare," *The Cambridge Companion to Shakespeare on Film* (ed.), Russell Jackson (Cambridge University Press, 2000), p. 214.

14. The convenient term "paratext" was apparently coined by Linda Charnes. See Eric S. Mallin,"'You Kilt My Foddah': or Arnold, Prince of Denmark," *SQ* 50.2. (Summer 1999), 128. It designates a film or stage version located "beyond or contrary to . . . the original text, while remaining broadly referential to it." A fine example would be the long running Off-Broadway, "The Donkey Show," which conceals behind its erotic, gay, hip-hop, façade debts to *A Midsummer Night's Dream*. Unfortunately, however, "paratext" still remains an umbrella term for a taxonomy that resembles Polonius's attempts at genre classification, or even the intricacy of sub-atomic particles (q.v. 208–18 above).

15. *Michael Almereyda* (adapt.), *William Shakespeare's "Hamlet"* (New York and London: Faber and Faber, 2000), p. xi.

16. *Shakespeare in Space: Recent Shakespeare Productions on Screen* (New York: Peter Lang, 2002), p. 156.

17. See Peter Donaldson, "Michael Almereyda's *Hamlet*: Video Art, Authenticity and 'Wisdom'," Unpub. Paper, "Shakespeare and the Movies" Seminar, Shakespeare Association of America, Victoria, BC, Apr. 2003.

18. Information from >http://elvis.rowan.edu/~cassidy/pixel/<

19. Almereyda, *Hamlet*, pp. 68–69.

20. Akira Kurosawa's modern dress Japanese language *The Bad Sleep Well* (1960) shares some similarities. See discussion above, pp. 182–84. See also Stephen Buhler's on *The Bad Sleep Well* in *Shakespeare in the Cinema: Ocular Proof* (Albany: State University Press of New York), pp. 170–72.

21. "*Hamlet*," *SB* 18.4 (Fall 2000), 39.

22. "'To Hear and See the Matter': Communicating Technology in Michael Almereyda's *Hamlet* (2000)," *Cinema Journal*, 42.3 (Spring 2003), 66.

23. M. S. Mason, "A *Hamlet* Fit for the Small Screen," *CSM*, Friday, Dec. 8, 2000, 20.

24. Richard Burt (ed.), *Shakespeare After Mass Media* (London: Palgrave, 2002), p. 8.

25. "O," *S&S* 12, 2 n.s. (Feb. 2002), 56–57.

26. "The PBS *Othello*: A Review Essay," *SB* 20.1 (Winter 2002), 38–39.

27. See Richard W. Schoch, "'Chopkins, Late Shakespeare': The Bard and His Burlesques. 1810–66," *ELH* 67 (2000), 973–91.

28. See *Shakespeare Remains: From Modernism to Postmodernism* (Ithaca: Cornell University Press, 2003), Lehmann, among others, has found a clever new vocabulary for talking about the problem of the disappearing text in Shakespeare movies.

29. See H. R. Coursen, "Winter of the Scottish Play," *SB* 10.2 (Spring 1992), 10–14.

30. *Ibid.*, quoted in, 14.

31. For information about Bogdanov's British television *Shakespeare on the Estate*, which in turn inspired Penny Woolcock's televised *Macbeth on the Estate* (1997), both productions having been designed to bridge the gap between *hoi polloi* and Shakespeare but neither of which has been easily available in North America, I am obliged to an unpublished paper by Peter Balderstone, "Who is Shakespeare? Who is Shakespeare? Nobody Knows. Nobody Cares. This is Ladywood." "Shakespeare and the Movies" Seminar. Shakespeare Association of America. Victoria, BC, Apr. 2003.

32. "A Spare *Lear* Influenced by Beckett and Brecht," *NYT* 9 Oct. 1998, B27.

33. "Bartlett's Evolving Shakespeare, " *Shakespeare After Mass Media* (ed.), Richard Burt (New York: Palgrave, 2002), pp. 287–94.

34. "Dismember Me: Shakespeare, Paranoia, and the Logic of Mass Culture," SQ 48.1 (Spring 1997), 1–16.

35. See Karen Durbin, "Making ' Lear' a 'Survivor' in the Desert," Arts and Leisure, *NYT*, Sunday 22 Apr. 2001, 1. 19.

36. See Gary Crowdus, "Cult Films, Commentary Tracks and Censorious Critics: An Interview with John Bloom," *Cineaste* 28.3 (Summer 2003), 32–34.

37. http://www.angelfire.com/movies/oc/titus.html

38. The debate about authorship never ceases. Most recently Brian Vickers, Jonathan Bate and others have revived the old hypothesis that George Peele, not William Shakespeare, wrote the play's labyrinthine first act. See Jonathan Bate, "In the Script Factory," Review of Brian Vickers, *Shakespeare Co-Author* in *TLS*, No. 5220 (18 Apr. 2003), 3–4.

39. See review by Patricia Lennox, "*Titus Andronicus*," *SB* 13.2 (Spring 1995), 35.

40. Interview with Taymor at Columbia University in the supplementary materials of the DVD version of *Titus* (2000), published by Twentieth-Century Fox Home Entertainment; and from the VHS "Behind the Scenes" with Julie Taymor, directed by Ellen Hovde and Muffie Meyer (First Run Features, 2000), distributed by Ambrose Video. See also Miranda Johnson-Haddad, "A Time for *Titus*: An Interview with Julie Taymor," *SB* 18.4 (Fall 2000), 34–36. Indispensable is Julie Taymor's *Titus: The Illustrated Screenplay* (New York: Newmarket Press, 2000).

41. "Bloody Arcades," *S&S* 10.7 n.s. (July 2000), 24.

42. I owe this concept to Mary Lindroth, "Some Device of Further Misery . . ," *LFQ* 29.2 (2001), 107–15.

43. Ben Brewster and Lea Jacobs, *Theatre to Cinema: Stage Pictorialism and the Early Feature Film* (New York: Oxford University Press, 1997), p. 35.

44. "Cinema of Cruelty: Powers of Horror in Julie Taymor's *Titus*," *The Reel Shakespeare: Alternative Cinema and Theory* (eds.), Lisa S. Starks and Courtney Lehmann (Madison and London: Fairleigh Dickinson University Press, 2002), pp. 121–42.

45. See also Richard Burt, "Shakespeare and the Holocaust: Julie Taymor's *Titus* Is Beautiful . . . ," *Shakespeare After Mass Media* (ed.), Burt, pp. 295–329; Samuel Crowl's perceptive review, "*Titus*," in *SB* 18.1 (Winter 2000), 46–47; and an unpublished essay by Elsie Walker, "'Now is a time to storm': Julie Taymor's *Titus* (2000)".

46. Notes from > http://www.maorimerchant of venice.com/the_production.html<, and from attendance at 2003 Victoria screening.

47. Yasunari Takahashi, *The Braggart Samurai*, an English version of *Hora-zamurai*, a Kyogen adaptation of Shakespeare's *Merry Wives of Windsor*. In *Shakespeare and the Japanese Stage* (eds.), Takashi Sasayama, J. R. Mulryne, and Margaret Shewring (Cambridge University Press, 1998), p. 229. I am indebted to Professor Tetsuo Kishi for his considerable pains in providing data about these Japanese performances.

48. Sasayama, pp. 257–331.

49. "A nose, a stride, a face, a guide," *TLS* no. 5232, July 11, 2003, 18–19.

50. http://pro.imdb.com/title/tt3011126/

51. Chris Hastings and Catherine Milner, "Hollywood Rivals Battle to Bring *The Merchant of Venice* to Screen," *The Telegraph*, 17 Aug. 2003. http://www.telegraph.co.uk/news/main. jhtml?xml=/news/2003/08/17/wshakes17.xml

– BIBLIOGRAPHY –

BOOKS

Abel, Richard, *The Cine Goes to Town: French Cinema 1896–1914*, University of California Press, 1994.
  French Cinema: The First Wave 1915–1929, Princeton University Press, 1984.
Addenbrooke, David, *The Royal Shakespeare Company. The Peter Hall Years*, London: William Kimber, 1974.
Alexander, Peter, *Hamlet Father and Son*, Oxford University Press, 1955.
Allen Robert C., *Vaudeville and Film 1895–1915: A Study in Media Interaction*, New York: Arno Press, 1980.
Almereyda, Michael (adapt.), *William Shakespeare's "Hamlet,"* New York and London: Faber and Faber, 2000.
Andrew, Dudley, *Film in the Aura of Art*, Princeton University Press, 1984.
Andrews, Cyrus, *Radio and TV Who's Who*, 3rd edn, London: George Young, 1954.
Atwell, David, *Cathedrals of the Movies: A History of British Cinema and Their Audiences*, London: The Architectural Press, 1980.
Ball, Robert Hamilton, *Shakespeare on Silent Film: A Strange Eventful History*, London: George Allen & Unwin, Ltd, 1968.
Barthes, Roland, *S/Z. An Essay*, trans. Richard Miller, New York: Hill & Wang, 1972.
Barton, Anne, "Love's Labour's Lost," in *Essays, Mainly Shakespearean*, Cambridge University Press, 1994.
Bernhardt, Sarah, *Memoirs of My Life*, rpt. 1908; New York: Benjamin Blom, 1968.
Boose, Lynda E. and Richard Burt (eds.), *Shakespeare, The Movie: Popularizing the Plays on Film, TV, and Video*, New York and London: Routledge, 1997.
Brady, Frank, *Citizen Welles: A Biography of Orson Welles*, New York: Charles Scribner's Sons, 1989.
Bragg, Melvyn, *Richard Burton, A Life*, Boston: Little, Brown and Company, 1988.
Branagh, Kenneth, *Beginning*, New York: W.W. Norton, 1989.
  Hamlet by William Shakespeare. Screenplay and Introduction by Kenneth Branagh. Film Diary by Russell Jackson, New York: W. W. Norton, 1996.
  Henry V by William Shakespeare. A Screen Adaptation by Kenneth Branagh, London: Chatto & Windus, 1989.
  Much Ado about Nothing by William Shakespeare. Screenplay, Introduction, and Notes on the Making of the Movie by Kenneth Branagh. Photographs by Clive Coote, New York: W. W. Norton, 1993.
Brewster, Ben and Lea Jacobs, *Theatre to Cinema: Stage Pictorialism and the Early Feature Film*, New York: Oxford University Press, 1997.

Brownlow, Kevin, *Hollywood the Pioneers*, New York: Knopf, 1979.

Buchman, Lorne, *Still in Movement: Shakespeare on Screen*, Oxford University Press, 1991.

Buhler, Stephen, *Shakespeare in the Cinema: Ocular Proof*, Albany: State University Press of New York, 2002.

Bullough, Geoffrey (ed.), *Narrative and Dramatic Sources of Shakespeare*, III, New York: Columbia University Press, 1975.

Bulman, J. C., and H. R. Coursen (eds.), *Shakespeare on Television*: *An Anthology of Essays and Reviews*, Hanover and London: University Press of New England, 1988.

Burnett, Mark Thornton and Ramona Wray (eds.), *Shakespeare, Film, Fin de Siècle*, Foreword by Peter Holland, New York: St. Martin's Press, 2000.

Burt, Richard, *Unspeakable ShaXXXspeares: Queer Theory and American Kiddie Culture*. New York: St. Martin's Press, 1998.

Callow, Simon, *Orson Welles: The Road to Xanadu*, London: Jonathan Cape, 1995.

Cameron, Ian (ed.), *The Book of Film Noir*, New York: Continuum, 1992.

Carroll, William C., *The Great Feast of Language in* Love's Labour's Lost, Princeton University Press, 1976.

Cartmell, Deborah, *Interpreting Shakespeare on Screen*, New York: St. Martin's Press, 2000.

Collick, John, *Shakespeare, Cinema and Society*, Manchester University Press, 1989.

Cook, David A., *A History of Narrative Film*, 3rd ed., New York: Norton, 1996.

Coursen, H.R., *Shakespeare in Production. Whose History?* Athens: Ohio University Press, 1996.

  Shakespearean Performance as Interpretation, Newark: Associated University Presses, 1992.

  Shakespeare in Space: Recent Shakespeare Productions on Screen, New York: Peter Lang, 2002.

Cross, Brenda (ed.), *The Film* Hamlet. *A Record of Its Production*, New York: Saturn Press, 1948.

Crowl, Samuel, *Shakespeare Observed: Studies in Performance on Stage and Screen*, Athens: Ohio University Press, 1992.

  At the Shakespeare Cineplex: The Kenneth Branagh Era, Athens: Ohio University Press, 2003.

Cubitt, Sean, *Videography: Video Media as Art and Culture*, New York: St. Martin's Press, 1993.

Davies, Anthony and Stanley Wells (eds.), *Shakespeare and the Moving Image: The Plays on Film and Television*, Cambridge University Press, 1994.

Davies, Anthony, *Filming Shakespeare's Plays: The Adaptations of Laurence Olivier, Orson Welles, Peter Brook and Akira Kurosawa*, Cambridge University Press, 1988.

De Mille, Agnes, *Dance to the Piper*, Boston: Little, Brown, 1952.

Donaldson, Peter S., *Shakespearean Films/Shakespearean Directors*, Boston: Unwin Hyman, 1990.

Drexler, Peter and Lawrence Guntner (eds.), *Negotiations with Hal: Multi-Media Perceptions of [Shakespeare's] Henry the Fifth*, Technische Universität Braunschweig: Braunschweiger Anglistische Arbeiten, 1995.

Eckert, Charles W. (ed.), *Focus on Shakespearean Films*, Englewood Cliffs: Prentice Hall, 1972.

Evans, G. Blakemore *et al.* (eds.), *The Riverside Shakespeare*, Boston: Houghton Mifflin, 1974.

Everson, William K., *American Silent Film,* Oxford University Press, 1978.

Forman, Maurice Buxton (ed.), *The Letters of John Keats*, 2nd ed. Oxford University Press, 1935.

France, Richard (ed.), *Orson Welles on Shakespeare: The W.P.A. and Mercury Theatre Playscripts*, New York: The Greenwood Press, 1990.

Fried, Albert, *The Rise and Fall of the Jewish Gangster in America,* New York: Holt, Rinehart and Winston, 1980.

Frye, Northrop, *A Natural Perspective: The Development of Shakespearean Comedy and Romance*, New York: Harcourt, Brace & World, 1965.

Gabler, Neal, *Winchell: Gossip, Power and the Culture of Celebrity,* New York: Knopf, 1994.

Geduld, Harry M., *Filmguide to* Henry V, Bloomington: Indiana University Press, 1973.

Giannetti, Louis D., *Understanding Movies*, 2nd ed., Englewood Cliffs [NJ]: Prentice-Hall, 1972.

Gielgud, Sir John (introd.), *Julius Caesar and the Life of William Shakespeare,* London: The Gawthorn Press, 1953.

Gilbert, Miriam, *"Love's Labour's Lost"*: *Shakespeare in Performance*, Manchester University Press, 1993.

Goodwin, James, *Akira Kurosawa and Intertextual Cinema,* Baltimore and London: Johns Hopkins University Press, 1994.

(ed.), *Perspectives on Akira Kurosawa*, New York: G.K. Hall & Co., 1994.

Gottesman, Ronald (ed.), *Focus on Orson Welles*, Englewood Cliffs: Prentice Hall, 1976.

Grant, Cathy (ed.), *As You Like It: Audio Visual Shakespeare*, London: British Universities Film & Video Council, 1992.

Greenaway, Peter, *The Belly of an Architect* [Film Script, 1987], London: Faber and Faber, 1988.

Prospero's Books: A Film of Shakespeare's The Tempest, New York: Four Walls Eight Windows, 1991.

Halio, Jay L., *"A Midsummer Night's Dream"*: *Shakespeare in Performance*, Manchester University Press, 1994.

Hall, Ben M., *The Best Remaining Seats: The Story of the Golden Age of the Movie Palace,* New York: Clarkson N. Potter, 1961.

Hatchuel, Sarah, *A Companion to the Shakespearean Films of Kenneth Branagh,* Winnipeg/Niagara Falls: Blizzard Publishing Inc., 2000.

Heston, Charlton, *In the Arena*: *An Autobiography,* New York: Simon & Schuster, 1995.

Hoffman, Michael (adapt.), *William Shakespeare's "A Midsummer Night's Dream,"* New York: HarperCollins, 1999.

Holderness, Graham, *"The Taming of the Shrew"*: *Shakespeare in Performance*, Manchester University Press, 1989.

Holland, Peter, *English Shakespeares, Shakespeare on the English Stage in the 1990's*, Cambridge University Press, 1997.

Howlett, Kathy, *Framing Shakespeare on Film*, Athens: Ohio University Press, 2000.

Ivory, James, *Savages/Shakespeare Wallah. A Film by James Ivory from a Screenplay by R. Prawer Jhabvala and James Ivory*, New York: Grove Press, 1973.

James, Nick (ed.), *360 Film Classics* [supplement to *S&S*]. London: BFI, 1998.

Jarman, Derek, *At Your Own Risk: A Saint's Testament*, Michael Christie (ed.), London: Vintage, 1993.

Dancing Ledge, Shaun Allen (ed.), London: Quartet Books, 1984.

Derek Jarman's Caravaggio, *The Complete Film Script and Commentaries*, London: Thames & Hudson, 1986.

Jorgens, Jack J., *Shakespeare on Film*, Bloomington: Indiana University Press, 1977.

Kantorowicz, Ernest, *The King's Two Bodies: A Study in Medieval Political Theology*, Princeton University Press, 1957.

Katz, Ephraim (ed.), *The Film Encyclopedia*, New York: Putnam, 1979.

Kennedy, Dennis (ed.), *Foreign Shakespeare, Contemporary Performance*, Cambridge University Press, 1993.

Kliman, Bernice W., *"Hamlet": Film, Television, and Audio Performance*, London and Toronto: Assoc. University Presses, 1988.

"Macbeth": Shakespeare in Performance, Manchester University Press, 1992.

Kotsilibas-Davis, James, *The Barrymores, the Royal Family in Hollywood*, New York: Crown Publishers, 1981.

Kott, Jan, *Shakespeare Our Contemporary*, New York: Anchor Books, 1966.

Kozintsev, Grigori, King Lear: *The Space of Tragedy: The Diary of a Film Director*, trans. Mary Mackintosh, Berkeley: University of California Press, 1977.

Shakespeare: Time and Conscience, trans. Joyce Vining, New York: Hill & Wang, 1966.

Kracauer, Siegfried, *From Caligari to Hitler: A Psychological History of the German Film*, Princeton University Press, 1947.

Kurosawa, Akira, *Ran*, ill. by Akira Kurosawa, screenplay by Akira Kurosawa, Hideo Oguni, Ide Masato, trans. Tadashi Shishido, Boston and London: Shambhala, 1986.

Lanier, Douglas, *Shakespeare and Modern Popular Culture*, New York: Oxford University Press, 2002.

Leaming, Barbara, *Orson Welles*, New York: Viking, 1985.

Lehmann, Courtney, *Shakespeare Remains: Theater to Film, Early Modern to Postmodern*, Ithaca: Cornell University Press, 2002.

Libby, M. F., *"Some New Notes on* Macbeth," in *Vindication of the Reading of the Folio of 1623*, Toronto: The Copp, Clark Co., Ltd., 1893.

Low, Rachel, *History of British Film 1906–1914*, London: George Allen & Unwin, 1949.

Lyons, Bridget Gellert (ed.), Chimes at Midnight: *Orson Welles, director*, New Brunswick and London: Rutgers University Press, 1988.

MacLiammóir, Micheál, *Put Money in Thy Purse: A Diary of the Film of* Othello, London: Methuen, 1952.

Manvell, Roger, *Shakespeare and the Film*, 2nd printing, South Brunswick and New York: A. S. Barnes, 1979.

　Theater and Film: A Comparative Study of the Two Forms of Dramatic Art, and of the Problems of Adaptation of Stage Plays into Films, London: Associated University Presses, 1979.

McBride, Joseph, *Orson Welles*, rev. ed., New York: Da Capo, 1996.

McCabe, Colin, *et al.*, *Godard: Images, Sounds, Politics*, Bloomington: Indiana University Press, 1980.

McFarlane, Brian, *An Autobiography of British Cinema, as told by the filmmakers and actors who made it*, Foreword by Julie Christie, London: Methuen, 1997.

McGilligan, Patrick, *George Cukor: A Double Life*, New York: St. Martin's Press, 1991.

McGuire, Philip C., *Speechless Dialect: Shakespeare's Open Silences*, Berkeley: University of California Press, 1985.

McKellen, Ian, *William Shakespeare's* Richard III: *A Screenplay*, New York: The Overlook Press, 1996.

McKernan, Luke and Olwen Terris, *Walking Shadows: Shakespeare in the National Film and Television Archive*, London: BFI, 1994.

McLean, Andrew M., *Shakespeare: Annotated Bibliographies and Media Guide for Teachers*, Urbana: NCTE, 1980.

Metallinos, Nikos, *Television Aesthetics: Perceptual, Cognitive, and Compositional Bases*, Mahwah [NJ]: Earlbaum Associates, 1996.

Miller, Jonathan, *Subsequent Performances*, New York: Elisabeth Sifton/Viking, 1986.

Morris, Beja (ed.), *Perspectives on Orson Welles*, New York: G. K. Hall & Co., 1995.

Morris, Peter (ed.), *Shakespeare on Film*, Ottawa: Canadian Film Institute, 1972.

Musser, Charles, *The Emergence of Cinema: The American Screen to 1907*, New York: Charles Scribner's Sons, 1990. Vol. 1 in *History of American Cinema*, gen. ed. Charles Harpole, New York: Charles Scribner's Sons, 1990–date.

Naremore, James, *The Magic World of Orson Welles*, rev. ed., Dallas: Southern Methodist University Press, 1989.

Nash, Jay Robert and Stanley Ralph Ross (eds.), *The Motion Picture Guide, 1927–1983*, Chicago: Cinebooks, 1987.

Nelson, Ralph (ed.), *"Hamlet". A Television Script*, New York: CBS, 1976.

Newman, Karen , *Fashioning Femininity and English Renaissance Drama*, University of Chicago Press, 1994.

Nowell-Smith, Geoffrey (ed.), *Oxford History of World Cinema*, Oxford University Press, 1996.

Nunn, Trevor (ed.), Twelfth Night *by William Shakespeare. A Screenplay*, London: Methuen Drama, 1996.

Palmer, Richard, *Hermeneutics: Interpretation Theory in Schleiermacher, Dilthey, Heidegger, and Gadamer*, Evanston: Northwestern University Press, 1969.

Parkinson, David (ed.), *The Graham Greene Film Reader: Reviews, Essays, Interviews and Film Stories*, New York: Applause Theatre Book Publishers, 1993.

Pearce, Craig and Baz Luhrmann, *William Shakespeare's* Romeo & Juliet: *The Contemporary Film, The Classic Play*, New York: Bantam Doubleday Books, 1996.

Pickford, Mary, *Sunshine and Shadow*, New York: Doubleday, 1955.

Pilkington, Ace G., *Screening Shakespeare from* Richard II *to* Henry V, Newark: University of Delaware Press, 1991.

Prince, Stephen, *The Warrior's Camera: The Cinema of Akira Kurosawa*, Princeton University Press, 1991.

Pudovkin, V. I., *Film Technique, Film Acting*, trans. Ivor Montagu, 1929; rpt Hackensack [NJ]: Wehman Brothers, 1968.

Rajadhyaksha, Ashish and Paul Willeman, *Encyclopedia of Indian Cinema*, New Delhi: Oxford University Press, 1994.

Richardson, Tony, *Long Distance Runner. A Memoir*, w. intro. by Lindsay Anderson, London: Faber & Faber, 1993.

Richie, Donald (w. additional material by Joan Mellen), *The Films of Akira Kurosawa*, 3rd ed., Berkeley: University of California Press, 1996.

Robbe-Grillet, Alain and Alain Resnais, *Last Year at Marienbad*, trans. Richard Howard, New York: Grove Press, 1962.

Rosabella. Italian Documentary Film, appended to *Othello* [1952]. Voyager Company Laserdisc, 1995.

Rosenbaum, Jonathan (ed.), *This Is Orson Welles*: *Orson Welles and Peter Bogdanovich*, New York: HarperCollins, 1992.

Rosenberg, Marvin, *The Masks of* King Lear, Berkeley: University of California Press, 1972.

Ross, Gordon, *Television Jubilee: The Story of 25 Years of BBC Television*, London: W. H. Allen, 1961.

Ross, Steven J., *Working-Class Hollywood: Silent Film and the Shaping of Class in America*, Princeton University Press, 1998.

Rothwell, Kenneth S., and Annabelle Henkin Melzer, *Shakespeare on Screen: An International Filmography and Videography*, New York: Neal-Schuman, 1990.

Sasayama, Takashi, J. R. Mulryne, and Margaret Shewring (eds.), *Shakespeare and the Japanese Stage*, Cambridge University Press, 1998.

Shakespeare, William, *Romeo and Juliet. With Designs by Oliver Messel* [Cukor *Rom.*], London: B. T. Batsford, 1936.

A Motion Picture Edition [Cukor *Rom.*], New York: Random House, 1936.

SIFT (Summary of Information on Film and Television), electronic data base in the British Film Institute Library.

Silviria, Dale, *Laurence Olivier and the Art of Film Making*, London and Toronto: Associated University Presses, 1985.

Sklar, Robert, *Movie-made America: A Social History of American Movies*, New York: Vintage, 1975.

Skovmand, Michael (ed.), *Screen Shakespeare*, Aarhus [Denmark]: Aarhus University Press, 1994.

Slide, Anthony, *The American Film Industry*, New York: Greenwood Press, 1986.

Smith, Anthony (ed.), *Television: An International History*, Oxford University Press, 1995.

Spoto, Donald, *Laurence Olivier: A Biography*, New York: HarperCollins, 1992.

Sterne, Richard L., *John Gielgud Directs Richard Burton in* Hamlet: *A Journal of Rehearsals*, New York: Random House, 1967.

Taranow, Gerda, *Sarah Bernhardt: The Art within the Legend*, Princeton University Press, 1972.

The Bernhardt Hamlet: Culture and Context, New York: Peter Lang, 1996.

Taylor, Geoffrey (ed.), *Paul Mazursky's* Tempest, New York: Zoetrope, 1982.

Taymor, Julie, *Titus: The Illustrated Screenplay*, New York: Newmarket Press, 2000.

Television Programme as Broadcast TPAB, 1937. BBC WAC, Caversham Park, Reading.

Thomson, David, *Rosebud: The Story of Orson Welles*, New York: Alfred Knopf, 1996.

Time-Out Film Guide, ed. Tom Milne, 3rd ed., London: Penguin, 1993.

Trimble, Marion Blackton, *J. Stuart Blackton, A Personal Biography*, Metuchen & London: The Scarecrow Press, 1985.

Trimble, Bjo, *StarTrek Concordance*, 1990, unpaged.

Tynan, Kenneth, *The Sound of Two Hands Clapping*, London: Jonathan Cape, 1975.

Uricchio, William and Roberta E. Pearson, *Reframing Culture: The Case of the Vitagraph Quality Films*, Princeton University Press, 1993.

Vardac, A. Nicholas, *Stage to Screen: Theatrical Method from Garrick to Griffith*, New York: Benjamin Blom, 1968 [c. 1949].

Vaughan, Alden T. and Virginia Mason Vaughan, *Shakespeare's Caliban: A Cultural History*, Cambridge University Press, 1991.

Warde, Frederick B., *Fifty Years of Make-Believe*, New York: International Press Syndicate, 1920.

Willis, Susan, *The BBC Shakespeare Plays: Making the Televised Canon*, Chapel Hill: University of North Carolina Press, 1991.

Worthen, W. B., *Shakespeare and the Force of Modern Performance*, Cambridge University Press, 2003.

Wyver, John, *The Moving Image: An International History of Film, Television and Video*, Oxford and New York: Basil Blackwell/BFI, 1989.

Zeffirelli, Franco, *Zeffirelli: The Autobiography of Franco Zeffirelli*, New York: Weidenfeld & Nicolson, 1986.

ARTICLES, REVIEWS, AND ESSAYS IN BOOKS, JOURNALS, NEWSPAPERS AND ANTHOLOGIES

Abramson, Albert, "The Invention of Television," in Anthony Smith (ed.), *Television: An International History*, Oxford University Press, 1995, pp. 13–34.

Agate, James, "Bergner as Rosalind," in *Around Cinemas*, London: Home & Van Thal, 1946; rpt. New York: Arno Press, 1972, pp. 73–77.

"Notes," *The Magazine Programme*, London Pavilion, 14 Nov. 1929.

Alkire, N. L., "Subliminal Masks in Olivier's *Hamlet*," *SFNL* 16.1 (Dec. 1991), 5.

Allen Robert C., "Manhattan Myopia, or Oh! Iowa!" *Cinema Journal* 35.3 (1996), 75–103.

American Film Institute Souvenir Program, 29 Oct. 1996, for Warde *Richard III* premiere.

Andrews, John F., "Kenneth Branagh's *Hamlet* Launched...," *SN* 46:3 No. 230 (Fall 1996), 61+.

Anikst, Alexander, "Grigori Kozintsev's *King Lear*," *Soviet Literature* 6 (1971), 176–82.

Arai, Yoshio, "Kurosawa's Three Shakespeare Films," in *Journal of the Faculty of Letters, Komazawa University*, 55 (March 1997), 23–36.

Balderstone, Peter, "Who is Shakespeare? Who is Shakespeare? Nobody Knows. Nobody Cares. This is Ladywood," Unpub. Paper. "Shakespeare and the Movies" Seminar. Shakespeare Association of American, Apr. 2003. Victoria, BC.

Ball, Robert Hamilton, "Tree's *King John* Film: An Addendum," *SQ* 24.4 (1973), 455–59.

Barker, Felix, "Review [Brook *Lear*]," *Evening Standard* 23 July 1971.

Barnes, Howard, "*As You Like It*," *NYHT* 6 Nov. 1936.

Barry, Michael, "Shakespeare on Television," *BBC Quarterly* 9.3 (Autumn 1954), 146.

Bate, Jonathan, "Words in a Quantum World," *TLS* 25 July 1997, 14–15.

"In the Script Factory," review of Brian Vickers, *Shakespeare Co-Author, TLS*, No. 5220 (18 Apr. 2003), 3–4.

BBC, "Floor Mistakes," Internal Circulating Memo, WAC T5/508, 6 Feb. 1939.

Berlin, Normand, "Peter Brook's Interpretation of *King Lear*: 'Nothing Will Come of Nothing'," *LFQ* 5.4 (1977), 299–303.

Biggs, Murray, "'He's Going to His Mother's Closet': Hamlet and Gertrude on Screen," *SS* 45 (1993), 53–62.

Bioscope, "Editorial," 25 June 1914, 1289.

"The Filming of *Hamlet*: Interview with Mr. Cecil Hepworth," 24 July 1913.

"Opening of Palace Electric," 5 Jan. 1911, 55; "Another Palace Opens," 12 Jan. 1911, 15; "Trade Ad for Globe *MV*," 12 June 1913, suppl. xxvi.

Blumenthal, J., "*Macbeth* into *Throne of Blood*," *S&S* 34.4 (Autumn 1965), 190–95.

Boddy, William, "The Beginnings of American Television," in *Television: An International History*, Anthony Smith (ed.), Oxford University Press, 1995, pp. 35–61.

Bradley, David, "Shakespeare on a Shoestring," *Movie Makers* (Apr. 1974), 146+.

Brien, Alan, "Review [Welles *Othello*]," *The Evening Standard* 23 Feb. 1956.

Brittain, Frederick (ed.), "2nd Vesper Services, Masses for the Virgin Mary," *Penguin Book of Latin Verses*, Baltimore: Peter Smith, 1962.

Brook, Peter, "Shakespeare and Kurosawa," in James Goodwin (ed.), *Perspectives on Akira Kurosawa*, New York: G. K. Hall & Co., 1994, pp. 31–32.

Brown, Constance A., "Olivier's *Richard III* – A Re-evaluation," *FQ* 20 (1967), 23–32.

Buhler, Stephen M., "'Who Calls Me Villain?': Blank Verse and the Black Hat," *Extrapolation* 36.1 (Spring 1995), 18–27.

Burnett, Mark Thornton, "'To Hear and See the Matter': Communicating Technology in Michael Almereyda's *Hamlet* (2000)," *Cinema Journal*, 42.3 (Spring 2003), 66.

Burt, Richard, "The Love that Dare Not Speak Shakespeare's Name: New Shakesqueer Cinema," in Boose and Burt (eds.), *Shakespeare, The Movie*, pp. 240–68.

"Shakespeare and the Holocaust: Julie Taymor's *Titus* Is Beautiful, or Shakesploi Meets (the) Camp," in *Shakespeare After Mass Media* (ed.), Richard Burt, London: Palgrave, 2002, pp. 295–329.

Bush, W. Stephen, "Our American Letter," *Bioscope* 16 Apr. 1914.

Cahir, Linda Costanzo, "The Artful Rerouting of *A Streetcar Named Desire*," *LFQ* 22.2 (1994), 72–77.

Callaghan, Dympna, "Resistance and Recuperation: Branagh's *Henry V*," *SFNL* 15.2 (Apr. 1991), 5.

Cameron-Wilson, James, "Review [Loncraine *R3*], *What's on in London?*" 24 Apr. 1996.

Canby, Vincent, "Reams on the Renaissance Fill 'Prospero's Books'," *NYT* 28 Sept. 1991, 9+.

"Screen: *The Tempest*," *NYT* 22 Sept. 1980, C.20.

"A House Party of Beatrice, Benedick and Friends," *NYT* 7 May 1993, C.16.

Carr [Vaughan],Virginia M., "The Second Season: *Twelfth Night*," *SFNL* 4.2 (Apr. 1980), 5.

Cartmell, Deborah, "Franco Zeffirelli and Shakespeare," in *The Cambridge Companion to Shakespeare on Film* (ed.), Russell Jackson, Cambridge University Press, 2000, pp. 212–21.

Caryn, James, "A Spare Lear Influenced by Beckett and Brecht," *NYT* 9 Oct. 1998: B27.

Castner, Tom, "*Et tu*, Charlton," *Village Voice* 25 Feb. 1971, 57.

Cavecchi, Mariacristina, "Peter Greenaway's *Prospero's Books*: A Tempest Between Word and Image," *LFQ* 25.2 (1997), 83–89.

Charnes, Linda, "Dismember Me: Shakespeare, Paranoia, and the Logic of Mass Culture," *SQ* 48.1 (Spring 1997), 1–16.

Cirillo, Albert R., "The Art of Franco Zeffirelli and Shakespeare's *Romeo and Juliet*," in Fred Marcus (ed.), *Film and Literature: Contrasts in Media*, Scranton: Chandler, 1971, 205–27.

Cobos, Juan and Miguel Rubio, "Welles and Falstaff: An Interview by Juan Cobos and Miguel Rubio," *S&S*, 35.4 (Autumn 1966), 158–63.

Cook, Page, "The Sound Track," *Films in Review* 19 (Nov. 1968), 570–73.

Corliss, Richard, "King Ken Comes to Conquer," *Time* 13 Nov. 1989, 119.

Coursen, H. R., "Not Fit to Live [Bard *Mac.*]," *SFNL* 13.1 (Dec. 1988).

"The Classic Theatre *Macbeth*," *Pulse* (Oct. 1976), in Bulman and Coursen (eds.), *Shakespeare on Television*: *An Anthology of Essays and Reviews*, pp. 247–48.

"The PBS *Othello*: A Review Essay," *SB* 20.1 (Winter 2002), 38–39.

"Winter of the Scottish Play," *SB* 10.2 (Spring 1992), 10–14.

"*Titus*," *SB* 18.1 (Winter 2000), 46–47.

Cowie, Peter, "Olivier at 75 Returns to Lear," *NYT* 1 May 1983.

Crane, Milton, "Shakespeare on Television," *SQ* 12.3 (Summer 1961), 323–27.

Crist, Judith,"Olivier Paints Othello Ridden by Neuroses," *NYHT*, 2 Feb. 1966.

Crowl, Samuel, "Chain Reaction: A Study of Roman Polanski's *Macbeth*," *Soundings* 59.2 (Summer 1976), 226–33.

"Changing Colors like the Chameleon: Ian McKellen's *Richard III* from Stage to Film," *Post Script* 17.1 (Fall 1997), 53–63.

"Review [Edzard *AYL*]," *SB* 11.3 (Summer 1993), 41.

"Stormy Weather: A New *Tempest* on Film," *SFNL* 5.1 (Dec. 1980), 1+.

"Review [Branagh *Ado*],"*SB* 11.3 (Summer 1993), 39–40.

"Review [Nunn *TN*]," *SB* 15.1 (Winter 1997), 36–37.

"Review [Branagh *Hamlet*]," *SB* 15.1. (Winter 1997), 34–35.

"The Bow Is Bent and Drawn: Kurosawa's *Ran* and the Shakespearean Arrow of Desire," *LFQ* 22.2 (1994), 109–16.

"Review [Taymor *"Titus"*]," *SB* 18.1 (Winter 2000): 46–47.

"Review [Almereyda *Hamlet*]," *SB* 18.4 (Fall 2000), 39.

Crowl, Samuel, and Mary Z. Maher, "Cambridgeshire *Hamlet*: Two Views,"*SFNL* 13.1 (Dec. 1988), 7.

Crowther, Bosley, "Minstrel Show *Othello* [Olivier]," *NYT* 2 Feb. 1966, 24.

"Review [Bradley *JC*]," *NYT* 25 Nov. 1952, 33.

"Review [Castellani *Romeo*]," *NYT* 22 Dec. 1954, 28.

"Review [Welles *Chimes*]," *NYT* 20 March 1967, 26.

"Review [Welles] *Macbeth*," *NYT* 28 Dec. 1950, 22.

"Review [Zeffirelli *Shrew*]," *NYT* 9 March 1967, 43.

Danson, Lawrence, "Gazing at Hamlet, or the Danish Cabaret," *SS* 45 (1993), 37–51.

David, Richard, "Shakespeare in Miniature: The BBC *Antony and Cleopatra*," in Bulman and Coursen (eds.), *Shakespeare on Television*, 139–44.

Davies, Brenda, "Review [Hall *MND*]," *MFB* 36. 422 (March 1969), 51.

Davy, Charles, "Films [Cukor *Rom.*]," *The London Mercury* 35 (Nov. 1936), 57–58.

Devlin, Polly, "I Know My Romeo and Juliet," *Vogue* 151 (1 Apr. 1968), 34+.

Díaz-Fernández, José Ramón, "The Reel Shakespeare: A Selective Bibliography of Criticism," in *The Reel Shakespeare: Alternative Cinema and Theory* (eds.), Lisa S. Starks and Courtney Lehmann, Cranbury (NJ): Assoc. University Presses, 2002, pp. 229–87.

Dews, Peter, "The Spread of the Eagle," *Radio Times* 25 Apr. 1963, 49.

Donaldson, Peter S., "Shakespeare in the Age of Post-Mechanical Reproduction: Sexual and Electronic Magic in *Prospero's Books*," in Boose and Burt (eds.), *Shakespeare, The Movie*, pp. 169–85.

"Taking on Shakespeare: Kenneth Branagh's *Henry V*," *SQ* 42.1 (Spring 1991), 60–71.

"Michael Almereyda's *Hamlet*: Video Art, Authenticity and 'Wisdom'," Unpub. Paper. "Shakespeare and the Movies" Seminar. Shakespeare Association of America, Apr. 2003. Victoria, BC.

Dukes, Ashley, "Televised Drama So Far: The English Scene," *TAM* 22.4 (Apr. 1938), 256–62.

Durbin, Karen, "Making 'Lear' a 'Survivor' in the Desert," Arts and Leisure, *NYT*, Sunday 22 Apr. 2001, 19.

Dworkin, Martin S., "'Stay Illusion!' Having Words about Shakespeare on Screen," *The Journal of Aesthetic Education* 11.1 (Jan. 1977), 51–61.

Edwards, Geoffrey, "*Julius Caesar* in Modern Dress," *News Chronicle* 25 July 1938.

Elley, Derek, "Review of Edzard *AYL*," *Variety* 5 Oct. 1992.

Felperin, Leslie, "*Hamlet*," *S&S* 7.2 n.s. (Feb. 1997), 46.

Fenwick, Henry, "The Production," in *The BBC-TV Shakespeare* Othello, London: BBC, 198, pp. 18–28.

"The Production," in *The BBC-TV Shakespeare* Troilus and Cressida, London: BBC, 1981, pp. 18–24.

Filmindia, "*Hamlet* Flops," 21.2 (Feb. 1955), 71–75.

Forbes, Jill, "Henry [Branagh *H5*]," *S&S* 58.4 (Autumn 1989), 258–59.

Fulton, Robert C., "*Love's Labour's Lost* and the Marx Brothers," *Upstart Crow* 5 (1984), 125–34.

Gelmis, Joseph, "Shakespeare's *Henry V* in Two Incarnations," *Newsday* 7 Dec. 1990, II. 153.

Gerlach, John, "Shakespeare, Kurosawa, and *Macbeth*: A Response to J. Blumenthal," *LFQ* 1.4 (Fall 1973), 352–59.

Gilbey, Brian, "Bard Therapy [Review of McKellen *R3*]," *Independent* 25 Apr. 1996, 2:11.

Gill, Brendan, "Not Lacking Gall [Richardson *Ham.*]," *TNY* 10 May 1969, 121–22.
"Black and White [Olivier *Oth.*]," *TNY* 19 Feb. 1966, 145.

Goldie, Grace Wyndham, "Critic on the Hearth," *The Listener* 29 Dec. 1938, 1428.

Gould, Jack, "Worthington Miner's Version [of *Julius Caesar*] in Modern Dress Proves Spectacular," *NYT* 13 March 1949, II. 11.
"Review: *Macbeth*," *NYT* 22 May 1949, II. 9.

Green, Juana, "Bicycles, Bustles and Brides in Michael Hoffman's *William Shakespeare's A Midsummer Night's Dream*," Unpub. Paper. "Shakespeare and the Movies" Seminar. Shakespeare Association of America, Apr. 2003. Victoria, BC.

Greenaway, Peter, "Movie Memories," *S&S* 6.5 suppl. (May 1996), 15, 16.

Griffin, Alice, "Shakespeare through the Camera's Eye: 1953–54," *SQ* 6.1 (Winter 1955), 63–66.
"Shakespeare through the Camera's Eye," *SQ* 17.4 (Autumn 1966), 383–87.

Griffiths, Michael, "Review Gay-Music [Coronado *MND*]," *Time-Out*, 1984, in Ritzy-Brixton Cinema Club p.r. handout.

Grilli, Peter, "Kurosawa Directs a Cinematic 'Lear'," *NYT* 15 Dec. 1985, sec. 2, 1+.

Gritten, David, "Bard with a Vengeance [McKellen *R3*]," *Daily Telegraph*, 19 Apr. 1996, 21+.

Guia de Filmes, "Review [Brazilian *a Heranca*]," 34 (July/Aug. 1971), 152–53.

Guntner J. Lawrence, "Expressionist Shakespeare: The Gade/Nielsen *Hamlet* (1920) and the History of Shakespeare on Film," *Post Script*, 17.2 (Winter/Spring 1998), 90–102.

Guthrie, Tyrone, "Shakespeare on the Modern Stage," *The Listener* 3 Feb. 1937, 207.

Hall, Mordaunt, "Review [Taylor *Shr.*]," *NYT* 29 Nov. 1929, 23.

Hapgood, Robert, "*Chimes at Midnight* from Stage to Screen: The Art of Adaptation," *SS* 39 (1987) 39–52.
"Shakespeare and the Included Spectator," in Norman Rabkin (ed.), *Reinterpretations of Elizabethan Drama*, New York: Columbia University Press, 1969: 117–36.
"Kurosawa's Shakespeare Films: *Throne of Blood, The Bad Sleep Well*, and*Ran*," in Davies and Wells (eds.), *Shakespeare and the Moving Image*, pp. 234–49.
"Popularizing Shakespeare: The Artistry of Franco Zeffirelli," in Boose and Burt (eds.), *Shakespeare, The Movie*, pp. 80–94.

Harris, Diana and MacDonald Jackson, "Stormy Weather: Derek Jarman's *The Tempest*," *LFQ* 25.2 (1997), 90–98.

Harrison, G. B., "Shakespeare in His Theatre," *The Listener* 20 Jan. 1937, 116–8.

Hastings, Chris and Catherine Milner, "Hollywood Rivals Battle to Bring *The Merchant of Venice* to Screen," *The Telegraph,* 17 Aug. 2003.

Hatch, Robert, "Films [Review Welles *Othello*]," *TN* 1 Oct. 1955, 81.

"Films [Review Castellani *Romeo*]," *TN* 8 Jan. 1955, 37.

Haughton, David, "Program Notes for the Lindsay Kemp Company," Sadler's Wells Theatre, 15 Apr.–11 May, 1985.

Hedrick, Donald K., "War Is Mud: Branagh's Dirty Harry V and the Types of Political Ambiguity," in Boose and Burt (eds.), *Shakespeare, The Movie,* pp. 45–66.

Henderson, Diana E., "A Shrew for the Times," in Boose and Burt (eds.), *Shakespeare, The Movie,* pp. 148–68.

Heston, Charlton, "Heston Directs Heston," Publicity Booklet, London, 1972, unpaged.

Hetherington, Robert A., "The *Lear*s of Peter Brook," *SFNL* 6.1. (1982), 7.

Higashi, Sumiko, "Dialogue: Manhattan's Nickelodeons," *Cinema Journal* 35.3 (1996), 72–74.

Hinson, Hal, "The Heart of 'Henry V'," *WP* 15 Dec. 1989, D.1.

Hinxman, Margaret, "Review [of Burton *Hamlet*]," *Sunday Telegraph* 9 July 1972.

Hoberman, J., "Review of Godard *Lear*," *Village Voice* 26 Jan. 1988, 53.

"Moor Better Blues [Review of Welles *Othello* Re-release]," *Village Voice* 31 March 1992, 5.

Hodgdon, Barbara, "Race-ing *Othello*, Re-Engendering White-Out," in Boose and Burt (eds.), *Shakespeare, The Movie,"* pp. 23–44.

"Two *King Lear*s: Uncovering the Filmtext," *LFQ* 11.3 (1983), 143–51.

Holderness, Graham, "Shakespeare Rewound," *SS* 45 (1993), 63–74.

Holland, Peter, "Two-Dimensional Shakespeare, *King Lear* on Film," in Davies and Wells (eds.), *Shakespeare and the Moving Image,* pp. 50–68.

Houseman, John, "Filming *Julius Caesar*," *S&S* 23.1 (July/Sept. 1953), 24–27.

Howard, Tony, "When Peter Met Orson: The 1953 CBS *King Lear*," in Boose and Burt (eds.), *Shakespeare, The Movie,* pp. 121–34.

Humphrey, A. R., "Introduction," *King Henry IV Part Two, The Arden Shakespeare,* London: Methuen, 1966.

Impastato, David, "Godard's *Lear* ... Why Is It So Bad?" *SB* 12.3 (Summer 1994), 38–41.

"Zeffirelli's *Hamlet* and the Baroque," *SFNL* 16.2 (Apr. 1992), 1+.

"Zeffirelli's *Hamlet*: Sunlight Makes Meaning" *SFNL* 16.1 (Dec. 1991), 1+.

Ingrams, Richard, "Review [Nunn *Mac.*]," *The Standard* 13 Jan. 1979.

Jackson, Russell, "Shakespeare's Comedies on Film," in Davies and Wells (eds.), *Shakespeare and the Moving Image,* pp. 99–120.

"A Shooting Script for the Reinhardt/Dieterle *Dream*," *SB* 16.4 (Fall 1998), 39–41.

James, Caryn, "A Mideast Variation," *NYT* 20 Apr. 1999, C.13.

Jarman, Derek, Derek Jarman Special Collection, British Film Institute Library, Ms., Item #23.

Jays, David, "In the Bleak Midwinter," *S&S* 5.12 n.s. (Dec. 1995), 47.

"Love's Labours' Lost," *S&S* 10.4 n.s. (Apr. 2000), 54.

"The Children's Midsummer Night's Dream," *S&S* 11.8 n.s. (Aug. 2001), 40.

Jensen, Michael P., "Mel Gibson on *Hamlet*," *SFNL* 15.2 (Apr. 1991), 1+.

Jewel, John, "A Defence of the Apologie of the Church of England, conteining an Answer to a Certain Book lately set forth by Mr. Harding..." in John Eyre (ed.), *Works of John Jewel*, III, The Parker Society, XXV, Cambridge University Press, 1848.

Johnson, S. F., "The Regeneration of Hamlet: A Reply to E. M. W. Tillyard...," *SQ* 3.3 (July 1952), 187–207.

Johnson, Vida, "Russia after the Thaw," in Nowell-Smith (ed.), *Oxford History of World Cinema*, 641–51.

Johnson, William, "*King Lear* and *Macbeth*," *FQ* 25.3 (1972), 41–48.

Johnson-Haddad, Miranda, "A Time for *Titus*: An Interview with Julie Taymor," *SB* 18.4 (Fall 2000), 34–36.

Johnston, Sheila, "Review of Godard *Lear*," *Independent* 28 Jan. 1988, 14.

Jones, Nicholas, "Gender and Voice in Hoffman's [i]*Dream*," Unpub. Paper. "Shakespeare and the Movies" Seminar. Shakespeare Association of America, Apr. 2003. Victoria, BC.

Jorgens, Jack J., "Kurosawa's *Throne of Blood*: Washizu and Miki Meet the Forest Spirit," *LFQ* 11.3. (1983), 167–72.

"The Opening Scene of Polanski's *Macbeth*," *LFQ* 3.3 (1975), 277–78.

Jorgenson, Paul. "Castellani's *Romeo and Juliet*: Intention and Response," *FQ* 10.1 (Fall 1955), 1–10. Reprinted in *Focus on Shakespearean Films* (ed.), Charles W. Eckert. Englewood Cliffs [NJ]: Prentice-Hall, 1972, pp. 108–15.

Kachur, B. A., 'The First Shakespeare Film: A Reconsideration and Reconstruction of Tree's *King John*," *TS* 32 (May 1991), 43–63.

Kael, Pauline, "Peter Brook's Night of the Living Dead," *TNY* 11 Dec. 1971, 135–37.

Kallet, Nathan, "Olivier and the Moor," *Holiday* 26 Apr. 1966, 143+.

Kehr, David, "Samurai *Lear*," *American Film* x (Sept. 1985), 21–26.

Kermode, Frank, "Shakespeare in the Movies," *NYRB* 18 (4 May 1972), 18–21.

Kimbrough, R. Alan, "The First Season [BBC Series]," *SFNL* 3.2 (Apr. 1979), 5.

Kinder, Marsha, "*Throne of Blood*: A Morality Dance," *LFQ* 5.4 (1977), 339–45.

Kissel, Howard, "*King Lear*," *Women's Wear Daily*, 4 Aug. 1975, 24.

Klawans, Stuart, "Holiday Celluloid Wrap-Up [Branagh *Ham.*]," *TN* 13/20 Jan. 1997, 36.

"Films [Branagh *Ado*]," *TN* 31 May 1993, 750–52.

Kliman, Bernice W., "Katharine Hepburn as Hamlet and Juliet," *SFNL* 13.2 (Apr. 1989), 6.

"Kozintsev's *Hamlet*: A Flawed Masterpiece," *Hamlet Studies* 1.2 (Oct. 1979), 117–28.

"Olivier's *Hamlet*: A Film-Infused Play," in *LFQ*, Michael Mullin (ed.), 5.4 (Fall 1977), 305–14.

"Swedish *Hamlet* Bursts into View," *SFNL* 11.2 (Apr. 1987), 1+.

"Welles's *Macbeth*, A Textual Parable," in Michael Skovmand (ed.), *Screen Shakespeare*, 25–38.

Knight, Arthur, "Review [of Burton *Hamlet*]," *Saturday Review* 17 Oct. 1964.

Kott, Jan, "The Edo *Lear*," *NYRB* xxxii. 7 (24 Apr. 1986), 13–15.

Kroll, Jack, "A *Henry V* for Our Time," *Newsweek* 20 Nov. 1989, 78.

MG, "The 'Othello' of Mr. Orson Welles," 25 Feb. 1956.

MPW, "Audience Applauds His Shrieks of Agony," 22 Feb. 1908.

Lake, James H., "Hands in Zeffirelli's *Romeo,*" SAA Abstracts, 1990, in *SFNL* 15.1. (Dec. 1990), 4.

Lane, Anthony, "Too Much Ado," *TNY* 69.12 (10 May 1993), 97–99.

Leavis, F. R., "Diabolic Intellect and the Noble Hero," in *Shakespeare* Othello. *A Casebook* (ed.), John Wain. London: Macmillan, 1971, pp. 123–46.

Lehmann, Courtney, "*Shakespeare in Love*: Romancing the Author, Mastering the Body," *Spectacular Shakespeare: Critical Theory and Popular Cinema* (eds.), Courtney Lehmann and Lisa S. Starks, Madison (NJ) and London: Associated University Presses, 2002, pp. 125–45.

Lennox, Patricia, "*Titus Andronicus,*" *SB* 13.2 (Spring 1995), 35.

Leonard, Harold, "Hollywood: Notes on *Macbeth,*" *S&S* 19.1 (March 1950), 15–17.

Levin, Harry, "General Introduction," *TRS,* pp. 1–25.

Lillich, Meredith, "Shakespeare on the Screen: A Survey of How His Plays Have Been Made into Movies," *FR* (June/July 1956), 247–60.

Lindroth, Mary, "'Some Device of Further Misery': Taymor's *Titus* Brings Shakespeare to Film Audiences with a Twist," *LFQ* 29.2 (2001), 107–15.

Loehlin, James N., "'Top of the World, Ma': *Richard III* and Cinematic Convention," in Boose and Burt, (eds.), *Shakespeare, The Movie,* pp. 67–79.

London Mercury, The "Films [Review of Cukor *Rom.*]," 35 (Nov. 1936), 57.

Look, "A New *Romeo and Juliet,*" 31 (17 Oct. 1967), 58+.

M. G. M., "M.G.M. Proudly Brings to the Screen [1953 *JC*]," Souvenir Book, n.d., p. 3.

MacArthur, Colin, "Review of Freeston *Macbeth,*" *S&S* 7.6 n.s. (June 1997), 56–57.

Macnab, Geoffrey, "Review: *Looking for Richard,*" *S&S* 7.2.n.s. (Feb. 1997), 48–49.

"Review: Nunn *Twelfth Night,*" *S&S* 6.11.n.s. (Nov. 1996), 60.

"Review: Parker *Othello,* " *S&S* 6.2 n.s. (Feb. 1996), 51–52.

Manheim, Michael, "Olivier's *Henry V* and the Elizabethan World Picture," *LFQ* (Kenneth S. Rothwell (ed.), Special Issue of Papers from Seminar 16, World Shakespeare Congress), 11.3 (1983), 179–84.

"The Shakespeare Plays on TV," *SFNL* 8.2. (Apr. 1984), 4.

Marks, Martin, "The Sound of Music," in *The Oxford History of World Cinema,* Oxford University Press, 1996: 248–59.

Marks, Peter, "So Young, So Fragile . . .[Nunn *TN*]," *NYT* 20 Oct. 1996, II. 13.

Maslin, Janet, "Royal Monster, Are You Out There?" *NYT* 11 Oct. 1996, C. 3.

"Soft! What Light? It's Flash, Romeo," *NYT* 1 Nov. 1996, C. 1.

Mason, M. S., "A *Hamlet* Fit for the Small Screen," *CSM* Friday, Dec. 8, 2000, 20.

Mathieson, Muir, "Note on *Hamlet,*" *Film Music* 13 (Jan./Feb. 1954), 19.

McCarthy, Todd, "*Much Ado about Nothing,*" *Variety* 3 May 1993.

McCloskey, Susan, "The Shakespeare Plays on TV [*Much Ado*]," *SFNL* 9.2 (Apr. 1985), 5.

McKernan, Luke, "Beerbohm Tree's *King John* Rediscovered: The First Shakespeare Film, September 1899," *SB* 11.1 (1993), 35–36.

"Further News on Beerbohm Tree's *King John,*" *SB* 11.2 (1993), 49–50.

Private letter, 4 Nov. 1994.

Megahey, Leslie (Interviewer), "With Orson Welles: Stories from a Life in Film," Television interview in 1980, Channel TNT, Monday, 5 Feb., 1990.

Meyer, David, Conversation at London Globe Theatre, October 1996.

MFB, "[J.G.] Review of Fried *TN*," 23. 269 (June 1956), 74.

MFB, "[P.H.] Review of *Forbidden Planet*," 23. 269 (June 1956), 71.

MFB, "[W.F.] *As You Like It* [Czinner]," 3.33 (Sept. 1936), 147.

MG, "The 'Othello' of Mr. Orson Welles," 25 Feb. 1956.

Middleton, Drew, "Review of Televised *Hamlet*," *NYT* 14 Dec. 1947, X. 11.

Millar, Sylvia, "*King Lear*," *MFB* 38 (1971), 182–83.

"Review [Heston *Ant.*]," *MFB* 39.459 (Apr. 1972), 67.

Miller, Edwin, "Love is the Sweetest Thing," *Seventeen* 27 (Jan. 1968), 82+.

Mirage Corp., "Essay on Dust Jacket," Laser Disc, *The Taming of the Shrew*. The Mary Pickford Co.© 1966; 1990.

MPW "Audience Applauds His Shrieks of Agony," 22 Feb. 1908.

Mullan, John, "Ken, Al and Will, too," *TLS* 21 Feb. 1997, 19.

Mullin, Michael, "Peter Hall's *Midsummer Night's Dream* on Film," *ETJ* 27 (1975), 529–34.

"Stage and Screen: The Trevor Nunn *Macbeth*," *SQ* 38.3 (Autumn 1987), 350–59.

"Tony Richardson's *Hamlet*: Script and Screen," *LFQ* 4.2 (Spring 1976), 123–33.

"Orson Welles' *Macbeth*: Script and Screen," in Gottesman (ed.), *Focus on Orson Welles*, 136–45.

Newman, Karen, "Chabrol's *Ophelia*," *SFNL* 6.2. (March 1982), 1+.

Newman, Kim, "Review of *Tromeo and Juliet*," *S&S* 6.12. (Dec. 1996), 54–55.

Nichols, Nina da Vinci, "Branagh's *Hamlet* Redux," *SB* 15.3 (Summer 1997), 38–41.

Nokes, David, "Echoes of Godard," *TLS* 29 Jan. 1988, 112.

Nouryeh, Andrea J., "Shakespeare and the Japanese Stage," in Dennis Kennedy (ed.), *Foreign Shakespeare*, 254–69.

NYT, "Edison's Film at Koster & Bial," 24, 26 Apr. 1896, 5, 19.

NYT, "Review of Asta Nielsen *Hamlet*," 9 Nov. 1921, 20.

NYT, "Review of Guazzoni's *JC*.," 12 Feb. 1922, II. 3.

NYT, Advertisement for Roxy Theatre, 6 March 1927, VIII. 9.

O'Connor, John, "Olivier as the Controversial Shylock in 1880's," *NYT* 15 March 1974, 67.

Occhiogrosso, Frank, "Cinematic Oxymoron in Peter Hall's *A Midsummer Night's Dream*," *LFQ* 11.3 (1983), 174–78.

"'Give Me Thy Hand': Manual Gesture in the Elliott/Olivier *King Lear*," *SB* 2.9 (May–June 1984), 16–19.

Olivier, Laurence, "An Essay in *Hamlet*," in Cross (ed.), *The Film* Hamlet, pp. 11–15.

Orbison, Tucker, "The Stone and the Oak: Olivier's TV Film of *King Lear*," *The CEA Critic* 47 1.2 (Fall-Winter 1984), 67–77.

Oruch, Jack, "Shakespeare for the Millions: Kiss Me, Petruchio," *SFNL* 11.2 (Apr. 1987), 7.

Osborne, Laurie E., "Poetry in Motion. Animating Shakespeare," in Boose and Burt (eds.), *Shakespeare, The Movie*, pp. 103–20.

Parker, Barbara L., "Review of George W. Williams' videocassette lecture, 'Feuding and Loving in Shakespeare's *Romeo and Juliet*'," in *SFNL* 16.1 (Dec. 1991), 8.

Parker, Elspeth, "*The Wars of the Roses*: Space, Shape, and Flow," *SB* 13.2 (Spring 1995), 40–41.

Parkinson, David, "Performance of Epic Proportions [Branagh *Ham.*]," *Oxford Times*, 2 May 1997.

Parr, Gus, "S for Smoking," *S&S* 7. 12 n.s. (Dec. 1997), 30–33.

Pasinetti, P. M., "The Role of the Technical Adviser," *QFRT* 8.2. (1953), 131–38.

Perret, Marion, "Kurosawa's *Hamlet*: Samurai in Business Dress,"*SFNL* 15.1 (Fall 1990), 6.

Petersen, Per Serritslev, "The 'Bloody Business' of Roman Polanski's *Macbeth*: A Case Study of the Dynamics of Modern Shakespeare [Reception] Appropriation," in Michael Skovmand (ed.), *Screen Shakespeare*, pp. 38–53.

Pilkington, Ace G., "Zeffirelli's Shakespeare," in Davies and Wells (eds.), *Shakespeare and the Moving Image*, 163–79.

Pomar, Mark, "Books in Review,"*SFNL* 4.1 (Dec. 1979), 10+.

Praz, Mario, "Shakespeare's Italy," in *SS* 7 (1954), 95–106.

Pulleine, Tim, "Review of Coronado *Hamlet*," *MFB* v.45 n.529 (Feb. 1978), 24.

Pursell, Michael, "Artifice and Authenticity in Zeffirelli's *Romeo and Juliet*," *LFQ* 14.4 (1986), 173–78.

"Zeffirelli's Shakespeare: The Visual Realization of Tone and Theme," *LFQ* 8.4 (1980), 210–18.

Quinn, Edward, "Zeffirelli's *Hamlet*," *SFNL* 15.2 (Apr. 1991), 1+.

Raban, Jonathan, "Peter Brook's *King Lear*," *New Statesman* 30 July 1971.

Rabkin, Norman, "Rabbits, Ducks and *Henry V*," *SQ* 28.3 (Summer 1977), 279–96.

Radio Times, "Interview with Janet Suzman," 188 (17 Sept. 1970), 6–7.

Rafferty, Terence, "Time Out of Joint [Review of McKellen *R3*]," *TNY* 22 Jan. 1996, 86.

Rajadhyaksha, Ashish, "India: Filming TN," in Nowell-Smith, (ed.), *Oxford History of World Cinema*, pp. 678–89.

Reed, Rex, "Parting, Like, Sucks! So Does *Romeo*," *NYO* 11 Nov. 1996, 41.

"On the Town [Loncraine *R3*]," *NYO* 8 Jan. 1996, 22.

Reed, Rex, "The Bard's Cabaret Act," *NYO* 12 June 2000, 20.

Riding, Alan, "The Royal Shakespeare: Renewing Itself under Fire," *NYT* 17 May 1998, II.1+.

Robinson, David, "Review [of Burton *Hamlet*]," *Financial Times* 7 July 1972.

Romney, Jonathan, "*Prospero's Books*," *S&S* 1.5 (Sept. 1991), 44–45.

Rosenbaum, Jonathan, "The Invisible Orson Welles: A First Inventory," *S&S* 55.3 (Summer 1986), 164–71.

Rothwell, Kenneth S., "In Search of Nothing: Mapping *King Lear*," in *Shakespeare, The Movie* (eds.), Lynda Boose and Richard Burt. London: Routledge, pp. 135–47.

"Kenneth Branagh's *Henry V*: The Gilt [Guilt] in the Crown Re-Examined," *CD* 24.2 (Summer 1990), 173–78.

"Psychiatry and the Freshman Theme," *College English* 20.7 (Apr. 1959), 338–42.

"Roman Polanski's *Macbeth*: Golgotha Triumphant," *LFQ* 1.4 (1973), 71–75.

"Roman Polanski's *Macbeth*: The 'Privileging' of Ross," *The CEA Critic* 46 1&2 (1983–84), 50–55.

"The Audience for the Blackfriars Playhouse in Shakespeare's London," *The Yearbook of the American Philosophical Society*, Philadelphia, 1969: 649–50.

"Zeffirelli's *Romeo and Juliet*: Words into Picture and Music," *LFQ* 5.4 (1977), 326–31.

"*Elizabeth* and *Shakespeare in Love,*" *Cineaste* 24. 2.3 (Spring/Summer, 1999), 78–80.

"*Much Ado About Something,*" *Cineaste* 27. 4.4 (Fall 2002), 64.

Rozsa, Miklos "*Julius Caesar,*" *Film Music* 13 (Sept./Oct. 1953), 7–13.

Sarris, Andrew, "At the Movies [Loncraine *R*3]," *NYO* 8 Jan. 1996, 17.

Schatz-Jacobsen, Claus, "'Knowing I Lov'd My Books': Shakespeare, Greenaway, and the Prosperous Dialectics of Word and Image," in Skovmand (ed.), *Screen Shakespeare*, pp. 132–47.

Schlueter, June, "Trivial Pursuit: The Casket Plot in the Miller/Olivier *Merchant of Venice,*" *SFNL* 10.1. (Dec. 1985), 7+.

Schoenbaum, S., "Looking for Shakespeare," in Philip Highfill (ed.,) *Shakespeare's Craft,* Carbondale: Southern Illinois University Press, 1982: 156–72.

Sharman, Leslie Felperin, "*Much Ado about Nothing,*" *S&S* 3. 9 n.s. (Sept. 1993), 50–51.

Shaw, William P., "Textual Ambiguities and Cinematic Certainties in *Henry V,*" *LFQ* 22.2 (1994), 117–28.

"Violence and Vision in Polanski's *Macbeth* and Brook's *King Lear,*" *LFQ* 14.4 (1986), 211–13.

Shenon, Philip, "A Hindu Romeo, A Muslim Juliet," *NYT* 5 Sept. 1991, A. 4.

Sherwood, A. M. Jr., "The Movies [Taylor *Shr.*]," *Outlook* 153 (18 Dec. 1929), 633–34.

Silver, Nathan, rev., Dennis Sharp, *The Picture Palace* (London (?): Hugh Evelyn, 1969) in *S&S* 38. 3 (Summer 1969), 160+.

Silverstein, Norman, "The Opening Shot of Roman Polanski's *Macbeth,*" *LFQ* 2.1 (1974), 88–90.

Simon, John, "Review [Brook *Lr.*]," *The New Leader* 27 Dec. 1971.

Simon, Ronald, "An Interview with George Schaefer," *Hallmark Hall of Fame: A Tradition of Excellence,* New York: Museum of Broadcasting, 1984: 23–30.

Singer, Ben, "New York, Just Like I Pictured It,"*Cinema Journal* 35.3 (1996), 104–128.

Sinker, Mark, "Review [Noble *MND*]," *S&S* 7.1 n.s. (Jan. 1997), 41.

Sokolov, Raymond A., "Angry Young Hamlet [Richardson *Hamlet*]," *Newsweek* 73, 12 May 1969, 119.

Speaight, Robert, "Shakespeare in Britain," *SQ* 23. 4 (Fall 1972) in Bulman and Coursen (eds.), *Shakespeare on Television,* pp. 246–47.

Starks, Lisa, "Cinema of Cruelty: Powers of Horror in Julie Taymor's *Titus,*" in *The Reel Shakespeare: Alternative Cinema and Theory* (eds.), Lisa S. Starks and Courtney Lehmann, Madison and London: Fairleigh Dickinson University Press, 2002, pp. 121–42.

Stenberg, Doug, "The Circle of Life and the Chain of Being: Shakespearean Motifs in *The Lion King,*" *SB* 14.2 (Spring 1996), 36–37.

Sterritt, David, "A *King Lear* Launched over Lunch," *CSM* 22 Jan. 1988.

Sunday Times, "*Julius Caesar* in Modern Dress: Television Version," 24 July 1938.

Taylor, John Russell, "Review [Burton *Hamlet*]," *Times* 7 July 1972.

"Shakespeare in Film, Radio and Television," in T. J. B. Spencer (ed.), *Shakespeare: A Celebration, 1564–1616*, Penguin: Baltimore, 1964, pp. 97–113.

Taylor, Neil, "The Films of *Hamlet,*" in Davies and Wells (eds.), *Shakespeare and the Moving Image,* pp. 180–95.

Thalberg, Irving, "Picturizing *Romeo and Juliet,*" in Romeo and Juliet *by William Shakespeare. A Motion Picture Edition*, New York: Random House, 1936: 13–15.

The Spectator, "Cinema [Castellani *Romeo*]," no. 6587 (24 Sept. 1954), 361.

Thompson, Ann, "Asta Nielsen and the Mystery of *Hamlet*," in Boose and Burt (eds.), *Shakespeare, The Movie*, pp. 215–224.

Thompson, Howard, "Jason Robards, *et al.* [Burge/Snell *JC*], " *NYT* 4 Feb. 1971, 30.

Tibbenham, Allwyn, "Shakespeare Today," in "Points from Letters," *The Listener* 17 March 1937, 521.

Tibbetts, John, "Breaking the Classical Barrier [Franco Zeffirelli Interviewed by John Tibbetts]," *LFQ* 22.2 (1994), 136–140.

Time, "*Macbeth* in Color," 13 Dec. 1954, 36.

"Review [Dieterle/Reinhardt *MND*]," 26 (21 Oct. 1935), 44–45.

"Review [Richardson *Hamlet*]," 93, 28 Feb. 1969, 74.

"The New Pictures [Review of Welles *Othello*]," 6 June 1955, 106.

Times, "A Shakespearian Experience on TV," 21 Apr. 1965, 13d.

"Continuity Problem of New B.B.C. Shakespeare Series," 4 May 1963, 5d.

"Review [*Hamlet* at Elsinore]," 20 Apr. 1964, 16.

"Review of BBC Old Vic *Macbeth*," 13 Dec. 1937.

"Televised Drama [Review of BBC *Othello*]," 15 Dec. 1937.

"Uneasy Lies the Head [Review *of An Age of Kings*]," 8 July 1960, 4g.

Tiruchelvam, Sharmini, "Encounter on the Field of Philippi," *The Daily Telegraph Magazine* 6 Feb. 1970, 14–17, 19, 21–22.

Variety, "Review [of Ghana *Hamile*]," 20.10 (1965).

"[Lor.] Review of Lange *Othello*," 31 May 1989.

"[Pit.] Review of Heston *Ant.*," 8 March 1972.

"[Pit.] Review of Coronado *Hamlet* at London Fest," 1 Dec. 1976.

"[Rich.] Starry Cast . . . Review Snell *JC*," 10 June 1970.

"[Strat.] Review of Kemp *MND*," 11 Nov. 1984.

"[Whit.] Review of Re-Release Taylor, *Shr.*," 2 Nov. 1966.

Vaughan, Virginia Mason, "The Forgotten Television *Tempest*," *SFNL* 9.1. (Dec. 1984), 3.

Walker, Alexander, "Review [Brook *Lr.*]," *Evening Standard*, 22 July 1971.

Walker, Elsie, "'Now is a time to storm': Julie Taymor's *Titus* (2000)". Unpub. Essay.

Walters, Ben, "O," *S&S* 12. 2 n.s. (Feb. 2002), 56–57.

Warner Brothers, Public relations kit in British Film Institute.

Wayne, Valerie, "*Shakespeare Wallah* and Colonial Specularity," in Boose and Burt (eds.), *Shakespeare, The Movie*, 95–101.

Weales, Gerald, "I Am Not Prince Hamlet," *Commonweal* 90, 30 May 1969, 319–20.

Weatherby, W. J., "Forgotten Heir of *Citizen Kane*," *Guardian* 28 Apr. 1992, 38.

Weiler, A. H., "Review [of Yutkevich *Oth.*]," *NYT* 16 May 1960, 39.

Weinraub, Bernard, "Interview with Polanski," *NYT Magazine* 12 Dec. 1971, 36+.

Welles, Orson ,"Interview," 1992 Voyager LD, Appendix #49.

Welsh, James M., "Shakespeare, With – and Without – Words," *LFQ* 1.1. (1973), 84–88.

Whitebait, William, "Romeo and Juliet at the Odeon," *New Statesman and Nation* (2 Oct. 1954), 390.

Wilds, Lillian, "On Film: Maximilian Schell's Most Royal *Hamlet*," *LFQ* 4.2 (1976), 134–40.

"One *King Lear* for Our Time: A Bleak Film Vision by Peter Brook," *LFQ* 4.2 (1976), 159–64.

Williams, Linda, "Sex and Sensation," in Nowell-Smith (ed.), *Oxford History of World Cinema*, pp. 490–96.

Willson, Robert F. Jr., "Disarming Scenes in *Richard III* & *Casablanca*," *SFNL* 10.1 (Dec. 1985), 4.

"Lubitsch's *To Be or Not to Be*," *SFNL* 1.1. (Dec. 1976), 2+.

"Shakespeare in *The Goodbye Girl*," *SFNL* 2.2. (Apr. 1978) 1+.

"The Opening of *Henry V*: Olivier's Visual Pun," *SFNL* 5.2. (May 1981): 1+.

Wilson, Richard, "*Macbeth* on Film [Welles]," *TA* 33.5 (June 1949), 53–55.

Wilson, J. Dover, "Shakespeare: The Scholar's Contribution," *The Listener*, 17 March 1937, 498+.

Wiseman, Susan, "The Family Tree Motel: Subliming Shakespeare in *My Own Private Idaho*," in Boose and Burt (eds.), *Shakespeare, The Movie*, 225–39.

World Film News, "Review of BBC *Julius Caesar*," 30 Aug. 1938.

Worthen, W. B., "Drama, Performativity, and Performance," *PMLA* 113.5 (Oct. 1998), 1093–1107.

Wrathall, John, "Bloody Arcades," *S&S* 10.7 n.s. (July 2000), 24.

Yardley, Jonathan, "The Metamorphosis of 'Henry'," *WP*, 26 Feb. 1990, C2.

WebSites

http://www.angelfire.com/movies/oc/titus.html

http://elvis.rowan.edu/~cassidy/pixel/

http://pro.imdb.com

http://www.telegraph.co.uk/news/main.jhtml?xml=/news/2003/08/17/wshakes17.xml

– CHRONOLOGICAL LIST OF FILMS –

Year	Title	Country	Director
1899	*Jn.*	UK	Dickson
1900	*Hamlet*	France	Maurice
1903	*Great Train Robbery*	USA	Porter
1907	*Ben Hur*	USA	n/a
1907	*Great Thaw Trial, The*	USA	n/a
1907	*Hamlet*	France	Méliès
1907	*JC (Shakespeare Writing Julius Caesar)*	France	Méliès
1908	*Ant*	USA	Kent
1908	*JC*	USA	Ranous
1908	*MV*	USA	Ranous
1908	*Nero and the Burning of Rome*	USA	Porter
1908	*Othello*	USA	Ranous
1908	*R3*	USA	Ranous
1908	*Rom.*	USA	Ranous
1909	*Cook Makes Madeira Sauce, The*	USA	n/a
1909	*Lr.*	USA	Ranous
1909	*Macbeth*	France	Calmettes
1909	*MND*	USA	Kent
1909	*Othello*	Italy	Savio
1910	*JC (Brutus)*	Italy	Guazzoni
1910	*Ant(Cleopatra)*	France	Zecca
1910	*MV (Mercante di Venezia, Il)*	Italy	Savio
1910	*Lr.*	Italy	Savio
1910	*Rom. (Romeo Turns Bandit)*	France	n/a
1910	*TN*	USA	Kent
1911	*JC*	UK	Benson/Barker
1911	*Lonedale Operator, The*	USA	Griffith
1911	*R3*	UK	Barker
1911	*Rom.*	Italy	Savio
1912	*AYL*	USA	Kent
1912	*H8 (Cardinal Wolsey)*	USA	Trimble
1912	*Quo Vadis*	Italy	Guazzoni
1912	*R3*	USA	Keane
1913	*Shr. (Bisbetica Domata, La)*	Italy	Ambrosio
1913	*Hamlet*	UK	Hepworth

Year	Title	Country	Director
1913	*Ant. (Marcantonio e Cleopatra)*	Italy	Guazzoni
1913	*MND*	Italy	Azzuri
1913	*MND*	Germany	Ewer
1913	*MV (Shylock)*	France	Desfontaines
1913	*WT (Tragedie alla Corte di Sicilia, Una)*	Italy	Negroni
1914	*Cabiria*	Italy	Pastrone
1914	*JC (Giulio Cesare) MV*	Italy	Guazzoni
1914	*Perils of Pauline, The*	USA	Gaznier/MacKenzie
1915	*Birth of a Nation, The*	USA	Griffith
1916	*Intolerance*	USA	Griffith
1916	*Lr.*	USA	Warde, E.
1916	*Macbeth*	USA	Griffith/Emerson
1916	*Rom.*	USA	Noble, J.
1916	*Rom.*	USA	Edwards
1917	*Hamlet*	Italy	Rodolfi
1919	*Cabinet of Dr. Caligari, The*	Germany	Wiene
1920	*Hamlet, The Drama of Vengeance*	Germany	Gade
1920	*Othello*	UK	Dyer
1921	*Carnival*	Uk	Knoles
1922	*Day Dreams*	USA	Keaton
1922	*Nosferatu*	Germany	Murnau
1922	*Othello*	Germany	Buchowetski
1923	*MV (Kaufmann von Venedig, Der)*	Germany	Felner
1924	*Last Laugh, The*	Germany	Murnau
1924	*Thief of Bagdad, The*	USA	Walsh
1925	*Street of Sorrow (Die freudlose Gasse)*	Germany	Pabst
1927	*Jazz Singer, The*	USA	Crosland
1927	*MV*	UK	Newman
1927	*Sunrise*	USA	Murnau
1927	*Way of All Flesh, The*	USA	Fleming
1928	*Passion of Joan of Arc*	France	Dreyer
1929	*Coquette*	USA	Taylor
1929	*Rom. (Hollywood Revue of 1929)*	USA	Reisner
1929	*H6 (Show of Shows (Excerpt))*	USA	Adolfi
1929	*Shr.*	USA	Taylor
1930	*Blue Angel, The*	Germany	von Sternberg
1930	*Man with Flower in Mouth*	UK	Baird
1930	*Hamlet (Royal Box, The)*	USA	Foy
1931	*M*	Germany	Lang
1933	*Hamlet (Morning Glory)*	USA	Sherman
1935	*Khoon Ka Khoon (Hamlet)*	India	Modi
1935	*MND*	USA	Dieterle/Reinhardt
1935	*Triumph of the Will*	Germany	Reifenstahl
1935	*Night at the Opera, A*	USA	Wood
1936	*AYL*	UK	Czinner
1936	*Oth. (Men Are Not Gods)*	UK	Reisch
1936	*Rom.*	USA	Cukor/Thalberg

Year	Title	Country	Director
1937	*AYL*	UK	Atkins
1937	*H5*	UK	O'Ferrall
1937	*Macbeth*	UK	O'Ferrall
1937	*Othello*	UK	O'Ferrall
1938	*Alexander Nevsky*	Russia	Eisenstein
1938	*JC*	UK	Bower
1939	*Gone with the Wind*	USA	Fleming
1939	*Stagecoach*	USA	Ford
1939	*Tmp.*	UK	Bower
1939	*Wizard of Oz*	USA	Fleming
1940	*Err. (Boys from Syracuse, The)*	USA	Sutherland
1941	*Citizen Kane*	USA	Welles
1942	*Magnificent Ambersons, The*	USA	Welles
1942	*Rom. (Shuhaddaa el Gharam)*	Egypt	Selim
1942	*Hamlet (To Be or Not to Be)*	USA	Lubitsch
1944	*Enfants du paradis, Les*	France	Carné
1944	*Grosse Künig, Der*	Germany	Harlan
1944	*H5*	UK	Olivier
1945	*Hamlet (Strange Illusion)*	USA	Ulmer
1946	*Lady from Shanghai, The*	USA	Welles
1946	*Hamlet (My Darling Clementine)*	USA	Ford
1947	*Oth. (Double Life, A)*	USA	Cukor
1947	*Hamlet*	UK	O'Farrell
1947	*Macbeth*	USA	Bradley
1948	*Rom. (Anjuman)*	India	Hussain
1948	*Hamlet*	UK	Olivier
1948	*Macbeth*	USA	Welles
1948	*Otello*	USA	Crotty
1948	*Terra trema, La*	Italy	Visconti
1949	*H5 (scene)*	USA	Demonstration for affiliates
1949	*JC*	USA	Miner/Nickell
1949	*Rom. (Les amants de Verone)*	France	Cayatte
1949	*Macbeth*	USA	Simpson/Brown
1949	*Third Man, The*	UK	Reed
1950	*Black Rose, The*	USA	Hathaway
1950	*JC*	USA	Bradley
1950	*Rashomon*	Japan	Kurosawa
1950	*Shr.*	USA	Miner/Nickell
1951	*Coriolanus*	USA	Miner/Nickell
1951	*Macbeth*	USA	Miner/Schaffner
1951	*Return to Glennascaul*	UK	Edwards
1952	*Othello*	Morocco Italy	Welles
1953	*Hamlet*	USA	Schaefer
1953	*JC*	USA	Mankiewicz/ Houseman

Year	Title	Country	Director
1953	*Shr. (Kiss Me Kate)*	USA	Sidney
1953	*Lr.*	USA	Brook
1954	*Macbeth*	USA	Schaefer
1954	*Prince of Players*	USA	Dunne
1954	*R2*	USA	Schaefer
1954	*Rom.*	UK/Italy	Castellani
1954	*Seven Samurai*	Japan	Kurosawa
1954	*La Strada*	Italy	Fellini
1955	*Hamlet*	India	Sahu
1955	*Mac. (Joe Macbeth)*	UK	Hughes
1955	*Othello*	Russia	Yutkevitch
1955	*R3*	UK	Olivier
1955	*TN*	Russia	Fried
1955	*Othello*	Russia	Yutkevitch
1955	*R3*	UK	Olivier
1955	*TN*	Russia	Fried
1956	*Tmp. (Forbidden Planet)*	USA	Wilcox
1956	*Shr.*	USA	Schaefer
1956	*Ten Commandments, The*	USA	DeMille
1957	*Mac. (Throne of Blood)*	Japan	Kurosawa
1957	*TN*	USA	Greene
1958	*Shr. (Kiss Me Kate)*	USA	Schaefer
1958	*Touch of Evil, A*	USA	Welles
1959	*Ben-Hur*	USA	Wyler
1959	*Hamlet (Der Rest ist Schweigen)*	Germany	Käutner
1959	*Hamlet*	USA	Nelson/Benthall
1959	*JC*	UK	Burge
1959	*MND*	CzechoSlovakia	Trnka
1959	*Some Like It Hot*	USA	Wilder
1960	*Hamlet (Bad Sleep Well, The)*	Japan	Kurosawa
1960	*Breathless*	France	Godard
1960	*Hamlet*	Germany	Wirth/Dmytryk
1960	*Macbeth*	USA	Schaefer
1960	*Magnificent Seven, The*	USA	Sturges
1960	*Tmp.*	USA	Schaefer
1961	*H6 (Age of Kings, An)*	UK	Dews/Hayes
1961	*Last Year at Marienbad*	France	Resnais
1961	*Rom. (Romanoff and Juliet)*	USA	Ustinov
1961	*Rom. (West Side Story)*	USA	Wise/Robbins
1961	*Yojimbo*	Japan	Kurosawa
1962	*Oth. (All Night Long)*	UK	Dearden
1962	*Rom. (And What If It's Love?)*	Russia	Raizman
1962	*Hamlet (Ophelia)*	France	Chabrol
1963	*Blowjob*	USA	Warhol
1963	*Ant. (Cleopatra)*	USA	Mankiewicz
1963	*Ricotta, La ("Curd-cheese")*	Italy	Pasolini
1963	*Cor. (Spread of the Eagle)*	UK	Dews

Year	Title	Country	Director
1964	*Dr. Strangelove*	USA	Kubrick
1964	*Hamlet (The Tongo Hamlet)*	Ghana	Bishop
1964	*Hamlet*	Russia	Kozintsev
1964	*Hamlet*	USA	Gielgud
1964	*Hamlet at Elsinore*	UK/Denmark	Luke/Saville
1964	*MND*	UK	Kemp-Welch
1964	*My Fair Lady*	USA	Cukor
1964	*Dr. Strangelove*	UK	Kubrick
1965	*Othello*	UK	Burge
1965	*Shakespeare Wallah*	India	Ivory
1965	*Sound of Music, The*	USA	Wise
1965	*H6 (Wars of the Roses)*	UK	Bakewell/Barton/ Hall
1966	*H4 (Chimes at Midnight)*	Spain/Switzerland	Welles
1966	*Conscience of the King*	USA	Oswald
1966	*Rom.*	UK	Drumm
1966	*Hamlet (Star Trek)*	USA	See *Hamlet*
1966	*Shr.*	USA	Zeffirelli
1967	*Dr. Faustus*	UK	Coghill, Burton
1967	*Elvira Madigan*	Sweden	Widerberg
1967	*Two or Three Things I Know about Her*	France	Godard
1968	*Blue Movie*	USA	Warhol
1968	*Rom.*	Italy/UK	Zeffirelli
1968	*Rosemary's Baby*	USA	Polanski
1969	*Hamlet*	UK	Richardson
1969	*Magic Show, The*	USA	Welles
1969	*MND*	UK	Birkett/Hall
1969	*MV*	n/a	Welles
1969	*Fellini Satyricon*	Italy	Fellini
1969	*Lr.*	Russia	Kozintsev
1970	*Hamlet*	UK	Wood
1970	*Hamlet,a Heranca*	Brazil	Candelas
1970	*JC*	UK	Snell/Burge
1970 (1975)	*Macbeth*	UK	Messina/Gorrie
1970	*MV*	UK	Miller
1970	*TN*	UK	Dexter/Sichel
1971	*Devils, The*	UK	Russell
1971	*Lr.*	UK	Brook
1971	*Macbeth*	UK	Polanski
1972 (1974)	*Ant.*	UK	Nunn/Scoffield
1972	*Ant.*	Spain/ Switzerland/UK	Heston
1972	*Discreet Charm of the Bourgeoisie*	France	Buñuel

Year	Title	Country	Director
1972	*TN*	USA	Wertheim
1973	*Ado*	USA	Papp/Antoon
1973	*Oth. (Catch My Soul: Santa Fe Satan)*	USA	McGoohan
1973	*F for Fake*	France	Welles
1973 (1977)	*Lr.*	USA	Papp/Sherin
1973	*R3 (Theater of Blood)*	UK	Hickox
1973	*MV*	UK	Miller/Olivier
1974	*Lr. (Harry and Tonto)*	USA	Mazurzky
1974	*Woman under the Influence, A*	USA	Cassavetes
1974	*Texas Chain Saw Massacre*	USA	Hooper
1975	*One Hundred Twenty Days of Sodom*	Italy	Pasolini
1975	*Sebastiane*	UK	Jarman/Humfress
1976 (1978)	*Err.*	UK	Nunn/Casson
1976	*Hamlet*	Spain/UK	Coronado
1976 (1979)	*Macbeth*	UK	Nunn/Casson
1976	*Rom.*	UK	Bosner
1976	*Shr.*	USA	Ball
1977	*R3 (Goodbye Girl, The)*	USA	Ross
1978 (1979)	*AYL*	UK	Messina/Coleman
1978	*Filming Othello*	Germany	Welles
1978	*Jubilee*	UK	Jarman
1978	*R2*	UK	Messina/Giles
1978 (1979)	*Rom.*	UK	Messina/Rakoff
1978	*Ti (I Spit on Your Grave)*	USA	Zarchi
1979 (1980)	*H41*	UK	Messina/Giles
1979 (1980)	*H42*	UK	Messina/Giles
1979 (1980)	*H5*	UK	Messina/Giles
1979	*H8*	UK	Messina/Billington
1979	*JC*	UK	Messina/Wise
1979	*MM*	UK	Messina/Davis
1979	*Wiv.*	USA	Taylor
1980	*Fame*	USA	Parker
1980	*Hamlet*	UK	Messina/Bennett
1980	*Mon oncle d'Amerique*	France	Resnais
1980 (1981)	*MV*	UK	Miller/Gold
1980	*Othello*	USA	White
1980	*Rom. (Romeu e Julieta)*	Brazil	Grisolli

Year	Title	Country	Director
1980	*Shadow Warrior, The*	Japan	Kurosawa
1980 (1981)	*Shr.*	UK	Miller
1980	*Tempest, The*	UK	Jarman
1980	*Tmp.*	UK	Messina/Gorrie
1980	*TN*	UK	Messina/Gorrie
1981	*Ant.*	UK	Miller
1981	*AWW*	UK	Miller/Moshinsky
1981	*Shr. (Kiss Me Petruchio)*	USA	Papp/Leach
1981	*Macbeth*	USA	Caldwell
1981	*Macbeth*	USA	Seidelman
1981 (1982)	*MND*	UK	Miller/Moshinsky
1981	*Othello*	UK	Miller
1981	*Shr.*	Canada	Dews
1981	*Tempest*	USA	Mazursky
1981	*Tim.*	UK	Miller
1981 (1982)	*Tro.*	UK	Miller
1981	*WT*	UK	Miller/Howell
1982	*Draughts-man's Contract,*	UK	Greenaway
1982	*The Fast Times at Ridgemont High School*	USA	Heckerling
1982	*Lr.*	UK	Sutton/Miller
1982	*MND*	USA	Papp/Lapine
1982	*R2*	USA	Woodman
1982	*Cymbeline*	UK	Sutton/Moshinsky
1983	*(Lr.) Dresser, The*	USA	Yates
1983 (1984)	*Err.*	UK	Sutton/Cellan-Jones
1983	*H6 (The Black Adder)*	UK	Atkinson
1983	*H6 1–3*	UK	Sutton/Howell
1983	*Lr.*	UK	Elliott
1983	*Macbeth.*	UK	Sutton/Gold
1983	*R3*	UK	Sutton/Howell
1983 (1984)	*TGV*	UK	Sutton/Taylor
1984	*Ado*	UK	Sutton/Burge
1984	*Coriolanus*	UK	Sutton/Moshinsky
1984	*Hamlet (Den tragiska historien om Hamlet, prinz av Danmark)*	Sweden	Lyth
1984	*Jewel in the Crown, The*	UK	Monahan/O'Brien
1984 (1985)	*Jn.*	UK	Sutton/Giles
1984	*MND*	Spain/UK	Coronado
1984	*Othello (Otelo de Oliveira)*	Brazil	Grisolli
1984	*Pericles.*	UK	Sutton/Jones
1984	*Playing Shakespeare*	UK	Barton
1985	*Ant.*	USA	Carra
1985	*LLL*	UK	Sutton/Moshinsky
1985	*Lr. (Ran)*	Japan	Kurosawa

Year	Title	Country	Director
1985	Tit.	UK	Sutton/Howell
1985	Tmp.	USA	Woodman
1986	Caravaggio	UK	Jarman
1986	Shr.	USA	MacKenzie
1986	Singing Detective, the	UK	Amiel
1987	Belly of an Architect, The	UK	Greenaway
1987	Err.	USA	Mosher/Woodruff
1987	Hamlet	UK	Kenyon/MacDonald
1987	Lr.	USA/Switzerland	Godard
1987	Rom.	USA	Thomas
1987	Othello (Otello)	USA/Italy	Zeffirelli
1988	Last of England, The	UK	Jarman
1988	Little Dorrit	UK	Edzard
1988	Othello	UK/South Africa	Suzman
1988	TN	UK	Branagh/Kafno
1988 (1989)	H6 (Wars of the Roses, The)	UK	Bogdanov
1989	MND (Dead Poets Society, The)	USA	Weir
1989	H5	UK	Branagh
1989	Jaded	USA	Kodar
1989	Othello	USA	Lange
1990	Tit. (Cook, the Thief, his Wife and Her Lover, The)	Nether-lands/France	Greenaway
1990	Hamlet (Discovering Hamlet)	UK	Olshaker
1990	Dreams	Japan	Kurosawa
1990	Lr. (Godfather III)	USA	Coppola
1990	Hamlet	USA	Kline/Browning
1990	Hamlet	USA	Zeffirelli
1990	Macbeth (Men of Respect)	USA	Reilly
1990	Rom. (Torn Apar)	USA	Fisher
1990's	Seinfeld	USA	Seinfeld
1991	Hamlet (Henna)	India/Pakistan	Kapoor
1991	Hamlet (L.A. Story)	USA	Jackson
1991	H4 (My Own Private Idaho)	USA	Van Sant
1991	Tmp. (Prospero's Books)	Netherlands/France/Italy	Greenaway
1991	Wiv.(The Braggart Samurai)	Japan	Nomura
1992	AYL	UK	Edzard
1992	Shakespeare: The Animated Tales	UK/Russia	Serebryakov/Edwards
1993	Ado	UK/USA	Branagh
1993	Blue	UK	Jarman
1993	Hamlet (Last Action Hero, The)	USA	McTiernan
1994	Hamlet (Lion King, The)	USA	Disney

Year	Title	Country	Director
1994	*Macbeth*	USA	Braunmuller/ Rodes
1994	*Natural Born Killers*	USA	Stone
1994	*Hamlet (Renaissance Man)*	USA	Marshall
1994	*Macbeth(Shakespeare on the Estate)*	UK	Bogdanov
1995	*Hamlet: For the Love of Ophelia*	USA (?)	Damiano
1995	*Hamlet (Midwinter's Tale, A) (In the Bleak Midwinter)*	UK	Branagh
1995	*MV*	UK	Horrox
1995	*Othello*	UK	Parker
1995	*R3*	UK	Loncraine
1995	*Clueless*	USA	Heckerling
1995	*Last Supper, The*	USA	Title
1996	*Evita*	USA	Parker
1996	*Hamlet*	UK	Branagh
1996	*R3 (Looking for Richard)*	USA	Pacino
1996	*MND*	UK	Noble
1996	*Romeo + Juliet; Romeo & Juliet*	USA	Luhrmann
1996	*TN*	UK	Nunn
1996	*Tromeo and Juliet*	USA	Kaufman
1997	*Macbeth*	Scotland	Freeston
1997	*Lr. (Thousand Acres, A)*	USA	Moorhouse
1997	*Macbeth on the Estate*	UK	Woolcock
1997	*Titus Andronicus: The Movie*	USA	Richey
1998	*Celebrity*	USA	Allen
1998	*Lr.*	UK	Eyre
1998	*Macbeth*	UK	Bogdanov
1998	*Tmp.*	USA	Bender
1999	*Elizabeth*	UK	Kapur
1999	*Hamlet (Let the Devil Wear Black)*	USA	Title
1999	*MND*	USA	Hoffman
1999	*Titus Andronicus*	USA	Dunne
1999	*Titus (Tit.)*	USA	Taymor
1999	*Shakespeare in Love*	UK	Madden
1999	*Shr.(10 Things I Hate about You)*	USA	Yunger
2000	*Hamlet*	USA	Simonson/ Budig
2000	*LLL*	UK/France/ USA	Branagh
2000	*Titus Andronicus*	USA	Griffin
2000	*Tit. (Behind the Scenes)*	USA	Hovde/ Meyer
2001	*Lr. (The King Is Alive)*	Denmark	Levring
2001	*Macbeth (Scotland,Pa)*	USA	Morrissette
2001	*MV*	UK	Nunn
2001	*MND Children's*	UK	Edzard
2001	*Much Ado about Something*	USA	Rubbo
2001	*Othello(O)*	USA	Nelson
2001	*Othello*	UK	Saxe

Year	Title	Country	Director
2002	*Lr. (King of Texas)*	USA	Edel
2002	*Maori MV*	New Zealand	Selwyn
2003	*Err. (Machiagini Kyogen)*	Japan	Nomura
2003	*In Search of Shakespeare (Doc.)*	UK	Wood
2004	*MV*	USA	Radford
2004	*MV*	USA	Stewart
n/a	*Mid-Slumber Night's Dream*	n/a	n/a
n/a	*Much Ado about Humping*	n/a	n/a

Abbreviations for multi-word Shakespeare titles follow the standard MLA format, e.g., *MND=A Midsummer Night's Dream*, but single word titles like *Othello* are not abbreviated. For several reasons, release dates may vary slightly from one country to another but an attempt has been made to select a plausible one when reliable sources are in conflict. When two dates appear, as with the BBC The Shakespeare Plays series, the first is the UK release date, the second the U.S. date. Surnames only of directors and key actors are given to help identify the film or television program. For ease of reference "Derivatives" have been filed under the titles of the Shakespearean plays that they grew out of (e.g., *The King Is Alive* will be found under *King Lear*), though in some instances (e.g., *The Prince of Players* and *Shakespeare Wallah*), for economy when segments from different plays appear in the production the title of only one may be listed. Non-Shakespearean films listed individually appear because they have been mentioned in the text to clarify cinematic contexts. Early silent films, some sound films, and primitive television prior to the use of the Kinescope may be permanently lost or archived in remote places so full information is not available. Only surnames of directors and actors appear but in most cases the given names will be found in the name index.

Other abbreviations are as follows:

Fsibw	Film silent black-and-white
Fsit	Film silent tinted
Fsdbw	Film sound black-and-white
Fsdc	Film sound color
Tvbw	Television black-and-white
Tvc	Television color. Tvbw and Tvc are also used for black-and-white or color videos that have never been transmitted on the air.
DVD	Many films listed as TV are now also available on DVD.
Prod. Co/Dist.	Denotes one or two, of what may be several, companies involved with either making or marketing the film.
Mins.	Duration, though running times will vary depending on the condition of the print and the speed of projection. Allow for some leeway, especially for older films.
n/a	Information unavailable.

Title	Country	Year	Director	Actor(s)	Type	Prod. Co/Dist.	Mins.	Pages
Ado	USA	1973	Papp/ Antoon	Waterston/ Widdoes/ Watson	Tvc	NY Shakespeare Fest./CBS	120	101
Ado	UK	1984	Sutton/ Burge	Lunghi/ Lindsay	Tvc	BBC Shakespeare Plays	150	114
Ado	UK/USA	1993	Branagh	Branagh/ Thompson	Fsdc	Goldwyn	111	238–41, 242, 244
Ado (Much Ado about Humping)	n/a	n/a	n/a	n/a	CD-ROM	n/a	n/a	218
Alexander Nevsky	Russia	1938	Eisenstein	Cherkassov	Fsdbw	Mosfilm	112	53, 71, 73, 87, 154
Ant.	USA	1908	Kent	Chapman	Fsibw	Vitagraph	10	7
Ant. (Cleopatra)	France	1910	Zecca	Roch	Fsibw	Pathé	12	4
Ant. (Marcantonio e Cleopatra)	Italy	1913	Guazzoni	Novelli/ Gonzales	Fsibw	Kleine	63	16
Ant. (Cleopatra)	USA	1963	Mankiewicz	Burton/Taylor	Fsdc	20th Cent. Fox	243	4
Ant. (Spread of the Eagle)	UK	1963	Dews	Pettingell	Tvbw	BBC	Serial	95, 96
Ant.	UK	1972 (1974)	Nunn/ Scoffield	Suzman/ Johnson	Tvc	ATV	162	105

Title	Country	Year	Director	Actor(s)	Type	Prod. Co/Dist.	Mins.	Pages
Ant.	Spain/Switzerland/UK	1972	Heston	Heston/Neil	Fsdc	Folio Films	160	153, 155–59
Ant.	UK	1981	Miller	Blakely/Lapotaire	Tvc	BBC Shakespeare Plays	177	109, 156
Ant.	USA	1985	Carra	Redgrave/Dalton	Tvc	Bard Prod.	183	116
AWW	UK	1981	Miller/Moshinsky	Johnson/Charleson	Tvc	BBC Shakespeare Plays	160	109–10
AYL	USA	1912	Kent	Coghlan	Fsibw	Vitagraph	30	7
AYL	UK	1936	Czinner	Olivier	Fsdbw	20th Century Fox	97	47–50
AYL	UK	1937	Atkins	Scott/Swinlay	Tvbw	BBC	11	91
AYL	UK	1978 (1979)	Messina/Coleman	Mirren/Pasco	Tvc	BBC Shakespeare Plays	150	107
AYL	UK	1992	Edzard	Cusack/Fox/Croft	Fsdc	Sands Films	117	47, 205–07, 220
Behind the Scenes (Tit.)	USA	2000	Hovde/Meyer	Taymor	Doc	First Run Features	30	27

Title	Country	Year	Director	Actor(s)	Type	Prod. Co/Dist.	Mins.	Pages
Belly of an Architect, The	UK	1987	Greenaway	Dennehy	Fsdc	Hemdale Releasing	118	199
Ben Hur	USA	1907	n/a	n/a	Fsibw	Kalem	10	12
Birth of a Nation, The	USA	1915	Griffith	Gish	Fsit	Mutual Film	120	20
Black Rose, The	USA	1950	Hathaway	Welles	Fsdbw	20th-Century Fox	120	76
Blowjob	USA	1963	Warhol	n/a	Fsdbw	The Factory	30	192
Blue	UK	1993	Jarman	Jarman	Fsdc	Basilisk Communications	76	198
Blue Angel, The	Germany	1930	Von Sternberg	Dietrich/ Jannings	FsdBw	UFA	98	25
Blue Movie	USA	1968	Warhol	Waldron, V & L.	Fsdbw	The Factory	133	192
Breathless	France	1960	Godard	Belmondo/ Seberg	Fsdbw	Imperia Films	89	202
Cabinet of Dr. Caligari, The	Germany	1919	Wiene	Krauss	Fsibw	Decla-Bioscop	60	22, 25, 74
Cabiria	Italy	1914	Pastrone	Pagano	Fsibw	Itala Film	140	16, 42
Caravaggio	UK	1986	Jarman	Terry/Cooper	Fsdc	British Film Institute	97	195

[331]

Title	Country	Year	Director	Actor(s)	Type	Prod. Co/Dist.	Mins.	Pages
Celebrity	USA	1998	Allen	Branagh	Fsdbw	Sweet-land/Miramax	113	234
Citizen Kane	USA	1941	Welles	Welles	Fsdbw	RKO Mercury	n/a	42, 57, 69, 70, 73, 74, 75, 76, 122
Clueless	USA	1995	Heckerling	Silverstone	Fsdc	Paramount	97	250
Cook Makes Madeira Sauce, The	USA	1909	n/a	n/a	Fsibw	n/a	n/a	6
Coquette	USA	1929	Taylor	Pickford	Fsdbw	United Artists	75	28
Coriolanus	USA	1951	Miner/Nickell	Greene/Evelyn	Tvbw	Westing-House Studio One, CBS	60	100
Coriolanus (Spread of the Eagle)	UK	1963	Dews	Pettingell	Tvbw	BBC	50	94, 95, 96
Coriolanus	UK	1984	Sutton/Moshinsky	Howard/Worth	Tvc	BBC Shakespeare Plays	150	113
Cymbeline	UK	1983 1982	Sutton/Moshinsky	Johnson/Bloom/Mirren	Tvc	BBC Shakespeare Plays	175	112
Devils, The	UK	1971	Russell	Reed/Redgrave	Fsdc	Warner Bros.	109	198

Title	Country	Year	Director	Actor(s)	Type	Prod. Co/Dist.	Mins.	Pages
Discreet Charm of the Bourgeoisie	France	1972	Buñuel	Rey	Fsdc	20th Century Fox	120	220
Dr. Faustus	UK	1967	Coghill/Burton	Taylor/Burton	Fsdc	Oxford Drama/Columbia	92	123
Dr. Strangelove	UK	1964	Kubrick	Sellers/Scott	Fsdc	Hawk Films	93	192, 258
Dreams	Japan	1990	Kurosawa	Terao/Scorsese	Fsdc	Warner/Spielberg	120	183
Elvira Madigan	Sweden	1967	Widerberg	Degermark	Fsdc	Jance Film	95	39
Elizabeth	UK	1999	Kapur	Blanchett	Fsdc	Gramercy Pictures	124	273
Enfants du paradis, Les	France	1944	Carné	Barrault	Fsdbw	Tricolore Films	144	125
Err. (The Boys from Syracuse)	USA	1940	Sutherland	Jones/Penner/Raye	Fsdbw	Universal	73	104, 215, 249
Err.	UK	1976 (1978)	Nunn/Casson	Dench/Annis	Tvc	ATV/RSC	130	104
Err.	UK	1983 1984	Sutton/Cellan-Jones	Gray/Cusack/Daltrey	Tvc	BBC Shakespeare Plays	110	113, 207
Err.	USA	1987	Mosher/Woodruff	Karamazov Brothers	Tvc	Lincoln Center/PBS	120	117

Title	Country	Year	Director	Actor(s)	Type	Prod. Co/Dist.	Mins.	Pages
Err.(Machiagino Kyogen)	Japan	2003	Nomura	Nomura	Tvc DVD	Hosaka, Chieko, and Mansuku Co.	100	272
Evita	USA	1996	Parker	Madonna	Fsdc	Cinergi Pictures	134	221
Fame	USA	1980	Parker	Cara	Fsdc	MGM/United Artists	130	217
Fast Times at Ridgemont High School	USA	1982	Heckerling	Penn	Fsdc	Refugee Films	90	254
Fellini Satyricon	Italy	1969	Fellini	Potter/Keller	Fsdc	Produzioni Europee Associati (PEA)	120	271
Forbidden Planet (Tmp.)	USA	1956	Wilcox	Pidgeon	Fsdc	MGM	96	210
Gone with the Wind	USA	1939	Fleming	Gable/Leigh	Fsdc	Selznick International	222	29
Great Thaw Trial, The	USA	1907	n/a	n/a	Fsibw	n/a	n/a	6
Great Train Robbery	USA	1903	Porter	Anderson	Fsibw	Edison	10	7
Grosse König, Der	Germany	1944	Harlan	n/a	Fsdbw	n/a	n/a	51

Title	Country	Year	Director	Actor(s)	Type	Prod. Co/Dist.	Mins.	Pages
H41–2 (Chimes at Midnight)	Spain/Switzerland	1966	Welles	Welles	Fsdbw	Internacionale/Peppercorn (US)	119	69, 84–85, 103, 108, 237
H41	UK	1979 (1980)	Messina/Giles	Finch/Gwillim	Tvc	BBC Shakespeare Plays	155	108
H42	UK	1979 (1980)	Messina/Giles	Finch/Gwillim	Tvc	BBC Shakespeare Plays	155	108
H41 and 2 (My Own Private Idaho)	USA	1991	Van Sant	Rhoenix/Reeves	Fsdc	Fine Line Features	102	192, 214
H5	UK	1937	O'Ferrall	Arnaud	Tvbw	BBC	16	92
H5	UK	1944	Olivier	Olivier	Fsdc	Two Cities	137	50–54, 58, 68, 75, 81, 87, 119, 156
H5 (scene)	USA	1949	Demonstration for affiliates	Wanamaker	Tvbw	NBC	n/a	100
H5	UK	1979 (1980)	Messina/Giles	McCowen Gwillim	Tvc	BBC Shakespeare Plays	170	108
H5	UK	1989	Branagh	Branagh/Thompson	Fsdc	Sam Goldwyn	135	135, 219, 234–38

Title	Country	Year	Director	Actor(s)	Type	Prod. Co/Dist.	Mins.	Pages
H6 3 (Show of Shows: Excerpt)	USA	1929	Adolfi	Barrymore	Fsdbw	Warner Bros.	120	38, 217
H6–R3 (Wars of the Roses)	UK	1965	Bakewell/ Barton/Hall	Warner, Holm, Ashcroft	Tvbw	BBC	Series	97
H6–R3 (The Black Adder)	UK	1983	BBC	Atkinson	Tv	BBC	Series	117
H6 1–3	UK	1983	Sutton/ Howell	Benson/ Cook/Foster	Tvc	BBC Shakespeare Plays	1–185 2–201 3–200	112
H6–H5 (Wars of the Roses)	UK	1988 (1989)	Bogdanov	Jarvis/ Pennington	Tvc	English Shakespeare Co.	Series	97
H8 (Cardinal Wolsey)	USA	1912	Trimble	Young	Fsibw	Vitagraph	10	7
H8	UK	1979	Messina/ Billington	Stride/Bloom	Tvc	BBC Shakespeare Plays	145	108
Hamlet	France	1900	Maurice	Bernhardt	Fsibw	Maurice	3	3
Hamlet	France	1907	Méliès	Méliès	Fsibw	Méliès	5	4
Hamlet	UK	1913	Hepworth	Forbes-Robertson	Fsibw	Gaumont	59	17
Hamlet	Italy	1917	Rodolfi	Ruggeri	Fsibw	Rodolfi-Film	40	14

Title	Country	Year	Director	Actor(s)	Type	Prod. Co/Dist.	Mins.	Pages
Hamlet (The Drama of Vengeance)	Germany	1920	Gade	Nielsen	Fsibw	Art-Film	117	21–25
Hamlet (Day Dreams)	USA	1922	Keaton	Keaton	Fsibw	Buster Keaton Prod.	30	216–17
Hamlet (The Royal Box)	USA	1930	Foy	Moissi	Fsibw	Warner Bros.	89	216
Hamlet (Morning Glory)	USA	1933	Sherman	Hepburn	Fsdbw	RKO	74	209, 217
Hamlet (Khoon Ka Khoon)	India	1935	Modi	Banu	Fsdbw	Stage Film	122	161
Hamlet (To Be or Not to Be)	USA	1942	Lubitsch	Benny	Fsdbw	United Artists	99	213
Hamlet (Strange Illusion)	USA	1945	Ulmer	Lydon	Fsdbw	PRC Pictures	80	210
Hamlet (My Darling Clementine)	USA	1946	Ford	Fonda/Mowbray	Fsdbw	20th-Century Fox	97	217
Hamlet	UK	1947	O'Ferrall	Byron/Shaw	Tvbw	BBC	180	57, 94
Hamlet	UK	1948	Olivier	Olivier	Fsdbw	Two Cities	155	54–59, 95, 108, 137, 139, 169

Title	Country	Year	Director	Actor(s)	Type	Prod. Co/Dist.	Mins.	Pages
Hamlet	USA	1953	Schaefer	Evans/Churchill	Tvbw	Hallmark	98	98
Hamlet (Prince of Players)	USA	1954	Dunne	Burton	Fsdc	20th-Century Fox	105	209, 216
Hamlet	India	1955	Sahu	Sahu/Sinha	Fsdbw	Hindustan Chitra	n/a	160–61
Hamlet	USA	1959	Nelson/Benthall	Neville/Jefford	Tvbw	DuPont Show of Month	90	99, 101
Hamlet (Der Rest ist Schweigen)	Germany	1959	Käutner	Kruger/Andree	Fsdbw	Frele Film	106	164
Hamlet	Germany	1960	Wirth/Dmytryk	Schell/Movar	Tvbw/Fsdbw	Bavaria Attelier	127	164
Hamlet (The Bad Sleep Well)	Japan	1960	Kurosawa	Mifune	Fsdbw	Toho	135	182–85, 187, 257
Hamlet (Ophelia)	France	1962	Chabrol	Valli/Jocelyn	Fsdbw	Boreal Pictures	105	169
Hamlet	Russia	1964	Kozintsev	Smoktunovsky/Vertinskaya	Fsdbw	LenFilm	148	170, 175–78
Hamlet	USA	1964	Gielgud	Burton/Cronan/Drake/Herlie	Electrono-vision	Classic Cinemas	199	102–03

Title	Country	Year	Director	Actor(s)	Type	Prod. Co/Dist.	Mins.	Pages
Hamlet (at Elsinore)	UK/Denmark	1964	Luke/Saville	Plummer/Shaw/Caine	Tvc	BBC/Danmark Radio	80	103
Hamlet (Hamile: The Tongo Hamlet)	Ghana	1964	Bishop	Kofi/Yirenki	Fsdbw	Ghana Film	120	161–62
Hamlet (Conscience of the King; The Undiscovered Country)	USA	1966 1991	Oswald	Adams/Moss	Tvc	Star Trek	30	117, 217
Hamlet	UK	1969	Richardson	Williamson/Parfitt/Hopkins	Fsdc	Woodfall	117	113, 131, 136–38, 166
Hamlet	UK	1970	Wood	Chamberlain/Redgrave	Tvc	Hallmark	115	98
Hamlet (a Heranca)	Brazil	1970	Candelas	Cardoso/Fazio	Fsdc	Longfilm	87	162
Hamlet	Spain/UK	1976	Coronado	Meyer/Mirren	Tvc	Cabochon	67	23, 192–94
Hamlet	UK	1980	Messina/Bennett	Jacobi/Bloom/Porter/Stewart	Tvc	BBC Shakespeare Plays	210	109

Title	Country	Year	Director	Actor(s)	Type	Prod. Co/Dist.	Mins.	Pages
Hamlet (Den tragiska historien om Hamlet, prinz av Danmark)	Sweden	1984	Lyth	Skarsgaard/Malm	Tvc	Rundquist	160	165–68
Hamlet	UK	1987	Kenyon/MacDonald	Hitchcock/Spaul	Tvc	Cambridge CCAT	96	117
Hamlet	USA	1990	Zeffirelli	Gibson/Close	Fsdc	Warner Bros.	135	131–35, 223, 243
Hamlet (Discovering Hamlet)	UK	1990	Olshaker	Branagh/Jacobi	Tvc	Renaissance Theatre Co.	53	217
Hamlet (Henna)	India/Pakistan	1991	Kapoor	Bakhtiar/Kapoor	Fsdc	n/a	n/a	162
Hamlet (L.A. Story)	USA	1991	Jackson	Martin	Fsdc	Rastar Prod.	95	217
Hamlet (The Last Action Hero)	USA	1993	McTiernan	Schwarzenegger	Fsdc	Columbia Tristar	131	132
Hamlet (Renaissance Man)	USA	1994	Marshall	DeVito	Fsdc	Cinergi Pictures	128	217
Hamlet (The Lion King)	USA	1994	Disney	Goldberg, Whoopi (Voice)	Animation	Disney	87	209, 217

Title	Country	Year	Director	Actor(s)	Type	Prod. Co/Dist.	Mins.	Pages
Hamlet (A Midwinter's Tale; In the Bleak Midwinter)	UK	1995	Branagh	Briers	Fsdbw	Rank	98	214, 234
Hamlet (For the Love of Ophelia)	USA (?)	1995	Damiano	Young	Tvc	n/a	n/a	218
Hamlet	UK	1996	Branagh	Branagh	Fsdc	Castle Rock/Columbia	242	58, 155, 255
Hamlet (Let the Devil Wear Black)	USA	1999	Title	Penner	Fsdc	New Moon Productions	89	255, 259, 263
Hamlet	USA	2000	Almereyda	Hawke/Stiles	Fsdc	Double A Films/Miramax	122	254–58
Hamlet	USA	2000	Simonson/Budig	Scott	Tvc	Hallmark Entertainment	178	258
In Search of Shakespeare	UK	2003	Wood	Wood	TvDoc	BBC1	c.180	273
Intolerance	USA	1916	Griffith	Gish	Fsibw	Griffith	123	16
Jaded	USA	1989	Kodar	Brady	Fsdc	Olpal Prod.	93	89
Jazz Singer, The	USA	1927	Crosland	Jolson	Fsdbw	Warner Brothers	89	27

Title	Country	Year	Director	Actor(s)	Type	Prod. Co/Dist.	Mins.	Pages
JC (Shakespeare Writing Julius Caesar)	France	1907	Méliès	Méliès	Fsibw	Méliès	10	4
JC	USA	1908	Ranous	Kent	Fsibw	Vitagraph	13	7, 9, 16
JC (Brutus)	Italy	1910	Guazzoni	Novelli	Fsibw	Cines	8	16
JC	UK	1911	Benson/ Barker	Benson	Fsibw	Co-op Cine-matographer	10	17
JC (Quo Vadis)	Italy	1912	Guazzoni	n/a	Fsibw	n/a	n/a	17, 20
JC (Giulio Cesare)	Italy	1914	Guazzoni	Gonzales	Fsibw	Cines	60	16
JC	UK	1938	Bower	Milton	Tvbw	BBC	141	92
JC	USA	1949	Miner/ Nickell	Keith/Heston	Tvbw	CBS Studio One	60	100
JC	USA	1950	Bradley	Heston	Fsdbw	Avon Prod.	90	156
JC	USA	1953	Mankiewicz/ Houseman	Brando/ Gielgud	Fsdbw	MGM	121	27, 42–46, 208, 209
JC	UK	1959	Burge	Sylvester/Porter	Tvbw	BBC	115	153
JC (Spread of the Eagle)	UK	1963	Dews	Pettingell	Tvbw	BBC	Serial	94–96

Title	Country	Year	Director	Actor(s)	Type	Prod. Co/Dist.	Mins.	Pages
JC	UK	1970	Snell/Burge	Heston/Rigg/Robards/Gielgud	Fsdc	Commonwealth United	117	89, 153–55
JC (Theatre of Blood)	UK	1973	Hickox	Price	Tvc	United Artists	104	209, 216
JC	UK	1979	Messina/Wise	Pasco/Michell/Gray	Tvc	BBC Shakespeare Plays	180	107, 110
Jewel in the Crown, The	UK	1984	Monahan/O'Brien	Pigott-Smith/Ashcroft	Tvc	BBC	700 (14 Episodes)	220
Jn.	UK	1899	Dickson	Tree	Fsibw	British Mutoscope	1	1
Jn.	UK	1984 1985	Sutton/Giles	Rossiter/Bloom	Tvc	BBC Shakespeare Plays	155	114
Jubilee	UK	1978	Jarman	Runacre	Fsdc	Cinegate	103	195
Lady from Shanghai, The	USA	1946	Welles	Hayworth	Fsdbw	Columbia	155/86	70
La Strada	Italy	1954	Fellini	Quinn/Baseheart	Fsdc	Ponti-De Laurentiis Cinematografica	115	271
Last Laugh, The	Germany	1924	Murnau	Jannings	Fsibw	UfA	n/a	10

Title	Country	Year	Director	Actor(s)	Type	Prod. Co/Dist.	Mins.	Pages
Last of England, The	UK	1988	Jarman	Swinton	Fsdbw	BFI (?)	87	140, 197, 207
Last Supper, The	USA	1995	Title	Diaz/Penner	Fsdc	Columbia	92	259
Last Year at Marienbad	France	1961	Resnais	Seyrig	Fsdbw	Astor Pictures	93	199
Little Dorrit	UK	1988	Edzard	Guinness/Jacobi	Fsdc	Sands Film	356–2 parts	206
LLL	UK	1985	Sutton/Moshinsky	Gwilym/Warner	Tvc	BBC Shakespeare Plays	120	114
LLL	UK/France/USA	2000	Branagh	Branagh	Fsdc	Arts Council/Miramax	93	249
Lonedale Operator, The	USA	1911	Griffith	Sweet	Fsibw	Biograph	10	7
Looking for Richard (R3)	USA	1996	Pacino	Pacino/Baldwin	Fsdc	20th Century Fox	109	209, 216
Lr.	USA	1909	Ranous	Ranous	Fsibw	Vitagraph	15	7, 9
Lr.	Italy	1910	Savio	Novelli	Fsibw	Film d'Arte Italiana	11	14
Lr.	USA	1916	Warde, E.	Warde, F.	Fsibw	Thanhouser	43	22, 146, 180, 182

Title	Country	Year	Director	Actor(s)	Type	Prod. Co/Dist.	Mins.	Pages
Lr.	USA	1953	Brook	Welles	Tvbw	Omnibus	73	79–80, 142, 182
Lr.	Russia	1969	Kozintsev	Yarvet/Shendrikova	Fsdbw	USSR	140	170, 174, 178–82
Lr.	UK	1971	Brook	Scofield	Fsdbw	Filmways/Athene	137	79, 142–46, 178
Lr.	USA	1973 (1977)	Papp/Sherin	Jones/Julia/Watson	Tvbw	Theatre in America; NY Shakespeare Fest.	120	101
Lr. (Harry and Tonto)	USA	1974	Mazurzky	Carney	Fsdc	20th-Century Fox	115	211
Lr.	UK	1983	Elliott	Olivier	Tvc	Granada TV	158	67–68, 111
Lr. (The Dresser)	USA	1983	Yates	Finney/Courtenay	Fsdc	Columbia	118	111
Lr. (Ran)	Japan	1985	Kurosawa	Nakadai	Fsdc	Greenway Film/Nippon	160	188–91, 203
Lr.	USA/Switzerland	1987	Godard	Meredith	Fsdc	Cannon	95	202–05
Lr. (Godfather III)	USA	1990	Coppola	Pacino	Fsdc	Paramount	163	210, 216
Lr. (A Thousand Acres)	USA	1997	Moorhouse	Lange	Fsdc	Beacon Comm.	105	214

Title	Country	Year	Director	Actor(s)	Type	Prod. Co/Dist.	Mins.	Pages
Lr.	UK	1998	Eyre	Holm	Tvc	BBC/Masterpiece Theatre	150	264
Lr. (The King Is Alive)	Denmark	2001	Levring	Anderson	Fsdc	IFC Films	118	266
Lr. (King of Texas)	USA	2002	Edel	Stewart	Tvc	TNT (Turner Network)	93	267
M	Germany	1931	Lang	Lorre	Fsdbw	A. G. Ver/Star Film	89	144
Macbeth	France	1909	Calmettes	Mounet	Fsibw	Film d'Art	10	4
Macbeth	USA	1916	Griffith/Emerson	Tree	Fsibw	Triangle	45 (?)	102
Macbeth	UK	1937	O'Ferrall	Olivier/Anderson	Tvbw	BBC/Old Vic	30	66, 92
Macbeth	USA	1947	Bradley	Bradley	Fsdbw	Willow Prod.	73	70, 153
Macbeth	USA	1948	Welles	Welles	Fsdbw	Republic	89	27, 45, 69, 70–74, 76
Macbeth	USA	1949	Simpson/Brown	Hampden, Bellamy	Tvbw	NBC TV	60	100

Title	Country	Year	Director	Actor(s)	Type	Prod. Co/Dist.	Mins.	Pages
Macbeth	USA	*1951*	Miner/Schaffner	Heston/Evelyn	Tvbw	Westinghouse Studio One, CBS	60	100
Macbeth	USA	*1954*	Schaefer	Evans/Anderson	Tvc	Hallmark	103	98, 99
Macbeth (Joe Macbeth)	UK	*1955*	Hughes	Douglas/Roman	Fsdbw	Columbia	107	209
Macbeth (Throne of Blood)	Japan	*1957*	Kurosawa	Mifune	Fsdbw	Toho Productions	110	160, 182, 185–89, 190, 197, 208
Macbeth	USA	*1960*	Schaefer	Evans/Anderson	Fsdc/For TV	Hallmark	107	98, 99
Macbeth	UK	*1970 (1975)*	Messina/Gorrie	Porter/Suzman	Tvc	PBS Classic Theatre	137	105
Macbeth	UK	*1971*	Polanski	Finch/Annis	Fsdc	Playboy	140	108, 133, 146–53, 187
Macbeth	UK	*1976 (1979)*	Nunn/Casson	Dench/McKellen	Tvc	Thames TV	120	106
Macbeth	USA	*1981*	Caldwell	Anglim/Anderman	Tvc	Lincoln Center	148	117

Title	Country	Year	Director	Actor(s)	Type	Prod. Co/Dist.	Mins.	Pages
Macbeth	USA	1981	Seidelman	Brett/Piper	Tvc	Bard Prod.	150	116
Macbeth	UK	1983	Sutton/Gold	Williamson/Lapotaire	Tvc	BBC Shakespeare Plays	150	73, 113, 137
Macbeth (Men of Respect)	USA	1990	Reilly	Turturro/Steiger	Fsdc	Central City/Columbia	107	210
Macbeth	USA	1994	Braunmuller/Rodes	Rodes	CD/ROM	Voyager	n/a	118
Macbeth on the Estate	UK	1997	Woolcock	Winstone	Tvc	n/a	n/a	27
Macbeth	UK	1998	Bogdanov	Pertwee	Tvc	Channel 4 Granada TV	87	263
Macbeth (Scotland, PA)	USA	2001	Morrissette	Walken/LeGros/Tierney	Fsdc	Lot 47 Films	104	261
Magic Show, The	USA	1969	Welles	n/a	n/a	n/a	Unfinished	69
Magnificent Ambersons, The	USA	1942	Welles	Welles/Cotton/Costello	Fsdbw	Republic/RKO	131/88	69, 70, 73, 74, 84
Magnificent Seven, The	USA	1960	Sturges	Brynner/McQueen	Fsdc	Alpha/Mirisch	126	238, 239, 241
Man with Flower in Mouth	UK	1930	Baird	Pirandello	Tvbw	Baird	n/a	91

Title	Country	Year	Director	Actor(s)	Type	Prod. Co/Dist.	Mins.	Pages
MM	UK	1979	Messina/Davis	Nelligan/Pigott-Smith	Tvc	BBC Shakespeare Plays	150	107, 109
MND	USA	1909	Kent	Costello	Fsibw	Vitagraph	11	6, 10
MND	Italy	1913	Azzuri	Tommasi	Fsibw	Artistic Cinema Negatives	22	14, 16
MND	Germany	1913	Ewer	Berger	Fsibw	Deutsche Bioscop	45	22
MND	USA	1935	Dieterle/Reinhardt	Cagney/Rooney	Fsdbw	Warner Bros.	132	22, 27, 33–37, 141, 194
MND	Czecho-slovakia	1959	Trnka	Burton (Voice)	Fsibw	Cescoslovensky	74	217
MND	UK	1964	Kemp-Welch	Hill	Tvbw	Rediffusion	111	104
MND	UK	1969	Birkett/Hall	Warner/Rigg/Mirren	Fsdc	RSC Ent./Alan Clore	124	136, 140–42
MND	UK	1981 1982	Miller/Moshinsky	Mirren/Davenport	Tvc	BBC Shakespeare Plays	120	110, 194
MND	USA	1982	Papp/Lapine	Venora/DeMunn	Tvc	ABC Video	165	114
MND	Spain/UK	1984	Coronado	Kemp/Testory/Meyer	Fsdc	Cabochon	72	35, 192, 194–95

Title	Country	Year	Director	Actor(s)	Type	Prod. Co/Dist.	Mins.	Pages
MND	UK	1996	Noble	Jennings/Duncan	Fsdc	Channel Four Films	103	232–34
MND	USA	1999	Hoffman	Kline	Fsdc	Fox Searchlight	115	251
MND (Mid-Slumber Night's Dream)	n/a	n/a	n/a	n/a	CD-ROM	n/a	n/a	218
MND (The Dead Poets Society)	USA	1989	Weir	Williams	Fsdc	Touchstone	129	217
MND Children's	UK	2001	Edzard	Peachey	Fsdc	Sands Films	115	253
Mon oncle d'Amérique	France	1980	Resnais	Depardieu	Fsdc	Home Film Festival	123	199
Much Ado about Something	USA	2001	Rubbo	Ryelance	Doc.	The Helpful Eye/Chili Films/Australian Broadcasting Co.	93	273
MV	USA	1908	Ranous	Turner	Fsibw	Vitagraph	10	7
MV(Il Mercante di Venezia)	Italy	1910	Savio	Bertini	Fsit	Film d'Arte Italiana	10	14
MV (Shylock)	France	1913	Desfontaines	Baur	Fsibw	Film d'Art	22	13

Title	Country	Year	Director	Actor(s)	Type	Prod. Co/Dist.	Mins.	Pages
MV (Der Kaufmann von Venedig)	Germany	1923	Felner	Krauss/Porten	Fsibw	Felner	64	26
MV	UK	1927	Newman	Casson	Fsdbw	DeForest Phonofilms	10	28
MV	n/a	1969	Welles	Gray	Fsd	Never completed	n/a	89
MV	UK	1973	Miller	Olivier	Tvc	Precision Video	120	66, 104
MV	UK	1980 (1981)	Miller/Gold	Mitchell/Jones	Tvc	BBC Shakespeare Plays	160	110
MV	UK	1995	Horrox	Peck/Gwynne	Tvc	Tetra Films	81	117
MV	UK	2001	Nunn	Goodman/Crotty	Tvc	Ntl. Theatre/PBS	120	268
MV (Maori)	New Zealand	2002	Selwyn	Shortland	Fsdc	He Taonga Films	170	272
MV	USA	2004	Radford	Pacino/McKellen/Fiennes	Fsdc	In production	n/a	274
MV	USA	2004	Stewart	Stewart	Fsdc	In production	n/a	274
My Fair Lady	USA	1964	Cukor	Harrison/Hepburn	Fsdc	MGM	170	58

Title	Country	Year	Director	Actor(s)	Type	Prod. Co/Dist.	Mins.	Pages
Natural Born Killers	USA	1994	Stone	Harrelson/Lewis	Fsdc	Warner Bros.	119	40
Nero and the Burning of Rome	USA	1908	Porter	n/a	Fsibw	Edison	10	5
Night at the Opera, A	USA	1935	Wood	Marx Bros.	Fsdc	MGM	96	250
Nosferatu	Germany	1922	Murnau	Schreck	Fsibw	Prana-Film	63	33, 196
One Hundred Twenty Days of Sodom	Italy	1975	Pasolini	Bonacelli/Cataldi	Fsdc	Peppercorn/Wormser	117	192
Othello	USA	1908	Ranous	Ranous	Fsibw	Vitagraph	10	7
Othello	Italy	1909	Savio	Garavaglia	Fsibw	Film d'Arte Italiana	16	14
Othello	UK	1920	Dyer	Animation	Fsibw	Hepworth	10	217
Othello (Carnival)	UK	1921	Knoles	Lang/Bayley	Fsibw	Alliance Films	54	212
Othello	Germany	1922	Buchowetski	Jannings	Fsibw	Wörner-Film	98	21, 25, 226
Othello (Men Are Not Gods)	UK	1936	Reisch	Hopkins/Harrison	Fsdbw	United Artists	110	212
Othello	UK	1937	O'Ferrall	Johnson/Holloway	TVbw	BBC	67	94

Title	Country	Year	Director	Actor(s)	Type	Prod. Co/Dist.	Mins.	Pages
Othello (A Double Life)	USA	1947	Cukor	Colman	Fsdbw	Universal	103	209, 213
Othello (Otello)	USA	1948	Crotty	Albanese/Warren	Tvbw	ABC TV	240	98
Othello	Morocco Italy	1952	Welles	Welles	Fsdbw	Mogador/Mercury	91	69, 72, 74–80, 172, 174, 224, 226
Othello	Russia	1955	Yutkevitch	Bondarchuk/Skobtseva	Fsdc	MosFilm	108	170, 172–74
Othello (All Night Long)	UK	1962	Dearden	McGoohan/Michell	Fsdbw	Rank	82	163, 212, 215
Othello	UK	1965	Burge	Olivier	Fsdc	BHE/Eagle	166	64–66, 208–09
Othello (Shakespeare Wallah)	India	1965	Ivory	Kendal/Kapoor	Fsdc	Merchant/Ivory	124	160, 214
Othello (Catch My Soul: Santa Fe Satan)	USA	1973	McGoohan	Havens/LeGault	Fsdc	Metro-media	100	215
Othello (Filming)	Germany	1978	Welles	Welles	Tvbw	Hellwig	84	79
Othello	USA	1980	White	Kotto/Dixon	Fsdc	Howard University	115	205–06

Title	Country	Year	Director	Actor(s)	Type	Prod. Co/Dist.	Mins.	Pages
Othello	UK	1981	Miller	Hopkins/Hoskins	Tvc	BBC Shakespeare Plays	210	110
Othello (Otelo de Oliveira)	Brazil	1984	Grisolli	Bonfim/Lemmertz	Tvc	TV Globo	120	163
Othello (Otello)	USA/Italy	1987	Zeffirelli	Domingo	Fsdc	Cannon Group	123	123, 209
Othello	UK/South Africa	1988	Suzman	Kani/Haines	Tvc	Focus/Portobello	199	114, 205
Othello	USA	1989	Lange	Lange/James	Fsdc	Rockbottom Productions	120	206
Othello	UK	1995	Parker	Fishburne/Jacob/Branagh	Fsdc	Rank/Castle Rock	123	135, 224–26, 234
Othello	UK	2001	Sax	Hawes	Tvc	CBC/Masterpiece Theatre	100	260–61
Othello (O)	USA	2001	Nelson	Stiles/Phifer	Fsdc	Lions Gate Films	91	256, 259
Passion of Joan of Arc	France	1928	Dreyer	Falconetti	Fsibw	Société Generale de film	114	169
Pericles	UK	1984	Sutton/Jones	Gwilym/Peacock	Tvc	BBC Shakespeare Plays	180	113
Perils of Pauline, The	USA	1914	Gaznier/MacKenzie	Panzer/White	Fsibw	Pathé	Serial	8

Title	Country	Year	Director	Actor(s)	Type	Prod. Co/Dist.	Mins.	Pages
Playing Shakespeare	UK	1984	Barton	Multiple actors	Tvc	Channel Four	30 (each)	118, 218
Prince of Players	USA	1954	Dunne	Burton	Fsdc	20th-Century Fox	105	209, 216
R2	USA	1954	Schaefer	Evans/Churchill	Tvbw	Hallmark	120	98, 99
R2	UK	1978 (1979)	Messina/Giles	Jacobi/Gielgud	Tvc	BBC/ShakeSpeare Plays	180	103, 107, 108–09, 110
R2	USA	1982	Woodman	Birney/Hammond	Tvc	Bard Prod.	172	116
R2–R3 (Age of Kings)	UK	1961	Dews/Hayes	Atkins/Warner	Tvbw	BBC	Series	95–96
R3	USA	1908	Ranous	Turner	Fsibw	Vitagraph	10	7
R3	UK	1911	Barker	Benson	Fsibw	Cooperative Cinematographer	15	19
R3	USA	1912	Keane	Warde	Fsibw	Dudley	55	17–20
R3	UK	1955	Olivier	Olivier	Fsdc	London Film Prod.	158	59–64, 68, 101, 134
R3 (The Goodbye Girl)	USA	1977	Ross	Dreyfuss	Fsdc	Rastar	110	213

Title	Country	Year	Director	Actor(s)	Type	Prod. Co/Dist.	Mins.	Pages
R3	UK	1983	Sutton/ Howell	Cook/ Wanamaker	Tvc	BBC Shakespeare Plays	230	112
R3	UK	1995	Loncraine	McKellen/ Smith	Fsdc	United Artists	104	115, 219–24
R3 (Looking for Richard)	USA	1996	Pacino	Pacino/ Baldwin	Fsdc	20th Century Fox	109	209, 216
Rashomon	Japan	1950	Kurosawa	Mifune	Fsdbw	Daiei Productions	88	183
Return to Glennascaul	UK	1951	Edwards	Welles	Fsdbw	n/a	n/a	76
Ricotta, La (Curd-cheese)	Italy	1963	Pasolini	n/a	Fsdbw	n/a	15 (?)	192
Rom.	USA	1908	Ranous	Panzer/ Lawrence	Fsibw	Vitagraph	15	7, 8
Rom. (Romeo Turns Bandit)	France	1910	n/a	n/a	Fsibw	Pathé	6	4
Rom.	Italy	1911	Savio	Bertini	Fsibw	Film d'Arte Italiana	25	15
Rom.	USA	1916	Noble, J.	Bushman/ Bayne	Fsibw	Metro	80	21
Rom.	USA	1916	Edwards	Hilliard/Bara	Fsibw	Fox	50	21, 231

Title	Country	Year	Director	Actor(s)	Type	Prod. Co/Dist.	Mins.	Pages
Rom. (Hollywood Revue of 1929)	USA	1929	Reisner	Gilbert/Shearer	Fsdbw	MGM	113	217
Rom.	USA	1936	Cukor/Thalberg	Shearer/Howard	Fsdbw	MGM	126	27, 37–42, 127, 136
Rom. (Shuhaddaa el Gharam)	Egypt	1942	Selim	Mourad	Fsdbw	Films el Nil	90	162
Rom. (Anjuman)	India	1948	Hussain	Nargis/Jaraj	Fsdbw	Nargis Art	140	162
Rom. (Les amants de Verone)	France	1949	Cayatte	Reggiani/Aimée	Fsdbw	Films de France	110	169
Rom.	UK/Italy	1954	Castellani	Harvey/Shentall	Fsdc	Verona Productions	138	119–26, 162, 231
Rom. (Romanoff and Juliet)	USA	1961	Ustinov	Ustinov/Dee	Fsdc	Universal/International	112	221
Rom. (West Side Story)	USA	1961	Wise/Robbins	Wood	Fsdc	United Artist	151	162, 168, 209, 215
Rom. (And What If It's Love?)	Russia	1962	Raizman	n/a	Fsdc (?)	USSR	n/a	170
Rom.	UK	1966	Drumm	Francis/Scoular	Fsdbw	RADA	107	208

Title	Country	Year	Director	Actor(s)	Type	Prod. Co/Dist.	Mins.	Pages
Rom.	Italy/UK	1968	Zeffirelli	Hussey/Whiting	Fsdc	BHE/Dino De Laurentiis	152	107, 126–31, 135, 136, 162, 215, 229, 231
Rom.	UK	1976	Bosner	McEnery/Badel	Tvc	St. George's Playhouse	170	107
Rom.	UK	1978 (1979)	Messina/Rakoff	Ryecart/Saire/Johnson	Tvc	BBC Shakespeare Plays	170	107
Rom. (*Romeu e Julieta*)	Brazil	1980	Grisolli	Junior/Santos	Tvc	TV Globo	94	162–63
Rom.	USA	1987	Thomas	n/a	Tvc	n/a	n/a	218
Rom.(*Torn Apart*)	USA	1990	Fisher	Pasdar/Peck	Fsdc	Castle Hill	95	162
Rom. (*Romeo + Juliet; Romeo & Juliet*)	USA	1996	Luhrmann	DiCaprio/Danes	Fsdc	20th-Century Fox	120	135, 215, 229–34
Rom. (*Tromeo and Juliet*)	USA	1996	Kaufman	Jensen/Keenan	Fsdc	Troma Inc.	107	218

Title	Country	Year	Director	Actor(s)	Type	Prod. Co/Dist.	Mins.	Pages
Rosemary's Baby	USA	1968	Polanski	Farrow/Cassavetes/Gordon	Fsdc	Paramount	136	147
Sebastiane	UK	1975	Jarman/Humfress	Treviglio	Fsdc	Discopat	85	195
Seinfeld	USA	1990s	NBC	Seinfeld	Tv	NBC	Series	98
Seven Samurai	Japan	1954	Kurosawa	Mifune	Fsdbw	Toho	207	193–194, 184–85
Shadow Warrior, The	Japan	1980	Kurosawa	Nakadai	Fsdbw	Kurosawa/Toho	162	183
Shakespeare in Love	UK	1999	Madden	Fiennes/Paltrow	Fsdc	Miramax/Universal	113	248
Shakespeare on the Estate	UK	1994	Bogdanov	n/a	Tvc	n/a	n/a	264
Shakespeare Wallah	India	1965	Ivory	Kendal/Kapoor	Fsdc	Merchant/Ivory	124	160, 214
Shakespeare: The Animated Tales	UK/Russia	1992	Serebryakov/Edwards	Animations	Tvc	Island World Video	30 (each)	217
Shr. (La Bisbetica Domata)	Italy	1913	Ambrosio	Rodolfi	Fsibw	Ambrosio.	40	14
Shr.	USA	1929	Taylor	Pickford/Fairbanks	Fsdbw	United Artists	68	5, 27–32, 48, 118

Title	Country	Year	Director	Actor(s)	Type	Prod. Co/Dist.	Mins.	Pages
Shr. (Kiss Me Kate)	USA	*1950*	Miner/Nickell	Heston/Kirk	Tvbw	Westinghouse Studio One, CBS	60	100
Shr.	USA	*1953*	Sidney	Keel/Grayson	Fsdc	MGM	109	215
Shr.	USA	*1956*	Schaefer	Evans/Palmer	Tvc	Hallmark	90	98, 99
Shr. (Kiss Me Kate)	USA	*1958*	Schaefer	Drake/Morrison	Tvbw	Hallmark	90	98
Shr.	USA/Italy	*1966*	Zeffirelli	Taylor/Burton	Fsdc	Royal Films	121	28, 123–26, 132, 133
Shr.	USA	*1976*	Ball	Singer/Olster	Tvc	Am. Cons. Theatre	82	101
Shr.	UK	*1980 1981*	Miller	Cleese/Badel	Tvc	BBC Shakespeare Plays	125	125
Shr. (Kiss Me Petruchio)	USA	*1981*	Papp/Leach	Streep/Julia	Tvc	NY Shakespeare Fest.	58	118
Shr.	Canada	*1981*	Dews	Cariou/Flett	Tvc	Stratford Fest.	153	116
Shr.	USA	*1986*	MacKenzie	Willis/Shepherd	Tvc	ABC-TV "Moonlighting"	20 (?)	117

Title	Country	Year	Director	Actor(s)	Type	Prod. Co/Dist.	Mins.	Pages
Shr. (*10 Things I Hate about You*)	USA	1999	Yunger	Stiles	Fsdc	Touchstone Pictures	97	254, 256
Singing Detective, The	UK	1986	Amiel	Gambon	Tvc	BBC	360 (6 episodes)	220
Some Like It Hot	USA	1959	Wilder	Lemmon/ Monroe	Fsdc	Ashton Productions	120	271
Sound of Music, The	USA	1965	Wise	Andrews	Fsdc	20th Century Fox	172	245
Spread of the Eagle (*Ant., Cor., JC*)	UK	1963	Dews	Hardy/ Michell	Tvbw	BBC	Series	96
Stagecoach	USA	1939	Ford	Wayne	Fsdbw	United Artists	99	70
Star Trek	USA	1966 1991						See *Hamlet*
Street of Sorrow (*Die freudlose Gasse*)	Germany	1925	Pabst	Garbo/ Nielsen	Fsibw	n/a	n/a	21
Sunrise	USA	1927	Murnau	Gaynor	Fsibw	Fox	90	21
Ten Commandments	USA	1956	DeMille	Heston/ Brynner	Fsdbw	MGM	219	42, 156

Title	Country	Year	Director	Actor(s)	Type	Prod. Co/Dist.	Mins.	Pages
Terra trema, La	Italy	1948	Visconti	Non-professionals	Fsdbw	Universalis	160	127
Texas Chain Saw Massacre	USA	1974	Hooper	Burns/Danziger	Fsdc	Vortex	83	271
TGV	UK	1983 1984	Sutton/Taylor	Hudson/Butterworth	Tvc	BBC Shakespeare Plays	135	113
Theatre of Blood	UK	1973	Hickox	Price	Tvc	United Artists	104	209, 216
Thief of Bagdad, The	USA	1924	Walsh	Fairbanks	Fsibw	United Artists	140	28, 29, 123
Third Man, The	UK	1949	Reed	Welles	Fsdbw	London Films	104	76
Tim.	UK	1981	Miller	Price/Sharpnel	Tvc	BBC Shakespeare Plays	130	110
Tit.	UK	1985	Sutton/Howell	Peacock/Calder-Marshall	Tvc	BBC Shakespeare Plays	150	114
Tit. (The Cook, the Thief, His Wife and Her Lover)	Netherlands/France	1990	Greenaway	Gambon/Mirren	Fsdc	Allarts/Cook/Era to	123	199
Tit. (Andronicus: The Movie)	USA	1997	Richey	n/a	Tvc	Lorne Richey Productions	n/a	269

Title	Country	Year	Director	Actor(s)	Type	Prod. Co/Dist.	Mins.	Pages
Tit. (I Spit on Your Grave)	USA	1978	Zarchi	Keaton	Fsdc	Cinemagic Films	100	269
Tit. (Titus Andronicus)	USA	1999	Dunne	Reece/Raleigh	Tvc	Joe Redner Film & Productions	147	269
Tit. (Titus)	USA	1999	Taymor	Hopkins/Lange	Fsdc	Fox Searchlight/Clear Blue Sky Productions.	163	269
Tit. (Titus Andronicus)	USA	2000	Griffin	Gore	Tvc	South Main Street Productions	167	269
Tit. (Behind the Scenes)	USA	2000	Hovde/Meyer	Taymor	Doc	First Run Features	30	27
Tmp.	UK	1939	Bower	Ashcroft	Tvbw	BBC	100	94
Tmp. (Forbidden Planet)	USA	1956	Wilcox	Pidgeon	Fsdc	MGM	96	210
Tmp.	USA	1960	Schaefer	Remick/Burton	Tvc	Hallmark	90	98, 99, 196
Tmp.	UK	1980	Jarman	Wilcox/Birkett	Fsdc	World Northal	90	99, 110, 195–98
Tmp.	UK	1980	Messina/Gorrie	Hordern/Guard	Tvc	BBC Shakespeare Plays	125	109, 196

Title	Country	Year	Director	Actor(s)	Type	Prod. Co/Dist.	Mins.	Pages
Tmp.	USA	1981	Mazursky	Cassavetes	Fsdc	Columbia	140	204, 211
Tmp.	USA	1985	Woodman	Zimbalist/Taylor	Tvc	Bard Prod.	126	116
Tmp. (Prospero's Books)	Netherlands/France/Italy	1991	Greenaway	Gielgud	Fsdc	Allarts/Cine/Camera One	129	103, 198–202, 209
Tmp.	USA	1998	Bender	Fonda	Tvc	Bonnie Raskin Productions	90	254
TN	USA	1910	Kent	Gordon	Fsibw	Vitagraph	12	7, 10, 170
TN	Russia	1955	Fried	Luchko/Larionova	Fsdc	LenFilm	90	108, 170–72, 173, 174
TN	USA	1957	Greene	Evans/Harris	Tvbw	Hallmark	90	98, 99
TN	UK	1970	Dexter/Sichel	Guinness/Richardson/Plowright	Tvc	ATV TV	105	104, 226
TN	USA	1972	Wertheim	n/a	Tvc	Playboy	n/a	218
TN	UK	1980	Messina/Gorrie	McCowen/Peacock/Kendal	Tvc	BBC Shakespeare Plays	130	108, 161

Title	Country	Year	Director	Actor(s)	Type	Prod. Co/Dist.	Mins.	Pages
TN	UK	1988	Branagh/ Kafno	Barber/Lesser	Tvc/ Disk	Renaissance Theatre Co.	165	118, 234, 244
TN	UK	1996	Nunn	Carter	Fsdc	Fine Line Features	105	226–29
Touch of Evil, A	USA	1958	Welles	Heston	Fsdbw	Universal	108/93	77, 90
Triumph of the Will	Germany	1935	Reifenstahl	Documentary	Fsdbw	UFA	80	51
Tro.	UK	1981 1982	Miller	Lesser/Burden	Tvc	BBC Shakespeare Plays	180	110
Two or Three Things I Know about Her	France	1967	Godard	Vlady	Fsdbw	Anouchka Films	95	202
Way of All Flesh, The	USA	1927	Fleming	Jannings	Fsibw	Paramount/Lasky	90	25
Wiv.	USA	1979	Taylor	Charles/ Grahame	Tvc	Los Angeles Globe	120	116
Wiv.	UK	1982 1983	Sutton/Jones	Griffiths/ Kingsley	Tvc	BBC Shakespeare Plays	150	112
Wiv. (The Braggart Samurai)	Japan	1991	Nomura	Nomura	Tvc	Panasonic Globe Theatre, Tokyo	60	272
Wizard of Oz	USA	1939	Fleming	Garland	Fsdc	MGM	119	196

Title	Country	Year	Director	Actor(s)	Type	Prod. Co/Dist.	Mins.	Pages
Woman Under the Influence, A	USA	1974	Cassavetes	Rowlands	Fsdc	Faces International	155	133
WT (Una Tragedie alla Corte di Sicilia)	Italy	1913	Negroni	Fabbri	Fsit	Milano-Film	40	15
WT	UK	1981	Miller/ Howell	Kemp/ Calder-Marshall	Tvc	BBC Shakespeare Plays	185	110, 164
Yojimbo	Japan	1961	Kurosawa	Mifune	Fsdbw	Kurosawa/Toho	110	184